College Writing Skills with Readings

College Writing Skills with Readings

NINTH EDITION

John Langan

Atlantic Cape Community College

Mc Graw Hill

Connect
Learn
Succeed™

Connect
Learn
Succeed™

COLLEGE WRITING SKILLS WITH READINGS, NINTH EDITION
Published by McGraw-Hill, a business unit of The McGraw-Hill Companies, Inc., 1221 Avenue of the Americas, New York, NY 10020. Copyright © 2014 by The McGraw-Hill Companies, Inc. All rights reserved. Printed in the United States of America. Previous editions © 2011 and 2008. No part of this publication may be reproduced or distributed in any form or by any means, or stored in a database or retrieval system, without the prior written consent of The McGraw-Hill Companies, Inc., including, but not limited to, in any network or other electronic storage or transmission, or broadcast for distance learning.

Some ancillaries, including electronic and print components, may not be available to customers outside the United States.

This book is printed on acid-free paper.
5 6 7 8 9 0 DOC 21 20 19 18 17 16

ISBN 978-0-07-803627-9
MHID 0-07-803627-5

ISBN 978-0-07-7531249 (Annotated Instructor's Edition)
MHID 0-07-753124-8

Senior Vice President, Products & Markets: *Kurt L. Strand*
Vice President and General Manager: *Michael Ryan*
Vice President, Content Production & Technology Services: *Kimberly Meriwether David*
Managing Director: *David S. Patterson*
Director: *Paul Banks*
Executive Brand Manager: *Kelly Villella-Canton*
Director of Development: *Dawn Groundwater*
Development Editor: *Merryl Maleska Wilbur*
Senior Marketing Manager: *Jaclyn Elkins*
Director, Content Production: *Terri Schiesl*
Content Project Manager: *Jolynn Kilburg*
Buyer: *Susan K. Culbertson*
Designer: *Debra Kubiak*
Cover/Interior Designer: *Preston Thomas, Cadence Design Studio*
Cover Images: *Laptop on desk © Marnie Burkhart/Corbis; Coffee cup, digital tablet and documents on desk © John Smith/Corbis.*
Content Licensing Specialist: *Ann Marie Jannette*
Photo Researcher: *Emily Tietz/Editorial Image, LLC.*
Compositor: *MPS Limited*
Typeface: *11/13 Times*
Printer: R. R. Donnelley

Library of Congress Cataloging-in-Publication Data

Cataloging-in-Publication Data has been requested from the Library of Congress.

The Internet addresses listed in the text were accurate at the time of publication. The inclusion of a website does not indicate an endorsement by the authors or McGraw-Hill, and McGraw-Hill does not guarantee the accuracy of the information presented at these sites

www.mhhe.com

John Langan has taught reading and writing at Atlantic Cape Community College near Atlantic City, New Jersey, for more than twenty-five years. The author of a popular series of college textbooks on both writing and reading, John enjoys the challenge of developing materials that teach skills in an especially clear and lively way. Before teaching, he earned advanced degrees in writing at Rutgers University and in reading at Rowan University. He also spent a year writing fiction that, he says, "is now at the back of a drawer waiting to be discovered and acclaimed posthumously." While in school, he supported himself by working as a truck driver, a machinist, a battery assembler, a hospital attendant, and an apple packer. John now lives with his wife, Judith Nadell, near Philadelphia. In addition to his wife and Philly sports teams, his passions include reading and turning on nonreaders to the pleasure and power of books. Through Townsend Press, his educational publishing company, he has developed the nonprofit "Townsend Library"—a collection of more than one hundred new and classic stories that appeal to readers of any age.

BRIEF CONTENTS

PART 1 Essay Writing 1

1. An Introduction to Writing   2
2. The Writing Process   22
3. The First and Second Steps in Essay Writing   50
4. The Third Step in Essay Writing   83
5. The Fourth Step in Essay Writing   110
6. Four Bases for Revising Essays   144

PART 2 Patterns of Essay Development   173

7. Introduction to Essay Development   174
8. Description   182
9. Narration   203
10. Exemplification   222
11. Process   242
12. Cause and/or Effect   260
13. Comparison and/or Contrast   281
14. Definition   304
15. Division-Classification   325
16. Argument   343

PART 3 Special Skills   365

17. Taking Essay Exams   366
18. Writing a Summary   375
19. Writing a Report   387
20. Writing a Résumé and Cover Letter   392
21. Using the Library and the Internet   399
22. Writing a Research Paper   413

PART 4 Handbook of Sentence Skills   439

SECTION I Grammar   440

23. Subjects and Verbs   441

24. Fragments   447

25. Run-Ons   460

26. Regular and Irregular Verbs   473

27. Subject-Verb Agreement   484

28. Additional Information about Verbs   490

29. Pronoun Agreement and Reference   494

30. Pronoun Types   500

31. Adjectives and Adverbs   507

32. Misplaced Modifiers   513

33. Dangling Modifiers   517

SECTION II Mechanics   522

34. Manuscript Form   523

35. Capital Letters   526

36. Numbers and Abbreviations   534

SECTION III Punctuation   538

37. Apostrophe   539

38. Quotation Marks   546

39. Comma   554

40. Other Punctuation Marks   564

SECTION IV Word Use   569

41. Spelling Improvement   570

42. Commonly Confused Words   575

43. Effective Word Choice   585

44. Editing Tests   592

45. ESL Pointers   605

PART 5 Readings for Writers   621

INTRODUCTION TO THE READINGS   622

LOOKING INWARD   627

OBSERVING OTHERS   674

CONFRONTING PROBLEMS   707

Credits   764

Index   766

CONTENTS

About the Author   v

Preface   xxii

PART 1 Essay Writing   1

1. An Introduction to Writing   2
Point and Support   3
Structure of the Traditional Essay   6
Benefits of Writing the Traditional Essay   11
Writing as a Skill   11
Writing as a Process of Discovery   12
Writing as a Way to Communicate with Others   13
Keeping a Journal   14
Tips on Using a Computer   15
Review Activities   17
Using This Text   20

2. The Writing Process   22
Prewriting   23
Writing a First Draft   31
Revising   33
Editing   35
Review Activities   38

3. The First and Second Steps in Essay Writing   50
Step 1: Begin with a Point, or Thesis   51
Step 2: Support the Thesis with Specific Evidence   60
Practice in Advancing and Supporting a Thesis   67

4. The Third Step in Essay Writing   83
Step 3: Organize and Connect the Specific Evidence   84
Introductions, Conclusions, and Titles   94
Practice in Organizing and Connecting
Specific Evidence   102

5. The Fourth Step in Essay Writing   110

Revising Sentences   111

Editing Sentences   130

Practice in Revising Sentences   133

6. Four Bases for Revising Essays   144

Base 1: Unity   145

Base 2: Support   148

Base 3: Coherence   152

Base 4: Sentence Skills   155

Practice in Using the Four Bases   159

PART 2 Patterns of Essay Development   173

7. Introduction to Essay Development   174

Important Considerations in Essay
Development   175

Patterns of Essay Development   180

8. Description   182

READING *Lou's Place* by Beth Johnson   192

9. Narration   203

READING *The Yellow Ribbon* by Pete Hamill   214

10. Exemplification   222

READING *Dad* by Andrew H. Malcolm   233

11. Process   242

READING *How to Do Well on a Job Interview* by Glenda Davis   251

12. Cause and/or Effect   260

READING *Taming the Anger Monster* by Anne Davidson   269

13. **Comparison and/or Contrast   281**
    READING *Born to Be Different?*
    by Camille Lewis   293

14. **Definition   304**
    READING *Television Addiction*
    by Marie Winn   313

15. **Division-Classification   325**
    READING *Wait Divisions*
    by Tom Bodett   334

16. **Argument   343**
    READING *Ban the Things. Ban Them All.*
    by Molly Ivins   356

PART 3 Special Skills   365

17. **Taking Essay Exams   366**

18. **Writing a Summary   375**
    How to Summarize an Article   376
    How to Summarize a Book   385

19. **Writing a Report   387**
    A Model Report   389

20. **Writing a Résumé and Cover
    Letter   392**
    Résumé   392
    Cover Letter   396

21. Using the Library and the Internet   399

Using the Library   400

Using the Internet   407

Practice in Using the Library and the Internet   411

22. Writing a Research Paper   413

A Model Paper   427

PART 4 Handbook of Sentence Skills   439

SECTION I Grammar   440

CONNECT WRITING PLUS 2.0 PERSONAL LEARNING PLAN CORRELATION GUIDE

UNIT	TOPIC IN PERSONAL LEARNING PLAN
Writing Clear Sentences	Subjects and Verbs
Fixing Common Problems	Fragments Run-Ons Regular and Irregular Verbs Subject-Verb Agreement Additional Information about Verbs
	Pronoun Agreement and Reference Pronoun Types Adjectives and Adverbs Misplaced Modifiers Dangling Modifiers

23. Subjects and Verbs   441

A Simple Way to Find a Subject   442

A Simple Way to Find a Verb   442

More about Subjects and Verbs   443

24. Fragments   447

Dependent-Word Fragments   447

-ing and *to* Fragments   451

Added-Detail Fragments   453

Missing-Subject Fragments   455

25. Run-Ons   460
What Are Run-Ons?   460
Three Ways to Correct Run-Ons   461

26. Regular and Irregular Verbs   473
Regular Verbs   473
Irregular Verbs   476

27. Subject-Verb Agreement   484
Words between Subject and Verb   485
Verb before Subject   485
Compound Subjects   486
Indefinite Pronouns   487

28. Additional Information about Verbs   490
Verb Tense   490
Helping Verbs   491
Verbals   492

29. Pronoun Agreement and Reference   494
Pronoun Agreement   495
Pronoun Reference   497

30. Pronoun Types   500
Subject and Object Pronouns   500
Possessive Pronouns   504
Demonstrative Pronouns   505

31. Adjectives and Adverbs   507
Adjectives   507
Adverbs   509

32. Misplaced Modifiers   513

33. Dangling Modifiers   517

SECTION II Mechanics   522

CONNECT WRITING PLUS 2.0 PERSONAL LEARNING PLAN CORRELATION GUIDE	
UNIT	TOPIC IN PERSONAL LEARNING PLAN
Addressing Mechanics	Manuscript Form Capital Letters Numbers and Abbreviations

34. Manuscript Form   523

35. Capital Letters   526
Main Uses of Capital Letters   526
Other Uses of Capital Letters   529
Unnecessary Use of Capitals   532

36. Numbers and Abbreviations   534
Numbers   535
Abbreviations   536

SECTION III Punctuation   538

CONNECT WRITING PLUS 2.0 PERSONAL LEARNING PLAN CORRELATION GUIDE	
UNIT	TOPIC IN PERSONAL LEARNING PLAN
Punctuating Correctly	Commas Apostrophe Quotation Marks Comma Other Punctuation Marks

37. Apostrophe   539
Apostrophe in Contractions   540
Apostrophe to Show Ownership or Possession   541

38. Quotation Marks   546

Quotation Marks to Set Off the Words of
a Speaker or Writer   546

Quotation Marks to Set Off Titles of
Short Works   550

Other Uses of Quotation Marks   552

39. Comma   554

Six Main Uses of the Comma   554

40. Other Punctuation Marks   564

Colon (:)   564

Semicolon (;)   565

Dash (—)   565

Parentheses ( )   566

Hyphen (-)   567

SECTION IV Word Use   569

CONNECT WRITING PLUS 2.0 PERSONAL LEARNING PLAN CORRELATION GUIDE	
UNIT	TOPIC IN PERSONAL LEARNING PLAN
Using Words Effectively	Spelling Improvement Commonly Confused Words
	Effective Word Choice Editing Tests ESL Pointers

41. Spelling Improvement   570

42. Commonly Confused Words   575

Homonyms   575

Other Words Frequently Confused   580

43. Effective Word Choice   585

Slang   585

Clichés   587

Pretentious Words   589

44. Editing Tests   592

45. ESL Pointers   605

Articles with Count and Noncount Nouns   606

Subjects and Verbs   610

Adjectives   615

Prepositions Used for Time and Place   617

Correction Symbols   620

PART 5   Readings for Writers   621

INTRODUCTION TO THE READINGS   622

The Format of Each Selection   622

How to Read Well: Four General Steps   623

How to Answer the Comprehension Questions: Specific Hints   625

LOOKING INWARD   627

from *Self-Reliance*
Ralph Waldo Emerson   627

Three Passions
Bertrand Russell   632

Shame
Dick Gregory   636

I Became Her Target
Roger Wilkins   643

Stepping into the Light
Tanya Savory   650

A Hanging
George Orwell   658

What Your Closet Reveals about You
Amy Tan   667

OBSERVING OTHERS   674

The Professor Is a Dropout
Beth Johnson   674

The Certainty of Fear
Audra Kendall   684

What's Wrong with Schools? Teacher Plays Student,
Learns to Lie and Cheat
Casey Banas   691

Propaganda Techniques in Today's Advertising
Ann McClintock   697

CONFRONTING PROBLEMS   707

Chief Seattle's Speech of 1854
Chief Seattle   707

Single-Sex Schools: An Old Idea Whose Time
Has Come
Diane Urbina   715

Here's to Your Health
Joan Dunayer   722

Mayor of Rust
Sue Halpern   728

How to Make It in College, Now That You're Here
Brian O'Keeney   740

College Lectures: Is Anybody Listening?
David Daniels   749

Is Sex All That Matters?
Joyce Garity   756

Reading Comprehension Chart   763

Credits   764

Index   766

READINGS Listed by Rhetorical Mode

Note: Some selections are cross-listed because they illustrate more than one rhetorical method of development.

DESCRIPTION

Lou's Place   Beth Johnson   192

A Hanging   George Orwell   658

Stepping into the Light   Tanya Savory   650

What Your Closet Reveals about You   Amy Tan   667

The Certainty of Fear   Audra Kendall   684

Is Sex All That Matters?   Joyce Garity   756

NARRATION

Lou's Place   Beth Johnson   192

The Yellow Ribbon   Pete Hamill   214

Shame   Dick Gregory   636

I Became Her Target   Roger Wilkins   643

A Hanging   George Orwell   658

What Your Closet Reveals about You   Amy Tan   667

Chief Seattle's Speech of 1854   Chief Seattle   707

Mayor of Rust   Sue Halpern   728

EXEMPLIFICATION

Dad   Andrew H. Malcolm   233

How to Do Well on a Job Interview   Glenda Davis   251

Taming the Anger Monster   Anne Davidson   269

Born to Be Different?   Camille Lewis   293

Television Addiction   Marie Winn   313

Wait Divisions   Tom Bodett   334

Ban the Things. Ban Them All.   Molly Ivins   356

Three Passions   Bertrand Russell   632

The Professor Is a Dropout   Beth Johnson   674

Propaganda Techniques in Today's Advertising   Ann McClintock   697

Here's to Your Health   Joan Dunayer   722

Mayor of Rust   Sue Halpern   728

Is Sex All That Matters?   Joyce Garity   756

PROCESS

How to Do Well on a Job Interview   Glenda Davis   251

Taming the Anger Monster   Anne Davidson   269

from *Self-Reliance*   Ralph Waldo Emerson   627

Mayor of Rust   Sue Halpern   728

How to Make It in College, Now That You're Here   Brian O'Keeney   740

CAUSE AND/OR EFFECT

How to Do Well on a Job Interview   Glenda Davis   251

Taming the Anger Monster   Anne Davidson   269

Born to Be Different?   Camille Lewis   293

Television Addiction   Marie Winn   313

Three Passions   Bertrand Russell   632

Shame   Dick Gregory   636

Stepping into the Light   Tanya Savory   650

The Professor Is a Dropout   Beth Johnson   674

What's Wrong with Schools? Teacher Plays Student, Learns to Lie and Cheat   Casey Banas   691

Propaganda Techniques in Today's Advertising   Ann McClintock   697

Is Sex All That Matters?   Joyce Garity   756

COMPARISON AND/OR CONTRAST

Born to Be Different?   Camille Lewis   293

Ban the Things. Ban Them All.   Molly Ivins   356

A Hanging   George Orwell   658

Chief Seattle's Speech of 1854   Chief Seattle   707

Here's to Your Health   Joan Dunayer   722

Mayor of Rust   Sue Halpern   728

Is Sex All That Matters?   Joyce Garity   756

DEFINITION

Television Addiction   Marie Winn   313

Shame   Dick Gregory   636

Propaganda Techniques in Today's Advertising   Ann McClintock   697

DIVISION-CLASSIFICATION

Wait Divisions   Tom Bodett   334

What Your Closet Reveals about You   Amy Tan   667

Propaganda Techniques in Today's Advertising   Ann McClintock   697

ARGUMENT

Ban the Things. Ban Them All.   Molly Ivins   356

from *Self-Reliance*   Ralph Waldo Emerson   627

Chief Seattle's Speech of 1854   Chief Seattle   707

Single-Sex Schools: An Old Idea Whose Time Has Come   Diane Urbina   715

Here's to Your Health   Joan Dunayer   722

College Lectures: Is Anybody Listening?   David Daniels   749

Is Sex All That Matters?   Joyce Garity   756

Preface

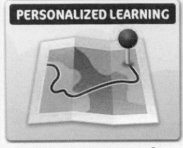

Personalized Learning

College Writing Skills with Readings 9/e emphasizes personalized learning. Powered by *Connect Writing Plus 2.0*, students gain access to our groundbreaking personal learning plan, which helps students become aware of what they already know and what they need to practice. A self-study tool, its cutting-edge, continually adaptive technology, and exclusive time-management features make students more productive, keep them on track, and give them the writing skills needed for all their college courses.

With a baseline adaptive diagnostic that assesses student proficiencies in five core areas of grammar and mechanics, students can generate a unique learning plan tailored to address their specific needs and help them determine what they want to study. Students receive a personalized program of lessons, videos, animations, and interactive exercises to improve their skills, as well as immediate feedback on their work. With an engine that incorporates metacognitive learning theory and provides ongoing diagnosis for each learning objective, the personal learning plan continually adapts with each student interaction, while built-in time management tools ensure that students work on pace to master all required learning objectives by the end of the course. This personalized, constantly adapting online environment increases student readiness, motivation, and confidence and allows classroom instruction to focus on thoughtful and critical writing processes.

Personalized learning icons, like the one above, are integrated throughout the chapters. The detailed Table of Contents also contains a *Connect Writing Plus 2.0* Personal Learning Plan Correlation Guide. It lists related individual learning topics in the *Connect* personal learning plan.

Personal, Academic, and Workplace Writing

College Writing Skills with Readings 9/e is flexible. Students are exposed to examples of writing that reflect the three key realms of their lives—personal, academic, and workplace. They will find models, activities, and examples for any writing situation. This variety provides great flexibility in the kinds of assignments you prefer to give. Icons identifying personal, academic, and workplace writing are integrated throughout the chapters.

Mastering the Four Bases: Unity, Support, Coherence, Sentence Skills

College Writing Skills with Readings 9/e emphasizes writing skills and process. By referring to a set of four skills for effective writing, *College Writing Skills with Readings 9/e* encourages new writers to see writing as a skill that can be learned and a process that must be explored. The four skills, or bases, for effective writing are as follows:

- **Unity:** Discover a clearly stated point, or topic sentence, and make sure that all other information in the paragraph or essay supports that point.

- **Support:** Support the points with specific evidence, and plenty of it.

- **Coherence:** Organize and connect supporting evidence so that paragraphs and essays transition smoothly from one bit of supporting information to the next.

- **Sentence skills:** Revise and edit so that sentences are error-free for clearer and more effective communication.

The four bases are essential to effective writing, whether it be a narrative paragraph, a cover letter for a job application, or an essay assignment.

UNITY

Discover a clearly stated point, or topic sentence, and make sure that all other information in the paragraph or essay supports that point.

SUPPORT

Support the points with specific evidence, and plenty of it.

COHERENCE

Organize and connect supporting evidence so that paragraphs and essays transition smoothly from one bit of supporting information to the next.

SENTENCE SKILLS

Revise and edit so that sentences are error-free for clearer and more effective communication.

In addition to incorporating the personal learning plan, maintaining the four bases framework, and continuing to build in many familiar personal writing examples, *College Writing Skills with Readings 9/e* includes the following chapter-by-chapter changes:

Part 1: Essay Writing

- New sample paragraphs that reflect academic and workplace writing
- Revised writing samples to eliminate use of second-person
- Revised presentation of the term "essay," including fuller explanation of "thesis" and coverage of essays with more than three supporting paragraphs
- Greater emphasis on the role of mixed modes in essay writing
- Revised full-length essay with focus on adding details
- Revised treatment of the use of questions in essay structuring
- Inclusion of multiple across-chapter cross-references to related topics

Part 2: Patterns of Essay Development

- New sample paragraphs and Writing Assignments that reflect academic and workplace writing
- Updated personal writing examples
- New explanation about limited use of second-person in writing
- Revised writing samples to eliminate use of second-person
- Greater coverage of essays with more than three supporting paragraphs
- Inclusion of multiple across-chapter cross-references to related topics
- Revised introductory text for each pattern with explanation of how multiple modes function together in one essay

Part 3: Special Skills

- Updated formatting for sample student paper to better represent academic expectations

- Revised exposition to reflect updated MLA standards

- Revised exposition to reflect updated Internet and library skills

Part 4: Handbook of Sentence Skills

- Grammar activities and exercises rewritten to incorporate academic and workplace-related themes

- Review Tests reworked to incorporate academic and workplace-related themes

- Revised material frequently focused on one issue so that it reads as a unified passage rather than a set of disconnected statements

- Improved coverage of certain key grammar topics, such as subordinating words and verb forms

- Inclusion of multiple across-chapter cross-references to related topics

Part 5: Readings for Writers

- Readings updated to include four new selections by diverse and well-respected authors:

  "Mayor of Rust" by Sue Halpern

  "What Your Closet Reveals about You" by Amy Tan

  from *Self-Reliance* by Ralph Waldo Emerson

  "Chief Seattle's Speech of 1854" by Chief Seattle

- Each new reading accompanied by new full set of questions and assignments

- All assignments reflect either personal, academic, or workplace-related themes

Book-Specific Supplements for Instructors

The **Annotated Instructor's Edition** consists of the student text, complete with answers to all activities and tests.

The **Online Learning Center** (**www.mhhe.com/langan**) offers a number of instructional materials including an instructor's manual, test bank, and PowerPoint ® slides that may be tailored to course needs.

Create the Perfect Course Materials with Create™

create With McGraw-Hill Create™, you can easily arrange your book to align with the syllabus, eliminate chapters you do not assign, combine material from other content sources, and quickly upload content you have written, such as your course syllabus or teaching notes, to enhance the value of course materials for your students. You control the net price of the book as you build it and have the opportunity to choose format: color, black and white, and eBook. When you build a CREATE book, you'll receive a complimentary print review copy in three to five business days or a complimentary electronic review copy (eComp) via e-mail in about one hour.

Go to www.mcgrawhillcreate.com and register today!

Customize *College Writing Skills* in Create™ with Bonus Content

In addition to reordering and eliminating chapters in *College Writing Skills with Readings,* adding your own materials or adding chapters from other McGraw-Hill textbooks, you may customize the readings in Part Five by eliminating or adding readings from other Langan titles or from other McGraw-Hill collections.

McGraw-Hill Create™ *ExpressBooks* facilitate customizing your book more quickly and easily. To quickly view the possibilities for customizing your book, visit **www.mcgrawhillcreate.com** and enter "College Writing Skills with Readings" under the Find Content tab. Once you select the current edition of the book, click on the "View Related ExpressBooks" button or ExpressBooks tab to see options. ExpressBooks contain a combination of pre-selected chapters, articles, cases, or readings that serve as a starting point to help you quickly and easily build your own text. These helpful templates are built using content available on Create and organized in ways that match various course outlines. We understand that you have a unique perspective. Use McGraw-Hill Create ExpressBooks to build the book you've only imagined!

Connect Learning Management System Integration

Connect Writing Plus 2.0 integrates with your local Learning Management System (Blackboard, Desire2Learn, and others.)

McGraw-Hill Campus™ is a new one-stop teaching and learning experience available to users of any learning management system. This complimentary integration allows faculty and students to enjoy single sign-on (SSO) access to all McGraw-Hill Higher Education materials and synchronized grade-books with our award-winning McGraw-Hill *Connect* platform. For more information on McGraw-Hill Campus please visit our website at **www.mhcampus.com** or contact your local McGraw-Hill representative to find out more about installations on your campus.

Tegrity

Tegrity Campus is a service that makes class time available all the time by automatically capturing every lecture in a searchable format for students to review when they study and complete assignments. With a simple one-click start and stop process, users capture all computer screens and corresponding audio. Students replay any part of any class with easy-to-use browser-based viewing on a PC or Mac. Educators know that the more students can see, hear, and experience class resources, the better they learn. With Tegrity Campus, students quickly recall key moments by using Tegrity Campus's unique search feature. This search helps students efficiently find what they need, when they need it, across an entire semester of class recordings. Help turn all your students' study time into learning moments immediately supported by your lecture.

Coursesmart™

This text is available as an eTextbook at **www. CourseSmart.com.** At CourseSmart your students can take advantage of significant savings off the cost of a print textbook, reduce their impact on the environment, and gain access to powerful tools for learning. CourseSmart eTextbooks can be viewed online or downloaded to a computer. CourseSmart offers free Apps to access the textbooks on SmartPhones and iPads. The eTextbooks allow students to do full text searches, add highlighting and notes, and share notes with classmates. CourseSmart has the largest selection of eTextbooks available anywhere. Visit **www.CourseSmart.com** to learn more and to try a sample chapter.

ACKNOWLEDGMENTS

Without the contributions and diligence of Zoe L. Albright of Metropolitan Community College—Longview, this edition would not have come to fruition. The quality of *College Writing Skills with Readings 9/e* is a testament to the suggestions and insights from instructors around the country. Many thanks to all of those who helped improve this project.

Steven R. Acree, *College of the Desert*

Marty Ambrose, *Edison State College*

James M. Andres, *Harper College*

Marcia Backos, *Bryant & Stratton College*

Elizabeth Barnes, *Daytona Beach Community College—Daytona Beach*

Michalle Barnett, *Gulf Coast Community College*

Carolyn Barr, *Broward College*

Elizabeth Bass, *Camden County College*

Elaine Bassett, *Troy University*

Glenda Bell, *University of Arkansas Community College at Batesville*

Victoria S. Berardi-Rogers, *Northwestern Community College*

Manette Berlinger, *Queensborough Community College*

Jennifer Black, *McLennan Community College*

Christian Blum, *Bryant and Stratton College*

Kathleen S. Britton, *Florence-Darlington Technical College*

Marta Brown, *Community College of Denver*

Shanti Bruce, *Nova Southeastern University*

Jennifer Bubb, *Illinois Valley Community College*

Alexandra C. Campbell-Forte, *Germanna Community College*

Jessica Carroll, *Miami Dade College—Wolfson*

Patti Casey, *Tyler Junior College*

Helen Chester, *Milwaukee Area Technical College*

Cathy Clements, *State Fair Community College*

Patricia Colella, *Bunker Hill Community College*

Donna-Marie Colonna, *Sandhills Community College*

Linda Austin Crawford, *McLennan Community College*

Dena DeCastro, *Clark College*

Beverly F. Dile, *Elizabethtown Community and Technical College*

Carrie Dorsey, *Northern Virginia Community College*

Thomas Dow, *Moraine Valley Community College*

Michelle Downey, *Florence-Darlington Technical College*

Joyce Anne Dvorak, *Metropolitan Community College—Longview*

Kevin Dye, *Chemeketa Community College*

Marie Eckstrom, *Rio Hondo College*

Claudia Edwards, *Piedmont Technical College*

Amy England, *University of Cincinnati*

Susan Ertel, *Dixie State College of Utah*

Lori Farr, *Oklahoma City Community College*

Karen Feldman, *Seminole Community College*

Jim Fields, *Iowa Western Community College*

Alexander Fitzner, *Pellissippi State Technical Community College*

Karen Fleming, *Sinclair Community College*

Deborah Fontaine, *Okaloosa-Walton College*

Billy Fontenot, *Louisiana State University—Eunice*

H. L. Ford, *Pellissippi State Technical Community College*

Jaquelyn Gaiters-Jordan, *Pikes Peak Community College*

Valerie Gray, *Harrisburg Area Community College*

Jennifer Green, *Southern University at Shreveport*

Roxanne Hannon-Odom, *Bishop State Community College*

Linda H. Hasty, *Motlow State Community College*

Dawn Hayward, *Delaware County Community College*

Angela Hebert, *Hudson County Community College*

Catherine Higdon, *Tarrant County College—South Campus*

Rita Higgins, *Essex County College*

Desha S. Hill, *Tyler Junior College*

Lee Nell W. Hill, *Tyler Junior College*

Elizabeth Holton, *Frederick Community College*

Sharyn L. Hunter, *Sinclair Community College*

Michael Jaffe, *El Camino College*

Kaushalya Jagasia, *Illinois Valley Community College*

Leslie Johnston, *Pulaski Technical College*

Leigh Jonaitis, *Bergen Community College*

Billy Jones, *Miami Dade College—Kendall*

Julie Kelly, *St. Johns River State College*

Heather Kichner, *Lorain County Community College*

Laura Kingston, *South Seattle Community College*

Trudy Krisher, *Sinclair Community College*

Dianne Krob, *Rose State College*

Kristin Le Veness, *Nassau Community College*

Amy Lerman, *Mesa Community College*

Keming Liu, *Medgar Evers College*

Paulette Longmore, *Essex County College*

Breanna Lutterbie, *Germanna Community College*

Suzanne Lynch, *Hillsborough Community College*

Teri Maddox, *Jackson State Community College*

Jeanette Maurice, *Illinois Valley Community College*

Linda McCloud, *Broward College*

Diane McDonald, *Montgomery County Community College—Blue Bell*

Sarah McFarland, *Northwestern State University*

Candace C. Mesa, *Dixie State College*

Theresa Mohamed, *Onondaga Community College*

Susan Monroe, *Housatonic Community College*

Christopher Morelock, *Walters State Community College*

Lori Renae Morrow, *Rose State College*

Steven Mullis, *Central Piedmont Community College*

Julie Nichols, *Okaloosa-Walton College*

Julie Odell, *Community College of Philadelphia*

Ellen Olmstead, *Montgomery College*

Kelly Ormsby, *Cleveland State Community College*

Robin Ozz, *Phoenix College*

Jay Peterson, *Atlantic Cape Community College*

Susie Peyton, *Marshall Community and Technical College*

Tracy Peyton, *Pensacola Junior College*

Jacklyn R. Pierce, *Lake-Sumter Community College*

Lydia Postell, *Dalton State College*

Teresa Prosser, *Sinclair Community College*

Danielle Reites, *Lake-Sumter Community College*

Charles A. Riley II, *Baruch College, City University of New York*

Michael Roberts, *Fresno City College*

Dawnielle B. Robinson-Walker, *Metropolitan Community College—Longview*

Patty Rogers, *Angelina College*

Stephanie Sabourin, *Montgomery College—Takoma Park/Silver Spring*

Jamie Sadler, *Richmond Community College*

Jim Sayers, *University of New Mexico—Gallup Campus*

Joseph Scherer, *Community College of Allegheny—South*

Anna Schmidt, *Lonestar College—CyFair*

Caroline Seefchak, *Edison State College*

Linda Shief, *Wake Technical Community College*

Lori Smalley, *Greenville Technical College*

Anne Smith, *Northwest Mississippi Community College*

Hank Smith, *Gulf Coast Community College*

James R. Sodon, *St. Louis Community College—Florissant Valley*

Crystal Stallman, *Hawkeye Community College*

James Suderman, *Okaloosa-Walton College*

Holly Susi, *Community College of Rhode Island—Flanagan*

Karen Taylor, *Belmont Technical College*

Lisa Telesca, *Citrus College*

Douglas Texter, *Minneapolis Community and Technical College*

Caryl Terrell-Bamiro, *Chandler-Gilbert Community College*

Connie Kendall Theado, *University of Cincinnati*

Sharisse Turner, *Tallahassee Community College*

Christine Tutlewski, *University of Wisconsin—Parkside*

Kathryn Y. Tyndall, *Wake Technical Community College*

Cynthia VanSickle, *McHenry County College*

Maria Villar-Smith, *Miami Dade College—Wolfson*

Nikka Vrieze, *Rochester Community and Technical College*

Ross Wagner, *Greenville Technical College*

Mark Walls, *Jackson State Community College*

Arthur Wellborn, *McLennan Community College*

Stephen Wells, *Community College of Allegheny—South*

Marjorie-Anne Wikoff, *St. Petersburg College*

Sheila Wiley, *Santa Barbara City College*

Debbie Wilke, *Daytona State College*

Kelli Wilkes, *Valdosta Technical College*

Jim Wilkins-Luton, *Clark College*

Julia Williams, *Harrison College*

Jeff Wheeler, *Long Beach City College*

Mary Joyce Whiteside, *El Paso Community College*

Shonda Wilson, *Suffolk County Community College*

Mary Katherine Winkler, *Blue Ridge Community College*

Xuewei Wu, *Century Community and Technical College*

Deborah Yaden, *Richland Community College*

William Young, *University of South Alabama*

Betsy Zuegg, *Quinsigamond Community College*

Essay Writing

Have yourself a merry little Christmas
It may be your last
Next year we may all be living in the past
Have yourself a merry little Christmas
Pop the champagne cork
Next year we may all be living in New York.
No good times like the olden days,
Happy golden days of yore,
Faithful friends who were dear to us
Will be near to us no more.
But at least we all will be together
If the Lord allows.
From now on we'll have to muddle through somehow.
So have yourself a merry little Christmas now.

Have yourself a merry little Christmas,
Let your heart be light
From now on, our troubles will be out of sight
Have yourself a merry little Christmas
Make your yuletide gay
From now on our troubles will be miles away.
Here we are as in olden days,
Happy golden days of yore.
Faithful friends who were dear to us
Gather near to us once more.
Through the years we all will be together
If the fates allow.
Until then, we'll have to muddle through somehow
So have yourself a merry little Christmas now.

PREVIEW

1 An Introduction to Writing

2 The Writing Process

3 The First and Second Steps in Essay Writing

4 The Third Step in Essay Writing

5 The Fourth Step in Essay Writing

6 Four Bases for Revising Essays

Even songwriters often have to write several drafts of lyrics before producing an effective song. Compare this excerpted draft of "Have Yourself a Merry Little Christmas" by Hugh Martin with its final version; what has changed? Choose one revision and explain why and how it makes the lyrics more effective.

An Introduction to Writing

This chapter will explain and illustrate

- the importance of supporting a point in writing
- the structure of the traditional essay
- the benefits of writing the traditional essay

This chapter also

- presents writing as both a skill and a process of discovery
- suggests keeping a journal

What is your ideal job? Write two or more paragraphs about what your ideal job would be and what your daily activities on the job would entail. Be sure to include your reasons for wanting such a job.

The experience I had writing my first college essay helped shape this book. I received a C– for the essay. Scrawled beside the grade was the comment "Not badly written, but ill-conceived." I remember going to the instructor after class, asking about his comment as well as the word *Log* that he had added in the margin at various spots. "What are all these logs you put in my paper?" I asked, trying to make a joke of it. He looked at me a little wonderingly. "Logic, Mr. Langan," he answered, "logic." He went on to explain that I had not thought out my paper clearly. There were actually two ideas rather than one in my thesis, one supporting paragraph had nothing to do with either idea, another paragraph lacked a topic sentence, and so on. I've never forgotten his last words: "If you don't think clearly," he said, "you won't write clearly."

I was speechless, and I felt confused and angry. I didn't like being told that I didn't know how to think. I went back to my room and read over my paper several times. Eventually, I decided that my instructor was right. "No more logs," I said to myself. "I'm going to get these logs out of my papers."

My instructor's advice was invaluable. I learned that clear, disciplined thinking is the key to effective writing. *College Writing Skills with Readings* develops this idea by breaking down the writing process into a series of four logical, easily followed steps. These steps, combined with practical advice about prewriting and revision, will help you write strong papers.

Here are the four steps in a nutshell:

1. Discover a clearly stated point, or thesis.
2. Provide logical, detailed support for your thesis.
3. Organize and connect your supporting material.
4. Revise and edit so that your sentences are effective and error-free.

Part 1 of this book explains each of these steps in detail and provides many practice materials to help you master them.

Point and Support

An Important Difference between Writing and Talking

In everyday conversation, you make all kinds of points or assertions. You say, for example, "My boss is a hard person to work for," "It's not safe to walk in our neighborhood after dark," or "Poor study habits keep getting me into trouble." The points that you make concern personal matters as well as, at times, outside issues:

"That trade will be a disaster for the team," "Lots of TV commercials are degrading to women," "Students are better off working for a year before attending college."

The people you are talking with do not always challenge you to give reasons for your statements. They may know why you feel as you do, or they may already agree with you, or they simply may not want to put you on the spot; and so they do not always ask why. But the people who read what you write may not know you, agree with you, or feel in any way obliged to you. If you want to communicate effectively with readers, you must provide solid evidence for any point you make. An important difference, then, between writing and talking is this: *In writing, any idea that you advance must be supported with specific reasons or details.*

Think of your readers as reasonable people. They will not take your views on faith, but they are willing to accept what you say as long as you support it. Therefore, remember to support with specific evidence any point that you make.

Point and Support in a Paragraph

In conversation, you might say to a friend who has suggested a movie, "No, thanks. Going to the movies is just too much of a hassle. Parking, people, everything." From shared past experiences, your friend may know what you are talking about so that you will not have to explain your statement. But in writing, your point would have to be backed up with specific reasons and details.

Below is a paragraph, written by a student named Diane Woods, on why moviegoing is a nuisance. A *paragraph* is a short paper of around 150 to 200 words. It usually consists of an opening point, called a *topic sentence,* followed by a series of sentences that support that point.

The Hazards of Moviegoing

Although I love movies, I've found that there are drawbacks to moviegoing. One problem is just the inconvenience of it all. To get to the theater, I have to drive for at least fifteen minutes, or more if traffic is bad. It can take forever to find a parking spot, and then I have to walk across a huge parking lot to the theater. There I encounter long lines, sold-out shows, and ever-increasing prices. And I hate sitting with my feet sticking to the floor because of other people's spilled snacks. Another problem is my lack of self-control at the theater. I often stuff myself with unhealthy calorie-laden snacks. My choices might include a bucket of popcorn, a box of Milk Duds, a giant soda, or all three. The worst problem is some of the other moviegoers. Kids run up and down the aisle. Teenagers laugh and shout at the screen. People of all ages drop soda cups and popcorn tubs, cough and burp, and talk to one another. All in all, I would rather stay home and watch a DVD in the comfort of my own living room.

Personal

Notice what the supporting evidence does here. It provides you, the reader, with a basis for understanding *why* the writer makes the point that is made. Through this specific evidence, the writer has explained and successfully communicated the idea that moviegoing can be a nuisance.

The evidence that supports the point in a paper often consists of a series of reasons followed by examples and details that support the reasons. That is true of the paragraph above: three reasons are provided, with examples and details that back up those reasons. Supporting evidence in a paper can also consist of anecdotes, personal experiences, facts, studies, statistics, and the opinions of experts.

The paragraph on moviegoing, like almost any piece of effective writing, has two essential parts: (1) a point is advanced, and (2) that point is then supported. Taking a minute to outline "The Hazards of Moviegoing" will help you understand these basic parts. Write in the following space the point that has been advanced in the paragraph. Then add the words needed to complete the paragraph's outline.

ACTIVITY 1

Point Support

_____

1. _____
   a. Fifteen-minute drive to theater
   b. _____
   c. Long lines, sold-out shows, and increasing prices
   d. _____
2. Lack of self-control
   a. Often stuff myself with unhealthy snacks
   b. Might have popcorn, candy, soda, or all three
3. _____
   a. _____
   b. _____
   c. People of all ages make noise.

Point and Support in an Essay

An excellent way to learn how to write clearly and logically is to practice composing the traditional college *essay*—a paper of about five hundred words that typically consists of an introductory paragraph, three or more supporting paragraphs, and a concluding paragraph. The central idea, or point, developed in any essay is called a *thesis statement* (rather than, as in a paragraph, a *topic sentence*). The thesis appears in the introductory paragraph, and the specific support for the thesis appears in the paragraphs that follow. The supporting paragraphs allow for a fuller treatment of the evidence that backs up the central point than would be possible in a single-paragraph paper. Unlike paragraphs that are usually developed using one mode of writing, like description, essays are usually developed using several modes of writing to support the single point.

Structure of the Traditional Essay
A Model Essay

The following model will help you understand the form of an essay. Diane Woods, the writer of the paragraph on moviegoing, later decided to develop her subject more fully. Here is the essay that resulted.

Introductory paragraph

First supporting paragraph

Second supporting paragraph

The Hazards of Moviegoing

I am a movie fanatic. My friends count on me to know movie trivia (who was the pigtailed little girl in *E.T.: The Extra-Terrestrial*? Drew Barrymore) and to remember every big Oscar awarded since I was in grade school (Best Picture, 1994? *Forrest Gump*). My friends, though, have stopped asking me if I want to go out to the movies. While I love movies as much as ever, the inconvenience of going out, the temptations of the concession stand, and the behavior of some patrons are reasons for me to wait and rent the DVD.

To begin with, I just don't enjoy the general hassle of the evening. Since small local movie theaters are a thing of the past, I have to drive for fifteen minutes to get to the nearest multiplex. The parking lot is shared with several restaurants and a supermarket, so it's always jammed. I have to drive around at a snail's pace until I spot another driver backing out. Then it's time to stand in an endless line, with the constant threat that tickets for the show I want will sell out. If we do get tickets, the theater will be so crowded that I won't be able to sit with my friends, or we'll have to sit in a front row gaping up at a giant screen. I have to shell out a ridiculous amount of money—up to $11—for a ticket. That entitles me to sit while my shoes seal themselves to a sticky floor coated with spilled soda, bubble gum, and crushed Raisinets.

Second, the theater offers tempting snacks that I really don't need. Like most of us, I have to battle an expanding waistline. At home I do pretty well by simply not buying stuff that is bad for me. I can make do with snacks like celery and carrot sticks because there is no ice cream in the freezer. Going to the theater, however, is like spending my evening in a 7-Eleven that's been equipped with a movie screen and comfortable seats. As I try to persuade myself to just have a Diet Coke, the smell of fresh popcorn dripping with butter soon overcomes me. Chocolate bars the size of small automobiles seem to jump into my hands. I risk pulling out my fillings as I chew enormous

continued

mouthfuls of Milk Duds. By the time I leave the theater, I feel disgusted with myself.

Many of the other patrons are even more of a problem than the concession stand. Little kids race up and down the aisles, usually in giggling packs. Teenagers try to impress their friends by talking back to the screen, whistling, and making what they consider to be hilarious noises. Adults act as if they were at home in their own living room. They comment loudly on the ages of the stars and reveal plot twists that are supposed to be a secret until the film's end. And people of all ages create distractions. They crinkle candy wrappers, stick gum on their seats, and drop popcorn tubs or cups of crushed ice and soda on the floor. They also cough and burp, squirm endlessly in their seats, file out for repeated trips to the restrooms or concession stands, and elbow me out of the armrest on either side of my seat.

Third supporting paragraph

After arriving home from the movies one night, I decided that I was not going to be a moviegoer anymore. I was tired of the problems involved in getting to the theater, resisting unhealthy snacks, and dealing with the patrons. The next day, I arranged to have premium movie channels added to my cable TV service, and I also got a Netflix membership. I may now see movies a bit later than other people, but I'll be more relaxed watching box office hits in the comfort of my own living room.

Concluding paragraph

Parts of an Essay

"The Hazards of Moviegoing" is a good example of the standard short essay you will write in college English. It is a composition of over five hundred words that consists of a one-paragraph introduction, a three-paragraph body, and a one-paragraph conclusion. The roles of these paragraphs are described and illustrated below.

Introductory Paragraph

The introductory paragraph of an essay should start with several sentences that attract the reader's interest. It should then advance the central idea, or *thesis*, that will be developed in the essay. The thesis often includes a *plan of development*—a "preview" of the major points that will support the thesis. These supporting points should be listed in the order in which they will appear in the essay. Such a thesis might assert, "Winter is my favorite season because I like the weather, the holidays, and the sports," leading to an essay that has a paragraph about weather, followed by a paragraph about winter holidays, and so on. In some cases, however, the plan of development is omitted. For example, a thesis that claims, "Education can be a key to socioeconomic security," doesn't state how the essay will be developed, but still advances a central idea.

ACTIVITY 2

1. In "The Hazards of Moviegoing," which sentence or sentences are used to attract the reader's interest?

   a. First sentence

   b. First two sentences

   c. First three sentences

2. In which sentence is the thesis of the essay presented?

   a. Third sentence

   b. Fourth sentence

3. Does the thesis include a plan of development?

   a. Yes

   b. No

4. Write the words in the thesis that announce the three major supporting points in the essay:

   a. _____

   b. _____

   c. _____

Body: Supporting Paragraphs

Many essays have three supporting points, developed at length over three separate paragraphs. However, more developed essays require four or more body paragraphs to support the thesis. This is very common in essays with thesis statements that omit a plan of development. Each of the supporting paragraphs should begin with a *topic sentence* that states the point to be detailed in that paragraph. Just as a thesis provides a focus for the entire essay, the topic sentence provides a focus for a supporting paragraph.

ACTIVITY 3

1. What is the topic sentence for the first supporting paragraph of the model essay?

   _____

   _____

2. The first topic sentence is then supported by the following details (fill in the missing details):

   a. Have to drive fifteen minutes

   b. _____

   c. Endless ticket line

d. _____

e. _____

f. Sticky floor

3. What is the topic sentence for the second supporting paragraph of the essay?

_____

_____

4. The second topic sentence is then supported by the following details:

   a. At home, only snacks are celery and carrot sticks.

   b. Theater is like a 7-Eleven with seats.

      (1) Fresh popcorn

      (2) _____

      (3) _____

5. What is the topic sentence for the third supporting paragraph of the essay?

_____

_____

_____

6. The third topic sentence is then supported by the following details:

   a. _____

   b. _____

   c. Adults talk loudly and reveal plot twists.

   d. People of all ages create distractions.

Concluding Paragraph

The concluding paragraph often summarizes the essay by briefly restating the thesis and, at times, the main supporting points. In addition, the writer often presents a concluding thought about the subject of the paper.

1. Which two sentences in the concluding paragraph restate the thesis and supporting points of the essay?

   a. First and second

   b. Second and third

   c. Third and fourth

ACTIVITY 4

2. Which sentence in the concluding paragraph contains the final thought of the essay?

    a. Second

    b. Third

    c. Fourth

Diagram of an Essay

The following diagram shows you at a glance the different parts of a standard college essay, also known as a *one-three-one-essay*. This diagram will serve as a helpful guide when you are writing or evaluating essays.

TITLE OF THE ESSAY

Introduction

Opening remarks to catch reader's interest
Thesis statement
Plan of development (optional)

Body

Topic sentence 1 (supporting point 1)
Specific evidence

Topic sentence 2 (supporting point 2)
Specific evidence

Topic sentence 3 (supporting point 3)
Specific evidence

Conclusion

Summary (optional)
General closing remarks
(Or both)

You now have an overview of the traditional form of the essay. In Chapter 2, you will learn *how* to go about writing an effective essay. First, though, it will be helpful to consider the following: the benefits of writing traditional essays, the advantage of seeing writing as both a skill and a process of discovery, the value of keeping a journal, and the ways a computer can enhance the writing process.

Benefits of Writing the Traditional Essay

Learning to write a traditional essay offers at least three benefits. First of all, mastering the traditional essay will help make you a better writer. For other courses, you'll often compose papers that will be variations on the essay form—for example, examination essays, reports, and research papers. Becoming comfortable with the basic structure of the traditional essay, with its emphasis on a clear point and well-organized, logical support, will help with almost every kind of writing that you have to do.

Second, the discipline of writing an essay will strengthen your skills as a reader and listener. As a reader, you'll become more critically aware of other writers' ideas and the evidence they provide (or fail to provide) to support those ideas. Essay writing will also help you become a better speaker. You'll be more prepared to develop the three basic parts of an effective speech—an appealing introduction, a solidly developed body, and a well-rounded conclusion—because of your experience writing three-part essays.

Most important, essay writing will make you a stronger thinker. Writing a solidly reasoned traditional essay requires mental discipline and close attention to a set of logical rules. Creating an essay in which there is an overall thesis statement and in which each of three supporting paragraphs begins with a topic sentence is more challenging than writing a free-form or expressive paper. Such an essay obliges you to carefully sort out, think through, and organize your ideas. You'll learn to discover and express just what your ideas are and to develop those ideas in a logical, reasoned way. Traditional essay writing, in short, will train your mind to think clearly, and that ability will prove to be of value in every phase of your life.

Writing as a Skill

A realistic attitude about writing must build on the idea that *writing is a skill,* not a "natural gift." It is a skill like driving, typing, or cooking; and, like any skill, it can be learned. If you have the determination to learn, this book will give you the extensive practice needed to develop your writing skills.

People often fear they are the only ones for whom writing is unbearably difficult. They believe that everyone else finds writing easy or at least tolerable. Such people typically say, "I'm not any good at writing," or "English was not one of my good subjects." They imply that they simply do not have a talent for writing, while others do. Often, the result of this attitude is that people try to avoid writing, and when they do write, they don't try their best. Their attitude becomes a self-fulfilling prophecy: their writing fails chiefly because they have brainwashed themselves into thinking that they don't have the "natural talent" needed to write.

Many people find it difficult to do the intense, active thinking that clear writing demands. It is frightening to sit down before a blank sheet of paper or computer screen and know that an hour later, nothing on it may be worth keeping. It is frustrating to discover how much of a challenge it is to transfer thoughts and feelings from one's head onto the page. It is upsetting to find that an apparently simple subject often turns out to be complicated. But writing is not an automatic process: we will not get something for nothing—and we should not expect to. For almost everyone, competent writing comes from plain hard work—from determination, sweat, and head-on battle. The good news is that the skill of writing can be mastered, and if you are ready to work, you will learn what you need to know.

Writing as a Process of Discovery

In addition to believing that writing is a natural gift, many people falsely believe that writing should flow in a simple, straight line from the writer's head onto the written page. But writing is seldom an easy, one-step journey in which a finished paper comes out in a first draft. The truth is that *writing is a process of discovery* involving a series of steps, and those steps are very often a zigzag journey. Look at the following illustrations of the writing process:

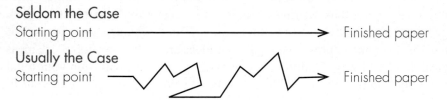

Very often, writers do not discover just what they want to write about until they explore their thoughts in writing. For example, Diane Woods (the author of the paragraph and essay on moviegoing) had been assigned to write about an annoyance in everyday life. She did not know what annoyance she would choose; instead, she just began writing about annoyances in general, in order to discover a topic. One of those annoyances was traffic, which seemed promising, so she began putting down ideas and details that came to her about traffic. One detail was the traffic she had to deal with in going to the movies. That made her think of the traffic in the parking lot at the theater complex. At that point, she realized that moviegoing itself was an annoyance. She switched direction in midstream and began writing down ideas and details about moviegoing.

As Diane wrote, she realized how much other moviegoers annoyed her, and she began thinking that other movie patrons might be her main idea in a paper. But when she was writing about patrons who loudly drop popcorn tubs onto the floor, she realized how much all the snacks at the concession stand tempted her. She changed direction again, thinking now that maybe she could talk about patrons and tempting snacks. She kept writing, just putting down more and more details about her movie experiences, still not having figured out exactly how she would fit both patrons and snacks into the paper. Even though her paper had not quite jelled, she was not worried, because she knew that if she kept writing, it would eventually come together.

The point is that writing is often a process of continuing discovery; as you write, you may suddenly switch direction or double back. You may be working on a topic sentence and realize suddenly that it could be your concluding thought. Or you may be developing a supporting idea and then decide that it should be the main point of your paper. Chapter 2 will treat the writing process more directly. What is important to remember here is that writers frequently do not know their exact destination as they begin to write. Very often they discover the direction and shape of a paper during the process of writing.

Writing as a Way to Communicate with Others

When you talk, chances are you do not treat everyone the same. For example, you are unlikely to speak to your boss in the same way that you chat with a young child. Instead, you adjust what you say to suit the people who are listening to you—your *audience*. Similarly, you probably change your speech each day to suit whatever *purpose* you have in mind when you are speaking. For instance, if you wanted to tell someone how to get to your new apartment, you would speak differently than if you were describing your favorite movie.

To communicate effectively, people must constantly adjust their speech to suit their purpose and audience. This same idea is true for writing. When you write for others, it is crucial to know both your purpose for writing and the audience who will be reading your work. The ability to adjust your writing to suit your purpose and audience will serve you well not only in the classroom but also in the workplace and beyond.

> TIP   Purpose and audience, further explained on page 176, are special focuses of each of the nine patterns of essay development in Part 2.

Keeping a Journal

Because writing is a skill, it makes sense that the more you practice writing, the better you will write. One excellent way to get practice in writing, even before you begin composing essays, is to keep a daily or almost daily journal. Writing in a journal will help you develop the habit of thinking on paper and will show you how ideas can be discovered in the process of writing. A journal can make writing a familiar part of your life and can serve as a continuing source of ideas for papers.

At some point during the day—perhaps during a study period after your last class of the day, or right before dinner, or right before going to bed—spend fifteen minutes or so writing in your journal. Keep in mind that you do not have to plan what to write about, or be in the mood to write, or worry about making mistakes as you write; just write down whatever words come out. You should write at least one page in each session.

You may want to use a notebook that you can easily carry with you for on-the-spot writing. Or you may decide to write on loose-leaf paper that can be transferred later to a journal folder on your desk. Many students choose to keep their journals on their home computer or laptop. No matter how you proceed, be sure to date all entries.

Your instructor may ask you to make journal entries a specific number of times a week, for a specific number of weeks. He or she may have you turn in your journal every so often for review and feedback. If you are keeping the journal on your own, try to make entries three to five times a week every week of the semester.

Tips on Using a Computer

- If you are using your school's computer center, allow enough time. You may have to wait for a computer or printer to be free. In addition, you may need several sessions at a computer and printer to complete your paper.

- Every word-processing program allows you to save your writing by pressing one or more keys. Save your work frequently as you write your draft. A saved file is stored safely on the computer or network. A file that is not saved will be lost if the computer crashes or if the power is turned off.

- Keep your work in two places—the hard drive or network you are working on and a backup USB drive. At the end of each session with a computer, copy your work onto the USB drive or e-mail a copy to yourself. Then, if the hard drive or network fails, you'll have the backup copy.

- Print out your work at least at the end of every session. Then you will have not only your most recent draft to work on away from the computer but also a copy in case something should happen to your electronic file.

- Work in single spacing so that you can see as much of your writing on the screen at one time as possible. Just before you print out your work, change to double spacing.

- Before making major changes in a paper, create a copy of your file. For example, if your file is titled "Worst Job," create a file called "Worst Job 2." Then make all your changes in that new file. If the changes don't work out, you can always go back to the original file.

Using a Computer at Each Stage of the Writing Process

Following are some ways to make word processing a part of your writing. Note that this section may be more meaningful *after* you have worked through Chapter 2 of this book.

Prewriting

If you're a fast typist, many kinds of prewriting will work well on a computer. With freewriting in particular, you can get ideas onto the screen almost as quickly as they occur to you. A passing thought that could be productive is not likely to get lost. You may even find it helpful, when freewriting, to dim the monitor screen so that you can't see what you're typing. If you temporarily can't see the screen, you won't have to worry about grammar or spelling or typing errors (all of which do not matter in prewriting); instead, you can concentrate on getting down as many ideas and details as possible about your subject.

After any initial freewriting, questioning, and list-making on a computer, it's often very helpful to print out a hard copy of what you've done. With a clean print-out in front of you, you'll be able to see everything at once and revise and expand your work with handwritten comments in the margins of the paper.

If you have prepared a list of items, you may be able to turn that list into an outline right on the screen. Delete the ideas you feel should not be in your paper (saving them at the bottom of the page in case you change your mind), and add any new ideas that occur to you. Then use the cut and paste functions to shuffle the supporting ideas around until you find the best order for your paper.

Word processing also makes it easy for you to experiment with the wording of the point of your paper. You can try a number of versions in a short time. After you have decided on the version that works best, you can easily delete the other versions—or simply move them to a temporary "leftover" section at the end of the paper.

Writing Your First Draft

Like many writers, you may want to write out your first draft by hand and then type it into the computer for revision. Even as you type your handwritten draft, you may find yourself making some changes and improvements. And once you have a draft on the screen, or printed out, you will find it much easier to revise than a handwritten one.

If you feel comfortable composing directly on a computer, you can benefit from its special features. For example, if you have written an anecdote in your freewriting that you plan to use in your paper, simply copy the story from your freewriting file and insert it where it fits in your paper. You can refine it then or later. Or if you discover while typing that a sentence is out of place, cut it out from where it is and paste it wherever you wish. And if while writing you realize that an earlier sentence can be expanded, just move your cursor back to that point and type in the additional material.

Revising

It is during revision that the virtues of word processing really shine. All substituting, adding, deleting, and rearranging can be done easily within an existing file. All changes instantly take their proper places within the paper, not scribbled above the line or squeezed into the margin. You can concentrate on each change you want to make, because you never have to type from scratch or work on a messy draft. You can carefully go through your paper to check that all your supporting evidence is relevant and to add new support as needed here and there. Anything you decide to eliminate can be deleted in a keystroke. Anything you add can be inserted precisely where you choose. If you change your mind, all you have to do is delete or cut and paste. Then you can sweep through the paper, focusing on other changes, such as improving word choice, increasing sentence variety, and eliminating wordiness.

> **TIP** If you are like many students, you might find it convenient to print out a hard copy of your file at various points throughout the revision. You can then revise in longhand—adding, crossing out, and indicating changes—and later quickly make those changes in the document.

Editing and Proofreading

Editing and proofreading also benefit richly from word processing. Instead of crossing out mistakes, using correction fluid, or rewriting an entire paper to correct numerous errors, you can make all necessary changes within the most recent draft. If you find editing or proofreading on the screen hard on your eyes, print out a copy. Mark any corrections on that copy, and then transfer them to the final draft.

If the word-processing program you're using includes spelling and grammar checks, by all means use them. The spell-checker function tells you when a word is not in the program's dictionary. Keep in mind, however, that the spell-checker cannot tell you how to spell a name correctly or when you have mistakenly used, for example, *their* instead of *there*. To a spell-checker, *Thank ewe four the complement* is as correct as *Thank you for the compliment*. Also, use the grammar-checker with caution. Any errors it doesn't uncover are still your responsibility.

A word-processed paper, with its clean appearance and handsome formatting, looks so good that you may feel it is in better shape than it really is. Do not be fooled. Take sufficient time to review your grammar, punctuation, and spelling carefully.

Even after you hand in your paper, save the computer file. Your teacher may ask you to do some revising, and then the file will save you from having to type the paper from scratch.

Review Activities

Answering the following questions will help you evaluate your attitude about writing.

ACTIVITY 5

1. How much practice were you given writing compositions in high school?

    _____ Much _____ Some _____ Little

2. How much feedback (positive or negative comments) from teachers were you given on your compositions?

    _____ Much _____ Some _____ Little

3. How did your teachers seem to regard your writing?

    _____ Good _____ Fair _____ Poor

4. Do you feel that some people simply have a gift for writing and others do not?

    _____ Yes _____ Sometimes _____ No

5. When do you start writing a paper?

    _____ Several days before it is due

    _____ About a day before it is due

    _____ At the last possible minute

EXPLANATION: Many people who answer *Little* to questions 1 and 2 often answer *Poor, Yes,* and *At the last possible minute* to questions 3, 4, and 5. On the other hand, people who answer *Much* or *Some* to questions 1 and 2 also tend to have more favorable responses to the other questions. The point is that people with little practice in the skill of writing often have understandably negative feelings about their writing ability. They need not have such feelings, however, because writing is a skill that they can learn with practice.

---

6. What kinds of writing do you do on a computer? What additional types of writing might you want to undertake on the computer?

    _____

    _____

    _____

7. Have you ever kept a diary or journal like the one explained in this chapter? If so, what kinds of ideas, images, or other information have you put into your journal? If you have never kept a journal, why not? Does this fact have anything to do with how you think of writing?

    _____

    _____

    _____

8. In your own words, explain what it means to say that writing is often a zigzag journey rather than a straight-line journey.

    _____

    _____

    _____

    _____

    _____

Following is an excerpt from one student's journal. As you read, look for a general point and supporting material that could be the basis for an interesting paper.

ACTIVITY 6

Personal

September 12

   I received the results of my first history test today. I really thought I had studied a lot, but my grade was terrible. In high school, I never needed to study much, and I still received As and Bs. My teachers always provided a study guide of some sort and working through it usually guaranteed a good grade. My history professor didn't give us anything to study from. When I asked about a study guide, I was told that our text, notes, and PowerPoints were the study guide. How was I supposed to figure out what was and wasn't important? At first I was really angry at my professor that she hadn't helped me more. It was hard to sit through the class listening to her go over the exam and reprimanding the class for not doing well. I felt like telling her that maybe it was her fault if so many people did poorly. When class was over, I ended up storming out, promising myself that I was going to complain to the dean. I headed to the dean's office to formally complain, but was told by the assistant that if I hadn't spoken to my professor first, the dean wasn't going to listen to my complaint. As upset as I was, I headed back to my professor's office and waited for her. When she arrived, she seemed really pleased to see me. I was totally surprised! She told me she was happy that I was coming in to talk about my test and would be more than pleased to show me where I had gone

continued

wrong. After forty-five minutes, I completely understood what I had missed and what I needed to do for future tests. Our meeting ended with my professor making me promise to visit her again—before the next exam—to make sure I understood the material. I learned a lot more from this test than just history! I now realize that professors expect us to take responsibility for our learning, which means going to see them for help and not waiting for them to spoon-feed us.

1. If the writer of the journal entry above was looking for ideas for an essay, she could probably find several in this single entry. For example, she might write a story about the differences between high school teachers and college professors. See if you can find an idea in the entry that might be the basis for an interesting essay, and write your point in the space below.

_____

2. Take fifteen minutes now to write a journal entry on this day in your life. On a separate sheet of paper, just start writing about anything that you have seen, said, heard, thought, or felt today, and let your thoughts take you where they may.

Using This Text

Here is a suggested sequence for using this book if you are working on your own.

1. After completing this introduction, read Chapters 2 through 6 in Part 1 and work through as many of the activities as you need to master the ideas in these chapters. By the end of Part 1, you will have covered all the basic theory needed to write effective papers.

2. Work through some of the chapters in Part 2, which describe a number of ways to organize and develop essays. You may want to integrate "Exemplification," "Process," and "Argument." Each chapter opens with a brief introduction to a specific pattern, followed by two student essays and one professional essay written in a way that emphasizes that pattern. Included are a series of questions so that you can evaluate the essays in terms of the basic principles of writing explained in Part 1. Finally, a number of writing topics are presented, along with hints about prewriting and revising to help you plan and write an effective paper.

3. Turn to Part 3 as needed for help with types of writing you will do in college: exam essays, summaries, reports, the résumé and cover letter, and the research paper. You will see that these kinds of writing are variations of the essay form you have already learned.

4. In addition, refer to Part 4 as needed for review and practice in the skills needed to write effective, error-free sentences.

5. Finally, read some of the selections in Part 5 and respond to the activities that follow the selections.

For your convenience, the book includes the following:

- On the inside back cover, there is a checklist of the four basic steps in effective writing.
- On page 620, there is a list of commonly used correction symbols.

Get into the habit of regularly referring to these guides; they'll help you produce clearly thought-out, well-written essays.

College Writing Skills with Readings will help you learn, practice, and apply the thinking and writing skills you need to communicate effectively. But the starting point must be your own determination to do the work needed to become a strong writer. The ability to express yourself clearly and logically can open doors of opportunity for you, both in school and in your career. If you decide—and only you can decide—that you want such language power, this book will help you reach that goal.

The Writing Process

This chapter will explain and illustrate
- the sequence of steps in writing an effective essay
- prewriting
- revising
- editing

Think about an electronic device you use everyday; it could be your cell phone, radio, computer, iPod, iPad, etc. See if you can write for ten minutes about why you couldn't live without it. Don't worry about spelling and punctuation; just get your thoughts down on paper.

Chapter 1 introduced you to the essay form and to some basics of writing. This chapter explains and illustrates the sequence of steps in writing an effective essay. In particular, the chapter focuses on prewriting and revising—strategies that can help with every essay you write.

For many people, writing is a process that involves the following steps:

1. Discovering a thesis—often through prewriting.

2. Developing solid support for the thesis—often through more prewriting.

3. Organizing the thesis and supporting material and writing it out in a first draft.

4. Revising and then editing carefully to ensure an effective, error-free essay.

Learning this sequence will help give you confidence when the time comes to write. You'll know that you can use prewriting as a way to think on paper and to gradually discover just what ideas you want to develop. You'll understand that there are four clear-cut goals—unity, support, organization, and error-free sentences—to aim for in your writing. You'll realize that you can use revision to rework an essay until it is a strong and effective piece of writing. And you'll be able to edit your writing so that your sentences are clear and error free.

Prewriting

If you are like many people, you may have trouble getting started with writing. A mental block may develop when you sit down before a blank sheet of paper. You may not be able to think of an interesting topic or thesis. Or you may have trouble coming up with relevant details to support a possible thesis. And even after starting an essay, you may hit snags—moments when you wonder, What else can I say? or Where do I go next?

The following pages describe five prewriting techniques that will help you think about and develop a topic and get words on paper: (1) freewriting, (2) questioning, (3) making a list, (4) clustering, and (5) preparing a scratch outline. These techniques help you think about and create material, and they are a central part of the writing process.

Technique 1: Freewriting

Freewriting means jotting down in rough sentences or phrases everything that comes to mind about a possible topic. See if you can write nonstop for ten minutes or more. Do not worry about spelling or punctuating correctly, about erasing mistakes, about organizing material, or about finding exact words. Instead, explore an idea by putting down whatever pops into your head. If you get stuck for words, repeat yourself until more words come. There is no need to feel inhibited, since mistakes *do not count* and you do not have to hand in your freewriting.

Freewriting will limber up your writing muscles and make you familiar with the act of writing. It is a way to break through mental blocks about writing. Since you do not have to worry about mistakes, you can focus on discovering what you want to say about a subject. Your initial ideas and impressions will often become clearer after you have gotten them down on paper, and they may lead to other impressions and ideas. Through continued practice in free-writing, you will develop the habit of thinking as you write. And you will learn a helpful technique for getting started on almost any writing you have to do.

Freewriting: A Student Model

Diane Woods's essay "The Hazards of Moviegoing" on pages 6–7 was developed in response to an assignment to write about some annoyance in everyday life. Diane began by doing some general freewriting and thinking about things that annoy her. Here is her freewriting:

Personal

> There are lots of things I get annoyed by. One of them that comes to mind is politishans, in fact I am so annoyed by them that I don't want to say anything about them the last thing I want is to write about them. Another thing that bothers me are people who keep complaining about everything. If you're having trouble, do something about it just don't keep complaining and just talking. I am really annoyed by traffic. There are too many cars in our block and its not surprising. Everyone has a car, the parents have cars and the parents are just too induljent and the kids have cars, and theyre all coming and going all the time and often driving too fast. Speeding up and down the street. We need a speed limit sign but here I am back with politiks again. I am really bothered when I have to drive to the movies all the congestion along the way plus there are just so many cars there at the mall. No space even though the parking lot is huge it just fills up with cars. Movies are a bother anyway because the people can be annoying who are sitting there in the theater with you, talking and dropping popcorn cups and acting like they're at home when they're not.

At this point, Diane read over her notes and, as she later commented, "I realized that I had several potential topics. I said to myself, 'What point can I make that I can cover in an essay? What do I have the most information about?' I decided that maybe I could narrow my topic down to the annoyances involved in going to the movies. I figured I would have more details for that topic." Diane then did more focused freewriting to accumulate details for an essay on problems with moviegoing:

> I really find it annoying to go see movies anymore. Even though I love films. Traffic to Cinema Six is awful. I hate looking for a parking place, the lot isn't big enough for the theaters and other stores. You just keep driving to find a parking space and hoping someone will pull out and no one else will pull in ahead of you. Then you don't want there to be a long line and to wind up in one of the first rows with this huge screen right in front of you. Then I'm in the theater with the smell of popcorn all around. Sitting there smelling it trying to ignore it and just wanting to pour a whole bucket of popcorn with melted butter down my throat. I can't stop thinking about the choclate bars either. I love the stuff but I don't need it. The people who are there sometimes drive me nuts. Talking and laughing, kids running around, packs of teens hollaring, who can listen to the movie? And I might run into my old boyfriend—the last thing I need. Also sitting thru all the previews and commercals. If I arrive late enough to miss that junk the movie may be selled out.

Notice that there are errors in spelling, grammar, and punctuation in Diane's freewriting. Diane is not worried about such matters, nor should she be. At this stage, she just wants to do some thinking on paper and get some material down on the page. She knows that this is a good first step, a good way of getting started, and that she will then be able to go on and shape the material.

You should take the same approach when freewriting: explore your topic without worrying at all about being correct. Figuring out what you want to say and getting raw material down on the page should have all of your attention at this early stage of the writing process.

To get a sense of the freewriting process, take a sheet of paper and freewrite about some of the everyday annoyances in your life. See how much material you can accumulate in ten minutes. And remember not to worry about mistakes; you're just thinking on paper.

ACTIVITY 1

Technique 2: Questioning

In *questioning,* you generate ideas and details by asking questions about your subject. Such questions include *why, when, where, who, what,* and *how.* Ask as many questions as you can think of.

Questioning: A Student Model

Here are some questions that Diane Woods might have asked while developing her essay.

Questions	Answers
<u>Why</u> don't I like to go to a movie?	Just too many problems involved.
<u>When</u> is going to the movies a problem?	Could be any time—when a movie is popular, the theater is too crowded; when traffic is bad, the trip is a drag.
<u>Where</u> are problems with moviegoing?	On the highway, in the parking lot, at the concession stand, in the theater itself.
<u>Who</u> creates the problems?	I do by wanting to eat too much. The patrons do by creating disturbances. The theater owners do by not having enough parking space and showing too many commercials.
<u>How</u> can I deal with the problem?	I can stay home and watch movies on DVD or cable TV.

Asking questions can be an effective way of getting yourself to think about a topic from a number of different angles. The questions can really help you generate details about a topic.

ACTIVITY 2

To get a sense of the questioning process, use a sheet of paper to ask yourself a series of questions about a good or bad experience that you have had recently. See how many details you can accumulate in ten minutes. And remember again not to be concerned about mistakes, because you are just thinking on paper.

Technique 3: Making a List

In *making a list*, also known as *brainstorming*, you collect ideas and details that relate to your subject. Pile these items up, one after another, without trying to sort out major details from minor ones or trying to put the details in any special order. Your goal is just to make a list of everything about your subject that occurs to you.

Making a List: A Student Model

After Diane did her freewriting about moviegoing, she made up the following list
of details.

Traffic is bad between my house and theater

Noisy patrons

Don't want to run into Jeremy

Hard to be on a diet

Kids running in aisles

I'm crowded into seats between strangers who push me off armrests

Not enough parking

Parking lot needs to be expanded

Too many previews

Can't pause or fast-forward as you can with a DVD

Long lines

High ticket prices

Too many temptatons at snack stand

Commercials for food on the screen

Can prepare healthy snacks for myself at home

Tubs of popcorn with butter

Huge choclate bars

Candy has always been my downfall

Movie may be sold out

People who've seen movie before talk along with actors and give away plot twists

People coughing and sneezing

Icky stuff on floor

Teenagers yelling and showing off

One detail led to another as Diane expanded her list. Slowly but surely, more
details emerged, some of which she could use in developing her paper. By the time

she was done with her list, she was ready to plan an outline of her paragraph and
then to write her first draft.

ACTIVITY 3

To get a sense of list-making, list on a sheet of paper a series of realistic goals,
major or minor, that you would like to accomplish between today and one year
from today. Your goals can be personal, academic, or career-related.

Technique 4: Clustering

Clustering, also known as *diagramming* or *mapping*, is another strategy that can be
used to generate material for an essay. This method is helpful for people who like
to do their thinking in a visual way. In clustering, you use lines, boxes, arrows, and
circles to show relationships among the ideas and details that occur to you.

Begin by stating your subject in a few words in the center of a blank sheet of
paper. Then, as ideas and details come to you, put them in boxes or circles around
the subject and draw lines to connect them to each other and to the subject. Put
minor ideas or details in smaller boxes or circles, and use connecting lines to show
how they relate as well.

Clustering: A Student Model

Keep in mind that there is no right or wrong way of clustering or diagramming. It
is a way to think on paper about how various ideas and details relate to one another.
Below is an example of what Diane might have done to develop her ideas.

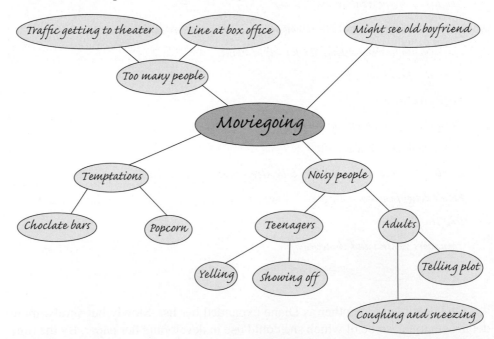

> ## TIP
> In addition to helping generate material, clustering can give you an early sense of how ideas and details relate to one another. For example, the cluster for Diane's essay suggests that different kinds of noisy people could be the focus of one paragraph and that different kinds of temptations could be the focus of another paragraph.

Use clustering (diagramming) to organize the list of year-ahead goals that you created for the previous activity (page 28).

ACTIVITY 4

Technique 5: Preparing a Scratch Outline

A *scratch outline* is an excellent sequel to the first four prewriting techniques. A scratch outline often follows freewriting, questioning, list-making, or diagramming; or it may gradually emerge in the midst of these strategies. In fact, trying to make a scratch outline is a good way to see if you need to do more prewriting. If you cannot come up with a solid outline, then you know you need to do more prewriting to clarify your main point or its several kinds of support.

In a scratch outline, you think carefully about the point you are making, the supporting items for that point, and the order in which you will arrange those items. The scratch outline is a plan or blueprint to help you achieve a unified, supported, well-organized essay.

When you are planning a traditional essay consisting of an introduction, three supporting paragraphs, and a conclusion, a scratch outline is especially important. It may be only a few words, but it will be the framework on which your whole essay will be built.

Scratch Outline: A Student Model

As Diane was working on her list of details, she suddenly realized what the plan of her essay could be. She could organize many of her details into one of three supporting groups: (1) annoyances in going out, (2) too many tempting snacks, and (3) other people. She then went back to the list, crossed out items that she now saw did not fit, and numbered the items according to the group where they fit. Here is what Diane did with her list:

1   *Traffic is bad between my house and the theater*

3   *Noisy patrons*

~~*Don't want to run into Jeremy*~~

continued

2   Hard to be on a diet

3   Kids running in aisles

3   I'm crowded into seats between strangers who push me off armrests

1   Not enough parking

1   Parking lot needs to be expanded

1   Too many previews

~~Can't pause or fast-forward as you can with a DVD~~

1   Long lines

1   High ticket prices

2   Too many temptations at snack stand

~~Commercials for food on the screen~~

2   Can prepare healthy snacks for myself at home

2   Tubs of popcorn with butter

~~Candy has always been my downfall~~

2   Huge choclate bars

1   Movie may be sold out

3   People who've seen movie before talk along with actors and give away plot twists

3   People coughing and sneezing

1   Icky stuff on floor

3   Teenagers yelling and showing off

Under the list, Diane was now able to prepare her scratch outline:

Going to the movies offers some real problems.

1.   Inconvenience of going out

2.   Tempting snacks

3.   Other moviegoers

After all her prewriting, Diane was pleased. She knew that she had a promising essay—one with a clear point and solid support. She saw that she could organize the material into a traditional essay consisting of an introduction, several supporting paragraphs, and a conclusion. She was now ready to write the first draft of her essay, using her outline as a guide.

> **TIP** Chances are that if you do enough prewriting and thinking on paper, you will eventually discover the point and support of your essay.

Create a scratch outline that could serve as a guide if you were to write an essay about your year-ahead goals.

ACTIVITY 5

Writing a First Draft

When you write a first draft, be prepared to put in additional thoughts and details that did not emerge during prewriting. And don't worry if you hit a snag. Just leave a blank space or add a comment such as "Do later" and press on to finish the essay. Also, don't worry yet about grammar, punctuation, or spelling. You don't want to take time correcting words or sentences that you may decide to remove later. Instead, make it your goal to state your thesis clearly and develop the content of your essay with plenty of specific details.

Writing a First Draft: A Student Model

Here is Diane's first draft:

Even though I love movies, my friends have stopped asking me to go. There are just too many problems involved in going to the movies.

There are no small theaters anymore, I have to drive fifteen minutes to a big multaplex. Because of a supermarket and restarants, the parking lot is filled. I have to keep driving around to find a space. Then I have to stand in a long line. Hoping that they do not run out of tickets. Finally, I have to pay too much money for a ticket. Putting out that much money, I should not have to deal with a floor that ~~is sticky~~ seems coated with rubber cement. By the end of a movie, my shoes are often sealed to a mix of spilled soda, bubble gum, and other stuff.

continued

The theater offers temptations in the form of snacks I really don't need. Like most of us I have to worry about weight gain. At home I do pretty well by simply watching what I keep in the house and not buying stuff that is bad for me. I can make do with healthy snacks because there is nothing in the house. Going to the theater is like spending my evening in a ~~market~~ 7-Eleven that's been equiped with a movie screen and there are seats which are comfortable. I try to persuade myself to just have a diet soda. The smell of popcorn soon overcomes me. My friends are as bad as I am. Choclate bars seem to jump into your hands, I am eating enormous mouthfuls of milk duds. By the time I leave the theater I feel sick and tired of myself.

Some of the other moviegoers are the worst problem. There are teenagers who try to impress their friends in one way or another. Little kids race up and down the aisles, gigling and laughing. Adults act as if they're watching the movie at home. They talk loudly about the ages of the stars and give away the plot. Other people are droping popcorn tubs or cups of soda crushed ice and soda on the floor. Also coughing a lot and doing other stuff—bms!

I decided one night that I was not going to be a moviegoer anymore. I joined Netflix, and I'll watch movies comfortable in my own living room.

TIP After Diane finished the first draft, she was able to put it aside until the next day. You will benefit as well if you can allow some time between finishing a draft and starting to revise.

ACTIVITY 6

Team up with someone in your class and see if you can fill in the missing words in the following explanation of Diane's first draft.

1. Diane has a very brief introduction—no more than an opening sentence and a

   second sentence that states the _____. She knows she can develop the introduction more fully in a later draft.

2. Of Diane's three supporting paragraphs, only the _____ paragraph lacks a topic sentence. She realizes that this is something to work on in the next draft.

3. There are some misspellings—for example, _____. Diane doesn't worry about spelling at this point. She just wants to get down as much of the substance of her paper as possible.

4. There are various punctuation errors, such as the run-on sentences in the _____ paragraphs. Again, Diane is focusing on content; she knows she can attend to punctuation and grammar later.

5. At several points in the essay, Diane revises on the spot to make images more _____: she changes "is sticky" to "seems coated with rubber cement," "market" to "7-Eleven," and "cups of soda" to "cups of crushed ice and soda."

6. Near the end of her essay, Diane can't think of added details to insert so she simply puts the letters "_____" at that point to remind herself to "be more specific" in the next draft. She then goes on to finish her first draft.

7. Her _____ is as brief as her introduction. Diane knows she can round off her essay more fully during revision.

Revising

Revising is as much a stage in the writing process as prewriting, outlining, and doing the first draft. *Revising* means rewriting an essay, building on what has already been done, to make it stronger. One writer has said about revision, "It's like cleaning house—getting rid of all the junk and putting things in the right order." But it is not just "straightening up"; instead, you must be ready to roll up your sleeves and do whatever is needed to create an effective essay. Too many students think that the first draft *is* the essay. They start to become writers when they realize that revising a rough draft three or four times is often at the heart of the writing process.

Here are some quick hints that can help make revision easier. First, set your first draft aside for a while. A few hours will do, but a day or two would be better. You can then come back to the draft with a fresh, more objective point of view. Second, work from typed or printed text. You'll be able to see the essay more impartially in this way than if you were just looking at your own familiar handwriting. Next, read your draft aloud. Hearing how your writing sounds will help you pick up problems with meaning as well as with style. Finally, as you do all these things, add your thoughts and changes above the lines or in the margins of your essay. Your written comments can serve as a guide when you work on the next draft.

There are three stages to the revising process:

- revising content
- revising sentences
- editing

Revising Content

To revise the content of your essay, ask these questions:

1. Is my essay **unified**?
   - Do I have a thesis that is clearly stated or implied in the introductory paragraph of my essay?
   - Do all my supporting paragraphs truly support and back up my thesis?
2. Is my essay **supported**?
   - Are there three separate supporting points for the thesis?
   - Do I have specific evidence for each of the three supporting points?
   - Is there plenty of specific evidence for each supporting point?
3. Is my essay **organized**?
   - Do I have an interesting introduction, a solid conclusion, and an accurate title?
   - Do I have a clear method of organizing my essay?
   - Do I use transitions and other connecting words?

Chapters 3 and 4 will give you practice in achieving **unity, support,** and **organization** in your writing.

Revising Sentences

To revise sentences in your essay, ask yourself the following questions:

1. Do I use parallelism to balance my words and ideas?
2. Do I have a consistent point of view?
3. Do I use specific words?
4. Do I use active verbs?
5. Do I use words effectively by avoiding slang, clichés, pretentious language, and wordiness?
6. Do I vary my sentences?

Chapter 5 will give you practice in revising sentences.

Editing

After you have revised your essay for content and style, you are ready to *edit*—check for and correct—errors in grammar, punctuation, capitalization, sentence structure, word usage, and spelling. Students often find it hard to edit their writing carefully. They have put so much, or so little, work into their writing that it's almost painful for them to look at the essay one more time. You may simply have to *will* yourself to perform this important closing step in the writing process. Remember that eliminating sentence-skill mistakes will improve an average essay and help ensure a strong grade on a good essay. Further, as you get into the habit of checking your writing, you will also get into the habit of using the sentence skills consistently. They are an integral part of clear and effective writing.

Chapter 5 and Part 4 of this book will serve as a guide while you are editing your essay for mistakes in **sentence skills.**

An Illustration of the Revising and Editing Processes

Revising with a Second Draft: A Student Model

Since Diane Woods was using a word-processing program on a computer, she was able to print out a double-spaced version of her essay about movies, leaving her plenty of room for revisions. Here is one of her revised paragraphs:

second,
The theater offers ~~temptations in the form of~~ *tempting* snacks I really don't need. Like most of us I have to ~~worry about weight gain.~~ *battle an expanding waistline.* At home I do pretty well by simply ~~watching what I keep in the house and~~ not buying stuff that is bad for me. I can make do with ~~healthy~~ *like celery and carrot sticks* snacks because there is ~~nothing~~ *no ice cream* in the freezer. Going to the theater is like spending my evening in a 7-Eleven *however* that's been equiped with a movie screen and ~~there are~~ *comfortable* seats ~~which are comfortable.~~ *As* I try to persuade myself to just have a diet soda, *t*The smell of fresh popcorn *dripping with butter* soon overcomes me. ~~My friends are as bad as I am.~~ Choclate bars seem to jump into ~~your~~ *my* hands. I ~~am eating~~ *risk pulling out my fillings as I chew* enormous mouthfuls of milk duds. By the time I leave the theater I feel ~~out of sorts~~ *disgusted* with myself.

Diane made her changes in longhand as she worked on the second draft. As you will see when you complete the activity below, her revision serves to make the paragraph more unified, better supported, and better organized.

ACTIVITY 7   Fill in the missing words.

1. To achieve better organization, Diane adds at the beginning of the paragraph the transitional phrase "_____," making it very clear that her second supporting idea is tempting snacks.

2. Diane also adds the transition "_____" to show clearly the difference between being at home and being in the theater.

3. In the interest of (*unity, support, organization*) _____, Diane crosses out the sentence "_____." She realizes this sentence is not a relevant detail but really another topic.

4. To add more (*unity, support, organization*) _____, Diane changes "healthy snacks" to "_____"; she changes "nothing in the freezer" to "_____"; she adds "_____" after "popcorn"; and she changes "am eating" to "_____."

5. In the interest of eliminating wordiness, she removes the words "_____ _____" from the third sentence.

6. In the interest of parallelism, Diane changes "and there are seats which are comfortable" to "_____."

7. For greater sentence variety, Diane combines two short sentences, beginning the first sentence with the subordinating word "_____."

8. To create a consistent point of view, Diane changes "jump into your hands" to "_____."

9. Finally, Diane replaces the vague "out of sorts" with the more precise "_____."

Editing: A Student Model

After typing into her word-processing file all the changes in her second draft, Diane printed out another clean draft of the essay. The paragraph on tempting snacks required almost no more revision, so Diane turned her attention mostly to editing changes, illustrated below with her work on the second supporting paragraph:

> Second, the theater offers tempting snacks I really don't need. Like most of us, I have to battle an expanding waistline. At home I do pretty well by simply not buying stuff that is bad for me. I can make do with snacks like celery and carrot sticks because there is no ice cream in the freezer. Going to the theater, however, is like spending my evening in a 7-Eleven that's been ~~equiped~~ *equipped* with a movie screen and comfortable seats. As I try to persuade myself to just have a Diet ~~soda~~ *Coke*, the smell of fresh popcorn dripping with butter soon overcomes me. ~~Choclate~~ *Chocolate* bars *the size of small automobiles* seem to jump into my hands. I risk pulling out my fillings as I chew enormous mouthfuls of *M*ilk *D*uds. By the time I leave the theater, I feel disgusted with myself.

Once again, Diane makes her changes in longhand right on the printout of her essay. To note these changes, complete the activity below.

Fill in the missing words.

ACTIVITY 8

1. As part of her editing, Diane checked and corrected the _____ of two words, *equipped* and *chocolate*.

2. She added _____ to set off two introductory phrases ("Like most of us" in the second sentence and "By the time I leave the theater" in the final sentence) and also to set off the interrupting word *however* in the fifth sentence.

3. She realized that "milk duds" is a brand name and added _____ to make it "Milk Duds."

4. And since revision can occur at any stage of the writing process, including editing, she made one of her details more vivid by adding the descriptive words "_____."

Review Activities

You now have a good overview of the writing process, from prewriting to first draft to revising to editing. The remaining chapters in Part 1 will deepen your sense of the four goals of effective writing: unity, support, organization or coherence, and sentence skills.

To reinforce the information about the writing process that you have learned in this chapter, you can now work through the following activities:

- taking a writing inventory
- prewriting
- outlining
- revising

Taking a Writing Inventory

ACTIVITY 9

Answer the questions below to evaluate your approach to the writing process. This activity is not a test, so try to be as honest as possible. Becoming aware of your writing habits will help you realize changes that may be helpful.

1. When you start work on an essay, do you typically do any prewriting?

   _____ Yes   _____ Sometimes   _____ No

2. If so, which prewriting techniques do you use?

   _____ Freewriting   _____ Diagramming

   _____ Questioning   _____ Scratch outline

   _____ List-making   _____ Other (please describe)

   _____

3. Which prewriting technique or techniques work best for you, or which do you think will work best for you?

4. Many students say they find it helpful to handwrite a first draft and then type that draft on a computer. They then print out the draft and revise it by hand. Describe the way you proceed in drafting and revising an essay.

5. After you write the first draft of an essay, do you have time to set it aside for a while so that you can come back to it with a fresh eye?

   _____ Yes   _____ No

6. How many drafts do you typically write when working on an essay? _____

7. When you revise, are you aware that you should be working toward an essay that is unified, solidly supported, and clearly organized? Has this chapter given you a better sense that unity, support, and organization are goals to aim for?

8. Do you revise an essay for the effectiveness of its sentences as well as for its content?

   _____ Yes   _____ No

9. Do you typically do any editing of the almost-final draft of an essay, or do you tend to "hope for the best" and hand it in without careful checking?

   _____ Edit   _____ Hope for the best

10. What (if any) information has this chapter given you about *prewriting* that you will try to apply in your writing?

11. What (if any) information has this chapter given you about *revising* that you will try to apply in your writing?

12. What (if any) information has this chapter given you about *editing* that you will try to apply in your writing?

Prewriting

On the following pages are examples of how the five prewriting techniques could be used to develop the topic "Problems of Combining Work and College." Identify each technique by writing F (for freewriting), Q (for questioning), L (for list-making), C (for clustering), or SO (for the scratch outline) in the answer space.

ACTIVITY 10

_____   Never enough time

Miss campus parties

Had to study (only two free hours a night)

Give up activities with friends

No time to rewrite papers

Can't stay at school to play video games or talk to friends

Friends don't call me to go out anymore

Sunday no longer relaxed day—have to study
Missing sleep I should be getting
Grades aren't as good as they could be
Can't watch favorite TV shows
Really need the extra money
Tired when I sit down to study at nine o'clock

_____ __What__ are some of the problems of combining work and school?	Schoolwork suffers because I don't have time to study or rewrite papers. I've had to give up things I enjoy, like sleep and touch football. I can't get into the social life at college, because I have to work right after class.
__How__ have these problems changed my life?	My grades aren't as good as they were when I didn't work. Some of my friends have stopped calling me. My relationship with a girl I liked fell apart because I couldn't spend much time with her. I miss TV.
__What__ do I do in a typical day?	I get up at 7 to make an 8 A.M. class. I have classes till 1:30, and then I drive to the super-market where I work. I work till 7 P.M., and then I drive home and eat dinner. After I take a shower and relax for a half hour, it's about 9. This gives me only a couple of hours to study—read textbooks, do math exercises, write essays. My eyes start to close well before I go to bed at 11.
__Why__ do I keep up this schedule?	I can't afford to go to school without working, and I need a degree to get the accounting job I want. If I invest my time now, I'll have a better future.

_____ Juggling a job and college has created major difficulties in my life.

1. Little time for studying
   a. Not reading textbooks
   b. No rewriting papers
   c. Little studying for tests
2. Little time for enjoying social side of college
   a. During school
   b. After school
3. No time for personal pleasures
   a. Favorite TV shows
   b. Sunday football games
   c. Sleeping late

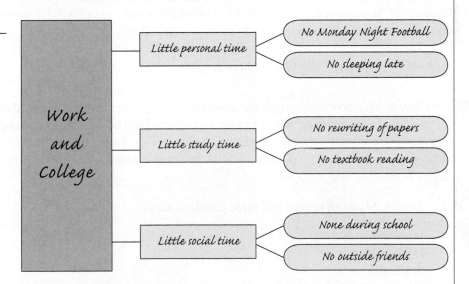

_____ It's hard working and going to school at the same time. I never realized how much I'd have to give up. I won't be quitting my job because I need the money. And the people are friendly at the place where I work. I've had to give up a lot more than I thought. We used to play touch football games every Sunday. They were fun and we'd go out for drinks afterwards. Sundays now are for catch-up work with my courses. I have to catch up because I don't get home every day until 7, I have to eat dinner first before studying. Sometimes I'm so hungry I just eat cookies or chips. Anyway, by the time I take a shower it's 9 P.M. or later and I'm already feeling tired. I've been up since 7 A.M. Sometimes I write an

> English paper in twenty minutes and don't even read it over. I feel that I'm missing out on a lot in college. The other day some people I like were sitting in the cafeteria listening to music and talking. I would have given anything to stay and not have to go to work. I almost called in sick. I used to get invited to parties, I don't much anymore. My friends know I'm not going to be able to make it, so they don't bother. I can't sleep late on weekends or watch TV during the week.

Outlining

As already mentioned (see page 29), outlining is central to writing a good essay. An outline lets you see, and work on, the bare bones of an essay, without the distraction of a clutter of words and sentences. It develops your ability to think clearly and logically. Outlining provides a quick check on whether your essay will be *unified*. It also suggests right at the start whether your essay will be adequately *supported*. And it shows you how to plan an essay that is *well organized*.

The following two exercises will help you develop the outlining skills so important to planning and writing a solid essay.

ACTIVITY 11

One key to effective outlining is the ability to distinguish between major ideas and details that fit under those ideas. In each of the four lists below, major and supporting items are mixed together. Working in pairs, put the items into logical order by filling in the outline that follows each list. In items 3 and 4, one of the three major ideas is missing and must be added.

1. Thesis: My high school had three problem areas.

    Involved with drugs   a. _____
    Leaky ceilings
    Students   (1) _____
    Unwilling to help after class   (2) _____
    Formed cliques
    Teachers   b. _____
    Buildings
    Ill-equipped gym   (1) _____
    Much too strict   (2) _____

                                                c. _____

                                                    (1) _____
                                                    (2) _____

2. Thesis: Working as a dishwasher in a restaurant was my worst job.

Ten-hour shifts   a. _____
Heat in kitchen
Working conditions   (1) _____
Minimum wage   (2) _____
Hours changed every week
No bonus for overtime   b. _____
Hours   (1) _____
Pay   (2) _____
Noisy work area
                                                 c. _____
                                                     (1) _____
                                                     (2) _____

3. Thesis: Running is an ideal way to get needed exercise.

Great way to keep fit   a. _____
No special equipment needed/
    no gym fees   (1) _____
Can run while listening to music   (2) _____
    on headphones   _____
Can run with friends
Burns calories/weight loss   b. _____
Great for heart/lungs/builds leg
    muscles   (1) _____
Inexpensive   _____
No special clothing needed,   (2) _____
    except sneakers
Not boring   _____
                                                 c. _____
                                                     (1) _____
                                                         _____
                                                     (2) _____

4. Thesis: The Internet is an invaluable tool for college students.

E-mail instructor/classmates
Research
Take online courses
Access online learning centers/
   extra help
Find information for term
   papers
Test preparation/practice
   exercises
Schedule more flexible if the
   studying is online
Read more about important
   topics
Save money/time traveling to
   class
Keep up even if absent

a. _____

(1) _____

(2) _____

     _____

(3) _____

     _____

b. _____

(1) _____

     _____

(2) _____

     _____

c. _____

(1) _____

     _____

(2) _____

     _____

ACTIVITY 12 Read the following essay and outline it in the spaces provided. Write out the central point and topic sentences, and summarize in a few words the supporting material that fits under each topic sentence. One item is summarized for you as an example.

Losing Touch

    Steve, a typical American, stays home on workdays. He logs onto his e-mail. In the evenings, he listens to his iPod, watches a DVD, or surfs the Internet. On many days, Steve doesn't talk to any other human beings, and he doesn't see any people except those on television. Steve is imaginary, but his lifestyle is very common. More and more, the inventions of modern technology seem to be cutting us off from contact with our fellow human beings.

Thesis: _____

_____

> The world of business is one area in which technology is isolating us. Many people now work alone at home. With access to a large central computer, employees such as secretaries, insurance agents, and accountants do their jobs at display terminals in their own homes. They no longer have to actually see the people they're dealing with. In addition, employees are often paid in an impersonal way. Workers' salaries are automatically credited to their bank accounts, eliminating the need for paychecks. Fewer people stand in line with their coworkers to receive their pay or cash their checks. Finally, personal banking is becoming a detached process. Customers interact with machines rather than people to deposit or withdraw money from their accounts. Even some bank loans are approved or rejected, not in an interview with a loan officer, but by a computer program.

First topic sentence: _____

_____

Support: 1. Many people now work alone at home.

2. _____

_____

3. _____

_____

a. _____

_____

b. _____

_____

Another area that technology is changing is entertainment. Music, for instance, was once a group experience. People listened to music in concert halls or at small social gatherings. For many people now, however, music is a solitary experience. Walking along the street or sitting in their living rooms, they wear headphones to build a wall of music around them. Movie entertainment is changing, too. Movies used to be social events. Now, some people are not going out to see a movie. Some are choosing to wait for a film to appear on cable television or DVD. Instead of being involved with the laughter, applause, or hisses of the audience, viewers watch movies in the isolation of their own living rooms.

_____

_____

Support: 1. _____

_____

2. _____

_____

Education is a third important area in which technology is separating us from others. From elementary schools to colleges, students spend more and more time sitting by themselves in front of computers. The computers give them feedback, while teachers spend more time tending the computers and less time interacting with their classes. A similar problem occurs in homes. As more families buy computers, increasing numbers of students practice their math and reading skills with software programs instead of with their friends, brothers and sisters, and parents. Last, alienation is occurring as a result of DVDs. People are buying DVDs on subjects such as cooking, real estate investment, speaking, and speed-reading. They then practice their skills at home rather than by taking group classes in which a rich human interaction can occur.

Third topic sentence: _____

_____

Support: 1. _____

2. _____

3. _____

> Technology, then, seems to be driving human beings apart. Soon, we may
> no longer need to communicate with other human beings to do our work,
> entertain ourselves, or pursue an education. Machines will be the coworkers
> and companions of the future.

Revising

Following is the second supporting paragraph from an essay called "Problems of
Combining School and Work." The paragraph is shown in four different stages of
development: (1) first draft, (2) revised second draft, (3) edited next-to-final draft,
(4) final draft. The four stages appear in scrambled order. Write the number 1 in
the answer blank for the first draft, and number the remaining stages in sequence.
To help you get started, a few comments about the changes made in draft 2 are
included here. Add to these, but also record the changes made in drafts 3 and 4.

ACTIVITY 13

Changes in draft 2: _Adds information about sports he/she used to play._

Removes sentence beginning "Psychologists say . . ."

_____

Changes in draft 3: _____

_____

_____

Changes in draft 4: _____

_____

_____2_____ I have also given up some personal pleasures in my life. On sundays for example I used to play softball or football, now I use the entire day to study. Good old-fashioned sleep is another lost pleasure for me now. I never get as much as I like because their just isn't time. Finally I miss having the chance to just sit in front of the TV, on weeknights. In order to watch the whole lineup of movies and sports that I used to watch regularly. These sound like small pleasures, but you realize how important they are when you have to give them up.

_____1_____ I've had to give up pleasures in my life. I use to spend sundays playing games, now I have to study. Im the sort of person who needs a lot of sleep, but I dont have the time for that either. Sleeping nine or ten hours a night woul'dnt be unusual for me. Psycologists say that each individual need a different amount of sleep, some people need as little as five hours, some need as much as nine or ten. So I'm not unusual in that. But Ive given up that pleasure too. And I can't watch the TV shows I use to enjoy. This is another personal pleasure Ive lost because of doing work and school. These may seem like small things, but you realize how good they are when you give them up.

_____4_____ Besides missing the social side of college life, I've also had to give up some of my special personal pleasures. I used to spend Sunday afternoons, for example, playing lob-pitch softball or touch football depending on the season. Now I use Sunday as a catch-up day for my studies. Another pleasure I've lost is sleeping late on days off and weekends. I once loved mornings when I could check the clock, bury my head in the pillow, and drift off for another hour. These days I'm forced to crawl out of bed the minute the alarm lets out its piercing ring. Finally, I no longer have the chance to just sit watching the movies and sports programs that I enjoy. A leisurely night of *Monday Night Football* or a network premiere of a Tom Hanks movie is a pleasure of the past for me now.

_____3_____ Besides missing the social side of college life, I've also had to give up some of my special personal pleasures. I used to spend sunday afternoons, for example playing lob-pitch softball or touch football depending on the season. Now I use the day as a catch-up day for my studies. Another pleasure I've lost is sleeping late on days off and weekends. I once loved mornings when I could check the clock, then burying my head in the pillow, and you drift off to sleep for another hour. These days I'm forced to get out of bed the minute the alarm lets out it's ring. Finally I no longer have the chance to just sit watching the movies and also programs with sports that I enjoy. A leisurely night of Monday Night Football or a network premiere of a Tom Hanks movie is a pleasure of the past for me now.

After you have done that, explain why you think that drafts 2, 3, and 4 are each better than the one that preceded them. In other words, explain what improvements that writer has made to each. As you do this, consider the following questions:

1. Is this version of the paragraph better unified, supported, and organized than the previous one? (Review the Revising Content questions on page 34.)

2. Has the student revised sentences? (Review the Revising Sentences questions on page 34.)

3. Has the student edited for mistakes in grammar, punctuation, and spelling? Which ones?

The First and Second Steps in Essay Writing

This chapter will show you how to

- start an essay with a point, or thesis

- support that point, or thesis, with specific evidence

Describe a favorite childhood place that made you feel secure, safe, private, or in a world of your own. Begin with a thesis statement, something like this: "_____ was a place that made me feel _____ when I was a child." Remember to keep the point of your thesis statement in mind as you describe this place. Include only details that will support the idea that your place was one of security, safety, privacy, or the like.

Chapter 2 emphasized how prewriting and revising can help you become an effective writer. This chapter focuses on the first two steps in writing an effective essay:

1. Begin with a point, or thesis.

2. Support the thesis with specific evidence.

The chapters that follow will focus on the third and fourth steps in writing:

3. Organize and connect the specific evidence (pages 83–109).

4. Write clear, error-free sentences (pages 110–143).

Step 1: Begin with a Point, or Thesis

Your first step in writing is to discover what point you want to make and to write that point out as a single sentence. There are two reasons for doing this. You want to know right from the start if you have a clear and workable thesis. Also, you will be able to use the thesis as a guide while writing your essay. At any stage you can ask yourself, Does this support my thesis? With the thesis as a guide, the danger of drifting away from the point of the essay is greatly reduced.

Understanding Thesis Statements

In Chapter 1, you learned that effective essays center around a thesis, or main point, that a writer wishes to express. This central idea is usually presented as a *thesis statement* in an essay's introductory paragraph.

A good thesis statement does two things. First, it tells readers an essay's *topic*. Second, it presents the writer's *attitude, opinion, idea,* or *point* about that topic. This is often referred to as the *author's claim*. For example, look at the following thesis statement:

Owning a pet has several important benefits.

In this thesis statement, the topic is *owning a pet;* the writer's main point is that owning a pet *has several important benefits.*

For each thesis statement below, <u>single-underline</u> the topic and <u>double-underline</u> the main point that the writer wishes to express about the topic.

ACTIVITY 1

EXAMPLES   <u>Our company president</u> <u><u>should be fired for three main reasons.</u></u>

<u>The Internet</u> <u><u>has led to new kinds of frustration in everyday life.</u></u>

1. Having to care for a child requires hard work, commitment, and patience.
2. Celebrities are often poor role models because of the ways they dress, talk, and behave.
3. My first night as a security guard turned out to be one of the most frightening experiences of my life.
4. SUVs are inferior to cars because they are harder to control, more expensive, and dangerous to the environment.
5. The twentieth century produced three inventions that dramatically changed the lives of all Americans.

6. Stress in the fast-food workplace has led to serious physical, psychological, and emotional problems for employees.

7. Advertisers target young people when marketing cigarettes, alcohol, and adult movies.

8. Christian Bale's varied film roles demonstrate his versatility as an actor.

9. American carmakers need to produce vehicles that are fuel efficient, safe, and less expensive.

10. Being successful at any job requires punctuality, dependability, and ambition.

Writing a Good Thesis I

Now that you know how thesis statements work, you can begin writing your own. To start, you need a topic that is neither too broad nor too narrow. Suppose, for example, that an instructor asks you to write a paper on marriage. Such a subject is too broad to cover in a five-hundred-word essay. You would have to write a book to support adequately any point you might make about the general subject of marriage. What you would need to do, then, is limit your subject. Narrow it down until you have a thesis that you can deal with specifically in about five hundred words. In the box that follows are (1) several general subjects, (2) a limited version of each general subject, and (3) a thesis statement about each limited subject.

General Subject	Limited Subject	Thesis
Marriage	Honeymoon	A honeymoon is perhaps the worst way to begin a marriage.
Family	Older sister	My older sister helped me overcome my shyness.
Television	TV preachers	TV evangelists use sales techniques to promote their messages.
Children	Disciplining of children	My husband and I have several effective ways of disciplining our children.
Sports	Players' salaries	Players' high salaries are bad for the game, for the fans, and for the values our children are developing.

Sometimes a subject must go through several stages of limiting before it is narrow enough to write about. Below are four lists reflecting several stages that writers went through in moving from a general subject to a narrow thesis statement. Number the stages in each list from 1 to 5, with 1 marking the broadest stage and 5 marking the thesis.

ACTIVITY 2

LIST 1

_____ Major league baseball players

_____ Athletes

_____ Major league pitchers' salaries too high

_____ Professional athletes

_____ Major league pitchers

LIST 3

_____ Retail companies

_____ Supermarkets

_____ Dealing with customers

_____ Working in a supermarket

_____ I've learned how to handle unpleasant supermarket customers.

LIST 2

_____ John Philip Souza

_____ American composers

_____ Music 101 taught me to appreciate Souza's band music.

_____ Music

_____ Band music

LIST 4

_____ Camping

_____ First camping trip

_____ Summer vacation

_____ My first camping trip was a disastrous experience.

_____ Vacations

Later in this chapter, you will get more practice in narrowing general subjects to thesis statements.

How to Limit and Focus Your Thesis

You have just learned that it is important to *limit* a topic. One way to do this is by clustering, which is also a good way to gather information. (If necessary, turn back to page 28 to review how to cluster.) Let's say your instructor assigns a paper on physical exercise. Obviously, this is far too broad a topic for a short paper. Therefore, you can try to cluster ideas around this topic as a way to limit it to an aspect of the topic that you know most about or that you are most interested in. Here's an example of how one student began to use this method to limit her topic:

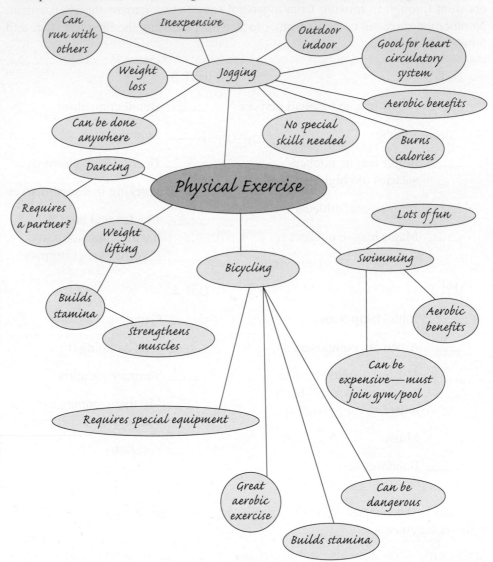

Immediately after completing this exercise, the student realized that the type of physical exercise she knew most about was running. So, she decided to limit her essay to that topic. However, she also knew that she would have to *focus* on a main point about running and that her clustering suggested several different main points. Here are just three:

- Running <u>is an easy way to get needed exercise</u>: it is inexpensive, can be done almost anywhere, and requires few special skills.

- Running <u>benefits the lungs, circulatory system, and the leg muscles.</u>
- Running <u>burns calories and helps maintain a healthy weight.</u>

To determine which of these three main points she could most easily write about, the student used another prewriting technique, making a list. (If necessary, turn back to pages 26–28 to review list making.) In fact, she listed everything she knew about each of her three potential thesis statements:

Easy way to get exercise	Benefits circulatory system, lungs, muscles	Helps maintain a healthy weight
Can be done outside or inside	Strengthens heart muscle	Lost 20 pounds in one year jogging three times a week
No special training needed	Strengthens lungs, improves breathing	
Inexpensive	Slows pulse rate	
No special location needed	Increases blood supply	
No uniform or special clothing required		
Can be done with others		
Can be done while listening to music on headset		

It is obvious from what we see here that the interests of the student favor writing about why running is an easy way to get exercise.

As you can see, limiting or narrowing a topic is extremely important. However, you will also have to *focus* on a main point. Writers should always be committed to the ideas they are discussing. So, if possible, always write about the main point that you know most about, that you are most interested in, or that you are most passionate about.

Below is a list of thesis statements that make or focus on different main points about the same topic. Each can be the foundation of a very different essay.

Topic	Main Point
Some professional athletes	act as negative role models for young people.
Some professional athletes	have to train year round.

Topic	Main Point
Some professional athletes	have caused themselves harm by taking steroids.
Some professional athletes	contribute time and money to worthy causes.
Some professional athletes	forget they are members of a team that needs to work together.
Going to college	demands careful time management.
Going to college	enables people to appreciate different cultures and lifestyles.
Going to college	provides students with analytical skills that can lead to rewarding careers.
Going to college	requires study habits different from those used in high school.
Conserving energy at home	saves residents a great deal of money.
Conserving energy at home	reduces air pollution caused by the burning of fossil fuels.
Conserving energy at home	doesn't require a change in lifestyle.
Conserving energy at home	reduces our dependence on foreign sources of energy.
The Internet	should be regulated to protect children.
The Internet	is an inexpensive way to transmit information.
The Internet	is a valuable academic tool.
The Internet	enables millions of people to speak out on important social and political issues.

As you can see, you can write several different thesis statements about the same topic. In each case, of course, your purpose will help determine your main point and may even help shape the organization of your paper. Below is a list of several different thesis statements written on "heating costs." Each serves a different purpose.

Purpose	Thesis
To analyze	A home energy audit revealed that we can reduce home heating costs by $500 a year.
To explain a cause	Our home heating costs were high because of poor insulation, drafty windows, and an inefficient furnace.

Purpose	Thesis
To contrast	Homes using passive solar energy have lower heating bills than others.
To explain an effect	Higher heating costs have made architects design more energy-efficient homes.
To explain a process	Lowering home heating costs is easy if one follows three basic steps.
To offer a solution	People who own older homes should have an energy audit to find ways to reduce heating costs.
To classify	Heating costs can be reduced by using fossil-fuel alternatives: solar, wind, and geothermal.
To explain advantages	Reducing heating costs not only saves money, but it also increases the value of a home and helps the environment.
To explain disadvantages	Installing solar panels will reduce heating costs, but they are unsightly and expensive.

Writing a Good Thesis II

When writing thesis statements, people often make mistakes that undermine their chances of producing an effective essay. One mistake is to simply announce the subject rather than state a true thesis. A second mistake is to write a thesis that is too broad, and a third is to write a thesis that is too narrow. A fourth error is to write a thesis containing more than one idea. Here are tips for avoiding such mistakes and writing good thesis statements.

1 Write Statements, Not Announcements

The subject of this paper will be my parents.

I want to talk about the crime wave in our country.

The baby-boom generation is the concern of this essay.

In this first group, the sentences are not thesis statements but announcements of a topic. For instance, "The subject of this paper will be my parents" does not make a point about the parents but merely tells, in a rather weak and unimaginative way, the writer's general subject. Remember, a thesis statement must make a point about a limited subject. Effective thesis statements based on the above sentences could be as follows:

My parents each struggled with personal demons.

The recent crime wave in our city has several apparent causes.

The baby-boom generation has changed American society in key ways.

2 Avoid Statements That Are Too Broad

Disease has shaped human history.

Insects are fascinating creatures.

Men and women are very different.

In the preceding examples, each statement is too broad to be supported adequately in a student essay. For instance, "Disease has shaped human history" would require far more than a five-hundred-word essay. In fact, there are many lengthy books written on the exact same topic. Remember, your thesis statement should be focused enough that it can be effectively supported in a five-paragraph essay. Revised thesis statements based on the topics in the above sentences could be as follows:

In the mid-1980s, AIDS changed people's attitudes about dating.

Strength, organization, and communication make the ant one of nature's most successful insects.

Men and women are often treated very differently in the workplace.

3 Avoid Statements That Are Too Narrow

Here are three statements that are too narrow:

The speed limit near my home is sixty-five miles per hour.

A hurricane hit southern Florida last summer.

A person must be at least thirty-five years old to be elected president of the United States.

In this third group, there is no room in any of the three statements for support to be given. For instance, "The speed limit near my home is sixty-five miles per hour" is too narrow to be expanded into a paper. It is a simple fact that does not require any support. Such a statement is sometimes called a *dead-end statement:* there is no place to go with it. Remember, a thesis statement must be broad enough to require support in an essay. Successful thesis statements based on the preceding sentences are as follows:

The speed limit near my home should be lowered to fifty-five miles per hour for several reasons.

Federal officials made a number of mistakes in their response to the recent Florida hurricane.

The requirement that a U.S. president must be at least thirty-five years old is unfair and unreasonable.

4 Make Sure Statements Develop Only One Idea

Here are three statements that contain more than one idea:

One of the most serious problems affecting young people today is bullying, and it is time more kids learned the value of helping others.

Studying with others has several benefits, but it also has drawbacks and can be difficult to schedule.

Teachers have played an important role in my life, but they were not as important as my parents.

In this fourth group, each statement contains more than one idea. For instance, "One of the most serious problems affecting young people today is bullying, *and* it is time more kids learned the value of helping others" clearly has two separate ideas ("One of the most serious problems affecting young people today is bullying" *and* "it is time more kids learned the value of helping others"). The reader is asked to focus on two separate points, each of which more logically belongs in an essay of its own. Remember, the point of an essay is to communicate a *single* main idea to readers. To be as clear as possible, then, try to limit your thesis statement to the single key idea you want your readers to know. Revised thesis statements based on each of the examples above are as follows:

One of the most serious problems affecting young people today is bullying.

Studying with others has several benefits.

Teachers have played an important role in my life.

Write *TN* in the space next to the two statements that are too narrow to be developed in an essay. Write *TB* beside the two statements that are too broad to be covered in an essay. Then, in the spaces provided, revise one of the too-narrow statements and one of the too-broad statements to make them each an effective thesis.

ACTIVITY 3

_____   1. The way our society treats elderly people is unbelievable.

            _____

_____   2. Enrollment at Freestone State College increased by 10 percent.

            _____

_____   3. California has much to offer the tourist.

            _____

_____   4. I failed my biology course.

_____

_____

Step 2: Support the Thesis with Specific Evidence

The first essential step in writing a successful essay is to formulate a clearly stated thesis. The second basic step is to support the thesis with specific reasons or details.

To ensure that your essay will have adequate support, you may find an informal outline very helpful. Write down a brief version of your thesis idea, and then work out and jot down the three points that will support the thesis.

Here is the scratch outline that was prepared by the author of the earlier essay on moviegoing:

Moviegoing is a problem.

1. *Inconvenience of going out*

2. *Tempting snacks*

3. *Other moviegoers*

A scratch outline like this one looks simple, but developing it often requires a great deal of careful thinking. The time spent on developing a logical outline is invaluable, though. Once you have planned the steps that logically support your thesis, you will be in an excellent position to go on to write an effective essay.

Activities in this section will give you practice in the crucial skill of planning an essay clearly.

ACTIVITY 4

Following are ten informal outlines. Working with a partner, complete any five of them by adding a third logical supporting point (*c*) that will parallel the two already provided (*a* and *b*).

1. The first day on a new job can be nerve-racking.

    a. Meeting new people

    b. Finding your way around a new place

    c. _____

2. My stepmother has three qualities I admire.

   a. Patience

   b. Thoughtfulness

   c. _____

3. My summer job on a landscaping crew had several advantages.

   a. Learned how to follow directions

   b. Great people to work for

   c. _____

4. College students should live at home.

   a. Stay in touch with family

   b. Avoid distractions of dorm or apartment life

   c. _____

5. Bussing tables is the worst job I've ever had.

   a. Difficult boss

   b. Poor pay

   c. _____

6. College is stressful for many people.

   a. Worry about grades

   b. Worry about being accepted

   c. _____

7. My high school algebra teacher was excellent.

   a. Extra help after class

   b. Great practice handouts for tests

   c. _____

8. The college library is the best place to study.

   a. Quiet and well lit

   b. Nothing to tempt me away from my books

   c. _____

9. Buying a used car is better than buying a new one.

   a. Used cars are less likely to be stolen than new cars.

   b. Used cars don't lose their value as quickly as most new cars.

   c. _____

10. Many companies use annoying practices to increase sales.

   a. Junk mail

   b. Spam e-mail

   c. _____

The Importance of *Specific* Details

Just as a thesis must be developed with at least three supporting points, each supporting point must be developed with specific details. Specific details are valuable in two key ways. First, details excite the reader's interest. They make writing a pleasure to read, for we all enjoy learning particulars about people, places, and things. Second, details serve to explain a writer's points. They give the evidence needed for us to see and understand general ideas.

All too often, the body paragraphs in essays contain only vague generalities, rather than the specific supporting details that are needed to engage and convince a reader. Here is what one of the paragraphs in "The Hazards of Moviegoing" would have looked like if the writer had not detailed her supporting evidence vividly:

> Some of the other patrons are even more of a problem than the theater itself. Many people in the theater often show themselves to be inconsiderate. They make noises and create disturbances at their seats. Included are people in every age group, from the young to the old. Some act as if they were at home in their own living room watching TV. And people are often messy, so that you're constantly aware of all the food they're eating. People are also always moving around near you, creating a disturbance and interrupting your enjoyment of the movie.

The following box contrasts the vague support in the preceding paragraph with the specific support in the essay.

Vague Support	Specific Support
1. Many people in the theater show themselves to be inconsiderate. They make noises and create disturbances at their seats. Included are people in every age group, from the young to the old. Some act as if they were at home in their own living room watching TV.	1. Little kids race up and down the aisles, usually in giggling packs. Teenagers try to impress their friends by talking back to the screen, whistling, and making what they consider to be hilarious noises. Adults act as if they were at home in their own living room and comment loudly on the ages of the stars or why movies aren't as good anymore.
2. And people are often messy, so that you're constantly aware of all the food they're eating.	2. And people of all ages crinkle candy wrappers, stick gum on their seats, and drop popcorn tubs or cups of crushed ice and soda on the floor.
3. People are also always moving around near you, creating a disturbance and interrupting your enjoyment of the movie.	3. They also cough and burp, squirm endlessly in their seats, file out for repeated trips to the restrooms or concession stand, and elbow you out of the armrest on either side of your seat.

The effective paragraph from the essay provides details that make vividly clear the statement that patrons are a problem in the theater. The writer specifies the exact age groups (little kids, teenagers, and adults) and the offenses of each (giggling, talking and whistling, and loud comments). She specifies the various food excesses (crinkled wrappers, gum on seats, dropped popcorn and soda containers). Finally, she provides concrete details that enable us to see and hear other disturbances (coughs and burps, squirming, constant trips to restrooms, jostling for elbow room). The ineffective paragraph asks us to guess about these details; the effective paragraph describes the details in a specific and lively way.

In the strong paragraph, then, sharp details capture our interest and enable us to share the writer's experience. They provide pictures that make us feel we are there. The particulars also enable us to understand clearly the writer's point that patrons are a problem. Aim to make your own writing equally convincing by providing detailed support.

ACTIVITY 5

Write *S* in front of the two selections below that provide specific evidence to support the opening point. Write *X* in front of the two selections in which the opening point is followed by vague, general, wordy sentences.

_____ 1. The tree house my father and I built was a masterpiece.

It had three floors, each of which was about 75 square feet. There were two windows made of real glass on each floor, allowing sunlight to flood in and making the place pleasant and cheerful. The walls were made of sweet-smelling cedar planks Dad and I salvaged from a landfill. On the bottom floor was a small cast-iron stove, which gave off enough heat to keep us toasty on the coldest winter day. The second floor had an old rocking chair on which I read my favorite comics every summer afternoon. On the top floor, Dad had set up a telescope from which we observed the glories of the night sky.

_____ 2. Our first camping trip in Keystone State Forest was disappointing.

Many of the animals we had hoped to see on our walk just weren't there. Some smaller animals were, but we had seen them before in our backyards. The forest was rather quiet. It was not what we had expected. The weather didn't cooperate either. It was dreadful for most of our stay. Then there were the bugs! We had planned for the trip well, spending a lot of money on provisions and special equipment. But much of it was a waste because we left much earlier than we had intended. We came home frustrated and soured on the whole idea of camping.

_____ 3. Some things are worse when they're "improved."

A good cheesecake, for one thing, is perfect. It doesn't need pineapple, cherries, blueberries, or whipped cream smeared all over it. Plain old American blue jeans, the ones with five pockets and copper rivets, are perfect too. Manufacturers only made them worse when they added flared legs, took away the pockets, tightened the fit, and plastered white logos and designers' names all over them.

_____ 4. Pets can be more trouble than children.

My dog, unlike my children, has never been completely housebroken. When he's excited or nervous, he still has an occasional problem. My dog, unlike my children, has never learned how to take care of himself when we're away, despite the fact that we've given him plenty of time to do so. We don't have to worry about our grown children anymore. However, we still have to hire a dog-sitter.

The Importance of *Adequate* Details

One of the most common and most serious problems in students' writing is inadequate development. You must provide *enough* specific details to fully support the point in a body paragraph of an essay. You could not, for example, include a paragraph about a friend's unreliability and provide only a one- or two-sentence example. You would have to extend the example or add several other examples showing your friend as an unreliable person. Without such additional support, your paragraph would be underdeveloped.

Students may try to disguise unsupported paragraphs through repetition and generalities. Do not fall into this "wordiness trap." Be prepared to do the plain hard work needed to ensure that each paragraph has solid support.

Both of the following body paragraphs were written on the same topic, and each has a clear opening point. Which paragraph is adequately developed? Which one has only several particulars and uses mostly vague, general, wordy sentences to conceal that it is starved for specific details?

ACTIVITY 6

Eternal Youth?—No, Thanks

I wouldn't want to be a teenager again, first of all, because I wouldn't want to worry about talking to girls. I still remember how scary it was to call up a girl and ask her out. My heart would race, my pulse would pound, and perspiration would trickle down my face, adding to my acne by the second. I never knew whether my voice would come out deep and masculine, like a television anchorman's, or squeaky, like a little boy's. Then there were the questions: Would she be at home? If she was, would she want to talk to me? And if she did, what would I say? The one time I did get up the nerve to take a girl in my homeroom to a movie, I was so tongue-tied that I stared silently at the box of popcorn in my lap until the feature finally started. Needless to say, I wasn't very interesting company.

Terrors of My Teenage Years

I wouldn't want to be a teenager again, first of all, because I wouldn't want to worry about talking to girls. Calling up a girl to ask her out was something that I completely dreaded. I didn't know what words to express or how to express them. I would have all the symptoms of nervousness when I got on the phone. I worried a great deal about how I would sound, and I had a lot of doubts about the girl's reaction. Once, I managed to call up a girl to go out, but the evening turned out to be a disaster. I was too unsure of myself to act in a confident way. I couldn't think of anything to say and just kept quiet. Now that I look back on it, I really made a fool of myself. Agonizing over my attempts at relationships with the opposite sex made adolescence a very uncomfortable time.

The first paragraph offers a series of well-detailed examples of the author's nerve-racking experiences, as a teenager, with girls. The second paragraph, on the other hand, is underdeveloped. For instance, the second paragraph makes only the general observation "I would have all the symptoms of nervousness when I got on the phone," but the first paragraph states, "My heart would race, my pulse would pound, and perspiration would trickle down my face."

The second paragraph makes the general statement "I worried a great deal about how I would sound," but in the first paragraph the author wonders if his voice will "come out deep and masculine, like a television anchorman's, or squeaky, like a little boy's." And the second paragraph has no specific description of the evening that turned into a disaster. In summary, the second paragraph lacks the full, detailed support needed to develop its opening point convincingly.

ACTIVITY 7   Write a paragraph supporting one of the following points:

1. My room is a mess.
2. Our cafeteria offers a variety of ethnic foods.
3. My friend is a dangerous driver.
4. Shirley is the most helpful neighbor on our street.

Afterward, consider reading your paragraph to a small group of classmates. The best paragraphs are sure to be those with plenty of specific details.

Practice in Advancing and Supporting a Thesis

Identifying the Parts of an Essay

Each cluster below contains one topic, one thesis statement, and two supporting sentences. In the space provided, label each item as follows:

ACTIVITY 8

> T—topic
> TH—thesis statement
> S—supporting sentence

GROUP 1

_____ a. Films based on historical events are sometimes shown in class.

_____ b. Making history more interesting

_____ c. Some history teachers use innovative methods to increase student interest.

_____ d. Instructors ask students to write short plays dramatizing historical events.

GROUP 2

_____ a. Vegetarian diets

_____ b. Staying away from meat can reduce intake of fat and cholesterol.

_____ c. Eating vegetables helps the environment because raising veggies uses less energy than raising animals.

_____ d. Vegetarianism benefits both the individual and the environment.

GROUP 3

_____ a. Medicine

_____ b. Antibiotics have enabled doctors to control many diseases that were once fatal.

_____ c. Organ transplants have prolonged the lives of tens of thousands of people.

_____ d. Advances in modern medicine have had great success in helping people.

GROUP 4

_____ a. Reading

_____ b. Parents can take steps to encourage their children to enjoy reading.

_____ c. The adults' own behavior can influence children to become readers.

_____ d. Parents can make sure the physical environment of the home encourages reading.

GROUP 5

_____ a. Insects perform many helpful functions for human beings.

_____ b. Insects are essential to the growth of many important crops.

_____ c. Insects

_____ d. Insects protect the environment by removing wastes and controlling
disease-causing germs.

ACTIVITY 9   This activity will sharpen your sense of the parts of an essay. The essay that follows, "Coping with Old Age," has no indentations starting new paragraphs. Read
this essay carefully, and then double-underline the thesis and single-underline the
topic sentence for each of the three supporting paragraphs and the first sentence
of the conclusion. Write the numbers of those sentences in the spaces provided at
the end.

Coping with Old Age

¹I recently read about an area of the former Soviet Union where many
people live to be well over a hundred years old. ²Being 115 or even
125 isn't considered unusual there, and these old people continue to do
productive work right up until they die. ³The United States, however, isn't such
a healthy place for older people. ⁴Since I retired from my job, I've had to
cope with the physical, mental, and emotional stresses of being "old." ⁵For
one thing, I've had to adjust to physical changes. ⁶Now that I'm over sixty,
the trusty body that carried me around for years has turned traitor. ⁷Aside
from the deepening wrinkles on my face and neck, and the wiry gray hairs
that have replaced my brown hair, I face more frightening changes. ⁸I don't
have the energy I used to. ⁹My eyes get tired. ¹⁰Once in a while, I miss
something that's said to me. ¹¹My once faithful feet seem to have lost their
comfortable soles, and I sometimes feel I'm walking on marbles. ¹²In order
to fight against this slow decay, I exercise whenever I can. ¹³I walk, I stretch,

continued

and I climb stairs. [14]I battle constantly to keep as fit as possible. [15]I'm also trying to cope with mental changes. [16]My mind was once as quick and sure as a champion gymnast. [17]I never found it difficult to memorize answers in school or to remember the names of people I met. [18]Now, I occasionally have to search my mind for the name of a close neighbor or favorite television show. [19]Because my mind needs exercise, too, I challenge it as much as I can. [20]Taking a college course like this English class, for example, forces me to concentrate. [21]The mental gymnast may be a little slow and out of shape, but he can still do a backflip or turn a somersault when he has to. [22]Finally, I must deal with the emotional impact of being old. [23]Our society typecasts old people. [24]We're supposed to be unattractive, senile, useless leftovers. [25]We're supposed to be the crazy drivers and the cranky customers. [26]At first, I was angry and frustrated that I was considered old at all. [27]And I knew that people were wrong to stereotype me. [28]Then I got depressed. [29]I even started to think that maybe I was a castoff, one of those old animals that slow down the rest of the herd. [30]But I have now decided to rebel against these negative feelings. [31]I try to have friends of all ages and to keep up with what's going on in the world. [32]I try to remember that I'm still the same person who sat at a first-grade desk, who fell in love, who comforted a child, who got a raise at work. [33]I'm not "just" an old person. [34]Coping with the changes of old age has become my latest full-time job. [35]Even though it's a job I never applied for, and one for which I had no experience, I'm trying to do the best I can.

Thesis statement in "Coping with Old Age": _____

Topic sentence of first supporting paragraph: _____

Topic sentence of second supporting paragraph: _____

Topic sentence of third supporting paragraph: _____

First sentence of the conclusion: _____

Evaluating Thesis Statements

As was explained on pages 57–59, some writers announce a subject instead of stating a true thesis idea. Others write a dead-end thesis statement that is too narrow to need support or development. Contrasting with such a dead-end statement is the statement that is wide open—too broad to be adequately supported in the limited space of a five-hundred-word essay. Other thesis statements are vague or contain more than one idea. They suggest that the writer has not thought out the main point sufficiently.

ACTIVITY 10

Write *A* beside the sentence in each pair that is an announcement rather than a thesis statement. Write *OK* beside the statement in each pair that is a clear, limited point that could be developed in an essay.

1. _____ a. I want to discuss what it means to be a good citizen.

   _____ b. Being a good citizen means becoming informed about important social, environmental, and political issues.

2. _____ a. I made several mistakes in the process of trying to win the respect and affection of my teenage stepson.

   _____ b. My thesis in this paper is relationships between stepparents and stepchildren.

3. _____ a. Successfully purchasing a good used car requires four simple steps.

   _____ b. This paper explains how to purchase a good used car.

4. _____ a. This paper will be about sharing housework.

   _____ b. Deciding who will perform certain unpleasant household chores can be the crisis that makes or breaks a marriage.

5. _____ a. I want to show how cardiology has changed in the last 20 years.

   _____ b. The advances in cardiology in the last 20 years have been miraculous.

ACTIVITY 11

Write *TN* beside the statement in each pair that is too narrow to be developed in an essay. Write *OK* beside the statement in each pair that is a clear, limited point.

1. _____ a. It snowed last winter.

   _____ b. The snow last winter caused many hardships.

2. _____ a. The library is located in the center of town.

   _____ b. The library is conveniently located in the center of town.

3. _____ a. The addition of a fifty-seat computer lab at our college has made it possible to expand the computer-science, mathematics, and English curricula.

   _____ b. Our college just added a fifty-seat computer lab.

4. _____ a. Nathaniel Hawthorne's novel *The Scarlet Letter* is about the Puritans.

   _____ b. Nathaniel Hawthorne's novel *The Scarlet Letter* criticizes Puritan morality.

5. _____ a. Americans are living longer than before because of better diets, a cleaner environment, and advanced medical care.

   _____ b. The average American can now expect to live longer than before.

Write *TB* beside the statement in each pair that is too broad to be developed in an essay. Write *OK* beside the statement in each pair that is a clear, limited point.

ACTIVITY 12

1. _____ a. After-school art and athletic clubs provide healthy outlets for young people.

   _____ b. After-school art and athletic clubs at Garfield Junior High School have helped reduce the number of thefts, gang wars, and acts of vandalism once common in our community.

2. _____ a. The educational system in the United States needs to be improved.

   _____ b. The educational system in my hometown could be improved by eliminating the current school board, hiring more teachers, and holding parents accountable.

3. _____ a. The attacks of 9/11 dramatized the heroism we have come to expect from our police and firefighters.

   _____ b. Americans responded well during the attacks of 9/11.

4. _____ a. College classes can be very challenging.

   _____ b. Completing a college course requires organization, persistence, and patience.

5. _____ a. The history of the Puritan faith is very interesting.

   _____ b. The persecution of the Puritans in England led to their immigration to the New World.

For each pair, write *2* beside the statement that contains more than one idea. Write *OK* beside the statement that is a clear, limited point.

ACTIVITY 13

1. _____ a. Working with old people changed my stereotypical ideas about the elderly.

   _____ b. My life has moved in new directions since the rewarding job I had working with older people last summer.

2. _____   a. The police officers in our town do their jobs very well and the police chief is really nice.

_____   b. Our town's police department is efficient, nice, and professional.

3. _____   a. Forest fires are one way nature creates new habitats.

_____   b. Forest fires destroy lives and property, but they do provide some benefits to the environment.

4. _____   a. My roommate and I are compatible in most ways, but we still have conflicts at times.

_____   b. My roommate has his own unique systems for studying, writing term papers, and cleaning our room.

5. _____   a. Although the Modern Language Department offers first-rate instruction in several European languages, many professors and students see the need to offer Arabic, Chinese, and Hindi as well.

_____   b. Many professors and students believe there is a need for courses in Arabic, Chinese, and Hindi.

Completing Thesis Statements

ACTIVITY 14

Complete the following thesis statements by adding a third supporting point that will parallel the two already provided. You might want to first check the section on parallelism in Chapter 5 (page 111) to make sure you understand parallel form.

1. A successful camping trip requires familiarity with the terrain, a good tent and

   sleeping bag, and _____.

2. Our new college library building is massive, overwhelming, and _____.

3. Successful TV shows have good actors, great writers, and _____

   _____.

4. School cafeteria food should include non-fried foods, fruits, and _____

   _____.

5. A good teacher should be compassionate, patient, and _____.

6. Drinking tea promotes good health, a relaxed state of mind, and _____

   _____.

7. The loss of a job can result in depression, weight gain, and _____.

8. Before beginning an exercise program, a person should get a thorough physical examination, decide on his or her exercise goals, and _____ _____.

9. The sights, sounds, and _____ of the amusement park made the visit very interesting.

10. Cats make great pets because they are easy to care for, quiet, and_____.

Writing a Thesis Statement

Write a thesis for each group of supporting statements. This activity will give you practice in writing an effective essay thesis—one that is neither too broad nor too narrow. It will also help you understand the logical relationship between a thesis and its supporting details.

ACTIVITY 15

1. Thesis: _____

   a. Most animals in animal shelters have been abandoned; therefore, they look at potential families with very sad, longing eyes.

   b. Seeing animals in cages can make a visitor feel sympathy for all the animals.

   c. Puppies and kittens are usually very cute and can easily work their way into a person's heart.

2. Thesis: _____

   a. The actors were very stiff and unbelievable.

   b. The costumes were very poorly designed.

   c. The plot was predictable and boring.

3. Thesis: _____

   a. First, I tried simply avoiding the snacks aisle of the supermarket.

   b. Then I started limiting myself to only five units of any given snack.

   c. Finally, in desperation, I began keeping the cellophane bags of snacks in a padlocked cupboard.

4. Thesis: _____

    a. Thomas Jefferson wrote the Declaration of Independence and helped lead the American Revolution.

    b. As third president of the United States, he negotiated the Louisiana Purchase, which doubled the size of the country.

    c. He provided many books to the Library of Congress in its early years.

5. Thesis: _____

    a. Many students who intend to go to law school major in English.

    b. Studying writing and literature is excellent preparation for a career in teaching.

    c. After earning undergraduate degrees in English, some students pursue a master's degree in business administration.

Limiting a Topic and Writing a Thesis Statement

The following two activities will give you practice in distinguishing general from limited subjects and in writing a thesis.

ACTIVITY 16 Look carefully at the ten general subjects and ten limited subjects below. Then write a thesis statement for any five of them.

> **HINT** To create a thesis statement for a limited subject, ask yourself, What point do I want to make about _____ (*my limited subject*)?

GENERAL SUBJECT

1. Apartment
2. Self-improvement
3. Family
4. Eating
5. Automobiles
6. Health

LIMITED SUBJECT

1. Sharing an apartment with a roommate
2. Behavior toward others
3. My mother
4. Fast-food restaurants
5. Bad driving habits
6. Regular exercise

7. Owning a house
8. Baseball
9. Religion
10. Pollution

7. Do-it-yourself home repairs
8. Free-agent system
9. Religious celebrations
10. Noise pollution

Thesis statements for five of the limited subjects:

_____

_____

_____

_____

_____

_____

_____

_____

_____

_____

_____

_____

_____

_____

_____

_____

Here is a list of ten general subjects. Limit five of the subjects. Then write a thesis statement about each of the five limited subjects.

ACTIVITY 17

GENERAL SUBJECT

1. Parenting
2. Cell Phones
3. Homework
4. Happiness
5. Weather

LIMITED SUBJECT

_____

_____

_____

_____

_____

GENERAL SUBJECT	LIMITED SUBJECT
6. Career	_____
7. Foreign Languages	_____
8. Leadership	_____
9. Math	_____
10. Change	_____

Thesis statements for five of the limited subjects:

_____

_____

_____

_____

_____

_____

_____

_____

_____

_____

_____

_____

_____

_____

_____

_____

_____

_____

Providing Specific Evidence

ACTIVITY 18

Provide three details that logically support each of the following points. Your details can be drawn from your own experience, or they can be invented. In each case,
the details should show *specifically* what the point expresses only generally. State
your details briefly in several words rather than in complete sentences.

EXAMPLE

We quickly spruced up the apartment before our guest arrived.

1. *Hid toys and newspapers in spare closet*

2. *Vacuumed pet hairs off sofa*

3. *Sprayed air freshener around living room*

1. The hike up to the mountain lookout was exciting.

   _____

   _____

   _____

2. My hometown is worth visiting.

   _____

   _____

   _____

   _____

3. There are several reasons why I put off studying.

   _____

   _____

   _____

4. Working at the hospital has taught me many valuable skills.

   _____

   _____

   _____

5. I have several ways to earn extra cash.

   _____

   _____

   _____

6. My car needs repairs.

_____

_____

_____

7. Friday evening, I didn't sit still for a minute.

_____

_____

_____

8. My best friends are very different, but I love each of them.

_____

_____

_____

_____

Identifying Adequate Supporting Evidence

ACTIVITY 19

The following body paragraphs were taken from student essays. Two of the paragraphs provide sufficient details to support their topic sentences convincingly. Write *AD* for *adequate development* beside those paragraphs. Three paragraphs use vague, wordy, general, or irrelevant sentences instead of real supporting details. Write *U* for *underdeveloped* beside those paragraphs.

_____ 1.   Another consideration in adopting a dog is the cost. Initial fees for shots and a license might add up to $50. Annual visits to the vet for heartworm pills, rabies and distemper shots, and general checkups could cost $100 or more. Then there is the cost of food. A twenty-five-pound bag of dry food (the cheapest kind) costs around $15. A large dog can eat that much in a couple of weeks.

_____ 2.   People can be cruel to pets simply by being thoughtless. They don't think about a pet's needs, or they simply ignore those needs. It never occurs to them that their pet can be experiencing a great deal of discomfort as a result of their failure to be sensitive. The cruelty is a result of the basic lack of attention and concern—qualities that should be there, but aren't.

_____ 3.   If I were in charge of the nighttime programming on a TV network, I would make changes. I would completely eliminate some shows. In fact, all the shows that proved to be of little interest would be canceled. Commercials would also change so that it would be possible to watch them without wanting to turn off the TV. I would expand the good shows so that people would come away with an even better experience. My ideal network would be a great improvement over the average lineup we see today on any of the major networks.

_____ 4.   A friend's rudeness is much more damaging than a stranger's. When a friend says sharply, "I don't have time to talk to you just now," it can hurt deeply. When a friend shows up late for lunch or a shopping trip, with no good reason, it can make a person feel as if he or she is being taken for granted. Worst, though, is when a friend pretends to be listening but his or her wandering eyes show a lack of attention. This often feels like betrayal. Friends, after all, are supposed to make up for the thoughtless cruelties of strangers.

_____ 5.   Giving my first shampoo and set to a real person, after weeks of practicing on wigs, was a nerve-racking experience. The customer was a woman who acted very sure about what she came for. She tried to describe what she wanted, and I tried without much success to understand what she had in mind. Every time I did something, she seemed to be indicating in one way or another that it was not what she wanted. I got more and more nervous as I worked on her hair, and the nervousness showed. The worst part of the ordeal happened at the very end, when I added the final touches. Nothing, to this woman, had turned out right.

Adding Details to Complete an Essay

The following essay needs specific details to back up the ideas in the supporting paragraphs. Using the spaces provided, add a sentence or two of clear, convincing details for each supporting idea. This activity will give you practice at supplying specific details and an initial feel for writing an essay.

ACTIVITY 20

Life Off-Line

When my family's Internet provider had some mechanical problems that interrupted our service for a week, my parents, my sister, and I thought we would never make it. Getting through long evenings without streaming movies,

Introduction

continued

e-mails, Twitter updates, and Internet searches seemed impossible. We soon realized, though, that living off-line for a while was a stroke of good fortune. It became easy for each of us to enjoy some activities alone, to complete some postponed chores, and to spend rewarding time with each other and friends.

First support-ing paragraph

First of all, now that we were disconnected, we found plenty of hours for personal interests. We all read more that week than we had read during the six months before. _____

_____

_____

We each also enjoyed some hobbies we had ignored for ages._____

_____

_____

_____

In addition, my sister and I both stopped procrastinating with our

homework._____

_____

_____

_____

Second supporting paragraph

Second, we did chores that had been hanging over our heads for too long. There were many jobs around the house that had needed attention for some time._____

_____

_____

continued

We had a chance to do some long-postponed shopping._____

_____

_____

_____

Also, each of us did some paperwork that was long overdue._____

_____

_____

_____

    Finally, and probably most important, we spent time with each other. Instead of just being in the same room together while we stared at different screens, we actually talked for many pleasant hours._____

_____

_____

Moreover, for the first time in years my family played some card games and board games together._____

_____

_____

_____

Because we couldn't keep up with everyone electronically, we had some family friends over one evening and spent an enjoyable time with them._____

_____

_____

_____

Third support-ing paragraph

Conclusion

Once our Internet provider got the problems fixed, we were not prepared to go back to our previous ways. We had gained a sense of how our online activities had not only taken over our lives, but had also interrupted our family's life. We still spend time streaming movies, gaming, e-mailing, and tweeting, but we make sure to spend at least two evenings a week focusing on each other. As a result, we have found that we can enjoy our virtual lives and still have time left over for our real lives!

What are some ways besides using electronic media that you and your family or friends spend quality time together? Write about one of these activities and why you enjoy it.

The Third Step in Essay Writing

This chapter will show you how to

- organize and connect specific evidence in the body paragraphs of an essay

- begin and end an essay with effective introductory and concluding paragraphs

In the previous chapter, you helped complete one student's essay about life without electronic media. Without Internet access, the student had time to enjoy a host of other activities he or she otherwise would not have had time to do. Write an essay about what, in your life, keeps you from completing tasks or doing what you enjoy. Also include what you would do with your time if this obstacle was removed.

You know from Chapter 3 that the first two steps in writing an effective essay are advancing a thesis and supporting it with specific evidence. This chapter deals with the third step: organizing and connecting the supporting information in a paper. You'll also learn how to start an essay with a suitable introductory paragraph and how to finish it with a well-rounded concluding paragraph.

Step 3: Organize and Connect the Specific Evidence

As you are generating the specific details needed to support a thesis, you should be thinking about ways to organize and connect those details. All the details in your essay must *cohere,* or stick together, so that your reader will be able to move smoothly from one bit of supporting information to the next. This section shows you how to organize and connect supporting details by using (1) common methods of organization, (2) transitions, and (3) other connecting words.

Common Methods of Organization

Two common methods used to organize the supporting material in an essay are time order and emphatic order. (You will learn more specific methods of development in Part 2 of this book.)

Time order, or *chronological order,* simply means that details are listed as they occur in time. *First* this is done; *next* this; *then* this; *after* that, this; and so on. Here is an outline of an essay in this book that uses time order:

Thesis

> In order to effectively market the preschool, promoting the center needs to remain at the top of our priority list and should include proper advertising, publicity, and referrals.
>
> 1. The first step is proper advertising that must start with a well-designed multi-layered Web site that includes general information, enrollment forms, and profiles of teachers and staff.
>
> 2. A second step to increasing enrollment is through concerted publicity.
>
> 3. The final and best way to increase enrollment is to utilize our currently enrolled families.

Fill in the missing words: The topic sentences in the essay use the words or phrases _____, and _____ to help show time order.

Here is one supporting paragraph from the essay:

> A second step to increasing enrollment is through concerted publicity. Publicity could include a monthly column in the local newspaper that highlights what is currently going on at the preschool. Because our curriculum is a blend of Montessori and Carden methods, we have a unique offering; calling attention to the special achievements, programs, and students in our school would offer the positive publicity needed to interest potential families. Each column's publication should be followed by an open house, so potential families can actually visit our school. These open houses should also occur during key enrollment periods to encourage greater attendance. Finally, hosting one or two major events such as a school picnic or music program will continue to raise awareness of our school within the community.

Fill in the missing words: The paragraph uses the following words to help show time order: _____, and _____.

Emphatic order is sometimes described as "saving the best till last." It is a way to put *emphasis* on the most interesting or important detail by placing it in the last part of a paragraph or in the final supporting paragraph of an essay.

> **TIP**   In cases where all the details seem equal in importance, the writer should impose a personal order that seems logical or appropriate.

The last position in a paper is the most emphatic position because the reader is most likely to remember the last thing read. *Finally, last of all,* and *most important* are typical words or phrases showing emphasis. Here is an outline of an essay in this book that uses emphatic order:

> *When I compare the two restaurants, the advantages of eating at McDonald's are clear.*
> 1.   *For one thing, going to the Chalet is more difficult than going to McDonald's.*
> 2.   *Eating at the Chalet is, to me, less enjoyable than eating at McDonald's.*
> 3.   *The most important difference between the Chalet and McDonald's, though, is price.*

Thesis

Fill in the missing words: The topic sentences in the essay use the words or phrases _____, _____, _____ to help show emphatic order.

Here is the third supporting paragraph from the essay:

> The most important difference between the Chalet and McDonald's, though, is price. Dinner for two at the Chalet, even without appetizers or desserts, would easily cost $100. And the $100 doesn't include the cost of parking the car and tipping the waiter, which can come to an additional $20. Once, I forgot to bring enough money. At McDonald's, a filling meal for two will cost around $10. With the extra $110, my wife and I can eat at McDonald's eleven more times, or go to the movies five times, or buy tickets to a football game.

Fill in the missing phrase: The words _____ are used to mark the most emphatic detail in the paragraph.

Some essays use a combination of time order and emphatic order. For example, the essay on moviegoing in Chapter 1 (page 4) includes time order: the writer first describes getting to the theater, then the theater itself, and finally the behavior of audience members during the movie. At the same time, the writer uses emphatic order, ending with the most important reason for her dislike of moviegoing: "Some of the other patrons are even more of a problem than the theater itself."

ACTIVITY 1

Part A Read the essays listed below (page numbers are in parentheses) and identify their method of organizing details—time order, emphatic order, or a combination of both.

1. "Taking on a Disability" (page 204)

    _____

2. "A Vote for McDonald's" (page 284)

    _____

3. "Look on the Bright Side" (page 223)

    _____

Part B Now see if you can complete the explanations that follow.

The essay titled "Taking on a Disability" uses (*add the missing word*)

_____ order. The author begins with the challenge of learning to sit properly in the wheelchair, then moves on to learning to move in the wheelchair, and ends with several problems that occurred next, during the church service. "A Vote for McDonald's" uses (*add the missing word*) _____ order. The writer presents three advantages of eating at McDonald's and ends with the most important one: reasonable prices. "Look on the Bright Side" uses a combination of (*add the missing words*) _____ and _____ order. It moves from something that took place one morning, to one that took place at lunchtime, to one that took place one evening. It ends with one of "the worst and best examples of human behavior" that the author witnessed.

Transitions

Transitional Words

Transitions signal the direction of a writer's thoughts. They are like the road signs that guide travelers. In the box that follows are some common transitions, grouped according to the kind of signal they give to readers. Note that certain words provide more than one kind of signal.

Common Transitions

Addition Signals: one, first, second, the third reason, also, next, and, in addition, moreover, further, furthermore, finally, last, similarly, likewise, as well, too, besides.

Time Signals: first, then, next, after, as before, while, meanwhile, soon, now, during, finally, after a while, as soon as, at that time, by then, since, suddenly, then, thereafter, by then, in a few hours, by that time.

Space Signals: next to, across, on the opposite side, to the left, to the right, above, below, near, nearby, beside, on top of, under, over, underneath, far from.

Change-of-Direction Signals: but, however, yet, in contrast, although, otherwise, still, on the contrary, on the other hand, nevertheless, instead, nonetheless, otherwise, even though.

Illustration Signals: for example, for instance, specifically, as an illustration, once, such as.

Conclusion Signals: therefore, consequently, thus, then, as a result, in summary, to conclude, last, finally.

Other Transitions: Conjunctive Adverbs and Transitional Phrases

A conjunctive adverb is a word that, when used after a semicolon, connects two independent (main) clauses. A transitional phrase is a group of words that, when used after a semicolon, connects two independent (main) clauses.

Conjunctive adverb: Napoleon successfully invaded Russia in 1812; **however,** he did not occupy it for long.

Transitional phrase: Jean Piaget made major contributions to child psychology; **in fact,** he proved that children and adults reason differently.

Like transitional words, conjunctive adverbs and transitional phrases signal the direction of the writer's thoughts and guide the reader.

ACTIVITY 2

1. Underline the four *addition* signals in the following selection:

> Applying for financial aid is a very detailed process. First, students should fill out the Free Application for Federal Student Aid (FAFSA). This may require gathering a lot of specific information, but once it has been completed, the Student Aid Report (SAR) should arrive quickly. Second, students should review their SAR to find out how much they will be expected to pay for college and how much aid they qualify for. Next, they should compare financial aid packages offered by each of their chosen colleges. Finally, students should decide which financial aid package they are going to accept, contact the college, and prepare to fill out more paperwork to receive their financial aid.

2. Underline the three *time* signals in the following selection:

> To set up a realistic exercise regime, people need to follow a simple plan consisting of arranging time, making preparations, and starting off at a sensible pace. The first step is arranging time. Most people who don't regularly exercise have excuses for not exercising: a heavy schedule at work

continued

or school; being rushed in the morning and exhausted at night; or too many other responsibilities. One simple solution is to get up half an hour earlier in the morning. The next step is making preparations. Having necessary items like workout clothes, videos, and exercise equipment laid out and ready makes it much easier to get started. Finally, people who are just beginning an exercise regime should start off at a sensible pace. Many workout videos have different levels of exercise programs and new exercisers should always start with level one to avoid injuries. Through careful planning and common sense, anyone can start exercising.

3. Underline the three *space* signals in the following selection:

The vegetable bin in my refrigerator contained an assortment of weird-looking items. Next to a shriveled, fuzz-coated lemon were two oranges covered with blue fur. To the right of the oranges was a bunch of carrots that had begun to sprout points, spikes, knobs, and tendrils. The carrots drooped into U shapes as I picked them up with the tips of my fingers. Near the carrots was a net bag of onions; each onion had sent curling shoots through the net until the whole thing resembled a mass of green spaghetti. The most horrible item, though, was a head of lettuce that had turned into a pool of brown goo. It had seeped out of its bag and coated the bin with a sticky, evil-smelling liquid.

4. Underline the two *change-of-direction* signals in the following selection:

Taking small children on vacation, for instance, sounds like a wonderful experience for the entire family. But vacations can be scary or emotionally overwhelming times for children. When children are taken away from their usual routine and brought to an unfamiliar place, they can become very frightened. That strange bed in the motel room or the unusual noises

continued

in Grandma's spare bedroom may cause nightmares. On vacations, too, children usually clamor to do as many things in one day as they can and to stay up past their usual bedtime. And since it is vacation time, parents may decide to give in to the children's demands. A parental attitude like this, however, can lead to problems. After a sixteen-hour day of touring the amusement park, eating in a restaurant, and seeing a movie, children can experience sensory and emotional overload. They become cranky, unhappy, or even rebellious and angry.

5. Underline the two *illustration* signals in the following selection:

Supermarkets also use psychology to encourage people to buy. For example, in most supermarkets, the milk and the bread are either at opposite ends of the store or located far away from the first aisle. Even if a shopper stopped at the market only for staples like these, he or she must first pass hundreds of items. The odds are that instead of leaving with just a quart of milk, additional purchases will be made. Special displays, such as a pyramid of canned green beans in an aisle or a large end display of cartons of paper towels, also increase sales. Because the shopper assumes that these items are a good buy, he or she may pick them up. However, the items may not even be on sale. Store managers know that the customer is automatically attracted to a display like this, and they will use it to move an overstocked product.

6. Underline the two *conclusion* signals in the following selection:

Finally, my grandmother was extremely thrifty. She was one of those people who hoard pieces of used aluminum foil after carefully scrubbing off the cake icing or beef gravy. She had a drawer full of old eyeglasses that dated back at least thirty years. The lens prescriptions were no longer accurate, but Gran couldn't bear to throw away "a good pair of glasses." She kept them "just in case," but we could never figure out what situation would involve a desperate need for a dozen pairs of old eyeglasses. We never realized the true extent of Gran's thriftiness, though, until after she died. Her house was to be sold, and therefore we cleaned out its dusty attic. In one corner was a cardboard box filled with two- and three-inch pieces of string. The box was labeled, in Gran's spidery hand, "String too short to be saved."

Transitional Sentences

Transitional sentences, or *linking sentences*, are used between paragraphs to help tie together the supporting paragraphs in an essay. They enable the reader to move smoothly from the idea in one paragraph to the idea in the next paragraph.

Here is the linking sentence used in the essay on moviegoing:

Many of the other patrons are even more of a problem than the concession stand.

The words *concession stand* remind us of the point of the first supporting paragraph, while *Many of the other patrons* presents the point to be developed in the second supporting paragraph.

Following is a brief sentence outline of an essay. The second and third topic sentences serve as transitional, or linking, sentences. Each reminds us of the point in the preceding paragraph and announces the point to be developed in the current paragraph. In the spaces provided, add the words needed to complete the second and third topic sentences.

ACTIVITY 3

Personal

> The most memorable sites I visited in Washington, D.C., were the Capitol Building, the Lincoln Memorial, and the Vietnam Memorial.
>   Our first stop was Capitol Hill, the very symbol of our democratic system. . . .

Thesis

After leaving the _____, we walked along the Mall to the

_____

_____ . . . .

First supporting paragraph

A short distance to the right of the _____ is the

_____

_____ . . . .

Second supporting paragraph

Other Connecting Words

In addition to transitions, there are three other kinds of connecting words that help tie together the specific evidence in a paper: *repeated words*, *pronouns*, and *synonyms*.

Repeated Words

Many of us have been taught—correctly—not to repeat ourselves in writing. However, repeating *key* words helps tie together the flow of thought in a paper. Below, repeated words remind readers of the selection's central idea.

> One good reason for studying <u>psychology</u> is to help parents deal with their children. Perhaps a young daughter refuses to go to bed when she should and bursts into tears at the least mention of "lights out." A little knowledge of <u>psychology</u> comes in handy. If she is given a choice of staying up until 7:30 with the family or going upstairs and playing until 8:00, she gets to make the decision. In this way, she does not feel so powerless and will not resist. <u>Psychology</u> is also useful in rewarding a child for a job well done. Instead of telling a ten-year-old son what a good boy he is when he makes his own bed, good <u>psychology</u> says to focus on how neat it is and the fact that he did it by himself. The <u>psychology</u> books say that being a good boy is much harder to live up to than doing one job well.

Pronouns

Pronouns (*he, she, it, you, they, this, that,* and others) are another way to connect ideas. Also, using pronouns in place of other words can help you avoid needless repetition. (Note, however, that pronouns should be used with care to avoid the problems described on pages 495–498.) Here is a selection that makes good use of pronouns:

> Another way for people to economize at an amusement park is to bring <u>their</u> own food. If <u>they</u> pack a nourishing, well-balanced lunch of cold chicken, carrot sticks, and fruit, <u>they</u> will avoid having to pay high prices for hamburgers and hot dogs. <u>They</u> will also save on calories. Also, instead of filling up on soft drinks, <u>they</u> should bring a thermos of iced tea. Iced tea is more refreshing than soda, and <u>it</u> is a great deal cheaper. Every dollar that is not spent at a refreshment stand is <u>one</u> that can be spent on another ride.

Synonyms

Synonyms are words alike in meaning. Using synonyms can also help move the reader easily from one thought to the next. In addition, the use of synonyms increases variety and interest by avoiding needless repetition.

Note the synonyms for *method* in the following selection:

> Several methods of fund-raising work well with small organizations. One <u>technique</u> is to hold an auction, with everyone either contributing an item from home or obtaining a donation from a sympathetic local merchant. Because all the merchandise and the services of the auctioneer have been donated, the entire proceeds can be placed in the organization's treasury. A second fund-raising <u>procedure</u> is a car wash. Club members and their children get together on a Saturday and wash all the cars in the neighborhood for a few dollars apiece. A third, time-tested <u>way</u> to raise money is to hold a bake sale, with each family contributing homemade cookies, brownies, layer cakes, or cupcakes. Sold by the piece or by the box, these baked goods will satisfyingly fill both the stomach and the pocketbook.

Read the selection below and then answer the questions about it that follow.

ACTIVITY 4

> [1]When I think about my childhood in the 1930s, life today seems like the greatest of luxuries. [2]In our house, we had only a wood-burning cookstove in the kitchen to keep us warm. [3]In the morning, my father would get up in the icy cold, go downstairs, and light a fire in the black iron range. [4]When he called us, I would put off leaving my warm bed until the last possible minute and then quickly grab my school clothes. [5]The water pitcher and washing basin in my room would be layered with ice, and my breath would come out as white puffs as I ran downstairs. [6]My sisters and I would all dress—as quickly as possible—in the chilly but bearable air of the kitchen. [7]Our schoolroom, once we had arrived, didn't provide much relief from the cold. [8]Students wore woolen mitts that left their fingers free but covered their palms and wrists. [9]Even with these, we occasionally suffered chilblains. [10]The throbbing swellings on our hands made writing a painful process. [11]When we returned home in the afternoon, we spent all our indoor hours in the warm kitchen. [12]We hated to leave it at bedtime to make the return trip to those cold bedrooms and frigid sheets. [13]My mother made up hot-water bottles and gave us hot bricks to tuck under the covers, but nothing could eliminate the agony of that penetrating cold when we first slid under the bedclothes.

1. How many times is the key word *cold* used? _____

2. Write here the pronoun that is used for *father* (sentence 4): _____

3. Write here the words in sentence 3 that are used as a synonym for *cookstove:*
_____; write in the words in sentence 10 that are used as a synonym for *chilblains:* _____; write in the word in sentence 12 that is used as a synonym for *cold:* _____.

Introductions, Conclusions, and Titles

So far, this chapter has discussed ways to organize and connect the supporting paragraphs of an essay. A well-organized essay, however, also needs a strong introductory paragraph, an effective concluding paragraph, and a good title.

Introductory Paragraph

Functions of the Introduction

A well-written introductory paragraph performs four important roles:

1. It attracts the reader's interest, encouraging him or her to continue reading the essay.

2. It supplies any background information that the reader may need to understand the essay.

3. It presents a thesis statement. This clear, direct statement of the main idea of the paper usually appears near the end of the introductory paragraph.

4. It indicates a plan of development. In this preview, the major supporting points for the thesis are listed in the order in which they will be presented. In some cases, the thesis and plan of development appear in the same sentence. However, writers sometimes choose not to describe the plan of development.

Common Methods of Introduction

Here are some common methods of introduction. Use any one method, or a combination of methods, to introduce your subject to the reader in an interesting way.

- **Begin with a broad, general statement of your topic and narrow it down to your thesis statement.** Broad, general statements ease the reader into your thesis statement by first introducing the topic. In the following example, the writer talks generally about categories of students and then narrows down to comments on a specific type.

Schools divide people into categories. From first grade on up, students are labeled "advanced" or "deprived" or "remedial" or "antisocial." Students pigeonhole their fellow students, too. We've all known the "brain," the "jock," the "dummy," and the "teacher's pet." In most cases, these narrow labels are misleading and inaccurate. But there is one label for a certain type of college student that says it all: "zombie."

- **Start with an idea or a situation that is the opposite of the one you will develop.** This approach works because your readers will be surprised, and then intrigued, by the contrast between the opening idea and the thesis that follows it.

Most Americans are not alcoholics. Most do not cruise seedy city streets looking to score crack cocaine or heroin. Relatively few try to con their doctors into prescribing unneeded mood-altering medications. And yet, many Americans are traveling through life with their minds slightly out of kilter. In its attempt to cope with modern life, the human mind seems to have evolved some defense strategies. Confronted with inventions like television, the shopping center, and the Internet, the mind will slip—all by itself—into an altered state.

- **Explain the importance of your topic to the reader.** If you can convince your readers that the subject in some way applies to them, or is something they should know more about, they will want to keep reading.

Happy Child Preschool is a valuable and cherished part of our campus, but enrollment has declined dramatically over the past two years. Thus, a task force was commissioned to analyze the causes. The comparative analysis conducted by the task force uncovered numerous ways that other campus childcare centers have achieved success through advertising. The task force agrees that promotion is the number one issue that has been overlooked in the past and the area where major and immediate improvements are essential to the long-term success of the center. In order to effectively market the preschool, promoting the center needs to remain at the top of the priority chart and should include proper advertising, publicity, and referrals.

- **Use an incident or a brief story.** Stories are naturally interesting. They appeal to a reader's curiosity. In your introduction, an anecdote will grab the reader's attention right away. The story should be brief and should be related to your main idea. The incident in the story can be something that happened to you, something you have heard about, or something you have read about in a newspaper or magazine.

> Early Sunday morning, the young mother dressed her little girl warmly and gave her a candy bar, a picture book, and a well-worn stuffed rabbit. Together, they drove downtown to a Methodist church. There the mother told the little girl to wait on the stone steps until children began arriving for Sunday school. Then the young mother drove off, abandoning her five-year-old because she couldn't cope with being a parent anymore. This incident is one of thousands of cases of child neglect and abuse that occur annually. Perhaps the automatic right to become a parent should no longer exist. Would-be parents should be forced to apply for parental licenses for which they would have to meet three important conditions.

- **Use a quotation.** A quotation can be something you have read in a book or an article. It can also be something that you have heard: a popular saying or proverb ("Never give advice to a friend"), a current or recent advertising slogan ("Can you hear me now?"), or a favorite expression used by friends or family ("My father always says . . ."). Using a quotation in your introductory paragraph lets you add someone else's voice to your own.

> "Fish and visitors," wrote Benjamin Franklin, "begin to smell after three days." Last summer, when my sister and her family came to spend their two-week vacation with us, I became convinced that Franklin was right. After only three days of my family's visit, I was thoroughly sick of my brother-in-law's lame jokes, my sister's endless complaints about her boss, and their children's constant invasions of our privacy.

ACTIVITY 5   The box that follows summarizes the five kinds of introductions. Read the introductions that come after it and, in the space provided, write the letter of the kind of introduction used in each case.

> A. General to narrow
> B. Starting with an opposite
> C. Stating importance of topic
> D. Incident or story
> E. Quotation

_____ 1. The ad, in full color on a glossy magazine page, shows a beautiful kitchen with gleaming counters. In the foreground, on one of the counters, stands a shiny new food processor. Usually, a feminine hand is touching it lovingly. Around the main picture are other, smaller shots. They show mounds of perfectly sliced onion rings, thin rounds of juicy tomatoes, heaps of matchstick-sized potatoes, and piles of golden, evenly grated cheese. The ad copy proclaims how wonderful, how easy, food preparation will be with a processor. Don't believe it. My processor turned out to be expensive, difficult to operate, and very limited in its use.

_____ 2. My father stubbornly says, "You <u>can</u> often tell a book by its cover," and when it comes to certain paperbacks, he's right. Whenever a person is browsing in the drugstore or supermarket and he or she sees a paperback featuring an attractive young woman in a low-cut dress fleeing from a handsome dark figure in a shadowy castle, it is obvious what the book will be about. Every romance novel has the same elements: an innocent heroine, an exotic setting, and a cruel but fascinating hero.

_____ 3. Americans are incredibly lazy. Instead of cooking a simple, nourishing meal, we pop a frozen dinner into the oven. Instead of studying a daily newspaper, we are contented with the capsule summaries on the network news. Worst of all, instead of walking even a few blocks to the local convenience store, we jump into our cars. This dependence on the automobile, even for short trips, has robbed us of a valuable experience—walking. If we drove less and walked more, we would save money, become healthier, and discover fascinating things about our surroundings.

Concluding Paragraph

A concluding paragraph is your chance to remind the reader of your thesis idea and bring the paper to a natural and graceful end.

Common Methods of Conclusion

You may use any one of the methods below, or a combination of methods, to round off your paper.

- **End with a summary and final thought.** When army instructors train new recruits, each of their lessons follows a three-step formula:

  1. Tell them what you're going to tell them.

  2. Tell them.

  3. Tell them what you've told them.

An essay that ends with a summary is not very different. After you have stated your thesis ("Tell them what you're going to tell them") and supported it ("Tell them"), you restate the thesis and supporting points ("Tell them what you've told them"). However, don't use the exact wording you used before. Here is a summary conclusion:

> Online shopping at home, then, has several advantages. Such shopping is convenient, saves money, and saves time. It is not surprising that growing numbers of people are doing the majority of their shopping on the Internet for everything from turnip seeds to televisions.

Note that the summary is accompanied by a final comment that rounds off the paper and brings the discussion to a close. This combination of a summary and a final thought is the most common method of concluding an essay.

- **Include a thought-provoking quotation.** A well-chosen quotation can be effective in re-emphasizing your point. Here is an example:

> Rude behavior has become commonplace and needs to stop. People no longer treat each other with the respect and courtesy they should. People talk on their cell phones at inappropriate times and places. Cutting off other drivers in order to save mere seconds happens more and more often. As the Dalai Lama said, "Love and kindness are the very basis of society. If we lose these feelings, society will face tremendous difficulties; the survival of humanity will be endangered."

- **End with a prediction or recommendation.** Predictions and recommendations encourage the reader to continue thinking about the essay. A prediction states what may happen in the future:

> It is believed that as many as two million people are currently undiagnosed with celiac disease, or gluten sensitivity. There is currently no medication to cure the disease. If doctors disregard patients who complain of symptoms of the disease, serious physical damage can occur. But if doctors listen to their patients and administer the appropriate tests, proper diagnosis can be made in a timely manner.

A recommendation suggests what should be done about a situation or problem:

> Stereotypes such as the ditzy blonde, harried executive, and annoying in-law are insulting enough to begin with. In magazine ads or television commercials, they become even more insulting. Now these unfortunate characters are not just being laughed at; they are being turned into hucksters to sell products to an unsuspecting public. Consumers should boycott companies whose advertising continues to use such stereotypes.

In the space provided, note how each concluding paragraph ends: with a summary and final thought (write *S* in the space), with a prediction or recommendation (write *P/R*), or with a quotation (write *Q*).

ACTIVITY 6

_____ 1. Disappointments are unwelcome, but regular, visitors in everyone's life. We can feel depressed about them, or we can try to escape from them. The best thing, though, is to accept a disappointment and then try to use it somehow: step over the unwelcome visitor and then get on with life.

_____ 2. Saving the environment is up to each of us. Levels of harmful emissions would drop dramatically if we chose to carpool or take public transportation more often. Conserving fuel and electricity at home by sealing up leaky windows and using energy-saving light bulbs would help, too. As David Orr once wrote, "When we heal the Earth, we heal ourselves."

_____ 3. Some people dream of starring roles, their names in lights, and their pictures on the cover of *People* magazine. I'm not one of them, though. A famous person gives up private life, feels pressured all the time, and is never completely safe. So let someone else have that cover story. I'd rather lead an ordinary, but calm, life than a stress-filled one.

Titles

A title is usually a very brief summary of what your paper is about. It is often no more than several words. You may find it easier to write the title *after* you have completed your paper.

Following are the introductory paragraphs for two of the essays in this text, along with the titles of the essays.

Introductory paragraph

> I'm not just a consumer—I'm a victim. If I order a product, it is sure to arrive in the wrong color, size, or quantity. If I hire people to do repairs, they never arrive on the day scheduled. If I owe a bill, the computer is bound to overcharge me. Therefore, in self-defense, I have developed the following consumer's guide to complaining effectively.

Title: How to Complain

Introductory paragraph

> Schools divide people into categories. From first grade on up, students are labeled "advanced" or "deprived" or "remedial" or "antisocial." Students pigeonhole their fellow students, too. We've all known the "brain," the "jock," the "dummy," and the "teacher's pet." In most cases, these narrow labels are misleading and inaccurate. But there is one label for a certain type of college student that says it all: "zombie."

Title: Student Zombies

Note that you should not underline the title. Nor should you put quotation marks around it. On the other hand, you should capitalize all but small connecting words in the title. Also, you should skip a space between the title and the first line of the text. (See "Manuscript Form," page 523.)

ACTIVITY 7

Write an appropriate title for each of the introductory paragraphs that follow.

1. Returning to my hometown of Mercyville after five years, I discovered several newcomers on the same street as the pharmacy, hardware store, and restaurants I had patronized. A store selling African art had opened next to my favorite pizzeria. A few doors down was a Thai take-out restaurant, and across the street a Hindu grocer had set up shop. In the storefront where Charlie's Hamburgers was once located, I found a fancy Hungarian bistro featuring an elegant New Year's Eve dinner for $65.

Title: _____

Personal

2. When my parents bought a new home in a small town outside Chicago, they decided to fence in our yard so that our two Labrador retrievers wouldn't wander off. The contractor they hired informed them that they would have to apply for a building permit, which would cost $150. After the shock wore off, my father went to town hall with the check, but the clerk informed him that he would have to submit a written request for the permit as well as a plot plan of our property. When he returned two hours later, the office was closed, and he had to return on Monday. After submitting everything, he learned that the town planning committee would not meet to consider our application for two months. When they did meet, they refused to grant our permit because the proposed fence crossed a "designated wetlands" area, and they refused to refund our $150.

Title: _____

For further practice in writing titles, write an appropriate title for the image pictured here.

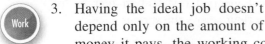
Work

3. Having the ideal job doesn't depend only on the amount of money it pays, the working conditions, or the opportunities for advancement. It also has to do with one's fellow employees and, of course, the boss. While most people realize that bosses need to exercise careful supervision over the workplace and the employees, they prefer bosses who socialize with workers, make few demands, and look the other way when they don't perform well. Unfortunately, such supervisors too often turn out to be inefficient, disorganized, and unpredictable. A better alternative is someone who enforces rules predictably and demands that workers meet reasonable expectations.

Title: _____

Practice in Organizing and Connecting Specific Evidence

You now know the third step in effective writing: organizing the specific evidence used to support the thesis of a paper. This closing section will expand and strengthen your understanding of the third step in writing. You will work through the following series of activities:

- organizing through time or emphatic order
- providing transitions
- identifying transitions and other connecting words
- completing transitional sentences
- identifying introductions and conclusions

Organizing through Time or Emphatic Order

ACTIVITY 8

Use time order to organize the scrambled lists of supporting ideas below. Write *1* beside the supporting idea that should come first in time, *2* beside the idea that logically follows, and *3* beside the idea that comes last in time.

1. Thesis: When I was a child, Disney movies frightened me more than any other kind.

   _____ As a five-year-old, I was terrified by the movie *Pinocchio,* about a puppet transformed into a boy.

   _____ Although I saw *Bambi* when I was old enough to begin poking fun at "baby movies," the scene during which Bambi's mother is killed has stayed with me to this day.

   _____ About a year after *Pinocchio,* I gripped my seat in fear as the witches and goblins of *Fantasia* flew across the screen.

2. Thesis: Observing three important rules will help you write better research papers.

   _____ Follow the format for including researched material required by your instructor.

   _____ Start the project early, immediately after it is assigned.

   _____ Use note cards, not notebook paper, to record the facts and ideas you research.

3.   Thesis: Applying for unemployment benefits was a confusing, frustrating experience.

_____   It was difficult to find both the office and a place to park.

_____   When I finally reached the head of the line after four hours of waiting, the clerk had problems processing my claim.

_____   There was no one to direct or help me when I entered the large office, which was packed with people.

Use emphatic order (order of importance) to arrange the following scrambled lists of supporting ideas. For each thesis, write 1 in the blank beside the point that is perhaps less important or interesting than the other two, 2 beside the point that appears more important or interesting, and 3 beside the point that should be most emphasized.

ACTIVITY 9

1.   Thesis: My part-time job has been an invaluable part of my life this year.

_____   Better yet, it has taught me how to get along with many kinds of people.

_____   Since it's in the morning, it usually keeps me from staying up too late.

_____   Without it, I would have had to drop out of school.

2.   Thesis: Our soccer team was awarded three special honors for winning the state championship.

_____   Three of our team members won college athletic scholarships

_____   Our victory was written up in major newspapers.

_____   Each team member received a gold medal.

3.   Thesis: Donna is my most loyal friend.

_____   She has taken time to do special favors for me.

_____   She's always there in real emergencies or emotional crises.

_____   She once lent me her favorite necklace to wear on a date.

Providing Transitions

In the spaces provided, add appropriate transitions to tie together the sentences and ideas in the following essay. Draw from the words given in the boxes above the paragraphs. Use each word only once.

ACTIVITY 10

Personal

Annoying People

President Richard Nixon used to keep an enemies list of all the people he didn't especially like. I'm ashamed to confess it, but I, too, have an enemies list—a mental one. On this list are all the people I would gladly live without, the ones who cause my blood pressure to rise to the boiling point. The top three places on the list go to people with annoying nervous habits, people who talk in movie theaters, and people who talk on cell phones while driving.

For example	First of all	Another	However

_____, there are the people with annoying nervous habits.

_____, there are the ones who make faces. When in deep thought, they twitch, squint, and frown, and they can be a real distraction when I'm

trying to concentrate during an exam. _____ type of nervous character makes useless designs. These people bend paper clips into abstract sculptures or string the clips into necklaces as they talk.

_____, neither of these groups is as bad as the people who make noises. These individuals, when they are feeling uncomfortable, bite their fingernails or crack their knuckles. If they have a pencil in their hands, they tap it rhythmically against whatever surface is handy—a desk, a book, a head. Lacking a pencil to play with, they jingle the loose change or keys in their pockets. These people make me wish I were hard of hearing.

On the contrary	Then	As a result	After	Second

A _____ category of people I would gladly do away with is the ones who talk in movie theaters. These people are not content to sit back,

relax, and enjoy the film they have paid to see. _____, they feel compelled to comment loudly on everything from the hero's hairstyle to the

appropriateness of the background music. _____, no one hears a

word of any dialogue except theirs. _____ these people have been in the

theater for a while, their interest in the movie may fade. _____ they will start discussing other things, and the people around them will be treated to an instant replay of the latest family scandal or soap-opera episode. These stories may be entertaining, but they don't belong in a movie theater.

continued

In addition	But	Last of all

_____, there are the people who talk on the phone while they're driving. One of the things that irritates me about them is the way they seem to be showing off. They're saying, "Look at me! I'm so important I have to make phone calls in my <u>car</u>." _____, such behavior is just plain dangerous. Instead of concentrating on adjusting carefully to everchanging traffic conditions, they're weaving all over the road or getting much too close to the car in front of them as they gossip with a friend, make an appointment with a doctor, or order a pizza.

So long as murder remains illegal, the nervous twitchers, movie talkers, and cell-phone users of the world are safe from me. _____ if ever I am granted the power of life or death, these people had better think twice about annoying me. They might not have long to live.

Identifying Transitions and Other Connecting Words

The following sentences use connecting words to help tie ideas together. The connecting words you are to identify are set off in italics. In the space, write T for *transition*, RW for *repeated word*, S for *synonym*, or P for *pronoun*.

_____ 1. The Statue of Liberty stands watch in New York Harbor. In *her* right hand she holds the torch of freedom.

_____ 2. Plants like poinsettias and mistletoe are pretty. *They* are also poisonous.

_____ 3. A strip of strong cloth can be used as an emergency fan-belt replacement. *In addition,* a roll of duct tape can be used to patch a leaky hose temporarily.

_____ 4. The battleship *Arizona* was sunk during the attack on Pearl Harbor in 1941. Entombed in the *vessel* are the bodies of sailors who made the ultimate sacrifice for their country.

_____ 5. The molded plastic chairs in the classrooms are hard and uncomfortable. When I sit in one of these *chairs,* I feel as if I were sitting in a bucket.

_____ 6. One way to tell if skin is aging is to pinch a fold of skin on the back of the hand. If *it* doesn't smooth out quickly, the skin is losing its youthful tone.

_____ 7. I never eat sloppy joes. *They* look as if they've already been eaten.

_____ 8. Clothing intended just for children seems to have vanished. *Instead,* children wear scaled-down versions of everything adults wear.

_____ 9. Naturalism was the literary movement that described the individual's struggle in a hostile world. Among those writers who embraced *naturalism* were Theodore Dreiser and Upton Sinclair.

_____ 10. The giant cockroaches in Florida are the subject of local legends. A visitor, according to one tale, saw one of the *insects*, thought it was a Volkswagen, and tried to drive it away.

_____ 11. Some thieves scour garbage cans for credit-card receipts. *Then* they use the owner's name and card number to order merchandise by phone.

_____ 12. Switzerland did not take sides in World War I or II. *It* remained neutral in both.

_____ 13. There are many phobias other than the ones described in psychology textbooks. I have *phobias,* for instance, about toasters and lawn mowers.

_____ 14. My back problems seem to be getting better because I am trying the exercises the team trainer taught me. *As a result,* I might not have to have surgery.

Completing Transitional Sentences

ACTIVITY 12

Following are brief sentence outlines from two essays. In each outline, the second and third topic sentences serve as transitional, or linking, sentences. Each reminds us of the point in the preceding paragraph and announces the point to be developed in the current paragraph. In the spaces provided, add the words needed to complete the second and third topic sentences.

Thesis 1

To prepare for a long automobile trip, a driver should check tire pressure and condition, replace worn belts and hoses, and make sure the engine oil and other fluids are at proper levels.

First supporting paragraph

To ensure safety on the trip, the tire pressure and condition of the tires should be checked first.

After making sure that _____

_____, the driver should _____

_____ . . . .

Second supporting paragraph

Once he or she is certain that _____

_____ . . . .

Third supporting paragraph

Cheaper cost, greater comfort, and superior electronic technology make watching football at home more enjoyable than attending a game at the stadium.

Thesis 2

Personal

For one thing, watching the game on TV eliminates the cost of attending the game. . . .

First supporting paragraph

In addition to saving me money, watching the game at home is more _____ than sitting in a stadium. . . .

Second supporting paragraph

Even more important than _____ and _____ , though, is the _____ that makes a televised game better than the "real thing." . . .

Third supporting paragraph

Identifying Introductions and Conclusions

The following box lists five common kinds of introductions and three common kinds of conclusions. Read the three pairs of introductory and concluding paragraphs that follow. Then, in the space provided, write the letter of the kind of introduction and conclusion used in each paragraph.

ACTIVITY 13

Introductions	Conclusions
A. General to narrow	F. Summary and final thought
B. Starting with an opposite	G. Quotation
C. Stating importance of topic	H. Prediction or recommendation
D. Incident or story	
E. Quotation	

Pair 1

_____ Shortly before Easter, our local elementary school sponsored a fund-raising event at which classroom pets and their babies—hamsters, guinea pigs, and chicks—were available for adoption. Afterward, as I was driving home, I saw a hand drop a baby hamster out of the car ahead of me. I couldn't avoid running over the tiny creature. One of the parents had taken the pet, regretted the decision, and decided to get rid of it. Such people have never stopped to consider the real obligations involved in owning a pet.

_____ A pet cannot be thrown onto a trash heap when it is no longer wanted or tossed into a closet if it begins to bore its owner. A pet, like us, is a living thing that needs attention and care. Would-be owners, therefore, should think seriously about their responsibilities before they acquire a pet.

Pair 2

_____ All animals communicate. Some forms of communication, like that of the bee, are through movement while others include sound and movement. Humans naturally communicate through a variety of methods including body language and sounds, but they also communicate through methods that don't require physical proximity. Letters, phone calls, and e-mails are such forms of communication, often entailing serious drawbacks.

_____ Neither letters, phone calls, nor e-mails guarantee perfect communication. With all our sophisticated skills, we human beings often communicate less effectively than howling wolves or chattering monkeys. We always seem to find some way to foul up the message.

Pair 3

Personal

_____   "Few things are harder to put up with," said Mark Twain, "than the annoyance of a good example." Twain obviously knew the problems faced by siblings cursed with older brothers or sisters who are models of perfection. All our lives, my older sister Shelley and I have been compared. Unfortunately, in competition with my sister's virtues, my looks, talents, and accomplishments always ended up on the losing side.

_____   Although I always lost in the sibling contests of looks, talents, and accomplishments, Shelley and I have somehow managed not to turn into deadly enemies. Feeling like the dud of the family, in fact, helped me to develop a drive to succeed and a sense of humor. In our sibling rivalry, we both managed to win.

The Fourth Step in Essay Writing

This chapter will show you how to

- revise so that your sentences flow smoothly and clearly

- edit so that your sentences are error free

What differences do you notice about the two students in the photograph above? Most likely, you can identify with both of them. Thinking about your own experiences in the classroom, write an essay about one or more teachers or instructors who have conducted classes that made you glad to learn or, alternatively, left you daydreaming in class. Once you have written your first draft, read it aloud to make sure all your sentences flow smoothly and clearly.

Up to now, this book has emphasized the first three goals in effective writing: unity, support, and coherence. This chapter focuses on the fourth goal of writing effectively: sentence skills. You'll learn how to revise an essay so that your sentences flow smoothly and clearly. Then you'll review how to edit a paper for mistakes in grammar, punctuation, and spelling.

Revising Sentences

These strategies will help you to revise your sentences effectively:

- Use parallelism.
- Use a consistent point of view.
- Use specific words.
- Use active verbs.
- Use concise words.
- Vary your sentences.

Use Parallelism

Words in a pair or a series should have parallel structure. By balancing the items in a pair or a series so that they have the same kind of structure, you will make the sentence clearer and easier to read. Notice how the parallel sentences that follow read more smoothly than the nonparallel ones.

NONPARALLEL (NOT BALANCED)	PARALLEL (BALANCED)
My job includes checking the inventory, initialing the orders, and *to call* the suppliers.	My job includes checking the inventory, initialing the orders, and calling the suppliers. (A balanced series of -*ing* words: *checking, initialing, calling*)
The game-show contestant was told to be cheerful, charming, and *with enthusiasm*.	The game-show contestant was told to be cheerful, charming, and enthusiastic. (A balanced series of descriptive words: *cheerful, charming, enthusiastic*)
Grandmother likes to read mystery novels, to do needlepoint, and *surfing* the Internet.	Grandmother likes to read mystery novels, to do needlepoint, and to surf the Internet. (A balanced series of *to* verbs: *to read, to do, to surf*)
We painted the trim in the living room; *the wallpaper was put up by a professional*.	We painted the trim in the living room; a professional put up the wallpaper. (Balanced verbs and word order: *We painted . . . ; a professional put up . . .*)

Balanced sentences are not a skill you need worry about when writing first drafts. But when you rewrite, you should try to put matching words and ideas into matching structures. Such parallelism will improve your writing style.

Cross out and revise the unbalanced part of each of the following sentences.

EXAMPLE   Chocolate makes me gain weight, lose my appetite, and ~~breaking~~ *break* out in hives.

1. Florida is famous for its wonderful weather, theme parks that are family oriented, and great fishing.

2. Many people share the same three intense fears: being in high places, working with numbers, and speeches.

3. The garden boasted a line of fruit trees that were mature, several rows of vegetables, and a large stand of rose bushes.

4. The History Channel offers many programs that are timely, well researched, and that people find interesting.

5. To become a dancer, Lola is taking lessons, working in amateur shows, and auditioned for professional companies.

6. Juan's last job offered security; a better chance for advancement is offered by his new job.

7. Cell phones allow us to communicate, store important information, and they can even be used to take photographs.

8. Because the dying woman was dignified and with courage, she won everyone's respect.

9. The candidate for governor promised that she would cut taxes, reform public education, and do something to rebuild roads and bridges.

10. If we're not careful, we'll leave the next generation polluted air, contaminated water, and forests that are dying.

Use a Consistent Point of View

Consistency with Verbs

Do not shift verb tenses unnecessarily. If you begin writing a paper in the present tense, do not shift suddenly to the past. If you begin in the past, do not shift without reason to the present. Notice the inconsistent verb tenses in the following example:

> *Incorrect:* The gardener breaks up the hard earth with a shovel, added peat moss and other compost, then blends the soil evenly.

> *Correct:* The gardener breaks up the hard earth with a shovel, adds peat moss and other compost, then blends the soil evenly.

> *Correct:* The gardener broke up the hard earth with a shovel, added peat moss and other compost, then blended the soil evenly.

Make the verbs in each sentence consistent with the *first* verb used. Cross out the incorrect verb and write the correct form in the space at the left.

ACTIVITY 2

EXAMPLE

_____ran_____   Aunt Flo tried to kiss her little nephew, but he ~~runs~~ out of the room.

_____   1. An aggressive news photographer knocked a reporter to the ground as the movie stars arrive for the Academy Awards.

_____   2. The winning wheelchair racer in the marathon slumped back in exhaustion and asks for some ice to soothe his blistered hands.

_____   3. George Washington won his first battle when he defeats the Hessians in Trenton, New Jersey.

_____   4. Charles Conrad and Alan Bean landed on the moon in 1969 and gathered rock samples, which they bring back to Earth for examination.

_____   5. John Steinbeck wrote his masterpiece *The Grapes of Wrath* in 1939, but he does not win the Nobel Prize until 1962.

_____   6. Galileo (1564–1642) did not invent the telescope, but he improves upon it in order to observe the heavens better.

_____ 7. Ralph ripped open the bag of cheese puffs with his teeth, grabs handfuls of the salty orange squiggles, and stuffed them into his mouth.

_____ 8. From his perch high up on the rocky cliff, the eagle spots a whitetailed rabbit and swooped down toward his victim.

_____ 9. An American physicist was the first to measure the speed of light accurately when he calculates it at just over 186,000 miles per second.

_____ 10. When the great earthquake struck San Francisco in 1906, the entire city burns to the ground in less than twenty-four hours.

Consistency with Pronouns

When writing a paper, you should not shift your point of view unnecessarily. Be consistent in your use of first-, second-, or third-person pronouns.

Point of View

	Singular	Plural
First-person pronouns	I (my, mine, me)	we (our, us)
Second-person pronouns	you (your)	you (your)
Third-person pronouns	he (his, him)	they (their, them)
	she (her)	
	it (its)	

TIP Any person, place, or thing, as well as any indefinite pronoun such as *one, anyone, someone,* and so on (page 496), is a third-person word.

For instance, if you start writing in the first person, *I,* do not jump suddenly to the second person, *you.* Or if you are writing in the third person, *they,* do not shift unexpectedly to *you.* Look at the following examples.

INCONSISTENT

One of the fringe benefits of my job is that *you* can use a company credit card for gasoline.

(The most common mistake people make is to let *you* slip into their writing after they start with another pronoun.)

Though *we* like most of *our* neighbors, there are a few *you* can't get along with.

(The writer begins with the first-person pronouns *we* and *our* but then shifts to the second-person *you*.)

CONSISTENT

One of the fringe benefits of my job is that *I* can use a company credit card for gasoline.

Though *we* like most of *our* neighbors, there are a few *we* can't get along with.

Cross out inconsistent pronouns in the following sentences, and revise with the correct form of the pronoun above each crossed-out word.

ACTIVITY 3

EXAMPLE   When I examined the used car, ~~you~~ *I* could see that one of the front fenders had been replaced.

1. Many people are ignorant of side effects that diets can have on your health.

2. I am always nervous when the dentist examines my teeth because you never know what she will find.

3. It is expensive for us to take public transportation to work every day, but what choice do you have if you can't afford a car?

4. During the border crisis, each country refused to change their aggressive stance.

5. If you go to Chicago, one should visit the Art Institute.

6. We don't have enough money to travel to Egypt, but you can learn about the pyramids on the Discovery Channel.

7. Maria loves algebra problems because solving them gives you a sense of accomplishment.

8. It's hard for us to pay for health insurance, but you don't dare go without it.

9. People often take a first-aid course so that we can learn how to help choking and heart attack victims.

10. There are several ways you can impress your new boss. For example, one should dress well, arrive at work on time, and complete tasks efficiently.

Use Specific Words

To be an effective writer, you must use specific words rather than general words. Specific words create pictures in the reader's mind. They help capture interest and make your meaning clear. Compare the following sentences:

GENERAL	SPECIFIC
The plane landed at the airport.	The United Airlines 747 landed at Reagan National Airport.
Animals came into the place.	Hungry lions padded silently into the sawdust-covered arena.
The man signed the paper.	The biology teacher hastily scribbled his name on the course withdrawal slip.

The specific sentences create clear pictures in our minds. The details *show* us exactly what has happened.

Here are four ways to make your sentences specific.

1. Use exact names.

   Luke fixed the muffler on his car.

   Luke fixed the muffler on his *2007 Chevrolet Impala*.

2. Use lively verbs.

   The flag *moved* in the breeze.

   The flag *fluttered* in the breeze.

3. Use descriptive words (modifiers) before nouns.

   A man strained to lift the crate.

   A *heavyset, perspiring* man strained to lift the *heavy wooden* crate.

4. Use words that relate to the senses—sight, hearing, taste, smell, touch.

   The tourists enjoyed a picnic lunch of cheese, bread, and olives.

   The tourists enjoyed a picnic lunch of *sharp* cheese, *crusty* bread, and *spicy* olives. (*taste*)

   The campers built a fire of pine and cedar.

   The campers built a fire of *aromatic* pine and cedar. (*smell*)

   A noise told the crowd that there were two minutes left to play.

A *piercing whistle* told the *cheering* crowd that there were two minutes left to play. (*hearing*)

When he returned, all he found in the refrigerator was bread and milk.

When he returned, all he found in the refrigerator was *stale* bread and *sour* milk. (*taste*)

Neil stroked the kitten's fur until he felt its tiny claws on his hand.

Neil stroked the kitten's *velvety* fur until he felt its tiny, *needle-sharp* claws on his hand. (*touch*)

Fran placed a sachet in her bureau drawer.

Fran placed a *lilac-scented* sachet in her bureau drawer. (*smell*)

Revise the following sentences, replacing vague, indefinite words with sharp, specific ones.

ACTIVITY 4

EXAMPLE   *Several of our appliances* broke down at the same time.

Our washer, refrigerator, and television broke . . .

1. The new home came with *energy-saving appliances*.

    _____

    _____

    _____

2. I swept aside the *things* on my desk to spread out the road map.

    _____

    _____

    _____

3. Large *trees* shaded the valley.

    _____

    _____

    _____

4. *Several sections* of the newspaper were missing.

    _____

    _____

    _____

5. The doctor examined *various parts of my body* before diagnosing my illness as bronchitis.

_____

_____

_____

ACTIVITY 5 Again, you will practice changing vague, indefinite writing into lively, image-filled writing that helps capture the reader's interest and makes your meaning clear. With the help of the methods described on pages 116–117, add specific details to the five sentences that follow. Note the two examples.

EXAMPLES   The person got off the bus.

The teenage boy bounded down the steps of the shiny yellow school bus.

_____

She worked hard all summer.

All summer, Eva sorted peaches and blueberries in the hot, noisy canning

factory.

1. The car would not start.

_____

_____

_____

2. The desk was cluttered.

_____

_____

_____

3. The woman was overjoyed at finding her lost son.

_____

_____

_____

4. My room needs cleaning.

_____

_____

_____

5. A vehicle blocked traffic.

_____

_____

_____

Rewrite the sign pictured here using lively, image-filled writing that will grab people's attention.

Use Active Verbs

When the subject of a sentence performs the action of the verb, the verb is in the *active voice*. When the subject of a sentence receives the action of a verb, the verb is in the *passive voice*.

Passive voice uses a form of the verb *to be* (*am, is, are, was, were*) and the past participle of the main verb (usually the same as its past-tense form). Look at the following active and passive forms.

PASSIVE	ACTIVE
The computer *was turned on* by Hakim.	Hakim *turned on* the computer.
The car's air conditioner *was fixed* by the mechanic.	The mechanic *fixed* the car's air conditioner.
The stream *was diverted* by the engineers.	The engineers *diverted* the stream.
A Country Doctor, a novel by Sarah Orne Jewett, *was written* in 1884.	Sarah Orne Jewett *wrote* the novel *A Country Doctor* in 1884.
In World War II, France, Holland, Norway, Hungary, Poland, Russia, and other countries *were invaded* by Germany.	In World War II, Germany *invaded* France, Holland, Norway, Hungary, Poland, Russia and other countries.

In general, active verbs are more effective than passive verbs. Active verbs give your writing a simpler and more vigorous style.

ACTIVITY 6   Revise the following sentences, changing verbs from the passive to the active voice and making any other word changes necessary.

EXAMPLE   Fruits and vegetables are painted often by artists.

Artists often paint fruits and vegetables.
_____

1. Many unhealthy foods are included in the typical American diet.

    _____

2. The North Atlantic Treaty Organization (NATO) was established by the United States, Great Britain, and nine other countries in 1949.

    _____

    _____

3. The soldier's wounds were attacked by gangrene-producing bacteria.

    _____

4. A second Nobel Prize was won by Marie Curie in 1911.

   _____

5. Final grades will be determined by the instructor on the basis of class performance.

   _____

Use Concise Words

Wordiness—using more words than necessary to express a meaning—is often a sign of lazy or careless writing. Your readers may resent the extra time and energy they must spend when you have not done the work needed to make your writing direct and concise.

Here are two examples of wordy sentences:

In this paper, I am planning to describe the hobby that I enjoy of collecting old comic books.   **Wordy**

In Ben's opinion, he thinks that cable television will change and alter our lives in the future.

Omitting needless words improves these sentences:

I enjoy collecting old comic books.   **Clear**

Ben thinks that cable television will change our lives.

Following is a list of some wordy expressions that could be reduced to single words.

Wordy Form	Shorter Form
at this time	now
in the present	now
in the event that	if
due to the fact that	because
for the reason that	because
in every instance	always
in this day and age	today
during the time that	while
a large number of	many

continued

Wordy Form	Shorter Form
big in size	big
red in color	red
five in number	five
12 midnight/12 noon	midnight/noon
return back	return
good benefit	benefit
cooperate together	cooperate
completely unanimous	unanimous
commute back and forth	commute
postponed until later	postponed

ACTIVITY 7   Revise the following sentences, omitting needless words.

1. The bird was purple, red, orange, and yellow in color, and its body was extremely large in size.

   _____

   _____

2. Controlling the quality and level of the television shows that children watch is a continuing challenge to parents that they must meet on a daily basis.

   _____

   _____

3. A large number of people are now seeking out various electronic devices as presents to give to others on their birthdays.

   _____

   _____

4. In 1962, Linus Pauling, who was an American, was awarded the Nobel Prize, which was given to him for his attempts to limit the making of nuclear arms and to curtail the spread of nuclear testing.

   _____

   _____

5. I found out recently that Benito Mussolini (1883–1945), the dictator of the fascist nation of Italy for a period lasting nearly twenty-one years, was named after the Mexican political leader who went by the name of Benito Juarez (1806–1872).

_____

_____

_____

6. In today's uncertain economic climate, it is clear that people, namely, average middle-class working people, have great difficulty saving much money or putting anything aside for emergencies.

_____

_____

7. We thought the television program that was on last night was enjoyable, whereas our parents reacted with dislike to the content of the show.

_____

_____

8. Because of the bad weather, the school district felt it would be safer to cancel classes and let everyone stay home than to risk people having accidents on the way to school.

_____

_____

9. Out of all the regrets in my life so far, one of my greatest ones to the present time is that I did not take additional art classes when I was still in high school and had a chance to do so.

_____

_____

10. It seems obvious to me, and it should be to everyone else, too, that people can be harmed as much by emotional abuse as by physical abuse, even if you don't lay a hand on them.

_____

_____

Vary Your Sentences

One part of effective writing is to vary the kinds of sentences you write. If every sentence follows the same pattern, writing may become monotonous to read. This section explains four ways you can create variety and interest in your writing style. It also describes coordination and subordination—two important techniques for achieving different kinds of emphasis in writing.

The following are four methods you can use to revise simple sentences, making them more complex and sophisticated:

- Add a second complete thought (coordination).
- Add a dependent thought (subordination).
- Begin with a special opening word or phrase.
- Place adjectives or verbs in a series.

Revise by Adding a Second Complete Thought

When you add a second complete thought to a simple sentence, the result is a *compound* (or double) sentence. The two complete statements in a compound sentence are usually connected by a comma and a joining or coordinating word (*and, but, for, or, nor, so, yet*).

A compound sentence is used to give equal weight to two closely related ideas. The technique of showing that ideas have equal importance is called *coordination*. Following are some compound sentences. In each case, the sentence contains two ideas that the writer considers equal in importance.

Greg worked on the engine for three hours, but the car still wouldn't start.

Bananas were on sale this week, so I bought a bunch for the children's lunches.

We laced up our roller blades, and then we moved cautiously onto the rink.

ACTIVITY 8   Combine the following pairs of simple sentences into compound sentences. Use a comma and a logical joining word (*and, but, for, so*) to connect each pair of statements.

 HINT   If you are not sure what *and, but, for,* and *so* mean, check pages 463–464.

EXAMPLE   The weather was cold and windy.
Al brought a thick blanket to the football game.

The weather was cold and windy, so Al brought a thick blanket to the

football game.

1. My son can't eat peanut butter snacks or sandwiches.
    He is allergic to peanuts.

    _____

    _____

2. I tried to sleep.
    The thought of tomorrow's math exam kept me awake.

    _____

    _____

3. The poet Ezra Pound left America in 1908.
    He was dissatisfied with the artistic climate of his native country.

    _____

    _____

4. My philosophy professor believes that every student can learn.
    He spends much of his extra time tutoring his students.

    _____

    _____

5. I didn't have enough money to buy my parents an anniversary present.
    I offered to mow their lawn for the whole summer.

    _____

    _____

Revise by Adding a Dependent Thought

When you add a dependent thought to a simple sentence, the result is a *complex* sentence.* A dependent thought begins with one of the following subordinating words:

---

*The two parts of a complex sentence are sometimes called an *independent clause* and a *dependent clause*. A *clause* is simply a word group that contains a subject and a verb. An independent clause expresses a complete thought and can stand alone. A dependent clause does not express a complete thought in itself and depends on the independent clause to complete its meaning. Dependent clauses always begin with a dependent or subordinating word.

Subordinating Words

after	if, even if	when, whenever
although, though	in order that	where, wherever
as	since	whether
because	that, so that	which, whichever
before	unless	while
even though	until	who
how	what, whatever	whose

A complex sentence is used to emphasize one idea over another. Look at the following complex sentence:

Although the exam room was very quiet, I still couldn't concentrate.

The idea that the writer wishes to emphasize here—*I still couldn't concentrate*—is expressed as a complete thought. The less important idea—*Although the exam room was very quiet*—is subordinated to the complete thought. The technique of giving one idea less emphasis than another is called *subordination*.

Following are other examples of complex sentences. In each case, the part starting with the dependent word is the less emphasized part of the sentence.

Even though I was tired, I stayed up to watch the horror movie.

Before I take a bath, I check for spiders in the tub.

When Ivy feels nervous, she pulls on her earlobe.

ACTIVITY 9   Use logical subordinating words to combine the following pairs of simple sentences into sentences that contain a dependent thought. Place a comma after a dependent statement when it starts the sentence.

EXAMPLE   Rita bit into the hard taffy.
She broke a filling.
When Rita bit into the hard taffy, she broke a filling.

1. Many Americans blamed President Herbert Hoover for the Great Depression, which began in 1929.
    They elected Franklin Roosevelt president in 1932.

2. The bear turned over the rotten log.
   Fat white grubs crawled in every direction.

3. Europe had suffered a great deal of damage during World War II.
   The United States helped rebuild its infrastructure and economy.

4. Some people are allergic to wool.
   They buy sweaters made only from synthetic fibers.

5. An older woman in my typing class can type almost one hundred words a minute.
   She is having trouble landing a secretarial job.

Revise by Beginning with a Special Opening Word or Phrase

Among the special openers that can be used to start sentences are *-ed* words, *-ing* words, *-ly* words, *to* word groups, and prepositional phrases. Additional information can be found in Chapters 23, 24, and 28. Here are examples of all five kinds of openers:

-ed WORD

Concerned about his son's fever, Paul called a doctor.

-ing WORD

Humming softly, the woman browsed through the rack of dresses.

-ly WORD

Hesitantly, Sue approached the instructor's desk.

to WORD GROUP

To protect her hair, Eva uses the lowest setting on her blow dryer.

PREPOSITIONAL PHRASE

During the exam, drops of water fell from the ceiling.

ACTIVITY 10

Combine each of the following pairs of simple sentences into one sentence by using the opener shown at the left and omitting repeated words. Use a comma to set off the opener from the rest of the sentence.

EXAMPLE   *-ing* word   The pelican scooped small fish into its baggy bill. It dipped into the waves.

Dipping into the waves, the pelican scooped small fish into its baggy bill.

-ly word

1. Shirley signed the repair contract.
   She was reluctant.

   _____

   _____

to word group

2. Eva and Olaf wanted to find the shortest route over the mountain.
   They bought a map of the local hiking trails.

   _____

   _____

Prepositional phrase

3. The accused murderer grinned at the witnesses.
   He did this during the trial.

   _____

   _____

-ed word

4. The vet's office was noisy and confusing.
   It was crowded with nervous pets.

   _____

   _____

-ing word

5. Barry tried to find something worth watching,
   He flipped from channel to channel.

_____

_____

Revise by Placing Adjectives or Verbs in a Series

Various parts of a sentence may be placed in a series. Among these parts are adjectives (descriptive words) and verbs. (Additional information can be found in Chapter 31.) Here are examples of both in a series:

ADJECTIVES

I gently applied a *sticky new* Band-Aid to the *deep, ragged* cut on my finger.

VERBS

The truck *bounced* off a guardrail, *sideswiped* a tree, and *plunged* down the embankment.

Combine the simple sentences into one sentence by using adjectives or verbs in a series and by omitting repeated words. Use a comma when necessary between adjectives or verbs in a series.

ACTIVITY 11

EXAMPLE   Jesse spun the basketball on one finger.
He rolled it along his arms.
He dribbled it between his legs.

esse spun the basketball on one finger, rolled it along his arms, and dribbled it between his legs.

1. The bobcat sat high on a rock.
It stared down at the unsuspecting rodent.
It leaped upon its prey.

_____

_____

2. Some Native Americans lived in the desert.
They built permanent homes.
These homes were usually made of adobe.
Adobe resembles stucco.

_____

_____

3. By 6 A.M., I had read the textbook chapter.
    I had taken notes on it.
    I had studied the notes.
    I had drunk eight cups of coffee.

    _____

    _____

4. The exterminator approached the wasps' nests hanging under the eaves.
    The nests were large.
    The nests were papery.
    The eaves were old.
    The eaves were wooden.

    _____

    _____

5. Reeds bordered the pond.
    The reeds were slim.
    The reeds were brown.
    The pond was green.
    The pond was stagnant.

    _____

    _____

Editing Sentences

After revising sentences in a paper so that they flow smoothly and clearly, you need to edit the paper for mistakes in grammar, punctuation, mechanics, usage, and spelling. Even if a paper is otherwise well written, it will make an unfavorable impression on readers if it contains such mistakes. To edit a paper, check it against the agreed-upon rules, or conventions, of written English—simply called *sentence skills* in this book. Here are the most common of these conventions:

> ✓ Write complete sentences rather than fragments.
> ✓ Do not write run-on sentences.
> ✓ Use verb forms correctly.
> ✓ Make sure that subject, verbs, and pronouns agree.

continued

✓   Eliminate faulty modifiers.

✓   Use pronoun forms correctly.

✓   Use capital letters when needed.

✓   Use the following marks of punctuation correctly: apostrophe, quotation marks, comma, semicolon, colon, hyphen, dash, parentheses.

✓   Use correct manuscript form.

✓   Eliminate slang, clichés, and pretentious words.

✓   Check for possible spelling errors.

✓   Eliminate careless errors.

These sentence skills are treated in detail in Part 4 of this book, and they can be referred to easily as needed. Both the list of sentence skills on the inside back cover of this book and the correction symbols on page 620 include page references so that you can turn quickly to any skill you want to check.

Hints about Editing

These hints can help you edit the next-to-final draft of a paper for sentence-skill mistakes:

1. Have at hand two essential tools: a good dictionary and a grammar handbook (you can use the one in this book beginning on page 439).

2. Use a sheet of paper to cover your essay so that you will expose only one sentence at a time. Look for errors in grammar, spelling, and typing. It may help to read each sentence out loud. If a sentence does not read clearly and smoothly, chances are something is wrong.

3. Pay special attention to the kinds of errors you tend to make. For example, if you tend to write run-ons or fragments, be especially on the lookout for those errors.

4. Try to work on a typewritten or word-processed draft, where you'll be able to see your writing more objectively than you can on a handwritten page; use a pen with colored ink so that your corrections will stand out.

TIP   A series of editing tests appears on pages 593–604. You will probably find it most helpful to take these tests after reviewing the sentence skills in Part 4.

Proofreading

Proofreading means closely checking the final, edited draft of your paper for typos and other careless errors. A helpful strategy is to read your paper backward, from the last sentence to the first. This helps keep you from getting caught up in the flow of the paper and missing small mistakes. Here are six helpful proofing symbols:

Proofing Symbol	Meaning	Example
^	insert missing letter or word	achéve
___ℓ	omit	draw two ~~two~~ conclusions
⌒⌒	reverse order of words or letters	lived happily ⁀after ever⁀
#	add space	all‸right
‿	close up space	base‿ball
Ⓒⓐⓟ = ⓛⓒ /	Add a capital (or a lowercase) letter	ⒸⓐⓟMy english Çlass ⓛⓒ

After you mark corrections on the page, enter them into your word processer file, then reprint the page.

Personal

ACTIVITY 12   In the spaces below this paragraph, write the numbers of the ten word groups that contain fragments or run-ons. Then, in the spaces between the lines, edit by making the necessary corrections. One is done for you as an example.

A unique object in my family's living room is an ashtray, Ẅhich I made ⓛⓒ

in second grade. I can still remember the pride I felt. When I presented

it to my mother. Now, I'm amazed that my parents didn't hide it away at

the back of a shelf it is a remarkably ugly object. The ashtray is made out

of brown clay that I had tried to mold into a perfect circle, unfortunately my

class was only forty-five minutes long. The best I could do was to shape

it into a lopsided oval. Its most distinctive feature, though, is the grooves

carved into its rim. I had theorized that each groove could hold a cigarette or cigar, I made at least fifty of them.   I somehow failed to consider that the only person who smoked in my family was my father.   Who smoked about five cigars a year.   Further, although our living room is decorated in sedate tans and blues, my ashtray is bright purple.   My favorite color at the time.

   For variety, it has stripes around its rim they are colored neon green.   My parents have proudly displayed my little masterpiece on their coffee table for the past ten years.   If I ever wonder if my parents love me.   I look at that ugly ashtray, the answer is plain to see.

1. _____   3. _____   5. _____   7. _____   9. _____

2. _____   4. _____   6. _____   8. _____   10. _____

Practice in Revising Sentences

You now know the fourth step in effective writing: revising and editing sentences. You also know that practice in *editing* sentences is best undertaken after you have worked through the sentence skills in Part 4. The focus in this section, then, will be on *revising* sentences—using a variety of methods to ensure that your sentences flow smoothly and are clear and interesting. You will work through Review Tests on the following:

- using parallelism
- using a consistent point of view
- using specific words
- using active verbs
- using concise words
- varying your sentences

Using Parallelism

REVIEW TEST 1

Cross out the unbalanced part of each sentence. In the space provided, revise the unbalanced part so that it matches the other item or items in the sentence.

EXAMPLE   In many ways, starting college at forty is harder than ~~to start~~ at eighteen.
                starting

1. Langston Hughes (1902–1967) wrote plays, poetry, and he was an essayist.

   _____

2. Alex Haley's career included writing several short stories and essays, authoring *Roots*, the novel that made him famous, and he also edited *The Autobiography of Malcolm X.*

   _____

3. Melissa likes reading mystery novels, to listen to bluegrass, and playing golf.

   _____

4. Thomas impressed the audience because of his clear, reasonable presentation
   with friendliness as well.

   _____

5. Janine is very talented: she is a gourmet cook, a published poet, and she takes
   great photographs.

   _____

6. Studying a little every day is more effective than to cram.

   _____

7. The keys to improving grades are to take effective notes in class, to plan study
   time, and preparing carefully for exams.

   _____

8. Paying college tuition and not studying is as sensible as to buy tickets to a
   movie and not watching it.

   _____

9. The college provides three ways to earn extra money while attending school:
   serve as a lab assistant, tutoring fellow students in the learning lab, and working in one of the many federally sponsored work-study programs.

   _____

10. While waiting for the exam to start, small groups of nervous students glanced
    over their notes, drank coffee, and were whispering to each other.

    _____

REVIEW TEST 2

Cross out the unbalanced part of each sentence. In the space above, revise the un-balanced part so that it matches the other item or items in the sentence.

Although there are many different majors, students who desire to be in the top one percent of income earners should plan on majoring in economics, biochemistry, zoology, or biology, or to follow a pre-med program.

Students who go into pre-med will then need to decide what specific sector to specialize in. General practitioners are usually paid less than oncologists, doctors who do surgery, and dermatologists. Economics majors can choose a wide variety of careers like economic consulting, law, or becoming a professor. Biochemistry majors can enter careers such as pharmacist, research scientist, or they can even become doctors of medicine. It is a degree that offers many pathways to different graduate degrees. Studying zoology doesn't mean just to work in a zoo. States like Oregon, Washington, and Maryland hire zoologists to study the management of wildlife or how the wildlife is encroaching on urban areas. Biology degrees offer the best chance of earning wages at the high end of the spectrum. Many biology majors get medical degrees, but they might choose other high-paying careers like pharmaceutical sales representative, biological scientist, or microbiologist. These majors require years of study and hard-working, but they may lead to careers with big salaries.

Using a Consistent Point of View

REVIEW TEST 3

Change verbs as needed in the following selection so that they are consistently in the past tense. Cross out each incorrect verb and write the correct form above it, as shown in the example. You will need to make ten additional corrections.

My uncle's shopping trip last Thursday was discouraging to him. First of all, he had to drive around for fifteen minutes until he ~~finds~~ *found* a parking space.

There was a half-price special on paper products in the supermarket, and every spot is taken. Then, when he finally got inside, many of the items on his list were not where he expected. For example, the pickles he wanted are not on the same shelf as all the other pickles. Instead, they were in a refrigerated case next to the bacon. And the granola was not on the cereal shelves but in the health-food section. Shopping thus proceeds slowly. About halfway through his list, he knew there would not be time to cook dinner and decides to pick up a barbecued chicken. The chicken, he learned, was available at the end of the store he had already passed. So he parks his shopping cart in an aisle, get the chicken, and came back. After adding half a dozen more items to his cart, he suddenly realizes it contained someone else's food. So he retraced his steps, found his own cart, transfers the groceries, and continued to shop. Later, when he began loading items onto the checkout counter, he notices that the barbecued chicken was missing. He must have left it in the other cart, certainly gone by now. Feeling totally defeated, he returned to the deli counter and says to the clerk, "Give me another chicken. I lost the first one." My uncle told me that when he saw the look on the clerk's face, he felt as if he'd flunked Food Shopping.

REVIEW TEST 4

Cross out inconsistent pronouns in the following sentences, and revise with the correct form of the pronoun above each crossed-out word.

EXAMPLE   MLA format is a way for students to format ~~your~~ *their* documents in English classes.

Students who are required to lay out his or her documents in MLA format often don't know what to do. This can be frustrating for both professors and you. However, by following a few simple rules, you can be successful. The first thing a student needs to do is open their word processing program. The next thing you should do is go to the page formatting tool. MLA standards require that the page margins are one inch around, lines are double-spaced, and the type size is a legible twelve-point font. After checking that this is correct, we should then create a header that numbers all pages in the upper-right-hand corner. Once the page layout is correct, the student should type their heading, which includes their name, instructor's name, course, and date. The final thing the student will need to do is type your essay title and essay. Following these steps won't guarantee that the essay gets an A but will mean that they will be formatted correctly.

Using Specific Words

REVIEW TEST 5

Revise the following sentences, changing vague, indefinite words to sharp, specific ones.

1. *We were exhausted* after shoveling snow all day.

   _____

   _____

   _____

2. The *food choices* in the cafeteria were unappetizing.

   _____

   _____

   _____

3. *Bugs* invaded our kitchen and pantry this summer.

   _____

   _____

   _____

4. All last week, *the weather was terrible*.

   _____

   _____

   _____

5. My mathematics teacher *is excellent*.

_____

_____

_____

REVIEW TEST 6

With the help of the methods described on pages 116–117, add specific details to the sentences that follow.

1. The salesperson was obnoxious.

_____

_____

_____

2. The kitchen was cheery.

_____

_____

_____

3. My city is a cultural paradise.

_____

_____

_____

4. The lounge area was busy.

_____

_____

_____

5. A passenger on the bus was acting strangely.

_____

_____

_____

Using Active Verbs

Revise the following sentences, changing verbs from the passive to the active voice and making any other necessary word changes.

EXAMPLE   Soccer is played by children all over the world.

Children all over the world play soccer.

1. The pizza restaurant was closed by the health inspector.

   _____

2. Huge stacks of donated books were sorted by the workers in the library.

   _____

3. A poem about Chicago entitled "City of Big Shoulders" was written by Carl Sandburg.

   _____

4. In 1928, the antibiotic penicillin was discovered by Sir Alexander Fleming.

   _____

5. Nearly a million tons of tobacco are grown by American farmers each year.

   _____

6. An additional charge was placed on our phone bill by the telephone company.

   _____

7. The building of a new community library was made possible by a grant from a large corporation.

   _____

   _____

8. Stress is relieved by physical activity, meditation, and relaxation.

   _____

9. Taxes will be raised by the federal government to pay for highway improvements.

   _____

10. Studies show that violent behavior among young children is increased by watching violent TV programs.

_____

_____

Using Concise Words

Revise the following sentences, omitting needless words.

1. At this point in time, we are not exactly sure what the causes of Alzheimer's disease are, but we are aware of the fact that it rarely attacks younger people who are below the age of sixty.

_____

_____

2. The two identical twins wore exactly the same shoes, shirt, pants, and socks.

_____

_____

3. The salesperson advised us not to buy the laptop at this time because it was going to have a drop in price in the very near future.

_____

_____

4. Scientists who study botany classify or think of the tomato as a type of fruit, but most other people today think of it as a vegetable.

_____

_____

5. Many people are of the opinion that children should be required by law to attend school until they reach the age of sixteen years old.

_____

_____

6. Majoring in liberal arts during the first year in college can help a student explore various types of academic majors, and doing so will help a student decide what discipline he or she might want to study.

_____

_____

7. Many uneducated people who have never attended school wish they could get an education.

_____

_____

8. The primary focus of today's class will be the critiquing of one student's essay by another student.

_____

_____

9. It is the belief of the professor that all students enrolled in her class need to be aware of the due date for the essay focusing on the film.

_____

_____

10. At around the time that the clock strikes seven in the evening, we will be meeting together to view a movie.

_____

_____

Varying Your Sentences

REVIEW TEST 9

Combine each of the following groups of simple sentences into one longer sentence. Omit repeated words. Various combinations are often possible, so try to find the combination in each group that flows most smoothly and clearly.

1. Jane Austen is an author.
   She is English.
   She is well known and beloved.

_____

_____

2. Austen wrote *Emma*.
   Emma is a novel.
   The novel is about Emma Woodhouse.

_____

_____

3. Emma was a matchmaker.
   Emma meant well.
   Emma's matches were usually wrong.

   _____

   _____

4. Jane Austen wrote *Sense and Sensibility*.
   Sense and Sensibility is about Miss Elinor Dashwood.
   Sense and Sensibility is about Miss Marianne Dashwood.

   _____

   _____

5. The book focuses on Elinor's quest for love.
   The book focuses on Marianne's quest for love.
   The book is about the two sisters' quest for marriage.

   _____

   _____

6. Austen wrote *Mansfield Park*.
   Mansfield Park is about Fanny Price.
   Fanny Price is involved with the Bertram family.

   _____

   _____

7. Fanny Price is poor.
   She is young.
   Fanny Price is sent to live with relatives.
   Her relatives are wealthy.

   _____

   _____

8. Austen wrote *Pride and Prejudice*.
   Pride and Prejudice is Jane Austen's most famous novel.
   Pride and Prejudice is about the Bennet family.

   _____

   _____

9. Elizabeth Bennet is the main character.
   She is kind and smart.
   She is a loving person.

She falls in love with Mr. Fitzwilliam Darcy.
Mr. Darcy is arrogant and proud.

_____

_____

10. Critics used to consider Austen's books frivolous.
Critics used to dismiss Austen's books.
Critics now see her books as progressive and distinctive.

_____

_____

REVIEW TEST 10

Combine the sentences in the following paragraph into four sentences. Omit repeated words. Try to find combinations in each case that flow as smoothly and clearly as possible.

Lena and Miles wanted a vacation. They wanted a vacation that was nice. They wanted one that was quiet. They wanted one that was relaxing. They rented a small lakeside cabin. Their first day there was very peaceful. The situation quickly changed. A large family moved into a nearby cabin. They played music at top volume. They raced around in a speedboat with a loud whining engine. Lena and Miles were no longer very relaxed. They packed up their things. They drove off. They returned to their quiet apartment.

_____

_____

_____

_____

_____

_____

_____

_____

Four Bases for Revising Essays

This chapter will show you how to evaluate an essay for

- unity
- support
- coherence
- sentence skills

What emotions come to mind as you look at this photograph taken in the aftermath of the 2011 earthquake and tsunami in Japan? Write an essay about a tragedy you have experienced in your own life. What was the experience like and how did it change you—for better or worse? After writing the first draft of your essay, check that you have covered the four bases of writing: unity, support, coherence, and sentence skills.

In the preceding chapters, you learned four essential steps in writing an effective paper. The box below shows how the steps lead to four standards, or bases, you can use in revising an essay.

Four Steps	→	Four Bases
1 If you advance a single point and stick to that point,		your paper will have *unity*.
2 If you support the point with specific evidence,		your paper will have *support*.
3 If you organize and connect the specific evidence,		your paper will have *coherence*.
4 If you write clear, error-free sentences,		your paper will demonstrate effective *sentence skills*.

This chapter discusses these four bases—unity, support, coherence, and sentence skills—and shows how the four bases can be used to evaluate and revise a paper.

Base 1: Unity

Understanding Unity

The following student essays are on the topic "Problems or Pleasures of My Teenage Years." Which one makes its point more clearly and effectively, and why?

Teenage Pranks

Essay 1

Personal

1   Looking back at some of the things I did as a teenager makes me break out in a sweat. The purpose of each adventure was fun, but occasionally things got out of hand. In my search for good times, I was involved in three notable pranks, ranging from fairly harmless to fairly serious.

2   The first prank proved that good, clean fun does not have to be dull. As a high school student, I was credited with making the world's largest dessert. With several friends, I spent an entire year collecting boxes of Jell-O. Entering our school's indoor pool one night, we turned the water temperature up as high as it would go and poured in box after box of the strawberry powder. The next morning, school officials arrived to find the pool filled with thirteen thousand gallons of the quivering, rubbery stuff. No one was hurt by the prank, but we did suffer through three days of a massive cleanup.

---

continued

Not all my pranks were harmless, and one involved risking my life. 　3
As soon as I got my driver's license, I wanted to join the Fliers' Club.
Membership in this club was limited to those who could make their cars fly a
distance of at least ten feet. The qualifying site was an old quarry field where
friends and I had built a ramp made of dirt. I drove my battered Ford Pinto up
this ramp as fast as it would go. The Pinto flew ten feet, but one of the tires
exploded when I landed. The car rolled on its side, and I luckily escaped with
only a bruised arm.

Risking my own life was bad enough, but there was another prank 　4
in which other people could have been hurt, too. On this occasion, I
accidentally set a valley on fire. Two of my friends and I were sitting on a hill
sharing a few beers. It was a warm summer night, and there was absolutely
nothing to do. The idea came like a thunderclap. We collected a supply of
large plastic trash bags, emergency highway flares, and a half tank of helium
left over from a science-fair experiment. Then we began to construct a fleet
of UFOs. Filling the bags with helium, we tied them closed with wire and
suspended several burning flares below each bag. Our UFOs leaped into the
air like an army of invading Martians. Rising and darting in the blackness,
they convinced even us. Our fun turned into horror, though, as we watched
the balloons begin to drop onto the wooded valley of expensive homes
below. Soon, a brushfire started and, quickly sobered, we hurried off to call
the fire department anonymously.

Every so often, I think back on the things that I did as a teenager. I 　5
chuckle at the innocent pranks and feel lucky that I didn't harm myself or
others with the not-so-innocent ones. Those years were filled with wild times.
Today I'm older, wiser—and maybe just a little more boring.

Essay 2

Personal

Problems of My Adolescence

In the unreal world of television situation comedies, teenagers are 　1
carefree, smart, funny, wisecracking, secure kids. In fact, most of them are
more "together" than the adults on the shows. This, however, isn't how I recall
my teenage years at all. As a teen, I suffered. Every day, I battled the terrible
physical, family, and social troubles of adolescence.

For one thing, I had to deal with a demoralizing physical problem— 　2
acne. Some days, I would wake up in the morning with a red bump the size
of a taillight on my nose. Since I worried constantly about my appearance
anyway, acne outbreaks could turn me into a crying, screaming maniac.
Plastering on a layer of (at the time) orange-colored Clearasil, which didn't

continued

fool anybody, I would slink into school, hoping that the boy I had a crush on would be absent that day. Within the last few years, however, treatments for acne have improved. Now, skin doctors prescribe special drugs that clear up pimples almost immediately. An acne attack could shatter whatever small amount of self-esteem I had managed to build up.

In addition to fighting acne, I felt compelled to fight my family. As a teenager, I needed to be independent. At that time, the most important thing in life was to be close to my friends and to try out new, more adult experiences. Unfortunately, my family seemed to get in the way. My little brother, for instance, turned into my enemy. We are close now, though. In fact, Eddie recently painted my new apartment for me. Eddie used to barge into my room, make calls on my cell phone, and read my e-mail. I would threaten to tie him up and leave him in a garbage dumpster. He would scream, my mother would yell, and all hell would break loose. My parents, too, were enemies. They wouldn't let me stay out late, wear the clothes I wanted to wear, or hang around with the friends I liked. So I tried to get revenge on them by being miserable, sulky, and sarcastic at home.

3

Worst of all, I had to face the social traumas of being a teenager. Things that were supposed to be fun, like dates and dances, were actually horrible. On the few occasions when I had a real date, I agonized over everything—my hair, my weight, my pimples. After a date, I would come home, raid the kitchen, and drown my insecurities in a sea of junk food. Dances were also stressful events. My friends and I would sneak a couple of beers just to get up the nerve to walk into the school gym. Now I realize that teenage drinking is dangerous. I read recently that the number-one killer of teenagers is drunk driving. At dances, I never relaxed. It was too important to look exactly right, to act really cool, and to pretend I was having fun.

4

I'm glad I'm not a teenager anymore. I wouldn't ever want to feel so unattractive, so confused, and so insecure again. I'll gladly accept the crow's-feet and stomach bulge of adulthood in exchange for a little peace of mind.

5

Fill in the blanks.

Essay _____ makes its point more clearly and effectively because _____

_____

_____

_____

ACTIVITY 1

EXPLANATION: Essay 1 is more effective because it is unified. All the details in this essay are on target; they support and develop each of its three topic sentences ("The first prank proved that good, clean fun does not have to be dull"; "Not all my pranks were harmless, and one involved risking my life"; and "Risking my own life was bad enough, but there was another prank where other people could have been hurt, too").

On the other hand, essay 2 contains some details irrelevant to its topic sentences. In the first supporting paragraph (paragraph 2), for example, the sentences "Within the last few years, however, treatments for acne have improved. Now, skin doctors prescribe special drugs that clear up pimples almost immediately" do not support the writer's topic statement that she had to deal with the physical problem of acne. Such details should be left out in the interest of unity.

The difference between these first two essays leads us to the first base, or standard, of effective writing: *unity*. To achieve unity is to have all the details in your paper related to your thesis and to your three supporting topic sentences. Each time you think of something to put into your paper, ask yourself whether it relates to your thesis and your supporting points. If it does not, leave it out. For example, if you were writing a paper about the problems of being unemployed and then spent a couple of sentences talking about the pleasures of having a lot of free time, you would be missing the first and most essential base of good writing.

Revising for Unity

ACTIVITY 2

Go back to essay 2 and cross out the two sentences in the first supporting paragraph (paragraph 2), the one sentence in the second supporting paragraph (paragraph 3), and the two sentences in the third supporting paragraph (paragraph 4) that are off target and do not support their topic sentences.

Base 2: Support

Understanding Support

The following essays were written on "Dealing with Disappointment." Both are unified, but one communicates more clearly and effectively. Which one, and why?

Dealing with Disappointment

1 One way to look at life is as a series of disappointments. Life can certainly appear that way because disappointment crops up in the life of everyone more often, it seems, than satisfaction. How disappointments are handled can have a great bearing on how life is viewed. People can react negatively by sulking or by blaming others, or they can try to understand the reasons behind the disappointment.

2 Sulking is one way to deal with disappointment. This attitude—Why does everything always happen to me?—is common because it is easy to adopt, but it is not very productive. Everyone has had the experience of meeting people who specialize in feeling sorry for themselves. A sulky manner will often discourage others from wanting to lend support, and it prevents the sulker from making positive moves toward self-help. It becomes easier just to sit back and sulk. Unfortunately, feeling sorry for oneself does nothing to lessen the pain of disappointment. It may, in fact, increase the pain. It certainly does not make future disappointments easier to bear.

3 Blaming others is another negative and unproductive way to cope with disappointment. This all-too-common response of pointing the finger at someone else doesn't help one's situation. This posture will lead only to anger, resentment, and, therefore, further unhappiness. Disappointment in another's performance does not necessarily indicate that the performer is at fault. Perhaps expectations were too high, or there could have been a misunderstanding as to what the performer actually intended to accomplish.

4 A positive way to handle disappointment is to try to understand the reasons behind the disappointment. An analysis of the causes of disappointment can have an excellent chance of producing desirable results. Often understanding alone can help alleviate the pain of disappointment and can help prevent future disappointments. Also, it is wise to try to remember that what would be ideal is not necessarily what is reasonable to expect in any given situation. The ability to look disappointment squarely in the face and then go on from there is the first step on the road back.

5 Continuous handling of disappointment in a negative manner can lead to a negative view of life itself. Chances for personal happiness in such a state of being are understandably slim. Learning not to expect perfection in an imperfect world and keeping in mind those times when expectations were actually surpassed are positive steps toward allowing the joys of life to prevail.

Essay 2

Reactions to Disappointment

Ben Franklin said that the only sure things in life are death and taxes. He   1
left something out, however: disappointment. No one gets through life without
experiencing many disappointments. Strangely, though, most people seem
unprepared for disappointment and react to it in negative ways. They feel
depressed or try to escape their troubles instead of using disappointment as
an opportunity for growth.

One negative reaction to disappointment is depression. For example,   2
Helen, a woman trying to win a promotion, works hard for over a year in
her department. Helen is so sure she will get the promotion, in fact, that she
has already picked out the car she will buy when her salary increase comes
through. However, the boss names one of Helen's coworkers to the spot. The
fact that all the other department employees tell Helen that she is the one
who really deserved the promotion doesn't help her deal with the crushing
disappointment. Deeply depressed, Helen decides that all her goals are
doomed to defeat. She loses her enthusiasm for her job and can barely force
herself to show up every day. Helen tells herself that she is a failure and that
doing a good job just isn't worth the work.

Another negative reaction to disappointment, and one that often follows   3
depression, is the desire to escape. Jamal fails to get into the college his
brother is attending, the college that was the focus of all his dreams, and
decides to escape his disappointment. Why worry about college at all?
Instead, he covers up his real feelings by giving up on his schoolwork and
getting completely involved with friends, parties, and "good times." Or
Carla doesn't make the varsity basketball team—something she wanted very
badly—and so refuses to play sports at all. She decides to hang around with
a new set of friends who get high every day; then she won't have to confront
her disappointment and learn to live with it.

The positive way to react to disappointment is to use it as a chance   4
for growth. This isn't easy, but it's the only useful way to deal with an
inevitable part of life. Helen, the woman who wasn't promoted, could have
handled her disappointment by looking at other options. If her boss doesn't
recognize her talent and hard work, perhaps she could transfer to another
department. Or she could ask the boss how to improve her performance
so that she would be a shoo-in for the next promotion. Jamal, the boy who
didn't get into the college of his choice, should look into other schools.
Going to another college may encourage him to be his own person, step
out of his brother's shadow, and realize that being turned down by one
college isn't a final judgment on his abilities or potential. Rather than escape
into drugs, Carla could improve her basketball skills for a year or pick up

continued

another sport—like swimming or tennis—that would probably turn out to be more useful to her as an adult.

Disappointments are unwelcome but regular visitors to everyone's life. 5
We can feel depressed about them, or we can try to escape from them.
The best thing, though, is to accept a disappointment and then try to use
it somehow: step over the unwelcome visitor on the doorstep and get on
with life.

Fill in the blanks.

ACTIVITY 3

Essay _____ makes its point more clearly and effectively because _____

_____

_____

EXPLANATION: Here, essay 2 is more effective, for it offers specific examples of the ways people deal with disappointment. We see for ourselves the kinds of reactions people have to disappointment.

Essay 1, on the other hand, gives us no specific evidence. The writer tells us repeatedly that sulking, blaming others, and trying to understand the reasons behind a disappointment are the reactions people have to a letdown. However, the writer never *shows* us any of these responses in action. Exactly what kinds of disappointments is the writer talking about? And how, for instance, does someone analyze the causes of disappointment? Would a person write a list of causes on a piece of paper, or review the causes with a concerned friend, or speak to a professional therapist? In an essay like this, we would want to see *examples* of how sulking and blaming others are negative ways of dealing with disappointment.

Consideration of these two essays leads us to the second base of effective writing: *support*. After realizing the importance of specific supporting details, one student writer revised a paper she had done on being lost in the woods as the worst experience of her childhood. In the revised paper, instead of talking about "the terror of being separated from my parents," she referred to such specifics as "tears streamed down my cheeks as I pictured the faces I would never see again" and

"I clutched the locket my parents had given me as if it were a lucky charm that could help me find my way back to the campsite." All your papers should include such vivid details.

Revising for Support

On a separate sheet of paper, revise one of the three supporting paragraphs in "Dealing with Disappointment" by providing specific supporting examples.

Base 3: Coherence

Understanding Coherence

The following two essays were written on the topic "Positive or Negative Effects of Television." Both are unified, and both are supported. However, one communicates more clearly and effectively. Which one, and why?

Essay 1

Harmful Effects of Watching Television

In a recent cartoon, one character said to another, "When you think of   1
the awesome power of television to educate, aren't you glad it doesn't?"
It's true that television has the power to educate and to entertain, but
unfortunately, these benefits are outweighed by the harm it does to dedicated
viewers. Television is harmful because it creates passivity, discourages
communication, and presents a false picture of reality.

Television makes viewers passive. Children who have an electronic   2
babysitter spend most of their waking hours in a semiconscious state. Older
viewers watch tennis matches and basketball games with none of the
excitement of being in the stands. Even if children are watching *Sesame Street*
or *Barney & Friends,* they are being educated passively. The child actors
are going on nature walks, building crafts projects, playing with animals,
and participating in games, but the little viewers are simply watching. Older
viewers watch guests discuss issues with Oprah Winfrey, but no one will turn
to the home viewers to ask their opinion.

Worst of all, TV presents a false picture of reality that leaves viewers   3
frustrated because they don't have the beauty or wealth of the characters
on television. Viewers absorb the idea that everyone else in the United
States owns a lavish apartment, a suburban house, a sleek car, and an

continued

expensive wardrobe. Every detective, police officer, oil baron, and lawyer, male or female, is suitable for a pinup poster. The material possessions on TV shows and commercials contribute to the false image of reality. News anchors and reporters, with their perfect hair and makeup, must fit television's standard of beauty. From their modest homes or cramped apartments, many viewers tune in daily to the upper-middle-class world that TV glorifies.

Television discourages communication. Families watching television do very little talking except for brief exchanges during commercials. If Uncle Bernie or the next-door neighbors drop in for a visit, the most comfortable activity for everyone may be not conversation but watching ESPN. The family may not even be watching the same set; instead, in some households, all the family members head for their own rooms to watch their own sets. At dinner, plates are plopped on the coffee table in front of the set, and the meal is wolfed down during *NBC Nightly News*. During commercials, the only communication a family has all night may consist of questions like "Do we have any popcorn?" and "Where's *TV Guide*?"   **4**

Television, like cigarettes or saccharin, is harmful to our health. We are becoming isolated, passive, and frustrated. And, most frightening, the average viewer now spends more time watching television than ever before.   **5**

The Benefits of Television

We hear a lot about the negative effects of television on the viewer. Obviously, television can be harmful if it is watched constantly to the exclusion of other activities. It would be just as harmful to listen to CDs all the time or to eat constantly. However, when television is watched in moderation, it is extremely valuable, as it provides relaxation, entertainment, and education.   **1**

First of all, watching TV has the value of sheer relaxation. Watching television can be soothing and restful after an eight-hour day of pressure, challenges, or concentration. After working hard all day, people look forward to a new episode of a favorite show or yet another showing of *Casablanca* or *Anchorman*. This period of relaxation leaves viewers refreshed and ready to take on the world again. Watching TV also seems to reduce stress in some people. This benefit of television is just beginning to be recognized. One doctor, for example, advises his patients with high blood pressure to relax in the evening with a few hours of television.   **2**

Essay 2

continued

In addition to being relaxing, television is entertaining. Along with the standard comedies, dramas, and game shows that provide enjoyment to viewers, television offers a variety of movies and sports events. Moreover, viewers can pay a monthly fee and receive special cable programming or Direct TV. Viewers can watch first-run movies, rock and classical music concerts, and specialized sports events, like international soccer and Grand Prix racing. Viewers can also buy or rent movies and TV shows on DVD. Still another growing area of TV entertainment is video games. PlayStation, Xbox, and Nintendo consoles allow the owner to have a video-game arcade in the living room.   3

Most important, television is educational. Preschoolers learn colors, numbers, and letters from public television programs, like *Sesame Street*, that use animation and puppets to make learning fun. On the Discovery Channel, science shows for older children go on location to analyze everything from volcanoes to rocket launches. Adults, too, can get an education (college credits included) from courses given on television. Also, television widens our knowledge by covering important events and current news. Viewers can see and hear presidents' speeches, state funerals, natural disasters, and election results as they are happening.   4

Perhaps because television is such a powerful force, we like to criticize it and search for its flaws. However, the benefits of television should not be ignored. We can use television to relax, to have fun, and to make ourselves smarter. This electronic wonder, then, is a servant, not a master.   5

ACTIVITY 5

Fill in the blanks.

Essay _____ makes its point more clearly and effectively because _____

_____

_____

EXPLANATION: In this case, essay 2 is more effective because the material is organized clearly and logically. Using emphatic order, the writer develops three positive uses of television, ending with the most important use: television as an educational tool. The writer includes transitional words that act as signposts, making movement from one idea to the next easy to follow. The major transitions include *First of all*, *In addition*, and *Most important*;

continued

transitions within paragraphs include such words as *Moreover, Still another, too,* and *Also.* And this writer also uses a linking sentence ("In addition to being relaxing, television is entertaining") to tie the first and second supporting paragraphs together clearly.

Although essay 1 is unified and supported, the writer does not have any clear and consistent way of organizing the material. The most important idea (signaled by the phrase *Worst of all*) is discussed in the second supporting paragraph instead of being saved for last. None of the supporting paragraphs organizes its details in a logical fashion. The first supporting paragraph, for example, discusses older viewers, then goes to younger viewers, then jumps back to older people again. The third supporting paragraph, like the first, leaps from an opening idea (families talking only during commercials) to several intervening ideas and then back to the original idea (talking during commercials). In addition, essay 1 uses practically no transitional devices to guide the reader.

These two essays lead us to the third base of effective writing: *coherence.* All the supporting ideas and sentences in a paper must be organized so that they cohere, or "stick together." As has been discussed in Chapter 4, key techniques for tying together the material in a paper include a clear method of organization (such as time order or emphatic order), transitions, and other connecting words.

Revising for Coherence

On a separate sheet of paper, revise one of the three supporting paragraphs in "Harmful Effects of Watching Television" by providing a clear method of organizing the material and transitional words.

ACTIVITY 6

Base 4: Sentence Skills

Understanding Sentence Skills

Following are the opening paragraphs from two essays. Both are unified, supported, and organized, but one version communicates more clearly and effectively. Which one, and why?

**Essay 1,
First Part**

"revenge"

[1]Revenge is one of those things that everyone enjoy. [2]People don't like to talk about it, though. [3]Just the same, there is nothing more tempting, more satisfying, or with the reward of a bit of revenge. [4]The purpose is not to harm the victims. [5]But to let them know that they have been doing something that is upsetting. [6]Careful plotting can provide relief from bothersom coworkers, gossiping friends, or nagging family members.

[7]Coworkers who make comments about the fact that a person is always fifteen minutes late for work can be taken care of very simply. [8]The first thing that a person seeking revenge should do is to get up extra early one day. [9]Before the sun comes up, he or she should drive to each coworker's house, park near the coworker's car, reach under the hood of the car, and disconnected the center wire that leads to the distrib. cap. [10]The car will be unharmed, but it will not start. [11]All of the victims will be late for work on the same day. [12]If the person seeking revenge is really lucky, his or her boss might notice that no one else is on time and will reward the person who did show up. [13]Later if guilt becomes an issue anonymous calls to the coworkers to tell them how to get their car running again may help ease those feelings. . . .

1

2

A Bit of Revenge

Revenge is one of those things that everyone enjoys. People don't like to talk about it, though. Just the same, there is nothing more tempting, more satisfying, or more rewarding than a bit of revenge. The purpose is not to harm the victims but to let them know that they have been doing something that is upsetting. Careful plotting can provide relief from bothersome coworkers, gossiping friends, or nagging family members.

Coworkers who make comments about the fact that a person is always fifteen minutes late for work can be taken care of very simply. The first thing that a person seeking revenge should do is to get up extra early one day. Before the sun comes up, he or she should drive to each coworker's house, park near the coworker's car, reach under the hood of the car, and disconnect the center wire that leads to the distributor cap. The car will be unharmed, but it will not start. All of the victims will be late for work on the same day. If the person seeking revenge is really lucky, his or her boss might notice that no one else is on time and will reward the person who did show up. Later, if guilt becomes an issue, anonymous calls to the coworkers to tell them how to get their cars running again may help ease those feelings. . . .

1

2

**Essay 2,
First Part**

Fill in the blanks.

Essay _____ makes its point more clearly and effectively because _____

_____

_____

EXPLANATION: Essay 2 is more effective because it uses *sentence skills,* the fourth base of competent writing. Here are the sentence-skills mistakes in essay 1:

- The title should not be set off in quotation marks.
- The first letter of the title should be capitalized.
- The singular subject *everyone* in sentence 1 should have a singular verb: *enjoy* should be *enjoys.*
- There is a lack of parallelism in sentence 3: *with the reward* of should be *more rewarding.*
- Word group 5 is a fragment; it can be corrected by attaching it to the previous sentence.
- The word *bothersom* in sentence 6 is misspelled; it should be *bothersome.*
- The word *disconnected* in sentence 9 should be *disconnect* to be consistent in tense with *reach,* the other verb in the sentence.
- The word *distrib.* in sentence 9 should be spelled out in full: *distributor.*
- Commas must be added in sentence 13 to set off the interrupting words.
- The word *car* in sentence 13 needs to be changed to agree with *their* and *coworkers.*

Revising for Sentence Skills

Here are the final three paragraphs from the two essays. Edit the sentences in the first essay to make the corrections needed. Note that comparing essays 1 and 2 will help you locate the mistakes. This activity will also help you identify some of the sentence skills you may want to review in Part 4.

Essay 1, Last Part

. . . ¹Gossiping friends at school are also perfect targets for a simple act   3
of revenge. ²A way to trap either male or female friends are to leave phony
messages on their lockers. ³If the victim is male, the person seeking revenge
should leave a message setting up a meeting with a certain girl at her home
later that day. ⁴With any luck, her boyfriend will be there. ⁵The girl won't know
what's going on, and the victim will be so embarrassed that he probably won't
leave his home for a month. ⁶The plan works just as well for female friends, too.

⁷Parents and siblings can also be victims of harmless revenge, especially   4
when they have been really annoying. ⁸It may be just the way to make
them quite down for a while. ⁹The dinner table, where most of the nagging
probably happens, is a likely place. ¹⁰Just before the meal begins, you
should throw a handful of raisins into the food. ¹¹After about 5 minutes, once
everyone has began to eat, the person should then begin to make odd noises
and yell, "Bugs!" ¹²Dumping the food in the disposal, the car, will head
quickly for mcdonald's. ¹³After they leave, the meal will be quiet and peaceful.

¹⁴Well-planned revenge does not have to hurt anyone. ¹⁵The object is   5
simply to let other people know that they are being a bother. ¹⁶Anyone who
plans revenge should remember, though, to stay on his or her guard after
completing the revenge. ¹⁷The reason for this is simple, ¹⁸coworkers, friends,
and family can also plan revenge.

Essay 2, Last Part

. . . Gossiping friends at school are also perfect targets for a simple act   3
of revenge. A way to trap either male or female friends is to leave phony
messages on their lockers. If the victim is male, the person seeking revenge
should leave a message setting up a meeting with a certain girl at her home
later that day. With any luck, her boyfriend will be there. The girl won't know
what's going on, and the victim will be so embarrassed that he probably
won't leave his home for a month. The plan works just as well for female
friends, too.

continued

Parents and siblings can also be victims of harmless revenge, especially   **4**
when they have been really annoying. It may be just the way to make
them quiet down for a while. The dinner table, where most of the nagging
probably happens, is a likely place. Just before the meal begins, the person
should throw a handful of raisins into the food. After about five minutes, once
everyone has begun to eat, the person should then begin to make odd noises
and yell, "Bugs!" The others will all dump their food in the disposal, jump into
the car, and head quickly for McDonald's. After they leave, the meal will be
quiet and peaceful.

Well-planned revenge does not have to hurt anyone. The object is   **5**
simply to let other people know that they are being a bother. Anyone who
plans revenge should remember, though, to stay on his or her guard after
completing the revenge. The reason for this is simple. Coworkers, friends, and
family can also plan revenge.

Practice in Using the Four Bases

You are now familiar with four standards, or bases, of effective writing: *unity, support, coherence,* and *sentence skills*. In this section you will expand and strengthen your understanding of the four bases as you evaluate and revise essays for each of them.

Revising Essays for Unity

Both of the following essays contain irrelevant sentences that do not relate to the thesis of the essay or support the topic sentence of the paragraph in which they appear. Cross out the irrelevant sentences and write the numbers of those sentences in the spaces provided.

ACTIVITY 9

Playing on the Browns

Essay 1

Personal

¹For the past three summers, I have played first base on a softball team   **1**
known as the Browns. ²We play a long schedule, including playoffs, and
everybody takes the games pretty seriously. ³In that respect, we're no different
from any other of the thousand or so teams in our city. ⁴But in one respect, we
<u>are</u> different. ⁵In an all-male league, we have a woman on the team—me.
⁶Thus I've had a chance to observe something about human nature by seeing

continued

how the men have treated me. ⁷Some have been disbelieving; some have been patronizing; and, fortunately, some have simply accepted me.

    ⁸One new team in the league was particularly flabbergasted to see me start the game at first base. ⁹Nobody on the Comets had commented one way or the other when he saw me warming up, but playing in the actual game was another story. ¹⁰The Comets' first-base coach leaned over to me with a disbelieving grin and said, "You mean, you're starting, and those three guys are on the bench?" ¹¹I nodded and he shrugged, still amazed. ¹²He probably thought I was the manager's wife. ¹³When I came up to bat, the Comet pitcher smiled and called to his outfielders to move way in on me. ¹⁴Now, I don't have a lot of power, but I'm not exactly feeble. ¹⁵I used to work out on the exercise machines at a local health club until it closed, and now I lift weights at home a couple of times a week. ¹⁶I wiped the smirks off their faces with a line drive double over the left fielder's head.

2

The number of the irrelevant sentence: _____

    ¹⁷The next game, we played another new team, the Argyles, and their attitude was patronizing. ¹⁸The Argyles had seen me take batting practice, so they didn't do anything so rash as to draw their outfield way in. ¹⁹They had respect for my ability as a player. ²⁰However, they tried to annoy me with phony concern. ²¹For example, a redheaded Argyle got on base in the first inning and said to me, "You'd better be careful, hon. ²²When you have your foot on the bag, somebody might step on it. ²³You can get hurt in this game." ²⁴I was mad, but I have worked out several mental techniques to control my anger because it interferes with my playing ability. ²⁵Well, this delicate little girl survived the season without injury, which is more than I can say for some of the he-men on the Argyles.

3

The number of the irrelevant sentence: _____

    ²⁶Happily, most of the teams in the league have accepted me, just as the Browns did. ²⁷The men on the Browns coached and criticized me (and occasionally cursed me) just like anyone else. ²⁸Because I'm a religious person, I don't approve of cursing, but I don't say anything about it to my

4

continued

teammates. [29]They are not amazed when I get a hit or stretch for a wide throw. [30]My average this year was higher than the averages of several of my teammates, yet none of them acted resentful or threatened. [31]On several occasions I was taken out late in a game for a pinch runner, but other slow players on the team were also lifted at times for pinch runners. [32]Every woman should have a team like the Browns!

The number of the irrelevant sentence: _____

[33]Because I really had problems only with the new teams, I've concluded that it's when people are faced with an unfamiliar situation that they react defensively. [34]Once a rival team has gotten used to seeing me on the field, I'm no big deal. [35]Still, I suspect that the Browns secretly feel we're a little special. [36]After all, we won the championship with a woman on the team.

5

The Power of the Vote

Essay 2

[1]Since 1971, voter turn-out in America has been less than 60 percent during a presidential election year and 40 percent during a non-presidential election year. [2]Those who don't vote claim that their vote wouldn't make any difference and they are powerless to change anything. [3]However, in January 2012, Web sites like Wikipedia and Google demonstrated just how powerful the voices of the American people really are.

1

[4]In October 2011, two bills, the Stop Online Piracy Act (SOPA) and the Protect Intellectual Property Act (PIPA), were introduced. [5]Bills are regularly introduced in both the House and the Senate. [6]The purpose of these bills was to make it easier for the U.S. Department of Justice to block sites that sell or distribute pirated copyrighted material like music and movies as well as sites that sell counterfeit items like purses and watches. [7]Neither of the bills would have necessarily shut down the sites, but it would have allowed the U.S. Department of Justice to require Internet service providers to block access to the sites and stop providers, search engines, and advertisers from doing business with such sites. [8]Those in favor of the bills claimed the bills would protect jobs and revenue, but those against the bills saw them as an infringement of freedom of information.

2

The number of the irrelevant sentence: _____

> [9]Those in favor of the bill, like many of the major Hollywood studios and   **3**
> several news corporations, claimed the bills would protect jobs and revenue.
> [10]In December 2011, Chris Dodd, Chair of the Motion Picture Association of
> America (MPAA) wrote, "Indeed, the theft of intellectual property (which costs
> our nation 373,000 jobs and $58 billion in economic output each year) is
> itself the true threat to free speech, because it threatens to silence the artists
> whose creations—and livelihoods—are being stolen." [11]Dodd's support of the
> bill demonstrates his concern for those he represents—the film industry. [12]Art
> industries have also been victims of piracy. [13]The White House also maintains
> that online piracy is problematic and does threaten American jobs and the
> economy. [14]However, on January 14, 2012, in response to a petition against
> the SOPA bill that had over 50,000 signatures, the White House released
> a statement that said, "Online piracy by foreign Web sites is a serious
> problem that requires a serious legislative response, [but] we will not support
> legislation that reduces freedom of expression, increases cybersecurity risk, or
> undermines the dynamic, innovative global Internet."

The number of the irrelevant sentence: _____

> [15]On January 18, 2012, a coordinated service blackout was led by the   **4**
> English Wikipedia and Reddit. [16]Reddit is a social news Web site founded
> in 2005. [17]Other sites like Google offered a link to sign a petition, but
> didn't stop service. [18]Still other sites like Twitter, MoveOn.org, and Mozilla
> vocalized their protest, but didn't participate in the blackout. [19]NetCoalition,
> a group that provides a platform for and represents companies like Google,
> eBay, Expedia, and Amazon.com, released national radio and print ads
> against SOPA and PIPA. [20]In a statement, Google's news team said, "Like
> many businesses, entrepreneurs and Web users, we oppose these bills
> because there are smart, targeted ways to shut down foreign rogue Web sites
> without asking American companies to censor the Internet. [21]So tomorrow we
> will be joining many other tech companies to highlight this issue on our U.S.
> home page."

The number of the irrelevant sentence: _____

> [22]More than four and a half million people signed Google's anti-   **5**
> SOPA/PIPA petition. [23]As a result of the outpouring of opinion, both bills
> lost congressional support and the votes were postponed pending further
> discussion and resolution. [24]There were a lot of people who expressed angry

continued

reactions about the bills going back to the discussion table. [25]The blackout of January 18 is a strong example of the power of the people; it is something that should inspire more people to participate in the civic responsibility of voting.

The number of the irrelevant sentence: _____

Revising Essays for Support

Both of the essays below lack supporting details at certain key points. In each essay, identify the spots where details are needed.

ACTIVITY 10

The Formula for Happiness

[1]The study of happiness and what creates it has become a multi-million-dollar business. [2]Some people say that happiness comes from wealth, but most researchers say that happiness comes from within. [3]In pursuit of happiness, many people create goals, but often find once they have achieved them, the expected contentment is not present. [4]Martha Beck, a life coach with a Ph.D. from Harvard, writes that "Over and over, researchers studying happiness have found that the situational elements people crave—money, social status, possessions—don't reliably lead to an experience of well-being. [5]Learning to find joy in the present moment . . . increases life satisfaction, improves health, and allows us to live longer more fulfilling lives." [6]Finding joy in the present moment might be difficult at first, but if one focuses on what truly matters, this joy can lead to a better life.

[7]The first step in learning to find joy is to learn to be in the present. [8]Instead of seeing a rainy day as a negative thing, they see a rainy day and think about splashing and jumping in puddles. [9]They see caterpillars as fascinating, not gross, objects to observe and follow. [10]They see life as a series of exciting gifts that need to be experienced. [11]Instead of always focusing on what is coming next, learning to find joy means pausing. [12]Whether it is taking a moment to deeply breathe in the aroma of that first cup of coffee or marveling at the way toothpaste foams, finding satisfaction in the little moments of the day will lead to a more positive outlook.

1

2

Essay 1

Academic

The spot where supporting details are needed occurs after sentence _____.

> ¹³The second step in finding joy is to focus on experiences instead of things. ¹⁴Buying a television might be exciting at first, but sitting in a room watching television alone isn't going to contribute to a sense of happiness. ¹⁵According to Thomas A. Glass, professor at Johns' Hopkins Bloomberg School of Public Health, studies show that people who live longer lives have strong social connections and that people who have weak or no social connections will die earlier, despite seemingly good health.
>
> 3

The first spot where supporting details are needed occurs after sentence _____.
The second spot occurs after sentence _____.

> ¹⁶Finally, it is important to live generously. ¹⁷Many people report that when they spend more time volunteering or learning something new, they find happiness. ¹⁸This intrinsic desire to better themselves or the world around them leads people to a sense of worth and happiness.
>
> 4

The spot where supporting details are needed occurs after sentence _____.

> ¹⁹Pursuing happiness can always remain a goal, or it can become a reality. ²⁰All a person needs to do is focus on the present, focus on experiences, and live generously. ²¹Together these actions can lead to a longer, happier life.
>
> 5

Essay 2

> ### International Student Orientation Program
>
> ¹With the increase of international students on campus, it is important that the academic community be aware of the major issues these students face. ²Many international students struggle with language barriers, cultural barriers, and social barriers. ³In order to effectively educate our students, the counseling department, in conjunction with the College Orientation department and the Honors Student Ambassador Program, will be implementing an orientation program that all international students will be required to attend.
>
> 1
>
> ⁴To address the language barriers, all international students will be tested on their English language skills. ⁵If they have already taken the TOESL, that score will be used in place of the added testing. ⁶Students who are more proficient will be partnered with students in the Student Ambassador program. ⁷These pairings will allow students to work with a peer to ask questions, have subjects clarified, and seek the necessary resources that will offer help. ⁸This peer
>
> 2

continued

mentoring will be a way to increase student engagement, thus enhancing student success. ⁹Students who are less fluent in English will be linked up with all the helpful elements that our ESL program can offer. ¹⁰Not only will the orientation program offer students an opportunity to improve their English language skills, but it will offer them connections with other students and professors who are aware of the added struggles faced by international students.

The spot where supporting details are needed occurs after sentence _____.

¹¹To address the cultural barriers, the orientation classes will focus specifically on American culture in comparison to the cultures represented by the students in the class. ¹²Many students come from countries that view education and professors differently. ¹³Specific focus will be placed on American classroom culture and the expected behavior of student-professor interaction. ¹⁴Students will also be instructed about the many differing aspects of American social culture. ¹⁵Students will be encouraged to share their cultures and customs to create a deeper understanding and bond within the class. ¹⁶This type of learning will create a strong learning community that will aid in students' acclimation.

3

The spot where supporting details are needed occurs after sentence _____.

¹⁷The final problems many international students face are social barriers. ¹⁸Most students attending college are forging new social connections. ¹⁹However, it is generally much harder for international students as they are also trying to learn new customs, languages, and etiquette. ²⁰Within the safety of the orientation class, students will be able to form a cohort of other international students who are also facing social barriers. ²¹For many reasons, the Student Ambassadors will be vital to this part of the orientation class.

4

The spot where supporting details are needed occurs after sentence _____.

²²Our international students face many added challenges, and they give much to our college community. ²³Studies show that students who attend orientation programs often are far more successful in school. ²⁴Offering an orientation that is specifically geared toward the obstacles our international students face will help them to have a more positive experience, which in turn should greatly improve our retention of our international students.

5

Revising Essays for Coherence

Both of the essays that follow could be revised to improve their coherence. Answer the questions about coherence that come after each essay.

Essay 1

Noise Pollution

[1] ¹Natural sounds—waves, wind, birdsong—are so soothing that companies sell recordings of them to anxious people seeking a relaxing atmosphere at home or in the car. ²One reason why "environmental sounds" are big business is that ordinary citizens, especially city dwellers, are bombarded by noise pollution. ³On the way to work, on the job, and on the way home, the typical urban resident must cope with a continuing barrage of unpleasant sounds.

[2] ⁴The noise level in an office can be unbearable. ⁵From nine to five o'clock, phones and fax machines ring, computer keyboards chatter, intercoms buzz, and copy machines thump back and forth. ⁶Every time the receptionists can't find people, they resort to a nerve-shattering public address system. ⁷And because the managers worry about the employees' morale, they graciously provide the endless droning of canned music. ⁸This effectively eliminates any possibility of a moment of blessed silence.

[3] ⁹Traveling home from work provides no relief from the noisiness of the office. ¹⁰The ordinary sounds of blaring taxi horns and rumbling buses are occasionally punctuated by the ear-piercing screech of car brakes. ¹¹Taking a shortcut through the park will bring the weary worker face to face with chanting religious cults, freelance musicians, screaming children, and barking dogs. ¹²None of these sounds can compare with the large radios many park visitors carry. ¹³Each radio blasts out something different, from heavy-metal rock to baseball, at decibel levels so strong that they make eardrums throb in pain. ¹⁴If there are birds singing or wind in the trees, the harried commuter will never hear them.

[4] ¹⁵Even a trip to work at 6 or 7 a.m. isn't quiet. ¹⁶No matter which route a worker takes, there is bound to be a noisy construction site somewhere along the way. ¹⁷Hard hats will shout from third-story windows to warn their coworkers below before heaving debris out and sending it crashing to earth. ¹⁸Huge front-end loaders will crunch into these piles of rubble and back up, their warning signals letting out loud, jarring beeps. ¹⁹Air hammers begin an earsplitting chorus of rat-a-tat-tat sounds guaranteed to shatter sanity as well as concrete. ²⁰Before reaching the office, the worker is already completely frazzled.

[5] ²¹Noise pollution is as dangerous as any other kind of pollution. ²²The endless pressure of noise probably triggers countless nervous breakdowns, vicious arguments, and bouts of depression. ²³And imagine the world problems we could solve, if only the noise stopped long enough to let us think.

1. In "Noise Pollution," what is the number of the sentence to which the transition word *Also* could be added in paragraph 2? _____

2. In the last sentence of paragraph 2, to what does the pronoun *This* refer? _____

3. What is the number of the sentence to which the transition word *But* could be added in paragraph 3? _____

4. What is the number of the sentence to which the transition word *Then* could be added in paragraph 4? _____

5. What is the number of the sentence to which the transition word *Meanwhile* could be added in paragraph 4? _____

6. What word is used as a synonym for *debris* in paragraph 4? _____

7. How many times is the key word *sounds* used in the essay? _____

8. The time order of the three supporting paragraphs is confused. What is the number of the supporting paragraph that should come first? _____ Second? _____ Third? _____

Weight Loss

Essay 2

Personal

1   ¹The big fraternity party turned out to be the low point of my first year at college. ²I was in heaven until I discovered that my date with handsome Greg, the fraternity vice president, was a hoax: he had used me to win the "ugliest date" contest. ³I ran sobbing back to the dorm, wanting to resign from the human race. ⁴Then I realized that it was time to stop kidding myself about my weight. ⁵Within the next two years, I lost forty-two pounds and turned my life around. ⁶Losing weight gave me self-confidence socially, emotionally, and professionally.

2   ⁷I am more outgoing socially. ⁸Just being able to abandon dark colors, baggy sweaters, and tent dresses in favor of bright colors, T-shirts, and designer jeans made me feel better in social situations. ⁹I am able to do more things. ¹⁰I once turned down an invitation for a great camping trip with my best friend's family, making up excuses about sun poisoning and allergies. ¹¹Really, I was too embarrassed to tell them that I couldn't fit into the bathroom in their Winnebago! ¹²I made up for it last summer when I was one of the organizers of a college backpacking trip through the Rockies.

3   ¹³Most important, losing weight helped me seek new professional goals. ¹⁴When I was obese, I organized my whole life around my weight, as if it

continued

were a defect I could do nothing about. ¹⁵With my good grades, I could have chosen almost any major the college offered, but I had limited my goal to teaching kindergarten because I felt that little children wouldn't judge how I looked. ¹⁶Once I was no longer fat, I realized that I love working with all sorts of people. ¹⁷I became a campus guide and even had small parts in college theater productions. ¹⁸As a result, last year I changed my major to public relations. ¹⁹The area fascinates me, and I now have good job prospects there.

²⁰I have also become more emotionally honest. ²¹Rose, at the college counseling center, helped me see that my "fat and jolly" personality had been false. ²²I was afraid others would reject me if I didn't always go along with their suggestions. ²³I eventually put Rose's advice to the test. ²⁴My roommates were planning an evening at a Greek restaurant. ²⁵I loved the restaurant's atmosphere, but there wasn't much I liked on the menu. ²⁶Finally, in a shaky voice I said, "Actually, I'm not crazy about lamb. ²⁷How about Chinese food?" ²⁸They scolded me for not mentioning it before, and we had dinner at a Chinese restaurant. ²⁹We all agreed it was one of our best evenings out.

4

³⁰Fortunately, the low point of my first year turned out to be the turning point, leading to what promises to be an exciting senior year. ³¹Greg's cruel joke became a strange sort of favor, and I've gone from wanting to resign from the human race to welcoming each day as a source of fresh adventure and self-discovery.

5

1. In "Weight Loss," what is the number of the sentence to which the transition words *For one thing* could be added in paragraph 2? _____

2. What is the number of the sentence to which the transition word *Also* could be added in paragraph 2? _____

3. What is the number of the sentence to which the transition word *But* could be added in paragraph 2? _____

4. In sentence 11, to what does the pronoun *them* refer? _____

5. What is the number of the sentence to which the transition word *However* could be added in paragraph 3? _____

6. What word is used as a synonym for *obese* in paragraph 3? _____

7. How many times is the keyword *weight* used in the essay? _____

8. What is the number of the supporting paragraph that should be placed in the emphatic final position? _____

Revising Essays for All Four Bases: Unity, Support, Coherence, and Sentence Skills

In this activity, you will evaluate and revise two essays in terms of all four bases: unity, support, coherence, and sentence skills. Comments follow each supporting paragraph. Circle the letter of the statement that applies in each case.

Chiggers

Essay 1

Personal

1   I had lived my whole life not knowing what chiggers are. I thought they were probably a type of insect Humphrey Bogart encountered in *The African Queen*. I never had any real reason to care, until one day last summer. Within twenty-four hours, I had vividly experienced what chigger bites are, learned how to treat them, and learned how to prevent them.

2   First of all, I learned that chiggers are the larvae of tiny mites found in the woods and that their bites are always multiple and cause intense itching. A beautiful summer day seemed perfect for a walk in the woods. I am definitely not a city person, for I couldn't stand to be surrounded by people, noise, and concrete. As I walked through the ferns and pines, I noticed what appeared to be a dusting of reddish seeds or pollen on my slacks. Looking more closely, I realized that each speck was a tiny insect. I casually brushed off a few and gave them no further thought. I woke up the next morning feeling like a victim staked to an anthill by an enemy wise in the ways of torture. Most of my body was speckled with measlelike bumps that at the slightest touch burned and itched like a mosquito bite raised to the twentieth power. When antiseptics and calamine lotion failed to help, I raced to my doctor for emergency aid.

a.   Paragraph 2 contains an irrelevant sentence.

b.   Paragraph 2 lacks supporting details at one key spot.

c.   Time order in paragraph 2 is confused.

d.   Paragraph 2 contains two run-ons.

3   Healing the bites of chiggers, as the doctor diagnosed them to be, is not done overnight. It seems that there is really no wonder drug or commercial product to help. The victim must rely on a primitive home remedy and mostly wait out the course of the painful bites. First, the doctor explained, the skin must be bathed carefully with warm soapy water. An antihistamine spray applied several hours later will not cure the bites but will soothe the intense itching and help prevent infection. A few days after the treatment, the bites

continued

finally healed. Although I was in pain, and desperate for relief, I followed the doctor's instructions.

a.   Paragraph 3 contains an irrelevant sentence.

b.   Paragraph 3 lacks supporting details at one key spot.

c.   Time order in paragraph 3 is confused.

d.   Paragraph 3 contains one fragment.

Most important of all, I learned what to do to prevent getting chigger   4
bites in the future. Mainly, of course, stay out of the woods in the summertime. But if the temptation is too great on an especially beautiful day, I'll be sure to wear the right type of clothing, like a long-sleeved shirt, long pants, knee socks, and closed shoes. In addition, I'll cover myself with clouds of superstrength insect repellent. I will then shower thoroughly as soon as I get home, I also will probably burn all my clothes if I notice even one suspicious red speck.

a.   Paragraph 4 contains an irrelevant sentence.

b.   Paragraph 4 lacks supporting details at one key spot.

c.   Paragraph 4 lacks transitional words.

d.   Paragraph 4 contains a run-on and a fragment.

I will never forget my lessons on the cause, cure, and prevention of   5
chigger bites. I'd gladly accept the challenge of rattlesnakes and scorpions in the wilds of the West but will never again confront a siege of chiggers in the pinewoods.

Essay 2

Navigating the Hunt for a Job

As economies fluctuate and job markets change, it is important for people   1
to know how to navigate the process of job hunting. Getting a new job starts long before the résumé or cover letter, although they are both very important. Good hunters learn about the companies they are applying to, put together strong application packets, and extensively prepare for the interviews.

Securing a good job begins even before the application process. Seekers   2
should learn about the company they are applying to because knowing information about the company shows interest and conscientiousness. Applicants who know what the company's history is, what the company does, and what is expected of employees will demonstrate desired attitudes

continued

that many companies want. Also, through research, a job seeker might learn that a potential employer spends 10 percent of the gross income each year on a specific program for underprivileged children. One company in Chicago spent 20 percent of its gross income on a program for inner city children. People who really want a job with that company will then learn about the charitable programs that are important to that company, understand that program, and accept that a job with this company will mean possibly working with that program.

a. Paragraph 2 contains an irrelevant sentence.

b. Paragraph 2 lacks supporting details at one key spot.

c. Paragraph 2 lacks transitional words.

d. Paragraph 2 contains one fragment and one run-on.

Once job seekers have researched potential employers, the next step is to prepare strong application packets. This means that an applicant must understand the skills and education requirements listed in the job descriptions and properly fill out the applications. If a job requires a degree in engineering, but the applicant doesn't have a degree. This may not be the right job. After the applicant has found a job that is a right fit, it is important to properly fill out the application. An applicant should double check that every question is answered, all the information is correct, and no spelling or grammar mistakes are made. Leaving off a signature or forgetting to fill in areas will not impress the potential employer. Cover letters should also be included in the packet they are the first introduction to the applicant and should address the specifics of the job, laying out why the candidate is the best choice. Cover letters should be error free and well-articulated. Weak application packets that include cover letters and applications that are filled with spelling mistakes, grammar errors, and irrelevant material will hold the applicant back. Strong application packets will increase the chance of applicants' moving on to the final step in job hunting.   3

a. Paragraph 3 contains an irrelevant sentence.

b. Paragraph 3 lacks supporting details at one key spot.

c. Paragraph 3 lacks transitional words.

d. Paragraph 3 contains one fragment and one run-on.

The final step in navigating the process is preparing for the interviews, which includes proper grooming and practiced interviewing skills. Clothes should be appropriate for the interview, shoes should be polished, and bodies should be groomed. It isn't necessary to go out and buy a $5000   4

continued

suit, but it is important not to wear flip-flops and shorts. By visiting the work place ahead of time, if possible, the interviewee can assess how employees are dressed and then wear a similar—or slightly nicer—outfit. Specific interviewing skills should be practiced so that when questioned, the interviewee can eloquently and intelligently respond. Proper preparation will increase the candidate's chance of being offered a job because a prepared interviewee often means that he or she will be a prepared employee.

a.   Paragraph 4 contains an irrelevant sentence.

b.   Paragraph 4 lacks supporting details at one key spot.

c.   Paragraph 4 lacks transitional words.

d.   Paragraph 4 contains one fragment and one run-on.

By properly navigating the process of job hunting, people who are   5
seeking a new job will stand out to potential employers. There are thousands of people looking for jobs every day, but by taking hints from the successfully employed, job seekers will have the opportunity to move from seeker to employee.

Patterns of Essay Development

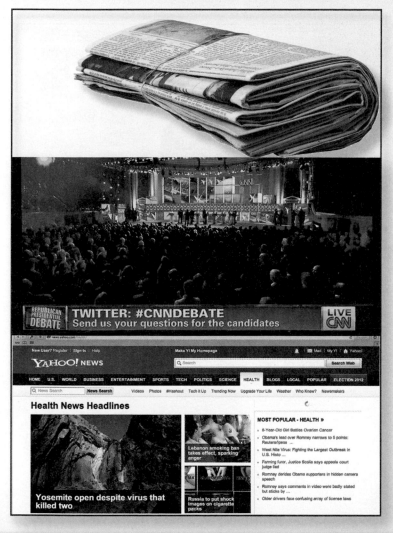

PART 2

PREVIEW

7 Introduction to Essay Development

8 Description

9 Narration

10 Exemplification

11 Process

12 Cause and/or Effect

13 Comparison and/or Contrast

14 Definition

15 Division-Classification

16 Argument

What do all of the images shown here have in common? They can all be classified as news sources. Think about the many different formats available for getting the news today. Then select three formats and write an essay in which you discuss the unique qualities of each.

Introduction to Essay Development

This chapter will

- introduce you to nine patterns of essay development

- explain the importance of understanding the nature and length of an assignment

- explain the importance of knowing your subject, your purpose, and your audience

- explain the three different points of view used in writing

- show you how to conduct a peer review and personal review

Who do you believe is the intended audience of this advertisement? Write a description of that intended audience.

Important Considerations in Essay Development

When you begin work on particular types of essays, keep in mind several general considerations about writing; they are discussed in the following pages.

Understanding the Nature and Length of an Assignment

In all likelihood, your college writing assignments will have a good deal of variety. Sometimes you will be able to write on a topic of your own choosing or on a point you discover within a given topic; at other times you may be given a very specific assignment. In any case, do not start writing a paper until you know exactly what is expected.

First of all, be clear about *what kind of paper* the instructor has in mind. Should it be primarily a research paper summarizing other people's ideas? Should it consist entirely of your own ideas? Should it consist of a comparison of your ideas with those of a given author? Should it be something else? If you are not sure about the nature of an assignment, other students may be confused as well. Do not hesitate, then, to ask an instructor about an assignment. Most instructors are more than willing to provide an explanation. They would rather spend a few minutes of class time explaining an assignment than spend hours reading student essays that miss the mark.

Second, find out right at the start *how long* a paper is expected to be. Many instructors will indicate the approximate length of the papers they assign. Knowing the expected length of a paper will help you decide exactly how detailed your treatment of a subject should be.

Knowing Your Subject

Whenever possible, try to write on a subject that interests you. You will then find it easier to put more time into your work. Even more important, try to write on a subject that you already know something about. If you do not have direct experience with the subject, you should at least have indirect experience—knowledge gained through thinking, reading, or talking about the subject as well as from prewriting.

If you are asked to write on a topic about which you have no experience or knowledge, do whatever research is required to gain the background information you may need. Chapter 21, "Using the Library and the Internet," will show you how to look up relevant information. Without direct or indirect experience, or the information you gain through research, you may not be able to provide the specific evidence needed to develop an essay.

Knowing Your Purpose and Audience

The three most common purposes of writing are *to inform, to persuade*, and *to entertain*. As noted previously, much of the writing you do in this book will involve some form of argumentation or persuasion. You will advance a point or thesis and then support it in a variety of ways. To some extent, also, you will write papers to inform—to provide readers with information about a particular subject. And since, in practice, writing often combines purposes, you might also find yourself at times providing vivid or humorous details to entertain your readers.

Your audience will be primarily your instructor and sometimes other students. Your instructor is really a symbol of the larger audience you should see yourself writing for—educated adult readers who expect you to present your ideas in a clear, direct, organized way. If you can learn to write to persuade or inform such a general audience, you will have accomplished a great deal.

It will also be helpful for you to write some papers for a more specific audience. By doing so, you will develop an ability to choose words and adopt a tone and point of view that are just right for a given audience. This part of the book includes assignments asking you to write with very specific purposes in mind and for very specific audiences.

Determining Your Point of View

When you write, you can take any of three approaches, or points of view: first person, second person, or third person.

First-Person Approach

In the first-person approach—a strongly individualized point of view—you draw on your own experience and speak to your audience in your own voice, using pronouns like *I, me, mine, we, our*, and *us*.

The first-person approach is most common in narrative essays based on personal experience. It also suits other essays where most of the evidence presented consists of personal observation.

Here is a first-person supporting paragraph from an essay on camping:

First of all, I like comfort when I'm camping. My motor home, with its completely equipped kitchen, shower stall, toilet, double bed, and flatscreen television, resembles a mobile motel room. I can sleep on a real mattress, clean sheets, and fluffy pillows. Next to my bed are devices that make me feel at home: a Bose radio, an alarm clock, and a remote control. Unlike the poor campers huddled in tents, I don't have to worry about cold, rain, heat,

continued

or annoying insects. After a hot shower, I can slide into my best nightgown, sit comfortably on my down-filled quilt, and read the latest best seller while a thunderstorm booms outside.

Second-Person Approach

In the second-person approach, the writer speaks directly to the reader, using the pronoun *you*. The second-person approach is considered appropriate for giving direct instructions and explanations to the reader. That is why *you* is used throughout this book.

You should plan to use the second-person approach only when writing a process essay, although even for this type of essay, the third-person approach is effective. Otherwise, as a general rule, never use the word *you* in writing.

TIP If using *you* has been a common mistake in your writing, you should review the rule about pronoun point of view on pages 114–116.

Third-Person Approach

The third-person approach is by far the most common point of view in academic writing. In the third person, the writer includes no direct references to the reader (*you*) or the self (*I, me*). Third person gets its name from the stance it suggests— that of an outsider or "third person" observing and reporting on matters of public rather than private importance. In this approach, you draw on information achieved through observation, thinking, or reading.

Here is a similar paragraph on camping, recast in the third person. Note the third-person pronouns *their, them,* and *they,* which all refer to *campers* in the first sentence.

First of all, modern campers bring complete bedrooms with them. Winnebagos, Airstream motor homes, and Fleetwood recreational vehicles lumber into America's campgrounds every summer like mobile motel rooms. All the comforts of home are provided inside. Campers sleep on real mattresses with clean sheets and fluffy pillows. Next to their beds are the same gadgets that litter their night tables at home—Bose radios, alarm clocks, and remote controls. It's not necessary for them to worry about

Academic

continued

annoyances like cold, heat, rain, or buzzing insects, either. They can sit comfortably in bed and read the latest best sellers while a thunderstorm booms outside.

Using Peer Review

In addition to having your instructor as an audience for your writing, you will benefit from having other students in your class as an audience. On the day a paper is due, or on a day when you are writing papers in class, your instructor may ask you to pair up with another student (or students). That student will read your paper, and you will read his or her paper.

Ideally, read the other paper aloud while your peer listens. If that is not practical, read it in a whisper while your peer looks on. As you read, both you and your peer should look and listen for spots where the paper does not read smoothly and clearly. Check or circle the trouble spots where your reading snags.

Your peer should then read your paper, marking possible trouble spots. Then each of you should do three things.

1 Identification

At the top of a separate sheet of paper, write the title and author of the paper you have read. Under it, write your name as the reader of the paper.

2 Scratch Outline

"X-ray" the paper for its inner logic by making up a scratch outline. The scratch outline need be no more than twenty words or so, but it should show clearly the logical foundation on which the essay is built. It should identify and summarize the overall point of the paper and the three areas of support for the point.

Your outline can look like this:

Point: _____

Support:

(1) _____

(2) _____

(3) _____

For example, here is a scratch outline of the essay on moviegoing on page 4:

Point: _____

Support:

(1) _____

(2) _____

(3) _____

3 *Comments*

Under the outline, write a heading: "Comments." Here is what you should comment on:

- Look at the spots where your reading of the paper snagged. Are words missing or misspelled? Is there a lack of parallel structure? Are there mistakes with punctuation? Is the meaning of a sentence confused? Try to figure out what the problems are and suggest ways to fix them.

- Are there spots in the paper where you see problems with *unity, support,* or *organization*? (You'll find it helpful to refer to the Four Bases checklist on the inside back cover of this book.) If so, offer comments. For example, you might say, "More details are needed in the first supporting paragraph," or, "Some of the details in the last supporting paragraph don't really back up your point."

- Finally, note something you really liked about the paper, such as good use of transitions or an especially realistic or vivid specific detail.

After you have completed your evaluation of the paper, give it to your peer. Your instructor may give you the option of rewriting a paper in light of the feedback you get. Whether or not you rewrite, be sure to hand in the peer-evaluation form with your paper.

Doing a Personal Review

1. While you're writing and revising an essay, you should be constantly evaluating it in terms of *unity, support*, and *coherence*. Use as a guide the detailed checklist on the inside back cover of the book.

2. After you've finished the next-to-final draft of an essay, check it for the *sentence skills* listed on the inside back cover. It may also help to read the paper out loud. If a given sentence does not sound right—that is, if it does

not read clearly and smoothly—chances are something is wrong. Then revise or edit as needed until your paper is error-free.

Patterns of Essay Development

Traditionally, essay writing has been divided into the following patterns of development. However, it's important to remember that essays often emphasize one pattern while employing additional patterns to help support the thesis.

- Description
- Narration
- Exposition

    Exemplification   Comparison or contrast

    Process   Definition

    Cause and effect   Division-classification

- Argument

Description emphasizes verbal pictures of people, places, or things. *Narration* is used when a writer tells the story of something that happened.

In *exposition*, the writer provides information about and explains a particular subject. Patterns of development often used within exposition include giving examples (*exemplification*); detailing a *process* of doing or making something; analyzing *causes* and *effects*; *comparing* or *contrasting*; *defining* a term or concept; and *dividing* something into parts or *classifying* it into categories.

Finally, in *argument*, a writer attempts to support a controversial point or to defend a position on which there is a difference of opinion.

The pages ahead present individual chapters that describe how to write essays that emphasize each pattern. You will have a chance, then, to learn nine different patterns or methods for organizing material in your papers. As you practice writing essays, keep these two points in mind:

- **While each essay that you write will involve one predominant pattern, very often one or more additional patterns may be involved**. For example, consider the two student essays in Chapter 10, "Exemplification." The first essay there, "Look on the Bright Side" (pages 223–225), is developed through a series of *examples*. But there is also an element of *narration,* because the writer presents examples that occur as he proceeds through his day. In the second essay, "Altered States" (pages 225–226), *exemplification* is again the predominant pattern, but in a lesser way the author is also explaining the *causes* of altered states of mind.

- **No matter which pattern or patterns you use, each essay will probably involve some form of argumentation**. You will advance a point and then go on to support that point. In "Look on the Bright Side," for instance, the author uses *exemplification* to support his point that people inflict little cruelties on each other. In "A Description of Celiac Disease," a writer supports the point that celiac disease needs to be diagnosed and controlled by providing a number of *descriptive details* (see pages 184–185). In "A Night of Violence," another writer claims that a certain experience in his life was frightening and then uses a *narrative* to persuade us of the truth of this statement (see pages 205–206). Yet another author states that a fast-food restaurant can be preferable to a fancy one and then supplies *comparative information* about both to support his statement (see pages 284–285, "A Vote for McDonald's"). Much of your writing, in short, will have the purpose of persuading your reader that the idea you have advanced is valid.

The Progression in Each Chapter

In Chapters 8 through 16, after each pattern is explained, student essays and a professional essay illustrating that emphasized pattern are presented, followed by questions about the essays. The questions relate to unity, support, and coherence— principles of effective writing explained earlier in this book and outlined on the inside back cover. You are then asked to write your own essay. In most cases, the first assignment has a personal focus, is fairly structured, and provides a good deal of guidance for the writing process. The other assignments typically have academic and work focuses and frequently require you to write with a specific purpose and for a specific audience. In some instances, the academic assignments require outside reading of literary works; a student model is provided for each of these assignments. Finally, some of the work assignments ask you to research local and campus issues, and in a few instances, write about your own work place.

Description

This chapter will explain and illustrate how to

- develop an essay with emphasis on description

- write an essay with emphasis on description

- revise an essay with emphasis on description

In addition, you will read and consider

- two student essays that emphasize description

- one professional essay that emphasizes description

Think about your college graduation day and write an essay about what you imagine it will be like. How will you feel? What sights and sounds will surround you? Will your family and friends be there to congratulate you? Describe the day and bring it to life in your essay.

When you describe someone or something, you give your readers a picture in words. To make the word picture as vivid and real as possible, you must observe and record specific details that appeal to your readers' senses (sight, hearing, taste, smell, and touch). More than any other type of essay, a paper that emphasizes description needs sharp, colorful details.

Here is a sentence in which there is almost no appeal to the senses: "In the window was a fan." In contrast, here is a description rich in sense impressions: "The blades of the rusty window fan clattered and whirled as they blew out a stream of warm, soggy air." Sense impressions in this second example include sight (*rusty window fan, whirled*), hearing (*clattered*), and touch (*warm, soggy air*). The vividness and sharpness provided by the sensory details give us a clear picture of the fan and enable us to share the writer's experience.

In this chapter, you will be asked to describe a person, place, or thing sharply, by using words rich in sensory details. To prepare for this assignment, read the student essays and the professional essay that follow and work through the questions that accompany each piece of writing.

Student Essays to Consider

Family Portrait

My great-grandmother, who is ninety-five years old, recently sent me a photograph of herself that I had never seen before. While cleaning out the attic of her Florida home, she came across a studio portrait she had taken about a year before she married my great-grandfather. This picture of my great-grandmother as a twenty-year-old girl and the story behind it have fascinated me from the moment I began to consider it.   1

The young woman in the picture has a face that resembles my own in many ways. Her face is a bit more oval than mine, but the softly waving brown hair around it is identical. The small, straight nose is the same model I was born with. My great-grandmother's mouth is closed, yet there is just the slightest hint of a smile on her full lips. I know that if she had smiled, she would have shown the same wide grin and down-curving "smile lines" that appear in my own snapshots. The most haunting feature in the photo, however, is my great-grandmother's eyes. They are an exact duplicate of my own large, dark brown ones. Her brows are plucked into thin lines, which are like two pencil strokes added to highlight those fine, luminous eyes.   2

I've also carefully studied the clothing and jewelry in the photograph. Although the photo was taken seventy-five years ago, my great-grandmother is wearing a blouse and skirt that could easily be worn today. The blouse is made of heavy eggshell-colored satin and reflects the light in its folds and hollows. It has a turned-down cowl collar and smocking on the shoulders and below the collar. The smocking (tiny rows of gathered material) looks hand-done. The skirt, which covers my great-grandmother's calves, is straight and made of light wool or flannel. My great-grandmother is wearing silver drop earrings. They are about two inches long and roughly shield-shaped. On her   3

continued

left wrist is a matching bracelet. My great-grandmother can't find this bracelet now, despite our having spent hours searching through the attic for it. On the third finger of her left hand is a ring with a large, square-cut stone.

The story behind the picture is as interesting to me as the young woman it captures. Great-Grandmother, who was earning twenty-five dollars a week as a file clerk, decided to give her boyfriend (my great-grandfather) a picture of herself. She spent almost two weeks' salary on the skirt and blouse, which she bought at a fancy department store downtown. She borrowed the earrings and bracelet from her older sister, Dorothy. The ring she wore was a present from another young man she was dating at the time. Great-Grandmother spent another chunk of her salary to pay the portrait photographer for the hand-tinted print in old-fashioned tones of brown and tan. Just before giving the picture to my great-grandfather, she scrawled at the lower left, "Sincerely, Beatrice."   4

When I study this picture, I react in many ways. I think about the trouble that my great-grandmother went to in order to impress the young man who was to be my great-grandfather. I laugh when I look at the ring, which was probably worn to make him jealous. I smile at the serious, formal inscription my great-grandmother used at this stage of the budding relationship. Sometimes, I am filled with a mixture of pleasure and sadness when I look at this frozen long-ago moment. It is a moment of beauty, of love, and—in a way—of my own past.   5

A Description of Celiac Disease

It is estimated that one person in one hundred suffers from celiac disease, a genetic disorder that causes digestive problems. These problems occur when gluten, a protein composite found in grains like wheat and barley, is ingested. The symptoms of celiac disease can range from irritability and abdominal pain to severe weight loss and fatigue. Also called celiac sprue, non-tropical sprue, gluten-sensitive enteropathy, and coeliac disease, the disease can cause serious damage that ranges from malnutrition to cancer. I have been suffering celiac symptoms, so I am interested in this disease. Doctors currently don't know exactly what causes the disease, but they do understand that people who have the disease have an overreaction to gluten in food, and it needs to be diagnosed and controlled.   1

Diagnosing celiac disease can be difficult because many of the symptoms are similar to other diseases like Crohn's, anemia, or irritable bowel syndrome. The obvious symptoms of celiac disease are abdominal pain and bloating. Other less obvious symptoms can be mouth blisters, joint irritation, and painful nerve damage. More serious symptoms include weight loss,   2

continued

stunted growth, and osteoporosis. These symptoms result from what is physically occurring within the small intestine. The small intestine is lined with tiny finger-like projections called villi, and the villi are covered with microvilli, which look like tendrils. The villi and microvilli increase the surface space within the intestines, thus increasing absorption of nutrients. Celiac disease destroys the villi and obstructs nutrient absorption. Without the villi, nutrients like vitamins and protein are not absorbed and are quickly eliminated, often resulting in painful diarrhea.

A blood test to screen for transglutaminase antibody (tTG) is the primary   3
test used to screen for celiac. Several other tests, like a total immunoglobulin A test or the anti-giadan antibody, may be ordered if the tTG test is positive for celiac disease. These tests will be positive in celiac sufferers because their bodies see gluten as an enemy substance and produce elevated levels of antibodies to fight the substance. If blood tests are positive, doctors will often test a sample of the small intestine to check for damaged villi. Some doctors may have patients swallow a camera pill to examine the entire small intestine. Proper diagnosis of celiac disease often requires several tests and procedures.

There is currently no cure for celiac disease, but it can be effectively   4
managed through a rigid diet. Any foods that contain gluten must be avoided. This includes barley, bulgur, durum, farina, graham flour, rye, semolina, spelt, triticale, and wheat. Most gluten is found in food, but people diagnosed with celiac disease should also be aware of medicines, vitamins, and lip balms that may contain gluten. Once a person has started on a gluten-free diet, the body will begin to recover. The inflammation within the intestine will subside within several weeks. Full healing and regrowth of the villi may take as long as two to three years. Trace amounts of gluten can be damaging, so it is important that once a person is diagnosed with celiac he or she avoid all forms of gluten.

It is believed that as many as two million people are currently   5
undiagnosed with celiac disease or gluten sensitivity. It is imperative that doctors understand this disease and do not disregard patients who complain of symptoms of the disease. Doctors need to listen to the patients' complaints and administer the proper tests. Since there is currently no medication to help heal patients, it is crucial that doctors diagnose patients before serious physical damage occurs.

ABOUT UNITY

QUESTIONS 1

1. In which supporting paragraph of "A Description of Celiac Disease" does the topic sentence appear at the paragraph's end, rather than the beginning?
   a. paragraph 2
   b. paragraph 3
   c. paragraph 4

2. Which sentence in paragraph 1 of "A Description of Celiac Disease" should be eliminated and why should it be eliminated? (*Write your answer here.*)

_____

_____

3. Which sentence in paragraph 3 of "Family Portrait" should be eliminated and why? (*Write your answer here.*)

_____

_____

ABOUT SUPPORT

4. In paragraph 3 of "Family Portrait," the writer goes beyond the mere mention of clothing and jewelry. Focus on one item and summarize the details she includes to make the object clearer to the reader. (*Write your answer here.*)

_____

_____

_____

5. Label as sight, touch, hearing, or smell all the sensory details in the following sentences taken from the two essays. The first one is done for you as an example.

                sight   *touch*   *sight*

   a. "Her face is a bit more oval than mine, but the softly waving brown hair around it is identical."

   b. "The small intestine is lined with tiny finger-like projections called villi, and the villi are covered with microvilli, which look like tendrils."

   c. "The blouse is made of heavy eggshell-colored satin and reflects the light in its folds and hollows."

   d. Her brows are plucked into thin lines, which are like two pencil strokes added to highlight those fine, luminous eyes.

6. The author could have added further descriptive details to provide a more specific picture of how celiac disease makes a person feel or look. Suggest two or three you would add. (*Write your answer here.*)

_____

ABOUT COHERENCE

7. Which method of organization does paragraph 2 of "Family Portrait" use?
   a. Time order
   b. Emphatic order

8. What sentence in paragraph 3 of "Family Portrait" serves as a transition? (*Write the first words.*)

_____

9. Find at least three transitions and connecting words in paragraph 2 of "A Description of Celiac Disease." Remember that repeated words, pronouns, and synonyms can act as connectors.

_____

_____

ABOUT THE INTRODUCTION AND CONCLUSION

10. What method discussed in Chapter 4 is used in the introduction to "A Description of Celiac Disease"?

_____

_____

Developing an Essay with Emphasis on Description

Considering Purpose and Audience

The main purpose of an essay with an emphasis on description is to make readers see—or hear, taste, smell, or feel—what you are writing about. Vivid details are the key to good descriptions, enabling your audience to picture and, in a way, experience what you describe.

Unlike a descriptive paragraph that focuses *only* on describing the topic, an essay that emphasizes description may also contain cause and effect, comparison or contrast, or narration.

As you start to think about your own essay, choose a topic that will allow you to write descriptions that appeal strongly to at least one of your senses. Also, when selecting your topic, consider how much your audience already knows about it. If your topic is a familiar one, you can assume your audience already understands the general idea. However, if you are presenting something new or unfamiliar to your readers—perhaps a description of one of your relatives or a place where you've lived—you must provide background information.

Once you have selected your topic, focus on the goal or purpose of your essay. It is important to use the specific modes and writing techniques where and when needed. The purpose of your essay will determine what events should be told, what events should be eliminated, and what strategies should be employed when writing. What message do you hope to convey to your audience? For instance, if you chose as your topic a playground you used to visit as a child, decide what dominant impression you want to communicate. Is your goal to make readers see the park as a pleasant play area, or do you want them to see it as a dangerous place? If you choose the second option, focus on conveying that sense of danger to your audience. Then jot down any details that support that idea. You might describe broken beer bottles on the asphalt, graffiti sprayed on the metal jungle gym, or a pack of loud teenagers gathered on a nearby street corner. In this case, the details support your overall purpose, creating a threatening picture that your audience can see and understand.

Visualizing the Subject

Physical description relies solely on sense impressions. Of course, all five senses can be used when describing. However, perhaps the most important sense is sight, and many of us can be classified as visual learners. Therefore, one advantage that description has over other methods of development is that it allows the writer to visualize his or her subject before describing it in words.

If you like to draw or paint, make an image of your subject before you start writing about him, her, or it. If possible, use different colors to reveal the complexity of your subject, apply perspective to give your picture depth and contrast, or add small details like a tiny mole, a button on a shirt, or a stain on a tie.

When you are done, use the picture as inspiration as you gather information during prewriting.

Including People and Events in the Description of a Place

Discussing the type of people who are in a place can sometimes give clues to its character and help describe it. The same can be said for what happens there. For example, a bar where middle-aged men quietly drink beer and watch a hockey game on TV is one thing; a bar where young people dance to loud music is quite another.

You might even describe animals and their actions to enliven your description of a place. Say you're writing about a zoo. It might be worth discussing the antics of chimpanzees or the majestic pacing of a tiger as it struts within its habitat.

Finally, consider including dialogue. You will learn more about creating dialogue in Chapter 9, "Narration." For now just remember that dialogue can sometimes reveal a great deal about a person or a place. For example, our first clue that the owner of the café in "Lou's Place" (an essay appearing later in this chapter) is rather feisty is his response to a woman who wants to know if he's open: "I'm here, aren't I?" Later, when another customer asks for breakfast, Lou says, "I'm reading the paper. . . . Eggs are in the refrigerator."

Development through Prewriting

When Cindy, the author of "Family Portrait," sat down to think about a topic for her essay, she looked around her apartment for inspiration. First she thought about describing her own bedroom. But she had moved into the apartment only recently and hadn't done much in the way of decorating, so the room struck her as too bare and sterile. Then she looked out her window, thinking of describing the view. That seemed much more promising: she noticed the sights and sounds of children playing on the sidewalks and a group of older men playing cards, as well as smells— neighbors' cooking and exhaust from passing traffic. She was jotting down some details for such an essay when she glanced up at the framed portrait of her great-grandmother on her desk. "I stopped and stared at it, as I often do, wondering again about this twenty-year-old girl who became my great-grandmother," she said. "While I sat there studying it, I realized that the best topic of all was right under my nose."

As she looked at the photograph, Cindy began to freewrite. This is what she wrote:

> Great-Grandma is twenty in the picture. She's wearing a beautiful skirt and blouse and jewelry she borrowed from Dorothy. Looks a lot like me— nose, eyes, mouth. She's shorter than I am but you really can't tell in picture. Looks a lot like old photos I've seen of Grandma too—all the Diaz women resemble each other. Earrings and bracelet are of silver and they match. Ring might be amber or topaz? We've laughed about the "other man" who gave it to her. Her brown hair is down loose on her shoulders. She's smiling a little. That doesn't really look like her—her usual smile is bigger and opens her mouth. Looking at the photo makes me a little sad even though I really like it. Makes me realize how much older she's getting and I wonder how long she'll be with us. It's funny to see a picture of your great-grandmother at a younger age than you are now—stirs up all kinds of weird feelings. Picture was taken at a studio in Houston to give to Great-Grandpa. Signed "Sincerely, Beatrice." So serious! Hard to imagine them being so formal with each other.

Cindy looked over her notes and thought about how she might organize her essay. First she thought only of describing how the photograph *looked*. With that in mind, she thought her main points might be (1) what her great-grandmother's face looked like and (2) what her great-grandmother was wearing. But she was stuck for a third main point.

Studying her notes again, Cindy noticed two other possible main points. One was her own emotional reaction to the photo—how it made her feel. The other was the story of the photo—how and why it was taken. Not sure which of those two she would use as her third main point, she began to write. Her first draft follows.

First Draft

Family Portrait

I have a photograph of my great-grandmother that was taken seventy-five years ago, when she was only twenty. She sent it to me only recently, and I find it very interesting.

In the photo, I see a girl who looks a good deal like I do now at twenty-two. Like most of the women in her family, including me, the girl in the picture has the Diaz family nose, waving brown hair, and large brown eyes. Her mouth is closed and she is smiling slightly. That isn't my great-grandmother's usual big grin that shows her teeth and her "smile lines."

In the photo, Great-Grandmother is wearing a very pretty skirt and blouse. They look like something that would be fashionable today. The blouse is made of heavy satin. The satin falls in lines and hollows that reflect the light. It has a turned-down cowl collar and smocking on the shoulders and under the collar. Her skirt is below her knees and looks like it is made of light wool. She is wearing jewelry. Her silver earrings and bracelet match. She had borrowed them from her sister. Dorothy eventually gave them both to her, but the bracelet has disappeared. On her left hand is a ring with a big yellow stone.

When I look at this photo, I feel conflicting emotions. It gives me pleasure to see my great-grandmother as a pretty young woman. It makes me sad, too, to think how quickly time passes and realize how old she is getting. It amuses me to read the inscription to my great-grandfather, her boyfriend at the time. She wrote, "Sincerely, Beatrice." It's hard for me to imagine them ever being so formal with each other.

My great-grandmother had the photograph taken at a studio near where she worked in Houston. She spent nearly two weeks' salary on the outfit she wore for it. She must have really wanted to impress my great-grandfather to go to all that trouble and expense.

Development through Revising

Cindy showed this first draft to her classmate Elena, who read it and returned it with these notes jotted in the margin:

Reader's Comments

Was this the first time you'd seen it? Where's it been? And "very interesting" doesn't really say anything. Be more specific about why it interests you.

The "Diaz family nose" isn't helpful for someone who doesn't know the Diaz family—describe it!

Nice beginning, but I still can't quite picture her. Can you add more specific detail? Does anything about her face really stand out?

Color?

This is nice—I can picture the material.

What is smocking?

How—what are they like?

Family Portrait

I have a photograph of my great-grandmother that was taken seventy-five years ago, when she was only twenty. She sent it to me only recently, and I find it very interesting.

In the photo, I see a girl who looks a good deal like I do now at twenty-two. Like most of the women in her family, including me, the girl in the picture has the Diaz family nose, waving brown hair, and large brown eyes. Her mouth is closed and she is smiling slightly. That isn't my great-grandmother's usual big grin that shows her teeth and her "smile lines."

In the photo, Great-Grandmother is wearing a very pretty skirt and blouse. They took like something that would be fashionable today. The blouse is made of heavy satin. The satin falls in lines and hollows that reflect the light. It has a turned-down cowl collar and smocking on the shoulders and under the collar. Her skirt is below her knees and looks like it is made of light wool. She is wearing jewelry. Her silver earrings and bracelet match. She had borrowed them from her sister. Dorothy eventually gave them both to her, but the bracelet has disappeared. On her left hand is a ring with a big yellow stone.

continued

It'd make more sense for the main points of the essay to be about your great-grandma and the photo. How about making this—your reaction— the conclusion of the essay?

This is interesting stuff—she really did go to a lot of trouble to have the photo taken. I think the story of the photograph deserves to be a main point.

When I look at this photo, I feel conflicting emotions. It gives me pleasure to see my great-grandmother as a pretty young woman. It makes me sad, too, to think how quickly time passes and realize how old she is now. It amuses me to read the inscription to my great-grandfather, her boyfriend at the time. She wrote, "Sincerely, Beatrice." It's hard for me to imagine them ever being so formal with each other.

My great-grandmother had the photograph taken at a studio near where she worked in Houston. She spent nearly two weeks' salary on the outfit she wore for it. She must have really wanted to impress my great-grandfather to go to all that trouble and expense.

Making use of Elena's comments and her own reactions upon rereading her essay, Cindy wrote the final draft that appears on pages 183–184.

A Professional Essay to Consider

Read the following professional essay. Then answer the questions and read the comments that follow.

Lou's Place

by Beth Johnson

Imagine a restaurant where your every whim is catered to, your every want   1
satisfied, your every request granted without hesitation. The people on the staff
live to please you. They hover anxiously as you sample your selection, waiting for your judgment. Your pleasure is their delight, your dissatisfaction their
dismay.

Lou's isn't that kind of place.   2

At Lou's Kosy Korner Koffee Shop, the mock abuse flows like a cup of spilled 3
Folgers. Customers are yelled at, lectured, blamed, mocked, teased, and ignored.
They pay for the privilege of pouring their own coffee and scrambling their own
eggs. As in a fond but dysfunctional family, Lou displays his affection through
criticism and insults, and his customers respond in kind. If Lou's had a slogan, it
might be, "If I'm polite to you, ask yourself what's wrong."

Lou's is one of three breakfast joints located in the business district of a small 4
mid-Atlantic town. The county courthouse is nearby, supplying a steady stream of
lawyers, jurors, and office workers looking for a bite to eat. A local trucking firm
also provides Lou with customers as its drivers come and go in town. Lou's is on
the corner. Beside it is a jewelry shop ("In Business Since 1946—Watch Repairs
Our Speciality") and an upscale home accessories store that features bonsai trees
and hand-painted birdhouses in its window. There's a bus stop in front of Lou's.
Lou himself has been known to storm out onto the sidewalk to shoo away people
who've dismounted from the bus and lingered too long on the corner.

The sign on Lou's front door says "Open 7 A.M.–3 P.M." But by 6:40 on a 5
brisk spring morning, the restaurant's lights are on, the door is unlocked, and Lou
is settled in the booth nearest the door, with the *Philadelphia Inquirer* spread over
the table. Lou is sunk deep into the booth's brown vinyl seat, its rips neatly mended
with silver duct tape. He is studying the box scores from the night before as a
would-be customer pauses on the sidewalk, unsure whether to believe the sign or
her own eyes. She opens the door enough to stick her head in.

"Are you open?" she asks.   6

Without lifting his eyes from the paper, Lou answers. "I'm here, aren't I?"   7

Unsure how to interpret this remark, the woman enters and sits at a booth. Lou 8
keeps studying the paper. He begins to hum under his breath. The woman starts
tracing a pattern on the glass-topped table with her fingernail. She pulls out her
checkbook and pretends to balance it. After a few long minutes, Lou apparently
reaches a stopping point in his reading. He rises, his eyes still on the folded newspaper he carries with him. His humming breaks into low-volume song as he trudges
behind the counter. "Maaaaaaaake someone happy . . . Make-make-maaaaaake
someone happy," he croons as he lifts the steaming pot that has infused the room
with the rich aroma of freshly brewed coffee. He carries it to the woman's table,
fills her cup, and drops two single-serving containers of half-and-half nearby. He
then peers over the tops of his reading glasses at his customer. "You want anything
else, dear?" he asks, his bushy gray eyebrows rising with the question.

She shakes her head. "I'm meeting someone. I'll order when he gets here."   9

Lou nods absently, his eyes back on his paper. As he shuffles back to his seat, 10
he mutters over his shoulder, "Hope he shows up before three. I close then."

Lou reads his paper; the woman drinks her coffee and gazes around the room. 11
It's a small restaurant: just an eight-seat counter and seven padded booths. A grill,
coffeepots, and a huge stainless-steel refrigerator line the wall behind the counter.

Under the glass top of the tables is the breakfast menu: it offers eggs, pancakes, home fries, bacon, and sausage. A wall rack holds Kellogg's Jumbo Packs of single-serving cereals: smiling toucans and cheerful tigers offer Froot Loops and Frosted Flakes.

Two poster-size photographs hang side by side at the far wall. One is of Lou and 12 his wife on their wedding day. They appear to be in their midtwenties. He is slim, dark-haired, beaming; his arm circles the shoulders of his fair-haired bride. The other photo shows the same couple in an identical pose—only in this one, Lou looks much as he is today. His short white hair is parted at the side; a cropped white beard empha-sizes his prominent red mouth. His formerly slim figure now expands to take up much of the photograph. But the smile is the same as he embraces his silver-haired wife.

The bell at the door tinkles; two sleepy-eyed men in flannel shirts, work boots, 13 and oil-company caps walk in. Lou glances up and grunts at them; they nod. One picks up an *Inquirer* from the display stand and leaves two quarters on the cash register. They drop onto seats at the counter, simultaneously swivel to look at the woman in the booth behind them, and then turn back. For a few minutes, they flip through the sports section. Lou doesn't move. One man rises from his seat and wanders behind the counter to find cups and the coffeepot. He fills the cups, returns to his seat, and immerses himself in the paper. There is no noise but the occasional slurping of men sipping hot coffee.

Minutes pass. Finally one of the men speaks. "Lou," he says. "Can I maybe get 14 some breakfast?"

"I'm reading the paper," says Lou. "Eggs are in the refrigerator."   15

The man sighs and lumbers behind the counter again. "In some restaurants, 16 they actually cook for ya," he says, selecting eggs from the carton.

Lou doesn't raise his eyes. "In some restaurants, they wouldn't let a guy with 17 a face like yours in."

The room falls silent again, except for the splatter of grease on the grill and 18 the scrape of the spatula as the customer scrambles his eggs. He heaps them onto his plate, prepares some toast, and returns to his seat. The bell at the door begins tinkling as the breakfast rush begins—men, mostly, about half in work clothes and the rest in suits. They pour in on a wave of talk and laughter. Lou reluctantly rises and goes to work behind the counter, volleying comments with the regulars:

"Three eggs, Lou," says one.   19

"Three eggs. One heart attack wasn't enough for you? You want some bacon 20 grease on top of that?"

A large red-haired man in blue jeans and a faded denim shirt walks in with 21 a newspaper, which he reads as he waits for his cup of takeout coffee. "Anything good in the paper, Dan?" Lou asks.

"Not a thing," drawls Dan. "Not a *damn* thing. The only good thing is that the 22 machine down the street got my fifty cents instead of you."

Lou flips pancakes as the restaurant fills to capacity. The hum of voices fills 23 the room as the aromas of coffee, bacon, eggs, and toasting bread mingle in the air. A group of suits* from the nearby courthouse slide into the final empty booth. After a moment one rises, goes behind the counter, and rummages in a drawer.

"Whatcha need, Ben?" Lou asks, pouring more batter. 24

"Rag," Ben answers. He finds one, returns to the booth, and wipes crumbs off 25 the tabletop. A minute later he is back to drop a slice of ham on the hot grill. He and Lou stand side by side attending to their cooking, as comfortable in their silence as an old married couple. When the ham is sizzling and its rich fragrance reaches the far corners of the room, Ben slides it onto a plate and returns to his booth.

Filled plate in hand, Lou approaches a woman sitting at the counter. Her golden 26 hair contrasts with her sunken cheeks and her wrinkled lips sucking an unfiltered Camel. "You wanna I put this food in your ashtray, or are you gonna move it?" Lou growls. The woman moves the ashtray aside.

"Sorry, Lou," she says. 27

"I'm not really yelling at you, dear," he answers. 28

"I know," says the woman. "I'm glad *you're* here this morning." She lowers her 29 voice. "That girl you've got working here sometimes, Lou—she doesn't *like* me." Lou rolls his eyes, apparently at the poor taste of the waitress, and moves down to the cash register. As he rings up a bill, a teenage girl enters and walks by silently. Lou glares after her. "Start the day with a 'Good morning,' please," he instructs.

"Good morning, Lou," she replies obediently. 30

"*Very* nice," he mutters, still punching the cash-register buttons. "Thank you *so* 31 much for your concern. I get up at the crack of dawn to make your breakfast, but don't bother saying 'good morning' to *me*."

The day's earliest arrival, the woman in the booth, has been joined by a com- 32 panion. They order eggs and hash browns. As Lou slides the filled plates before them, he reverts briefly to the conventional manners he saves for first-timers. "Enjoy your meal," he says.

"Thank you," says the woman. "May I have some hot sauce?" 33

Lou's reserve of politeness is instantly exhausted. "Hot sauce. Jeez. She wants *hot* 34 *sauce*!" he announces to the room at large. "Anything else? Some caviar on the side, maybe?" He disappears behind the counter, reemerging with an enormous red bottle. "Here you are. It's a new bottle. Don't use it all, please. I'd like to save a little for other customers. Hey, on second thought, use it all if you want. Then I'll know you'll like my chili." Laughing loudly at his own joke, he refills the woman's coffee cup without being asked. Golden-brown coffee splashes into her saucer. Lou ignores it.

Lou's waitress, Stacy, has arrived, and begins taking orders and delivering 35 meals. Lou alternates between working the grill and clearing tables. Mid-stride, he halts before the golden-haired woman at the counter, who has pushed her plate aside and is lighting another cigarette. "What? What is this?" he demands.

"Looouuu …" she begins soothingly, a stream of smoke jetting from her mouth 36 with the word.

---

suits: business executives or professionals (people wearing business suits).

"Don't 'Lou' me," he retorts. "You don't eat your toast, you don't eat your 37 potatoes, you barely touch your eggs. Whatcha gonna live on? Camels?"

"Awww, Lou," she says, but she pulls her plate back and eats a few more bites. 38

As the rush of customers slows to a trickle, Lou returns to the register, mak- 39 ing change and conversation, talking Phillies and the weather. One of the flannel-shirted men rises from his counter seat and heads for the door, dropping his money on the counter. " 'Bye, Stacy," he says to the waitress. "Have a nice day."

"'Bye, Mel," she replies. "You too."   40

"What about me?" Lou calls after Mel.   41

Mel doesn't pause. "Who cares what kind of a day *you* have?"   42

Mel disappears into the morning sunshine; the Camel lady pulls a crossword 43 puzzle out of her purse and taps an unlit cigarette rapidly against the counter. Stacy wipes the tables and empties a wastebasket of its load of dark, wet coffee grounds. Lou butters a piece of toast and returns to his favorite booth. He spreads out his newspaper again, then glances up to catch the eye of the hot-sauce woman. "Where's your friend?" he asks.

"He left," she replies.   44

"He left you, eh?" Lou asks.   45

"No, he didn't *leave* me. He just had to go to work …"   46

"Dump him," Lou responds automatically. "And now, if you don't mind *very* 47 much, I would like to finish my newspaper."

QUESTIONS 2

ABOUT UNITY

1. What is the thesis of Johnson's essay? If it is stated directly, locate the relevant sentence or sentences. If it is implied, state the thesis in your own words.

   _____

2. Which statement would best serve as a topic sentence for paragraph 13?

   a. Many of Lou's customers are, like him, interested in the Philadelphia sports teams.

   b. Lou doesn't mind if customers serve themselves coffee.

   c. Lou apparently disliked the two men in oil-company caps who came into the restaurant.

   d. Regular customers at Lou's are used to taking care of themselves while Lou reads his paper.

ABOUT SUPPORT

3. In paragraph 3, Johnson claims that Lou and his customers are fond of one another. How does she support that claim in the case of the golden-haired woman who is first mentioned in paragraph 26?

   _____

   _____

4. We are told that customers enjoy the unusual atmosphere of Lou's coffee shop. What detail in paragraph 25 supports this idea?

_____

_____

5. Find a paragraph that appeals to three senses and identify those senses.

_____

ABOUT COHERENCE

6. Which sentence in paragraph 31 contains a change-of-direction signal?

_____

_____

7. Which sentence in paragraph 23 begins with a time signal? (*Write the opening words of that sentence.*)

_____

8. The sentence that makes up paragraph 38 includes which of the following types of transition?
   a. time
   b. addition
   c. change of direction
   d. conclusion

ABOUT THE INTRODUCTION AND CONCLUSION

9. Johnson begins with a situation that is the opposite of the one that will be developed. Rewrite paragraph 1 using another method for introducing essays explained in Chapter 4: a broad statement that gets narrowed or a brief story.

_____

_____

10. "Lou's Place" ends with a comment by Lou that characterizes the mood of his shop. Rewrite this conclusion by using another method for concluding essays as explained in Chapter 4, summarizing the description of the shop or predicting something about the future of the shop or its owner.

_____

_____

Writing an Essay with Emphasis on Description

WRITING ASSIGNMENT 1

Write an essay that describes your strengths and weaknesses as a student. You will want to use specific details that support your purpose. You may also want to look ahead to Chapter 13, "Comparison or Contrast" and Chapter 16, "Argument."

PREWRITING

a. Like all essays, this essay must have a thesis. It should state your dominant impression of yourself as a college student. Write a short sentence that summarizes what kind of student you think you are. Don't worry if your thesis doesn't feel just right—you can always revise later. For now, just express your opinion. Here are a couple of examples:

I am a model college student.

Although I am in college, I haven't yet acquired good study habits.

b. Once you have written your sentence, make a list of as many details as you can to support that general impression. For example, this could be a list made by a student who thought she was a great college student:

always study assigned homework

schedule study time every day

participate in class

attend class every day

meet with professors regularly

seek tutoring when necessary

participate in several clubs

c. After creating a list, organize your paper to effectively support your purpose. If you choose emphatic order, start with your least important example and end with your most important example. This will help create a more persuasive tone to your essay.

d. Use as many specific details as possible to create a full picture for your reader. For example, instead of saying, "I study at the same time every day," you might say, "Each night, I study from 7:00 P.M. until 11:00 P.M. because it is the most quiet time in my house."

e. Proceed to write the first draft of your essay.

REVISING

After you have completed the first draft of the paper, set it aside for a while—if possible, until the next day. When you review the draft, try to do so as critically as you would if it were not your own work. Ask yourself these questions:

Description Checklist: THE FOUR BASES

ABOUT *UNITY*

✔ Does my essay have a clearly stated thesis, including a dominant impression?

✔ Is there any irrelevant material that should be eliminated or rewritten?

ABOUT *SUPPORT*

✔ Have I provided rich, specific details that appeal to a variety of senses (sight, hearing, smell, taste, touch)?

ABOUT *COHERENCE*

✔ Have I organized my essay in a consistent manner that is appropriate to my subject?

✔ Have I used transition words to help readers follow my train of thought?

✔ Do I have a concluding paragraph that provides a summary, a final thought, or both?

ABOUT *SENTENCE SKILLS*

✔ Have I used a consistent point of view throughout my essay?

✔ Have I used specific rather than general words?

✔ Have I avoided wordiness and used concise wording?

✔ Are my sentences varied?

✔ Have I proofread my essay for spelling and other sentence skills, as listed on the inside back cover of the book?

As you revise your essay through one or more additional drafts, continue to refer to this checklist until you can answer "yes" to each question.

WRITING ASSIGNMENT 2

Write an essay that describes and summarizes the key ideas in a chosen book or essay. The work you choose may be assigned by your instructor, or it may require your instructor's approval. You may want to check Chapter 22, "Writing a Research Paper" for proper citation of the material you reference from your work.

PREWRITING

a. Find a quote that expresses the main principle of the author's thesis.

b. Answer the following questions:
    a. What does the author want you to understand?
    b. What is the author's main purpose?
    c. What ideas does the author use to support his/her purpose?

c. Decide how you will organize your essay. Your decision will depend on what seems appropriate for the chosen work. You may want to describe the main ideas in the same order as they are originally presented, or you may choose to describe the ideas in emphatic order, saving the most important idea for last.

d. Make a scratch outline for your essay, based on the organization you have chosen.

e. Using your scratch outline as a guide, make a list of details that support each of your main points.

f. Use your scratch outline and list of details to write your first draft.

REVISING

> **HINT** Refer to the FOUR BASES Checklist provided on page 199 with Writing Assignment 1.

Writing for a Specific Purpose and Audience

WRITING ASSIGNMENT 3

Imagine that you are working for a travel agency and have been asked to write a letter to prospective clients advertising a wonderful vacation destination you have already visited yourself. It might be a large city, a seaside town, an archeological site, a theme park that caters to families, a resort for honeymooners, a dude ranch, a lake, or a mountain hideaway. Then again, you might want to advertise a cruise or even a vacation that involves public service, like the kinds sponsored by Habitat for Humanity. Your purpose is, of course, to get your clients to sign up for the vacation you are advertising.

Focus on a particular type of audience: college students, young professionals, families, singles, or senior citizens, for example. You may want to check Chapter 10, "Exemplification" and Chapter 16, "Argument" to create a persuasive tone that will sell your destination.

PREWRITING

a. First, gather details about the physical appearance, sounds, smells, and even tastes of the setting your clients will visit. Talk about how it feels to swim in a crystal-clear lagoon or describe the taste of a crab sandwich you bought at a straw-covered beach shack. Describe the natural setting, as well the kind of weather your clients can expect.

   Discuss what the living and dining accommodations are like as well. By the way, if you are advertising a public-service vacation, you might have to tell them about the tents they'll be sleeping in or the outdoor toilets they'll use. In any case, use as many senses as possible.

b. Keeping the type of audience you have chosen in mind, tell your readers about the kinds of people they are likely to meet, both the tourists and permanent residents. Ask yourself questions such as:

   Are the tourists mostly single, young married couples, families?

   Are most of the people young, middle-aged, older? Or is there a mix of ages?

   Are these people friendly, helpful, interesting?

   Where do they come from?

   What do they talk about?

   Are they fun-loving and active or more private and sedate?

   What about the people who work or live at the place? Are they friendly, helpful, etc.?

c. Finally, provide details about the activities your clients might pursue during the vacation. Does the place offer hang gliding, scuba diving, tours of famous landmarks? Again, if this is a public-service vacation, will your readers be digging wells, framing houses, or constructing schoolhouses?

d. After reading the notes you have gathered, write a rough outline that might look like this:

A. The place
   1. Location
   2. Accommodations
   3. Food

B. The people
   1. Other tourists
   2. Staff
   3. Locals

C. Activities
   1. Water sports
   2. Guided tours
   3. Tennis/golf

e. Now, plan your introductory and concluding sections. In your introduction, state a thesis that is intended to persuade your readers. In addition, prepare them for the points you are going to cover and the order in which you will cover them. For example, you might write:

The setting and accommodations, the people, and the activities make a week at Crystal Bay Resort the ideal family beach vacation.

Your conclusion might summarize or remind your readers of the best reasons to book the vacation. Naturally, you will have to mention the cost of accommodations and travel as well.

DRAFTING

Write your rough draft by following your outline closely, but don't be a slave to it. If new ideas or details pop into your mind, put them down. You can fix any inconsistencies or repetitions when it comes time to revise. Just be as detailed as you can at this point.

REVISING

Read your first draft to a classmate who is willing to listen carefully and work hard at providing valuable feedback. Turn back to the FOUR BASES Checklist on page 199 for questions to consider while revising.

Narration

This chapter will explain and illustrate how to

- develop an essay with emphasis on narration

- write an essay with emphasis on narration

- revise an essay with emphasis on narration

In addition, you will read and consider

- two student essays that emphasize narration

- one professional essay that emphasizes narration

Imagine that you are the owner of your own very successful company, which you have built from the ground up. You have been asked to share your experience with a group of young entrepreneurs who have hopes of owning their own businesses someday. Write a narrative of your success story, including the type of business you own, how you came up with the idea, and how you managed to make it a success.

Children beg to hear a beloved story read again and again. Over dinner, tired adults tell each other about their day. A restless class is hushed when a teacher says, "Let me tell you something strange that happened to me once." Whatever our age, we never outgrow our hunger for stories. Just as our ancestors entertained and instructed each other with tales of great hunts and battles, of angry gods and foolish humans, we still love to share our lives and learn about others through storytelling.

Narration is storytelling, whether we are relating a single story or several related ones. Through narration, we make a statement clear by relating in detail something that has happened to us. In the story we tell, we present the details in the order in which they happened. A person might say, for example, "I was really embarrassed the day I took my driver's test," and then go on to develop that statement with an account of the experience. If the story is sharply detailed, we will be able to see and understand just why the speaker felt that way.

In this chapter, you'll be asked to tell a story that illustrates a specific point. To prepare for this assignment, first read the student essays and the professional essay that follow and work through the questions that accompany each piece of writing. All three essays emphasize narration to develop their points.

Student Essays to Consider

Taking on a Disability

My church recently staged a "Sensitivity Sunday" to make our congregation   1
more aware of the problems faced by people with physical disabilities. We
were asked to "take on a disability" for several hours one Sunday morning.
Some members, like me, chose to use wheelchairs. Others wore sound-blocking
earplugs, hobbled around on crutches, or wore blindfolds.

Just sitting in the wheelchair was instructive. I had never considered   2
before how awkward it would be to use one. As soon as I sat down, my
weight made the chair begin to roll. Its wheels were not locked, and I
fumbled clumsily to correct that. Another awkward moment occurred when I
realized I had no place to put my feet. I fumbled some more to turn the metal
footrest into place. I felt psychologically awkward as well, as I took my first
uneasy look at what was to be my only means of transportation for several
hours. I realized that for many people, using a wheelchair is not a temporary
experiment. That was a sobering thought as I sank back into my seat.

Once I sat down, I had to learn how to cope with the wheelchair. I   3
shifted around, trying to find a comfortable position. I thought it might be
restful, even kind of nice, to be pushed around for a while. I glanced around
to see who would be pushing me and then realized I would have to navigate
the contraption by myself! My palms reddened and my wrist and forearm
muscles started to ache as I tugged at the heavy metal wheels. I realized,

continued

as I veered this way and that, that steering and turning were not going to be easy tasks. Trying to make a right-angle turn from one aisle to another, I steered straight into a pew. I felt as though everyone was staring at me and commenting on my clumsiness.

When the service started, other problems cropped up to frustrate me further. Every time the congregation stood up, my view was blocked. I could not see the minister, the choir, or the altar. Also, as the church's aisles were narrow, I seemed to be in the way no matter where I parked myself. For instance, the ushers had to squeeze by me to pass the collection plate. This made me feel like a nuisance. Thanks to a new building program, however, our church will soon have the wide aisles and well-spaced pews that will make life easier for the disabled. After the service ended, when people stopped to talk to me, I had to strain my neck and look up at them. This made me feel like a little child being talked down to and added to my sense of powerlessness. **4**

My wheelchair experiment was soon over. It's true that it made an impression on me. I no longer resent large tax expenditures for ramp-equipped buses, and I wouldn't dream of parking my car in a space marked "Handicapped Only." But I also realize how little I know about the daily life of a truly disabled person. A few hours of voluntary "disability" gave me only a hint of the challenges, both physical and emotional, that people with handicaps must overcome. **5**

A Night of Violence

According to my history instructor, Adolf Hitler once said that he wanted to sign up "brutal youths" to help him achieve his goals. If Hitler were still alive, he wouldn't have any trouble recruiting the brutal youths he wanted; he could get them right here in the United States. I know, because I was one of them. As a teenager, I ran with a gang. And it took a frightening incident for me to see how violent I had become. **1**

The incident was planned one Thursday night when I was out with my friends. I was still going to school once in a while, but most of my friends weren't. We spent our days on the streets, talking, showing off, sometimes shoplifting a little or shaking people down for a few dollars. My friends and I were close, maybe because life hadn't been very good to any of us. On this night, we were drinking wine and vodka on the corner. For some reason, we all felt tense and restless. One of us came up with the idea of robbing one of the old people who lived in the high-rise close by. We would just knock him or her over, grab the money, and party with it. **2**

continued

The robbery did not go as planned. After about an hour, and after more   3
wine and vodka, we spotted an old man. He came out of the glass door of
the building and started up the street. Pine Street had a lot of antique stores
as well as apartment buildings. Stuffing our bottles in our jacket pockets,
we closed in behind him. Suddenly, the old man whipped out a homemade
wooden club from under his jacket and began swinging. The club thudded
loudly against Victor's shoulder, making him yelp with pain. When we heard
that, we went crazy. We smashed our bottles over the old man's head. Not
content with that, Victor kicked him savagely, knocking him to the ground. As
we ran, I kept seeing him sprawled on the ground, blood from our beating
trickling into his eyes. Victor, the biggest of us, had said, "We want your
money, old man. Hand it over."

Later, at home, I had a strong reaction to the incident. My head would   4
not stop pounding, and I threw up. I wasn't afraid of getting caught; in fact,
we never did get caught. I just knew I had gone over some kind of line. I
didn't know if I could step back, now that I had gone so far. But I knew I
had to. I had seen plenty of people in my neighborhood turn into the kind of
people who hated their lives, people who didn't care about anything, people
who wound up penned in jail or ruled by drugs. I didn't want to become one
of them.

That night, I realize now, I decided not to become one of Hitler's   5
"brutal youths." I'm proud of myself for that, even though life didn't get
any easier and no one came along to pin a medal on me. I just decided,
quietly, to step off the path I was on. I hope my parents and I will get along
better now, too. Maybe the old man's pain, in some terrible way, had a
purpose.

QUESTIONS 1

ABOUT UNITY

1. Which essay lacks an opening thesis statement? *Write a thesis statement that might work for that essay.*

_____

_____

2. Which sentence in paragraph 4 of "Taking on a Disability" should be omitted in the interest of paragraph unity? (*Write the opening words.*)

_____

_____

3. What sentence in paragraph 3 of "A Night of Violence" should be omitted in the interest of paragraph unity? (*Write the opening words.*)

_____

4. Reread the conclusions to both essays. Which one contains a sentence introducing a new topic and should be eliminated? (*Write the opening words of that sentence.*)

_____

_____

ABOUT SUPPORT

5. a. Find a sentence in "Taking on a Disability" that contains words appealing to both sight and touch. (*Write the opening words.*)

_____

   b. Find a sentence in "A Night of Violence" that contains words appealing to hearing. (*Write the opening words.*)

_____

6. In a narrative, the main method of organization is time order. Which sentence in paragraph 3 of "A Night of Violence" is placed out of order? (*Write the opening words.*)

_____

7. Reread paragraph 4 of "Taking on a Disability." Then, record three details that support that paragraph's topic sentence.

_____

_____

_____

ABOUT COHERENCE

8. The first stage of the writer's experience in "Taking on a Disability" might be called *sitting down in the wheelchair*. What are the other two stages of the experience?

_____

_____

9. List four transitions in paragraph 3 of "A Night of Violence." What type of transitions are they?

_____   _____   _____   _____

_____

ABOUT THE INTRODUCTION AND CONCLUSION

10. What method of writing introductions explained in Chapter 4 is used in the first paragraph of "A Night of Violence"?

_____

Developing an Essay with Emphasis on Narration

Considering Purpose and Audience

The main purpose of an essay that emphasizes narration is to make a point by incorporating one central story or several brief stories as support. Colorful details and interesting events that build up to a point of some kind make narrative essays enjoyable for readers and writers alike.

At one time or another, you have probably listened to someone tell a rambling story that didn't seem to go anywhere. You might have impatiently wondered, "Where is this story going?" or "Is there a point here?" Keep such questions in mind as you think about your own essay. To satisfy your audience, your story must have some overall purpose and point.

Also keep in mind that your essay should deal with an event or a topic that will appeal to your audience. A group of young children, for example, would probably be bored by an essay about your first job interview. They might, however, be very interested if you wrote about a time you were chased by a pack of mean dogs or when you stood up to a bully in your school. In general, essays that emphasize narration involve human conflict—internal or external—and are entertaining to readers of all ages.

Using Dialogue

In Chapter 8, you learned that including people in an essay about a place is important to communicating something about its character or atmosphere. Of course, people are essential to narration as are what they do and what they say. You can convey much about a person through the dialogue he or she has with others or even through the interior conversations he or she has while thinking silently. But dialogue can also be used to move the plot or action of the story along, to tell what happened before the story began, and to reveal other important facts that will make the story clearer, more suspenseful, or more meaningful.

For example, in "A Night of Violence" Victor's brutal tendencies become clear when he says, "We want your money, old man. Hand it over." You will see a great deal more dialogue in Pete Hamill's essay "The Yellow Ribbon" (pages 214–215). Here, dialogue reveals much about the plot: that Vingo had been sentenced to four years in prison, that he had given his wife the option to "forget" him, and that he asked her to tie a yellow handkerchief on a large oak near their home if she intended to welcome him home. It also reveals a lot about Vingo's character. Fair minded and reasonable, he admits that he deserved to have been in prison: "I did it and I went to jail. If you can't do the time, don't do the crime."

Some Rules for Using Dialogue

Use dialogue especially in the narrative essays you write, but remember to observe a few simple rules:

1. Place quotation marks around the words, and start a new paragraph when a new character begins speaking. For this reason, it is easy to tell that there are two different speakers in the following exchange between Vingo and a young girl he has met on the bus. The girl asks:

   "Are you married?"
   "I don't know."
   "You don't know?" she said.
   "Well, when I was in the can I wrote to my wife," he said. "I told her, I said, Martha, I understand if you can't stay married to me. I told her that I was gonna be away for a long time, and if she couldn't stand it, if the kids kept askin' questions, if it hurt her too much, well, she could just forget about me. Get a new guy—she's a wonderful woman, really something—and forget about me. I told her she didn't have to write me or nothing. And she didn't. Not for three and a half years."
   "And you're going home now, not knowing?"
   "Yeah," he said shyly.

2. Record people's words exactly as they speak them, complete with slang and errors in grammar and pronunciation. Notice that, in the dialogue quoted above, Vingo says "gonna" rather than "going to" and "askin'" rather than "asking." He also uses a double negative when he says "I told her she didn't have to write me or nothing." This is not the kind of writing expected in a college essay, but it is completely appropriate when you are recording dialogue. Remember that you are trying to capture the words—the very sounds—that the character uttered just as he or she said them.

3. Make sure your reader knows who is speaking at any given time. In "The Yellow Ribbon" passage quoted above, Hamill uses tag lines like "she

said" to explain that the girl is the speaker. Later, when we read "he said shyly," we know it's Vingo who is talking. One way to make sure that readers can identify the speaker is to use tag lines like "she said," "Johann replied," or "the man shouted."

4. Set off tag lines from quotations with commas, as in *"Yeah," he said shyly*. However, if a tag line is used in the middle of a quotation that is composed of two distinct sentences, place a comma before and a period after it, as in paragraph 6 of "The Yellow Ribbon": *"I've never been there," she said. "I hear it's beautiful."*

As you can see from the previous example, commas and periods appear within quotation marks, but colons and semicolons appear outside of them. Finally, if the quotation is a question, end it with a question mark without the comma, as in *"You don't know?" she said*.

Development through Prewriting

Freewriting is a particularly helpful prewriting technique as you're planning your essay. As you think about the story you want to relate, many ideas will crowd into your mind. Simply writing them down in free-form style will jog loose details you may have forgotten and also help you determine what the central point of your story really is.

 For more about freewriting, see pages 23–25.

Lisa, the writer of "Taking on a Disability," spent a half hour freewriting before she wrote the first draft of her essay. Here is what she came up with:

Our church was planning a building renovation to make the church more accessible to people with disabilities. Some people thought it was a waste of money and that the disabled could get along all right in the church the way it was. Not many disabled people come to our church anyway. Pastor Henry gave a sermon about disabilities. He suggested that we spend one Sunday pretending to be disabled ourselves. We got to choose our disability. Some people pretended to be blind or deaf or in need of crutches. I chose to use a wheelchair. I thought it might be fun to have someone push me around. It was a lot scarier and more disturbing than I expected. We borrowed

continued

wheelchairs and crutches from the local nursing home. I didn't like sitting down in the wheelchair. I didn't know how to work it right. It rolled when I didn't want it to. I felt clumsy trying to make it move. I even ran into a pew. I felt silly pretending to be disabled and also sort of disrespectful because for most people sitting in a wheelchair isn't a choice. It also bothered me to think what it'd be like if I couldn't get up again. It turned out that nobody was going to push me around. I thought Paula would, but instead she put on a blindfold and pretended to be blind. She knocked over a cup of coffee before the morning was over. She told me later she felt really panicky when that happened. Sitting down so low in the wheelchair was weird. I couldn't see much of anything. People ignored me or talked to me like I was a little kid. I was glad when the morning was over. Making the wheels turn hurt my hands and arms.

As Lisa read over her freewriting passage, she decided that the central point of her story was her new realization of how challenging it would be to be truly disabled. To support that central point, she realized, she would need to concentrate on details that demonstrated the frustrations she felt. She created a scratch outline for the first draft of her essay:

Thesis statement: A church experiment led to my spending the morning in a wheelchair.

1. *Sitting in the wheelchair*
   a. *Awkward because it rolled*
   b. *Awkward because footrest was out of place*
   c. *Psychologically awkward*
2. *Moving the wheelchair*
   a. *I thought someone would push me.*
   b. *It was hard to make the chair move and it hurt my hands.*
   c. *It was difficult to steer.*

continued

> 3. *Ways the wheelchair affected me*
>
>   a. *I couldn't see.*
>
>   b. *I felt in the way.*
>
>   c. *I felt funny talking to people as they bent down over me.*

Development through Revising

Lisa based her first draft on her scratch outline. Here is the draft:

First Draft

Taking on a Disability

The pastor at our church suggested that we each "take on a disability" for a few hours on Sunday morning. Some members, like me, chose to use wheelchairs. Others wore earplugs, used crutches, or wore blindfolds.

It surprised me that I felt nervous about sitting down in my wheelchair. I'm not sure why I felt scared about it. I guess I realized that most people who use wheelchairs don't do it by choice—they have to.

When I sat down, I thought my friend Paula would push me around. We had talked about her doing that earlier. But she decided instead to "assume" her own disability and she pretended to be blind. I saw her with a blindfold on, trying to fix herself a cup of coffee and knocking it off the table as she stirred it. So I had to figure out how to make the chair move by myself. It wasn't so easy. Pushing the wheels made my hands and arms sore. I also kept bumping into things. I felt really awkward. I even had trouble locking the wheels and finding the footrest.

I couldn't see well as I sat down low in my chair. When the rest of the congregation stood up, I could forget about seeing entirely. People would nod or chuckle at something that had happened up at the front of the church and I could only guess what was going on. Instead of sitting in the pew with everyone else, I was parked out in the aisle, which was really too narrow for the chair. The new building program our church is planning will make that problem better by widening the aisles and making the pews farther apart. It's going to be expensive, but it's a worthwhile thing. Another thing I disliked was how I felt when people talked to me. They had to lean down as though I was a kid, and I had to stare up at them as though I was too. One person I talked to who seemed to understand what I was experiencing was Don Henderson, who mentioned that his brother-in-law uses a wheelchair.

Lisa read over her first draft. Then she showed it to her roommate. After hearing her roommate's comments, Lisa read the essay again. This time she made a list of comments about how she thought it could be improved:

* *The introduction should explain why the pastor wanted us to take on disabilities.*

* *The second paragraph is sort of weak. Instead of saying, "I'm not sure why I felt scared," I should try to put into specific words what was scary about the experience.*

* *The stuff about Paula doesn't really add to my main point. The story is about me, not Paula.*

* *Maybe I shouldn't talk so much about the new building program. It's related to people with disabilities, but it doesn't really support the idea that my morning in a wheelchair was frustrating.*

* *Eliminate the part about Don Henderson. It doesn't contribute to my feeling frustrated.*

* *The essay ends too abruptly. I need to wrap it up with some sort of conclusion.*

With that list of comments in hand, Lisa returned to her essay. She then wrote the version that appears on pages 204–205.

A Professional Essay to Consider

Read the following professional essay. Then answer the questions and read the comments that follow.

The Yellow Ribbon

by Pete Hamill

They were going to Fort Lauderdale, the girl remembered later. There were six 1
of them, three boys and three girls, and they picked up the bus at the old terminal
on 34th Street, carrying sandwiches and wine in paper bags, dreaming of golden
beaches and the tides of the sea as the gray cold spring of New York vanished behind them. Vingo was on board from the beginning.

As the bus passed through Jersey and into Philly, they began to notice that 2
Vingo never moved. He sat in front of the young people, his dusty face masking
his age, dressed in a plain brown ill-fitting suit. His fingers were stained from cigarettes and he chewed the inside of his lip a lot, frozen into some personal cocoon
of silence.

Somewhere outside of Washington, deep into the night, the bus pulled into a 3
Howard Johnson's, and everybody got off except Vingo. He sat rooted in his seat,
and the young people began to wonder about him, trying to imagine his life: Perhaps he was a sea captain, maybe he had run away from his wife, he could be an
old soldier going home. When they went back to the bus, the girl sat beside him
and introduced herself.

"We're going to Florida," the girl said brightly. "You going that far?"   4

"I don't know," Vingo said.   5

"I've never been there," she said. "I hear it's beautiful."   6

"It is," he said quietly, as if remembering something he had tried to forget.   7

"You live there?"   8

"I did some time there in the Navy. Jacksonville."   9

"Want some wine?" she said. He smiled and took the bottle of Chianti and took 10
a swig. He thanked her and retreated again into silence. After a while, she went
back to the others, as Vingo nodded into sleep.

In the morning they awoke outside another Howard Johnson's, and this time 11
Vingo went in. The girl insisted that he join them. He seemed very shy and ordered
black coffee and smoked nervously, as the young people chattered about sleeping
on the beaches. When they went back on the bus, the girl sat with Vingo again,
and after a while, slowly and painfully and with great hesitation, he began to tell
his story. He had been in jail in New York for the last four years, and now he was
going home.

"Four years!" the girl said. "What did you do?"   12

"It doesn't matter," he said with quiet bluntness. "I did it and I went to jail. If 13
you can't do the time, don't do the crime. That's what they say and they're right."

"Are you married?"   14

"I don't know."   15

"You don't know?" she said.   16

"Well, when I was in the can I wrote to my wife," he said. "I told her, I said, 17 Martha, I understand if you can't stay married to me. I told her that. I said I was gonna be away a long time, and that if she couldn't stand it, if the kids kept askin' questions, if it hurt her too much, well, she could just forget me. Get a new guy— she's a wonderful woman, really something—and forget about me. I told her she didn't have to write me or nothing. And she didn't. Not for three and a half years."

"And you're going home now, not knowing?"   18

"Yeah," he said shyly. "Well, last week, when I was sure the parole was com- 19 ing through I wrote her. I told her that if she had a new guy, I understood. But if she didn't, if she would take me back she should let me know. We used to live in this town, Brunswick, just before Jacksonville, and there's a great big oak tree just as you come into town, a very famous tree, huge. I told her if she would take me back, she should put a yellow handkerchief on the tree, and I would get off and come home. If she didn't want me, forget it, no handkerchief, and I'd keep going on through."

"Wow," the girl said. "Wow."   20

She told the others, and soon all of them were in it, caught up in the approach 21 of Brunswick, looking at the pictures Vingo showed them of his wife and three children, the woman handsome in a plain way, the children still unformed in a cracked, much-handled snapshot. Now they were twenty miles from Brunswick and the young people took over window seats on the right side, waiting for the approach of the great oak tree. Vingo stopped looking, tightening his face into the ex-con's mask, as if fortifying himself against still another disappointment. Then it was ten miles, and then five and the bus acquired a dark hushed mood, full of silence, of absence, of lost years, of the woman's plain face, of the sudden letter on the breakfast table, of the wonder of children, of the iron bars of solitude.

Then suddenly all of the young people were up out of their seats, screaming 22 and shouting and crying, doing small dances, shaking clenched fists in triumph and exaltation. All except Vingo.

Vingo sat there stunned, looking at the oak tree. It was covered with yellow 23 handkerchiefs, twenty of them, thirty of them, maybe hundreds, a tree that stood like a banner of welcome blowing and billowing in the wind, turned into a gorgeous yellow blur by the passing bus. As the young people shouted, the old con slowly rose from his seat, holding himself tightly, and made his way to the front of the bus to go home.

ABOUT UNITY

1. The thesis of Hamill's essay is implied rather than stated directly. See if you can state the thesis in your own words.

_____

_____

2. The main point in paragraph 2 is not stated; it is implied. Write a topic sentence for that paragraph.

_____

3. What is the topic sentence of paragraph 11? (*Write the opening words.*)

_____

ABOUT SUPPORT

4. "His fingers were stained from cigarettes and he chewed the inside of his lip a lot, frozen in some personal cocoon of silence." This line from paragraph 2 supports the idea that
   a. Vingo had been drinking.
   b. Vingo was nervous.
   c. Vingo was a hostile person.
   d. Vingo knew the young peope were watching him.

5. Hamill writes in paragraph 11 that Vingo seemed very shy. Find at least two pieces of evidence in the essay to support the idea that Vingo was shy.

_____

_____

_____

6. Hamill implies that despite his crime, Vingo was an honorable man. Find evidence that supports that point.

_____

_____

ABOUT COHERENCE

7. Because this is the story of a trip, it is appropriate that Hamill uses place names to signal the passing of time. But he also uses other types of transitions like those appearing on pages 87–90. List four place names and four other transitions used in this essay.

Place Names	**Other Transitions**
_____	_____
_____	_____
_____	_____
_____	_____

8. What sentence in paragraph 19 begins with a transition word that indicates contrast? (*Write the opening words*.)

_____

ABOUT THE INTRODUCTION AND CONCLUSION

9. Reread the introduction. How do you think Hamill learned about this story?

_____

10. The author does not use one of the methods for writing conclusions discussed on pages 98–100. How does he end this essay? What kind of welcome might we expect Vingo to receive when he walks into his home? Why didn't Hamill tell us about this?

_____

_____

_____

_____

Writing an Essay with Emphasis on Narration

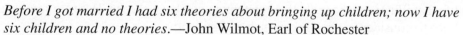

WRITING ASSIGNMENT 1

Think of an experience in your life that supports one of the statements below:

If you never have a dream, you'll never have a dream come true.
—popular saying

Before I got married I had six theories about bringing up children; now I have six children and no theories.—John Wilmot, Earl of Rochester

There are some things you learn best in calm, and some in storm.
—Willa Cather

Success is 99 percent perspiration and 1 percent inspiration.
—Thomas Edison

What a tangled web we weave / When first we practice to deceive.
—Walter Scott

There's a sucker born every minute.—P. T. Barnum

We lie loudest when we lie to ourselves.—Eric Hoffer

All marriages are happy. It's the living together afterward that causes all the trouble.—Raymond Hul

Hoping and praying are easier but do not produce as good results as hard work.—Andy Rooney

A little learning is a dangerous thing.—Alexander Pope

Nothing is as good as it seems beforehand.—George Eliot

Life shrinks or expands in proportion to one's courage.—Anaïs Nin

When I got to the end of my long journey in life / I realized I was the architect of my own destiny.—Amado Nervo

A fool and his money are soon parted.—popular saying

From what we get, we can make a living; what we give, however, makes a life.—Arthur Ashe

No matter how lovesick a woman is, she shouldn't take the first pill that comes along.—Dr. Joyce Brothers

Fear not those who argue but those who dodge.—Marie von Ebner-Eschenback

Trust in Allah, but tie your camel.—old Muslim proverb

Use one of the above statements or another noteworthy saying—perhaps one that has been a guidepost for your life—to write a thesis statement for an essay with emphasis on narration about that experience. As you develop and write the essay, refer to the suggestions in the following prewriting strategies and rewriting strategies. You may also want to review Chapter 8, "Description," to help create a strong narrative with strong support.

PREWRITING

The key to the success of your essay will be your choice of an incident from your life that illustrates the truth of the statement you have chosen. Here are some guidelines to consider as you choose such an incident:

- The incident should include a *conflict,* or a source of tension. That conflict does not need to be dramatic, such as a fistfight between two characters. Equally effective is a quieter conflict, such as a conflict between a person's conscience and desires, or a decision that must be made, or a difficult situation that has no clear resolution.

- The incident should be limited in time. It would be difficult to do justice in such a brief essay to an experience that continued over several weeks or months.

- The incident should evoke a definite emotional response in you so that it might draw a similar response from your reader.

- The incident must *fully support* the statement you have chosen, not merely be linked by some of the same ideas. Do not, for example, take the statement "We lie loudest when we lie to ourselves" and then write about an incident in which someone just told a lie. The essay should demonstrate the cost of being untruthful to oneself.

Here is how one student tested whether her plan for her narrative essay was a good one:

- What statement have I chosen as my thesis?
  The chains of habit are too weak to be felt until they are too strong to be broken.—Samuel Johnson

- Does the incident I have chosen include some kind of tension?

  Yes. I am going to write about the day I tried to purchase an expensive new shirt but was told that I had maxed out my credit card. When I tried a second card and then a third, I was told that they too had reached their balance limits. What an embarrassment. That day I realized something about myself—I get the urge to buy things whenever I am lonely, depressed, or just bored. I also learned that in order to battle that urge, I would have to change my values, my outlook on life. I would have to learn that happiness does not result simply from having nice things.

- Is the incident limited in time?

  Yes. I am going to write about events that happened in one day.

- Does the incident evoke an emotional response in me?

  Yes. I was embarrassed and ashamed of myself.

- Does the incident support the statement I have chosen?

  Yes. I was a "shopaholic," but I did not realize that I was caught in the "chains" of this habit until I was embarrassed into making major changes in my outlook on life.

REVISING

After you have put your essay away for a day, read it to a friend or classmate who will give you honest feedback. You and your reader should consider the questions in the checklist that follows:

Narration Checklist: THE FOUR BASES

ABOUT *UNITY*

✔ Have I included the essay's thesis (my chosen statement) in my introductory paragraph, or is it clearly implied?

✔ Does each paragraph, and each sentence within that paragraph, help either to keep the action moving or to reveal important things about the characters?

✔ Are there portions of the essay that do not support my thesis and therefore should be eliminated or rewritten?

ABOUT *SUPPORT*

✔ Do I have enough details, including dialogue?

✔ Have I included enough vivid, exact details that will help my readers experience the event as it actually happened?

ABOUT *COHERENCE*

✔ Do transitional words and phrases, and linking sentences between paragraphs, help make the sequence of events clear?

✔ Should I break up the essay by using bits of interesting dialogue instead of narration?

ABOUT *SENTENCE SKILLS*

✔ Have I used a consistent point of view throughout my essay?

✔ Have I used specific rather than general words?

✔ Have I avoided wordiness and used concise wording?

✔ Are my sentences varied?

✔ Have I checked for spelling and other sentence skills, as listed on the inside back cover of the book?

Continue revising your work until you and your reader can answer "yes" to each question.

WRITING ASSIGNMENT 2

Write an essay in which you research a historical figure and come to a conclusion about that figure. The person you choose may be assigned by your instructor, or may be of your own choosing and require your instructor's approval. Options could include Malcolm X, Eva Peron, President Andrew Johnson, or Queen Victoria. You may want to check Chapter 16, "Argument" and Chapter 22, "Writing a Research Paper."

PREWRITING

a. After choosing your topic, you will want to research as much information as possible. Not only should you develop a biographical understanding of your subject, but you will also want to learn about some of the more controversial ideas or actions that this figure was known for.

b. After researching, you should come to some sort of conclusion about this person. Was she maligned? Was he really as good as people thought? Did she do underhanded things to get her way? Was he really altruistic? Your conclusion should become the basis for your thesis statement.

c. You will then want to create an outline that organizes the story of your subject's life in a manner that supports your thesis.

d. Using your outline as a guide, prepare a rough draft of your paper.

REVISING

Once you have a first draft of your essay completed, turn back to the FOUR BASES Checklist on page 220 to help you with your revision process.

Writing for a Specific Purpose and Audience

WRITING ASSIGNMENT 3

In this essay, you will write with a specific purpose and for a specific audience.

The Yellow Ribbon is used as a symbol for many things, including teen suicide awareness, symbols of support for soldiers, and, in the story, as a symbol of homecoming. In this assignment, you are to write an essay that creates a campaign, complete with symbol, to improve something in your community. First, you will want to find out what issues are affecting your community, like teen suicide, homeless veterans, or decaying parks. After you have decided on your topic, you will need to explain what the problem is and why it is important, what your campaign will be like, and what you hope to accomplish with your campaign. You may want to review Chapter 10, "Exemplification" and Chapter 12, "Cause and/or Effect."

Exemplification

This chapter will explain and illustrate how to

- develop an essay with emphasis on exemplification

- write an essay with emphasis on exemplification

- revise an essay with emphasis on exemplification

In addition, you will read and consider

- two student essays that emphasize exemplification

- one professional essay that emphasizes exemplification

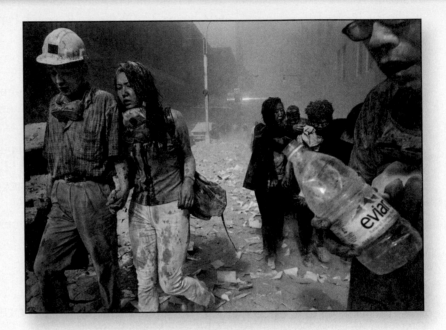

Did the events of 9/11 bring people in the United States together or are we a more divided nation? Use examples found in the media, in this photograph, or in your own daily observations to support your point.

In our daily conversations, we often provide examples—details, particulars, and specific instances—to explain statements that we make. Here are several statements and supporting examples:

Statement	Examples
The first day of school was frustrating.	My sociology course was canceled. Then, I couldn't find the biology lab. And the lines at the bookstore were so long that I went home without buying my textbooks.

| That washing machine is unreliable. | The water temperature can't be predicted; it stops in midcycle; and it sometimes shreds my clothing. |
| My grandfather is a thrifty person. | He washes and reuses aluminum foil. He wraps gifts in newspaper. And he's worn the same Sunday suit for twenty years. |

In each case, exemplification helps us see for ourselves the truth of the statement that has been made. In essays, too, explanatory examples help your audience fully understand your point. Lively, specific examples also add interest to your paper.

In this chapter, you will be asked to emphasize exemplification to support your thesis. First read the student essays and the professional essay that follow and work through the questions that accompany the essays. All three essays emphasize exemplification to develop their points.

Student Essays to Consider

Look on the Bright Side

Some people have a tendency to look for and remember the worst in life. Don't get me wrong; I do not wear rose-colored glasses. Yes, there's plenty of filth, evil, and corruption in the world to make anyone depressed. However, if you focus on the negative, you will never win the battle to achieve happiness. In fact, for every corrupt politician there is one who is an honest and dedicated public servant; for every doctor who is in it for the money, there is one who truly cares about patients, and for every stock-market cheat, there is a business executive who works hard, makes money honestly, and has a conscience. But a person doesn't have to work on Wall Street or in Washington to see that there are pluses and minuses to being human. Both good and evil can be seen in people anywhere.

1

continued

Every day I walk from the bus stop to the office where I work. On my way is a tiny patch of ground that was once strewn with rubbish and broken glass. The city is trying to make a "pocket park" out of it by planting trees and flowers. Every day this spring, I watched the skinny saplings put out tiny leaves. When I walked past I always noted how big the tulips were getting and made bets with myself on when they should bloom. To pass time as I walk, I often make silly little bets with myself such as predicting that the next man I see will be wearing a blue tie. But last Wednesday, I noticed that someone had uprooted the trees and trampled the budding tulips. I felt sick that some people can destroy such beauty for no apparent reason. However, the following Saturday, when I was downtown shopping, I saw a group of Boy Scouts cleaning up another empty lot. There were twelve of them accompanied by two adults, and everyone seemed to be having a great time picking up glass, throwing old mattresses into a dumpster, and repainting a wall that was covered with graffiti.   **2**

At lunchtime last Friday, I witnessed another example of meanness and stupidity, but this too was tempered by good will and kindness. I was waiting in a long line at McDonald's. Also in the line was a young mother with two tired, impatient children clinging to her legs. She was trying to calm them down, but it was obvious that their whining was about to give way to full-fledged tantrums. The lines barely moved, and the lunchtime tension increased. Then, one of the children began to cry and scream. As people stared angrily at the helpless mother, the little boy's screams echoed through the restaurant. Finally, a man shouted in the mother's face: "Lady, don't bring your kids to a public place if you can't control them!" A young woman chimed in with another piece of cruel criticism. Out of nowhere, however, came an elderly gentleman who stopped, knelt down next to the child, and started making funny faces. I learned later that he was an experienced grandfather who knew how to entertain the little ones. Within seconds tears and screams turned into smiles and giggles, and even the lines seemed to be moving faster. Meanwhile, the elderly man's companion waited for him near the exit.   **3**

Among the worst and best examples of human behaviour came one evening as I was heading home after a double shift at work. It was about 11 P.M. when I passed an old woman huddled in a doorway. Wrapped in a dirty blanket and clutching a cheap vinyl bag packed with her belongings, she was one of the "street people" our society leaves to fend for themselves. Approaching the woman from the opposite direction were three teenagers. Talking and laughing loudly, they began to shout crude remarks at her. Then they did even more cruel things to torment her. The woman stared helplessly at them, like a wounded animal surrounded by hunters. In a few seconds, however, two police officers in a patrol car arrived and quickly scared the   **4**

continued

scoundrels away. While one of the men went into a nearby Starbucks to get her some coffee, the other asked her if she wanted to be taken to a shelter. Then helping her to her feet, he wrapped her in a clean blanket he had taken from the trunk of the car and sat her carefully in the back seat. In a few moments, the second officer came out with the coffee as well as a bountiful sandwich he had purchased with his own money. It was probably the first meal she had in days.

    That night, I went home and began to think about what I had just witnessed. The world may be filled with mean-spirited creeps, but it doesn't take much work to find good-hearted, cheerful people who love their fellow human beings and are willing to help whenever they can. That idea, and the belief that with a little effort I too might be able to make a difference, made me sleep a lot better that night.   **5**

Altered States

    Most Americans are not alcoholics. Most do not cruise seedy city streets looking to score crack cocaine or heroin. Relatively few try to con their doctors into prescribing unneeded mood-altering medications. And yet, many Americans are traveling through life with their minds slightly out of kilter. In its attempt to cope with modern life, the human mind seems to have evolved some defense strategies. Confronted with inventions like television, the shopping center, and the Internet, the mind will slip—all by itself—into an altered state.   **1**

    Never in the history of humanity have people been expected to sit passively for hours, staring at moving pictures emanating from an electronic box. Since too much exposure to flickering images of police officers, detectives, and talk-show hosts can be dangerous to human sanity, the mind automatically goes into a state of TV hypnosis. The eyes see the sitcom or the dog-food commercial, but the mind goes into a holding pattern. None of the televised images or sounds actually enter the brain. This is why, when questioned, people cannot remember commercials they have seen five seconds before or why the TV cops are chasing a certain suspect. In this hypnotic, trancelike state, the mind resembles an armored armadillo. It rolls up in self-defense, letting the stream of televised information pass by harmlessly.   **2**

    If the TV watcher arises from the couch and goes to a shopping mall, he or she will again cope by slipping into an altered state. In the mall, the mind is bombarded with the sights, smells, and sounds of dozens of   **3**

continued

stores, restaurants, and movie theaters competing for its attention. There are hundreds of questions to be answered. Should I start with the upper or lower mall level? Which stores should I look in? Should I bother with the sweater sale at J. Crew? Should I eat fried chicken or try the healthier sounding Pita Wrap? Where is my car parked? To combat this mental overload, the mind goes into a state resembling the whiteout experienced by mountain climbers trapped in a blinding snowstorm. Suddenly, everything looks the same. The shopper is unsure where to go next and cannot remember what he or she came for in the first place. The mind enters this state deliberately so that the shopper has no choice but to leave. Some kids can be in a shopping mall for hours, but they are exceptions to the rule.

But no part of everyday life so quickly triggers the mind's protective   4
shutdown mode as that favorite pastime of the new millennium: Internet surfing. A computer user sits down with the intention of briefly checking his or her e-mail or looking up a fact for a research paper. But once tapped into the immense storehouse of information, entertainment, and seemingly intimate personal connections that the Internet offers, the user loses all sense of time and priorities. Prospects flood the mind: Should I explore the rise of Nazi Germany? Play a trivia game? Hear the life story of a lonely stranger in Duluth? With a mind dazed with information overload, the user numbly hits one key after another, leaping from topic to topic, from distraction to distraction. Hours fly by as he or she sits hunched over the keyboard, unable to account for the time that has passed.

These poor victims are merely trying to cope with the mind-numbing   5
inventions of modern life and are not responsible for their glazed eyes and robotic motions. People need to be aware of them and treat them with kindness and understanding. Going out of the way to bring these coma sufferers back to real life is the job of all those who have managed to avoid the side effects of television, shopping, and the Internet; otherwise, humanity will suffer.

QUESTIONS 1   ABOUT UNITY

1. Which sentence in paragraph 3 of "Altered States" should be omitted in the interest of paragraph unity? (*Write the opening words.*)

_____

2. Which supporting paragraph in one of the essays lacks a topic sentence?

_____

3. Find a sentence in one of the paragraphs of "Look on the Bright Side" that does not belong in the eassy. Write the opening words below, and explain why it doesn't belong.

_____

_____

ABOUT SUPPORT

4. Which idea in paragraph 4 of "Look on the Bright Side" is not supported with details? Write the opening words below and explain how would you fix this problem.

_____

_____

5. The last sentence in paragraph 3 of "Look on the Bright Side" seems out of place. Rewrite it so that it actually helps support that paragraph's topic sentence. (Hint: You might want to combine it with a sentence that appears earlier in the paragraph.)

_____

_____

_____

6. What three pieces of evidence does the writer of "Altered States" offer to support the statement that the Internet is an "immense storehouse of information, entertainment, and seemingly intimate personal connections"?

_____

_____

ABOUT COHERENCE

7. In paragraph 3 of "Look on the Bright Side," which four *time* signals does the author begin sentences with? (*Write the four signals here.*)

_____   _____   _____   _____

8. What sentence in "Altered States" indicates that the author has used emphatic order, saving his most important point for last? (*Write the opening words.*)

_____

ABOUT THE INTRODUCTION AND CONCLUSION

9. Which of the two essays provides a clue to its development? Write the title of the essay and a brief outline of that plan below.

_____

_____

_____

_____

10. a. What method discussed in Chapter 4 is used in the conclusion of "Altered States"?

    _____

    b. What method discussed in Chapter 4 is used in the introduction of "Look on the Bright Side"?

    _____

Developing an Essay with Emphasis on Exemplification

Considering Purpose and Audience

Using Various Types of Examples   All examples act as concrete representations of the abstract idea you are trying to communicate, but there are several kinds you can choose from depending on your purpose and audience. Varying the types of examples will help make your writing interesting. Readers would certainly become bored if you simply listed the different kinds of sports or other extracurricular activities your college offers in an attempt to prove that there are many good ways to spend your time. So, you might also include a couple of anecdotes (brief stories) about the interesting club trips you have been on in the past year or the fascinating people you met while planning a language-club fundraiser last semester.

Mention People, Places, Actions, and Things   Some effective examples refer to people, places, actions, and things that readers recognize or can relate to. If you wanted to prove that your town is making a strong effort to improve the environment, you might mention actions like the building of the new sewer treatment plan, the reduction in bus fares to encourage the use of public transportation, or the funding of an empty-lot cleanup project. If you were trying to prove that Virginia contributed a great deal to the founding of our country, you might mention figures such as George Washington, Thomas Jefferson, and Patrick Henry.

Mention Facts and Events   You could use facts if you wanted to explain that ancient Athens was not a democracy in the modern sense because poor people could not participate in government, women had no voice in the affairs of the city, and Athenians owned slaves. You might discuss World War I, World War II, the Korean War, the Vietnam War, and the Persian Gulf War to prove that, in the twentieth century, Americans fought in many global conflicts.

Include Anecdotes   Anecdotes are brief, informative stories that can serve as examples. Although they are brief, they go beyond the mere mention of something and actually tell a complete story that serves to make an abstract idea more understandable. There are several such stories in "Look on the Bright Side," an essay that appeared earlier in this chapter.

Using Only Relevant Examples   Examples should always relate directly to the idea that they are being used to support. Let's say you are trying to prove that taking public transportation can sometimes be inconvenient. Telling your readers that you often read on the bus while traveling to work won't help you. In fact, being able to read while commuting is an advantage. Neither will it help to say that bus fares have risen lately. Remember that you are trying to explain the term "inconvenient," not "expensive." A better example would be the fact that three days this week the bus was so crowded you had to stand up for the entire half-hour trip.

Development through Prewriting

When Cedric, the student author of "Altered States," was considering a topic for his exemplification essay, he looked around his dorm for inspiration. He first considered writing about examples of some different types of people: jocks, dorks, goths. Then he thought about examples of housekeeping in dorm rooms: the Slob Kingdom, the Neat Freak Room, and the Packrat's Place.

"But that evening I was noticing how my roommate acted as he was cruising the Internet," Cedric said. "He sat down to write his brother a brief e-mail, and three hours later he was still there, cruising from Web site to Web site. His eyes were glassy and he seemed out of touch with reality. It reminded me of how spaced out I get when I go to a busy shopping mall. I began to think about how our minds have to adjust to challenges that our grandparents didn't grow up with. I added 'watching television' as the third category, and I had a pretty good idea what my essay would be about."

Cedric had his three categories, but he needed to do some more work to generate supporting details for each. He used the technique of clustering, or diagramming, to help inspire his thinking. Here is what his diagram looked like:

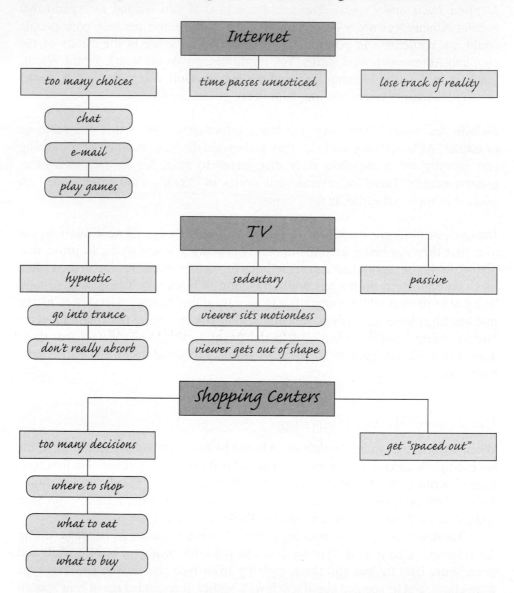

Looking at his diagram, Cedric saw that he would have no trouble supporting the thesis that people's minds go into an "altered state" when they watch TV, go to shopping centers, or use the Internet. As he quickly jotted down details in cluster form, he had easily come up with enough ideas for his essay. He started writing and produced this first draft.

Altered States

Modern life makes demands on the human mind that no other period of history has made. As society becomes more and more complex, the mind has developed some defense mechanisms. Confronted with inventions like the Internet, television, and the shopping center, the mind will slip—all by itself—into an altered state.

Surfing the Internet can quickly make the mind slip into a strange state. A computer user sits down to check his e-mail or look up something. But once tapped into the Internet, the user loses all sense of time. He can chat with strangers, research any topic, play a game, or shop for any product. Some people begin to think of the online world and online friends as more real than the people in their own homes. While my roommate is absorbed in the Internet, he can even have brief conversations with people who come into our room, yet not be able to remember the conversations later. He sits there in a daze from information overload. He seems numb as he hits key after key, going from Web site to Web site.

Then there's TV. Growing up, our grandparents could not have imagined the idea of sitting passively for hours, staring at moving pictures emanating from a box. It's not a normal state of affairs, so the mind goes into something like a hypnotic trance. You see the sitcom or the dog-food commercial, but your mind goes into a holding pattern. You don't really absorb the pictures or sounds. Five minutes after I watch a show I can't remember commercials I've seen or why the TV cops are chasing a certain suspect.

If the TV watcher arises from the couch and journeys into the real world, he often goes to the shopping center. Here, the mind is bombarded with the sights, smells, and sounds of dozens of stores, restaurants, and movie theaters competing for its attention. Dazed shoppers begin to feel like mountain climbers trapped in a blinding snowstorm. Suddenly, everything looks the same. My father is the worst of all when it comes to shopping in an altered state. He comes back from the mall looking like he'd been through a war. After about fifteen minutes of shopping, he can't concentrate enough to know what he's looking for.

Internet surfers, TV viewers, and shoppers all have one thing in common. They're just trying to cope with the mind-numbing inventions of modern life. I hope that someday we'll turn away from such inventions and return to a simpler and more healthy way of life.

Development through Revising

Cedric showed his first-draft essay to a classmate for her critique. She returned his essay with these comments:

Reader's Comments

This seems to me like a separate topic—people's relationships with people they meet on the Internet.

Sometimes you write about "a user," other times about "you," and then about "my roommate." It's confusing. Also, is the paragraph about your roommate on the Internet or what people in general are like?

These last two sentences are good. I'd like to read more about this "altered state" you think people go into.

The idea of the "hypnotic trance" is interesting, but you need more details to back it up.

The point of view is a problem again. You skip from "you" to "I."

Altered States

Modern life makes demands on the human mind that no other period of history has made. As society becomes more and more complex, the mind has developed some defense mechanisms. Confronted with inventions like the Internet, television, and the shopping center, the mind will slip—all by itself—into an altered state.

Surfing the Internet can quickly make the mind slip into a strange state. A computer user sits down to check his e-mail or look up something. But once tapped into the Internet, the user loses all sense of time. He can chat with strangers, research any topic, play a game, or shop for any product. Some people begin to think of the online world and online friends as more real than the people in their own homes. While my roommate is absorbed in the Internet, he can even have brief conversations with people who come into our room, yet not be able to remember the conversations later. He sits there in a daze from information overload. He seems numb as he hits key after key, going from Web site to Web site.

Then there's TV. Growing up, our grandparents could not have imagined the idea of sitting passively for hours, staring at moving pictures emanating from a box. It's not a normal state of affairs, so the mind goes into something like a hypnotic trance. You see the sitcom or the dog-food commercial, but your mind goes into a holding pattern. You don't really absorb the pictures or sounds. Five minutes after I watch a show I can't remember commercials I've seen or why the TV cops are chasing a certain suspect.

If the TV watcher arises from the couch and journeys into the real world, he often goes to the shopping center. Here, the mind is bombarded with the sights, smells, and sounds of dozens of stores, restaurants, and movie theaters competing for its attention. Dazed

continued

shoppers begin to feel like mountain climbers trapped in a blinding snowstorm. Suddenly, everything looks the same. My father is the worst of all when it comes to shopping in an altered state. He comes back from the mall looking like he'd been through a war. After about fifteen minutes of shopping, he can't concentrate enough to know what he's looking for.

Good image!

I don't think this works. The essay isn't about your father. It should be about modern shoppers, not just one man.

Internet surfers, TV viewers, and shoppers all have one thing in common. They're just trying to cope with the mind-numbing inventions of modern life. I hope that someday we'll turn away from such inventions and return to a simpler and more healthy way of life.

This final sentence seems to introduce a new topic—that we shouldn't get caught up in TV and the Internet, etc.

Cedric read his classmate's comments and reviewed the essay himself. He agreed with her criticisms about point of view and the need for stronger supporting details. He also decided that the Internet was his strongest supporting point and should be saved for the last paragraph. He then wrote the final version of his essay, the version that appears on pages 225–226.

A Professional Essay to Consider

Read the following professional essay. Then answer the questions and read the comments that follow.

Dad

by Andrew H. Malcolm

The first memory I have of him—of anything, really—is his strength. It was in 1 the late afternoon in a house under construction near ours. The unfinished wood floors had large, terrifying holes whose yawning darkness I knew led to nowhere good. His powerful hands, then age thirty-three, wrapped all the way around my tiny arms, then age four, and easily swung me up to his shoulders to command all I surveyed.

The relationship between a son and his father changes over time. It may grow 2 and flourish in mutual maturity. It may sour in resented dependence or independence. With many children living in single-parent homes today, it may not even exist.

But to a little boy right after World War II, a father seemed a god with strange 3 strengths and uncanny powers enabling him to do and know things that no mortal could do or know. Amazing things, like putting a bicycle chain back on, just like that. Or building a hamster cage. Or guiding a jigsaw so it formed the letter F; I learned the alphabet that way in those pretelevision days, one letter or number every other evening plus a review of the collection. (The vowels we painted red because they were special somehow.)

He seemed to know what I thought before I did. "You look like you could use   4 a cheeseburger and a chocolate shake," he would say on hot Sunday afternoons. When, at the age of five, I broke a neighbor's garage window with a wild curveball and waited in fear for ten days to make the announcement, he seemed to know about it already and to have been waiting for something.

There were, of course, rules to learn. First came the handshake. None of those   5 fishy little finger grips, but a good firm squeeze accompanied by an equally strong gaze into the other's eyes. "The first thing anyone knows about you is your hand-shake," he would say. And we'd practice it each night on his return from work, the serious toddler in the battered Cleveland Indians cap running up to the giant father to shake hands again and again until it was firm enough.

When my cat killed a bird, he defused the anger of a nine-year-old with a little   6 chat about something called "instinked." The next year, when my dog got run over and the weight of sorrow was just too immense to stand, he was there, too, with his big arms and his own tears and some thoughts on the natural order of life and death, although what was natural about a speeding car that didn't stop always escaped me.

As time passed, there were other rules to learn. "Always do your best." "Do   7 it now." "NEVER LIE!" And, most important, "You can do whatever you have to do." By my teens, he wasn't telling me what to do anymore, which was scary and heady at the same time. He provided perspective, not telling me what was around the great corner of life but letting me know there was a lot more than just today and the next, which I hadn't thought of.

When the most important girl in the world—I forget her name now—turned down   8 a movie date, he just happened to walk by the kitchen phone. "This may be hard to believe right now," he said, "but someday you won't even remember her name."

One day, I realize now, there was a change. I wasn't trying to please him so   9 much as I was trying to impress him. I never asked him to come to my football games. He had a high-pressure career, and it meant driving through most of Friday night. But for all the big games, when I looked over at the sideline, there was that familiar fedora. And, by God, did the opposing team captain ever get a firm hand-shake and a gaze he would remember.

Then, a school fact contradicted something he said. Impossible that he could 10 be wrong, but there it was in the book. These accumulated over time, along with personal experiences, to buttress[1] my own developing sense of values. And I could tell we had each taken our own, perfectly normal paths.

I began to see, too, his blind spots, his prejudices, and his weaknesses. I never 11 threw these up at him. He hadn't to me, and, anyway, he seemed to need protection. I stopped asking his advice; the experiences he drew from no longer seemed rel-evant to the decisions I had to make. On the phone, he would go on about politics at

---

[1]*buttress:* strengthen and support.

times, why he would vote the way he did or why some incumbent was a jerk. And I would roll my eyes to the ceiling and smile a little, though I hid it in my voice.

He volunteered advice for a while. But then, in more recent years, politics and 12 issues gave way to talk of empty errands and, always, to ailments—his friends', my mother's, and his own, which were serious and included heart disease. He had a bed-side oxygen tank, and he would ostentatiously² retire there during my visits, asking my help in easing his body onto the mattress. "You have very strong arms," he once noted.

From his bed, he showed me the many sores and scars on his misshapen body 13 and all the bottles of medicine. He talked of the pain and craved much sympathy. He got some. But the scene was not attractive. He told me, as the doctor had, that his condition would only deteriorate. "Sometimes," he confided, "I would just like to lie down and go to sleep and not wake up."

After much thought and practice ("You can do whatever you have to do"), one 14 night last winter, I sat down by his bed and remembered for an instant those ter-rifying dark holes in another house thirty-five years before. I told my father how much I loved him. I described all the things people were doing for him. But, I said, he kept eating poorly, hiding in his room, and violating other doctors' orders. No amount of love could make someone else care about life, I said: it was a two-way street. He wasn't doing his best. The decision was his.

He said he knew how hard my words had been to say and how proud he was 15 of me. "I had the best teacher," I said. "You can do whatever you have to do." He smiled a little, and we shook hands, firmly, for the last time.

Several days later, at about 4 A.M., my mother heard Dad shuffling about their 16 dark room. "I have some things I have to do," he said. He paid a bundle of bills. He composed for my mother a long list of legal and financial what-to-do's "in case of emergency." And he wrote me a note.

Then he walked back to his bed and laid himself down. He went to sleep, natu- 17 rally. And he did not wake up.

ABOUT UNITY

QUESTIONS 2

1. What is the thesis of Malcolm's essay, "Dad"? (Write the first words.)

_____

2. Which statement would best serve as a topic sentence for paragraph 6?
   a. My dad loved my dog as much as I did.
   b. Pets were a subject that drew my dad and me together.
   c. My dad helped me make sense of life's tragedies.
   d. I was angry at my cat for killing a bird.

3. Write a sentence that might serve as the topic sentence of paragraph 10.

_____

_____
²*ostentatiously:* dramatically.

ABOUT SUPPORT

4. List the details Malcolm uses in paragraph 3 to support the idea that his father "seemed a god with strange strengths and uncanny powers."

   _____

   _____

   _____

5. With which sentence does Malcolm support his statement in paragraph 14 that his father "wasn't doing his best"? (*Write the opening words.*)

   _____

6. What point or idea does the anecdote in paragraph 8 support?

   _____

ABOUT COHERENCE

7. What event makes Malcolm begin to see his father in more realistic, less idealized terms?

   _____

8. In paragraph 6, find each of the following:
   a. two time-transition signals

   _____   _____

   b. one addition-transition signal

   _____

   c. one change-of-direction transition signal

   _____

9. Which method of organization does Malcolm use in his essay?
   a. Time
   b. Emphatic

ABOUT THE CONCLUSION

10. The conclusion of "Dad" is made up of
    a. a summary of the narrative and a final thought.
    b. a quotation about fatherhood.
    c. the last event of the story about Malcolm and his father.
    d. a prediction of what kind of father Malcolm hopes to be himself.

Writing an Essay with Emphasis on Exemplification

In this assignment, write an essay that exemplifies how you best learn and should study.

PREWRITING

a. Using whatever prewriting method works best for you, write down past experiences, both good and bad, of studying for tests. Note what made the experiences positive and negative.

b. Visit http://www.vark-learn.com and click on "Questionnaire." Complete the questionnaire to discover what type of learner you are. Once you have determined your type, click on "Helpsheets" to read about studying suggestions geared toward that type.

c. In order to properly present the information you have gathered, read Chapter 22, "Writing a Research Paper," paying special attention to how to write your information and to how to avoid plagiarism.

d. Using all the information you have gathered, write a topic sentence that introduces your learner type and what it means. Sample topic sentences have been provided to get you started:
   • After reading the VARK Web site, I understand that I am a Read/Write learner and to be successful, I need to employ specific study skills.
   • I always struggled in school because I was terrible at studying, but since I now know that I am a kinesthetic learner, I have a better idea of how I should study.

e. Write the first draft of your essay and support your thesis sentence by incorporating a definition of your study type, facts from the helpsheets, and examples or anecdotes from past studying experiences.

REVISING

After you have completed the first draft of the paper, set it aside for a while if you can. When you review it, try to do so as critically as you would if it were not your own work. Better yet, read it aloud to a friend or classmate whose judgment you trust. Read the essay with these questions in mind:

Exemplification Checklist: THE FOUR BASES

ABOUT *UNITY*

✔ Do I have a clearly stated thesis?

ABOUT *SUPPORT*

✔ Have I provided *relevant* specific details?

✔ Have I provided *enough* specific details to support my thesis?

ABOUT *COHERENCE*

✔ Have I used transition words to help readers follow my train of thought?

✔ Do I have a concluding paragraph that provides a summary or final thought or both?

ABOUT *SENTENCE SKILLS*

✔ Have I used a consistent point of view throughout my essay?

✔ Have I used specific rather than general words?

✔ Have I avoided wordiness and used concise wording?

✔ Are my sentences varied?

✔ Have I proofread my essay for sentence skills, as listed on the inside back cover of the book?

As you revise your essay through one or more additional drafts, continue to refer to this checklist until you can answer "yes" to each question.

WRITING ASSIGNMENT 2

Write an essay that emphasizes exemplification based upon an outside reading. It might be a selection recommended by your instructor, or it might be a piece by one of the following authors, all of whom have written books of essays that should be available in your college library.

Annie Dillard	Andy Rooney
Malcolm Gladwell	David Sedaris
Ellen Goodman	Amy Tan
Aldous Huxley	Deborah Tannen
Molly Ivins	Henry David Thoreau
Maxine Hong Kingston	Calvin Trillin
Gabriel Garcia Marquez	Alice Walker
Vladimir Nabokov	E. B. White
George Orwell	Marie Winn
Anna Quindlen	Virginia Woolf
Richard Rodriguez	

Base your essay on an idea in the selection you have chosen, and provide a series of examples to back up your idea. Of course, you may want to draw information from the reading selection by quoting from it or making other types of references. However, you might also use examples from other sources, perhaps something else you have read, a movie you have seen, or a personal experience. You may want to review Chapter 18, "Writing a Summary," and Chapter 22, "Writing a Research Paper," to help you properly report and document the author's original information.

The following student essay on capital punishment was inspired by and takes information from George Orwell's essay, "A Hanging," which you can find on page 658.

However, the paper also uses examples from *The Green Mile,* a 1999 movie about the recollections of Paul Edgecomb during one year when he was a corrections officer in charge of inmates on death row.

Paying Attention to a Death

In "A Hanging" (1931), George Orwell narrates the execution of a   1
Burmese man in such a way that no reader can avoid realizing the enormity
of taking a human life. *The Green Mile* (1999), a movie based on a Stephen

continued

King novel, makes the same statement. The essay focuses on the last few moments in the life of a man we hardly get to know. The film covers the events of an entire year and allows us to see into the hearts of both prisoners and guards. But the messages are identical: no one, not even a legally constituted government, has the right to violate the sanctity of human life.

The moments leading to the hanging in Orwell's essay are filled with   **2** tension. Six tall guards, two of them armed with rifles, lead the prisoner, "a puny wisp of a man," who is both chained to their belts and handcuffed. Suddenly, the procession to the gallows is interrupted by a friendly dog that licks the prisoner's face and wags its "whole body wild with glee at finding so many human beings together." The scene is heavy with irony. This friendly animal, full of life and energy, contrasts markedly with the officials leading the prisoner to his death. "What is the point of all of this?" the presence of the dog suggests. In *The Green Mile*, a death-row prisoner called Del adopts a pet mouse that he names "Mr. Jingles." Del is a small, soft-spoken, endearing little man, who is able to train the mouse as if it were a very smart dog. He bonds with the tiny creature so poignantly that the silliness and brutality of his impending execution become clear. Here is a man who, literally, couldn't hurt a mouse—why not just keep him imprisoned for life?

Both essay and film defend the sanctity and dignity of human life. In "A   **3** Hanging," Orwell mentions that the prisoner moves to avoid a puddle on his way to the gallows. Why does he do this if not from some innate human need to keep his dignity intact, even to the last? Seconds before he is killed, he begins "crying out to his god." The repeated "Ram! Ram! Ram!" is his own death knell. The guards grow gray, finally realizing that the hooded, faceless little man on the platform is, after all, a human being. In *The Green Mile*, Del is finally electrocuted, but the manner in which he dies provides us a painful reminder of the sacredness that capital punishment violates. Guard Percy Wetmore, a sadistic coward, is given the job of preparing Del for the chair. This involves placing a wet sponge on his head so that electricity will flow more efficiently through his body and result in less pain. Demonically, Wetmore decides to leave the sponge dry. When the switch is thrown, Del writhes in agony, his suffering beyond belief. Then, the chair bursts into flame in a scene from which viewers will want to turn away.

Interestingly, the author of "A Hanging" never tells about the crime for   **4** which the prisoner was executed. He leaves this information out intentionally. For Orwell, capital punishment is wrong, no matter the crime. A similar statement is made in *The Green Mile*. John Coffee, an African American, sits on death row, having been wrongly convicted of killing two white girls. Coffee is a giant—seven feet tall and muscular—but he is as gentle as Del and his mouse. Moreover, he has magical healing powers that he uses to cure Paul Edgecomb, the death-row superintendent, of a severe urinary

continued

infection, to bring Mr. Jingles back to life, and even to save the warden's wife from a deadly cancer. Near the end of the movie, we discover that the girls' real killer is another death-row inmate, and we hope for John Coffee's release. But it is not to be; the real killer dies without confessing. Yes, Edgecomb gives Coffee the option to escape, but the gentle giant declines, explaining that the world is just too evil and that he is just "dog tired."

Only a few moments after the execution of the Burmese prisoner, Orwell's   5
prison officials attempt to forget that they have just killed a man. They make silly jokes, smoke cigarettes, and take a drink, even though it is still early morning. *The Green Mile* ends with Paul Edgecomb, now 108 years old, recalling Coffee's execution and explaining that living to see all of his friends and relatives die is his punishment for letting Coffee go to the chair. "We each owe a death," he says. "There are no exceptions. But, Oh God, sometimes the Green Mile seems so long." Standing only a few yards away from the body, Orwell's warders pretend to ignore the horror they have committed. They are trying to hide the moon with a sheet, as my grandmother would say. At least Paul Edgecomb accepts the enormous significance of Coffee's wrongful death. And for that reason, we too can feel his pain and regret as if they were our own.

Writing for a Specific Purpose and Audience

WRITING ASSIGNMENT 3

In this essay that emphasizes exemplification, you will write with a specific purpose and for a specific audience. Your essay should present a strong explanation to your boss about exactly what you do on a daily basis and why you should be given a raise. Strive to incorporate as many specific examples of the tasks you perform every day and describe why you are good at them. For instance, perhaps you work at an animal shelter and clean kennels every day, and you have streamlined the process to be quicker and less stressful on the animals. Possibly you work as a UPS package handler and have figured out a better route plan for your territory. You may want to review Chapter 8, "Description," to help you provide specific details explaining what your daily duties are. You may also want to check Chapter 16, "Argument," to help you create a persuasive tone to your essay.

Process

This chapter will explain and illustrate how to

- develop an essay with emphasis on process
- write an essay with emphasis on process
- revise an essay with emphasis on process

In addition, you will read and consider

- two student essays that emphasize process
- one professional essay that emphasizes process

Write an essay that informs a reader about how to perform a particular hobby or activity you enjoy. Depending on the hobby or activity you are writing about, you may prefer to use a humorous approach.

Every day we perform many activities that are *processes,* that is, series of steps carried out in a definite order. Many of these processes are familiar and automatic: for example, loading film into a camera, diapering a baby, or making an omelet. We are thus seldom aware of the sequence of steps making up each activity. In other cases—for example, when someone asks us for directions to a particular place, or when we try to read and follow directions for a new table game that someone has given us—we may be painfully conscious of the whole series of steps involved in the process.

In this chapter, you will be asked to write an essay with emphasis on process—one that explains clearly how to do or make something. To prepare for this assignment, you should first read the student papers and the professional essay and then answer the questions that follow them.

Student Essays to Consider

Marketing Plan: Happy Child Preschool

Happy Child Preschool is a valuable and cherished part of our campus, but enrollment has declined dramatically over the past two years. Thus, a task force was commissioned to analyze the causes. The comparative analysis conducted by the task force uncovered numerous ways that other campus childcare centers have achieved success through marketing. The task force agrees that promotion is the number one issue that has been overlooked in the past and the area where major and immediate improvements are essential to the long-term success of the center. In order to effectively market the preschool, promoting the center needs to remain at the top of the priority chart and should include proper advertising, publicity, and referrals.

The first step is proper advertising that must start with a well-designed multi-layered Web site that includes general information, enrollment forms, and profiles of teachers and staff. The general information page should contain the hours of operation, location, and contact information. The top of the page should include a banner with scrolling photos of children and staff at the center. Underneath the banner, several links, including the enrollment forms and profiles, should be prominently placed. Having a direct link to online enrollment and other business forms will encourage potential families to enroll because families can fill out the application forms when it is convenient for them, not when the center is open. Making the application process easier than the current process should increase interest. The page with teacher profiles is a great place to bring attention to our quality educators. Including pictures, background information, and education will help promote our facility because all the teachers at our center are highly qualified. All of this information will demonstrate our strengths and help potential families appreciate the top quality of education our center provides.

Publicity could include a monthly column in the local newspaper that highlights what is currently going on at the preschool. Because our curriculum is a blend of Montessori and Carden methods, we have a unique offering; calling attention to the special achievements, programs, and students in our school would offer the positive publicity needed to interest potential families. Each column's publication should be followed by an open house, so potential families can actually visit our school. These open houses should also occur during key enrollment periods to encourage greater attendance. In addition, hosting one or two major events will continue to raise awareness of our school within the community.

The final and best way to increase enrollment is to utilize our currently enrolled families. Word-of-mouth is one of the best ways to increase enrollment. Families who are pleased with their children's schools are often

continued

more than happy to tell others. Offering referral rewards to families will help encourage families to tell others about the school. The task force looked at several referral programs and determined that a program that offers families monetary rewards that are applied to monthly fees would be a cost-effective program. Partnering with local colleges' education programs would also be a cost-effective program.

By putting these approaches into place, we project that our enrollment should increase to capacity within the next two years. These key components have been overlooked in the past, so we are hopeful that the committee will accept this new direction. It will play a significant role in the future of the success of the school. 5

How to Complain

I'm not just a consumer—I'm a victim. If I order a product, it is sure to arrive in the wrong color, size, or quantity. If I hire people to do repairs, they never arrive on the day scheduled. If I owe a bill, the computer program is bound to overcharge me. Therefore, in self-defense, I have developed the following consumer's guide to complaining effectively. 1

The first step is getting organized. I save all sales slips and original boxes. Also, I keep a special file for warranty cards and appliance guarantees. This file does not prevent a product from falling apart the day after the guarantee runs out. One of the problems in our country is the shoddy workmanship that goes into many products. However, these facts give me the ammunition I need to make a complaint. I know the date of the purchase, the correct price (or service charge), where the item was purchased, and an exact description of the product, including model and serial numbers. When I compose my letter of complaint, I find it is not necessary to exaggerate. I just stick to the facts. 2

The next step is to send the complaint to the person who will get results quickly. My experience has shown that the president of the company is the best person to contact. I call the company to find out the president's name and make sure I note the proper spelling. Then I write directly to that person, and I usually get prompt action. For example, the head of AMF arranged to replace my son's ten-speed "lemon" when it fell apart piece by piece in less than a year. Another time, the president of a Philadelphia department store finally had a twenty-dollar overcharge on my bill corrected after I had spent three months arguing uselessly with a computer program. 3

If I get no response to a written complaint within ten days, I follow through with a personal telephone call. When I had a new bathtub installed a few years ago, the plumber left a gritty black substance on the bottom of the tub. No amount of scrubbing could remove it. I tried every cleanser on 4

continued

the supermarket shelf, but I still had a dirty tub. The plumber shrugged off my complaints and said to try Comet. The manufacturer never answered my letter or e-mail. Finally, I made a personal phone call to the president of the firm. Within days a well-dressed executive showed up at my door. In a business suit, white shirt, striped tie, and rubber gloves, he cleaned the tub. Before he left, he scolded me in an angry voice, "You didn't have to call the president." The point is, I did have to call the president. No one else cared enough to solve the problem.

Therefore, my advice to the consumer is to keep accurate records, and   5
if a complaint needs to be made, he or she should go right to the top. It has always worked for me.

ABOUT UNITY

1. The (*fill in the correct answer*: first, second, third) _____ supporting paragraph of "Marketing Plan" lacks a topic sentence. Write a topic sentence that expresses its main point:

   _____

   _____

2. Which sentence in paragraph 4 of "Marketing Plan" should be omitted in the interest of paragraph unity? (*Write the first words.*)

   _____

   _____

3. Which sentence in paragraph 2 of "How to Complain" should be omitted in the interest of paragraph unity? (*Write the opening words.*)

   _____

ABOUT SUPPORT

4. Which sentence in paragraph 3 of "Marketing Plan" needs more supporting details? (*Write the opening words.*)

   _____

5. Which supporting paragraph in "How to Complain" uses one extended example? Write the number of that paragraph and tell (in just a few words) what the example was about.

   _____

   _____

6. Which supporting paragraph in "How to Complain" depends on two short examples? Write the number of that paragraph and tell (in just a few words) what each example was about.

_____

_____

ABOUT COHERENCE

7. Paragraph 3 of "Marketing Plan" uses several transitions. What type of transitions are they? _____

List them here: _____

8. In "How to Complain" what transitions are used to maintain coherence between paragraphs 1 and 2? _____

Between 2 & 3? _____

ABOUT THE INTRODUCTION AND CONCLUSION

9. Which method for writing introductions discussed in Chapter 4 is used in "Marketing Plan"?

_____

10. Which method for writing conclusions discussed in Chapter 4 is used in "Marketing Plan"?

_____

Developing an Essay with Emphasis on Process

Considering Purpose and Audience

Glance at a newsstand and you'll see magazine cover stories with titles such as "How to Impress Your Boss," "How to Add Romance to Your Life," or "How to Dress Like a Movie Star." These articles promise to give readers directions or information they can follow; they are popular versions of essays that emphasize process.

In general, essays that emphasize process explain the steps involved in a particular action, process, or event. Some of these essays focus on giving readers actual instructions, others provide information, and still others focus on persuading readers. The type of essay you write depends on the specific topic and purpose you choose.

Begin by asking yourself what you want your readers to know. If, for example, you want your audience to know how to make the ultimate chocolate chip cookie, your essay would include directions telling them what to do and how to do it. On the other hand, if you want your readers to know how a cookie is digested, you would detail the events in the body as it turns food into energy.

No matter what your main purpose, keep your audience in mind as you work. As with any essay, select a topic that will interest readers. A group of college students, for example, might be interested in reading an essay that explains how and why to get financial aid but be bored by an essay on how and why to plan for retirement.

Finally, evaluate how much your readers already know about your topic. An audience unfamiliar with your topic might require you to explain technical terms. If you are explaining how to protect your computer from viruses, for example, you might have to define "firewall." If you are explaining how to check a car's tire pressure, you might have to describe a pressure gauge.

Deciding on Structure, Content, and Style

- As with other types of papers, include a thesis. Your thesis might explain your purpose—why it is important to learn how to change the oil in your car or why learning to prepare a room for painting is worth knowing. On the other hand, it might explain something definitive about the process. For example, you might begin a paper on the digestive process by stating that "the human body is a truly marvelous machine." Then, of course, you would have to show just how marvelous it is as you explain how it digests food.

- Use language that is easy to follow and not unnecessarily complex. If you are explaining how to do something, your readers may be executing your instructions as they read them for the first time. So be as clear as you can to avoid unintentionally misleading the reader.

- In most cases, list each step in chronological or time order. (See page 81 for words that signal time.)

- Explain each step in a separate paragraph. If two steps are done or occur simultaneously, connect separate paragraphs with phrases such as "At the same time."

- When giving information about a process, use the right verb tense. If you are explaining something that happened only once, use the past tense: "After Mount Vesuvius erupted, it covered the city of Pompeii with pumice and ash." However, if you are discussing something that recurs, use the present tense: "During the next phase of digestion, food passes down the esophagus to the stomach."

- If you are presenting information, as in the examples about Pompeii and digestion above, you should always write in the formal third person. If you are writing directions (something this book does), you may write in the second person, directly addressing your audience as "you," or in the third person. It's important to remember that the second person should be used very sparingly.

> TIP For more information about third- and second-person points of view, see pages 177–178.

Development through Prewriting

An essay that emphasizes process requires the writer to think through the steps involved in an activity. As Marian, the author of "How to Complain," thought about possible topics for her essay, she asked herself, "What are some things I do methodically, step by step?" A number of possibilities occurred to her, including getting herself and her children ready for school in the morning and shopping for groceries (from preparing a shopping list to organizing her coupons), and the one she finally settled on: effective complaining. "People tell me I'm 'so organized' when it comes to getting satisfaction on things I buy," Marian said. "I realized that I do usually get results when I complain because I go about complaining in an organized way. To write my essay, I just needed to put those steps into words."

Marian began by making a list of the steps she follows when she makes a complaint. This is what she wrote:

Save sales slips and original boxes

Engrave items with ID number in case of burglary

Write or e-mail letter of complaint

Save or make photocopy of letter

Create file of warranties and guarantees

Send complaint letter directly to president

Call company for president's name

Follow through with telephone call if no response

Make thank-you call after action is taken

Next, she numbered those steps in the order in which she performs them. She struck out some items she realized weren't really necessary to the process of complaining:

1   Save sales slips and original boxes

~~Engrave items with ID number in case of burglary~~

4   Write or e-mail letter of complaint

~~Save or make photocopy of letter~~

2   Create file of warranties and guarantees

5   Send complaint letter directly to president

3   Call company for president's name

6   Follow through with telephone call if no response

~~Make thank you call after action is taken~~

Next, she decided to group her items into three steps: (1) getting organized, (2) sending the complaint to the president, and (3) following up with further action.

With that preparation done, Marian wrote her first draft.

How to Complain

First Draft

Because I find that a consumer has to watch out for herself and be ready to speak up if a product or service isn't satisfactory, I have developed the following consumer's guide to complaining effectively.

The first step is getting organized. I save all sales slips, original boxes, warranty cards, and appliance guarantees. This file does not prevent a product from falling apart the day after the guarantee runs out. One of the problems in our country is the shoddy workmanship that goes into many products. That way I know the date of the purchase, the correct price, where the item was purchased, and an exact description of the product.

The next step is to send the complaint to the person who will get results quickly. I call the company to find out the president's name and then I write directly to that person. For example, the head of AMF arranged to replace

continued

my son's bike. Another time, the president of a Philadelphia department store finally had a twenty-dollar overcharge on my bill corrected.

If I get no response to a written complaint within ten days, I follow through with a personal telephone call. When I had a new bathtub installed a few years ago, the plumber left a gritty black substance on the bottom of the tub. I tried everything to get it off. Finally, I made a personal phone call to the president of the firm. Within days a well-dressed executive showed up at my door. In a business suit, white shirt, striped tie, and rubber gloves, he cleaned the tub. Before he left, he said, "You didn't have to call the president."

Therefore, my advice to consumers is to keep accurate records, and when you have to complain, go right to the top. It has always worked for me.

Development through Revising

After she had written the first draft, Marian set it aside for several days. When she reread it, she was able to look at it more critically. These are her comments:

I think this first draft is OK as the "bare bones" of an essay, but it needs to be fleshed out everywhere. For instance, in paragraph 2, I need to explain why it's important to know the date of purchase etc. And in paragraph 3, I need to explain more about what happened with the bike and the department store overcharge. In paragraph 4, especially, I need to explain how I tried to solve the problem with the bathtub before I called the president. I want to make it clear that I don't immediately go to the top as soon as I have a problem—I give the people at a lower level a chance to fix it first. All in all, my first draft looks as if I just rushed to get the basic ideas down on paper. Now I need to take the time to back up my main points with better support.

With that self-critique in mind, Marian wrote the version of "How to Complain" that appears on pages 244–245.

A Professional Essay to Consider

Read the following professional essay. Then answer the questions and read the comments that follow.

How to Do Well on a Job Interview
by Glenda Davis

Ask a random selection of people for a listing of their least favorite activities, **1** and right up there with "getting my teeth drilled" is likely to be "going to a job interview." The job interview is often regarded as a confusing, humiliating, and nerve-racking experience. First of all, you have to wait for your appointment in an outer room, often trapped there with other people applying for the same job. You sit nervously, trying not to think about the fact that only one of you may be hired. Then you are called into the interviewer's office. Faced with a complete stranger, you have to try to act both cool and friendly as you are asked all sorts of questions. Some questions are personal: "What is your greatest weakness?" Others are confusing: "Why should we hire you?" The interview probably takes about twenty minutes but seems like two hours. Finally, you go home and wait for days and even weeks. If you get the job, great. But if you don't, you're rarely given any reason why.

The job-interview "game" may not be much fun, but it is a game you *can* win if **2** you play it right. The name of the game is standing out of the crowd—in a positive way. If you go to the interview in a Bozo the Clown suit, you'll stand out of the crowd, all right, but not in a way that is likely to get you hired.

Here are guidelines to help you play the interview game to win: **3**

Present yourself as a winner. Instantly, the way you dress, speak, and move **4** gives the interviewer more information about you than you would think possible. You doubt that this is true? Consider this: a professional job recruiter, meeting a series of job applicants, was asked to signal the moment he decided *not* to hire each applicant. The thumbs-down decision was often made *in less than forty-five seconds—even before the applicant thought the interview had begun.*

How can you keep from becoming a victim of an instant "no" decision? **5**

- *Dress appropriately.* This means business clothing: usually a suit and tie or a conservative dress or skirt suit. Don't wear casual student clothing. On the other hand, don't overdress: you're going to a job interview, not a party. If you're not sure what's considered appropriate business attire, do some spying before the interview. Walk past your prospective place of employment at lunch or quitting time and check out how the employees are dressed. Your goal is to look as though you would fit in with that group of people.

- *Pay attention to your grooming.* Untidy hair, body odor, dandruff, un-shined shoes, a hanging hem, stains on your tie, excessive makeup or cologne, a sloppy job of shaving—if the interviewer notices any of these, your prospect of being hired takes a probably fatal hit.

- *Look alert, poised, and friendly.* When that interviewer looks into the waiting room and calls your name, he or she is getting a first impression of your behavior. If you're slouched in your chair, dozing or lost in the pages of a magazine; if you look up with an annoyed "Huh?"; if you get up slowly and wander over with your hands in your pockets, he or she will not be favorably impressed. What *will* earn you points is rising promptly and walking briskly toward the interviewer. Smiling and looking directly at that person, extend your hand to shake his or hers, saying, "I'm Lesley Brown. Thank you for seeing me today."

- *Expect to make a little small talk.* This is not a waste of time; it is the interviewer's way of checking your ability to be politely sociable, and it is your opportunity to cement the good impression you've already made. The key is to follow the interviewer's lead. If he or she wants to chat about the weather for a few minutes, do so. But don't drag it out; as soon as you get a signal that it's time to talk about the job, be ready to get down to business.

Be ready for the interviewer's questions. The same questions come up again   6 and again in many job interviews. *You should plan ahead for all these questions!* Think carefully about each question, outline your answer, and memorize each out-line. Then practice reciting the answers to yourself. Only in this way are you going to be prepared. Here are common questions, what they really mean, and how to answer them:

- *"Tell me about yourself."* This question is raised to see how organized you are. The *wrong* way to answer it is to launch into a wandering, disjointed response or—worse yet—to demand defensively, "What do you want to know?" or "What do you mean?" When this question comes up, you should be prepared to give a brief summary of your life and work experience— where you grew up, where your family lives now, where you went to school, what jobs you've had, and how you happen to be here now looking for the challenge of a new job.

- *"What are your strengths and weaknesses?"* In talking about your strong points, mention traits that will serve you well in this particular job. If you are well organized, a creative problem-solver, a good team member, or a quick learner, be ready to describe specific ways those strengths have served you in the past. Don't make the mistake of saying, "I don't have any real weaknesses." You'll come across as more believable if you admit a flaw—but make it one that an employer might actually like. For instance, admit that you are a workaholic or a perfectionist.

- *"Why should we hire you?"* Remember that it is up to *you* to convince the interviewer that you're the man or woman for this job. If you just sit there and hope that the interviewer will magically discern your good qualities, you are likely to be disappointed. Don't be afraid to sell yourself. Tell the recruiter that from your research you have learned that the interviewer's company is one you would like to work for, and that you believe the company's needs and your skills are a great match.

- *"Why did you leave your last job?"* This may seem like a great opportunity to cry on the interviewer's shoulder about what a jerk your last boss was or how unappreciated you were. It is not. The experts agree: never bad-mouth *anyone* when you are asked this question. Say that you left in order to seek greater responsibilities or challenges. Be positive, not negative. No matter how justified you may feel about hating your last job or boss, if you give voice to those feelings in an interview, you're going to make the interviewer suspect that you're a whiner and hard to work with.

- *"Do you have any questions?"* This is the time to stress one last time how interested you are in this particular job. Ask a question or two about specific aspects of the job, pointing out again how well your talents and the company's needs are matched. Even if you're dying to know how much the job pays and how much vacation you get, don't ask. There will be time enough to cover those questions after you've been offered the job. Today, your task is to demonstrate what a good employee you would be.

Send a thank-you note. Once you've gotten past the interview, there is one 7 more chance for you to make a fine impression. As soon as you can—certainly no more than one or two days after the interview—write a note of thanks to your interviewer. In it, briefly remind him or her of when you came in and what job you applied for. As well as thanking the interviewer for seeing you, reaffirm your interest in the job and mention again why you think you are the best candidate for it. Make the note courteous, businesslike, and brief—just a paragraph or two. If the interviewer is wavering between several equally qualified candidates, such a note could tip the scales in your favor.

No amount of preparation is going to make interviewing for a job your favorite 8 activity. But if you go in well-prepared and with a positive attitude, your potential employer can't help thinking highly of you. And the day will come when you are the one who wins the job.

ABOUT UNITY

1. Either of two sentences in "How to Do Well on a Job Interview" might serve as the thesis. Write the opening words of either of these sentences:

   _____

   _____

   _____

2. Which statement would make the best topic sentence for paragraph 4?
   a. Beauty is only skin-deep.
   b. Interviewers care only about how applicants dress.
   c. Professional job recruiters meet many applicants for a single job.
   d. You should present yourself as a winner because first impressions count a lot.

3. Write an appropriate topic sentence for the list item that talks about strengths and weaknesses in paragraph 6.

   _____

   _____

ABOUT SUPPORT

4. What does the author mean by "dress appropriately" in paragraph 5?

   _____

5. According to Davis, what is the best reason for sending a thank-you note?

   _____

   _____

ABOUT COHERENCE

6. In paragraph 1, what three transitional words or phrases are used to begin sentences as the author describes the process of interviewing?

   _____   _____   _____

7. The main method of organization of paragraph 1 is
   a. time order.
   b. emphatic order.

8. Find three change-of-direction signals in the listed items following paragraph 5. (*Write them here.*)

   _____   _____   _____

ABOUT THE INTRODUCTION AND CONCLUSION

9. Which statement best describes the introductory paragraph of "How to Do Well on a Job Interview"?

   a. It begins with a broad, general statement about job interviews and narrows it down to the thesis statement.

   b. It describes a typical job interview and its aftermath.

   c. It explains the importance of doing well on a job interview.

   d. It ends with a quotation about the importance of preparing for an interview.

10. What method for writing conclusions explained in Chapter 4 does Davis use?

Writing an Essay with Emphasis on Process

WRITING ASSIGNMENT 1

Everyone is an expert at something. Using your personal experiences and insights, write an essay with an emphasis on process. If you are a parent, you might write about how you taught your children to read. If you work as a sales representative, you might write about how monthly sales quotas are met. If you are a recovering addict, you might write about how the twelve-step recovery process works. If you know how to cook well, you could write about what it takes to make one of your favorite dishes. As a college student, you might write about how the registration process works at your school. Each of these topics will require you to incorporate several modes of writing, such as those discussed in Chapter 8, "Description," and Chapter 9, "Narration."

PREWRITING

a. Choose a prewriting technique that works for you, and for ten minutes use that technique to generate ideas on the topic you have tentatively chosen. Don't worry about spelling, grammar, organization, or anything other than getting your thoughts down on the page. If ideas are still flowing at the end of ten minutes, keep on writing. Once you have finished getting your thoughts down, you should have a base of raw material that you can draw on in the next phase of your work. Judging from what you have produced, do you think you have enough material to support your essay? If so, keep following the steps below. If not, choose another topic and spend about ten minutes generating ideas to see if this other topic might be a better choice.

b. Develop a single clear sentence that will serve as your thesis. Your thesis should demonstrate why it is important that your readers know about this process.

c. Make a list of the steps you are describing.

d. Number your items in time order. Strike out items that do not fit in the list; add others as they occur to you.

e. After making the list, decide how the items can be grouped into a minimum of three steps. With a topic like "How to Raise Good Children," you might divide the process into (1) infancy and toddlerhood; (2) elementary years; and (3) teen years.

f. Use your list as a guide to write the first rough draft of your paper. Do not expect to finish your paper in one draft. You should be ready to write a series of drafts as you work toward the goals of unity, support, and coherence.

REVISING

After you have completed the first draft of the paper, set it aside for a while if you can. Then read the paper out loud to a friend or classmate whose judgment you respect. Keep the following points in mind as you hear your own words, and ask your friend to respond to them as well:

Process Checklist: THE FOUR BASES

ABOUT *UNITY*

✔ Does my essay have a clearly stated thesis, including a dominant impression?

✔ Is there any irrelevant material that should be eliminated or rewritten?

✔ Does my essay describe the steps in a clear, logical way?

ABOUT *SUPPORT*

✔ Does the essay describe the necessary steps so that a reader could perform the task described, or is essential information missing?

ABOUT *COHERENCE*

✔ Have I organized my essay in a consistent manner that is appropriate to my subject?

✔ Have I used transition words to help readers follow my train of thought?

✔ Do I have a concluding paragraph that provides a summary, a final thought, or both?

ABOUT *SENTENCE SKILLS*

✔ Have I used a consistent point of view throughout my essay?

✔ Have I used specific rather than general words?

✔ Have I avoided wordiness and used concise wording?

✔ Are my sentences varied?

✔ Have I proofread my essay for spelling and other sentence skills, as listed on the inside back cover of the book?

As you revise your essay through one or more additional drafts, continue to refer to this list until you can answer "yes" to each question.

WRITING ASSIGNMENT 2

Write an essay in which you explain how something has happened or happens rather than how to do something. Focus on a limited subject. The topic you choose may be assigned by your instructor, or it may require your instructor's approval. For example, instead of trying to discuss the workings of the U.S. government, explain the process by which a bill presented in Congress eventually becomes law. Instead of explaining how World War II happened, focus on the events that led to America's involvement. You may want to check Chapter 12, "Cause and Effect," and Chapter 22, "Writing a Research Paper," for additional ways to support your thesis.

Here are other topics you might choose to explain:

- the process for conducting clinical trials of a new prescription drug
- how a virus like influenza can become a pandemic
- how a student theater production happens
- how a company like Apple became so profitable

PREWRITING

a. Select a topic you know a lot about. However, if necessary, gather more detail by reading about your topic in the library or on the Internet. Before researching, use freewriting, listing, or some other information-gathering technique to write down all the information and ideas in your head. This will help you remember what information should be cited and what information is your personal knowledge.

b. If you do need to do research, remember to check Chapter 22, "Writing a Research Paper," to properly cite your information and avoid plagiarism.

c. Look over your notes and make a list of steps involved in the process.

d. Organize your list to be chronological and orderly.

e. You have just prepared the beginnings of a scratch outline. Finish the outline by filling in information under each main point. Then use this outline as a guide as you write the first drafts of your paper.

REVISING

As you read through your first draft and subsequent drafts, ask yourself the following questions:

Process Checklist: THE FOUR BASES

ABOUT UNITY

✔ Have I introduced my essay with either a statement of the importance of the process or my opinion of the process?

ABOUT SUPPORT

✔ Have I provided a clear step-by-step description of the process?

ABOUT COHERENCE

✔ Have I used transitions to help readers follow my train of thought?

✔ Do I have a concluding paragraph that provides a summary, a final thought, or both?

ABOUT SENTENCE SKILLS

✔ Have I used a consistent point of view throughout my essay?

✔ Have I used specific rather than general words?

✔ Have I avoided wordiness and used concise wording?

✔ Are my sentences varied?

✔ Have I checked for spelling and other sentence skills, as listed on the inside back cover of the book?

As you revise your essay through one or more additional drafts, continue to refer to this checklist until you can answer "yes" to each question.

Work

WRITING ASSIGNMENT 3

Many jobs require people to provide reports that make recommendations. In this essay, you will write a report that analyzes and explains a process at your job and proposes a better, more effective process. For example, you could analyze the hiring process and suggest ways to make it more efficient, or you could analyze the process a restaurant customer's order goes through and propose ways to get the food to the customer more quickly. You may want to check Chapter 16, "Argument," to help you create a persuasive tone to your essay.

Cause and/or Effect

This chapter will explain and illustrate how to

- develop an essay with emphasis on cause and/or effect

- write an essay with emphasis on cause and/or effect

- revise an essay with emphasis on cause and/or effect

In addition, you will read and consider

- two student essays that emphasize cause and/or effect

- one professional essay that emphasizes cause and/or effect

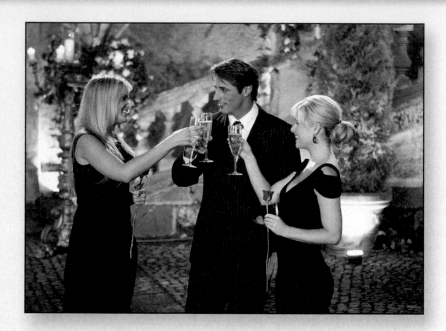

Write an essay in which you discuss the causes or effects of our society's fascination with reality TV. An essay on the causes would discuss why Americans are so intrigued with reality television shows. An essay on the effects would show how this fascination with reality TV has affected American society.

Why did Gail decide to move out of her parents' house? What made you quit a well-paying job? Why are horror movies so popular? Why has Ben acted so depressed lately? Why did our team fail to make the league play-offs?

Every day we ask questions like these and look for answers. We realize that many actions do not occur without causes, and we realize also that a given action can have a series of effects—good or bad. By examining the causes or effects of an action, we seek to understand and explain things that happen in our lives.

You will be asked in this chapter to do some detective work by examining the cause of something or the effects of something. First read the student essays and the professional essay that follow and work through the questions that accompany the essays. All three essays support their thesis statements by explaining a series of causes or a series of effects.

Student Essays to Consider

The Joys of an Old Car

1   Some of my friends can't believe that my car still runs. Others laugh when they see it parked outside the house and ask if it's an antique. But they aren't being fair to my twenty-year-old Toyota Corolla. In fact, my "antique" has opened my eyes to the rewards of owning an old car.

2   One obvious reward of owning my old Toyota is economy. Twenty years ago, when my husband and I were newly married and nearly broke, we bought the car—a shiny red year-old leftover—for a mere $4,200. Today it would cost four times as much. We save money on insurance, since it's no longer worthwhile for us to have collision coverage. Old age has even been kind to the Toyota's engine, which has required only three major repairs in the last several years. And it still delivers twenty-eight miles per gallon in the city and forty-one on the highway—not bad for a senior citizen.

3   I've heard that when a Toyota passes the twenty-thousand-mile mark with no problems, it will probably go on forever. I wouldn't disagree. Our Toyota breezed past that mark many years ago. Since then, I've been able to count on it to sputter to life and make its way down the driveway on the coldest, snowiest mornings. When my boss got stuck with his brand-new BMW in the worst snowstorm of the year, I sauntered into work on time. The single time my Toyota didn't start, unfortunately, was the day I had a final exam. The Toyota may have the body of an old car, but beneath its elderly hood hums the engine of a teenager.

4   Last of all, having the same car for many years offers the advantage of familiarity. When I open the door and slide into the driver's seat, the soft vinyl surrounds me like a well-worn glove. I know to the millimeter exactly how much room I have when I turn a corner or back into a curbside parking space. When my gas gauge points to "empty," I know that 1.3 gallons are still in reserve, and I can plan accordingly. The front wheels invariably begin to shake when I go more than fifty-five miles an hour, reminding me that I am exceeding the speed limit. With the Toyota, the only surprises I face come from other drivers.

5   I prize my twenty-year-old Toyota's economy and dependability, and most of all, its familiarity. It is faded, predictable, and comfortable, like a well-worn pair of jeans. And, like a well-worn pair of jeans, it will be difficult to throw away.

We Have Nothing to Fear

During the Great Depression, President Roosevelt claimed, "We have   1
nothing to fear but fear itself." He wanted to inspire citizens as a way
to spur the economy. In his Nobel Prize acceptance speech of 1949,
William Faulkner, the great American novelist, said, "The basest of
all things is to be afraid." Uttered more than a half century ago, both
these ideas still have relevance. Some young people make important
life decisions based on deep-seated anxieties. They fear that they won't
be accepted by others, that they won't find a mate, or that they just
aren't living life to the fullest. As a result, they pervert their identities,
becoming adults they don't want to become and living lives they
never intended.

A logical question is why so many people spend money—often money   2
they don't have—on costly toys they don't need. Deep in the pits of their
stomachs is the gnawing fear that, without such toys, their friends will
abandon them and they will have to sit home weekends watching sitcom
reruns. They are frightened they won't fit in, so frightened, in fact, that they
have become blind to the true meaning of friendship. They have forgotten
that, to those of character, possessions and image are far less important than
integrity, honesty, and compassion. Such people are worth knowing, and
they are everywhere. To find them, all people need to do is to show a little
character themselves.

Some individuals—both men and women—fear they will never be able   3
to attract and keep a lifelong partner. Therefore, they make gargantuan efforts
to re-create themselves in the Hollywood image. For example, they follow
ludicrous diets, exercise for hours each day, and drink expensive commercial
concoctions to curb their appetites and lose weight. Some even become
anorexic. Others, looking ahead to their more mature years, plan to get
collagen injections, hair plugs, and even breast implants. If people simply
trusted in the goodness of someone who might love them for who they are
and not for the smoothness of their skins or the fullness of their hair, their lives
could be so much easier.

However, the fear that causes the greatest damage to the human spirit   4
is the one that makes people question the value and fullness of their own
lives. Too many—young and old alike, if the truth be told—are afraid that
they might miss out on "the good life," which, the media tells us, is part of
a life fulfilled. Influenced by the glitz of Hollywood and Madison Avenue,
people equate happiness with owning the best of everything. So, they
take a second and even a third job to afford the sexiest car, the biggest
house, or the largest television set. This is the worst perversion of all, for
it turns human beings into slaves. They don't own the car, the house, the
television set; they are owned by the possessions. It cannot be called

continued

anything but slavery. The irony is, of course, that, in seeking the good life, people have lost the good life. Instead of having the luxury to relax at home, talk to family, enjoy dinner, go for long walks, or watch the sun set, too many men and women are rushing off to an evening of more work to pay off the bills.

Cowering to silly fears, getting and taking, or changing to fit in with the   5 ridiculous images created by a plastic society is harmful, and it is blurring American's moral vision. People need to realize once more that the true source of happiness, the measure of a life fulfilled, is the ability to see eternal beauty in the night sky, to become inspired by gently falling snow, and to make those ever important human connections.

ABOUT UNITY

1. Which supporting paragraph in "The Joys of an Old Car" lacks a topic sentence?
   a. 2
   b. 3
   c. 4

2. Which sentence in paragraph 3 of "The Joys of an Old Car" should be omitted in the interest of paragraph unity? (*Write the opening words.*)

   _____

3. Rewrite the thesis statement of "The Joys of an Old Car" to include a plan of development.

   _____

   _____

ABOUT SUPPORT

4. In paragraph 3 of "We Have Nothing to Fear," how does the author support the idea that some people are afraid they wont't be able to attract and keep lifelong partners?

   _____

   _____

   _____

5. After which sentence in paragraph 2 of "We Have Nothing to Fear" is more detail needed? (*Write the first words here.*)

_____

6. In "The Joys of an Old Car," what examples support the topic sentence in paragraph 2?

_____

_____

_____

_____

ABOUT COHERENCE

7. Which sentence in "We Have Nothing to Fear" serves as a linking sentence between paragraphs? (*Write the first words.*)

_____

8. Paragraph 3 of "We Have Nothing to Fear" contains two transitional words or phrases. List those words or phrases.

_____   _____

9. What are the two transition words or phrases in "The Joys of an Old Car" that signal two major points of support for the thesis?

_____   _____

ABOUT THE INTRODUCTION AND CONCLUSION

10. Which method for concluding essays explained in Chapter 4 does "The Joys of an Old Car" use?
    a. summary and final thought
    b. thought-provoking question
    c. recommendation

Developing an Essay with Emphasis on Cause and/or Effect

Considering Purpose and Audience

The primary purpose of an essay that emphasizes cause and/or effect is to support your main point by using examples that explain (1) the causes of a particular event or situation; (2) the effects of an event or a situation; or, more rarely (3) a combination of both.

The type of essay you write depends on your topic and main point. If you want to tell readers the impact a person had on your life, your essay would focus on *effects*. If you want to explain why you moved out of your family home, it would focus on *causes*.

Essays that emphasize cause and/or effect are like essays that emphasize process. However, while process explains how something happens, cause and/or effect discusses *the reasons for or results of* an event or situation. Exams in science, history, economics, and other courses include questions that demand the explanation of causes, effects, or both. For example, you might be asked to explain the economic causes of the Russian Revolution or the atmospheric effects of cutting down trees in the rain forest.

At first, this can seem simple. However, analyzing causes and effects is often complicated. For example, in the essay, "We Have Nothing to Fear," the writer claims that many young people desire to possess the same type of clothing or electronic gadgets that their friends have. This stems from an *ultimate* or primary cause: the fear of being alone. A more *proximate* cause (one that is closer to the effect) is the desire to be popular, part of a group. In short, the writer has not simply discussed a cause but has explained a causal chain: (1) fear of being alone (ultimate cause); (2) desire to be popular (proximate cause); (3) need to have what others have (effect). Of course, the author could have extended the chain to explain the cause behind the fear of being alone: low self-esteem, difficult family life, or peer pressure, for example.

Analyzing effects can also be tricky because one cause may lead to multiple effects. In addition, one cause may yield a long-term effect as well as an immediate effect. Take the case of a young construction worker who decided to go back to college to study architecture five years after having graduated from high school. The immediate effects of his decision include (1) having to budget his money more carefully because he had to quit his job; (2) having less time to socialize with friends; and (3) getting a lot less physical exercise. However, there are several long-term effects as well: (1) securing a high-paying, white-collar position after graduation; (2) making new friends at college and at his new job; and (3) developing new tastes in music and film as a result of taking college humanities courses.

Depending on your topic and purpose, you can decide whether to focus on causes or effects. If you want to balance your paper, you can discuss both. Consider each of the following scenarios and decide whether it requires discussing causes, effects, or both.

1. A young couple decides to buy a two-family house and rent out the top floor to tenants.

2. A new television reality show becomes an instant sensation, and the "actors" achieve instant fame.

3. Some patients of a local doctor demand she write them prescriptions for drugs when they know they can cure themselves by changing their diets and lifestyles.

Students writing on the first item might focus on effects; those writing on the second might discuss causes. The third item might be approached by writing about both.

Whichever approach you choose, remember that you can't discuss effects without at least mentioning causes, and vice versa. While discussing the problems that the young couple had with their tenants (effects of their decision to rent out the second floor), you might also explain their reason for becoming landlords in the first place: to earn rent money that would help them meet their mortgage payments.

As with all essays, pick a topic that appeals to your readers. An essay on the negative effects of steroids on professional athletes may interest sports fans; it might not appeal to people who dislike sports. In addition, make your main point clear so that your audience can follow the cause-and-effect relationship. You might even announce specific causes or effects by signaling them to readers: "One effect steroid use has on athletes is to . . ."

Development through Prewriting

The best essays are often those written about a topic that the author genuinely cares about. When Janine, the author of "The Joys of an Old Car," was assigned an essay with emphasis on cause and/or effect, she welcomed the assignment. She explains, "My husband and I believe in enjoying what we have and living simply, rather than 'keeping up with the Joneses.' Our beat-up old car is an example of that way of life. People often say to me, 'Surely you could buy a nicer car!' I enjoy explaining to them why we keep our old 'clunker.' So when I heard 'essay that emphasizes cause and/or effect,' I immediately thought of the car as a topic. Writing this essay was just an extension of a conversation I've had many times."

Although Janine had often praised the virtues of her old car to friends, she wasn't sure how to divide what she had to say into three main points. To get started, she made a list of all the good things about her car. Here is what she wrote:

Starts reliably

Has needed few major repairs

Reminder of Bill's and my first days of marriage

Gets good gas mileage

Don't need to worry about scratches and scrapes

continued

I know exactly how much room I need to turn and park

Saves money on insurance

I'm very comfortable in it

No car payments

Cold weather doesn't seem to bother it

Don't worry about its being stolen

Uses regular gas

Can haul anything in it—dog, plants—and not worry about dirt

Know all its little tics and shimmies and don't worry about them

When Janine reviewed her list, she saw that the items fell into three major categories. They were (1) the car's economy; (2) its familiarity; and (3) its dependability. She went back and noted which category each of the items best fit. Then she crossed out those items that didn't seem to belong in any of the categories.

3   *Starts reliably*

1   *Has needed few major repairs*

     ~~*Reminder of Bill's and my first days of marriage*~~

1   *Gets good gas mileage*

     ~~*Don't need to worry about scratches and scrapes*~~

2   *I know exactly how much room I need to turn and park*

1   *Saves money on insurance*

2   *I'm very comfortable in it*

1   *No car payments*

3   *Cold weather doesn't seem to bother it*

     ~~*Don't worry about its being stolen*~~

continued

> *1   Uses regular gas*
>
> ~~*Can haul anything in it — dog, plants — and not worry about dirt*~~
>
> *2   Know all its little tics and shimmies and don't worry about them*

Now Janine had three main points and several items to support each point. She produced this as a first draft:

First Draft

The Joys of an Old Car

When people see my beat-up old car, they sometimes laugh at it. But I tell them that owning a twenty-year-old Toyota has its good points.

One obvious reward is economy. My husband and I bought the car when we were newly married. We paid $4,200 for it. That seemed like a lot of money then, but today we'd spend four times that much for a similar car. We also save money on insurance. In the twenty years we've had it, the Toyota has needed only a few major repairs. It even gets good gas mileage.

I like the familiar feel of the car. I'm so used to it that driving anything else feels very strange. When I visited my sister recently, I drove her new Prius to the grocery store. Everything was so unfamiliar! I couldn't even figure out how to turn on the radio. I was relieved to get back to my own car.

Finally, my car is very dependable. No matter how cold and snowy it is, I know the Toyota will start quickly and get me where I need to go. Unfortunately, one day it didn't start, and naturally that day I had a final exam. But otherwise it just keeps on going and going.

My Toyota reminds me of a favorite piece of clothing that you wear forever and can't bear to throw away.

Development through Revising

Janine traded first drafts with a classmate, Sharon, and each critiqued the other's work before it was revised. Here is Janine's first draft again, with Sharon's comments in the margins.

The Joys of an Old Car

When people see my beat-up old car, they sometimes laugh at it. But I tell them that owning a twenty-year-old Toyota has its good points.

One obvious reward is economy. My husband and I bought the car when we were newly married. We paid $4,200 for it. That seemed like a lot of money then, but today we'd spend four times that much for a similar car. We also save money on insurance. In the twenty years we've had it, the Toyota has needed only a few major repairs. It even gets good gas mileage.

I like the familiar feel of the car. I'm so used to it that driving anything else feels very strange. When I visited my sister recently, I drove her new Prius to the grocery store. Everything was so unfamiliar! I couldn't even figure out how to turn on the radio. I was relieved to get back to my own car.

Finally, my car is very dependable. No matter how cold and snowy it is, I know the Toyota will start quickly and get me where I need to go. Unfortunately, one day it didn't start, and naturally that day I had a final exam. But otherwise it just keeps on going and going.

My Toyota reminds me of a favorite piece of clothing that you wear forever and can't bear to throw away.

Reader's Comments

How? Is the insurance less expensive just because the car is old?

Here would be a good place for a specific detail—how good is the mileage?

This topic sentence doesn't tie in with the others—shouldn't it say "Second," or "Another reason I like the car...."?

This is too much about your sister's car and not enough about yours.

This is a good comparison. But draw it out more—how is the car like comfortable old clothes?

Making use of Sharon's comments, Janine wrote the final version of "The Joys of an Old Car" that appears on page 261.

A Professional Essay to Consider

Read the following professional essay. Then answer the questions and read the comments that follow.

Taming the Anger Monster

by Anne Davidson

Laura Houser remembers the day with embarrassment.   1

"My mother was visiting from Illinois," she says. "We'd gone out to lunch and 2 done some shopping. On our way home, we stopped at an intersection. When the light changed, the guy ahead of us was looking at a map or something and didn't move right away. I leaned on my horn and automatically yelled—well, what I generally yell at people who make me wait. I didn't even think about what I was doing. One moment I was talking and laughing with my mother, and the next I was shouting curses at a stranger. Mom's jaw just dropped. She said, 'Well, I guess *you've* been living in the city too long.' That's when I realized that my anger was out of control."

Laura has plenty of company. Here are a few examples plucked from the headlines of recent newspapers: 3

- Amtrak's Washington–New York train: When a woman begins to use her cell phone in a designated "quiet car," her seatmate grabs the phone and smashes it against the wall.

- Reading, Mass.: Arguing over rough play at their ten-year-old sons' hockey practice, two fathers begin throwing punches. One of the dads beats the other to death.

- Westport, Conn.: Two supermarket shoppers get into a fistfight over who should be first in a just-opened checkout line.

Reading these stories and countless others like them which happen daily, it's hard to escape the conclusion that we are one angry society. An entire vocabulary has grown up to describe situations of out-of-control fury: road rage, sideline rage, computer rage, biker rage, air rage. Bookstore shelves are filled with authors' advice on how to deal with our anger. Court-ordered anger management classes have become commonplace, and anger-management workshops are advertised in local newspapers.

Human beings have always experienced anger, of course. But in earlier, more 4 civil decades, public displays of anger were unusual to the point of being aberrant. Today, however, whether in petty or deadly forms, episodes of unrepressed rage have become part of our daily landscape.

What has happened to us? Are we that much angrier than we used to be? Have 5 we lost all inhibitions about expressing our anger? Are we, as a society, literally losing our ability to control our tempers?

Why Are We So Angry?

According to Sybil Evans, a conflict-resolution expert in New York City, there are three 6 components to blame for our societal bad behavior: time, technology and tension.

What's eating up our time? To begin with, Americans work longer hours and 7 are rewarded with less vacation time than people in any other industrial society. Over an average year, for example, most British employees work 250 hours less than most Americans; most Germans work a full 500 hours less. And most Europeans are given four to six weeks vacation every year, compared to the average

American's two weeks. To make matters worse, many Americans face long stressful commutes at the beginning and end of each long workday.

Once we Americans finally get home from work, our busy day is rarely done. **8** We are involved in community activities; our children participate in sports, school programs, and extracurricular activities; and our houses, yards, and cars cry out for maintenance. To make matters worse, we are reluctant to use the little bit of leisure time we do have to catch up on our sleep. Compared with Americans of the nineteenth and early twentieth centuries, most of us are chronically sleep deprived. While our ancestors typically slept nine-and-a-half hours a night, many of us feel lucky to get seven. We're critical of "lazy" people who sleep longer, and we associate naps with toddlerhood. (In doing so, we ignore the example of successful people including Winston Churchill, Albert Einstein, and Napoleon, all of whom were devoted to their afternoon naps.)

The bottom line: we are time-challenged and just plain tired—and tired people **9** are cranky people. We're ready to blow—to snap at the slow-moving cashier, to tap the bumper of the slowpoke ahead of us, or to do something far worse.

Technology is also to blame for the bad behavior so widespread in culture. **10** Amazing gadgets were supposed to make our lives easier—but have they? Sure, technology has its positive aspects. It is a blessing, for instance, to have a cell phone on hand when your car breaks down far from home or to be able to "instant message" a friend on the other side of the globe. But the downsides are many. Cell phones, pagers, fax machines, handheld computers, and the like have robbed many of us of what was once valuable downtime. Now we're *always* available to take that urgent call or act on that last-minute demand. Then there is the endless pressure of feeling we need to keep up with our gadgets' latest technological developments. For example, it's not sufficient to use your cell phone for phone calls. Now you must learn to use the phone for text-messaging and downloading games. It's not enough to take still photos with your digital camera. You should know how to shoot ultra high-speed fast-action clips. It's not enough to have an enviable CD collection. You should be downloading new songs in MP3 format. The computers in your house should be connected by a wireless router, and online via high-speed DSL service. In other words, if it's been more than ten minutes since you've updated your technology, you're probably behind.

In fact, you're not only behind; you're a stupid loser. At least, that's how most **11** of us end up feeling as we're confronted with more and more unexpected technologies: the do-it-yourself checkout at the supermarket, the telephone "help center" that offers a recorded series of messages, but no human help. And feeling like losers makes us frustrated and, you guessed it, angry. "It's not any one thing but lots of little things that make people feel like they don't have control of their lives," says Jane Middleton-Moz, an author and therapist. "A sense of helplessness is what triggers rage. It's why people end up kicking ATM machines."

Her example is not far-fetched. According to a survey of computer users 12 in Great Britain, a quarter of those under age 25 admitted to having kicked or punched their computers on at least one occasion. Others confessed to yanking out cables in a rage, forcing the computer to crash. On this side of the Atlantic, a Wisconsin man, after repeated attempts to get his daughter's malfunctioning computer repaired, took it to the store where he had bought it, placed it in the foyer, and attacked it with a sledgehammer. Arrested and awaiting a court appearance, he told local reporters, "It feels good, in a way." He had put into action a fantasy many of us have had—that of taking out our feelings of rage on the machines that so frustrate us.

Tension, the third major culprit behind our epidemic of anger, is intimately con- 13 nected with our lack of time and the pressures of technology. Merely our chronic exhaustion and our frustration in the face of a bewildering array of technologies would be enough to cause our stress levels to skyrocket, but we are dealing with much more. Our tension is often fueled by a reserve of anger that might be the result of a critical boss, marital discord, or (something that many of today's men and women experience, if few will admit it) a general sense of being stupid and inadequate in the face of the demands of modern life. And along with the challenges of everyday life, we now live with a widespread fear of such horrors as terrorist acts, global warming, and antibiotic-resistant diseases. Our sense of dread may be out of proportion to actual threats because of technology's ability to so constantly bombard us with worrisome information. Twenty-four hours a day news stations bring a stream of horror into our living rooms. As we work on our computers, headlines and graphic images are never more than a mouseclick away.

The Result of Our Anger

Add it all together—our feeling of never having enough time; the chronic aggrava- 14 tion caused by technology; and our endless, diffuse sense of stress—and we become time bombs waiting to explode. Our angry outbursts may be briefly satisfying, but afterwards we are left feeling—well, like jerks. Worse, flying off the handle is a self-perpetuating behavior. Brad Bushman, a psychology professor at Iowa State University, says, "Catharsis is worse than useless." Bushman's research has shown that when people vent their anger, they actually become more, not less, aggressive. "Many people think of anger as the psychological equivalent of the steam in a pressure cooker. It has to be released, or it will explode. That's not true. The people who react by hitting, kicking, screaming, and swearing just feel more angry."

Furthermore, the unharnessed venting of anger may actually do us physical 15 harm. The vigorous expression of anger pumps adrenaline into our system and raises our blood pressure, setting the stage for heart attack and strokes. Frequently angry people have even been shown to have higher cholesterol levels than even-tempered individuals.

How to Deal with Our Anger

Unfortunately, the culprits behind much of our anger—lack of time, frustrating 16
technology, and mega-levels of stress—are not likely to resolve themselves anytime soon. So what are we to do with the anger that arises as a result?

According to Carol Tavris, author of *Anger: The Misunderstood Emotion,* the 17
keys to dealing with anger are common sense and patience. She points out that
almost no situation is improved by an angry outburst. A traffic jam, a frozen computer, or a misplaced set of car keys is annoying. To act upon the angry feelings
those situations provoke, however, is an exercise in futility. Shouting, fuming, or
leaning on the car horn won't make traffic begin to flow, the screen unlock, or the
keys materialize.

Patience, on the other hand, is a highly practical virtue. People who take the 18
time to cool down before responding to an anger-producing situation are far less
likely to say or do something they will regret later. "It is as true of the body as of
arrows," Tavris says, "that what goes up must come down. Any emotional arousal
will simmer down if you just wait long enough." When you are stuck in traffic, in
other words, turn on some soothing music, breathe deeply, and count to ten—or
thirty or forty, if need be.

Anger-management therapist Doris Wild Helmering agrees. "Like any feeling, 19
anger lasts only about three seconds," she says. "What keeps it going is your own
negative thinking." As long as you focus on the idiot who cut you off on the ex-
pressway, you'll stay angry. But if you let the incident go, your anger will go with
it. "Once you come to understand that you're driving your own anger with your
thoughts," adds Helmering, "you can stop it."

Experts who have studied anger also encourage people to cultivate activities 20
that effectively vent their anger. For some people, it's reading the newspaper or
watching TV, while others need more active outlets, such as using a treadmill,
taking a walk, hitting golf balls, or working out with a punching bag. People who
succeed in calming their anger can also enjoy the satisfaction of having dealt posi-
tively with their frustrations.

For Laura Houser, the episode in the car with her mother was a wake-up call. 21
"I saw myself through her eyes," she said, "and I realized I had become a chronically angry, impatient jerk. My response to stressful situations had become habit-
ual—I automatically flew off the handle. Once I saw what I was doing, it really
wasn't that hard to develop different habits. I simply decided I was going to treat
other people the way I would want to be treated." The changes in Laura's life
haven't benefited only her former victims. "I'm a calmer, happier person now,"
she reports. "I don't lie in bed at night fuming over stupid things other people
have done and my own enraged responses." Laura has discovered the satisfaction
of having a sense of control over her own behavior—which ultimately is all any
of us can control.

ABOUT UNITY

1. Which of the following statements best represents the implied thesis of "Taming the Anger Monster"?

    a. People today have lost their ability to control their anger and to behave in a civil fashion.

    b. Anger would last only a few seconds if we didn't keep it going with negative thinking.

    c. While technology has its positive aspects, it has made us constantly available to others and frustrates us with the need to master its endless new developments.

    d. Our out-of-control anger has understandable causes, but common sense and patience are more satisfying than outbursts of rage.

2. Write a topic sentence that covers what is discussed in paragraphs 3 and 4.

    _____

3. What sentence in paragraph 17 serves as the topic sentence for paragraphs 16 through 18? (*Write the first words.*)

    _____

    _____

ABOUT SUPPORT

4. The essay is about one main effect and three possible causes. What is the one main effect? What are the three causes?

    Effect: _____

    Three causes: _____

5. Trace the line of causation in paragraph 11. What is the ultimate cause, the proximate cause, and the effect?

    Ultimate cause: _____

    Proximate cause: _____

    Effect: _____

ABOUT COHERENCE

6. What is the best description of the organization of this essay?

    a. Introduction, Thesis, Three Supporting Parts, Conclusion

    b. Introduction, Thesis, Four Supporting Parts, Conclusion

    c. Introduction, Thesis, Five Supporting Parts

    d. Thesis, Six Supporting Parts, Conclusion

7. As shown by the outline below, "Taming the Anger Monster" bears a general resemblance to the traditional one-three-one essay model. Fill in the missing paragraph numbers.

Introduction: Paragraphs: _____

Supporting Point 1: Paragraph(s) _____

Supporting Point 2: Paragraph(s) _____

Supporting Point 3: Paragraph(s) _____

Supporting Point 4: Paragraphs   _____

Supporting Point 5: Paragraphs   _____

Conclusion: Paragraph: _____

8. What are the three addition signals used to introduce the three causes of anger?

_____ _____ _____

ABOUT THE INTRODUCTION AND CONCLUSION

9. What method best describes the introduction to "Taming the Anger Monster"?

a. quotation

b. broad, general statement narrowing to thesis

c. idea that is the opposite of the one to be developed

d. anecdote and questions

10. What is the relationship between the essay's first paragraph and its concluding paragraph?

_____

_____

Writing an Essay with Emphasis on Cause and/or Effect

WRITING ASSIGNMENT 1

Are you as good a writer as you want to be? Write an essay analyzing the reasons you have become a good writer or explaining why you are not as good as you'd like to be. Begin by considering some factors that may have influenced your writing ability.

Your family background: Did you see people writing at home? Did your parents respect and value the ability to write?

Your school experience: Did you have good writing teachers? Did you have a history of failure or success with writing? Was writing fun, or was it a chore? Did your school emphasize writing?

Social influences: How did your school friends do at writing? What were your friends' attitudes toward writing? What feelings about writing did you pick up from TV or the movies?

You might want to organize your essay by describing the three greatest influences on your skill (or your lack of skill) as a writer. Show how each of these has contributed to the present state of your writing. You will want to check Chapter 16, "Argument," to help create a persuasive and effective essay.

PREWRITING

a. Choose a prewriting technique that works for you, and for ten minutes use that technique to generate ideas. Don't worry about spelling, grammar, organization, or anything other than getting your thoughts down on the page. If ideas are still flowing at the end of ten minutes, keep on writing. Once you have finished getting your thoughts down, you should have a base of raw material that you can draw on in the next phase of your work. Judging from what you have produced, do you think you have enough material to support your essay? If so, keep following the steps below. If not, plan to spend at least another ten minutes generating additional ideas.

b. Develop a single clear sentence that will serve as your thesis. Your thesis should demonstrate how you feel about your writing and why.

c. Decide whether you will support each of your main points with short examples or one extended example.

d. Write a first draft of an introduction that attracts the reader's interest, states your thesis, and presents a plan of development.

REVISING

After you have completed the first draft of the paper, set it aside for a while (if possible). Then read it aloud to a friend or classmate. As you listen to your words, you should both keep these questions in mind:

Cause and/or Effect Checklist: THE FOUR BASES

ABOUT *UNITY*

✔ Does the essay have a clearly stated thesis, including a dominant impression?

✔ Is there any irrelevant material that should be eliminated or rewritten?

ABOUT *SUPPORT*

✔ Have I backed up each main point with one extended example or several shorter examples?

✔ Do I have enough detailed support?

ABOUT *COHERENCE*

✔ Have I used transition words to help readers follow my train of thought?

✔ Do I have a concluding paragraph that provides a summary, a final thought, or both?

ABOUT *SENTENCE SKILLS*

✔ Have I used a consistent point of view throughout my essay?

✔ Have I used specific rather than general words?

✔ Have I avoided wordiness and used concise wording?

✔ Are my sentences varied?

✔ Have I checked for spelling and other sentence skills, as listed on the inside back cover of the book?

As you revise your essay through one or more additional drafts, continue to refer to this list until you can answer "yes" to each question.

WRITING ASSIGNMENT 2

Write an essay in which you advance an idea about a poem, story, play, film, literary essay, or novel. The work you choose may be assigned by your instructor or may require your instructor's approval. To develop your idea, use a series of two or more reasons and specific evidence for each reason. You may want to check Chapter 8, "Description," Chapter 18, "Writing a Summary," and Chapter 22, "Writing a Research Paper," to properly present and cite your information. A student model follows.

Paul's Suicide

Paul, the main character in Willa Cather's short story, "Paul's Case," is a   1
young man on a collision course with death. As Cather reveals Paul's story,
we learn about elements of Paul's personality that inevitably come together
and cause his suicide. Paul takes his own life as a result of his inability to
conform to his society, his passive nature, and his emotional isolation.

First of all, Paul cannot conform to the standards of his own society.   2
At school, Paul advertises his desire to be part of another, more glamorous
world by wearing fancy clothes that set him apart from the other students.
At home on Cordelia Street, Paul despises everything about his middle-class
neighborhood. He hates the houses "permeated by kitchen odors," the
"ugliness and commonness of his own home," and the respectable neighbors
sitting on their front stoops every Sunday, "their stomachs comfortably
protruding." Paul's father hopes that Paul will settle down and become like the
young man next door, a nearsighted clerk who works for a corporate steel
magnate. Paul, however, is repelled by the young man and all he represents.
It seems inevitable, then, that Paul will not be able to cope with the office job
his father obtains for him at the firm of Denny & Carson; and this inability to
conform will, in turn, lead to Paul's theft of $1,000.

Paul's suicide is also due, in part, to his passive nature. Throughout his   3
life, Paul has been an observer and an onlooker. Paul's only escape from the
prison of his daily life comes from his job as an usher at Pittsburgh's Carnegie
Hall; he lives for the moments when he can watch the actors, singers, and
musicians. However, Paul has no desire to be an actor or musician. As Cather
says, "What he wanted was to see, to be in the atmosphere, float on the
wave of it, to be carried out ... away from everything." Although Paul steals
the money and flees to New York, these uncharacteristic actions underscore

continued

the desperation he feels. Once at the Waldorf in New York, Paul is again content to observe the glamorous world he has craved for so long: "He had no especial desire to meet or to know any of these people; all he demanded was the right to look on and conjecture, to watch the pageant." During his brief stay in the city, Paul enjoys simply sitting in his luxurious rooms, glimpsing the show of city life through a magical curtain of snow. At the end, when the forces of ordinary life begin to close in again, Paul kills himself. But it is typical that he does not use the gun he has bought. Rather, more in keeping with his passive nature, Paul lets himself fall under the wheels of a train.

Finally, Paul ends his life because he is emotionally isolated. Throughout   **4**
the story, not one person makes any real contact with Paul. His teachers do not understand him and merely resent the attitude of false bravado that he uses as a defense. Paul's mother is dead; he cannot even remember her. Paul is completely alienated from his father, who obviously cares for him but who cannot feel close to this withdrawn, unhappy son. To Paul, his father is only the man waiting at the top of the stairs, "his hairy legs sticking out of his nightshirt," who will greet him with "inquiries and reproaches." When Paul meets a college boy in New York, they share a night on the town. But the "champagne friendship" ends with a "singularly cool" parting. Paul is not the kind of person who can let himself go or confide in one of his peers. For the most part, Paul's isolation is self-imposed. He has drifted so far into his fantasy life that people in the "real" world are treated like invaders. As he allows no one to enter his dream, there is no one Paul can turn to for understanding.

The combination of these personality factors—inability to conform, passivity,   **5**
and emotional isolation—makes Paul's tragic suicide inevitable. Before he jumps in front of the train, Paul scoops a hole in the snow and buries the carnation that he has been wearing in his buttonhole. Like a hothouse flower in the winter, Paul has a fragile nature that cannot survive in its hostile environment.

Writing for a Specific Purpose and Audience

WRITING ASSIGNMENT 3

OPTION 1
Assume that there has been a series of large cuts in your school district's budget. What might be the causes of the cuts? Where are the cuts mostly taking place? Spend some time thinking about possible causes. Then, as a principal or superintendent, write a letter to the families in your school district explaining the causes of the cuts and the decisions behind what areas were affected. Your purpose is to provide information to the families so they understand the resulting cuts.

OPTION 2

Alternatively, think about how severe school district budget cuts would have an impact on your family. Write a letter to the principal or superintendent explaining how you see the consequences of the budget cuts affecting your family and the community at large. Your purpose is to provide administrators with useful information that may be used to persuade the school board to rethink where the budget has been cut.

Comparison and/or Contrast

This chapter will explain and illustrate how to

- develop an essay with emphasis on comparison and/or contrast

- write an essay with emphasis on comparison and/or contrast

- revise an essay with emphasis on comparison and/or contrast

In addition, you will read and consider

- two student essays that emphasize comparison and/or contrast

- one professional essay that emphasizes comparison and/or contrast

Looking at the two photographs above, write an essay in which you compare or contrast lecture classes with smaller classes.

Comparison and contrast are two thought processes we go through constantly in everyday life. When we *compare* two things, we show how they are similar; when we *contrast* two things, we show how they are different. We may compare or contrast two brand-name products (for example, Pepsi and Coca-Cola), two television shows, two cars, two teachers, two jobs, two friends, or two possible solutions to a problem we are facing. The purpose of comparing or contrasting is to understand each of the two things more clearly and, at times, to make judgments about them.

You will be asked in this chapter to write an essay that emphasizes comparison and/or contrast. To prepare for this assignment, first read about the two methods of development you can use in writing your essay. Then read the student essays and the professional essay that follow and work through the questions that accompany the essays.

Methods of Development

An essay that emphasizes comparison and/or contrast calls for one of two types of development. Details can be presented *one side at a time* or *point by point*. Each format is illustrated below.

One Side at a Time

Look at the following supporting paragraph from "A Vote for McDonald's," one of the model essays that will follow.

> For one thing, going to the Chalet is more difficult than going to McDonald's. The Chalet has a jacket-and-tie rule, which means I have to dig a sport coat and tie out of the back of my closet, make sure they're semiclean, and try to steam out the wrinkles somehow. The Chalet also requires reservations. Since it is downtown, I have to leave an hour early to give myself time to find a parking space within six blocks of the restaurant. The Chalet cancels reservations if a party is more than ten minutes late. Going to McDonald's, on the other hand, is easy. I can feel comfortable wearing my jeans or warm-up suit. I don't have to do any advance planning. I can leave my house whenever I'm ready and pull into a doorside parking space within fifteen minutes.

The first half of this paragraph fully explains one side of the contrast (the difficulty of going to the Chalet). The second half of the paragraph deals entirely with the other side (the ease of going to McDonald's). When you use this method, be sure to follow the same order of points of contrast (or comparison) for each side. An outline of the paragraph shows how the points for each side are developed in a consistent sequence.

One Side at a Time   Outline

Thesis: Going to the Chalet is more difficult than going to McDonald's.

1. *Chalet*

    a. *Dress code*

    b. *Advance reservations*

    c. *Leave an hour early*

    d. *Find parking space*

2. *McDonald's*

    a. *Casual dress*

    b. *No reservations*

    c. *Leave only fifteen minutes ahead of time*

    d. *Plenty of free parking*

Point by Point

Now look at the supporting paragraph below, which is taken from another essay you will read, "The Lone Ranger and Tonto Fistfight with Smoke Signals":

The book and film both illustrate how desperately Victor desires his father's love. *Smoke Signals* shows this desire only through Victor's eyes, whereas *The Lone Ranger and Tonto Fistfight in Heaven* uses the collective stories and emotions of the residents on the reservation to show that Victor's desires are shared by many. In "Because My Father Always Said He Was the Only Indian Who Saw Jimi Hendrix Play 'The Star Spangled Banner' at Woodstock," the reader sees Victor's pain and longing as he sits at his drunken father's feet while listening to Hendrix. In "A Train Is an Order of Occurrence Designed to Lead to Some Result," the reader's emotions are once again tugged as Samuel, isolated and distanced from his children, lies down in front of an oncoming train. These incidents demonstrate that the father-son connection is not just Victor's problem, but a reservation problem. Like most of the book's characters, Victor doesn't have a moment of enlightenment, a true happy ending. Instead, he continues to fumble through a series of good and bad moments, much as might happen in real life. In contrast, the film focuses only on Victor's path to enlightenment from broken-hearted angry boy needing his father to a healed mature adult. With the help of the

continued

> humorous Thomas, Victor travels to Phoenix to claim his father's belongings. After Victor is given his father's ashes, he realizes the anger he has clung to so tightly for fifteen years has been self-defeating. He lets the anger go and experiences a rebirth. The Victor that returns to the reservation is a new person and a man.

The paragraph contrasts a short story collection and a film point by point. The following outline illustrates the point-by-point method.

Outline

Point by Point

Thesis: Through Victor's story, the reader and the viewer are introduced to complex situations and emotions experienced by American Indians, but the book conveys a more comprehensive picture than the film.

1. *Victor's desire for his father's love*

   a. *Book*

   b. *Film*

2. *Victor's journey from child to adult*

   a. *Book*

   b. *Film*

When you begin writing an essay that emphasizes comparison and/or contrast, you should decide right away which format you will use: one side at a time or point by point. Use that format as you create the outline for your paper. Remember that an outline is an essential step in planning and writing a clearly organized paper.

Student Essays to Consider

A Vote for McDonald's

For my birthday this month, my wife has offered to treat me to dinner at the restaurant of my choice. I think she expects me to ask for a meal at the Chalet, the classiest, most expensive restaurant in town. However, I'm going to eat my birthday dinner at McDonald's. When I compare the two restaurants, the advantages of eating at McDonald's are clear.   1

continued

For one thing, going to the Chalet is more difficult than going to McDonald's. The Chalet has a jacket-and-tie rule, which means I have to dig a sport coat and tie out of the back of my closet, make sure they're semiclean, and try to steam out the wrinkles somehow. The Chalet also requires reservations. Since it is downtown, I have to leave an hour early to give myself time to find a parking space within six blocks of the restaurant. The Chalet cancels reservations if a party is more than ten minutes late. Going to McDonald's, on the other hand, is easy. I can feel comfortable wearing my jeans or warm-up suit. I don't have to do any advance planning. I can leave my house whenever I'm ready and pull into a doorside parking space within fifteen minutes.   **2**

The Chalet is a dimly lit, formal place. While I'm struggling to see what's on my plate, I worry that I'll knock one of the fragile glasses off the table. The waiters at the Chalet can be uncomfortably formal, too. As I awkwardly pronounce the French words on the menu, I get the feeling that I don't quite live up to their standards. Even the other diners can make me feel uncomfortable. And though the food at the Chalet is gourmet, I prefer simpler meals. I don't like unfamiliar food swimming in a pasty white sauce. Eating at the Chalet is, to me, less enjoyable than eating at McDonald's. McDonald's is a pleasant place where I feel at ease. It is well lit, and the bright-colored decor is informal. The employees serve with a smile, and the food is easy to pronounce and identify. I know what I'm going to get when I order a certain type of sandwich.   **3**

The most important difference between the Chalet and McDonald's, though, is price. Dinner for two at the Chalet, even without appetizers or desserts, would easily cost $100. And the $100 doesn't include the cost of parking the car and tipping the waiter, which can come to an additional $20. Once, I forgot to bring enough money. At McDonald's, a filling meal for two will cost around $10. With the extra $110, my wife and I can eat at McDonald's eleven more times, or go to the movies five times, or buy tickets to a football game.   **4**

So, for my birthday dinner, or any other time, I prefer to eat at McDonald's. It is convenient, friendly, and cheap. And with the money my wife saves by taking me to McDonald's, she can buy me what I really want for my birthday—a new Sears power saw.   **5**

The Lone Ranger and Tonto Fistfight with Smoke Signals

Sherman Alexie's short story collection, *The Lone Ranger and Tonto Fistfight in Heaven*, and the film, *Smoke Signals*, also written by Alexie, expose what life is like on an Indian Reservation in the twentieth century. Both the book and the film feature Victor Joseph, a young American Indian who is merely surviving, but continually grasping for something better. Through   **1**

continued

Victor's life, the reader and the viewer are introduced to complex situations and emotions experienced by American Indians, but the book conveys a more comprehensive picture than the film.

Each work demonstrates the anger and hatred Victor feels because of his situation. In *The Lone Ranger and Tonto Fistfight in Heaven*, the reader is carried through a series of short stories that detail the incidents that cause his anger and hatred. The book opens with "Every Little Hurricane," a story that describes Victor's parents' alcoholism, a problem rampant on the reservation. Subsequent stories like "Because My Father Always Said He Was the Only Indian Who Saw Jimi Hendrix Play 'The Star Spangled Banner' at Woodstock" and "This Is What It Means to Say Phoenix, Arizona" take the reader deeper into Victor's dysfunctional family and his emotional distress. The reader experiences the abuse and alcoholism from a profoundly first-person perspective. However, in *Smoke Signals*, based on one of the book's short stories, "This Is What It Means to Say Phoenix, Arizona," the viewer sees the alcoholism and abuse, but the scenes are often preceded or followed by humor, lightening the mood. Unlike the stories, which expose these problems as cultural and situational, the film leads the viewer to believe these are only Victor's problems.

2

The book and film both illustrate how desperately Victor desires his father's love. *Smoke Signals* shows this desire only through Victor's eyes, whereas *The Lone Ranger and Tonto Fistfight in Heaven* uses the collective stories and emotions of the residents on the reservation to show that Victor's desires are shared by many. In "Because My Father Always Said He Was the Only Indian Who Saw Jimi Hendrix Play 'The Star Spangled Banner' at Woodstock," the reader sees Victor's pain and longing as he sits at his drunken father's feet while listening to Hendrix. In "A Train Is an Order of Occurrence Designed to Lead to Some Result," the reader's emotions are once again tugged as Samuel, isolated and distanced from his children, lies down in front of the oncoming train. These incidents demonstrate that the father-son connection is not just Victor's problem, but also a reservation problem. Like most of the book's characters, Victor doesn't have a moment of enlightenment, a true happy ending. Instead, he continues to fumble through a series of good and bad moments, much as might happen in real life. In contrast, the film focuses only on Victor's path to enlightenment from broken-hearted angry boy needing his father to a healed mature adult. With the help of the humorous Thomas, Victor travels to Phoenix to claim his father's belongings. After Victor is given his father's ashes, he realizes the anger he has clung to so tightly for fifteen years has been self-defeating. He lets the anger go and experiences a rebirth. The Victor that returns to the reservation is a new person and a man.

3

Both works demonstrate the roller coaster of emotions that Victor experiences, but once again, the book gives a broader picture than the film. The book illustrates the fear, desperation, hope, and happiness that pervade

4

continued

not only Victor's life, but also the lives of those on the reservation. Many of the stories, no matter how dismal, end with the slightest bit of hope—the ever-present hope for something better. My favorite story was "Indian Education" because it actually reminded me of my education in rural Idaho. In the story, "The Only Traffic Signal on the Reservation Doesn't Flash Red Anymore," Adrian and Victor discuss how drinking has ruined so many lives, yet they demonstrate hope that someone from the younger generation will go on to play basketball beyond the reservation. In "The Approximate Size of My Favorite Tumor," Jimmy constantly tells jokes about his tumor, driving away his devastated wife. When she returns, it is with the knowledge that hope and humor can be found in anything—even an impending death. The film, however, omits these and other stories and focuses only on the roller coaster of Victor's growth as an adult. After Victor gains enlightenment, the film grows very positive. Life on the reservation no longer seems dismal. Victor and Thomas return home. They bond over the memory of Victor's father. Victor respects his father by spreading his ashes over the Spokane Falls, and as he does this, the viewer watches salmon jumping up the falls as they swim upstream, a reminder of new life. Victor's old life is ending and a new one is beginning.

The Lone Ranger and Tonto Fistfight in Heaven and Smoke Signals are   5
equally well-written pieces filled with multiple emotions. The film, however, focuses mostly on Victor and doesn't achieve the level of depth and profundity of the book. The multitude of characters created by Alexie and the clever organization of the book force the reader to experience Victor's life through many stories. Victor's story emerges as a representation of so many, and ultimately it is clear that the collective story of the reservation is what truly matters.

ABOUT UNITY

1. Which supporting paragraph in "A Vote for McDonald's" has its topic sentence within the paragraph, rather than at the beginning? (*Write the paragraph number and the opening words of the topic sentence.*)

_____

2. Which sentence in paragraph 4 of "A Vote for McDonald's" should be omitted in the interest of paragraph unity? (*Write the opening words.*)

_____

3. Which sentence in paragraph 4 in "The Lone Ranger and Tonto Fistfight with Smoke Signals" should be omitted in the interest of paragraph unity? (*Write the opening words.*)

_____

ABOUT SUPPORT

4. In paragraph 3 of "A Vote for McDonald's," what three points does the writer make to support his statement that, for him, dining at McDonald's is a more pleasant experience than dining at the Chalet?

   _____

   _____

   _____

5. In paragraph 3 of "A Vote for McDonald's," what sentence should be followed up by supporting details? (*Write the opening words of that sentence*.)

   _____

6. Which sentence in paragraph 2 of "The Lone Ranger and Tonto Fistfight with Smoke Signals" needs to be followed by more supporting details? (*Write the opening words*.)

   _____

   _____

ABOUT COHERENCE

7. In paragraph 2 of "A Vote for McDonald's," what "change of direction" signal does the author use to indicate that he has finished discussing the Chalet and is now going to discuss McDonald's? _____

8. Write the words in paragraph 4 of "A Vote for McDonald's" that indicate the writer has used emphatic order in organizing his supporting points.

   _____

ABOUT THE INTRODUCTION AND CONCLUSION

9. Which sentence best describes the opening paragraph of "The Lone Ranger and Tonto Fistfight with Smoke Signals"?

   a. It begins with a broad statement that narrows down to the thesis.

   b. It explains the importance of the topic to the reader.

   c. It uses an incident of a brief story.

   d. It begins with a quotation.

10. The conclusion of "The Lone Ranger and Tonto Fistfight with Smoke Signals" falls into which category?

    a. some observations and a prediction

    b. summary and final thought

    c. thoughtful quotation

Developing a Comparison or Contrast Essay

Considering Purpose and Audience

The purpose of an essay that emphasizes comparison and/or contrast is to make a point by including examples that show how distinct items or people are either similar or different. Whether you choose to use comparison or contrast depends on the specific point you want to convey to readers. Suppose, for instance, the main point of your essay is that home-cooked hamburgers are superior to fast-food burgers. To convince your audience of your claim, you might contrast the two items, pointing out those differences—price, taste, and nutrition—that make the homemade dish better. If, however, your main point is that tap water is just as good as store-bought bottled water, you could compare the two, pointing out the similarities that support your main point. Tap water and bottled water, for example, might be equally clean, fresh, and mineral-rich. In both examples above, comparing or contrasting is used to convince readers of a larger main point.

As you think about your own composition, ask yourself what type of essay would benefit from this type of support. Then determine whether you want to focus on the differences between the items or their similarities. You may even decide that you want to do both. If, say, you choose to persuade your reader that he or she should purchase a specific type of computer, you may include paragraphs on the similarities and differences between Mac and PC computers. But remember, no matter what topic you select, be sure that your comparison or contrast is connected to a main point that readers can see and understand.

Be sure to keep your audience in mind when planning your essay. If you were writing about Macs and PCs for computer majors, for example, you could assume your readers were familiar with the two systems. On the other hand, if your audience were made up of liberal arts majors, you could not make such an assumption, and it would be up to you to provide background information. Thinking about your audience will help you determine the tone of your essay as well. Once again, if you are writing for an audience of programmers, it is appropriate to write in an objective, technical tone. But if you are writing for a more general audience, you should assume a friendly, informal tone.

Development through Prewriting

When Jesse, one of the student writers featured earlier, had to choose a topic for his essay, the Chalet and McDonald's quickly came to mind: "My wife and I had been talking that morning about where I wanted to go for my birthday," he said. "I'd been thinking how I would explain to her that I'd really prefer McDonald's. So the comparisons and contrasts between the two restaurants were fresh in my mind."

To generate ideas for his paper, Jesse turned to the technique of freewriting. Without concerning himself with organization, finding the perfect word, or even spelling, he simply wrote whatever came into his mind as he asked himself, Why would I rather eat at McDonald's than at the Chalet? Here is what Jesse came up with:

> The Chalet is a beautiful restaurant and it's sweet of Lilly to want to take me there. But I honestly like McDonald's better. To me, food is food, and a meal at the Chalet is not eleven times better than a meal at McDonald's but that's what it costs. I like a plain cheeseburger better than something I can't pronounce or identify. The waiters at the Chalet are snooty and make me feel awkward—how can you enjoy eating when you're tensed up like that? Have to wear jacket and tie to the Chalet and I've gained weight; not sure jacket will even fit. Sweats or jeans are great at McDonald's. Desserts at Chalet are great, better than McCookies or whatever they're called. Parking is a hassle at the Chalet and easy at McD's. No tipping at McD's, either. I don't know why they keep it so dark at the Chalet—guess it's supposed to be relaxing, but seems creepy to me. McD's is bright and cheerful.

As Jesse looked over his freewriting, he saw that most of what he had written fell into three categories that he could use as the three supporting points of his essay. Using these three points, he prepared this first scratch outline for the essay:

> I'd rather eat my special dinner at McDonald's than at the Chalet.
>
> 1.   Can wear anything I want to McD's.
>
> 2.   Waiters, lighting, menu at Chalet make me feel awkward.
>
> 3.   Chalet is much more expensive than McD's.

Next, Jesse went back and inserted some supporting details that fit in with his three main points.

I'd rather eat my special dinner at McDonald's than at the Chalet.

1. *Going to the Chalet is a hassle.*

   a. *Have to wear jacket, tie to Chalet*

   b. *Have to make reservations*

   c. *Long drive; trouble parking*

2. *Waiters, lighting, menu at Chalet make me feel awkward.*

   a. *Waiters are snooty*

   b. *Lighting is dim*

   c. *French names on menu don't mean anything to me*

3. *Chalet is much more expensive than McD's.*

   a. *Meal costs eleven times as much*

   b. *Parking, tips on top of that*

   c. *Rather spend that money on other things*

Working from this scratch outline, Jesse wrote the following first draft of his essay.

A Vote for McDonald's

First Draft

Lilly has offered to take me anywhere I want for my birthday dinner. She thinks I'll choose the Chalet, but instead I want to eat at McDonald's.

The Chalet has a jacket-and-tie rule, and I hate wearing a jacket and tie, and the jacket's probably too tight for me anyway. I have to dig them out of the closet and get them cleaned. I can wear any old thing to McDonald's. We'd also have to leave the house early, since the Chalet requires reservations. Since it is downtown, I have to leave an hour early so I'm sure to have time to park. The Chalet cancels reservations if a party is more than ten minutes late. Going to McDonald's, on the other hand, is easy. I don't have to do any advance planning. I can leave my house whenever I'm ready.

McDonald's is a pleasant place where I feel at ease. It is bright and well lit. The employees serve with a smile, and the food is easy to pronounce and identify. I know what I'm going to get when I order a certain type of sandwich. I like simple meals more than gourmet ones. The Chalet is dimly lit. While I'm struggling to see what's on my plate, I worry that I'll knock one

continued

of the glasses off the table. The waiters at the Chalet can be uncomfortably formal, too. I get the feeling that I don't quite live up to their standards. Even the other diners can make me feel uncomfortable.

There's a big price difference between the Chalet and McDonald's. Dinner for two at the Chalet can easily cost $100, even without any "extras" like appetizers and dessert. And the $100 doesn't include the cost of parking the car and tipping the waiter. Once, I forgot to bring enough money. At McDonald's, a meal for two will cost around $10.

So, for my birthday dinner, or any other time, I prefer to eat at McDonald's. It is convenient, friendly, and cheap.

Development through Revising

Jesse put the first draft of his essay aside and took it to his writing class the next day. His instructor asked Jesse and the other students to work in small groups reading their drafts aloud and making suggestions for revision to one another. Here are the notes Jesse made on his group's comments:

- I need to explain that Lilly is my wife.

- I'm not consistent in developing my paragraphs. I forgot to do a "one side at a time" or "point by point" comparison. I think I'll try "one side at a time." I'll describe in each paragraph what the Chalet is like, then what McDonald's is like.

- I could use more support for some of my points, like when I say that the waiters at the Chalet make me uncomfortable. I should give some examples of what I mean by that.

- I want to say something about what I'd rather do with the money we save by going to McDonald's. For me that's important—we can "eat" that money at the Chalet, or do other things with it that we both enjoy.

After making these observations about his first draft, Jesse proceeded to write the version of his essay that appears on pages 284–285

A Professional Essay to Consider

Read the following professional essay. Then answer the questions and read the comments that follow.

Born to Be Different?

by Camille Lewis

Some years ago, when my children were very young, I cut a cartoon out of a maga-   1
zine and taped it to my refrigerator. It showed a young couple welcoming friends
over for Christmas. The hosts rather proudly announce that instead of dolls, they
have given their little daughter her own set of tools. And sure enough, the second
panel shows their little girl playing in her room, a wrench in one hand and a hammer in the other. But she's making the wrench say, "Would you like to go to the
prom, Barbie?" and the hammer answer, "Oh, Ken! I'd love to!"

Oh my, did that cartoon strike a chord. I grew up with *Ms.* magazine and the   2
National Organization of Women and a firm belief that gender differences were
learned, not inborn. Other parents may have believed that pink and baby dolls and
kindergarten teaching were for girls, and blue and trucks and engineering were for
boys, but by golly, *my* kids were going to be different. They were going to be raised
free of all that harmful gender indoctrination. They were just going to be *people.*

I don't remember exactly when I began to suspect I was wrong. Maybe it was   3
when my three-year-old son, raised in a "no weapons" household, bit his toast into
a gun shape and tried to shoot the cat. Maybe it was when his younger brother
nearly levitated out of his car seat, joyously crowing "backhoe!" upon spotting his
first piece of earth-moving equipment. Maybe it was when my little daughter first
lined up her stuffed animals and began teaching them their ABC's and bandaging
their boo-boos.

It wasn't that my sons couldn't be sweet and sensitive, or that my daughter   4
wasn't sometimes rowdy and boisterous. But I had to rethink my earlier assump-
tions. Despite my best efforts not to impose gender-specific expectations on them,
my boys and my girl were, well, different. *Really* different.

Slowly and hesitantly, medical and psychological researchers have begun con-   5
firming my observations. The notion that the differences between the sexes (beyond
the obvious anatomical ones) are biologically based is fraught[1] with controversy.
Such beliefs can easily be misinterpreted and used as the basis for harmful, oppressive stereotypes. They can be overstated and exaggerated into blanket statements about what men and women "can" and "can't" do; about what the genders

---

[1] *fraught:* filled.

are "good" and "bad" at. And yet, the unavoidable fact is that studies are making it ever clearer that, as groups, men and women differ in almost every measurable aspect. Learning about those differences helps us understand why men and women are simultaneously so attracted and fascinated, and yet so frequently stymied and frustrated, by the opposite sex. To dig into what it really means to be masculine and feminine helps to depersonalize our responses to one another's behavior—to avoid the "*My* perceptions and behaviors are normal; *yours* don't make sense" trap. Our differences are deep-rooted, hard-wired, and present from the moment of conception.

To begin with, let's look at something as basic as the anatomy of the brain. 6 Typically, men have larger skulls and brains than women. But the sexes score equally well on intelligence tests. This apparent contradiction is explained by the fact that our brains are apportioned differently. Women have about 15 percent more "gray matter" than men. Gray matter, made up of nerve cells and the branches that connect them, allows the quick transference of thought from one part of the brain to another. This high concentration of gray matter helps explain women's ability to look at many sides of an argument at once, and to do several tasks (or hold several conversations) simultaneously.

Men's brains, on the other hand, have a more generous portion of "white mat- 7 ter." White matter, which is made up of neurons, actually inhibits the spread of information. It allows men to concentrate very narrowly on a specific task, without being distracted by thoughts that might conflict with the job at hand. In addition, men's larger skulls contain more cerebrospinal fluid, which cushions the brain. Scientists theorize that this reflects men's history of engaging in warfare and rough sports, activities which bring with them a high likelihood of having one's head banged about.

Our brains' very different makeup leads to our very different methods of in- 8 teracting with the world around us. Simon Baron-Cohen, author of *The Essential Difference: Men, Women and the Extreme Male Brain,* has labeled the classic female mental process as "empathizing." He defines empathizing as "the drive to identify another person's emotions and thoughts, and to respond to these with an appropriate emotion." Empathizers are constantly measuring and responding to the surrounding emotional temperature. They are concerned about showing sensitivity to the people around them. This empathetic quality can be observed in virtually all aspects of women's lives: from the choice of typically female-dominated careers (nursing, elementary school teaching, social work) to reading matter popular mainly with women (romantic fiction, articles about relationships, advice columns about how people can get along better) to women's interaction with one another (which typically involves intimate discussion of relationships with friends and family, and sympathy for each others' concerns). So powerful is the empathizing mindset that it even affects how the typical female memory works. Ask a woman when a particular event happened, and she often pinpoints it in terms of an occurrence that had emotional content: "That was the summer my sister broke her leg," or "That was around the time Gene and Mary got into such an awful argument." Likewise, she is likely to bring her empathetic mind to bear on geography. She'll remember a particular address not as 11th and Market Streets but being "near the restaurant where we went on our anniversary," or "around the corner from Liz's old apartment."

In contrast, Baron-Cohen calls the typical male mindset "systemizing," which 9 he defines as "the drive to analyze and explore a system, to extract underlying rules that govern the behavior of a system." A systemizer is less interested in how people feel than in how things work. Again, the systematic brain influences virtually all aspects of the typical man's life. Male-dominated professions (such as engineering, computer programming, auto repair, and mathematics) rely heavily on systems, formulas, and patterns, and very little on the ability to intuit another person's thoughts or emotions. Reading material most popular with men includes science fiction and history, as well as factual "how-to" magazines on such topics as computers, photography, home repair, and woodworking. When they get together with male friends, men are far less likely to engage in intimate conversation than they are to share an activity: watching or playing sports, working on a car, bowling, golfing, or fishing. Men's conversation is peppered with dates and addresses, illustrating their comfort with systems: "Back in 1996 when I was living in Boston . . ." or "The best way to the new stadium is to go all the way out Walnut Street to 33rd and then get on the bypass. . . ."

One final way that men and women differ is in their typical responses to 10 problem-solving. Ironically, it may be this very activity—intended on both sides to eliminate problems—that creates the most conflict between partners of the opposite sex. To a woman, the *process* of solving a problem is all-important. Talking about a problem is a means of deepening the intimacy between her and her partner. The very anatomy of her brain, as well as her accompanying empathetic mindset, makes her want to consider all sides of a question and to explore various possible solutions. To have a partner who is willing to explore a problem with her is deeply satisfying. She interprets that willingness as an expression of the other's love and concern.

But men have an almost completely opposite approach when it comes to deal- 11 ing with a problem. Everything in their mental makeup tells them to focus narrowly on the issue, solve it, and get it out of the way. The ability to fix a problem quickly and efficiently is, to them, a demonstration of their power and competence. When a man hears his female partner begin to describe a problem, his strongest impulse is to listen briefly and then tell her what to do about it. From his perspective, he has made a helpful and loving gesture; from hers, he's short-circuited a conversation that could have deepened and strengthened their relationship.

The challenge that confronts men and women is to put aside ideas of 12 "better" and "worse" when it comes to their many differences. Our diverse brain development, our ways of interacting with the world, and our modes of dealing with problems all have their strong points. In some circumstances, a typically feminine approach may be more effective; in others, a classically masculine mode may have the advantage. Our differences aren't going to disappear: my daughter, now a middle-schooler, regularly tells me she loves me, while her teenage brothers express their affection by grabbing me in a headlock. Learning to understand and appreciate one another's gender-specific qualities is the key to more rich and rewarding lives together.

QUESTIONS 2

ABOUT UNITY

1. Which of the following statements best represents the implied thesis of "Born to Be Different"?
   a. Although the author believed that gender differences were learned rather than inborn, experience with her own children convinced her otherwise.
   b. Researchers have classified the typical female mental process as "empathizing" and the typical male process as "systemizing."
   c. Many of the differences in the ways men and women think and behave may be due to their biological makeup.
   d. In order to live together happily, men and women need to appreciate and understand their gender-based differences.

2. Which statement would best serve as a topic sentence for paragraphs 6 and 7?
   a. Because of their different construction, men's and women's brains function differently.
   b. Women are skilled at doing several tasks or holding several conversations simultaneously.
   c. Although men's brains are larger than women's, men and women score equally on tests of intelligence.
   d. Men's brains have a larger allocation of white matter, which contributes to the ability to focus narrowly on a particular task.

3. What statement below would best serve as the topic sentence of paragraph 11?
   a. Men solve problems quickly to demonstrate power and competence.
   b. Men's approach to solving problems usually involves giving instructions.
   c. Men's gestures of love are often unhelpful to women.
   d. Men's approach to problem solving is the opposite of women's.

ABOUT SUPPORT

4. Paragraph 8 states that the "empathizing" mindset "can be observed in virtually all aspects of women's lives." What evidence does Lewis provide to support that claim?

_____

_____

5. According to the author, what are the three major differences between men and women?

_____

_____

_____

ABOUT COHERENCE

6. Has the author presented her evidence one side at a time or point by point? Explain your answer.

_____

_____

_____

7. As shown by the outline below, the organization of "Born to Be Different?" resembles the traditional one-three-one essay model. Fill in the missing paragraph numbers.

Introduction: Paragraphs   _____

Supporting Point 1:   Paragraph(s)   _____

Supporting Point 2:   Paragraph(s)   _____

Supporting Point 3:   Paragraph(s)   _____

Conclusion: Paragraph   _____

8. What are the three contrast signals used to introduce the main supporting paragraphs in the essay? Where do they occur? (*Write the paragraph number after the signal.*)

_____   _____   _____

ABOUT THE INTRODUCTION AND CONCLUSION

9. What method best describes the introductory paragraph to the essay?
   a. broad, general statement narrowing to a thesis
   b. idea that is the opposite of the one to be developed
   c. anecdote

10. With which common method of conclusion does the essay end?

    a. a summary and final thought

    b. a quotation

    c. a prediction

Writing an Essay with Emphasis on Comparison and/or Contrast

WRITING ASSIGNMENT 1

Write an essay about a change (positive or negative) in a person you know and explain the causes and process of that change. You should provide a specific description of the person both before and after the change. You will want to review Chapter 8, "Description," Chapter 11, "Process," and Chapter 12, "Cause and/or Effect," to help you provide good support for your essay.

PREWRITING

a.   Gather information about the person you've selected by using a prewriting method of your choice. Write down as much information as possible within a ten-minute period. Don't worry about spelling, grammar, organization, or anything other than getting your thoughts down on the page. If ideas are still flowing at the end of ten minutes, keep on writing. Once you have finished getting your thoughts down, you should have a base of raw material that you can draw on in the next phase of your work. Judging from what you have produced, do you think you have enough material to support your essay? If so, keep following the steps below. If not, choose another person and spend about ten minutes generating ideas to see if he or she might be a better subject for your essay.

b.   Develop a single clear sentence that will serve as your thesis. Your thesis should demonstrate why it is important that your readers know about this person and the change he or she went through.

c.   Decide which method of development you will use to design your essay: one side at a time or point by point. Be consistent in your use of one method or the other in each of your paragraphs.

d.   Write the first draft of your essay.

REVISING

Reread your essay and then show it to a friend or classmate who will give you honest feedback. You should both review it with the following questions in mind:

Comparison and/or Contrast Checklist: THE FOUR BASES

ABOUT *UNITY*

✔ Does my essay have a clearly stated thesis, including a dominant impression of the person's change?

✔ Is there any irrelevant material that should be eliminated or rewritten?

ABOUT *SUPPORT*

✔ Does the essay describe what the person was like, what happened to change that person, and how the person was different after he or she changed?

ABOUT *COHERENCE*

✔ Have I consistently used a single method of development in each supporting paragraph?

✔ Have I organized my essay in a consistent manner that is appropriate to my subject?

✔ Have I used transition words to help readers follow my train of thought?

✔ Do I have a concluding paragraph that provides a summary, a final thought, or both?

ABOUT *SENTENCE SKILLS*

✔ Have I used a consistent point of view throughout my essay?

✔ Have I used specific rather than general words?

✔ Have I avoided wordiness and used concise wording?

✔ Are my sentences varied?

✔ Have I proofread my essay for spelling and other sentence skills, as listed on the inside back cover of the book?

As you revise your essay through one or more additional drafts, continue to refer to this list until you and your reader can answer "yes" to each question.

WRITING ASSIGNMENT 2

Academic

Write an essay in which you contrast two attitudes on a controversial subject. You may want to contrast your views with those of someone else, or contrast the way you felt about the subject in the past with the way you feel now. You might consider writing about one of these subjects:

Legalization of narcotics

Abortion

Men and women serving together in military units

Prayer in public schools

Nuclear power plants

Same-sex couples adopting children

Fertility methods that allow older women to have children

Gun control

The death penalty

Assisted suicide

Immigration policies

The public's right to know about elected officials' private lives

The war in Afghanistan

PREWRITING

a. To gather information for the point of view that contrasts with your own, you will need to do some research. In addition to the Internet, you'll find useful material if you go to the library and search through article indexes for recent newsmagazines. (If you need help, ask your instructor or the research librarian.) Or interview friends and acquaintances whose attitude on the subject is different from yours.

b. To generate ideas for your essay, try the following two-part exercise.

   • Part 1: Pretend that a visitor from Mars who has never heard of the topic of your paper has asked you to explain it, as well as why you take the attitude you do toward it. Using the technique of freewriting—not worrying about sentence structure, organization, spelling, repetition, etc.— write an answer for the Martian. Throw in every reason you can think of for your attitude.

- Part 2: Now the Martian asks you to do the same, taking the opposing point of view. Remember that it's up to you to make this interplanetary visitor understand both sides of the issue, so really try to put yourself in the other person's shoes as you represent the contrasting attitude.

c. As you look over the writing on both sides of the issue you've done for the Martian, note the strongest points on both sides. From them, select your three main supporting points. Are there other thoughts in your writing that can be used as supporting details for those points?

d. Write your three supporting paragraphs. Decide whether it is more effective to contrast your attitude and the opposing attitude point by point within each paragraph, or by devoting the first half of each paragraph to one side's attitude and then contrasting it with the other's.

e. In your concluding paragraph, summarize the contrast between your attitude and the other point of view. Consider closing with a final comment that makes it clear why you stand where you do.

REVISING

Refer to the guidelines for rewriting provided on page 299.

WRITING ASSIGNMENT 3

Write an essay that contrasts two characters or two points of view in one or more poems, stories, plays, or novels. The work you choose may be assigned by your instructor, or it may require your instructor's approval. For this assignment, your essay may have two supporting paragraphs, with each paragraph representing one side of the contrast. You will want to check Chapter 18, "Writing a Summary," and Chapter 22, "Writing a Research Paper," to ensure that you properly present and cite the information from your chosen works. A student model follows.

Warren and Mary

In "Death of the Hired Man," Robert Frost uses a brief incident—the return of Silas, an aging farmhand—to dramatize the differences between a husband and wife. As Warren and Mary talk about Silas and reveal his story, the reader learns their story, too. By the end of the poem, Warren and Mary emerge as contrasting personalities; one is wary and reserved, while the other is open and giving.   1

continued

Warren is a kindly man, but his basic decency is tempered by practicality **2** and emotional reserve. Warren is upset with Mary for sheltering Silas, who is barely useful and sometimes unreliable: "What use he is there's no depending on." Warren feels that he has already done his duty toward Silas by hiring him the previous summer and is under no obligation to care for him now. "Home," says Warren, "is the place where, when you have to go there/ They have to take you in." Warren's home is not Silas's home, so Warren does not have a legal or moral duty to keep the shiftless old man. Warren's temperament, in turn, influences his attitude toward Silas's arrival. Warren hints to Mary—through a condescending smile—that Silas is somehow playing on her emotions or faking his illness. Warren considers Silas's supposed purpose in coming to the farm—to ditch the meadow—nothing but a flimsy excuse for a free meal. The best that Warren can find to say about Silas is that he does have one practical skill: the ability to build a good load of hay.

Mary, in contrast, is distinguished by her giving nature and her **3** concentration on the workings of human emotion. In caring for Silas, Mary sees not his lack of ability or his laziness but the fact that he is "worn out" and needs help. To Mary, home represents not obligation ("They have to take you in") but unconditional love: "I should have called it/Something you somehow haven't to deserve." Mary is observant, not only of outer appearances but also of the inner person; this is why she thinks not that Silas is trying to trick them but that he is a desperate man trying to salvage a little self-respect. She realizes, too, that he will never ditch the meadow, and she knows that Silas's insecurity prompted his arguments with the college boy who helped with the haying. Mary is also perceptive enough to see that Silas could never humble himself before his estranged brother. Mary's attitude is more sympathetic than Warren's; whereas Warren wonders why Silas and his brother don't get along, Mary thinks about how Silas "hurt my heart the way he lay/And rolled his old head on that sharp-edged chairback."

In describing Silas, Warren and Mary describe themselves. We see a **4** basically good man whose spirit has been toughened by a hard life. Warren, we learn, would have liked to pay Silas a fixed wage but simply couldn't afford to. Life has taught Warren to be practical and to rein in his emotions. In contrast, we see a nurturing woman, alert to human feelings, who could never refuse to care for a lonely, dying man. Warren and Mary are both decent people. This is the reason why, as Mary instinctively feels, Silas chooses their home for his final refuge.

Writing for a Specific Purpose and Audience

WRITING ASSIGNMENT 4

In this comparison and/or contrast essay, you will write with a specific purpose and for a specific audience.

Write a letter to your boss in which you compare your abilities with those of the ideal candidate for a position to which you'd like to be promoted. Use the point-by-point method, discussing each desired qualification and then describing how well you measure up to it. Consider the requirements of a job you are familiar with, ideally a job you would really like to apply for. You may want to review Chapter 8, "Description," and Chapter 16, "Argument," to help you create a detailed persuasive essay.

Definition

This chapter will explain and illustrate how to

- develop an essay with emphasis on definition
- write an essay with emphasis on definition
- revise an essay with emphasis on definition

In addition, you will read and consider

- two student essays that emphasize definition
- one professional essay that emphasizes definition

What does it mean to be a successful student? What qualities and attributes does a successful student possess? Looking at the photograph above and thinking about these questions, write an essay in which you define what it means to be a successful student.

In talking with other people, we sometimes offer informal definitions to explain just what we mean by a particular term. Suppose, for example, we say to a friend, "Larry is really an inconsiderate person." We might then explain what we mean by "inconsiderate" by saying, "He borrowed my accounting book 'overnight' but didn't return it for a week. And when I got it back, it was covered with coffee stains." In a written definition, we make clear in a more complete and formal way our own personal understanding of a term. Such a definition typically starts with one meaning of a term. The meaning is then illustrated with a series of details.

In this chapter, you will be asked to write an essay in which you define and illustrate a term. To prepare for this assignment, first read the student essays and the professional essay that follow and work through the questions that accompany the essays.

Student Essays to Consider

Definition of a Football Fan

Not every person who likes football falls into the category of a football fan. The word "fan" is an abbreviation of "fanatic," meaning "an insane or crazy person." In the case of football fans, the term is appropriate. They behave insanely, they are insane about the past, and they are insanely loyal.   1

Football fans wear their official team T-shirts and warm-up jackets to the mall, the supermarket, the classroom, and even—if they can get away with it—to work. If the team offers a giveaway item, the fans rush to the stadium to claim the hat or sports bag or water bottle that is being handed out that day. Baseball fans go similarly nuts when their favorite teams give away some attractive freebie. Football fans just plain behave insanely. Even the fact that fans spend the coldest months of the year huddling on icy metal benches in places like Chicago proves it. In addition, football fans decorate their houses with football-related items of every kind. To them, team bumper stickers belong not only on car bumpers, but also on fireplace mantels and front doors. When they go to a game, which they do as often as possible, they also decorate their bodies. True football fans not only put on their team jackets and grab their pennants but also paint their heads to look like helmets or wear glow-in-the-dark cheeseheads. At the game, these fans devote enormous energy to trying to get a "wave" going.   2

Academic

Football fans are insanely fascinated by the past. They talk about William "Refrigerator" Perry's 1985 Super Bowl touchdown as though it had happened last week. They describe the "Fog Bowl" as if dense fog had blanketed yesterday's game, not 1988's playoff match between the Philadelphia Eagles and the Chicago Bears. They excitedly discuss John Elway's final game before retiring—when he won the 1999 Super Bowl and received MVP honors—as if it were current news. And if a person can't manage to get excited about such ancient history, he or she is looked at as insane.   3

continued

Last of all, football fans are insanely loyal to the team of their choice,   4
often dangerously so. Should their beloved team lose three in a row, fans
may begin to react negatively as a way to hide their broken hearts. They
still obsessively watch each game and spend the entire day afterward
reading and listening to the postgame commentary in newspapers, on TV
sports segments, and on sports radio. Further, this intense loyalty makes fans
dangerous. To anyone who dares to say to a loyal fan that another team
has better players or coaches or, God forbid, to anyone wandering near the
home cheering section wearing the jacket of the opposing team, physical
damage is a real possibility. Bloody noses, black eyes, and broken bones
are just some of the injuries inflicted on people cheering the wrong team
when fans are around. In 1997, one man suffered a concussion at a game in
Philadelphia when Eagles fans beat him up for wearing a jacket with another
team's insignia.

From February through August, football fans act like any other human   5
beings. They pay their taxes, take out the garbage, and complain about the
high cost of living. But when September rolls around, the colors and radios go
on, the record books come off the shelves, and the devotion returns. For the
true football fan, another season of insanity has begun.

Student Zombies

Schools divide people into categories. From first grade on up, students   1
are labeled "advanced" or "deprived" or "remedial" or "antisocial." Students
pigeonhole their fellow students, too. We've all known the "brain," the "jock,"
the "dummy," and the "teacher's pet." In most cases, these narrow labels are
misleading and inaccurate. But there is one label for a certain type of college
student that says it all: "zombie."

Zombies are the living dead. Most of us haven't known a lot of real   2
zombies personally, but we do know how they act. We have horror movies
to guide us. The special effects in horror movies are much better these days.
Over the years, we've learned from the movies that zombies stalk around
graveyards, their eyes glued open by Hollywood makeup artists, bumping
like cheap toy robots into living people. Zombie students in college do just
about the same thing. They stalk around campus, eyes glazed, staring off into
space. When they do manage to wander into a classroom, they sit down
mechanically and contemplate the ceiling. Zombie students rarely eat, talk,
laugh, or toss Frisbees on campus lawns. Instead, they vanish when class is
dismissed and return only when some mysterious zombie signal summons them
back into a classroom. The signal may not occur for weeks.

continued

Zombies are controlled by some mysterious force. According to   3
legend, real zombies are corpses that have been brought back to life to
do the bidding of a voodoo master. Student zombies, too, seem directed
by a strange power. They continue to attend school although they have no
apparent desire to do so. They show no interest in college-related activities
like tests, grades, papers, and projects. And yet some inner force compels
them to wander through the halls of higher education.

An awful fate awaits all zombies unless something happens to break the   4
spell they're under. In the movies, zombies are often shot, stabbed, drowned,
electrocuted, and run over by large vehicles, all to no avail. Finally the hero
or heroine realizes that a counterspell is needed. Once that spell is cast,
with the appropriate props of chicken feet, human hair, and bats' eyeballs,
the zombie-corpse can return peacefully to its coffin. The only hope for a
student zombie to change is for him or her to undergo a similarly traumatic
experience.

All college students know that it's not necessary to see *Night of the Living*   5
Dead or *Land of the Dead* in order to see zombies in action—or nonaction.
They can forget the campus film series or the late-late show. All they need
to do is just sit in a classroom and wait. They know what they're looking
for—the students who walk in without books or papers and sit in the very
last row of seats. The ones with iPods plugged into their ears don't count as
zombies—that's a whole different category of "student." *Day of the Living
Dead* is showing every day at a college nearby.

ABOUT UNITY

QUESTIONS 1

1. Which supporting paragraph in "Definition of a Football Fan" has a topic sentence buried within the paragraph, rather than at the paragraph's beginning? *(Write the paragraph number and the opening words of the topic sentence.)*

_____

2. What sentence in paragraph 2 of "Definition of a Football Fan" should be omitted in the interest of paragraph unity? *(Write the opening words.)*

_____

3. Which sentence in paragraph 2 of "Student Zombies" should be omitted in the interest of paragraph unity? *(Write the opening words.)*

_____

4. What sentence in the final paragraph of "Student Zombies" introduces a new topic and so should be eliminated? *(Write the opening words.)*

_____

ABOUT SUPPORT

5. Which essay develops its definitions through a series of comparisons?

   _____

6. After which sentence in paragraph 4 of "Definition of a Football Fan" is more support needed? *(Write the opening words.)*

   _____

7. In the second paragraph of "Definition of a Football Fan," how many examples are given of fans' "insane" behavior? *(Circle the letter of the answer.)*

   a. two   b. four   c. six

ABOUT COHERENCE

8. Which paragraph in "Definition of a Football Fan" begins with a transitional phrase? _____

9. Which sentence in paragraph 2 of "Student Zombies" begins with a change-of-direction transitional word? *(Write the opening words.)*

   _____

ABOUT THE INTRODUCTION AND CONCLUSION

10. Which method of introduction is used in the opening paragraph of "Student Zombies"? *(Circle the letter of the answer.)*

    a. anecdote
    b. idea that is the opposite of the one to be developed
    c. quotation
    d. broad, general statement narrowing to a thesis

Developing an Essay with Emphasis on Definition

Considering Purpose and Audience

When you write an essay that emphasizes definition, your main purpose is to explain to readers your understanding of a key term or concept, while your secondary purpose is to persuade them that your definition is a legitimate one. Keep in mind that when you present a definition in your essay, you should not simply repeat a word's dictionary meaning. Instead, you should convey what a particular term means *to you* by using persuasive examples. For example, if you were to write about the term *patriotism*, you might begin by presenting your definition of the word. You might say patriotism means turning out for Fourth of July parades, displaying the flag, or supporting the government. Or perhaps you think patriotism is about becoming politically active and questioning government policy. Whatever definition you choose, be sure to provide specific instances so that readers can fully understand your meaning of the term. For example, in writing an essay on patriotism, you might describe three people whom you see as truly patriotic. Writing about each person will help ensure that readers see and understand the term as you do.

As with other essay forms, keep your audience in mind. If, for instance, you were proposing a new definition of "patriotism," an audience of war veterans might require different examples than would an audience of college students.

Development through Prewriting

Brian, the author of "Definition of a Football Fan," spent a few minutes jotting down a number of possible essay topics, keeping in mind the question, "What do I know a good deal about, or at least have an interest in exploring?" Here is his list of topic ideas. Notice how they reflect Brian's interest in outdoor activities, sports, and history:

Definition of . . .

    A person who fishes

    A soccer goalie

    A reenactor of Civil War battles

    People who vacation at Gettysburg

    A bodybuilder

    A Green Bay Packers fan

    A history buff

    A Little League coach

After looking over his list, Brian selected "A Green Bay Packers fan" as the topic that interested him most. He thought it would lend itself well to a lighthearted essay that defined the sometimes nutty fans of the Wisconsin football team. After giving it further thought, however, Brian decided to broaden his topic to include all football fans. "I realized I just didn't know enough specifically about Green Bay fans to support an entire essay," he said.

A person who likes to think in visual terms, Brian decided to develop ideas and details about his topic by clustering his thoughts.

FOOTBALL FANS

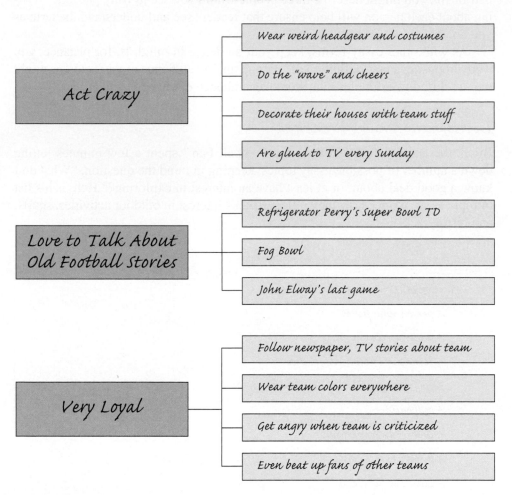

When he looked over his diagram, Brian realized that he could characterize each of his three main topics as a kind of "insanity." He decided on a thesis (he would define football fans as insane) that would indicate his essay's plan of development ("they behave insanely, they are insane about the past, and they are insanely loyal").

With that thesis and plan of development in mind, Brian wrote the first draft of his essay.

Definition of a Football Fan   **First Draft**

Football fans are by definition crazy. They behave insanely, they are insane about the past, and they are insanely loyal.

If their team gives away something free, the fans rush to the stadium to get the hat or whatever. Football fans just plain behave insanely. Baseball fans go similarly nuts when their favorite teams give away some attractive freebie. But football fans are even worse. Football fans freeze themselves in order to watch their favorite game. In addition, football fans decorate their houses with football-related items of every kind. When they go to a game, which they do as often as possible, the true football fans make themselves look ridiculous by decorating themselves in weird team-related ways. At the game, these fans do the "wave" more than they watch the game.

Football fans love to talk about the past. They talk about William "Refrigerator" Perry's 1985 Super Bowl touchdown as though it had happened last week. They still get all excited about 1988's "Fog Bowl." They talk about John Elway's final game as though it's today's news, though it happened in 1999. They think everyone should be as excited as they are about such old stories.

Last of all, football fans are insanely loyal to the team of their choice. Football fans wear their team T-shirts and warm-up jackets everywhere, even to work. Of course, if they have to dress up in business clothes, they can't do that. Should their beloved team lose three in a row, their fans may begin to criticize their team. But these reactions only hide their broken hearts. They still obsessively watch each game and read all the newspaper stories about it. This intense loyalty makes fans dangerous. To anyone who dares to say to a loyal fan that another team is better or, God forbid, to anyone wandering near the home cheering section wearing the jacket of the opposing team, physical damage is a real possibility. Incidents of violence in football stadiums have increased in recent years and are a matter of growing concern.

Football fans really act as if they're crazy. They behave insanely, they are crazy about the past, and they're too loyal.

Development through Revising

The next day, Brian showed his first draft to a study partner from his composition class. She returned it with comments noted in the margins.

Definition of a Football Fan

Football fans are by definition crazy. They behave insanely, they are insane about the past, and they are insanely loyal.

If their team gives away something free, the fans rush to the stadium to get the hat or whatever. Football fans just plain behave insanely. Baseball fans go similarly nuts when their favorite teams give away some attractive freebie. But football fans are even worse. Football fans freeze themselves in order to watch their favorite game. In addition, football fans decorate their houses with football-related items of every kind. When they go to a game, which they do as often as possible, the true football fans make themselves look ridiculous by decorating themselves in weird team-related ways. At the game, these fans do the "wave" more than they watch the game.

Football fans love to talk about the past. They talk about William "Refrigerator" Perry's 1985 Super Bowl touchdown as though it had happened last week. They still get all excited about 1988's "Fog Bowl." They talk about John Elway's final game as though it's today's news, though it happened in 1999. They think everyone should be as excited as they are about such old stories.

Last of all, football fans are insanely loyal to the team of their choice. Football fans wear their team T-shirts and warm-up jackets everywhere, even to work. Of course, if they have to dress up in business clothes, they can't do that. Should their beloved team lose three in a row, their fans may begin to criticize their team. But these reactions only hide their broken hearts. They still obsessively watch each game and read all the newspaper stories about it. This intense loyalty makes fans dangerous. To anyone who dares to say to a loyal fan that another team is better or, God forbid, to anyone wandering near the home cheering section wearing the jacket of the opposing team, physical damage is a real possibility. Incidents of violence in

Reader's Comments

Huh? I guess this is about the weather—make it clearer.

Like what? Details here.

Details needed. How do they decorate themselves?

I'm not a football fan, so I don't understand these references. Can you briefly explain them?

Shouldn't this be in the second paragraph? It seems to belong to "they behave insanely," not "loyalty."

This doesn't support your topic statement, so take it out.

continued

football stadiums have increased in recent years and are a matter of growing concern.

Football fans really act as if they're crazy. They behave insanely, they are crazy about the past, and they're too loyal.

Kind of a boring way to end it. You're just repeating your thesis.

After reading his classmate's comments, Brian went to work on his next draft. As he worked, he read his essay aloud several times and noticed places where his wording sounded awkward or too informal. (Example: "If their team gives away a freebie, the fans rush to the stadium to get the hat or whatever.") A few drafts later, he produced the version of "Definition of a Football Fan" that appears on pages 305–306.

A Professional Essay to Consider

Read the following professional essay. Then answer the questions and read the comments that follow.

Television Addiction
by Marie Winn

The word "addiction" is often used loosely and wryly in conversation. People will refer to themselves as "mystery book addicts" or "cookie addicts." E. B. White writes of his annual surge of interest in gardening, "We are hooked and are making an attempt to kick the habit." Yet nobody really believes that reading mysteries or ordering seeds by catalogue is serious enough to be compared to an addiction to heroin or alcohol. The word "addiction" is here used jokingly to denote a tendency to overindulge in some pleasurable activity.

People often refer to being "hooked on TV." Does this, too, fall into the light-hearted category of eating cookies and other pleasures that people pursue with unusual intensity, or is there a kind of television viewing that falls into the more serious category of destructive addiction?

When we think about addiction to drugs or alcohol, we frequently focus on negative aspects, ignoring the pleasures that accompany drinking or taking drugs. And yet the essence of any serious addiction is a pursuit of pleasure, a search for a "high" that normal life does not supply. It is only the inability to function without the addictive substance that is dismaying, the dependence of the organism upon a certain experience and an increasing inability to function without it. Thus a person will take two or three drinks at the end of the day not merely for the pleasure drinking provides, but also because he "doesn't feel normal" without them.

An addict does not merely pursue a pleasurable experience and need to experi- 4
ence it in order to function normally. He needs to repeat it again and again. Something about that particular experience makes life without it less than complete. Other potentially pleasurable experiences are no longer possible, for under the spell of the addictive experience, his life is peculiarly distorted. The addict craves an experience, and yet he is never really satisfied. The organism may be temporarily sated, but soon it begins to crave again.

Finally, a serious addiction is distinguished from a harmless pursuit of pleasure 5
by its distinctly destructive elements. A heroin addict, for instance, leads a damaged life: his increasing need for heroin in increasing doses prevents him from working, from maintaining relationships, from developing in human ways. Similarly, an alcoholic's life is narrowed and dehumanized by his dependence on alcohol.

Let us consider television viewing in the light of the conditions that define 6
serious addictions.

Not unlike drugs and alcohol, the television experience allows the participant 7
to blot out the real world and enter into a pleasurable and passive mental state. The worries and anxieties of reality are as effectively deferred by becoming absorbed in a television program as by going on a "trip" induced by drugs or alcohol. And just as alcoholics are only vaguely aware of their addiction, feeling that they control their drinking more than they really do ("I can cut it out any time I want—I just like to have three or four drinks before dinner"), people similarly overestimate their control over watching television. Even as they put off other activities to spend hour after hour watching television, they feel they could easily resume living in a different, less passive style. But somehow or other while the television set is present in their homes, the click doesn't sound. With television pleasures available, those other experiences seem less attractive, more difficult somehow.

A heavy viewer (a college English instructor) observes: "I find television al- 8
most irresistible. When the set is on, I cannot ignore it. I can't turn it off. I feel sapped, will-less, enervated. As I reach out to turn off the set, the strength goes out of my arms. I sit there for hours and hours."

The self-confessed television addict often feels he "ought" to do other things— 9
but the fact that he doesn't read and doesn't plant his garden or sew or crochet or play games or have conversations means that those activities are no longer as desirable as television. In a way the heavy viewer's life is as imbalanced by his television "habit" as a drug addict's or an alcoholic's. He is living in a holding pattern, as it were, passing up the activities that lead to growth or development or a sense of accomplishment. This is one reason people talk about their television viewing so ruefully, so apologetically. They are aware that it is an unproductive experience, that almost any other endeavor is more worthwhile by any human measure.

Finally, it is the adverse effect of television viewing on the lives of so many ¹⁰ people that defines it as a serious addiction. The television habit distorts the sense of time. It renders other experiences vague and curiously unreal while taking on a greater reality for itself. It weakens relationships by reducing and sometimes eliminating normal opportunities for talking, for communicating.

And yet television does not satisfy, else why would the viewer continue to ¹¹ watch hour after hour, day after day? "The measure of health," writes Lawrence Kubie, "is flexibility . . . and especially the freedom to cease when sated." But the television viewer can never be sated with his television experiences—they do not provide the true nourishment that satiation requires—and thus he finds that he cannot stop watching.

ABOUT UNITY

1. Winn's thesis is not presented directly in the essay. See whether you can state it in your own words.

   _____

QUESTIONS 2

2. Which statement would best serve as a topic sentence for paragraph 4?
   a. Addicts enjoy pleasurable experiences more than nonaddicts.
   b. Addicts feel that their lives are not really complete.
   c. Addicts would give up their addiction if other pleasurable experiences were available.
   d. Addicts need to endlessly repeat the experience on which they are dependent.

3. Which statement would best serve as a topic sentence for paragraph 7?
   a. People become television addicts because they have more troubled lives than most other people.
   b. Television addicts develop a distorted perception of reality and lose self-control.
   c. Few experiences in life are as pleasurable as watching television.
   d. Alcoholics often believe they have more control over their drinking than they really do.

ABOUT SUPPORT

4. The author defines TV as an addiction by first defining
   a. being hooked on TV.
   b. serious addiction.
   c. a heavy viewer.
   d. the real world.

5. The topic sentence of paragraph 5 states, "Finally, a serious addiction is distinguished from a harmless pursuit of pleasure by its distinctly destructive elements." What details does the author use to support this point?

_____

_____

6. Paragraph 8
   a. supports the idea in paragraph 7 that TV addicts overestimate their control over TV watching.
   b. raises a point not dealt with elsewhere.
   c. supports the idea in paragraph 9 that TV addicts are stuck in a living holding pattern.

ABOUT COHERENCE

7. Which paragraph fully signals the author's switch from discussing addiction in general terms to talking specifically about addiction to television? _____

8. What key transitional word is used twice in the essay? _____

ABOUT THE INTRODUCTION AND CONCLUSION

9. Which statement best describes the introductory paragraph of Winn's essay?
   a. It explains the importance of the topic of television addiction.
   b. It tells an anecdote that illustrates the nature of television addiction.
   c. It presents a type of "addiction" very different from the one discussed in the essay.

10. Which statement best describes the conclusion of "Television Addiction"?
    a. Winn recommends that the television addict try to "kick the habit."
    b. Winn summarizes the points made in the body of the essay.
    c. Winn comments on the damage television does to society at large.

Writing an Essay with Emphasis on Definition

WRITING ASSIGNMENT 1

Personal

The term *hero* is used so much that it has truly lost its meaning. In this extended definition essay, you are to identify someone who has been a hero in your life and explain why that person is a hero. Your definition may identify sensory characteristics of your hero, compare your hero to another person who is not a hero, and/or compare your hero to the dictionary definition. You may want to review Chapter 13, "Comparison and/or Contrast," Chapter 8, "Description," and Chapter 9, "Narration," to incorporate different types of support for your profile.

PREWRITING

a. Look up the dictionary definition of *hero* and decide if it does or doesn't support your idea of a hero.

b. Gather information about your subject by using a prewriting method of your choice. You will want to write down as much information as possible within a ten-minute period. Don't worry about spelling, grammar, organization, or anything other than getting your thoughts down on the page. If ideas are still flowing at the end of ten minutes, keep on writing.

c. Once you have finished getting your thoughts down, you should have a base of raw material that you can draw on in the next phase of your work. Judging from what you have produced, do you think you have enough material to support your essay? If so, keep following the steps below. If not, choose another person and spend about ten minutes generating ideas to see if he or she might be a better subject.

d. As you devise your opening paragraph, *don't* begin with the overused phrase "According to Webster. . . ."

e. Remember that the thesis of your definition is a version of "What a hero means to me." Your thesis should demonstrate why this person is a hero to you.

f. You may find outlining to be a helpful organizational strategy for this essay.

g. Now write the first draft of your essay.

REVISING

After you have completed the first draft of the paper, set it aside for a while if you can. Then read the paper out loud to a friend or classmate whose judgment you respect. Keep the following points in mind as you hear your own words, and ask your friend to respond to them as well:

Definition Checklist: THE FOUR BASES

ABOUT *UNITY*

✔ Does my essay have a clearly stated thesis, including a dominant impression of why my subject is a hero?

✔ Is there any irrelevant material that should be eliminated or rewritten?

ABOUT *SUPPORT*

✔ Have I supported my definition with an extended example?

ABOUT *COHERENCE*

✔ Have I consistently used a single method of development in each supporting paragraph?

✔ Have I organized my essay in a manner that is appropriate to my subject?

✔ Have I used transition words to help readers follow my train of thought?

✔ Does my concluding paragraph provide a summary or a final thought or both?

ABOUT *SENTENCE SKILLS*

✔ Have I used a consistent point of view throughout my essay?

✔ Have I used specific rather than general words?

✔ Have I avoided wordiness and used concise wording?

✔ Are my sentences varied?

✔ Have I checked my writing for spelling and other sentence skills, as listed on the inside back cover of the book?

As you revise your essay through one or more additional drafts, continue to refer to this list until you can answer "yes" to each question.

WRITING ASSIGNMENT 2

Choose one of the terms below as the subject of an essay that emphasizes definition. Each term refers to a certain kind of person.

Slob
Cheapskate
Loser
Good neighbor
Busybody
Whiner
Con artist
Optimist
Pessimist
Team player
Bully
Scapegoat
Religious person
Hypocrite
Snob
Tease
Practical joker
Procrastinator
Loner
Pig
Type A

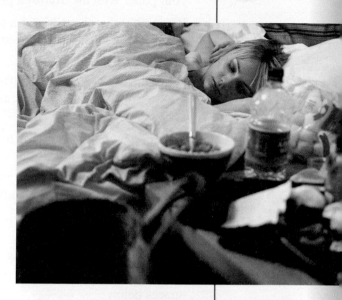

PREWRITING

a.   As you devise your opening paragraph, you may want to refer to the diction-ary definition of the term. If so, be sure to use only one meaning of the term. (Dictionaries often provide several different meanings for a term.) *Don't* begin your paper with the overused phrase "According to Webster. . . ."

b.   Remember that the thesis of a definition essay is a version of "What _____ means to me." The thesis presents what *your* experience has made *you* think the term actually means.

c.   As you plan your supporting paragraphs, think of different parts or qualities of your term. Here, for example, are the three-part divisions of the student essays considered in this chapter:

> Football fans are crazy in terms of their behavior, their fascination with the past, and their loyalty.

> Student zombies are the "living dead," are controlled by a "mysterious force," and are likely to suffer an "awful fate."

d.   Support each part of your division with either a series of examples or a single extended example.

e.   You may find outlining to be the most helpful prewriting strategy for your essay. As a guide, write your thesis and at least three supporting points in the spaces below.

Thesis: _____

Support: 1. _____

2. _____

3. _____

4. _____

REVISING

Once you have the first draft of your essay completed, read it aloud to a friend or classmate. The two of you should review it with these questions in mind:

Definition Checklist: THE FOUR BASES

ABOUT *UNITY*

✔ Does my thesis statement indicate how I define the term, and does it indicate my plan of development for the essay?

✔ Does each of my supporting paragraphs have a clear topic sentence?

ABOUT *SUPPORT*

✔ Have I supported each of my topic sentences with one extended example or a series of examples?

ABOUT *COHERENCE*

✔ Have I rounded off my essay with an appropriate concluding paragraph?

ABOUT *SENTENCE SKILLS*

✔ Have I used a consistent point of view throughout my essay?

✔ Have I used specific rather than general words?

✔ Have I avoided wordiness and used concise wording?

✔ Are my sentences varied?

✔ Have I proofread my essay for spelling and other sentence skills, as listed on the inside back cover of the book?

WRITING ASSIGNMENT 3

In this extended definition essay, you are to define a term from another course. For instance, if you are studying anthropology, you might define *culture*, or if you are studying criminal justice, you might define *environmental crime*. Not only will you need to write an extended definition, but you should also create a persuasive tone for your essay in order to convince your audience that you truly understand the term and that your definition is a correct one. You will want to check Chapter 16, "Argument," to help you create a persuasive tone.

PREWRITING

a. As you devise your opening paragraph, it would be helpful to refer to the class in which you are studying the term in order to provide an introduction for the reader and to establish a context for the term.

b. Your thesis should demonstrate why the term is important to understand in this field. It should also describe how your own experience has influenced your understanding of what the term actually means.

c. As you plan your supporting paragraphs, you may find outlining to be a helpful organizational strategy for this essay emphasizing definition.

d. Now write the first draft of your essay.

REVISING

After you have completed the first draft of the paper, set it aside for a while if you can. Then read the paper out loud to a friend or classmate whose judgment you respect. Keep the following points in mind as you hear your own words, and ask your friend to respond to them as well:

Definition Checklist: THE FOUR BASES

ABOUT *UNITY*

✔ Does my thesis statement indicate why the term is important and how I define the term?

✔ Is there any irrelevant material that should be eliminated or rewritten?

ABOUT *SUPPORT*

✔ Have I supported my definition with an extended example?

ABOUT *COHERENCE*

✔ Have I consistently used a single method of development in each supporting paragraph?

✔ Have I organized my essay in a consistent manner that is appropriate to my subject?

✔ Have I used transition words to help readers follow my train of thought?

✔ Have I rounded off my essay with an appropriate concluding paragraph?

ABOUT *SENTENCE SKILLS*

✔ Have I used a consistent point of view throughout my essay?

✔ Have I used specific rather than general words?

✔ Have I avoided wordiness and used concise wording?

✔ Are my sentences varied?

✔ Have I proofread my essay for spelling and other sentence skills, as listed on the inside back cover of the book?

As you revise your essay through one or more additional drafts, continue to refer to this checklist until you can answer "yes" to each question.

Writing for a Specific Purpose and Audience

WRITING ASSIGNMENT 4

In the past year, your school has had problems with parents demonstrating poor sportsmanship at school events. At one football game, two parents started yelling at a player because he missed a pass. At a theater production, several parents ridiculed a young girl who had forgotten her lines. At a chess tournament, a mother whose child was losing started accusing everyone else of cheating. The principal has decided to address this behavior, so he has asked you to create a hand-out, defining school standards and explaining what good sportsmanship is and how it applies to school events. Your definitions will need to focus on both attitudes and actions. You may want to review Chapter 8, "Description," and Chapter 10, "Exemplification," to help you develop and support your essay.

Division-Classification

This chapter will explain and illustrate how to

- develop an essay with emphasis on division-classification

- write an essay with emphasis on division-classification

- revise an essay with emphasis on division-classification

In addition, you will read and consider

- two student essays that emphasize division-classification

- one professional essay that emphasizes division-classification

Visit an online library like the Library of Congress at http://www. loc.gov and browse through the various categories. If you are more interested in music, visit Pandora at http://www.pandora.com and browse the different categories of music. Or, visit a site like Overstock at http://www.overstock.com and browse the categories of items for sale. Then design your own site selling, lending, or streaming something similar. (You can be as creative as you like.) Provide at least five categories for your "product" and explain what distinguishes each one.

When you return home from your weekly trip to the supermarket with five bags packed with your purchases, how do you sort them out? You might separate food items from nonfood items (like toothpaste, paper towels, and detergent). Or you might divide and classify the items into groups intended for the freezer compartment, the refrigerator, and the kitchen cupboards. You might even put the items into groups like "to be used tonight," "to be used soon," and "to be used last." Sorting supermarket items in such ways is just one simple example of how we spend a great deal of our time organizing our environment in one manner or another.

In this chapter, you will be asked to write an essay in which you divide or classify a subject according to a single principle. To prepare for this assignment, first read the student essays and the professional essay that follow and work through the questions that accompany the essays.

Student Essays to Consider

Mall People

Academic

People often question what goes into "having fun." For many, "fun" involves getting out of the house, seeing other people, having something interesting to look at, and enjoying a choice of activities, all at a reasonable price. Going out to dinner or to the movies may satisfy some of those desires, but often not all. But an attractive alternative does exist in the form of the free-admission shopping mall. Teenagers, couples on dates, and the nuclear family can all be observed having a good time at the mall.

Teenagers are drawn to the mall to pass time with pals and to see and be seen by other teens. The guys saunter by in sneakers, T-shirts, and blue jeans, complete with a package of cigarettes sticking out of a pocket. The girls stumble along in midriff-baring tank tops, with a cell phone tucked snugly in the rear pocket of their low-waisted jeans. Traveling in a gang that resembles a wolf pack, the teenagers make the shopping

1

2

continued

mall their hunting ground. Mall managers have obviously made a decision to attract all this teenage activity. The kids' raised voices, loud laughter, and occasional shouted obscenities can be heard from as far as half a mall away. They come to "pick up girls," to "meet guys," and just to "hang out."

Couples find fun of another sort at shopping malls. The young lovers are easy to spot because they walk hand in hand, stopping to sneak a quick kiss after every few steps. They first pause at a jewelry store window so that they can gaze at diamond engagement rings and platinum wedding bands. Then, they wander into furniture departments in the large mall stores. Finally, they drift away, their arms wrapped around each other's waist.   3

Mom, Dad, little Jenny, and Fred Jr., visit the mall on Friday and Saturday evenings for inexpensive recreation. Hearing the music of the antique carousel housed there, Jenny begs to ride her favorite pony with its shining golden mane. Shouting, "I'm starving!" Fred Jr., drags the family toward the food court, where he detects the seductive odor of pizza. Mom walks through a fabric store, running her hand over the soft velvets and slippery silks. Meanwhile, Dad has wandered into an electronics store and is admiring the sound system he'd love to buy someday. The mall provides something special for every member of the family.   4

Sure, some people visit the mall in a brief, businesslike way, just to pick up a specific purchase or two. But many more are shopping for inexpensive recreation. The teenagers, the dating couples, and the nuclear families all find cheap entertainment at the mall.   5

Genuine Draft

Personal

The other night, my six-year-old son turned to me and asked for a light beer. My husband and I sat there for a moment, stunned, and then explained to him that beer was only for grown-ups. I suddenly realized how many beer ads appear on television and how often they appear. To my little boy, it must seem that every American drinks beer after work, or after playing softball, or while watching a football game. Brewers have pounded audiences with all kinds of campaigns to sell beer. There seems to be an ad to appeal to the self-image of every beer drinker.   1

One type of ad attracts people who think of themselves as grown-up kids. Budweiser's animated frogs, squatting on lily pads and croaking, "Bud," "Weis," "Er," are a perfect example of this type. The frogs are an example of the wonders of computer animation, which is being increasingly mixed in with real-life action in advertisements. The campaign was an immediate hit with   2

continued

the underage set as well as with adult beer-drinkers. Within weeks, the frogs were as recognizable to children as Tony the Tiger or Big Bird. They became so popular that the new Bud ads were a feverishly anticipated part of the Super Bowl—as much a part of the entertainment as the game itself or the halftime show. These humorous ads suggest that beer is part of a lighthearted approach to life.

A second kind of ad is aimed not at wanna-be kids but at macho men,   3
guys who think of themselves as "men's men," doing "guy things" together. One campaign features men who see themselves as victims of their nagging wives. Ads in this series show men howling with laughter about how they've fooled their wives into thinking they're home doing chores (by leaving dummy-stuffed pants lying under leaky sinks or broken furnaces) while they're really out drinking. Beer is a man's drink, the ads seem to say, and women are a nuisance to be gotten around.

European and European-sounding beers such as Löwenbräu and   4
Heineken like to show handsome, wealthy-looking adults enjoying their money and leisure time. A typical scene shows such people enjoying an expensive hobby in a luxurious location. Beer, these ads tell us, is an essential part of the "good life." This type of ad appeals to people who want to see themselves as successful and upper class.

To a little boy, it may well seem that beer is necessary to every adult's   5
life. After all, we need it to make us laugh, to bond with our friends, and to celebrate our financial success. At least, that's what advertisers tell him—and us.

QUESTIONS 1

ABOUT UNITY

1. In which supporting paragraph in "Genuine Draft" is the topic sentence at the end rather than, as is more appropriate for student essays, at the beginning?

   _____

2. Which sentence in paragraph 2 of "Mall People" should be omitted in the interest of paragraph unity? (*Write the opening words.*)

   _____

3. What sentence in paragraph 2 of "Genuine Draft" should be omitted in the interest of paragraph unity? (*Write the opening words.*)

   _____

ABOUT SUPPORT

4. After which sentence in paragraph 3 of "Mall People" are more supporting details needed? (*Write the opening words.*)

_____

5. Which paragraph in "Genuine Draft" lacks sufficient specific details? _____

6. Label as *sight, touch, hearing,* or *smell* all the sensory details in the following sentences taken from "Mall People."

    a. "Hearing the music of the antique carousel housed there, Jenny begs to ride her favorite pony with its shining golden mane."

    b. "Shouting, 'I'm starving!' Fred Jr., drags the family toward the food court, where he detects the seductive odor of pizza."

    c. "Mom walks through a fabric store, running her hand over the soft velvets and slippery silks."

ABOUT COHERENCE

7. What are the time transition words used in paragraph 3 of "Mall People"?

_____   _____   _____

8. Which topic sentence in "Genuine Draft" functions as a linking sentence between paragraphs? (*Write the opening words.*)

_____

ABOUT THE INTRODUCTION AND CONCLUSION

9. What kind of introduction is used in "Genuine Draft"? (*Circle the appropriate letter.*)
    a. broad, general statement narrowing to a thesis
    b. idea that is the opposite of the one to be developed
    c. quotation
    d. anecdote

10. What conclusion technique is used in "Mall People"? (*Circle the appropriate letter.*)
    a. summary
    b. prediction or recommendation
    c. quotation

Developing an Essay with Emphasis on Division-Classification

Considering Purpose and Audience

When writing an essay that emphasizes division and classification, your purpose is to present your audience with your own unique way of dividing and classifying particular topics. In order to write a successful essay, you will need to first choose a topic that interests readers and lends itself to support that can be divided and classified. Once you pick your topic and decide on the support you will use, you will then have to come up with your own specific sorting system—one that readers will be able to understand.

For example, if your essay focuses on types of clothing, there are a number of ways to sort this topic into categories. You could divide clothing by the function it serves: shirts and jackets (to cover the upper body); pants and skirts (for the lower body); and shoes and socks (for the feet). Or you could divide clothes according to the materials they are made from: animal products, plant products, and synthetic materials. A more interesting, and potentially humorous, way to divide clothes is by fashion: clothes that are stylish, clothes that are going out of style, and clothes that are so unattractive that they never were in style. Notice that in all three of these cases, the broad topic of clothing has been divided into categories according to a particular principle (function, materials, and fashion). When you divide your topic for your essay, be sure to come up with your own division principle and make it clear to your readers.

Once you've selected your topic and figured out how to divide it, you will need to provide specific details so that readers fully understand the categories you created. For the example about fashion above, you might classify plaid bell-bottom pants as part of the "going out of style" category, while blue jeans might belong in the "clothes that are stylish" group and a mustard-yellow velour jacket might fit in the "never stylish" group. Whatever divisions you established, be sure to include enough details to make your division-classification method—your main point— clear to your readers. Equally important, keep your audience in mind. An audience of fashion-conscious young people, for instance, would probably have very different opinions about what is and isn't stylish than an audience of middle-aged bankers. Or an audience made up of the parents of middle-school students who are clamoring for "epic" clothes would have much more interest in clothing styles than the parents of students about to enter college.

Development through Prewriting

Julia, the writer of "Mall People," believed from her observations that "people at malls" would make a good topic for an essay that emphasizes division-classification.

But she did not immediately know how she wanted to group those people or what she wanted to say about them. She decided to begin her prewriting by making a list of observations about mall shoppers. Here is what she came up with:

Families with kids

Lots of snacking

Crowds around special displays—automobiles, kiddie rides

Older people walking in mall for exercise

Groups of teenagers

Women getting made over at makeup counter

Dating couples

Blind woman with Seeing Eye dog

Lots of people talking and laughing rather than shopping

Interviewers stopping shoppers to fill out questionnaires

Kids hanging out, meeting each other

As Julia reviewed her list, she concluded that the three largest groups of "mall people" were families with children, groups of teens, and dating couples. She decided to organize her essay around those three groups. To further flesh out her idea, she created a scratch outline that her essay would follow. Here is the scratch outline Julia prepared:

Thesis statement: Mall offers inexpensive fun for several groups.

1.   Teens

*   a.   Roam in packs*

*   b.   Dress alike*

*   c.   Meet new people*

continued

2. *Dating couples*

    a. *Act romantic*

    b. *Window-shop for future home*

    c. *Have lovers' quarrels*

3. *Families*

    a. *Kids' activities*

    b. *Cheap food*

    c. *Adults shop*

Julia's list and outline prepared her to write the first draft of her essay.

First Draft

Mall People

Malls aren't only places to go shopping. They also offer free or at least cheap fun and activities for lots of people. Teenagers, dating couples, and families all like to visit the mall.

Teenagers love to roam the mall in packs, like wolves. They often dress alike, depending on the latest fashion. They're noisy and sometimes rude, and mall security officers sometimes kick them out of the building. Then they find somewhere else to go, maybe one of the warehouse-sized amusement and video-game arcades that are springing up everywhere. Those places are fun, but they tend to be more expensive than just "hanging out" at the mall. Teens are usually not as interested in shopping at the mall as they are in picking up members of the opposite sex and seeing their friends.

Dating couples also enjoy wandering around the mall. They are easy to spot because they walk along holding hands and sometimes kissing. They stare at diamond rings and wedding bands and shop for furniture together. Sometimes they have spats and one of them stomps off to sulk on a bench for a while.

Little kids and their parents make up a big group of mall-goers. There is something for every member of the family there. There are usually some special displays that interest the kids, and Mom and Dad can always find things they like to window-shop for. Another plus for the family is that there is inexpensive food, like burgers and pizza, available at the mall's food court.

Development through Revising

After Julia completed her first draft, she put it aside. She knew from previous experience that she was a better critic of her own writing after she took a break from it. The following morning, when Julia read over her first draft, she noticed several places where it could be improved. Here are the observations she put in her writing journal:

- My first paragraph does present a thesis (malls offer inexpensive entertainment), and it tells how I'm going to develop that thesis (by discussing three groups of people). But it isn't very interesting. I think I could do a better job of drawing readers in by describing what is fun about malls.

- Some of the details in the essay aren't necessary; they don't support my main idea. For instance, the stuff about teens being kicked out of the mall and about dating couples having fights doesn't have anything to do with the entertainment malls provide. I'll eliminate this.

- Some of my statements that do support the main idea need more support. For example, when I say there are "special displays that interest the kids" in paragraph 4, I should give an example of such a display. I should also back up the idea that many teens dress alike.

With these observations in mind, Julia returned to her essay and revised it, producing the version that appears on pages 326–327.

A Professional Essay to Consider

Now read the following professional essay. Then answer the questions and read the comments that follow.

Wait Divisions
by Tom Bodett

I read somewhere that we spend a full third of our lives waiting. I've also read that   1
we spend a third of our lives sleeping, a third working, and a third at our leisure.
Now either somebody's lying, or we're spending all our leisure time waiting to go
to work or sleep. That can't be true or league softball and Winnebagos never would
have caught on.

So where are we doing all of this waiting, and what does it mean to an impa-   2
tient society like ours? Could this unseen waiting be the source of all our problems? A shrinking economy? The staggering deficit? Declining mental health
and moral apathy? Probably not, but let's take a look at some of the more classic
"waits" anyway.

The very purest form of waiting is what we'll call the *Watched-Pot Wait*. This   3
type of wait is without a doubt the most annoying of all. Take filling up the kitchen
sink. There is absolutely nothing you can do while this is going on but keep both
eyes glued to the sink until it's full. If you try to cram in some extracurricular activity, you're asking for it. So you stand there, your hands on the faucets, and wait.
A temporary suspension of duties. During these waits it's common for your eyes
to lapse out of focus. The brain disengages from the body and wanders around the
imagination in search of distraction. It finds none and springs back into action only
when the water runs over the edge of the counter and onto your socks.

The phrase "a watched pot never boils" comes of this experience. Pots don't   4
care whether they are watched or not; the problem is that nobody has ever seen a
pot actually come to a boil. While people are waiting, their brains turn off.

Other forms of the Watched-Pot Wait would include waiting for your dryer to   5
quit at the Laundromat, waiting for your toast to pop out of the toaster, or waiting
for a decent idea to come to mind at a typewriter. What they all have in common is
that they render the waiter helpless and mindless.

A cousin to the Watched-Pot Wait is the *Forced Wait*. Not for the weak of will,   6
this one requires a bit of discipline. The classic Forced Wait is starting your car in the
winter and letting it slowly idle up to temperature before engaging the clutch. This is
every bit as uninteresting as watching a pot, but with one big difference. You have a
choice. There is nothing keeping you from racing to work behind a stone-cold engine
save[1] the thought of the early demise of several thousand dollars' worth of equipment
you haven't paid for yet. Thoughts like that will help you get through a Forced Wait.

Properly preparing packaged soup mixes also requires a Forced Wait. Direc-   7
tions are very specific on these mixes. "Bring three cups of water to boil, add mix,

---

[1]*save:* except.

simmer three minutes, remove from heat, let stand five minutes." I have my doubts that anyone has actually done this. I'm fairly spineless when it comes to instant soups and usually just boil the bejeezus out of them until the noodles sink. Some things just aren't worth a Forced Wait.

8   All in all Forced Waiting requires a lot of a thing called patience, which is a virtue. Once we get into virtues I'm out of my element and can't expound on the virtues of virtue, or even lie about them. So let's move on to some of the more far-reaching varieties of waiting.

9   The *Payday Wait* is certainly a leader in the long-term anticipation field. The problem with waits that last more than a few minutes is that you have to actually do other things in the meantime. Like go to work. By far the most aggravating feature of the Payday Wait is that even

What, in your opinion, is worth waiting for? Think about this question and create a scratch outline for a division-classification essay on things you feel are worth waiting for.

though you must keep functioning in the interludes,[2] there is less and less you are able to do as the big day draws near. For some of us the last few days are best spent alone in a dark room for fear we'll accidentally do something that costs money. With the Payday Wait comes a certain amount of hope that we'll make it, and faith that everything will be all right once we do.

10   With the introduction of faith and hope, I've ushered in the most potent wait class of all, the *Lucky-Break Wait,* or the *Wait for One's Ship to Come In.* This type of wait is unusual in that it is for the most part voluntary. Unlike the Forced Wait, which is also voluntary, waiting for your lucky break does not necessarily mean that it will happen.

11   Turning one's life into a waiting game of these proportions requires gobs of the aforementioned faith and hope, and is strictly for the optimists among us. For these people life is the thing that happens to them while they're waiting for something to happen to them. On the surface it seems as ridiculous as following the directions

---

[2]*interludes:* times in between.

on soup mixes, but the Lucky-Break Wait performs an outstanding service to those who take it upon themselves to do it. As long as one doesn't come to rely on it, wishing for a few good things to happen never hurt anybody.

In the end it is obvious that we certainly do spend a good deal of our time wait- 12 ing. The person who said we do it a third of the time may have been going easy on us. It makes a guy wonder how anything at all gets done around here. But things do get done, people grow old, and time boils on whether you watch it or not.

The next time you're standing at the sink waiting for it to fill while cooking 13 soup mix that you'll have to eat until payday or until a large bag of cash falls out of the sky, don't despair. You're probably just as busy as the next guy.

QUESTIONS 2

ABOUT UNITY

1. The thesis of Bodett's essay is not presented directly. See if you can state it in your own words.

   _____

2. In paragraph 2, Bodett introduces several possible effects of waiting, then dismisses them with a "probably not." Is it a sign of careless writing that Bodett mentions irrelevant topics and then dismisses them? Or does he intend a particular effect by introducing unnecessary topics? If he does intend an effect, how would you describe it?

   _____

   _____

ABOUT SUPPORT

3. Bodett writes of four "classic waits": the Watched-Pot Wait, the Forced Wait, the Payday Wait, and the Lucky-Break Wait. For which two "waits" does he provide several examples?

   _____   _____

4. Bodett refers to the first two waits as cousins. How does he differentiate between them?

   _____

   _____

5. How does Bodett support his claim that the Forced Wait "requires a bit of discipline"?

   _____

   _____

ABOUT COHERENCE

6. Bodett's essay does not follow the strict one-three-one model (introduction, three supporting paragraphs, conclusion) often used in student essays. Instead, its form is a looser one that includes an introduction, four topics for development (the four "waits"), and a conclusion. Indicate in the following outline how the paragraphs of Bodett's essay are broken up:

   Introduction: Paragraph(s)   _____

   Topic 1:   Paragraph(s)   _____

   Topic 2:   Paragraph(s)   _____

   Topic 3:   Paragraph(s)   _____

   Topic 4:   Paragraph(s)   _____

   Conclusion: Paragraph(s)   _____

7. Which words in the first sentence of paragraph 6 link that sentence to the preceding three paragraphs?

   _____

8. Bodett organizes the waits
   a. from the most harmful to the least harmful.
   b. from the shortest waits to the longest.
   c. from the most difficult wait to the easiest one.
   d. in no particular order.

ABOUT THE INTRODUCTION AND CONCLUSION

9. Which method best describes the introduction to "Wait Divisions"?
   a. quotation
   b. idea that is the opposite of the one to be developed
   c. anecdote
   d. broad, general statement narrowing to thesis

10. In what way does the first sentence in paragraph 13 serve as a summary of Bodett's main points?

    _____

    _____

Writing an Essay with Emphasis on Division-Classification

In this essay, you are to organize the music on your iPod, smartphone, or other music medium into at least three categories and explain how these categories reflect who you are. You might have categories like "workouts" or "studying"; you

might even have more specific categories like "music to listen to after breaking up with a guy." You will want to review Chapter 8, "Description," and Chapter 9, "Narration," to help you create support and details that will appeal to your reader.

PREWRITING

a. For at least ten minutes, look at the songs you have on your iPod/MP3 player and group the songs into possible categories. You might create your categories by type (sad, soul, jazz) or group (U2, Adele, LMFAO) or by when you listen to the songs (with my parents, with friends, in the car). Whichever grouping principle you choose, be sure to come up with meaningful categories.

b. Decide on a thesis statement that will introduce your topic and claim. Two possible thesis statements follow:

> My iPod is filled with thousands of songs that can be categorized to explain my moods.

> My MP3 player is filled with songs that I listen to while I am with my parents, whenever I am alone, and when I am out with friends.

c. You may need to spend some extra time generating ideas to come up with additional support for your thesis. You do not want to simply inventory the songs that are on your iPod; instead, you want to highlight one or two songs in each category, and explain why those songs are good examples for that category. You may even want to incorporate a narrative with one or two songs in your essay as added support; gathering story ideas at this point will only help you as you draft your essay.

d. Now write the first draft of your essay.

REVISING

After you have completed the first draft of the paper, set it aside for a while if you can. Then read the paper out loud to a friend or classmate whose judgment you respect. Keep these points in mind as you hear your own words, and ask your friend to respond to them as well:

Division-Classification Checklist: THE FOUR BASES

ABOUT *UNITY*

✔ Does my essay have a clearly stated thesis, including the topic and a dominant impression or principle of division?

✔ Is there any irrelevant material that should be eliminated or rewritten?

ABOUT *SUPPORT*

✔ Have I backed up statements in my essay with specific relevant examples?

✔ Do I have enough detailed support?

ABOUT *COHERENCE*

✔ Is each one of the paragraphs in the body of my essay based on one of the categories I am describing?

✔ Have I used transition words to help readers follow my train of thought?

✔ Do I have a concluding paragraph that provides a sense of completion to the essay?

ABOUT *SENTENCE SKILLS*

✔ Have I used a consistent point of view throughout my essay?

✔ Have I used specific rather than general words?

✔ Have I avoided wordiness and used concise wording?

✔ Are my sentences varied?

✔ Have I checked my essay carefully for spelling and other sentence skills, as listed on the inside back cover of the book?

As you revise your essay, continue to refer to this list until you can answer "yes" to each question.

WRITING ASSIGNMENT 2

Many students find college to be more expensive than they expected, and as credit card companies continue to give cards away, more and more students are finding themselves deeper in debt than they need to be. The best way to save money, or not overspend, is to create a budget that helps you keep track of your cash flow. For this essay, you will need to classify common expenses that college students have and come up with a plan that helps students spend their money more wisely. You will want to review Chapter 10, "Exemplification," and Chapter 16, "Argument," to help you create an effective essay.

PREWRITING

a. First, you'll need to classify typical student expenses. You may want to break them down by month or semester to help organize them. You should then divide these expenses into necessary and unnecessary.

b. Once you have categorized students' typical expenses, generate some ideas that could help students save money. You should provide ideas for savings in both categories.

c. Create a thesis statement that introduces your topic and your proposal. Two possible thesis statements follow:

> Students in college often go deeper into debt than they need to and should follow a simple plan to avoid this pitfall.

> Students in college should organize and budget their expenses in order to avoid getting deeper in debt than necessary.

d. Now write the first draft of your essay.

REVISING

After you have completed the first draft of the paper, set it aside for a while if you can. Then read the paper out loud to a friend or classmate whose judgment you respect. Keep the following points in mind as you hear your own words, and ask your friend to respond to them as well:

Division-Classification Checklist: THE FOUR BASES

ABOUT *UNITY*

✔ Does my essay have a clearly stated thesis, including the topic and a dominant impression or principle of division?

✔ Is there any irrelevant material that should be eliminated or rewritten?

ABOUT *SUPPORT*

✔ Have I backed up statements in my essay with specific relevant examples?

✔ Do I have enough detailed support?

ABOUT *COHERENCE*

✔ Is each one of the paragraphs in the body of my essay based on one of the categories I am describing?

✔ Have I used transition words to help readers follow my train of thought?

✔ Do I have a concluding paragraph that provides a sense of completion to the essay?

ABOUT *SENTENCE SKILLS*

✔ Have I used a consistent point of view throughout my essay?

✔ Have I used specific rather than general words?

✔ Have I avoided wordiness and used concise wording?

✔ Are my sentences varied?

✔ Have I proofread my essay for spelling and other sentence skills, as listed on the inside back cover of the book?

As you revise your essay, continue to refer to this list until you and your reader can answer "yes" to each question.

Writing for a Specific Purpose and Audience

WRITING ASSIGNMENT 3

In this essay that emphasizes division-classification, you will write with a specific purpose and for a specific audience.

Imagine that your boss has asked you to prepare a section for the employee handbook. The purpose of this section is to explain to new employees the three main types of clients they can expect to deal with and how to properly handle those clients. For instance, if you work at a salon and spa, you may explain there are three kinds of clients that you must regularly handle: the over-demanding diva, the environmentally conscious client, and the customer who never knows what he or she wants. Or maybe you work at a restaurant and the regular clients are business people, senior citizens, and families with small children. Once you have identified the types, you will need to explain in detail how to effectively work with each specific group. You will want to review Chapter 8, "Description," Chapter 10, "Exemplification," and Chapter 12, "Cause and Effect," to help you create effective support for your essay.

Argument

Should cell phones be permitted in class? Look at the photograph above and write an essay in which you argue for or against the use of cell phones in the classroom. Include at least three separate reasons that support your point of view.

This chapter will explain and illustrate how to

- develop an essay with emphasis on argument

- write an essay with emphasis on argument

- revise an essay with emphasis on argument

In addition, you will read and consider

- two student essays that emphasize argument

- one professional essay that emphasizes argument

Do you know someone who enjoys a good argument? Such a person likes to challenge any sweeping statement we might make. For example, when we say something like "Ms. Lucci doesn't grade fairly," he or she comes back with "Why do you say that? What are your reasons?"

Our questioner then listens carefully as we state our case, judging if we really do have solid evidence to support our point of view. We realize that saying, "Ms. Lucci just doesn't, that's all," sounds weak and unconvincing, so we try to come up with stronger evidence to back up our statement. Such a questioner may make us feel uncomfortable, but we may also feel grateful to him or her for helping us clarify our opinions.

The ability to put forth sound and compelling arguments is an important skill in everyday life. You can use argument to make a point in a class discussion, persuade a friend to lend you money, or talk an employer into giving you a day off. Becoming skilled in clear, logical reasoning can also help you see through faulty arguments that others may make. You'll become a better critic of advertisements, newspaper articles, political speeches, and the other persuasive appeals you see and hear every day.

In this chapter, you will be asked to write an essay in which you defend a position with a series of solid reasons. In a general way, you have done the same thing—making a point and then supporting it—with all the essays in this book. The difference here is that argument advances a *controversial* point, a point that at least some of your readers will not be inclined to accept. To prepare for this assignment, first read about five strategies you can use in advancing an argument. Then read the student essays and the professional essay that follow and work through the questions that accompany the essays.

Strategies for Argument

Because argument assumes controversy, you have to work especially hard to convince readers of the validity of your position. Here are five strategies you can use to help win over readers whose viewpoint may differ from yours.

1 Use Tactful, Courteous Language

In an essay that emphasizes argument, you are attempting to persuade readers to accept your viewpoint. It is important, therefore, not to anger them by referring to them or their opinions in rude or belittling terms. Stay away from sweeping statements like "Everybody knows that . . ." or "People with any intelligence agree that. . . ." Also, keep the focus on the issue you are discussing, not on the people involved in the debate. Don't write, "*My opponents* say that orphanages cost less than foster care." Instead, write, "*Supporters of orphanages* say that orphanages cost less than foster care." Terms like *my opponents* imply that the argument is between you and anyone who disagrees with you. By contrast, a term such as *supporters of orphanages* suggests that those who don't agree with you are nevertheless reasonable people who are willing to consider differing opinions.

2 Point Out Common Ground

Another way to persuade readers to consider your opinion is to point out common ground—opinions that you share. Find points on which people on all sides of the argument can agree. Perhaps you are arguing that there should be an 11 P.M. curfew for juveniles in your town. Before going into detail about your proposal, remind readers who oppose such a curfew that you and they share certain goals: a safer city, a lower crime rate, and fewer gang-related tragedies. Readers will be more receptive to your idea once they have considered how you and they think alike.

3 Acknowledge Differing Viewpoints

It is a mistake to simply ignore points of view that conflict with yours. Acknowledging other viewpoints strengthens your position in several ways. First, it helps you spot flaws in the opposing position—as well as in your own argument. Second, and equally important, it gives the impression that you are a reasonable person, willing to look at an issue from all sides. Readers will be more likely to consider your point of view if you indicate a willingness to consider theirs.

At what point in your essay should you acknowledge opposing arguments? The earlier the better—ideally, in the introduction. By quickly establishing that you recognize the other side's position, you get your readers on board with you, ready to hear what else you have to say.

One effective technique is to *cite the opposing viewpoint in your thesis statement.* You do this by dividing your thesis into two parts. In the first part, you acknowledge the other side's point of view; in the second, you state your opinion, suggesting that yours is the stronger viewpoint. In the following example, the opposing viewpoint is underlined once; the writer's own position is underlined twice:

> Although some students believe that studying a foreign language is a waste of time, two years of foreign-language study should be required of all college graduates.

For another example of a thesis that acknowledges an opposing viewpoint, look at this thesis statement, taken from the essay titled "Once Over Lightly: Local TV News" (page 348):

> While local TV newscasts can provide a valuable community resource, too often such programs provide mere entertainment at the expense of solid news.

Another effective technique is to use one or two sentences (separate from the thesis) in the introduction to acknowledge the alternative position. Such sentences briefly state the "other side's" argument. To see this technique at work, look at the introduction to the essay "Teenagers and Jobs" (page 347), noting the sentence "Many people argue that working can be a valuable experience for the young."

A third technique is to *use a paragraph within the body of your essay to summarize opposing opinions in greater detail.* To do this successfully, you must spend some time researching those opposing arguments. A fair, evenhanded summary of the other side's ideas will help convince readers that you have looked at the issue from all angles before deciding where you stand. Imagine, for instance, that

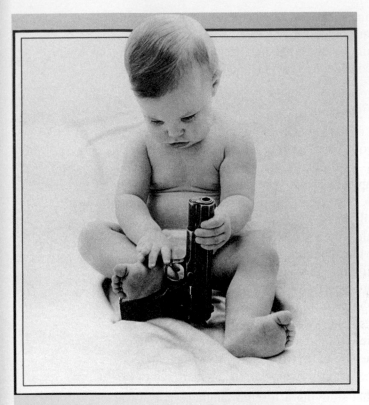

Arguments can be made through visual images as well. What visual argument is suggested by this photograph? Is it effective? Why or why not?

you are writing an essay arguing that the manufacture and sale of handguns should be outlawed. You would begin by doing some library research to find information on both sides of the issue, making sure to pay attention to material that argues against your viewpoint. You might also talk with local representatives of the National Rifle Association or other organizations that support gun ownership. Having done your research, you would be in a good position to write a paragraph summarizing the opposing viewpoints. In this paragraph, you might mention that many citizens believe that gun ownership is a right guaranteed by the Constitution and that gun owners fear that outlawing handguns would deprive law-abiding people of protection against gun-toting criminals. Once you had demonstrated that you understood opposing views, you would be in a stronger position to present your own point of view.

4 When Appropriate, Grant the Merits of Differing Viewpoints

Sometimes an opposing argument contains a point whose validity you cannot deny. What should you do then? The strongest strategy is to admit that the point is a good one. You will lose credibility if you argue against something that clearly makes sense. Admit the merit of one aspect of the other argument while making it clear that you still believe your argument to be stronger overall. Suppose that you were arguing against the use of computers in writing classrooms. You might say, "Granted, students who are already accustomed to computers can use them to write papers more quickly and efficiently"—admitting that the other side has a valid point. But you could quickly follow this admission with a statement making your own viewpoint clear: "But for students like me who write and think in longhand, a computer in the classroom is more a hindrance than a help; it would require too long a learning curve to be of any value to me."

5 Rebut Differing Viewpoints

Sometimes it may not be enough simply to acknowledge other points of view and present your own argument. When you are dealing with an issue that your readers feel strongly about, you may need to *rebut* the opposing arguments. To *rebut* means to point out problems with an opposing view, to show where an opponent's argument breaks down.

Imagine that you are writing an essay arguing that your college should use money intended to build a campus health and fitness center to upgrade the library instead. From reading the school paper, you know that supporters of the center say it will help attract new students to the college. You rebut that point by citing a study conducted by the admissions office that shows that most students choose a college because they can afford it and because they like its academic programs and facilities. You also emphasize that many students, already financially strapped, would have trouble paying the proposed fee for using the center.

A rebuttal can take two forms: (1) You can first mention all the points raised by the other side and then present your counterargument to each of those points. (2) You can present the first point raised by the opposition and rebut that point, then move on to the second opposing point and rebut that, and so on.

Student Essays to Consider

Teenagers and Jobs

1   "The pressure for teenagers to work is great, and not just because of the economic plight in the world today. Much of it is peer pressure to have a little bit of freedom and independence, and to have their own spending money. The concern we have is when the part-time work becomes the primary focus." These are the words of Roxanne Bradshaw, educator and officer of the National Education Association. Many people argue that working can be a valuable experience for the young. However, working more than about fifteen hours a week is harmful to adolescents because it reduces their involvement with school, encourages a materialistic and expensive lifestyle, and increases the chance of having problems with drugs and alcohol.

2   Schoolwork and the benefits of extracurricular activities tend to go by the wayside when adolescents work long hours. As more and more teens have filled the numerous part-time jobs offered by fast-food restaurants and malls, teachers have faced increasing difficulties. They must both keep the attention of tired pupils and give homework to students who simply don't have time to do it. In addition, educators have noticed less involvement in

continued

the extracurricular activities that many consider a healthy influence on young people. School bands and athletic teams are losing players to work, and sports events are poorly attended by working students. Those teens who try to do it all—homework, extracurricular activities, and work—may find themselves exhausted and prone to illness. A recent newspaper story, for example, described a girl in Pennsylvania who came down with mononucleosis as a result of aiming for good grades, playing on two school athletic teams, and working thirty hours a week.

Another drawback of too much work is that it may promote materialism   3
and an unrealistic lifestyle. Some parents claim that working helps teach adolescents the value of a dollar. Undoubtedly that can be true. It's also true that some teens work to help out with the family budget or to save for college. However, surveys have shown that the majority of working teens use their earnings to buy luxuries—computers, video-game systems, clothing, even cars. These young people, some of whom earn $500 or more a month, don't worry about spending wisely—they can just about have it all. In many cases, experts point out, they are becoming accustomed to a lifestyle they won't be able to afford several years down the road, when they no longer have parents paying for car insurance, food, lodging, and so on. At that point, they'll be hard-pressed to pay for necessities as well as luxuries.

Finally, teenagers who work a lot are more likely than others to get   4
involved with alcohol and drugs. Teens who put in long hours may seek a quick release from stress, just like the adults who need to drink a couple of martinis after a hard day at work. Stress is probably greater in our society today than it has been at any time in the past. Also, teens who have money are more likely to get involved with drugs.

Teenagers can enjoy the benefits of work while avoiding its drawbacks,   5
simply by limiting their work hours during the school year. As is often the case, a moderate approach will be the most healthy and rewarding.

Once Over Lightly: Local TV News

Unfortunately, local television newscasts are not a reliable source of news   1
and don't provide in-depth coverage and analysis of issues. While local TV newscasts can provide a valuable community resource, too often such programs provide mere entertainment at the expense of solid news. In their battle for high ratings, local programs emphasize news personalities at the expense of stories. Visual appeal has a higher priority than actual news. And stories and reports are too brief and shallow.

continued

Local TV newscasters are as much the subject of the news as are the stories they present. Nowhere is this more obvious than in weather reports. Weatherpersons spend valuable news time joking, drawing cartoons, chatting about weather fronts as "good guys" and "bad guys," and dispensing weather trivia such as statistics about relative humidity and record highs and lows for the date. Reporters, too, draw attention to themselves. Rather than just getting the story, the reporters are shown jumping into or getting out of helicopters to get the story. When reporters interview crime victims or the residents of poor neighborhoods, the camera angle typically includes them and their reaction as well as their subjects. When they report on a storm, they stand outside in the storm, their styled hair blowing, so we can admire how they "brave the elements." Then there are the anchorpersons, who are chosen as much for their looks as their skills. They, too, dilute the news by putting their personalities at center stage.

2

Often the selection of stories and the way they are presented are based on visual impact rather than news value. If a story is not accompanied by an interesting film clip, it is not likely to be shown on the local news. The result is an overemphasis on fires and car crashes and little attention to such important issues as the economy. A tractor-trailer spill on the highway slightly injures one person and inconveniences motorists for only an hour. But because it provides dramatic pictures—the big truck on its side, its load spilled, emergency personnel running around, lots of flashing lights—it is given greater emphasis in the local newscast than a rise in local taxes, which has far more lasting effect on the viewer. "If it bleeds, it leads" is the unofficial motto of many local news programs. A story that includes pictures of death and destruction, no matter how meaningless, is preferable on the local news to a solid, important story without flashy visuals. The mania for visuals is so strong that local news programs will even slap irrelevant visuals onto an otherwise strong story. A recent story on falling oil prices, for example, was accompanied by footage of a working oil well that drew attention away from the important economic information in the report.

3

On the average, about half a minute is devoted to a story. Clearly, stories that take less than half a minute are superficial. Even the longest stories, which can take up to several minutes, are not accompanied by meaningful analysis. Instead, the camera jumps from one location to another, and the newscaster simplifies and trivializes the issues. For instance, one recent "in-depth" story about the homeless consisted of a glamorous reporter talking to a homeless person and asking him what should be done about the problem. The poor man was in no condition to respond thoughtfully. The story then cut to an interview with a city

4

continued

bureaucrat who mechanically rambled on about the need for more government funding. Is raising taxes the answer to every social problem? There were also shots of homeless people sleeping in doorways and on top of heating vents, and there were interviews with people in the street, all of whom said that something should be done about the terrible problem of homelessness. There was, in all of this, no real exploration of the issue and no proposed solution. It was also apparent that the homeless were just the issue of the week. After the week's coverage was over, the topic was not mentioned again.

Because of the emphasis on newscasters' personalities and on   5
the visual impact of stories and the short time span for stories, local news shows provide little more than diversion. What viewers need instead is news that has real significance. Rather than being amused and entertained, we need to deal with complex issues and learn uncomfortable truths that will help us become more responsible consumers and citizens.

QUESTIONS 1

ABOUT UNITY

1. Which paragraph in "Once Over Lightly" lacks a topic sentence? _____
   Write a topic sentence for the paragraph:

   _____

2. What sentence in paragraph 4 of "Once Over Lightly" should be omitted in the interest of paragraph unity? *(Write the opening words.)*

   _____

3. Which sentence in paragraph 4 of "Teenagers and Jobs" should be omitted in the interest of paragraph unity? *(Write the opening words.)*

   _____

ABOUT SUPPORT

4. Which sentence in paragraph 4 of "Teenagers and Jobs" needs to be followed by more supporting details? Which sentence in paragraph 2 of "Once Over Lightly" needs to be followed by supporting details? *(Write the opening words of each sentence.)*

   _____

   _____

5. In "Teenagers and Jobs," which supporting paragraph raises an opposing idea and then argues against that idea? _____ What transition word is used to signal the author's change of direction? _____

6. In paragraph 2 of "Once Over Lightly," the topic sentence is supported by details about three types of newscasters. What are those three types?

   _____   _____   _____

ABOUT COHERENCE

7. Which two paragraphs of "Teenagers and Jobs" begin with an addition transition, and what are those words?

   _____   _____

8. Write the change-of-direction transition and the illustration transition in paragraph 3 of "Once Over Lightly."

   Change of direction: _____   *Illustration:* _____

ABOUT THE INTRODUCTION AND CONCLUSION

9. Two methods of introduction are used in "Teenagers and Jobs." Circle the letters of these two methods.
   a. broad, general statement narrowing to thesis
   b. idea that is the opposite of the one to be developed
   c. quotation
   d. anecdote

10. Both essays end with the same type of conclusion. What method do they use?
    a. summary only
    b. summary and recommendation
    c. prediction

Developing an Essay with Emphasis on Argument

Considering Purpose and Audience

When you write an essay that has an emphasis on argument, your main purpose is to convince readers that your particular view or opinion about a controversial issue or topic is correct. In addition, at times, you may have a second purpose for your essay: to persuade your audience to take some sort of action.

To convince readers, it is important to provide them with a clear main point and plenty of logical evidence to back it up. Say, for example, you want to argue that public schools should require students to wear uniforms. In this case, you might do research to gather as much evidence as possible to support your point. You may check to see, for instance, if uniforms are cheaper than the alternative. Perhaps you could find out if schools with uniforms have a lower rate of violence than those without them. You may even look for studies to see if students' academic performance improves when school uniforms are adopted. As you search for evidence, be sure that it clearly links to your topic and supports the main point you are trying to get across to your audience.

While consideration of your audience is important for all essay forms, it is absolutely critical to the success of an essay that is persuasive in tone. Depending on the main point you choose, your audience may be firmly opposed to your view or somewhat supportive of it. As you begin planning your essay, consider what your audience already knows, and how it feels about the main point of your essay. Using the example above, for instance, ask yourself what opinion your audience holds about school uniforms. What are likely to be their objections to your argument? Why would people not support your main point? What, if anything, are the merits of the opposing point of view? In order to "get inside the head" of your opposition, you might even want to interview a few people you're sure will disagree with you: say, for instance, a student with a very funky personal style who you know would dislike wearing a uniform. By becoming aware of the points of view your audience might have, you will know how to proceed in researching your rebuttal to their arguments.

> **TIP**   For more information on how to deal with opposing views in your essay, see pages 345–347. By directly addressing your opposition, you add credibility to your argument and increase the chances that others will be convinced that your main point is valid.

Development through Prewriting

Before choosing a topic for her essay, Anna, the writer of "Teenagers and Jobs," asked herself what controversial subject she was particularly well qualified to argue. She wanted to select something she cared about, something she could sink her teeth into. As a person who had been an active member of her high school community—she had worked on the newspaper, played basketball, and sung in a chorus—Anna first thought of writing about student apathy. It had always bothered her to see few students taking advantage of the opportunities available to them in school. But as she thought more about individual students she knew and their reasons for not getting more involved in school and extracurricular activities, she changed her opinion. "I realized that 'apathy' was not really the problem," she explained. "Many of them worked so much that they literally didn't have time for school life."

After narrowing her thesis to the idea of "teenagers and work," Anna made a list of what she perceived as the bad points of students' working too much:

No time for real involvement in school and school activities

Students leave right after school—can't stay for clubs, practices

Don't have time to attend games, other school functions

Students sleep in class and skip homework

Stress, extra money contribute to drug and alcohol use

Teachers frustrated trying to teach tired students

Having extra money makes teens materialistic

Some get so greedy they drop out of school to work full-time

Students miss the fun of being young, developing talents and social abilities

Students burn out, even get sick

Hanging around older coworkers can contribute to drug, alcohol use

Buying luxuries gives teens unrealistic idea of standard of living

As she reviewed and revised her list of points, Anna identified three main points to develop in her essay. Those she identified as points 1, 2, and 3. She realized that some of the other items she had jotted down were related ideas that might be used to support her main topics. She marked those with the number of the main idea they supported, in parentheses, like this: (1). She also crossed out points that did not fit.

1   No time for real involvement in school and school activities

(1) Students leave right after school—can't stay for clubs, practices

(1) Don't have time to attend games, other school functions

Students sleep in class and skip homework

continued

2   *Stress, extra money contribute to drug and alcohol use*

(1) *Teachers frustrated trying to teach tired students*

3   *Having extra money makes teens materialistic*

(3) *Some get so greedy for money they drop out of school to work full-time*

~~*Students miss the fun of being young, developing talents and social abilities*~~

~~*Students burn out, even get sick*~~

(2) *Hanging around older coworkers can contribute to drug, alcohol use*

(3) *Buying luxuries gives teens unrealistic idea of standard of living*

Referring to this list, Anna wrote the following first draft of her essay.

First Draft

Teenagers and Jobs

Many people think that working is a valuable experience for young people. But when teenagers have jobs, they are too likely to neglect their schoolwork, become overly materialistic, and get into trouble with drugs and alcohol.

Schoolwork and the benefits of extracurricular activities tend to go by the wayside when adolescents work long hours. As more and more teens have taken jobs, teachers have faced increasing difficulties. They must both keep the attention of tired pupils and give homework to students who simply don't have time to do it. In addition, educators have noticed less involvement in extracurricular activities. School bands and athletic teams are losing players to work, and sports events are poorly attended by working students. Those teens who try to do it all—homework, extracurricular activities, and work—may find themselves exhausted and burned out.

Another drawback of too much work is that it may promote materialism and an unrealistic lifestyle. Most working teens use their earnings to buy luxuries. These young people don't worry about spending wisely—they can just about have it all. They are becoming accustomed to a lifestyle they won't be able to afford several years down the road, when they have to support themselves.

continued

Finally, teenagers who work are more likely than others to get involved with alcohol and drugs. Teens who put in long hours may seek a quick release from stress, just like the adults who need to drink a couple of martinis after a hard day at work. Also, teens who have money are more likely to get involved with drugs.

In short, teens and work just don't mix.

Development through Revising

Anna's instructor had offered to look over students' first drafts and suggest improvements for revision. Here is the note she wrote at the end of Anna's work:

Anna—Good beginning. While I think your thesis is overstated, it and each of your main topics are on the right track. Here are some points to consider as you write your next draft:

- Many teenagers find working a <u>limited</u> number of hours a week to be a good experience. I think it's a mistake to state flatly that it's <u>always</u> a negative thing for teenagers to have jobs. Think about acknowledging that there can be good points to students' working part-time.

- You do a pretty good job of supporting your first main point ("School-work and the benefits of extracurricular activities tend to go by the wayside when adolescents work long hours") by noting the effect of too much work on scholastic achievement and extracurricular activities. You <u>less</u> effectively support points 2 and 3 ("Another drawback of too much work is that it may promote materialism and an unrealistic lifestyle" and "Finally, teenagers who work are more likely than others to get involved with alcohol and drugs"). <u>Show</u> how teens become too materialistic; don't just state that they do. And what evidence do you have that working teens use drugs and alcohol more than others?

- Throughout the essay, can you come up with evidence beyond your own observations to support the idea that too much working is detrimental to teens? Look in the magazine indexes in the library and on the Internet for studies or stories that might support your thesis.

I'll look forward to seeing your final draft.

After considering her instructor's comments, Anna wrote the version of "Teenagers and Jobs" that appears on pages 347–348.

A Professional Essay to Consider

Read the following professional essay. Then answer the questions and read the comments that follow.

Ban the Things. Ban Them All.

by Molly Ivins

Guns. Everywhere guns.   1

Let me start this discussion by pointing out that I am not anti-gun. I'm pro-   2
knife. Consider the merits of the knife.

In the first place, you have to catch up with someone to stab him. A general   3
substitution of knives for guns would promote physical fitness. We'd turn into a
whole nation of great runners. Plus, knives don't ricochet. And people are seldom
killed while cleaning their knives.

As a civil libertarian,[1] I of course support the Second Amendment. And I be- 4
lieve it means exactly what it says: "A well-regulated militia being necessary to the
security of a free state, the right of the people to keep and bear arms shall not be
infringed."[2] Fourteen-year-old boys are not part of a well-regulated militia. Members of wacky religious cults are not part of a well-regulated militia. Permitting
unregulated citizens to have guns is destroying the security of this free state.

I am intrigued by the arguments of those who claim to follow the judicial   5
doctrine of original intent. How do they know it was the dearest wish of Thomas
Jefferson's heart that teenage drug dealers should cruise the cities of this nation
perforating their fellow citizens with assault rifles? Channeling?[3]

There is more hooey spread about the Second Amendment. It says quite clearly   6
that guns are for those who form part of a well-regulated militia, i.e., the armed
forces including the National Guard. The reasons for keeping them away from
everyone else get clearer by the day.

The comparison most often used is that of the automobile, another lethal ob-   7
ject that is regularly used to wreak great carnage. Obviously, this society is full of
people who haven't got enough common sense to use an automobile properly. But
we haven't outlawed cars yet.

We do, however, license them and their owners, restrict their use to presum-   8
ably sane and sober adults and keep track of who sells them to whom. At a minimum, we should do the same with guns.

---

[1]*civil libertarian:* someone actively concerned with protecting rights guaranteed to the individual by law.
[2]*infringed:* violated.
[3]*channeling:* serving as a medium in order to communicate with spirits.

In truth, there is no rational argument for guns in this society. This is no longer 9 a frontier nation in which people hunt their own food. It is a crowded, overwhelmingly urban country in which letting people have access to guns is a continuing disaster. Those who want guns—whether for target shooting, hunting or potting⁴ rattlesnakes (get a hoe)—should be subjected to the same restrictions placed on gun owners in England, a nation in which liberty has survived nicely without an armed populace.

The argument that "guns don't kill people" is patent nonsense. Anyone who 10 has ever worked in a cop shop knows how many family arguments end in murder because there was a gun in the house. Did the gun kill someone? No. But if there had been no gun, no one would have died. At least not without a good footrace first. Guns do kill. Unlike cars, that is all they do.

Michael Crichton makes an interesting argument about technology in his 11 thriller *Jurassic Park*. He points out that power without discipline is making this society into wreckage. By the time someone who studies the martial arts becomes a master—literally able to kill with bare hands—that person has also undergone years of training and discipline. But any fool can pick up a gun and kill with it.

"A well-regulated militia" surely implies both long training and long disci- 12 pline. That is the least, the very least, that should be required of those who are permitted to have guns, because a gun is literally the power to kill. For years, I used to enjoy taunting my gun-nut friends about their psychosexual hangups—always in a spirit of good cheer, you understand. But letting the noisy minority in the National Rifle Association force us to allow this carnage to continue is just plain insane.

I do think gun nuts have a power hangup. I don't know what is missing in 13 their psyches that they need to feel they have the power to kill. But no sane society would allow this to continue.

Ban the damn things. Ban them all. 14

You want protection? Get a dog. 15

ABOUT UNITY

1. Which of the following statements best represents the implied thesis of the essay?
   a. The author is pro-knife.
   b. The Second Amendment is poorly understood.
   c. Despite arguments to the contrary, people without long training and discipline should not be allowed to have guns.
   d. In his novel *Jurassic Park,* Michael Crichton argues that power without discipline is wrecking society.

---

⁴*potting:* shooting with a potshot (an easy shot).

2. Which statement would best serve as a topic sentence for paragraphs 5 and 6?

   a. Drug dealers should not be allowed to purchase assault rifles.

   b. Ivins is interested in other people's points of view concerning gun ownership.

   c. Thomas Jefferson was opposed to the idea of a "well-regulated militia."

   d. Applying the original intent of the Second Amendment to modern circumstances is not clear-cut and must be done with common sense.

3. Which is the topic sentence of paragraph 9?

   a. "In truth, there is no rational argument for guns in this society."

   b. "This is no longer a frontier nation in which people hunt their own food."

   c. "It is a crowded, overwhelmingly urban country in which letting people have access to guns is a continuing disaster."

   d. "Those who want guns … should be subjected to the same restrictions placed on gun owners in England… ."

ABOUT SUPPORT

4. Why does Ivins contrast the use of martial arts with the use of guns?

   a. To support the idea that gun owners should be required to study the martial arts

   b. To support the idea that a martial arts master can kill with his bare hands

   c. To support the idea that power without discipline is dangerous

   d. To support the idea that guns are more practical than the martial arts

5. Which statement best expresses the implied point of paragraph 10?

   a. Guns kill people.

   b. Many family arguments are surprisingly violent.

   c. Many arguments end in death only because a gun was handy.

   d. Guns and cars are similar.

6. In what ways, according to Ivins, is the knife preferable to the gun? Is Ivins really "pro-knife," or is she making some other point in her discussion of knives versus guns?

   _____

   _____

   _____

ABOUT COHERENCE

7. In paragraph 3, Ivins uses three addition signals—one to introduce each of her three reasons for being pro-knife. What are those three signals? (Two are *not* in the list of addition signals on page 87.)

_____   _____   _____

8. In paragraph 7, Ivins acknowledges an opposing point of view when she mentions that automobiles, like guns, "wreak great carnage." In paragraph 8, what sentence includes a "change of direction" signal indicating that Ivins will present her argument against that point of view? (*Write the first few words of that sentence.*)

_____

ABOUT THE INTRODUCTION AND CONCLUSION

9. Ivins's introduction consists of three very brief paragraphs. Which statement best describes the style of her introduction?
   a. It presents an anecdote that is related to the topic of unregulated gun ownership.
   b. It presents a provocative quotation that grabs the reader's attention.
   c. It makes a startling point that at first seems unrelated to the topic.
   d. It presents a quotation that puts the topic in some sort of historical context.

10. Which of these best describes the conclusion of "Ban the Things"?
   a. It makes a blunt recommendation.
   b. It summarizes the essay.
   c. It narrates an anecdote about guns.
   d. It predicts what will happen if guns are not banned.

Writing an Essay with Emphasis on Argument

WRITING ASSIGNMENT 1

Find an editorial in your local newspaper with which you either strongly agree or strongly disagree. Write a letter to the editor responding to that editorial. State why you agree or disagree with the position taken by the paper. Provide several paragraphs of supporting evidence for your position. When you turn in the copy of your letter to your instructor, also turn in the editorial to which you are responding. Your instructor may want you to send your letter to the newspaper, but you will want instructor feedback before doing so. The topic of the editorial will determine the additional chapters you will need to review. For instance, if the editorial focuses on an implied definition, you will need to review Chapter 14, "Definition," but if the editorial focuses on the effects of a specific city project, you will need to review Chapter 12, "Cause and/or Effect."

PREWRITING

a. As you write your opening paragraph, make sure you include the title of the editorial and the date on which it appeared. Refer to Chapter 22, "Writing a Research Paper," to properly punctuate and cite this information.

b. If you are writing to disagree with the article, you will want to pay special attention to your tone, always keeping your words as respectful as possible. If you are writing to agree with the article, you should respectfully acknowledge the opposing point of view before stating your thesis. Often, an editorial is printed on the same page as another editorial or an op-ed piece that argues the opposite point; reading both articles will help you focus your introductory material to properly set up your reader.

c. As you organize your points, keep in mind that emphatic order (in which you end with your most important reason) is often the most effective way to organize an argument. Your reader is most likely to remember your final reason.

d. Proceed to write the first draft of your essay.

REVISING

After you have completed the first draft of the paper, set it aside for a while if you can. Then read the paper out loud to a friend or classmate whose judgment you respect. Keep the following points in mind as you hear your own words, and ask your friend to respond to them as well:

Argument Checklist: THE FOUR BASES

ABOUT *UNITY*

✔ Does my essay have a clearly stated thesis?

✔ Does each paragraph in my essay have a clear topic sentence?

✔ Are there portions of the essay that do not support my thesis and therefore should be eliminated or rewritten?

ABOUT *SUPPORT*

✔ Have I provided persuasive details to support my argument?

✔ Does my final supporting paragraph include a strong argument for my position?

ABOUT *COHERENCE*

✔ Have I acknowledged the opposing point of view, showing that I am a reasonable person willing to consider other arguments?

✔ Have I used transition words to help readers follow my train of thought?

✔ Have I provided a concluding paragraph to summarize my argument or add a final persuasive touch?

ABOUT *SENTENCE SKILLS*

✔ Is my language tactful and courteous in order to avoid insulting anyone who doesn't agree with me?

✔ Have I used specific rather than general words?

✔ Have I avoided wordiness and used concise wording?

✔ Are my sentences varied?

✔ Have I checked my writing for spelling and other sentence skills, as listed on the inside back cover of the book?

As you revise your essay through added drafts, continue to refer to this list until you and your reader can answer "yes" to each question.

WRITING ASSIGNMENT 2

Write an essay in which you argue *for* or *against* any one of the three comments below. Support and defend your argument by drawing on your reasoning ability and general experience.

OPTION 1

Until recently, junk food was available in school cafeterias and school vending machines across the nation. For decades, school cafeteria menus did not encourage the best eating habits. A 2012 federal mandate changed the kinds of foods offered in public schools so that, for the large part, junk food was no longer available, and there was a strong emphasis on healthy eating, including fruits and vegetables. This is only right. Schools are now practicing what they preach about the importance of healthy diets and it is commendable that they have stopped serving junk food.

OPTION 2

By the time many students reach high school, they have learned the basics in most subjects. Some still have much to gain from the education that high schools offer, but others might be better off spending the next four years in other ways. For their benefit, high school attendance should be voluntary.

OPTION 3

Many of today's young people are mainly concerned with prestigious careers, making money, and owning things. It seems we no longer teach the benefits of spending time and money to help the community, the country, or the world. Our country can strengthen these human values and improve the world by requiring young people to spend a year working in some type of community service.

WRITING ASSIGNMENT 3

Voting is a privilege that many Americans don't take advantage of. Choose one of the two options below as a topic for your essay. Support and defend your argument by drawing on your reasoning ability, general experience, and any necessary research. You may want to review Chapter 10, "Exemplification," Chapter 12, "Cause and/or Effect," and Chapter 13, "Comparison and/or Contrast," to help you focus your support. If you need to incorporate research, you will want to review Chapter 22, "Writing a Research Paper."

OPTION 1:
Since jury duty and taxes are compulsory, voting should also be required.

OPTION 2:
Persuade your audience of the importance of voting in all elections.

PREWRITING

a. Take a few minutes to think about the two options and decide which one you would most like to write about. Use a prewriting technique of your choice and write out as many ideas as possible about your chosen topic.

b. On a sheet of paper, organize your prewriting into a brief outline of support for your position. Preparing the outline will give you a chance to think further about your position.

c. Next, decide how you will develop each of your supporting points. Make brief outlines of the supporting paragraphs. If you need to generate more ideas for support, use the prewriting technique you have chosen.

d. Determine the order in which you want to present your paragraphs. Emphatic order (in which you end with your most important reason) is often the most effective way to organize an argument. Your reader is most likely to remember your final reason.

e. Now write the first draft of your essay.

REVISING
Use the suggestions for revision that follow Writing Assignment 1 on pages 360–361.

Writing for a Specific Purpose and Audience

In this essay with emphasis on argument, you will write with a specific purpose and for a specific audience.

The art of persuasion in the workplace is so important that many businesses bring in educational consultants to teach employees how, why, and when to be persuasive. Often these companies charge several thousands of dollars for their expertise; however, to save money, your boss has asked you to write an essay that will be given to all employees explaining the art of persuasion and why it is a necessary skill in your workplace.

In order for employees to understand what they are being asked to do, you should incorporate an extended definition of what good persuasion is, and possibly contrast it with what good persuasion is not. You may also want to incorporate scenarios that demonstrate both good and bad examples to help your audience fully understand how and when to be persuasive.

Perhaps you work at an advertising company. One of your jobs is to acquire new client accounts, and persuading them to sign with you usually involves a key presentation. As the writer of this essay, you could give an example of one of your best presentations, explaining what was done correctly and why it worked. You could also give an example of one of your worst presentations, emphasizing what was done incorrectly. You will want to review Chapter 8, "Description," Chapter 11, "Process," Chapter 13, "Comparison and/or Contrast," and Chapter 14, "Definition," to help create a strong, persuasive essay.

Special Skills

PART 3

PREVIEW

17 Taking Essay Exams

18 Writing a Summary

19 Writing a Report

20 Writing a Résumé and Cover Letter

21 Using the Library and the Internet

22 Writing a Research Paper

Write an essay about a skill you have learned outside of the classroom, which has helped you succeed in college. Maybe it is teamwork, persistence, time management, or something else. Be sure to provide specific examples of how this skill has been beneficial to you.

Taking Essay Exams

This chapter will explain and illustrate

- five steps in writing an effective exam essay

Visit AltaVista at http://www.altavista.com and enter the phrase "taking an essay exam" into the search box. Then visit a handful of the sites that AltaVista finds and choose one to recommend to your classmates. Write a one-paragraph review of the site to hand in to your instructor. Was it helpful? What advice did it offer?

Essay exams are perhaps the most common type of writing you will do in school. They include one or more questions to which you must respond in detail, writing your answers in a clear, well-organized manner. Many students have trouble with essay exams because they do not realize there is a sequence to follow that will help them do well on such tests. This section describes five basic steps needed to prepare adequately for an essay test and to take the test. It is assumed, however, that you are already doing two essential things: first, attending class regularly and taking notes on what happens in class; second, reading your textbook and other assignments and taking notes on them. If you are *not* consistently going to class, reading your text, and taking notes in both cases, you are likely to have trouble with essay exams and other tests as well.

To write an effective exam essay, follow these five steps:

Step 1: Anticipate ten probable questions.

Step 2: Prepare and memorize an informal outline answer for each question.

Step 3: Look at the exam carefully and do several things.

Step 4: Prepare a brief, informal outline before writing your essay answer.

Step 5: Write a clear, well-organized essay.

The following pages explain and illustrate these steps.

Step 1: Anticipate Ten Probable Questions

Because exam time is limited, the instructor can give you only several questions to answer. He or she will focus on questions dealing with the most important areas of the subject. You can probably guess most of them.

Go through your class notes with a colored pen and mark off those areas where your instructor has spent a good deal of time. The more time spent on any one area, the better the chance you will get an essay question on it. If the instructor spent a week talking about present-day changes in the traditional family structure, or the importance of the carbon molecule, or the advantages of capitalism, or key early figures in the development of psychology as a science, you can reasonably expect that you will get a question about the emphasized area.

In both your class notes and your textbooks, pay special attention to definitions and examples and to basic lists of items (enumerations). Enumerations in particular are often a key to essay questions. For instance, if your instructor spoke at length about causes of the Great Depression, effects of water pollution, or advantages of capitalism, you should probably expect a question such as What were the causes of the Great Depression? or What are the effects of water pollution? or What are the advantages of capitalism?

If your instructor has given you a study guide, look there for probable essay questions. (Some instructors choose essay questions from those listed in study guides.) Look for clues to essay questions on any short quizzes that you might have been given. Finally, consider very carefully any review that the instructor provides. Always write down such reviews—your instructor has often made up the test or is making it up at the time of the review and is likely to give you valuable hints about it. Take advantage of them! Note also that if the instructor does not offer to provide a review, do not hesitate to *ask* for one in a friendly way. Essay questions are likely to come from areas the instructor may mention.

An Illustration of Step 1

A psychology class was given one day to prepare for an essay exam on stress—a subject that had been covered in class and by a chapter in the textbook for the course. One student, Mark, read carefully through his class notes and the text-book chapter. On the basis of the headings, major enumerations, and definitions he noted, he decided that there were five likely essay questions:

1. What are the common sources of stress?
2. What are the types of conflict?
3. What are the defense mechanisms that people use to cope with stress?
4. What effects can stress have on people?
5. What are the characteristics of a well-adjusted person?

Step 2: Prepare and Memorize an Informal Outline Answer for Each Question

Write out each question you have made up and, under it, list the main points that need to be discussed. Put important supporting information in parentheses after each main point. You now have an informal outline that you can memorize.

Pick out a *key word* in each part, and then create a *catchphrase* to help you remember the key words.

> **TIP** If you have spelling problems, make up a list of words you might have to spell in writing your answers. For example, if you are having a psychology test on the principles of learning, you might want to study such terms as *conditioning, reinforcement, Pavlov, reflex, stimulus,* and so on.

An Illustration of Step 2

After identifying the likely questions on the exam, Mark made up an outline answer for each of the questions. For example, here is the outline answer that he made up for the first question:

Common sources of stress:

1. (Pressure) (internal and external)
2. (Anxiety) (sign of internal conflict)

3. (Frustration) (can't reach desired goal)

4. (Conflict) (three types of approach-avoidance)

   P A F C (People are funny creatures.)

See whether you can complete the following explanation of what Mark has done in preparing for the essay question.

ACTIVITY 1

First, Mark wrote down the heading and then numbered the sources of stress

under it. Also, in parentheses beside each point he added _____.

Then he circled the four key words, and he wrote down the first _____ of each word underneath his outline. Mark then used the first letter in each key word to make up a catchphrase that he could easily remember. Finally, he

_____ himself over and over until he could recall all four of the sources of stress that the first letters stood for. He also made sure that he recalled the supporting material that went with each idea.

PART 1

Make a list of the steps that Mark took in preparing for an essay test question on the common causes of stress.

_____

1. _____

2. _____

3. _____

   _____

4. _____

   _____

PART 2

After you have done that, pretend that you have been told that you will be tested on a particular chapter of a textbook in a history, sociology, biology, or other class you are taking. Write a list of five sample essay questions that might be on the test. Then, like Mark, write out an outline answer for each question.

_____

Step 3: Look at the Exam Carefully and Do Several Things

1. Get an overview of the exam by reading *all* the questions on the test.

2. Note *direction words (compare, illustrate, list,* and so on) for each question. Be sure to write the kind of answer that each question requires. For

example, if a question says "illustrate," do not "compare." The list on the next page will help clarify the distinctions among various direction words.

3. Budget your time. Write in the margin the number of minutes you should spend for each essay. For example, if you have three essays worth an equal number of points and a one-hour time limit, figure twenty minutes for each essay. Make sure you are not left with only a couple of minutes to do a high-point essay.

4. Start with the easiest question. Getting a good answer down on paper will help build up your confidence and momentum. Number your answers plainly so that your instructor knows what question you are answering first.

An Illustration of Step 3

When Mark received the exam, the question was "Describe the four common sources of stress in our lives." Mark circled the direction word *describe,* which meant he should explain in detail each of the four causes of stress. He also jotted a "30" in the margin when the instructor said that students would have a half hour to write the answer.

ACTIVITY 2   Complete the short matching quiz below. It will help you review the meanings of some of the direction words listed in the box below.

1. List _____   a.   Tell in detail about something.

2. Contrast _____   b.   Give a series of points and number them
                             1, 2, 3, etc.

3. Define _____   c.   Give a condensed account of the main points.

4. Summarize _____   d.   Show differences between two things.

5. Describe _____   e.   Give the normal meaning of a term.

Direction Words

Term	Meaning
Compare	Show similarities between things.
Contrast	Show differences between things.
Criticize	Give the positive and negative points of a subject as well as evidence for those positions.
Define	Give the formal meaning of a term.

continued

Describe	Tell in detail about something.
Diagram	Make a drawing and label it.
Discuss	Give details and, if relevant, the positive and negative points of a subject as well as evidence for those positions.
Enumerate	List points and number them 1, 2, 3, and so on.
Evaluate	Give the positive and negative points of a subject as well as your judgment about which outweighs the other and why.
Illustrate	Explain by giving examples.
Interpret	Explain the meaning of something.
Justify	Give reasons for something.
List	Give a series of points and number them 1, 2, 3, and so on.

Outline	Give the main points and important secondary points. Put main points at the margin and indent secondary points under the main points. Relationships may also be described with logical symbols, as follows:
	
	1. _____
	    a. _____
	    b. _____
	2. _____

Prove	Show to be true by giving facts or reasons.
Relate	Show connections among things.
State	Give the main points.
Summarize	Give a condensed account of the main points.
Trace	Describe the development or history of a subject.

Step 4: Prepare a Brief, Informal Outline before Writing Your Essay Answer

Use the margin of the exam or a separate piece of scratch paper to jot down quickly, as they occur to you, the main points you want to discuss in each answer. Then decide in what order you want to present these points in your response. Write 1 in front of the first item, 2 beside the second, and so on. You now have an informal outline to guide you as you answer your essay question.

If a question on the exam is similar to the questions you anticipated and outlined at home, quickly write down the catchphrase that calls back the content of the outline. Below the catchphrase, write the key words represented by each letter in the catchphrase. The key words, in turn, will remind you of the concepts they represent. If you have prepared properly, this step will take only a minute or so, and you will have before you the guide you need to write a focused, supported, organized answer.

An Illustration of Step 4

Mark immediately wrote down his catchphrase, "People are funny creatures." He next jotted down the first letters in his catchphrase and then the key words that went with each letter. He then filled in several key details and was ready to write his essay answer. Here is what his brief outline looked like:

> People are funny creatures.
>
> P   Pressure (internal and external)
>
> A   Anxiety (internal conflict)
>
> F   Frustration (prevented from reaching goal)
>
> C   Conflict (approach-avoidance)

Step 5: Write a Clear, Well-Organized Essay

If you have followed steps 1 through 4, you are ready to write an effective essay, keeping in mind the principles of good writing: unity, support, coherence, and clear, error-free sentences.

Start with a sentence that clearly states what your essay will be about. Then, make sure that everything in your essay relates to that sentence.

Second, although you must take time limitations into account, provide as much support as possible for each of your main points.

Third, use transitions such as *first, next, then, however,* and *finally* to guide your reader.

Last, leave time to proofread for sentence mistakes. Look for omitted, miswritten, or misspelled words (if you are allowed, bring a dictionary). Check for awkward phrasings or incorrect punctuation, or anything else that makes your writing unclear or distracts your reader. Cross out mistakes and make corrections neatly above them. To add or change a point, insert an asterisk at the appropriate spot, put another asterisk at the bottom of the page, and add the corrected material there.

An Illustration of Step 5

Read Mark's answer, reproduced below, and then do the activity that follows.

> There are four common sources of stress in our lives. The first one is pressure, which can be internal or external. Internal pressure occurs when a person tries to live

up to his or her own goals and standards. This kind of pressure can help (when a

person strives to be a better musician, for instance) or hurt (as when someone tries to

reach impossible standards of beauty). External pressure occurs when people must

compete, deal with rapid change, or cope with outside demands. Another source of stress

is anxiety. People who are ~~anxous~~ anxious often don't know why they feel this way. Some

psychologists think anxiety comes from some internal conflict, like feeling angry and

trying hard to repress this ~~angry feeling~~ anger. A third source of stress is frustration,

which occurs when people are prevented from reaching goals or obtaining certain

needs. For example, a woman may do poorly on an important exam because she has a

bad cold. She feels angry and frustrated because she could not reach her goal of an A

or B grade. The most common source of stress is conflict. Conflict results when a person

is faced with two incompatible ~~goals~~ desires. The person may want both goals (a demanding

career and motherhood, for instance). This is called approach-approach. Or a person

may want to avoid both choices (avoidance-avoidance). Or a person may be both

attracted to and repelled by a desire (as a woman who wants to marry a gambler).

This is approach-avoidance   .

The following sentences comment on Mark's essay. Fill in the missing word or words in each case.

ACTIVITY 3

1. Mark begins with a sentence that clearly states what his essay _____. Always begin with such a clear statement!

2. Notice the _____ that Mark made when writing and proofreading his paper. He neatly crossed out miswritten or unwanted words, and he used insertion signs (^) to add omitted words.

3. The four signal words that Mark used to guide his readers, and himself, through the main points of his answer are _____, _____, _____, and _____.

ACTIVITY 4

In Part 2 of Activity 1, you were asked to write five questions (as well as an informal outline for each) that you might use for an essay exam in another course you are taking. Use the outline you made for one of these questions as the basis for an answer you might provide on an essay exam.

Before you begin writing, read this sample essay, which responds to the following question: "Explain the major difference between ancient Athenian democracy and contemporary American democracy." Note that the essay begins with a clear thesis statement.

Ancient Athens had a direct form of democracy; America has a representative form of democracy. In Athens, all men could participate in the Assembly, the body where laws governing every aspect of Athenian life—from taxes to religious observances—were debated and voted upon. Each man, no matter how rich or poor, could speak his mind and cast a vote. In the United States, the people do not, as a rule, make laws directly. Instead, they elect representatives to legislative bodies to do that. In the federal government, for example, these two bodies are the House of Representatives and the Senate. Members of these groups can debate and decide on laws independent of the wishes of those who elected them. Although deliberations of the House and Senate are open, legislators usually hear from their constituents only when controversial laws are being discussed. However, no matter what the majority of people in a congressional district or state think about a particular proposal, a representative or senator may vote as he or she pleases. (Of course, he or she may pay a price for ignoring their opinions in the next election.) The closest thing we have to Athenian democracy is a referendum or plebiscite, which is also known as a ballot question. This is proposed law that every citizen can vote upon. Such questions appear on the ballot every two years when we vote in local, state, and national elections.

Writing a Summary

**This chapter will
explain and illustrate
how to**

- summarize an article
- summarize a book

*Find an article in your school or local newspaper about which
you can write an essay-length summary. Include an introductory
paragraph in which you state the article's thesis.*

At some point in a course, your instructor may ask you to write a summary
of a book, an article, a TV show, or the like. In a *summary* (also referred to
as a *précis* or an *abstract*), you reduce material in an original work to its
main points and key supporting details. Unlike an outline, however, a summary does not use symbols such as I, A, 1, 2, etc., to indicate the relations
among parts of the original material.

A summary may consist of a single word, a phrase, several sentences,
or one or more paragraphs. The length of any summary you prepare will
depend on your instructor's expectations and the length of the original
work. Most often, you will be asked to write a summary consisting of one
or more paragraphs.

Writing a summary brings together a number of important reading, study,
and writing skills. To condense the original assigned material, you must

preview, read, evaluate, organize, and perhaps outline it. Summarizing, then, can be a real aid to understanding; you must "get inside" the material and realize fully what is being said before you can reduce its meaning to a few words.

How to Summarize an Article

To write a summary of an article, follow the steps described below. If the assigned material is a TV show or film, adapt the suggestions accordingly.

1. Take a few minutes to preview the work. You can preview an article in a magazine by taking a quick look at the following:

   a. *Title*. A title often summarizes what an article is about. Think about the title for a minute and about how it may condense the meaning of the article.

   b. *Subtitle*. A subtitle, if given, is a short summary appearing under or next to the title. For example, in a *Newsweek* article titled "Growing Old, Feeling Young," the following caption appeared: "Not only are Americans living longer, they are staying active longer—and their worst enemy is not nature, but the myths and prejudices about growing old." In short, the subtitle, the caption, or any other words in large print under or next to the title often provide a quick insight into the meaning of an article.

   c. *First and last several paragraphs*. In the first several paragraphs, the author may introduce you to the subject and state the purpose of the article. In the last several paragraphs, the writer may present conclusions or a summary. The previews or summaries can give you a quick overview of what the entire article is about.

   d. *Other items*. Note any heads or subheads that appear in the article. They often provide clues to the article's main points and give an immediate sense of what each section is about. Look carefully at any pictures, charts, or diagrams that accompany the article. Page space in a magazine or journal is limited, and such visual aids are generally used only to illustrate important points in the article. Note any words or phrases set off in *italic type* or **boldface type;** such words have probably been emphasized because they deal with important points in the article.

2. Read the article for all you can understand the first time through. Do not slow down or turn back. Check or otherwise mark main points and key supporting details. Pay special attention to all the items noted in the preview. Also, look for definitions, examples, and enumerations (lists of items), which often indicate key ideas. You can also identify important points by turning any headings into questions and reading to find the answers to the questions.

3. Go back and reread more carefully the areas you have identified as most important. Also, focus on other key points you may have missed in your first reading.

4. Take notes on the material. Concentrate on getting down the main ideas and the key supporting points.

5. Prepare the first draft of your summary, keeping these points in mind:

   a. In the summary, identify the title and author of the work. If your summary is not part of an essay, with in-text citation and a "Works Cited" page, then you should also include the date of publication and publication name. The two examples below show the difference in format.

   b. The first sentence of your summary should also be written as a topic sentence and should contain the main idea or thesis of the original work in your own words.

   c. Do not write an overly detailed summary. Remember that the purpose of a summary is to reduce the original work to its main points and essential supporting details.

   d. Express the main points and key supporting details in your own words. Do not imitate the style of the original work.

   e. Quote from the material only to illustrate key points. Limit your quotations. A one-paragraph summary should not contain more than one quoted sentence or phrase.

   f. Preserve the balance and proportion of the original work. If the original devoted 70 percent of its space to one idea and only 30 percent to another, your summary should reflect that emphasis.

   g. Revise your final draft, paying attention to the four bases of effective writing (*unity*, *support*, *coherence*, and *sentence skills*) explained in Part 1.

   h. Write the final draft of the paper.

A Model Summary of an Article

Here is a model summary of a magazine article that would stand on its own:

> In the article, "Why the Campaign to Stop America's Obesity Crisis Keeps Failing," originally printed in the May 2012 *Newsweek*, Gary Taubes reports on the obesity epidemic and his beliefs that refined sugars are the cause of obesity. He begins his article by citing information from the 1930s that demonstrates children had obesity problems even during the Depression.

continued

He then goes on to demonstrate that despite government recommendations, Americans' dietary changes have not resulted in less obesity. He supports his ideas about refined sugars and carbohydrates by detailing the science of fat cells, insulin, and the liver. He concludes that the authorities like the Centers for Disease Control and Prevention and the National Institutes of Health may need to rethink what they are telling Americans (32–36).

Here is a model summary of a magazine article that is used in an essay containing a "Works Cited" page. Note that the publication information is not needed within the text, but it is available in the "Works Cited" entry. If this is the first time you are citing the article, you need to reference the article's title. However, if this is the second or subsequent time citing this article, you would refer only to the author's last name, as in "Taubes continues to remark. . . ."

In his article, "Why the Campaign to Stop America's Obesity Crisis Keeps Failing," Gary Taubes reports on the obesity epidemic and his beliefs that refined sugars are the cause of obesity. He begins his article by citing information from the 1930s that demonstrates children had obesity problems even during the Depression. He then goes on to demonstrate that despite government recommendations, Americans' dietary changes have not resulted in less obesity. He supports his ideas about refined sugars and carbohydrates by detailing the science of fat cells, insulin, and the liver. He concludes that the authorities like the Centers for Disease Control and Prevention and the National Institutes of Health may need to rethink what they are telling Americans (32–36).

Works Cited

Taubes, Gary. "Why the Campaign to Stop America's Obesity Crisis Keeps Failing." *Newsweek* 14 May 2012: 32–36.

ACTIVITY 1

Write an essay-length summary of the following article. Include a short introductory paragraph that states the thesis of the article. Then summarize in three supporting paragraphs the three important areas in which study skills can be useful. Your conclusion might be a single sentence restating the thesis.

Power Learning

Jill had not done as well in high school as she had hoped. Since college involved even more work, it was no surprise that she didn't do better there.   1

The reason for her so-so performance was not a lack of effort. She attended most of her classes and read her textbooks. And she never missed handing in any assignment, even though it often meant staying up late the night before homework was due. Still, she just got by in her classes. Before long, she came to the conclusion that she simply couldn't do any better.   2

Then one day, one of her instructors said something to make her think otherwise. "You can probably build some sort of house by banging a few boards together," he said. "But if you want a sturdy home, you'll have to use the right techniques and tools. Building carefully takes work, but it gets better results. The same can be said of your education. There are no shortcuts, but there are some proven study skills that can really help. If you don't use them, you may end up with a pretty flimsy education."   3

Jill signed up for a study-skills course and found out a crucial fact—that learning how to learn is the key to success in school. Certain dependable skills have made the difference between disappointment and success for generations of students. These techniques won't free you from work, but they will make your work far more productive. They include three important areas: time control, classroom note-taking, and textbook study.   4

Time Control

Success in college depends on time control. *Time control* means that you deliberately organize and plan your time, instead of letting it drift by. Planning means that you should never be faced with an overdue term paper or a cram session the night before a test.   5

Three steps are involved in time control. *First*, you should prepare a large monthly calendar. Buy a calendar with a large white block around each date, or make one yourself. At the beginning of the college semester, circle important dates on this calendar. Circle the days on which tests are scheduled; circle the days when papers are due. This calendar can also be used to schedule study plans. At the beginning of the week, you can jot down your plans for each day. An alternative method would be to make plans for each day the night before. On Tuesday night, for example, you might write down "Read Chapter 5 in psychology" in the Wednesday block. Hang this calendar where you will see it every day—your kitchen, bedroom, even your bathroom!   6

The *second step* in time control is to have a weekly study schedule for the semester—a chart that covers all the days of the week and all the waking hours in each day. Below is part of one student's schedule: 7

continued

Time	Mon.	Tue.	Wed.	Thurs.	Fri.	Sat.	
6:00 a.m.							
7:00	Breakfast	Breakfast	Breakfast	Breakfast	Breakfast		
8:00	Math	STUDY	Math	STUDY	Math	Breakfast	
9:00	STUDY	Biology	STUDY	Biology	STUDY	Job	
10:00	Psychology	↓	Psychology	↓	Psychology		
11:00		English		English			
12:00	Lunch		Lunch		Lunch	↓	

On your own schedule, fill in all the fixed hours in each day—hours for meals, classes, job (if any), and travel time. Next, mark time blocks that you can *realistically* use for study each day. Depending on the number of courses you are taking and the demands of these courses, you may want to block off five, ten, or even twenty or more hours of study time a week. Keep in mind that you should not block off time that you do not truly intend to use for study. Otherwise, your schedule will be a meaningless gimmick. Also, remember that you should allow time for rest and relaxation. You will be happiest, and able to accomplish the most, when you have time for both work and play.

The *third step* in time control is to make a daily or weekly to-do list. This may be the most valuable time-control method you ever use. On this list, write down the things you need to do for the following day or the following week. If you choose to write a weekly list, do it on Sunday night. If you choose to write a daily list, do it the night before. Here is part of one student's daily list:

8

To Do	Tuesday
1.	Review biology notes before class
2.	Proofread English paper due today
3.	See Dick about game on Friday
4.	Get gas for car
5.	Read next chapter of psychology text

You may use a three-by-five-inch notepad or a small spiral-bound notebook for this list. Carry the list around with you during the day. Always concentrate on doing the most important items first. To make the best use of your time, mark high-priority items with an asterisk and give them precedence over low-priority items. For instance, you may find yourself wondering what to do after dinner on Thursday evening. Among the items on your list are "Clean inside of car" and "Review chapter for math quiz." It is obviously more important for you to

continued

review your notes at this point; you can clean out the car some other time. As you complete items on your to-do list, cross them out. Do not worry about unfinished items. They can be rescheduled. You will still be accomplishing a great deal and making more effective use of your time.

Classroom Note-Taking

One of the most important single things you can do to perform well in a college course is to take effective class notes. The following hints should help you become a better note-taker.

9

First, attend class faithfully. Your alternatives—reading the text, reading someone else's notes, or both—cannot substitute for the class experience of hearing ideas in person as someone presents them to you. Also, in class lectures and discussions, your instructor typically presents and develops the main ideas and facts of the course—the ones you will be expected to know on exams.

10

Another valuable hint is to make use of abbreviations while taking notes. Using abbreviations saves time when you are trying to get down a great deal of information. Abbreviate terms that recur frequently in a lecture and put a key to your abbreviations at the top of your notes. For example, in sociology class, *eth* could stand for *ethnocentrism;* in a psychology class, *STM* could stand for *short-term memory.* (When a lecture is over, you may want to go back and write out the terms you have abbreviated.) Also, use *e* for *example; def* for *definition; info* for *information;* + for *and;* and so on. If you use the same abbreviations all the time, you will soon develop a kind of personal shorthand that makes taking notes much easier.

11

A third hint for taking notes is to be on the lookout for signals of importance. Write down whatever your instructor puts on the board. If he or she takes the time to put material on the board, it is probably important, and the chances are good that it will come up later on exams. Always write down definitions and enumerations. Enumerations are lists of items. They are signaled in such ways as "The four steps in the process are . . ."; "There were three reasons for . . ."; "The two effects were . . ."; "Five characteristics of . . ."; and so on. In your notes, always number such enumerations (1, 2, 3, etc.). They will help you understand relationships among ideas and organize the material of the lecture. Watch for emphasis words—words your instructor may use to indicate that something is important. Examples of such words are "This is an important reason . . ."; "A point that will keep coming up later . . ."; "The chief cause was . . ."; "The basic idea here is . . ."; and so on. Always write down the important statements announced by these and other emphasis words. Finally, if your instructor repeats a point, you can assume that it is important. You might put an *R* for *repeated* in the margin so that later you will know that your instructor stressed it.

12

continued

Next, be sure to write down the instructor's examples and mark them with **13**
an *e*. The examples help you understand abstract points. If you do not write
them down, you are likely to forget them later, when they are needed to help
make sense of an idea.

Also, be sure to write down the connections between ideas. Too many **14**
students merely copy terms the instructor puts on the board. They forget that,
as time passes, the details that serve as connecting bridges between ideas
quickly fade. You should, then, write down the relationships and connections
in class. That way you'll have them to help tie together your notes later on.

Review your notes as soon as possible after class. You must make them **15**
as clear as possible while they are fresh in your mind. A day later may be
too late, because forgetting sets in very quickly. Make sure that punctuation is
clear, that all words are readable and correctly spelled, and that unfinished
sentences are completed (or at least marked off so that you can check your
notes with another student's). Add clarifying or connecting comments wherever
necessary. Make sure that important ideas are clearly marked. Improve the
organization if necessary so that you can see at a glance main points and
relationships among them.

Finally, try in general to get down a written record of each class. You **16**
must do this because forgetting begins almost immediately. Studies have
shown that within two weeks you are likely to have forgotten 80 percent or
more of what you have heard. And in four weeks you are lucky if 5 percent
remains! This is so crucial that it bears repeating: To guard against the
relentlessness of forgetting, it is absolutely essential that you write down what
you hear in class. Later you can concentrate on working to understand fully
and to remember the ideas that have been presented in class. And then, the
more complete your notes are, the more you are likely to learn.

Textbook Study

In many college courses, success means being able to read and study **17**
a textbook skillfully. For many students, unfortunately, textbooks are heavy
going. After an hour or two of study, the textbook material is as formless and
as hard to understand as ever. But there is a way to attack even the most
difficult textbook and make sense of it. Use a sequence in which you preview
a chapter, mark it, take notes on it, and then study the notes.

Previewing

Previewing a selection is an important first step to understanding. Taking **18**
the time to preview a section or chapter can give you a bird's-eye view of
the way the material is organized. You will have a sense of where you are
beginning, what you will cover, and where you will end.

There are several steps in previewing a selection. First, study the title. **19**
The title is the shortest possible summary of a selection and will often tell

continued

you the limits of the material you will cover. For example, the title "FDR and the Supreme Court" tells you to expect a discussion of President Roosevelt's dealings with the Court. You know that you will probably not encounter any material dealing with FDR's foreign policies or personal life. Next, quickly read over the first and last paragraphs of the selection; these may contain important introductions to, and summaries of, the main ideas. Then briefly examine the headings and subheadings in the selection. Together, the headings and subheadings are a mini-outline of what you are reading. Headings are often main ideas or important concepts in capsule form; subheadings are breakdowns of ideas within main areas. Finally, read the first sentence of some paragraphs, look for words set off in **boldface** or *italics*, and look at pictures or diagrams. After you have previewed a selection in this way, you should have a good general sense of the material to be read.

Marking

You should mark a textbook selection at the same time that you read it through carefully. Use a felt-tip highlighter to shade material that seems important, or use a ballpoint pen and put symbols in the margin next to the material: stars, checks, or NB (*nota bene*, Latin for "note well"). What to mark is not as mysterious as some students believe. You should try to find main ideas by looking for clues: definitions and examples, enumerations, and emphasis words.   **20**

1. *Definitions and examples:* Definitions are often among the most important ideas in a selection. They are particularly significant in introductory courses in almost any subject area, where much of your learning involves mastering the specialized vocabulary of that subject. In a sense, you are learning the "language" of psychology or business or whatever the subject might be.   **21**

    Most definitions are abstract, and so they usually are followed by one or more examples to help clarify their meaning. Always mark off definitions and at least one example that makes a definition clear to you. In a psychology text, for example, we are told that "rationalization is an attempt to reduce anxiety by deciding that you have not really been frustrated." Several examples follow, among them: "A young man, frustrated because he was rejected when he asked for a date, convinces himself that the girl is not very attractive or interesting."   **22**

2. *Enumerations:* Enumerations are lists of items (causes, reasons, types, and so on) that are numbered 1, 2, 3, . . . or that could easily be numbered. They are often signaled by addition words. Many of the paragraphs in this book, for instance, use words like *First of all, Another, In addition,* and *Finally* to signal items in a series. Other textbooks also use this very common and effective organizational method.   **23**

continued

3. *Emphasis words:* Emphasis words tell you that an idea is important.   24
Common emphasis words include phrases such as *a major event, a key
feature, the chief factor, important to note, above all,* and *most of all.*
Here is an example: "The most significant contemporary use of marketing
is its application to nonbusiness areas, such as political parties."

Note-Taking

Next, you should take notes. Go through the chapter a second time,   25
rereading the most important parts. Try to write down the main ideas in a
simple outline form. For example, in taking notes on a psychology selection,
you might write down the heading "Defense Mechanisms." Below the
heading you would define them, number and describe each kind, and give
an example of each.

Defense Mechanisms

a.   *Definition: unconscious attempts to reduce anxiety*

b.   *Kinds:*

(1)   *Rationalization: An attempt to reduce anxiety by deciding that you
have not really been frustrated.*

*Example: A man turned down for a date decides that the woman was
not worth going out with anyway.*

(2)   *Projection: Projecting onto other people motives or thoughts of one's own.*

*Example: A wife who wants to have an affair accuses her husband of
having one.*

Studying Notes

To study your notes, use repeated self-testing. For example, look at the   26
heading "Defense Mechanisms" and say to yourself, "What are the kinds
of defense mechanisms?" When you can recite them, then say to yourself,
"What is rationalization?" "What is an example of rationalization?" Then ask
yourself, "What is projection?" "What is an example of projection?" After you
learn each section, review it, and then go on to the next section.

Do not simply read your notes; keep looking away and seeing if you can   27
recite them to yourself. This self-testing is the key to effective learning.

continued

Textbook Study Sequence

Remember this sequence for dealing with a textbook: preview, mark, take **28** notes, study the notes. Approaching a textbook in this methodical way will give you very positive results. You will no longer feel bogged down in a swamp of words, unable to figure out what you are supposed to know. Instead, you will understand exactly what you have to do and how to go about doing it.

Conclusion

Take a minute now to evaluate your own study habits. Do you practice **29** many of the above skills to take effective classroom notes, control your time, and learn from your textbooks? If not, perhaps you should. The skills are not magic, but they are too valuable to ignore. Use them carefully and consistently, and they will make academic success possible for you. Try them, and you won't need convincing.

Write an essay-length summary of a broadcast of the CBS television show *60 Minutes*. In your first sentence, include the date of the show. For example, "The September 8, 2013, broadcast of CBS's *60 Minutes* dealt with three subjects most people would find of interest. The first segment of the show centered on . . . ; the second segment examined . . . ; the final segment discussed. . . . " Be sure to use parallel form in describing the three segments of the show. Then summarize each segment in the three supporting paragraphs that follow.

ACTIVITY 2

Write an essay-length summary of a cover story of interest to you in a recent issue of *Time, Newsweek,* or *Consumer Reports.*

ACTIVITY 3

How to Summarize a Book

To write a summary of a book, first preview the book by briefly looking at the following:

1. *Title.* A title is often the shortest possible summary of what a book is about. Think about the title and how it may summarize the whole book.

2. *Table of contents.* The contents will tell you the number of chapters in the book and the subject of each chapter. Use the contents to get a general sense of how the book is organized. You should also note the number of pages in each chapter. If thirty pages are devoted to one episode or idea and an average of fifteen pages to other episodes or ideas, you should probably give more space in your summary to the contents of the longer chapter.

3. *Preface*. Here you will probably find out why the author wrote the book. Also, the preface may summarize the main ideas developed in the book and may describe briefly how the book is organized.

4. *First and last chapters*. In these chapters, the author may preview or review important ideas and themes developed in the book.

5. *Other items*. Note how the author has used headings and subheadings to organize information in the book. Check the opening and closing paragraphs of each chapter to see if these paragraphs contain introductions or summaries. Look quickly at charts, diagrams, and pictures in the book, since they are probably there to illustrate key points. Note any special features (index, glossary, appendices) that may appear at the end of the book.

Next, adapt steps 2 through 5 for summarizing an article on pages 376–377.

ACTIVITY 4   Write an essay-length summary of a book you have read.

Writing a Report

This chapter will explain and illustrate

- the two parts of a report

  Part 1: A summary of the work

  Part 2: Your reaction to the work

This chapter also includes

- points to keep in mind when writing a report

- a model report

To gain a sense of how to review a text, visit the New York Review of Books *Web site at http://www.nybooks.com and choose a review to read. Write a short paragraph explaining why you chose that review and what you've learned from it.*

Each semester, you will probably be asked by at least one instructor to read a book or an article and write a paper recording your response to the material. In these reports or reaction papers, your instructor will most likely expect you to do two things: *summarize the material* and *detail your reaction to it*. The following pages explain both parts of a report.

Part 1 of a Report: A Summary of the Work

To develop the first part of a report, do the following. (An example follows, on page 389.)

1. Identify the author and title of the work, and include in parentheses the publisher and publication date. With magazines, give the date of publication.

2. Write an informative summary of the material. Condense the content of the work by highlighting its main points and key supporting points. (See pages 376–377 for a complete discussion of summarizing techniques.) Use direct quotations from the work to illustrate important ideas.

Do *not* discuss in great detail any single aspect of the work while neglecting to mention other equally important points. Summarize the material so that the reader gets a general sense of *all* key aspects of the original work. Also, keep the summary objective and factual. Do not include in the first part of the paper your personal reaction to the work; your subjective impression will form the basis of the second part of the paper.

Part 2 of a Report: Your Reaction to the Work

To develop the second part of a report, do the following:

1. Focus on any or all of the questions below. (Check with your instructor to see whether you should emphasize specific points.)

   a. How is the assigned work related to ideas and concerns discussed in the course? For example, what points made in the course textbook, class discussions, or lectures are treated more fully in the work?

   b. How is the work related to problems in our present-day world?

   c. How is the work related to your life, experiences, feelings, and ideas? For instance, what emotions did it arouse in you? Did it increase your understanding of an issue or change your perspective?

2. Evaluate the merit of the work: the importance of its points; its accuracy, completeness, and organization; and so on. You should also indicate here whether you would recommend the work to others, and why.

Points to Keep in Mind When Writing a Report

Here are some important matters to consider as you prepare a report:

1. Apply the four basic standards of effective writing (unity, support, coherence, and clear, error-free sentences).

a. Make sure each major paragraph presents and then develops a single main point. For example, in the model report that follows, a paragraph summarizes the book, and the three paragraphs that follow detail three separate reactions that the student writer had. The student then closes the report with a short concluding paragraph.

b. Support with specific reasons and details any general points or attitudes you express. Statements such as "There are many good ideas in this article" and "This book is very interesting" are meaningless without specific evidence that shows why you feel as you do. Look at the model report to see how the main point or topic sentence of each paragraph is developed by specific supporting evidence.

c. Organize the material in the paper. Follow the basic *plan of organization* already described: an introduction, a summary consisting of one or more paragraphs, a reaction consisting of two or more paragraphs, and a conclusion. Use *transitions* to connect the parts of the paper.

d. Proofread the paper for grammar, mechanics, punctuation, and word use.

2. Document quotations from all works by giving the page number in parentheses after the quoted material (see the model report). You may use quotations in the summary and reaction parts of the paper, but do not rely too much on them. Use them only to emphasize key ideas.

A Model Report

Here is a report written by a student in an introductory sociology course. Look at the paper closely to see how it follows the guidelines for report writing described in this chapter.

I Know Why the Caged Bird Sings: Depth and Emotion Through Words

In *I Know Why the Caged Bird Sings* (New York: Bantam Books, 1971), 1
Maya Angelou tells the story of her earliest years. Angelou, a dancer, poet, and television producer as well as a writer, has continued her life story in three more volumes of autobiography. *I Know Why the Caged Bird Sings* is the start of Maya Angelou's story; in this book, she writes with extraordinary clarity about the pains and joys of being black in America.

Introductory paragraph

continued

**PART 1:
SUMMARY
Topic
sentence
for
summary
paragraph**

I Know Why the Caged Bird Sings covers Maya Angelou's life from   2
age three to age sixteen. When the book opens, she is a gawky little girl in
a white woman's cut-down lavender silk dress. She has forgotten the poem
she had memorized for the Easter service, and all she can do is rush out
of the church. At this point, Angelou is living in Stamps, Arkansas, with her
grandmother and uncle. The town is rigidly segregated: "People in Stamps
used to say that the whites in our town were so prejudiced that a Negro
couldn't buy vanilla ice cream" (40). Yet Angelou has some good things in
her life: her adored older brother Bailey, her success in school, and her pride
in her grandmother's quiet strength and importance in the black community.
There is laughter, too, as when a preacher is interrupted in mid-sermon by an
overly enthusiastic woman shouting, "Preach it, I say preach it!" The woman,
in a frenzied rush of excitement, hits the preacher with her purse; his false
teeth fly out of his mouth and land at Angelou's feet. Shortly after this incident,
Angelou and her brother are taken by her father to live in California with their
mother. Here, at age eight, she is raped by her mother's boyfriend, who is
mysteriously murdered after receiving only a suspended sentence for his crime.
She returns, silent and withdrawn, to Stamps, where the gloom is broken when
one of her mother's friends introduces her to the magic of great books. Later,
at age thirteen, Angelou returns to California. She learns how to dance. She
runs away after a violent family fight and lives for a month in a junkyard. She
becomes the first black female to get a job on the San Francisco streetcars.
She graduates from high school eight months pregnant. And she survives.

**PART 2:
REACTION
Topic
sentence
for first
reaction
paragraph**

Maya Angelou's writing style is impressive and vivid. For example, she   3
describes the lazy dullness of her life in Stamps: "Weekdays revolved in a
sameness wheel. They turned into themselves so steadily and inevitably that
each seemed to be the original of yesterday's rough draft" (93). She also
knows how to bring a scene to life, as when she describes her eighth-grade
graduation. For months, she has been looking forward to this event, knowing
she will be honored for her academic successes. She is even happy with her
appearance: her hair has become pretty, and her yellow dress is a miracle
of hand-sewing. But the ceremony is spoiled when the speaker—a white
man—implies that the only success available to blacks is in athletics. Angelou
remembers: "The man's dead words fell like bricks around the auditorium
and too many settled in my belly. . . . The proud graduating class of 1940
had dropped their heads" (152). Later, Angelou uses a crystal-clear image
to describe her father's mistress sewing: "She worked the thread through the
flowered cloth as if she were sewing the torn ends of her life together" (208).
With such vivid details and figures of speech, Maya Angelou re-creates her
life for her readers.

**Topic sentence
for second
reaction
paragraph**

The strong images of the injustices suffered by blacks two generations   4
ago are well done and incredibly powerful. The description of seven-year-old

continued

Maya—when some "powhitetrash" girls torment her dignified grandmother, calling her "Annie" and mimicking her mannerisms—is emotional and raw. In another incident, Mrs. Cullinan, Angelou's white employer, decides that Marguerite (Angelou's given name) is too difficult to pronounce and so renames her Mary. This loss of her name—a "hellish horror" (91)—is another humiliation suffered at white hands, and Angelou leaves Mrs. Cullinan's employ soon afterward. Later, Angelou encounters overt discrimination when a white dentist tells her grandmother, "Annie, my policy is I'd rather stick my hand in a dog's mouth than in a nigger's" (160)—and only slightly less obvious prejudice when the streetcar company refuses to accept her application for a conductor's job. Over and over again, Angelou is the victim of a white society.

Although these injustices are disheartening, Angelou's triumphs are ← 5   **Topic sentence for third reaction paragraph**
inspiring. Angelou is thrilled when she hears the radio broadcast of Joe Louis's victory over Primo Carnera: "A Black boy. Some Black mother's son. He was the strongest man in the world" (114). She weeps with pride when the class valedictorian leads her and her fellow eighth-graders in singing the Negro National Anthem. And there are personal victories, too. One of these comes after her father has gotten drunk in a small Mexican town. Though she has never driven before, she manages to get her father into the car and drives fifty miles through the night as he lies intoxicated in the backseat. Finally, she rejoices in the birth of her son: "He was beautiful and mine. Totally mine. No one had bought him for me" (245). Angelou shows, through these examples, that she is proud of her race—and of herself.

I Know Why the Caged Bird Sings is a remarkable book. Angelou ← 6   **Concluding paragraph**
could have been just another casualty of race prejudice. Yet by using her intelligence, sensitivity, and determination, she succeeds in spite of the odds against her. And by writing with such power, she lets the readers share her defeats and joys. She also teaches a vital lesson: With strength and persistence, all people can escape their cages—and sing their songs.

Writing a Résumé and Cover Letter

This chapter will provide

- a sample résumé and cover letter
- points to note when writing a résumé and cover letter

Write an essay about your first job interview. What was the job for? Did the interview go well? How did you feel before, during, and after the interview? Is there anything you would have done differently?

When applying for a job through the mail, you should ordinarily send (1) a résumé and (2) a cover letter.

Résumé

A résumé is a summary of your personal background and your qualifications. It helps potential employers see at a glance whether you are suited for a job opening. Two sample job résumés follow: a chronological résumé for someone just out of college; and a functional résumé for a more experienced person.

Chronological Résumé

ERIC KURLAND
27 Hawkins Road
Clarksboro, New Jersey 08020
609-723-2166

Ekurland@email.com

Professional objective	A challenging position in the computer technology field
Education	2009 to present: Rowan University, Glassboro, New Jersey Degree: B.S. (in June)
Major courses	Introduction to Computer Science I and II Data Structures and Algorithms I and II Programming Languages Assembly Language Operating Systems I and II
Related courses	Introduction to Discrete Mathematics I and II Calculus I and II Logic Entrepreneurship and Small Business Management Business Law Organizational Behavior
Special school project	Chaired study group that advised local business on advantages of installing computerized payroll system. The group projected comparative cost figures, developed a time-sharing purchase plan, and prepared a budget.
Work experience	2010 to present: Salesperson at the Shack (formerly RadioShack). Interact with customers, maintain inventory control, repair equipment. Wrote computer program in Visual Basic that demonstrates multimedia aspects of Dell Inspiron Laptop T6400 for use in homes and small businesses. 2007–2010: Word processor, theater usher, and child-care aide.

continued

<u>Skills</u>	Mastery of computer languages: C++, Visual Basic, Java, and PHP. Excellent math skills. Detail-oriented, dependable, relate easily to coworkers and customers, and show initiative for problem-solving.
<u>References</u>	Available upon request from Rowan University Placement Office, Glassboro, New Jersey 08028

Functional Résumé

MOLLY CORNELL
9061 Shadow Glen Way
Fort Myers, FL 33966
239-973-0987
<u>Mcornell@email.com</u>

<u>Objective</u>   Instructional designer in corporate training and development

<u>Summary of
Qualifications</u>

- Skilled in writing successful proposals that have secured $10 million in training contracts.
- Able to design and deliver successful training programs tailored to needs of IT professionals and sales personnel in the pharmaceutical and telecommunication industries.
- Able to address complex training issues and diverse client needs.
- Knowledge of all major design software programs including Microsoft Publisher, Lotus Notes, and ACT.

<u>Professional
Experience</u>

- Created thirteen new distance-learning programs, which increased client participation by between 15 percent and 30 percent.
- Designed a new product line that secured a two-year training contract with Merck, Inc.

continued

- Supervised delivery of two training programs for Verizon, Inc., which resulted in renewal of major contract.
- Wrote six proposals for new business that brought in $8 million in increased revenue for 2010–2012.

Employment History	
	2010 to present: Assistant Director of Training, Acme Consultants, Fort Myers, FL
	2009–2010: Proposal Writer, Instructional Design Systems, Alexandria, VA
Education	2009 to present: Completing MS in Instructional Design, Freewald Online University, Minneapolis, MN
	2008: BA in Technical Writing, St. Bonaventure University, St. Bonaventure, NY
	3.75/4.0 GPA
Special Skills	Speak and read Russian
References	Provided upon request

Points to Note about the Résumé

1. Your résumé, along with your cover letter, is your introduction to a potential employer. First impressions count, so make the resume neat!

   a. Prepare your résumé on a computer. This way you can change it easily if the need arises. Print it on good-quality letter paper (8½ by 11 inches).

   b. Proofread very carefully for sentence-skills and spelling mistakes. A potential employer will see such mistakes as signs of carelessness. In addition, get someone else to proofread the résumé for you.

   c. Be brief and to the point; limit it to one page if possible.

   d. Use a format like that of the model résumés (consider also the variations described below). Balance the résumé on the page so that you have roughly the same margins on all sides.

   e. Start with the most recent education/employment experience and work backward in time.

2. Point out strengths, not weaknesses. Don't include "Special Training" if you have had none. Don't refer to your grade-point average if it is less than a B. On the other hand, include a main heading like "Extracurricular Activities" if the activities or awards seem relevant. For example, if Eric Kurland had been vice president of the Computer Club in college he should have mentioned that.

    If you have no work experience related to the job for which you're applying, list the jobs you have had. Any job that shows a period of responsible employment may favorably impress a potential employer.

3. List the names of references on the résumé, but get the permission of people you cite before including their names. You can also give the address of a placement office file that holds references, as shown on Eric Kurland's résumé. Or you can simply say that you will provide references on request, as Molly Cornell did.

Cover Letter

The purpose of the cover letter that goes with your résumé is to introduce yourself briefly and to try to make an employer interested in you. You should include only the high points of the information in your résumé.

Following is the cover letter that Eric Kurland sent with his résumé.

27 Hawkins Road
Clarksboro, New Jersey 08020
May 13, 2013

Mr. George C. Arline
Personnel Manager, Indesco Associates
301 Sharptown Road
White Plains, New York 10019

Dear Mr. Arline:

I would like to be considered as a candidate for the assistant computer programmer position advertised in the *Philadelphia Inquirer* on May 5, 2013.

I am currently finishing my degree in Computer Science at Rowan University. I have taken every required computer course offered at Rowan and have a solid background in the following computer languages: C++, Visual Basic, Java, and PHP. In addition to my computer background, I have supplemented my education with business and mathematics courses.

continued

My knowledge of computers and the business field goes beyond my formal classroom education. For the past three years I have worked part-time at the Shack (formerly RadioShack), where I have gained experience in sales and inventory control. Also, on my own initiative, I designed a demonstration program for the Compaq Presario 5062 and developed promotional fliers about the program.

In short, I believe I have the up-to-date computer background and professional drive needed to contribute to your organization. I have enclosed a copy of my résumé to give you further details about my experience. Sometime next week, I'll give you a call to see whether I can come in for an interview at your convenience. I look forward to speaking with you then.

Sincerely,

Eric Kurland
Eric Kurland

Points to Note about the Cover Letter

1. Your letter should do the following:

   a. In the first paragraph, state that you are an applicant for a job and identify the source through which you learned about the job.

   Here is how Eric Kurland's letter might have opened if his source had been the college placement office: "I learned through the placement office at Rowan University of the assistant computer programmer position at your company. I would like to be considered as a candidate for the job."

   Sometimes an ad will list only a box number (such as Y 172) to reply to. Your inside address should then be:

   Y 172
   Philadelphia Inquirer
   Philadelphia, Pennsylvania 19101

   Dear Sir or Madam:

   b. In the second paragraph, briefly state your qualifications for the job and refer the reader to your résumé.

   c. In the last paragraph, state your willingness to come for an interview. If you can be available for an interview only at certain times, indicate this.

2. As with your résumé, neatness is crucial. Follow the same hints for the letter that you did for the résumé.

   a. Print the letter on good paper.

   b. Proofread *very carefully* for sentence-skills mistakes and spelling mistakes. Use the checklist of sentence skills on the inside back cover.

   c. Be brief and to the point: use no more than one page.

   d. Use a format like the model letter. Keep roughly the same margin on all sides.

   e. Use punctuation and spelling in the model letter as a guide. For example:

      (1) Skip two spaces between the inside address and the salutation ("Dear Mr. Arline").

      (2) Use a colon after the salutation.

      (3) Sign your name at the bottom, in addition to typing it.

ACTIVITY 1

Clip a job listing from a newspaper or copy a job description posted in your school placement office. The job should be one that you feel you are qualified for or that you would one day like to have.

Write a résumé and a cover letter for the job. Use the models already considered as guides.

Use the checklist on the inside back cover as a guide in your writing.

Using the Library and the Internet

This chapter will explain and illustrate how to

- research topics using the library
- research topics using the Internet
- evaluate Internet sources

Write a letter to a new student on campus in which you describe the various uses of the college library.

This chapter provides the basic information you need to use your college library and the Internet with confidence. You will learn that for most research topics there are two basic steps you should take:

1. Find books on your topic.
2. Find articles on your topic.

You will learn, too, that while the library is the traditional place for doing such research, a home computer with Internet access now enables you to thoroughly investigate any topic.

Using the Library

Most students know that libraries provide study space, computer workstations, and copying machines. They are also aware of a library's reading area, which contains recent copies of magazines and newspapers. But the true heart of a library consists of a *main desk, the library's catalog(s) of holdings, book stacks,* and *the periodicals storage area.* Each of these will be discussed in the pages that follow.

Main Desk

The main desk is usually located in a central spot. Check with the main desk to see whether a brochure describes the layout and services of the library. You might also ask whether the library staff provides tours. If not, explore your library to find each of the areas in the activity below.

ACTIVITY 1

Make up a floor plan of your college library. Label the main desk, catalogs (in print or computerized), book stacks, and periodicals storage area.

Library Catalog

The library catalog will be your starting point for almost any research project. In most libraries, the catalog can be accessed on computer terminals. Increasingly, local and college library catalogs can be accessed online, so you may be able to check their book holdings via your personal computer.

Finding a Book: Author, Title, and Subject

There are three ways to look up a book: according to *author, title,* or *subject.* Suppose you want to see if the library has the book *A Tribe Apart,* by Patricia Hersch. You could check for the book through:

1. An author search, in which you would look under *Hersch, Patricia.*

2. A title search, in which you would look under *Tribe Apart, A.*

3. A subject search. In this case, since the subject of the book is "teenagers," you would look under that term.

Here is the author entry in a computerized card catalog for Hersch's book *A Tribe Apart:*

Finding a Book: Author, Title, and Subject

Author	Hersch, Patricia.
Title	A tribe apart: a journey into the heart of American adolescence / Patricia Hersch.
Published	New York: Ballantine Books, 1999.
Edition	1st trade paperback ed.

Location	**Call #**	**STATUS**
RU Circ Top Floor	HQ796.H43 1999	Available

Description	x, 391, [13] p. ; 21 cm.
Note	Includes index.
	"Look for the reading group discussion guide at the back of this book" –P. 4 of cover.
LC SUBJECT	Teenagers – United States.
ISBN	034543594X (pbk.) :
OCLC#	42261321

Note that in addition to giving you the publisher (Ballantine) and year of publication (1999), the entry also tells you the book's physical location and its *call number*—each of which will help you find the book in the library. If the computerized catalog is part of a network of libraries, you may also learn at what branch or location the book is available. If the book is not at your library, you can probably arrange for an interlibrary loan.

Using Subject Headings to Research a Topic

Generally, if you are looking for a particular book, it is easier to search by *author* or *title*. On the other hand, if you are researching a topic, then you should search by *subject*.

The subject section performs three valuable functions:

- It will give you a list of books on a given topic.

- It will often provide related topics that might have information on your subject.

- It will suggest more-limited topics, helping you narrow your general topic.

Chances are you will be asked to do a research paper of about five to fifteen pages. You do not want to choose a topic so broad that it could be covered only by an entire book or more. Instead, you want to come up with a limited topic that can be adequately supported in a relatively short paper. As you search the subject section, take advantage of ideas that it might offer on how you can narrow your topic.

ACTIVITY 2

PART A

Team up with a partner in class and answer the following questions about your library's catalog.

1. Is your library's catalog an actual file of cards in drawers, or is it computerized?

   _____

2. Which type of catalog search will help you research and limit a topic?

   _____

PART B

Use your library's catalog to answer the following questions.

1. What is the title of one book by Anna Quindlen? _____

   _____

2. What is the title of one book by Bill Geist?

   _____

3. Who is the author of *A Tree Grows in Brooklyn?* (Remember to look up the title under *Tree,* not *A.*)

   _____

4. Who is the author of *Seven Habits of Highly Effective People?*

   _____

5. List two books and their authors dealing with the subject of adoption.

   a. _____

   b. _____

6. Look up a book titled *When Bad Things Happen to Good People* or *Silent Spring* and give the following information:

   a. Author _____

   b. Publisher _____

   c. Date of publication _____

   d. Call number _____

   e. One subject heading _____

7. Look up a book written by Deborah Tannen or Garrison Keillor and give the following information:

   a. Title _____

   b. Publisher _____

   c. Date of publication _____

d. Call number _____

e. One subject heading _____

Book Stacks

The book stacks are the library shelves where books are arranged according to their call numbers. The call number, as distinctive as a Social Security number, always appears on the catalog entry for any book. It is also printed on the spine of every book in the library.

   If your library has open stacks (ones that you are permitted to enter), here is how to find a book. Suppose you are looking for *A Tribe Apart,* which has the call number HQ796.H43 in the Library of Congress system. (Libraries using the Dewey decimal system have call letters made up entirely of numbers rather than letters and numbers. However, you use the same basic method to locate a book.) First, you go to the section of the stacks that holds the *H*'s. When you locate the *H*'s, you look for the *HQ*'s. After that, you look for *HQ796*. Finally, you look for *HQ796.H43,* and you have the book.

   If your library has closed stacks (ones you are not permitted to enter), you will have to write down the title, author, and call number on a request form. (Such forms will be available near the card catalog or computer terminals.) You'll then give the form to a library staff person, who will locate the book and bring it to you.

Use the book stacks to answer one of the following sets of questions. Choose the questions that relate to the system of classifying books used by your library.

ACTIVITY 3

SYSTEM 1: LIBRARY OF CONGRESS SYSTEM (LETTERS AND NUMBERS)

1. Books in the E184.6–E185.9 area deal with

   a. Benjamin Franklin.   c. American presidents.

   b. American Indians.   d. African Americans.

2. Books in the HM–HN65 area deal with

   a. sociology.   c. economics.

   b. history.   d. psychology.

3. Books in the M1–M220 area deal with

   a. painting.   c. music.

   b. sculpture.   d. architecture.

SYSTEM 2: DEWEY DECIMAL SYSTEM (NUMBERS)

1. Books in the 200–299 area deal with

   a. language.   c. religion.

   b. philosophy.   d. sports.

2. Books in the 370–372 area deal with

    a. education.   c. the military.

    b. death.   d. waste disposal.

3. Books in the 613 area deal with

    a. wildflowers.   c. drugs.

    b. health.   d. the solar system.

Periodicals

The second step in researching a topic is to locate relevant periodicals: *magazines, journals, and newspapers.* They contain recent or very specialized information about a subject, which may not be available in a book.

The library keeps a catalogue of the periodicals to which it subscribes. However, to find a particular article in periodical you will need to consult a periodical index.

Following are some widely used indexes.

Readers' Guide to Periodical Literature

One way to research is to use the volumes of the *Readers' Guide,* found in almost every libary. They list articles published in more than one hundred popular magazines, such as *Newsweek, Health, Ebony,* and *Popular Science.* Articles appear alphabetically under both subject and author. For example, if you wanted to learn the titles of articles published on the subject of child abuse within a certain time span, you would look under the heading "Child abuse." Following is a typical entry from the *Guide.*

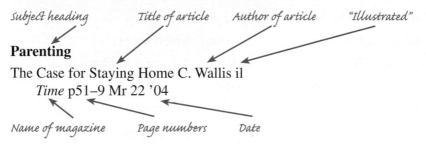

Note the sequence in which information is given about the article:

1. Subject heading.

2. Title of the article. In some cases, bracketed words ([ ]) after the title help make clear just what the article is about.

3. Author (if it is a signed article). The author's first name is always abbreviated.

4. Whether the article has a bibliography (*bibl*) or is illustrated with pictures (*il*). Other abbreviations sometimes used are shown in the front of the *Readers' Guide.*

5. Name of the magazine. Before 1988, the *Readers' Guide* used abbreviations for most of the magazines indexed. For example, the magazine *Popular Science* is abbreviated *Pop Sci*. If necessary, refer to the list of magazines in the front of the index to identify abbreviations.

6. Page numbers on which the article appears.

7. Date when the article appeared. Dates are abbreviated: for example, *Mr* stands for March, *Ag* for August, *O* for October. Other abbreviations are shown in the front of the *Guide*.

The *Readers' Guide* is published in monthly supplements. At the end of a year, a volume is published covering the entire year. You will see in your library large green volumes titled, for instance, *Readers' Guide 2000* or *Readers' Guide 2007*. You will also see the small monthly supplements for the current year.

The drawback of the *Readers' Guide* is that it gives you only a list of articles; you must then go to your library's catalog to see if the library actually has copies of the magazines that contain those articles. If you're lucky and it does, you must take the time to locate the relevant issue and then to read and take notes on the articles or to make copies of them.

The *Readers' Guide* may also be available at your library online. If so, you can quickly search for articles on a given subject simply by typing in a key word or key phrase.

Online Databases

Most college and public libraries now provide online computer-search services known as online databases or library subscription services. Using any of these services, you will be able to type in key words and quickly search many periodicals for articles on your subject. Some databases, such as General Science Index, are discipline specific, but others, such as Academic Search Premier, are more general.

Often, articles you find will be shown as "full text." That means that you can print out the entire article from your computer. In other cases, only an abstract (summary) of the article will be available. However, abstracts are valuable too, for they allow you to determine whether the article is relevant to your research and if you should continue searching for the full text.

Finally, database articles appear in *html* or *pdf* format or in both. Articles in .html (hypertext markup language) have been reformatted for publication on the Internet. Those in .pdf (portable document format) are exact reproductions of a print document. Note that some databases are among many compiled by the same provider. EBSCOhost, Infotrac, and ProQuest are such providers.

Following are a few online databases that have proven useful for new student researchers.

Academic Search Premier covers a variety of disciplines and includes full-text articles and abstracts of articles from over 4,400 periodicals.

Cumulative Index to Nursing and Allied Health Literature (CINAHL) provides access to articles found in over 1,800 professional journals in the health professions.

ERIC (Education Resources Information Center) makes available articles from professional journals, reports, and speeches having to do with education.

General Science Index lists articles on biology, chemistry, physics, and the other physical sciences.

Wilson Humanities Index covers over 500 English-language periodicals in disciplines such as archaeology, the classics, art, history, theater, music, literature, philosophy, and religion.

JSTOR (Journal Storage) provides full-text articles found in back issues of journals in the humanities, social sciences, and natural sciences.

CGP (Catalog of U.S. Government Publications) contains documents published by the U.S. government.

***New York Times* Index** lists articles published in this newspaper since 1913.

PsychInfo is published by the American Psychological Association. It includes abstracts of books, articles, and doctoral dissertations in psychology. It also provides access to full-text articles through PsycARTICLES.

ACTIVITY 4

At this point in the chapter, you now know the two basic steps in researching a topic in the library. What are the steps?

1. _____

2. _____

ACTIVITY 5

1. Look up a recent article on nursing home costs using one of your library's periodicals indexes or online databases, and fill in the following information:

    a.   Name of the index you used _____

    b.   Article title _____

    c.   Author (if given) _____

    d.   Name of magazine _____

    e.   Pages _____   f.   Date_____

2. Look up a recent article on organ donation using one of your library's periodicals indexes or online databases, and fill in the following information:

    a.   Name of the index you used _____

b. Article title _____

c. Author (if given) _____

d. Name of magazine _____

e. Pages _____ f. Date _____

Using the Internet

Before you begin searching the Internet, find out what databases your local and school libraries subscribe to. You may be able to do enough research using these online resources and print sources available in your library. If not, you can search for material on the Internet.

Finding Additional Books on Your Topic

To find current books on your topic, go online and search for one of the large commercial online booksellers such as Amazon or Barnes & Noble. They will list helpful books that you might want to buy. Many of these are used and are, therefore, discounted. However, if you dont't want to buy the book, just jot down the author's name, the title, the publisher, and the date of publication. Take this information to your college library and see if the book is on the shelves. If not, request an interlibrary loan. The librarian will forward your request to the nearest library that has the book. Be aware, however, that it may take a week or longer to get the book.

A Note on the Library of Congress

You can also find additional books on your topic by visiting the Library of Congress Web site (www.loc.gov). Located in Washington, D.C., the Library of Congress has copies of all books published in the United States. Its online catalog contains about twelve million entries. You can browse this catalog by subject or search by key words. The search form permits you to check just those books that interest you. After you find a given book, click on the "Full Record" option to view publication information and call number. You can then try to obtain the book from your college library or through an interlibrary loan.

Other Points to Note

After you have found the books you think might relate to your topic, print out a list of them. This way you can go to the library prepared to find just those you want to borrow. In fact, since many libraries are now accessible online, you might want to search your library's electronic catalogs on your home computer even when the library is closed. You can then go to the library as soon as it opens and start checking out the books you need right away.

Finding Articles on Your Topic

Online Magazines and Newspaper Articles

As already mentioned, your library probably subscribes to online databases such as Academic Search Premiere or JSTOR, which you can use to find relevant articles on your subject. Another online research service, one that you can subscribe to individually on a home computer, is eLibrary. You may be able to get a free seven-day trial subscription or pay for a monthly subscription at a limited cost. The service provides millions of newspaper and magazine articles as well as many thousands of book chapters and television and radio transcripts. After typing in one or more key words on the eLibrary Web site, you'll get long lists of articles that may relate to your subject.

Search Engines

An Internet search engine will help you go through a vast amount of information on the Web to find articles about almost any topic. As with other resources, choosing the appropriate key words is important to beginning a search. For example, if you are thinking of doing a paper on road rage, type "road rage." Within a second or so, you will get a list of over three million articles and sites on the Web about road rage!

You should then narrow your topic by adding other key words. For instance, if you typed "preventing road rage," you would get a list of over one million articles and sites. If you narrowed your potential topic further by typing "educational programs for preventing road rage," you would get a list of almost a half million items. Some search engines, such as Google, do good job of returning hits that are genuinely relevant to your search, so just scanning the early part of a list may be enough to provide you with the information you need.

As discussed above, sometimes you get too much information. So, try making your key words more specific, or use different combinations of key words. You might also try another search engine. Finally, many search engines have an Advanced Search feature for tips on successful searching.

Evaluating Internet Sources

Keep in mind that the quality and reliability of information you find on the Internet may vary widely. Anyone with a bit of computer know-how can create a Web site and post information there. That person may be a Nobel Prize winner, a leading authority in a specialized field, a high school student, or a crackpot. Be careful, then, to look closely at the source in the following ways:

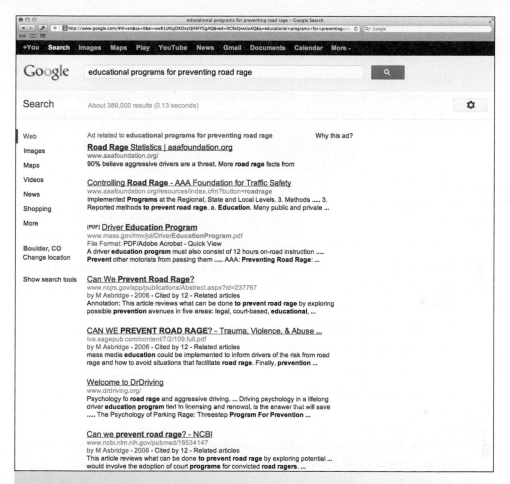

Results from a key word search on Google using "educational programs for preventing road rage" in the search box.

1. **Internet address**   In a Web address, the three letters following the "dot" are the domain. The most common domains are .com, .edu, .gov, .net, and .org. A common misconception is that a Web site's reliability can be determined by its domain. This is not the case, as almost anyone can get a Web address ending in .com, .edu, .org, or any of the other domains. Therefore, it is important that you examine every Web site carefully, considering the three points that follow.

2. **Author**   What credentials does the author have (if any)? Has the author published other material on the topic?

3. **Internal evidence**   Does the author seem to proceed objectively—presenting all sides of a topic fairly before arguing his or her own views? Does the author produce solid, adequate support for his or her views?

4. **Date**   Is the information up-to-date? Check at the top or bottom of the document for copyright, publication, or revision dates. Knowing such dates will help you decide whether the material is current enough for your purposes.

ACTIVITY 6

PART A

Go to www.google.com and search for "education." Then complete the items below.

1. How many items did your search yield? _____

2. In the early listings, you will probably find each of the following domains: edu, gov, org, and com. Pick one site with each domain and write its full address.

    a.   Address of one .com site you found: _____

    b.   Address of one .gov site: _____

    c.   Address of one .org site: _____

    d.   Address of one .edu site: _____

PART B

Circle *one* of the sites you identified above and use it to complete the following evaluation. Answers will vary.

3. Name of site's author or authoring institution: _____

4. Is site's information current (within two years)? _____

5. Does the site serve obvious business purposes (with advertising or attempts to sell products)? _____

6. Does the site have an obvious connection to a governmental, commercial, business, or religious organization? If so, which one?

    _____

7. Does the site's information seem fair and objective?

    _____

8. Based on the information above, would you say the site appears reliable?

    _____

Practice in Using the Library and the Internet

Use your library or the Internet to research a subject that interests you. Select one of the following areas or (with your instructor's permission) an area of your own choice:

ACTIVITY 7

Acid rain	Immigration-related issues
Alzheimer's disease	Interracial adoption
Animal rights movement	Mind-body medicine
Animals nearing extinction	New aid for people with disabilities
Antigay violence	New remedies for allergies
Best job prospects today	New treatments for AIDS
Cell phone use and health-related issues	New treatments for insomnia
Censorship on the Internet	Noise control
Child abuse	Nursing home costs
Cremation	Organ donation
Drug treatment programs	Origins of Kwanzaa or other holiday
Drug treatment programs for adolescents	Pollution of drinking water
Education-related issues	Prenatal care
Elections and voting	Prison reform
Ethical aspects of hunting	Problems of retirement
Everyday addictions	Recent consumer frauds
Fertility drugs	Ritalin and children
Food poisoning (salmonella)	Seat belt laws
Forecasting earthquakes	Self-help groups
Gambling and youth	Sex on television
Greenhouse effect	Sexual harassment
Hazardous substances in the home	Steroid use in sports
Health insurance reform	Stress reduction in the workplace
Heroes for today	Sudden infant death syndrome
Holistic healing	Surrogate mothers
Human rights	Telephone crimes
Identity theft	Toxic waste disposal
	Vegetarianism

Research the topic first through a subject search in your library's catalog or that of an online bookstore. Then research the topic through a periodicals index (print or online). On a separate sheet of paper, provide the following information:

1. Topic

2. Three books that either cover the topic directly or at least touch on the topic in some way. Include the following:

   Author

   Title

   Place of publication

   Publisher

   Date of publication

3. Three articles on the topic published in 2009 or later. Include the following:

   Title of article

   Author (if given)

   Title of magazine

   Date

   Pages (if given)

4. Finally, write a paragraph describing just how you went about researching your topic. In addition, include a photocopy or printout of one of the three articles.

Writing a Research Paper

If you were to write a research paper on war, what would you focus on? War itself is too broad a topic to cover in one research paper. You would need to select a more limited topic to write about, for example, the effect of war on the economy. Looking at the above photograph of American soldiers in Iraq, can you think of some other limited topics of war you might cover in a research paper?

This chapter will explain and illustrate

- the six steps in writing a research paper:

  Step 1: Select a topic that you can readily research.

  Step 2: Limit your topic and make the purpose of your paper clear.

  Step 3: Gather information on your limited topic.

  Step 4: Plan your paper and take notes on your limited topic.

  Step 5: Write the paper.

  Step 6: Use an acceptable format and method of documentation.

This chapter also provides

- a model research paper

Step 1: Select a Topic That You Can Readily Research

Researching at a Local Library

First of all, do a subject search of your library's catalog and see whether there are several books on your general topic. For example, if you initially choose the broad topic "parenting," try to find at least three books on being a parent. Make sure that the books are actually available on the library shelves.

Next, go to a periodicals index in your library to see if there are a fair number of magazine, newspaper, or journal articles on your subject. You can use the *Readers' Guide to Periodical Literature* (found in just about every library) to find articles that appear in the back issues of periodicals that your library may keep. But you may find that your library subscribes to a provider of electronic databases such as EBSCOhost, which will allow you access to articles published in a far greater range of publications. For instance, when Sonya Philips, author of the model research paper "Successful Families," visited her local library, she connected to EBSCOhost and typed "parenting" in the search box. In seconds, EBSCOhost came back with hundreds of hits—titles, publication information, and the complete text of articles about parenting.

Researching on the Internet

The first step is to go to the subjects section of a library's electronic catalog or large online bookseller to find relevant books (don't worry—you don't have to buy any books; you're just browsing for information). Two of the largest online booksellers are Barnes & Noble and Amazon.

As Sonya Philips explains, "Barnes and Noble's home page has a category called 'Books.' When I clicked on that, I found a subcategory called 'Subjects,' which included 'See All Subjects.' That led me to the topic I was looking for, 'Parenting and Family.' When I clicked on that, I got a bunch of subcategories, including one for 'Teenagers.' I clicked on 'Teenagers,' and that brought up a list of hundreds of books! I went through the list, and when I got to a book that sounded promising, I just clicked on that title and up like magic came reviews of the book—and sometimes a table of contents and a summary as well! This information helped me decide on the dozen or so books I eventually picked out that seemed relevant to my paper. I then went to my local library and found five of those titles on the shelves."

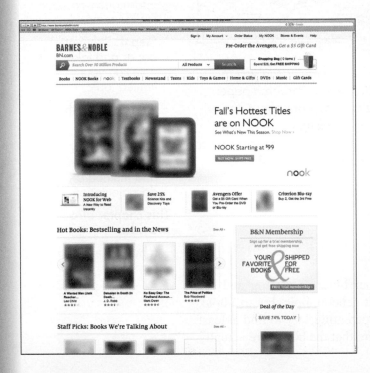

Next, determine whether magazine or newspaper articles on your topic are available online. The simplest way is to use an Internet search engine, such as Google. Here's what Sonya did.

"First I typed in the word 'parenting' in the key word box. I got more than eight million hits! So I tried more specific search terms. I tried 'parenting and teenagers' first, but that was still too general. So I narrowed the topic even more: 'parenting and teenagers and television' and 'parenting and teenagers and homeschooling.' This reduced the number of hits a lot. I was still getting thousands, but I could see that some of the first ones looked promising. In fact, I found some useful sites, like 'The Television Project,' which is an online resource that doesn't exist anywhere else.

"To look just for magazine and newspaper articles, I went directly to the site of some popular publications, such as *Time* and *Newsweek*. I was able to search for recent articles, but I saw that I would have to pay a fee of about two dollars to read each article online. So, I noted the date and page number of the articles, and I looked up the ones that were available in the library's reading room. Between doing that and using EBSCOhost, I found plenty of recent material related to my subject."

So, the first step in doing a research paper is to find out if both books and articles are available on your chosen topic. If so, pursue your topic. Otherwise, choose another one. You can't write a paper on a topic for which research materials are not available."

Step 2: Limit Your Topic and Make the Purpose of Your Paper Clear

A research paper should *thoroughly* develop a *limited* topic. The paper should be narrow and deep rather than broad and shallow. Therefore, as you read through books and articles, look for ways to limit your general topic.

For instance, as Sonya read materials on the general topic "parenting," she chose to limit her topic to the particular problems of parents raising children in today's culture. She then decided to limit it even more by focusing on what successful parents do to deal with those challenges. To take other examples, the general topic "drug abuse" might be narrowed to "successful drug treatment programs for adolescents." After reading about the worldwide problem of overpopulation, you might decide to limit your paper to the birth control policies enforced by the Chinese government.

The subject headings in your library's catalog and periodicals indexes will give you helpful ideas about how to limit your subject. For example, under the subject heading "parenting" in the book file were several related headings, such as "moral and ethical considerations of parenting" and "stepparenting." In addition, there was a list of seventy books, including several titles that suggested limited directions for research: parents and discipline, parenting and adolescent girls, how parents can protect their kids from violence. Under the subject heading "Parenting" in the library's periodicals index were subheadings and titles of many articles that suggested additional limited topics: how parents can limit the impact of TV on kids, keeping the lines of communication open between parents and teenagers, and secrets to raising a successful teen.

Do not expect to limit your topic and make your purpose clear all at once. You may have to do quite a bit of reading as you work out the limited focus of your paper. Note that many research papers have one of two general purposes: (1) to defend a point (for example, to provide evidence that elected officials should be limited to a single term) or (2) to present information (for example, to discuss the effects of diet on heart disease).

Step 3: Gather Information on Your Limited Topic

After limiting your topic, begin gathering relevant information. A helpful way to proceed is to sign out the books that you need from your library and photocopy relevant articles from magazines, newspapers, or journals. You should also print out articles directly from your library's databases or the Internet.

Then sit and work on these materials in a quiet, unhurried place.

Step 4: Plan Your Paper and Take Notes on Your Limited Topic

Preparing a Scratch Outline

As you carefully read through the material you have gathered, think about the content and organization of your paper. Begin deciding what information you will present and how you will arrange it. Prepare a scratch outline that shows both the paper's thesis and the areas that support the thesis. Try to include at least three areas of support.

Thesis: _____

Support: (1) _____

(2) _____

(3) _____

Following is the outline that Sonya Philips made for her paper on successful parenting.

Thesis: Parents can do things to overcome the negative influences hurting their families.

Support: (1) Create quality time with families

(2) Increase families' sense of community

(3) Minimize the impact of media and technology

Note-Taking

With this tentative outline in mind, you can begin taking notes on the information that you expect to include in your paper. Write your notes on four-by-six-inch or five-by-eight-inch cards, or in a computer file. Don't use loose-leaf or notebook paper; doing so makes it harder to organize your notes as you prepare to draft your paper. Notes should be in the form of *direct quotations and summaries in your own words*. At times, you may also *paraphrase*—use your own words in place of someone else's. Since most research involves condensing, you will probably summarize much more often than you will paraphrase. (For more information on summarizing, see pages 376–377.)

A *direct quotation* must be written *exactly* as it appears in the original work. But, you may omit words that are not relevant to your point as long as you don't change the meaning. To show such an omission, use three spaced periods (known as *ellipsis points*) in place of the deleted words:

We cannot guarantee that bad things will happen, but we can argue that good things are not happening. It is the contention of this report that increasing numbers of young people are left to their own devices at a critical time in their development.

Original passage

> "We cannot guarantee that bad things will happen, but we can argue that good things are not happening. . . . [I]ncreasing numbers of young people are left to their own devices at a critical time in their development."

(Note the four dots in the above example; the first dot is the period at the end of the sentence. The capital letter in brackets shows that the word was capitalized by the student and not by the author of the quotation.)

In a *summary,* you condense the original material and use your own words. Below is one of Sonya Philips's summary note cards.

Movie content

Study conducted in 2006 showed that of PG-13 movies, 91 percent had crude language, 89 percent had obscene language, 45 percent had actual or suggested sex. Worrisome because most parents assume PG-13 movies are OK for their kids.

Medved and Medved, 62

Remember that, in a *paraphrase,* you report the information in your own words and style without condensing it.

Keep the following in mind as you research:

- Write on only one side of each card.
- Write only one kind of information, from one source, on any one card. For example, the sample card on the previous page has information on only one idea (movie content) from one source (Medved and Medved).
- At the top of each card, write a heading that summarizes its content. This will help you organize different kinds of information.
- Identify the source and page number at the bottom.

Always record the exact source and page from which you take each piece of information. In a research paper, you must document all information that is not common knowledge or not a matter of historical record. For example, the birth and death dates of Dr. Martin Luther King, Jr. are established facts and do not need documenting. On the other hand, the average number of hours worked in the United States this year compared with the average number worked in 1980 is a specialized fact and should be documented. In addition, as you read several sources on a subject, you will develop a sense of what authors regard as generally shared, or common, information and what is more specialized information that requires documentation.

Read the following paragraphs from books that a student might use to gather material for a research paper. Then, using note cards, create three separate note cards for each:

1. In the first note card, use a direct quotation in which you indicate the omission of certain words or phrases by using ellipses.

2. In the second note card, write a paraphrase of the paragraph.

3. In the third note card, write a summary of the paragraph.

Provide a heading for each card and identify the author and the page number. You will end up with six complete note cards.

PARAGRAPH A
Taken from page 1 of *The Sea Around Us,* by Rachel Carson.

   Beginnings are apt to be shadowy, and so it is with the beginnings of the great mother of life, the sea. Many people have debated how and when the earth got its oceans, and it is not surprising that their explanations do not always agree. For the plain and inescapable truth is that no one was there to see, and in the absence of eyewitness accounts there is bound to be a certain amount of disagreement.

PARAGRAPH B
Taken from Robert Ramirez's "The Woolen Sarape," which appeared on page 53 of an essay anthology.

   Many lower-income families of the barrio manage to maintain a comfortable standard of living through the communal action of family members who contribute their wages to the head of the family. Economic need creates interdependence and closeness.

A Caution about Plagiarism

If you fail to document information that is not your own, you will be stealing. The formal term is *plagiarizing*—using someone else's work as your own, whether you borrow a single idea, a sentence, or an entire essay.

   One example of plagiarism is turning in a friend's paper as if it is your own. Another example is copying an article found in a magazine, newspaper, journal, or on the Internet and turning it in as your own. By copying someone else's work, you risk being failed or even expelled. Equally, plagiarism deprives you of what can be a most helpful learning and organization experience—researching and writing about a selected topic in detail.

Keep in mind, too, that while the Internet has made it easier for students to plagiarize, it has also made it riskier. Teachers can easily discover that a student has taken material from an Internet source by typing a sentence or two from the student's paper into a powerful search engine like Google; that source is then often quickly identified.

With the possibility of plagiarism in mind, then, be sure to take careful, documented notes during your research. Remember that if you use another person's material, *you must correctly acknowledge your source*. Failure to document correctly (even if appropriately summarized or paraphrased) also constitutes plagiarism. When you cite a source properly, you give credit where it is due, you provide your readers with a way to locate the original material on their own, and you demonstrate that your work has been carefully researched.

ACTIVITY 2

Here are three sets of passages. Each set begins with an original passage followed by notes on the passage. Both notes include a parenthetical citation, "(24)," crediting the original source. But while one note is an acceptable paraphrase or summary, the other is an unacceptable paraphrase or summary in which the sentences and ideas too closely follow the original, using some of the same structure and the same words as the original. Identify the acceptable note with an A and the unacceptable note with a U.

SET 1: ORIGINAL PASSAGE

The self-confessed television addict often feels he "ought" to do other things—but the fact that he doesn't read and doesn't plant his garden or sew or crochet or play games or have conversations means that those activities are no longer as desirable as television. In a way the heavy viewer's life is as imbalanced by his television "habit" as a drug addict's or an alcoholic's. He is living in a holding pattern, as it were, passing up the activities that lead to growth or development or a sense of accomplishment. This is one reason people talk about their television viewing so ruefully, so apologetically. They are aware that it is an unproductive experience, that almost any other endeavor is more worthwhile by any human measure.

—Marie Winn, from "Television Addiction," in *The Plug-In Drug* (Viking Penguin, 2002)

_____ a. Television addicts may feel they should do other things like play games or have conversations. But they pass up activities that might lead to a sense of accomplishment. Their lives are as imbalanced by their television watching as a drug addict's or alcoholic's. Aware of how unproductive television viewing is, they talk about it apologetically (24).

_____ b. TV addicts feel that they ought to spend their time doing more worthwhile activities. But like alcohol or drugs, TV has taken over their lives. The addicts' apologetic tone when they talk about their TV watching indicates that they know they're wasting time on a completely unproductive activity (24).

SET 2: ORIGINAL PASSAGE

Now, however, there is growing evidence that restorative naps are making a comeback. Recognizing that most of their employees are chronically sleep-deprived, some companies have set up nap rooms with reclining chairs, blankets and alarm clocks. If unions are truly interested in worker welfare, they should make such accommodations a standard item in contract negotiations. Workers who take advantage of the opportunity to sleep for twenty minutes or so during the workday report that they can go back to work with renewed enthusiasm and energy. My college roommate, Dr. Linda Himot, a psychiatrist in Pittsburgh, who has a talent for ten-minute catnaps between patients, says these respites help her focus better on each patient's problems, which are not always scintillating. And companies that encourage napping report that it reduces accidents and errors and increases productivity, even if it shortens the workday a bit. Studies have shown that sleepy workers make more mistakes and cause more accidents, and are more susceptible to heart attacks and gastrointestinal disorders.

—Jane Brody, from "New Respect for the Nap"
(*New York Times*, 2001)

_____ a. As employers realize that many workers are short on sleep, they are becoming more open to the idea of napping on the job. Some even provide places for workers to stretch out and nap briefly. Companies that allow napping find their employees are more alert and productive, and even suffer fewer physical ailments (24).

_____ b. Naps are becoming more acceptable. Some companies have done such things as set up nap rooms with reclining chairs and blankets. Naps provide workers with renewed enthusiasm and energy. Although naps shorten the workday a bit, they reduce accidents and increase productivity. Sleep-deprived workers are prone to heart attacks and gastrointestinal disorders (24).

SET 3: ORIGINAL PASSAGE

Chances are, you are going to go to work after you complete college. How would you like to earn an extra $950,000 on your job? If this sounds appealing, read on. I'm going to reveal how you can make an extra $2,000 a month between the ages of 25 and 65. Is this hard to do? Actually, it is simple for some, but impossible for others. All you have to do is be born a male and graduate from college. If we compare full-time workers, this is how much more the average male college graduate earns over the course of his career. Hardly any single factor pinpoints gender discrimination better than this total. The pay gap, which shows up at all levels of education, is so great that women who work full-time average only two-thirds (67 percent) of what men are paid. This gap does not occur only in the United States. All industrialized nations have it, although only in Japan is the gap larger than in the United States.

—James Henslin, from *Essentials of Sociology,* fourth edition (Allyn & Bacon, 2002)

_____ a. To make an extra $2,000 a month between the ages of 25 and 65, you need to be born male and graduate from college. This adds up to an additional $950,000. The pay gap between genders shows up at all levels of education. It is so great that women who work full time make only two-thirds what men make. The gender gap occurs in all industrialized nations, although only in Japan is it greater than in the U.S. (24).

_____ b. The effect of gender on salary is significant. At all levels of education, a woman who works full time earns about two-thirds as much as a man who works full time. For college graduates, this adds up to a difference of $950,000 over the course of a 40-year working life. The gender gap exists in all industrialized nations, but it is greatest in Japan and the U.S. (24).

Step 5: Write the Paper

Many instructors require an outline. So, start by making a *final outline* which you can use as a guide to write the first draft. You can prepare either a *topic outline* (thesis plus supporting words and phrases); or a *sentence outline* (complete sentences).

In the model paper shown (pages 427–436), a topic outline appears on pages 428–429. Note that roman numerals are used for first-level headings, capital letters for second-level headings, and arabic numbers for third-level headings.

In an *introduction,* include a thesis statement expressing your purpose and indicate the plan of development you will follow. Pages 94–97 contain information about writing introductions for both essays and research papers. The model research paper uses a two-paragraph introduction (page 429).

Always maintain unity and coherence and provide enough support to develop your thesis. Use the checklist on the inside back cover of this book to make sure that your paper follows all four bases of effective writing.

Step 6: Use an Acceptable Format and Method of Documentation

Format

The model paper in this chapter (pages 427–436) shows acceptable formats for a research paper using the style recommended by the Modern Language Association (MLA). Most English professors require this style. However, if you are writing in another class, such as psychology, sociology, or one of the physical sciences, your instructor may require a different style. So, always check with your professor first.

Documentation of Sources

You must reveal the sources (books, articles, and so on) of borrowed information in your paper. Whether you quote directly, or summarize ideas in your own words, you must acknowledge your sources. In the past, you may have used footnotes. However, the MLA now requires a simpler form of documentation.

Citations within a Paper

When citing a source, you must mention the author's name and the relevant page number. The author's name may appear either in the sentence you are writing or in parentheses following the sentence:

> In *The Way We Really Are,* Stephanie Coontz writes, "Right up through the 1940s, ties of work, friendship, neighborhood, ethnicity, extended kin, and voluntary organizations were as important a source of identity for most Americans . . ." (37).
>
> "Some . . . are looking for a way to reclaim family closeness in an increasingly fast-paced society. . . . Still others worry about unsavory influences in school—drugs, alcohol, sex, violence" (Kantrowitz and Wingert 66).

There are several points to note about citations within the paper:

- When the author's name is provided in parentheses, only the last name is given.
- There is no punctuation between the author's name and the page number.
- The parenthetical citation is placed after the borrowed material but before the period at the end of the sentence.
- If you are using more than one work by the same author, include a shortened version of the title in the citation. For example, your citation

for the quotation above would be (Coontz, *Way We Really* 39). Note that a comma appears between the author's name and the title.

- The abbreviation *qtd. in* is used when citing a quotation from another source. For example, a quotation from Edward Wolff on page 2 of the paper was found in a book not by Wolff but by Sylvia Ann Hewlett and Cornel West. The citation is as follows:

The economist Edward Wolff explains the loss of time:

> Over a thirty-year time span, parental time has declined 13 percent. The time parents have available for their children has been squeezed by the rapid shift of mothers into the paid labor force, by escalating divorce rates and the subsequent abandonment of children by their fathers, and by an increase in the number of hours required on the job. The average worker is now at work 163 hours a year more than in 1969, which adds up to an extra month of work annually (qtd. in Hewlett and West 48).

Citations at the End of a Paper

End your paper with a list of works cited that includes all the sources actually used in the paper. (Don't list other sources, no matter how many you have read.) Look at the "Works Cited" page in the model research paper (page 436) and note the following:

- The works-cited list begins on a new page, not on the last page of the paper's text.
- Entries are organized alphabetically according to the authors' last names. Entries are not numbered.
- Entries are double-spaced, with no extra spaces between entries.
- After the first line of an entry, a half-inch indentation separates each additional line in that entry. This arrangement is called a "hanging indent" in the formatting menus for most word processors.
- *Italicize* (do not underline) titles of books, periodicals, and other independently published works.
- Do not include URLs in Web entries.
- Include the publication medium, such as Print, Web, DVD, or TV.
- If no publisher's name appears in a Web source, write *n.p.* When no date appears in a Web site, write *n.d.*

Model Entries for a List of Works Cited

Use the following entries as a guide when you prepare your list.

> Bryson, Bill. *The Life and Times of the Thunderbolt Kid: A Memoir.*
>   New York: Broadway Books, 2006. Print.

Book by One Author

Note that the author's last name is written first.

> ---. *A Short History of Nearly Everything.* New York: Broadway Books,
>   2003. Print.

Two or More Entries by the Same Author

If you cite two or more entries by the same author (in the example above, a second book by Bill Bryson is cited), do not repeat the author's name. Instead, begin the line with three hyphens followed by a period. Then give the remaining information as usual. Arrange works by the same author alphabetically by title. The words *A, An,* and *The* are ignored in alphabetizing by title.

> Mortenson, Greg, and Greg Oliver Relin. *Three Cups of Tea.* New York:
>   Penguin Books, 2007. Print.

Book by Two or More Authors

For a book with two or more authors, give all the authors' names but reverse only the first author's name.

> Tumulty, Karen. "Maxed-Out Moms." *Time.* 29 Sept. 2008: 42–44. Print.

Magazine Article

> Wilson, Craig. "The Key to Saving Money: Just Don't Spend It." *USA Today.*
>   6 Aug. 2008: D1. Print.

Newspaper Article

The final letter and number refer to page 1 of section D. If the article is not printed on consecutive pages, simply list the first page followed by a plus sign ("+"). In that case, the above example would read "D1+").

> "Equality's Winding Path." Editorial. *New York Times.* 6 Nov. 2008: A28. Print.

Editorial

List an editorial as you would any signed or unsigned article, but indicate the nature of the piece by adding *Editorial* after the article's title.

> Andrews, Elmer. "The Gift and the Craft: An Approach to the Poetry of
>   Seamus Heaney." *Twentieth Century Literature* 31.4 (1985): 368–369. Print.

Article in a Professional Journal

> Dunne, Dominick. "Nightmare on Elm Drive." *True Crime: An American
>   Anthology.* Ed. Harold Schechter. New York: Library of America,
>   2008. 737. Print.

Selection in an Edited Collection

> Schaefer, Richard. *Sociology: A Brief Introduction.* 7th ed. New York:
>   McGraw Hill College, 2008. Print.

Revised or Later Edition

The abbreviations *Rev. ed., 2nd ed., 3rd ed.,* and so on, are placed right after the title.

Chapter or Section in a Book by One Author

> Clinton, Bill. "Model Gifts." *Giving.* New York: Alfred A. Knopf, 2007. 116–136.

Pamphlet	*Funding Your Education, 2007–2008.* Washington: Dept. of Education Office of Federal Student Aid, 2007. Print.
Television Program	"Following the Trail of Toxic E-Waste." *60 Minutes.* Report. Scott Pelle. CBS. 9 Nov. 2008. Television.
Film	*High School Musical 3: Senior Year.* Dir. Kenny Orts. Walt Disney Pictures, 2008. Film.
Sound Recording	Janet Jackson. "Feedback." *Discipline.* Island Def Jam Music Group, 2008. LP.
DVD	"UFOs—Seeing Is Believing." *Primetime* Narr. David Mu, ABC, WABC, New York. 16 September 2008. DVD. ABC/2008. DVD.
Personal Interview	Firbank, Matthew. Personal interview. 14 July 2009.
Article in an Online Magazine	Stone, Daniel. "Six Worst Kid Health Habits." *Newsweek.com.* 3 April 2008. 12 Oct. 2008.

The first date (3 April 2008) refers to the issue of the publication in which the article appeared; the second date (12 Oct. 2008) refers to the day when the student researcher accessed the source.

Article in an Online Web Site	"Sunbathing Spiders." *Urban Legends and Superstitions.* 2008. 17 Sept. 2008

The first date (2008) refers to when the material was electronically published, updated, or posted; the second date (17 Sept. 2008) refers to when the student researcher accessed the source.

Article in a Reference Database	Costa, Stefano. "Music in Dreams and the Emergence of the Self." *Journal of American Psychology* 54.1 (2009): 81–83. *Academic Search Premier.* Web. 3 Mar. 2009.

The first date (2009) refers to when the material was electronically published, updated, or posted; the second date (3 Mar. 2009) refers to when the student researcher accessed the source.

Electronic Mail (E-mail) Posting	Graham, Vanessa. "Re: Teenager Problems." Message to Sonya Philips. 12 Apr. 2004. E-mail.

ACTIVITY 3 On a separate sheet of paper, convert the information in each of the following into the correct form for a list of "Works Cited." Use the appropriate model above as a guide.

1. A book by David Carr called *The Longest Trip Home* and published in New York by HarperCollins in 2008.

2. An article by Julie Appleby titled "Drug Costs for Seniors Growing" on page 1A of the November 12, 2008 issue of *USA Today*.

3. A book by Michael W. Passer and Ronald E. Smith titled *Psychology: The Science of Mind and Behavior* and published in a second edition by McGraw-Hill in New York in 2007.

4. An article by Mark Miller titled "Parting with a Pet" found on May 16, 2007, in the October 8, 2007, issue of *Newsweek Online*.

5. An article titled "Depression in Teenagers" found on April 24, 2007, on the Web site titled *Troubled Teens* which is sponsored by the Aspen Education Group.

A Model Paper

While the *MLA Handbook* does not require a title page or an outline for a paper, your instructor may ask you to include one or both. Here is a model title page.

Model Title Page

Successful Families:

Fighting for Their Kids

by

Sonya Philips

English 101

Professor Lessing

5 May 2012

The title should begin about one-third of the way down the page. Center the title. Double-space the lines of the title and your name. Also center and double-space the instructor's name and the date.

Papers written in MLA style use the simple format shown below. There is no title page or outline.

Model First Page of MLA-Style Paper

1/2 inch

Philips 1

1 inch

Sonya Philips
Professor Lessing
English 101
5 May 2012

Double-space lines. Leave a one-inch margin on all sides.

Successful Families: Fighting for Their Kids

It's a terrible time to be a teenager, or even a teenager's parent. That message is everywhere. Television, magazines, and newspapers are all full of frightening stories about teenagers and families. They say that America's families are falling apart, that kids don't care about anything, and that parents have trouble doing anything. . . .

Use this format if your instructor asks you to submit an outline of your paper.

Model Outline Page

After the title page, number all pages in the upper-right corner, a half inch from the top. Place your name before the page number. Use small roman numerals on outline pages. Use arabic numerals on pages following the outline.

Outline

Thesis: Although these are difficult times to be raising teenagers, successful families are finding ways to cope with the challenges.

I.   Meeting the challenge of spending quality time together
    A.   Barriers to spending quality time
        1.   Increased working hours
        2.   Rising divorce rates
        3.   Women in workforce
    B.   Danger of lack of quality time
    C.   Ways found to spend time together
        1.   Working less and scaling back lifestyle
        2.   Homeschooling

II. Meeting the challenge of creating sense of community

    A. Lack of traditional community ties

    B. Ways found to create sense of community

        1. Intentional communities

        2. Religious ties

III. Meeting the challenge of limiting the negative impact of media and technology

    A. Negative impact of media and technology

        1. Creation of environment without protection

        2. Flood of uncontrolled, inappropriate information

    B. Ways of controlling media and technology

        1. Banning TV

        2. Using technology in beneficial ways

The word *Outline* (without underlining or quotation marks) is centered one inch from the top. Double-space lines. Leave a one-inch margin on all sides.

Here is a full model paper. It assumes the writer has included a title page.

Philips 1

Successful Families: Fighting for Their Kids

It's a terrible time to be a teenager, or even a teenager's parent. That message is everywhere. Television, magazines, and newspapers are all full of frightening stories about teenagers and families. They say that America's families are falling apart, that kids don't care about anything, and that parents have trouble doing anything about it. Bookstores are full of disturbing titles like these: *Parenting Your Out-of-Control Teenager*, *Teenage Wasteland*, *Unhappy Teenagers*, and *Teen Torment*. These books describe teenage problems that include apathy, violence, suicide, sexual abuse, depression, loss of values, poor mental health, crime, gang involvement, and drug and alcohol addiction.

Double-space lines of the text. Leave a one-inch margin all the way around the page. Your name and the page number should be typed one-half inch from the top of the page.

Common knowledge is not documented.

Naturally, caring parents are worried by all this. Their worry showed in a 2005 national poll in which 76% of parents said that raising children was "a lot harder" than it was when they were growing up ("A Lot Easier Said"). But just as most popular TV shows don't give a realistic view of American teens, these frightening books and statistics do not provide a complete picture of what's going on in families today. The fact is that not all teens and families are lost and without values. While they struggle with problems in our culture like everyone else, successful families are doing what they've always done: finding ways to protect and nurture their children. They are fighting the battle for their families in three ways: by fighting against the loss of quality family time, by fighting against the loss of community, and by fighting against the influence of the media.

It's true that these days parents face more challenges than ever before when it comes to finding quality time to spend with their children. The economist Edward Wolff explains the loss of time:

> Over a thirty-year time span, parental time has declined 13%. The time parents have available for their children has been squeezed by the rapid shift of mothers into the paid labor force, by escalating divorce rates and the subsequent abandonment of children by their fathers, and by an increase in the number of hours required on the job. The average worker is now at work 163 hours a year more than in 1969, which adds up to an extra month of work annually. (qtd. in Hewlett and West 48)

As a result, more children are at home alone than ever before. And this situation does leave children vulnerable to getting into trouble. Richardson and others, in their study of five thousand eighth graders in California, found that children who were home alone after school were twice as likely to experiment with drugs and alcohol as children who had a parent (or another adult) home in the after-school hours.

This typical citation shows the source by giving the author's last name or (as here, if no author is provided) the title of the article (and if relevant, a page number). "Works Cited" then provides full information about the source.

Thesis, followed by plan of development.

Source is identified by name and area of expertise.

Direct quotations of five typed lines or more are indented ten spaces (or one inch) from the left margin. Quotation marks are not used.

The abbreviation *qtd.* means *quoted.* No comma is used between the author name and the page number.

Philips 3

But creative parents still come up with ways to be there for their kids. For some, it's been a matter of cutting back on working hours and living more simply. For example, in her book *The Shelter of Each Other*, Mary Pipher tells the story of a couple with three-year-old twin boys. Eduardo worked sixty-hour weeks at a factory. Sabrina supervised checkers at a Kmart, cared for the boys, and tried to watch over her mother, who had cancer. Money was tight, especially, since day care was expensive and the parents felt they had to keep the twins stylishly dressed and supplied with new toys. The parents were stressed over money problems, their lack of time together, and especially, having so little time with their boys. It bothered them that the twins had begun to cry when their parents picked them up at day care, as if they'd rather stay with the day care workers. Finally, Sabrina and Eduardo made a difficult decision. Sabrina quit her job, and the couple invited her mother (whose illness was in remission) to live with them. With three adults pooling their resources, Sabrina and Eduardo found that they could manage without Sabrina's salary. The family no longer ate out, and they gave up their cable TV. Their sons loved having their grandmother in the house. Sabrina was able to begin doing relaxed, fun projects with the boys. They planted a garden and built a sandbox together. Sabrina observed, "I learned I could get off the merry-go-round" (195). Other parents have gotten off the merry-go-round by working at home, even if it means earning less money than they had previously.

Some parents even homeschool their children as a way to be sure they have plenty of time together. Homeschooling used to be thought of as a choice made only by very religious people or back-to-nature radicals. Now, teaching children at home is much less unusual. It's estimated that as many as two million American children are being homeschooled. Harvard even has an admissions officer whose job

When citing a work in general, not part of a work, it is best to include the author's name in the text instead of using a parenthetical citation. No page number is needed, as the citation refers to the overall findings of the study.

Only the page number is needed, as the author has already been named in the text.

it is to review applications from homeschooled kids. Parents who homeschool have different reasons, but according to a cover story in *Newsweek*, "some . . . are looking for a way to reclaim family closeness in an increasingly fast-paced society. . . . Still others worry about unsavory influences in school—drugs, alcohol, sex, violence" (Kantrowitz and Wingert 66). Homeschooling is no guarantee that a child will resist those temptations, but some families do believe it's a great way to promote family closeness. One fifteen-year-old, homeschooled since kindergarten, explained why he liked the way he'd been raised and educated. He ended by saying, "Another way I'm different is that I love my family. One guy asked me if I'd been brainwashed. I think it's spooky that liking my family is considered crazy" (Pipher 103).

Many parents can't quit their jobs or teach their children at home. But some parents find a second way to nurture their children, through building community ties. They help their children develop a healthy sense of belonging by creating links with positive, constructive people and activities. In the past, community wasn't so hard to find. In *The Way We Really Are*, Stephanie Coontz writes, "Right up through the 1940s, ties of work, friendship, neighborhood, ethnicity, extended kin, and voluntary organizations were as important a source of identity for most Americans, and sometimes a *more* important source of obligation, than marriage and the nuclear family" (37). Even when today's parents were teenagers, neighborhoods were places where kids felt a sense of belonging and responsibility. But today "parents . . . mourn the disappearance of neighborhoods where a web of relatives and friends kept a close eye on everyone's kids. And they worry their own children grow up isolated, knowing more about the cast of *Friends* than the people in surrounding homes" (Donahue D1).

Ellipsis points show where the student has omitted material from the original source. The quoted material is not capitalized because the student has blended it into a sentence with an introductory phrase.

Philips 5

One way that some families are trying to build old-fashioned community is through "intentional community," or "cohousing." Begun in Denmark in 1972, the cohousing movement is modeled after the traditional village. It brings together a number of families who live in separate houses but share some common space. For instance, families might share central meeting rooms, dining areas, gardens, day care, workshops, or office space. They might own tools and lawn mowers together, rather than each household having its own. The point is that they treat their neighbors as extended family, not as strangers. As described by the online site *Cohousing.org*, cohousing is "a type of collaborative housing that attempts to overcome the alienation of modern subdivisions in which no one knows their neighbors, and there is no sense of community." In its 2007 database, the Intentional Communities Web site estimates that over one thousand such communities exist in North America.

Other families turn to religion as a source of community. Michael Medved and Diane Medved, authors of *Saving Childhood*, are raising their family in a religious Jewish home. Their children attend Jewish schools, go to synagogue, and follow religious customs. They frequently visit, eat, play with, and are cared for by neighboring Jewish families. The Medveds believe their family is stronger because of their belief "in planting roots—in your home, in your family, in your community. That involves making a commitment, making an investment both physically and emotionally, in your surroundings" (200). Other religious traditions offer families a similar sense of community, purpose, and belonging. Marcus and Tracy Glover are members of the Nation of Islam. They credit the Nation with making their marriage and family strong and breaking a three-generation cycle of single motherhood (Hewlett and West 201–02).

Cited material extends from one page to another, so both page numbers are given.

A third way that families are fighting to protect their children is by controlling the impact of the media and technology. Hewlett and West and Pipher use similar words to describe this impact. As they describe growing up today, Hewlett and West write about children living "without a skin" (xiii), and Pipher writes about "houses without walls" (12). These authors mean that today—unlike in the old days, when children were protected from the outside world while they were in their homes—the home offers little protection. Even in their own living rooms, all children have to do is to turn on a TV, radio, or computer to be hit with a flood of violence, sick humor, and often weird sexuality. Children are growing up watching shows like *The Osbournes*, a program that celebrated two spoiled, foul-mouthed children and their father—a burned-out rock star slowed by years of carefree drug abuse. A recent article in *Science* magazine offered the most damning link yet between TV watching and antisocial behavior. Reporting on the results of its seventeen-year study that followed viewers from youth to adulthood, *Science* found that the more television a teen watched, the higher the chances he or she would commit violent acts later in life. Of kids who watched an hour or less of TV a day, fewer than 6% of teens went on to commit assaults, robberies, or other violent acts as adults. But nearly 28% of teens who watched TV three or more hours a day did commit crimes of violence (Anderson and Bushman 2377–79). Sadly, many parents seem to have given up even trying to protect their growing kids against the flood of televised garbage. They are like the mother quoted in *USA Today* as saying, "How can I fight five hundred channels on TV?" (Donahue D1).

Fortunately, some parents are still insisting on control over the information and entertainment that comes into their homes. Some subscribe to "The Television Project," an online educational organization

Philips 7

that helps parents "understand how television affects their families and community and proposes alternatives that foster positive emotional, cognitive and spiritual development within families and communities." Others ban TV entirely from their homes. More try to find a way to use TV and other electronics as helpful tools but not allow them to dominate their homes. One family in Nebraska, the Millers, who homeschool their children, described to Mary Pipher their attitude toward TV. They hadn't owned a TV for years, but they bought one so that they could watch the Olympics. The set is now stored in a closet unless a program is on that the family agrees is worthwhile. Some programs the Millers have enjoyed together include the World Cup soccer games, the TV drama *Sarah Plain and Tall*, and an educational TV course in sign language. Pipher was impressed by the Miller children, and she thought their limited exposure to TV was one reason why. In her words,

> Calm, happy children and relaxed, confident parents are so rare today. Probably most notable were the long attention spans of the children and their willingness to sit and listen to the grown-ups talk. The family had a manageable amount of information to deal with. They weren't stressed by more information than they could assimilate. The kids weren't overstimulated and edgy. Nor were they sexualized in the way most kids now are. (107)

Pipher's words describe children raised by parents who won't give in to the idea that their children are lost. Such parents structure ways to be present in the home, build family ties to a community, and control the impact of the media in their homes. Through their efforts, they succeed in raising nurtured, grounded, successful children. Such parents acknowledge the challenges of raising kids in today's America, but they are up to the job.

The conclusion provides a summary and restates the thesis.

Works cited should be double-spaced and should always appear on a separate, titled page.

Titles of books, magazines, and the like should be italicized.

Include the date you accessed a Web source—in the first case, October 4, 2007.

Several of these sources—*Public Agenda, Intentional Communities,* and the *Television Project*—are online. By going online and typing the letters after "www." in each citation, you can access any of the sources.

Works Cited

"A Lot Easier Said Than Done: Parents Talk about Raising Children in Today's America." *Public Agenda.* Oct 2005. Web. 4 Oct. 2007.

Anderson, Craig A., and Brad J. Bushman. "The Effects of Media Violence on Society." *Science* 29 Mar. 2002: 2377–79. Print.

Coontz, Stephanie. *The Way We Really Are.* New York: Basic Books, 1997. Print.

Donahue, Deirdre. "Struggling to Raise Good Kids in Toxic Times." *USA Today* 1 Oct. 1998: D1+. Print.

Hewlett, Sylvia Ann, and Cornel West. *The War Against Parents.* Boston: Houghton Mifflin, 1998. Print.

The Intentional Communities Home Page. Fellowship of Intentional Communities. Web. 2 Sept. 2007.

Kantrowitz, Barbara, and Pat Wingert. "Learning at Home: Does It Pass the Test?" *Newsweek* 5 Oct. 1998: 64–70. Print.

Medved, Michael, and Diane Medved. *Saving Childhood.* New York: Putnam, 1996. Print.

Pipher, Mary. *The Shelter of Each Other.* New York: Putnam, 1996. Print.

The Television Project Home Page. The Television Project. *n. d.* Web. 2 Feb. 2007.

"What Is Cohousing?" *Cohousing.* The Cohousing Association of the United States. 10 Sept. 2006. Web. 2 Feb. 2007.

Although the student writer of the research paper emphasized the impact of TV on children, she referred to the computer as another source of "violence, sick humor, and often weird sexuality." In your opinion, which do you feel is more dangerous for children when unsupervised, the computer or the TV? Why?

Handbook of Sentence Skills

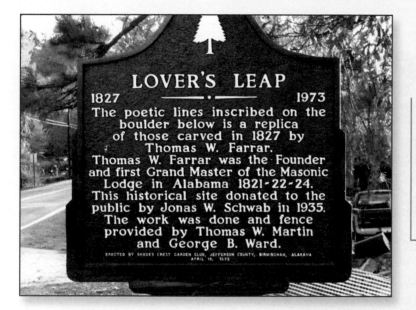

PART 4

LOVER'S LEAP
1827 ——————·—————— 1973
The poetic lines inscribed on the boulder below is a replica of those carved in 1827 by Thomas W. Farrar.
Thomas W. Farrar was the Founder and first Grand Master of the Masonic Lodge in Alabama 1821-22-24.
This historical site donated to the public by Jonas W. Schwab in 1935.
The work was done and fence provided by Thomas W. Martin and George B. Ward.
ERECTED BY SHADES CREST GARDEN CLUB, JEFFERSON COUNTY, BIRMINGHAM, ALABAMA
APRIL 18, 1973

PREVIEW

1 Grammar

2 Mechanics

3 Punctuation

4 Word Use

How could you change this sign's wording to make it grammatically correct? What specific errors have been made?

Grammar

SECTION PREVIEW

Chapter 23
Subjects and Verbs

Chapter 24
Fragments

Chapter 25
Run-Ons

Chapter 26
Regular and Irregular Verbs

Chapter 27
Subject-Verb Agreement

Chapter 28
Additional Information about Verbs

Chapter 29
Pronoun Agreement and Reference

Chapter 30
Pronoun Types

Chapter 31
Adjectives and Adverbs

Chapter 32
Misplaced Modifiers

Chapter 33
Dangling Modifiers

What sentence-skills errors can you find in the sign pictured above? How can you correct them?

Subjects and Verbs

This chapter will explain two of the basic building blocks of English sentences: subjects and verbs.

Key Terms

auxiliary verbs: verbs that work with the main verb to make up the complete verb in a sentence; also called helping verbs. Example: *The woman is working.* (Auxiliary verb: *is*)

linking verbs: verbs that help describe a subject by connecting it to another word. Example: *The man is handsome.* (Linking verb: *is*)

preposition: one of a group of words that precede a noun or pronoun and indicate direction, position, placement, duration, or another kind of connection to the other words in the sentence. Examples: *about, above, through, under, with.*

subject: who or what a sentence speaks about; usually a noun or pronoun that acts, is acted upon, or is described. Example: *The boy cries.* (Subject: *boy*)

verb: what the sentence says about the subject; a word that shows what a subject does or that helps describe the subject by linking it to an adjective. Example: *The boy cries.* (Verb: *cries*)

Every sentence has a subject and a verb. Who or what the sentence speaks about is called the *subject;* what the sentence says about the subject is the *verb.* In the following sentences, the subject is underlined once; the verb is underlined twice.

The boy cried.

That fish stinks.

Many people applied for the job.

The show is a documentary.

A Simple Way to Find a Subject

If you ask *who* or *what* the sentence is about, your answer will be the subject.

> *Who* is the first sentence about? The boy
>
> *What* is the second sentence about? That fish
>
> *Who* is the third sentence about? Many people
>
> *What* is the fourth sentence about? The show

A Simple Way to Find a Verb

If you ask what the sentence *says about* the subject, your answer will be the verb.

> What does the first sentence *say about* the boy? He cried.
>
> What does the second sentence *say about* the fish? It stinks.
>
> What does the third sentence *say about* the people? They applied.
>
> What does the fourth sentence *say about* the show? It is a documentary.

A second way to find the verb is to put *I, you, we, he, she, it,* or *they* in front of the word you think is a verb. If the result makes sense, you have a verb. For example, you could put *he* in front of *cried* in the first sentence, with the result, *he cried,* making sense. Thus, you know that *cried* is a verb.

Also remember that most verbs show action. In the sentences above, there are three action verbs: *cried, smells,* and *applied.* Other verbs, known as *linking verbs,* do not show action; they give information about the subject. In "The show is a documentary," the linking verb *is* joins the subject (*show*) with a word that identifies or describes it (*documentary*). Other common linking verbs include *am, are, was, were, feel, appear,* and *become.*

ACTIVITY 1

In each of the following sentences, draw one line under the subject and two lines under the verb.

1. The ripening tomatoes glistened on the sunny windowsill.

2. Acupuncture reduces the pain of my headaches.

3. Elena twisted a strand of hair around her fingers.

4. My brother built his bookshelves from cinder blocks and wood planks.

5. A jackrabbit bounds up to fifteen feet in one leap.

6. The singer's diamond earrings sparkled in the spotlight.

7. Walt Disney created the cartoon character Mickey Mouse.

8. The Federal Bureau of Investigation (FBI) pursues violators of federal laws.

9. Ferdinand and Isabella of Spain sponsored Columbus's voyages.

10. On April 9, 1865, General Robert E. Lee surrendered to General Ulysses S. Grant.

More about Subjects and Verbs

1. A sentence may have more than one verb, more than one subject, or several subjects and verbs.

   The <u>engine</u> <u>coughed</u> and <u>sputtered</u>.

   Broken <u>glass</u> and empty <u>cans</u> <u>littered</u> the parking lot.

   <u>Marta</u>, <u>Nilsa</u>, and <u>Robert</u> <u>met</u> after class and <u>headed</u> downtown.

2. The subject of the sentence never appears within a prepositional phrase. A *prepositional phrase* is simply a group of words that begins with a preposition. Following is a list of common prepositions.

Prepositions

about	before	by	inside	over
above	behind	during	into	through
across	below	except	like	to
among	beneath	for	of	toward
around	beside	from	off	under
at	between	in	on, onto	with

Crossing out prepositional phrases will help you find the sentence's subject or subjects.

A <u>stream</u> ~~of cold air~~ <u>comes</u> ~~through the space~~ ~~below the door~~.

<u>Specks</u> ~~of dust~~ <u>dance</u> gently ~~in a ray~~ ~~of sunlight~~.

The amber <u>lights</u> ~~on its sides~~ <u>outlined</u> the tractor-trailer ~~in the hazy dusk~~.

<u>Members</u> ~~of the club~~ <u>are entitled</u> to use the exercise room.

The golden <u>rays</u> ~~of the May sun~~ <u>reflect</u> ~~on the crystal-clear waters~~ ~~of the icy lake~~.

3. Many verbs consist of *helping, or auxiliary,* verbs, as seen here in several forms of the verb *work*. (See page 491 for a list of other helping verbs.)

Forms of *work*

work	worked	should work
works	were working	will be working
does work	have worked	can work
is working	had been working	could be working

---

4. Words like *not, just, never, only,* and *always* are not part of the verb, although they may appear within the verb.

    Ruby <u>has</u> never <u>liked</u> cold weather.

    Our boss <u>will</u> not <u>be singing</u> with the choir this year.

    The intersection <u>has</u> not always <u>been</u> this dangerous.

5. A verb preceded by *to* is never the verb of a sentence.

    At night, my son <u>likes</u> to read under the covers.

    Evelyn <u>decided</u> to separate from her husband.

6. An *-ing* word by itself is never the verb of a sentence. (It may be part of the verb, but it must have a helping verb in front of it.) The following is *not* a sentence, because the verb is not complete:

    They going on a trip this weekend.

    This *is* a sentence:

    They <u>are going</u> on a trip this weekend.

ACTIVITY 2

Draw a single line under subjects and a double line under verbs. Cross out prepositional phrases as necessary to find the subjects.

1. A large segment of the population supports the new legislation.

2. Two of the films we chose to write about were first released in the 1970s.

3. After more than 2,000 years, some Roman aqueducts are still supplying water to large European cities.

4. Every dog in the house barked as the mailman came to the door.

5. The fantastic advertisement about the new perfume inspired me to try the scent.

6. The novels of John Steinbeck portray the lives of the poor and powerless.

7. The smoke detector's tiny green light suddenly started to flicker.

8. A colleague of mine works at home and submits her reports by e-mail.

9. The large jar of marbles fell off the bookshelf and crashed on the floor.

10. A memorial of beautifully sculpted granite stands as tribute to Abraham Lincoln, our sixteenth president.

REVIEW TEST 1

Draw a single line under subjects and a double line under verbs. Cross out prepositional phrases as necessary to find the subjects. Many sentences contain multiple subjects and verbs.

1. Maria Sklodowka was born in 1867 in Warsaw in the country now known as Poland.

2. Her father was a mathematics and physics professor, and her mother managed a boarding school for girls.

3. Maria's mother died in 1878 of complications from tuberculosis.

4. Maria attended a clandestine university where she learned about Dostoevsky and Karl Marx.

5. Maria briefly moved to Paris to be a governess and to help her sister; her sister repaid Maria several years later when she insisted that Maria move back to Paris.

6. While in Paris, Maria met Pierre Curie and, after a courtship, married him in 1895, becoming Marie Curie.

7. Marie and Pierre worked together on the study of radiation.

8. In 1903, Marie and Pierre were awarded the Nobel Prize for physics, making Marie the first woman ever to win a Nobel Prize.

9. Pierre was killed in a wagon accident, and Marie began teaching at the Sorbonne.

10. When Marie was awarded a second Nobel Prize in 1911 for chemistry, she became the only woman to win two Nobel Prizes in different disciplines.

REVIEW TEST 2

Write five complete sentences that contain prepositional phrases that come between the subject and the verb. Remember that prepositional phrases begin with words such as *with, to, in, into, about,* and *for.* Then, draw a single line under the subject and a double line under the verb. Finally, draw a line through the prepositional phrase.

Fragments

This chapter will explain how to avoid the most common types of fragments. A fragment is a word group that lacks a subject or a verb and/or one that does not express a complete thought.

Fragment:

Whenever I go to school.

"Whenever," a dependent word, cannot introduce a complete thought, so it cannot stand alone.

Correct Sentence:

Whenever I go to school, I take the bus.

The fragment introduces a complete thought.

Every sentence must have a subject and a verb and must express a complete thought. A word group that lacks a subject or a verb and fails to express a complete thought is a *fragment*. Here are the most common types of fragments:

1. Dependent-word fragments
2. *-ing* fragments
3. Added-detail fragments
4. Missing-subject fragments

Dependent-Word Fragments

Some word groups that begin with *dependent words* are fragments. When you start a sentence with a dependent word, be careful not to create a fragment.

Dependent Words		
after	if, even if	when, whenever
although	in order that	where, wherever
as	since	whether

continued

because	that, so that	which, whichever
before	unless	while
even though	until	who, whom, whose
how	what, whatever	

Below, the word group beginning with *after* is a fragment:

After I cashed my paycheck. I treated myself to dinner.

A *dependent statement*—one starting with a dependent word like *after*—cannot stand alone. It depends on another statement to complete the thought. *After I cashed my paycheck* is a dependent statement. It leaves us hanging. We expect to find out, in the same sentence, *what happened after* the writer cashed the check. When a writer does not follow through and complete a thought, a fragment results.

To correct the fragment, simply follow through and complete the thought:

After I cashed my paycheck, I treated myself to dinner.

Remember, then, that *dependent statements by themselves are fragments*. They must be attached to a statement that makes sense standing alone.

Here are two other examples of dependent-word fragments:

I won't leave the house. Until I hear from you.

Rick finally picked up the socks. That he had thrown on the floor days ago.

Until I hear from you is a fragment; it does not make sense standing by itself. We want to know in the same statement what *until* refers to. The writer must complete the thought. Likewise, *That he had thrown on the floor days ago* is not in itself a complete thought. We want to know in the same statement what *that* refers to.

Additional information about dependent words and phrases can be found on pages 125–127. In this section, dependent words are also referred to as subordinating words.

How to Correct a Dependent-Word Fragment

Often, you correct a dependent-word fragment by attaching it to the sentence that comes after it or to the one that comes before it.

After I cashed my paycheck, I treated myself to dinner.

(The fragment has been attached to the sentence that comes after it.)

Rick finally picked up the socks that he had thrown on the floor days ago.

(The fragment has been attached to the sentence that comes before it.)

You can also connect a dependent-word fragment by removing the dependent word and rewriting the sentence:

I cashed my paycheck and then treated myself to dinner.

I will wait to hear from you.

He had thrown them on the floor days ago.

TIPS

a. Use a comma if a dependent-word group comes at the beginning of a sentence, but not generally if it comes at the *end* of a sentence.

Comma: After I cashed my paycheck, I treated myself to dinner.

No comma: I won't leave the house until I hear from you.

b. Sometimes *who, that, which,* or *where* appear not at the very start but near the start of a word group. A fragment can result:

I drove slowly past the old brick house. The place where I grew up.

The place where I grew up is not a complete thought. We want to know in the same statement *where was the place?* To correct the fragment attach it to the sentence that came before:

I drove slowly past the old brick house, the place where I grew up.

ACTIVITY 1

Turn each of the following dependent-word groups into a sentence by adding a complete thought. Use a comma after the dependent-word group if a dependent word starts the sentence. Note the examples.

EXAMPLES

Before I became a vegetarian.

Before I became a vegetarian, I would eat fish four times a week.

My neighbor who competitively barbeques.

My neighbor who competitively barbeques has won several prizes.

1. Unless I start practicing more.

_____

_____

2. Although I had studied for several hours.

_____

_____

3. Because I had just gotten paid.

_____

_____

4. Until the new mall opened.

_____

_____

5. The car that I bought.

_____

_____

ACTIVITY 2

Underline the dependent-word fragment in each item. Then rewrite the items, correcting each fragment by attaching it to the sentence that comes before or the sentence that comes after it—whichever sounds more natural. Use a comma after the dependent-word group if it starts the sentence.

1. My cat flattens herself and tries to get out of the room. Whenever I turn on the vacuum. Apparently, she thinks something is coming to eat her.

_____

_____

2. Philadelphia was originally a Quaker colony. That was founded by William Penn in 1681. By 1777, it had become the capital of the new United States.

_____

_____

3. Anna is the manager of the new neighborhood garden. That was started to encourage people to grow their own food. She has been making sure everyone is using only organic products.

_____

_____

4. Since Connor first began watching NOVA. He has been fascinated with space travel. He has decided to become an astronaut.

_____

_____

5. Roman law was first recorded in 450 B.C. in what was known as the "twelve tablets." It lasted for many centuries. Until the fall of the eastern Roman Empire nearly 2,000 years later.

_____

_____

-ing and *to* Fragments

When an *-ing* word appears at or near the start of a word group, a fragment may result. Such fragments often lack a subject and part of the verb. In the items on the following page, underline the word groups that contain *-ing* words. Each is a fragment.

1. Ellen walked all over the neighborhood yesterday. Trying to find her dog Bo. Several people claimed they had seen him only hours before.

2. We sat back to watch the movie. Not expecting anything special. To our surprise, we clapped, cheered, and cried for the next two hours.

3. I telephoned the balloon store. It being the day before our wedding anniversary. I knew my wife would be surprised to receive a dozen heart-shaped balloons.

People sometimes write *-ing* fragments because they think that the subject of one sentence will work for the next word group as well. Thus, in item 1 the writer thinks that the subject *Ellen* in the opening sentence will also serve as the subject for *Trying to find her dog Bo*. But the subject must be in the same sentence.

How to Correct *-ing* Fragments

1. Attach the fragment to the sentence that comes before it or the sentence that comes after it, whichever makes sense. Item 1 could read "Ellen walked all over the neighborhood yesterday trying to find her dog Bo."

2. Add a subject and change the *-ing* verb part to the correct form of the verb. Item 2 could read "We didn't expect anything special."

3. Change *being* to the correct form of the verb be *(am, are, is, was, were)*. Item 3 could read "It was the day before our wedding anniversary."

How to Correct *to* Fragments

When *to* appears at or near the start of a word group, a fragment sometimes results:

At the Chinese restaurant, Tim used chopsticks. To impress his date. He spent one hour eating a small bowl of rice.

The second word group is a fragment and can be corrected by adding it to the preceding sentence:

At the Chinese restaurant, Tim used chopsticks to impress his date.

ACTIVITY 3

Underline the *-ing* fragment in each of the following items. Then correct the item by using the method described in parentheses.

EXAMPLE

Including the Arctic Ocean and parts of Canada, the United States, and other countries. The Arctic Circle is the area that surrounds the Earth's North Pole. (Add the fragment to the sentence that comes after it.)

Including the Arctic Ocean and parts of Canada, the United States, and other countries, the

Arctic Circle is the area that surrounds the Earth's North Pole.

1. Ramses II ruled over Egypt from 1279 to 1212 B.C. Making his country stronger than ever before. He was both ambitious and intelligent.
   (Add the fragment to the preceding sentence.)

   _____

   _____

2. A noisy fire truck suddenly raced down the street. Coming to a stop at my house. My home security system had sent a false alarm.
   (Correct the fragment by adding the subject *it* and changing *coming* to the proper form of the verb, *came*.)

   _____

   _____

3. I couldn't find any books on Egyptian history in the library. They had all been checked out. The reason for this being that a research paper had just been assigned to students in an ancient history class.
   (Correct the fragment by changing *being* to the proper form of the verb, *was*.)

   _____

   _____

ACTIVITY 4

Underline the *-ing* or *to* fragment in each item. Then rewrite each item, correcting the fragment by using one of the three methods described above.

1. Knowing she had not finished the book. Madelyn was very nervous about going to class. She was sure the teacher was going to give a quiz.

   _____

   _____

2. I hired a neighbor boy. To mow my lawn and weed the garden. He has been doing a great job.

_____

_____

3. Searching for the right filament for his incandescent light bulb. Thomas Edison (1847–1931) found that a strip of carbonized bamboo could glow for 1,200 hours.

_____

_____

4. Cullen and Bryson have been friends since first grade. Graduating from high school this May.

_____

_____

5. To get his company to grow rapidly. Harvey Firestone launched a vigorous marketing campaign. In 1906, he sold 2,000 sets of tires to the Ford Motor Company.

_____

_____

Added-Detail Fragments

Added-detail fragments lack a subject and a verb. They often begin with one of the following words:

also	especially	except	for example
like	including	such as	

Underline the one added-detail fragment in each of the following items:

1. Before a race, I eat starchy foods. Such as bread and spaghetti. The carbohydrates provide quick energy.
2. Bob is taking a night course in auto mechanics. Also, one in plumbing. He wants to save money on household repairs.
3. My son keeps several pets in his room. Including hamsters and mice.

People often write added-detail fragments for much the same reason they write *-ing* fragments. They think the subject and verb in one sentence will serve for the next word group. But the subject and verb must be in *each* word group.

How to Correct Added-Detail Fragments

1. Attach the fragment to the complete thought that precedes it. Item 1 could read "Before a race, I eat starchy foods such as bread and spaghetti."

2. Add a subject and a verb to the fragment to make it a complete sentence. Item 2 could read "Bob is taking a night course in auto mechanics. Also, he is taking one in plumbing."

3. Insert the fragment within the preceding sentence. Item 3 could read "My son keeps several pets, including hamsters and mice, in his room."

ACTIVITY 5

Underline the fragment in each of the following items. Then make it a sentence by rewriting it, using the method described in parentheses.

EXAMPLE

My mother loves reading books written in the eighteenth and nineteenth centuries. Especially books by Jane Austen. She says they are more interesting than modern novels. (Add the fragment to the preceding sentence.)

My mother loves reading books written in the eighteenth and nineteenth centuries,

especially books by Jane Austen.

1. Mary Jane likes working at the department store. She enjoys the fringe benefits. For example, purchasing clothes at a discounted price.

   (Correct the fragment by adding the subject and verb *she purchases*.)

   _____

   _____

2. Henry Ford (1863–1947) is credited with the invention of the assembly line, not the automobile. Several nineteenth-century inventors had designed self-propelled vehicles. Like the one that ran on high-pressure steam.

   (Attach the fragment to the preceding sentence.)

   _____

   _____

3. I love to eat "b" vegetables because they are full of vitamins. Such as broccoli, Brussels sprouts, and beans. They also taste great.

   (Correct the fragment by inserting it in the preceding sentence.)

   _____

   _____

Underline the added-detail fragment in each item. Then rewrite to correct the fragment. Use one of the three methods described on the previous page.

ACTIVITY 6

1. The music festival had an amazing lineup. For example, The Black Eyed Peas, Maroon 5, and Coldplay. I was very excited when I was able to purchase tickets.

   _____

   _____

2. Some European countries remained neutral during World War II. Such as Switzerland and Portugal. Most South American countries refused to take sides as well.

   _____

   _____

3. The house was overrun with cats. At least twenty of them. It was incredibly smelly and filled with fur balls.

   _____

   _____

4. Chloé loves to collect rare pieces of pottery. Like jasperware. Her most prized piece is a Yixing teapot that is several hundred years old.

   _____

   _____

5. I know why I had to learn certain subjects in high school. Such as American history. Becoming a responsible citizen requires knowledge of our country's past and of its system of government.

   _____

   _____

Missing-Subject Fragments

In each item below, underline the word group in which the subject is missing:

1. Alicia loved getting wedding presents. But hated writing thank-you notes.

2. Mickey has orange soda and potato chips for breakfast. Then eats more junk food, like root beer and cookies, for lunch.

How to Correct Missing-Subject Fragments

1. Attach the fragment to the preceding sentence. Item 1 could read "Alicia loved getting wedding presents but hated writing thank-you notes."

2   Add a subject (which can often be a pronoun standing for the subject in the preceding sentence). Item 2 could read "Then he eats more junk food, like root beer and cookies, for lunch."

ACTIVITY 7

Underline the missing-subject fragment in each item. Then rewrite that part of the item needed to correct the fragment. Use one of the two methods of correction described above.

1. Ben loves to study math and science. But refuses to study history. He says he doesn't want to focus on the past.

   _____

   _____

2. My favorite pizza place is Sammy's Pizza and Pub. They have an amazing gluten-free spinach pizza. With fresh nut-free pesto.

   _____

   _____

3. Kendall is allergic to dairy. She goes into anaphylactic shock. And loses her ability to breathe.

   _____

   _____

4. When we arrived in Chicago, we took a train from the airport to the center of the city. Then walked a few blocks to our hotel. The trip was easy.

   _____

   _____

5. Next fall, I plan to take a course in calculus. And to join the mathematics club. By the time the year is over, I will have decided whether to become a mathematics teacher.

   _____

   _____

A Review: How to Check for Sentence Fragments

1. Read your paper aloud from the *last* sentence to the *first*. You will be better able to see and hear whether each word group you read is a complete thought.

2. If you think a word group may be a fragment, ask yourself, Does this contain a subject and a verb and express a complete thought?

3. More specifically, be on the lookout for the most common fragments:
   - Dependent-word fragments (starting with words like *after, because, since, when,* and *before*)
   - *-ing* and *to* fragments (*-ing* and *to* at or near the start of a word group)
   - Added-detail fragments (starting with words like *for example, such as, also,* and *especially*)
   - Missing-subject fragments (a verb is present but not the subject)

REVIEW TEST 1

Each word group in the following student paragraph is numbered. In the space provided, write C if a word group is a complete sentence; write F if it is a fragment. You will find eight fragments in the paragraph.

Personal

_____ 1. ¹For children in areas that get snow. ²There are stages of snow

_____ 2. days. ³The first day is always fun, exciting, and filled with

_____ 3. possibilities. ⁴It usually consists of sledding. ⁵Making snowmen,

_____ 4. drinking hot chocolate, and watching movies. ⁶The kids know

_____ 5. they have been given a gift of a day away from school. ⁷If the

_____ 6. first day is followed by more, days two through four continue

_____ 7. with the initial excitement of day one. ⁸But often lead into cabin

_____ 8. fever, boredom, and frustration. ⁹This is especially true if

_____ 9. days two through four are very cold. ¹⁰Although movies are

_____ 10. still an option. ¹¹Parents begin to feel guilty that their kids are not

_____ 11. learning anything; this begins a tug-o-war. ¹²And studying

_____ 12. suggested. ¹³If school is reopened, family sanity can be saved.

_____ 13. ¹⁴However, if more snow days occur. ¹⁵Reality sets in and

_____ 14. despondency grows in the parents. ¹⁶Parents' sanity is

_____ 15. jeopardized as they try to maintain normalcy. ¹⁷And

_____ 16. start bargaining with the school district by offering to

_____ 17. do whatever is necessary to reopen the schools. ¹⁸The final stage

_____ 18. for parents is despair. ¹⁹As the kids grow more and more

_____ 19. restless. ²⁰Countless families have been known to abandon hope

_____ 20. that the snow will ever melt and life will become normal.

Now (on separate paper) correct the fragments you have found. Attach the fragments to sentences that come before or after them or make whatever other change is needed to turn each fragment into a sentence.

REVIEW TEST 2

Underline the two fragments in each item below. Then make whatever changes are needed to turn the fragments into sentences.

EXAMPLE

Sharon was going to charge her new suit. ᵇBut then decided to pay cash instead. She remembered her New Year's resolution. ᵗTo cut down on her use of credit cards.

1. We both began to tire. As we passed the halfway mark in the race. But whenever I'd hear Reggie's footsteps behind me. I would pump my legs faster.

2. The American Southwest is home to several Native American nations. Such as the Navajo, the Apache, and the Pueblo. The East is the land of the Huron and Iroquois. Along with the Delaware and the Mohegan.

3. Punching all the buttons on his radio in sequence. Phil kept looking for a good song. He was in the mood to cruise down the highway. And sing at the top of his voice.

4. My children joke that we celebrate "Hanumas." With our Jewish neighbors. We share Hanukkah and Christmas activities. Including making potato pancakes at their house and decorating our tree.

5. Pop artists gained fame in the 1950s. Reacting to the more established art forms like expressionism, which preceded them. They portrayed common images from everyday life. Such as Coke bottles and soup cans.

6. Our landlord often invites her tenants to dinner. And allows them to use her washer and dryer. By doing such things. She has become known as the kindest person in our neighborhood.

7. The alley behind our house was flat. Except for a wide groove in the center. We used to sail paper boats down the groove. Whenever it rained hard enough to create a "river" there.

8. Don passed the computer school's aptitude test. Which qualifies him for nine months of training. Don kidded that anyone could be accepted. If he or she had $4,000.

REVIEW TEST 3

Read the paragraph below. In the space between the lines, correct each fragment.

It is very common for college students and young adults to find themselves in debt. As a result of poor spending habits. In order to learn how to effectively manage money. Students should be required to take economic classes. From elementary school all through high school. Starting in elementary school, students could learn how to budget allowances. How to save for items like toys and college, and how to run small businesses like lemonade stands or lawn mowing services. Games could be used in the classroom to allow students hands-on learning. As students get older. Classes could be more sophisticated. Students could learn about different concepts. Like compound interest, opportunity costs, and trade-offs. They could also be taught about the history of economics. How the government influences the economy, and how and why countries trade. High school students' courses would take economics even further. Explaining general investing, paying for college, and planning for retirement. Students could be required to intern at various businesses. To learn economics from the business side. Teaching economics on all educational levels could help many students avoid poor spending choices. And enjoy better financial situations throughout their lives.

Run-Ons

Run-ons are two complete thoughts that are run together with no adequate sign given to mark the break between them. In this text, the term "run-on" refers to both comma splices and fused sentences.

Key Terms

clause: a group of words having a subject and a verb.

comma splice: a comma incorrectly used to connect ("splice" together) two complete thoughts. Example:

> Comma splice: *I go to school, my brother stays home.*

> Correct sentences: *I go to school. My brother stays home.*

dependent clause: a group of words having a subject and a verb that does not express a complete thought and is not able to stand alone; also called a subordinate clause.

fused sentence: a run-on with no punctuation to mark the break between thoughts. Example:

> Fused sentence: *I go to school my brother stays home.*

> Correct sentences: *I go to school. My brother stays home.*

independent clause: a group of words having a subject and a verb that expresses a complete thought and is able to stand alone.

What Are Run-Ons?

A ***run-on*** consists of two complete thoughts run together without adequate punctuation to signal the break between them.[*] There are two types of run-ons: fused sentences and comma splices.

---

[*]Some instructors regard all run-ons as fused sentences. But for many other instructors, and for our purposes in this book, the term run-on applies equally to fused sentences and comma splices. The bottom line is that you do not want either fused sentences or comma splices in your writing.

Some instructors refer to each complete thought in a run-on as an independent clause. A clause is simply a group of words having a subject and a verb. A clause may be independent (expressing a complete thought and able to stand alone) or dependent (not expressing a complete thought and not able to stand alone). Using this terminology, we'd say that a run-on is two independent clauses run together with no adequate sign given to mark the break between them. Pages 124–127 in Chapter 5, "The Fourth Step in Essay Writing," demonstrate how to take simple sentences and make them compound or complex sentences without creating run-ons.

Fused sentences have no punctuation to mark the break between the two thoughts.

> The bus stopped suddenly I found myself in an old man's lap.

> We heard a noise in the garage two birds had flown in through the open window.

Comma splices are the most common kind of run-on. Students sense that some kind of connection is needed between two thoughts, so they often put a comma at the dividing point.

> The bus stopped suddenly, I found myself in an old man's lap.

> We heard a noise in the garage, two birds had flown in through the open window.

But the comma alone is *not sufficient*. A stronger, clearer mark is needed between the two complete thoughts.

TIP People often write run-ons when the second complete thought begins with one of the following words:

I	we	there	now
you	they	this	then
he, she, it	that	next	

Be on the alert for run-ons whenever you use one of these words.

Three Ways to Correct Run-Ons

Here are three common methods of correcting a run-on:

1. Use a period and a capital letter to separate sentences:

   The bus stopped suddenly. I found myself in an old man's lap.

   We heard a noise in the garage. Two birds had flown in through the open window.

2. Use a comma and a joining word *(and, but, for, or, nor, so, yet)*:

   The bus stopped suddenly, and I found myself in an old man's lap.

   We heard a noise in the garage, for two birds had flown in through the open window.

3. Use a semicolon to connect the two complete thoughts:

The bus stopped suddenly; I found myself in an old man's lap.

We heard a noise in the garage; two birds had flown in through the open window.

A fourth way to correct a run-on is to use *subordination*, which is discussed on page 469.

Method 1: Period and a Capital Letter

Use a period and a capital letter between two complete thoughts if the thoughts are not closely related or if another method would make the sentence too long.

ACTIVITY 1

In the following run-ons, locate the point at which one complete thought ends and another begins. Each is a fused sentence: two sentences joined with no punctuation. Reading a sentence aloud helps you hear where the break is. At this point, your voice may drop and pause. Correct each run-on by putting a period at the end of the first thought and a capital letter at the start of the next.

EXAMPLE

Molly's cell phone doesn't work anymore. She dropped it in the toilet.

1. I got stuck in rush hour traffic today it took me an extra hour to get home.

2. Bats have gotten a bad image they actually help reduce the mosquito population.

3. Since I got my smart phone, I spend too much time texting my friends i hardly ever send e-mails anymore.

4. The flower is the most important part of a plant it contains the seeds that enable the plant to reproduce.

5. Lucy has a unique sense of style her house is filled with brightly colored walls in oranges, yellows, and purples.

6. Galileo discovered that two solid objects of different weights fall at the same velocities he also made the first practical telescope for observing the heavens.

7. On our trip to Africa, we traveled to Mozambique and Zimbabwe then we went north to Zambia.

8. The man at the door was offering tree and lawn services he claimed to be the cheapest company in town.

9. Simeon is fluent in Chinese, French, Arabic, and Spanish he is often hired to help translate paperwork for immigrants.

10. Jessica loved to solve mysteries she entered college to become a forensic scientist.

Method 2: Comma and a Joining Word

Another way of correcting a run-on is to use a comma and a joining word to connect the two complete thoughts. Joining words (also called *conjunctions*) include *and, but, for, or, nor, so,* and *yet.* Here are what the four most common joining words mean:

and   in addition

Teresa works full time for an accounting firm, and she takes evening classes.

(*And* means *in addition:* Teresa works full time for an accounting firm; *in addition,* she takes evening classes.)

but   however, on the other hand

I turned to the want ads, but I knew my dream job wouldn't be listed.

(*But* means *however:* I turned to the want ads; *however,* I knew my dream job wouldn't be listed.)

for   because

Lizards become sluggish at night, for they need the sun's warmth to maintain an active body temperature.

(*For* means *because:* Lizards become sluggish at night *because* they need the sun's warmth to maintain an active body temperature.)

so   as a result, therefore

The canoe touched bottom, so Dave pushed it toward deeper water.

(*So* means *as a result:* The canoe touched bottom; *as a result,* Dave pushed it toward deeper water.)

yet   but, however, on the other hand

The defenders of the Alamo were vastly outnumbered, yet they refused to surrender.

(Yet means *however:* The defenders of the Alamo were vastly outnumbered; *however*, they refused to surrender.)

ACTIVITY 2

Insert the joining word *(and, but, for, so)* that logically connects the two thoughts in each sentence.

1. Jordan spends a lot of time doing his homework in his room, _____ he usually listens to his iPod at the same time.

2. King Macbeth of Scotland (1040–1057) defeated King Duncan in battle, _____ he later became the title character in one of Shakespeare's tragedies.

3. The school started a new organic garden, _____ the students don't like doing the weeding.

4. I needed to deposit the cash I made from my garage sale, _____ the ATM machine wasn't working.

5. Maria Montessori is known as a pioneer of modern education, _____ she created a system that included "learning games" designed especially for children.

6. The tomato is very popular today, _____ it was once thought to be poisonous.

7. We were awakened by a huge bang in the middle of the night, _____ it turned out to be our cats knocking over our large ficus plant.

8. My paycheck is not enough to pay all my bills, _____ I have started riding my bike to and from work.

9. My favorite restaurant serves steak and lobster, _____ I don't get to go very often because my husband is a vegetarian.

10. I lost fifteen pounds over the last three months, _____ I rewarded myself by purchasing a new dress.

Add a complete and closely related thought to go with each of the following statements. Use a comma and the indicated joining word when you write the second thought.

ACTIVITY 3

EXAMPLE

for I decided to leave school an hour early, _____

for I had a pounding headache.

1. The corner store is convenient _____ **but**

2. Leo attended night class _____ **for**

3. Aisha studied for an hour before dinner _____ **and**

4. Marcia was unable to take Prof. Samuelson's economics class _____ **so**

5. I had enough money to buy dinner _____ **but**

Correct each run-on with either (1) a period and a capital letter or (2) a comma and a logical joining word. Do not use the same method of correction for every sentence.

ACTIVITY 4

Some of the run-ons are fused sentences (there is no punctuation between the two complete thoughts), and some are comma splices (there is only a comma between the two complete thoughts). One sentence is correct.

EXAMPLE

There was a strange odor in the house, ^so Burt called the gas company immediately.

1. Oxygen is an odorless gas discovered independently by Joseph Priestly and Karl Scheele, it is the third most abundant element in the universe.

2. Cockroaches adapt to any environment they have even been found living inside nuclear reactors.

3. My dog was panting from the heat I decided to wet him down with the garden hose.

4. Our science class is working on a weather project with students from Russia we communicate by computer almost every day.

5. My grandfather is eighty-five years old, he goes to work every day.

6. The bristles of the paintbrushes were very stiff, soaking them in turpentine made them soft again.

7. Chen borrows cassettes from the library to listen to on the way to work, some are music, and some are recordings of best-selling books.

8. Thomas Paine, who supported the American Revolution, was accused of treason in England, he escaped to France in 1793.

9. Today, there are only eight major planets in our solar system, for astronomers have downgraded Pluto to a dwarf planet.

10. I volunteered to run the Meals on Wheels service in our city we deliver hot meals to sick or housebound people.

Method 3: Semicolon

A third way to correct a run-on is to use a semicolon to mark the break between thoughts. When used to correct run-ons, a semicolon can be used alone or with a transitional word.

Semicolon Alone   Unlike the comma alone, a semicolon can be used to connect the two complete thoughts:

> Lonnie heard a noise and looked out the window; the only thing he saw was his reflection.

> Lizards become sluggish at night; they need the sun's warmth to maintain an active body temperature.

> We knew a power failure had occurred; all the clocks were forty-seven minutes slow.

Using semicolons can add to sentence variety. For some people, however, the semicolon is a confusing punctuation mark. Keep in mind that if you are not comfortable using it, you can and should use one of the the first two methods of correcting run-ons.

Insert a semicolon where the break occurs between the two complete thoughts in each of the following sentences.

EXAMPLE

The plumber gave me an estimate of $260; I decided to repair the faucet myself.

1. The children stared at the artichokes on their plates they didn't know how to eat the strange vegetable.

2. Ecuador is in South America it is bordered by Colombia and Peru.

3. The Great Wall of China is immense it's the only human construction visible from the moon.

4. Elaine woke up at 3 A.M. to the smell of sizzling bacon her husband was having another insomnia attack.

5. Maya curled up under the covers she tried to get warm by grasping her icy feet with her chilly hands.

6. Honshu is the largest island in Japan it is also the most densely populated.

7. Ice had formed on the inside edge of our window Joey scratched a *J* in it with his finger.

8. Charles peered into the microscope he saw only his own eyelashes.

9. A man in a bear suit walked slowly down the street the children stopped their play to stare at him.

10. Ceylon was declared independent in 1948 later it became known as Sri Lanka.

Semicolon with a Transitional Word A semicolon can be used with a transitional word and a comma to join two complete thoughts.

I tried to cash my paycheck; however, I had forgotten to bring my identification.

Athletic shoes must fit perfectly; otherwise, wearers may injure their feet.

People use seventeen muscles when they smile; on the other hand, they use forty-three muscles when they frown.

Here is a list of transitional words, also known as *adverbial conjunctions*.

Transitional Word	Meaning
however	but
nevertheless	however
on the other hand	however

continued

Transitional Word	Meaning
instead	as a substitute
meanwhile	in the intervening time
otherwise	under other conditions
indeed	in fact
in addition	also, and
also	in addition
moreover	in addition
furthermore	in addition
as a result	thus, therefore
thus	as a result
consequently	as a result
therefore	as a result

ACTIVITY 6

For each sentence, choose a logical transitional word from the box above, and write it in the space provided. Use a semicolon *before* the connector and a comma *after* it.

EXAMPLE

I dread going to parties; ___*however*___, my husband loves meeting new people.

1. Lillian always attends every class session _____ she hopes to get the best grade possible.

2. Kryptonite is a fictitious substance that is supposed to be harmful to Superman _____ krypton is a real element, which was discovered in 1989.

3. Yoga is my favorite form of exercise _____ I enjoy running and hiking.

4. We were asleep in our tent _____ two bears crept into our campsite and began searching for food.

5. The sheriff was very popular _____ he won reelection quite easily.

A Note on Subordination

A fourth method of joining related thoughts is to use subordination. *Subordination* is a way of showing that one thought in a sentence is not as important as another thought. (Subordination is explained in full on pages 125–127.) Below are three earlier sentences, recast so that one idea is subordinated to (made less important than) the other idea. In each case, the subordinate (or less important) thought is underlined. Note that each subordinate clause begins with a dependent word.

Because the library had just closed, I couldn't get any of the reserved books.

When the canoe touched bottom, Dave pushed the craft toward deeper water.

I didn't make good time driving to work today because every traffic light along the way was red.

A Review: How to Check for Run-Ons

1. To see if a sentence is a run-on, read it aloud and listen for a break marking two complete thoughts. Your voice will probably drop and pause at the break.

2. To check an entire paper, read it aloud from the *last* sentence to the *first*. Doing so will help you hear and see each complete thought.

3. Be on the lookout for words that can lead to run-on sentences:

I	he, she, it	they	this	then	now
you	we	there	that	next	

4. Correct run-ons by using one of the following methods:

   Period and a capital letter

   Comma and a joining word *(and, but, for, or, nor, so, yet)*

   Semicolon, alone or with a transitional word

   Subordination

REVIEW TEST 1

Correct each run-on by using (1) a period and a capital letter; (2) a comma and a joining word; or (3) a semicolon. Do not use one method exclusively.

Some of the run-ons are fused sentences (there is no punctuation between the two complete thoughts), and some are comma splices (there is only a comma between the two complete thoughts). Two sentences are correct.

1. Slovakia, a country in Eastern Europe, was once ruled by the Austro-Hungarian Empire, it is now an independent country.

2. Slovakia has had a long history of being ruled by other countries in the fifth century, the kingdom of Greater Moravia was settled and founded by Slavic tribes.

3. In the tenth century, Magyar tribes invaded they formed Greater Hungary.

4. In 1526, Hungary was defeated by the Ottoman Turks, the Hapsburgs began their rule of Upper Hungary.

5. Pozony became the Hungarian capital the city is now known as Bratislava.

6. Austria-Hungary was formed in 1867, Franz Josef, the Hapsburg emperor, negotiated with Hungarian nobles to form the new country.

7. The Austro-Hungarian Empire was dissolved in 1918 at the end of World War I, Slovakia then became part of Czechoslovakia.

8. At the end of World War II, Czechoslovakia was ruled by Czech Communists in 1948 the Soviet Union tightened its control over the country.

9. In 1989, when the Soviet Union fell, Czechoslovakians demonstrated in the Velvet Revolution, which brought some democracy to the country.

10. In 1992, Czechoslovakia was known as the Czech and Slovak Federal Republics Prime Minister Meciar began talks to disband the confederation.

11. In 1993, the Slovak Republic and the Czech Republic became two separate countries, this was nicknamed the Velvet Divorce.

12. In 2000, Slovakia began the process to join the European Union and was granted membership in 2004.

Correct each run-on by using (1) a period and a capital letter; (2) a comma and a joining word; or (3) a semicolon. Do not use one method exclusively.

1. The nervous system works by transmitting signals from all parts of the body to the brain then it sends return signals to various organs and muscles.

2. With a groan, Margo pried off her high heels, then she plunged her swollen feet into a bucket of baking soda and hot water.

3. At 2 A.M. the last customer left the diner, a busboy began stacking chairs on the tables for the night.

4. Hypnosis has nothing to do with the occult. it is merely a state of deep relaxation.

5. Many young adults today live at home with their parents this allows them to save money.

6. Many politicians wanted America to remain neutral during World War II the attack on Pearl Harbor in 1941 made that impossible.

7. Early in life, Thomas Edison suffered with deafness, he taught his wife-to-be Morse code while he was courting her.

8. Originally, horses were too small to carry riders very far larger horses had to be bred for use in warfare.

9. The words *month, silver, purple,* and *orange* have something in common, no other English words rhyme with them.

10. I had heard that the Taj Mahal was one of the wonders of the world I planned a special excursion to visit this magnificent tomb.

REVIEW TEST 3

Locate and correct the five run-ons in the passage that follows.

My worst experience of the week was going home for lunch, rather than eating at work. My children didn't know I was coming, they had used most of the bread. All I had to make a sandwich with were two thin, crumpled pieces of crust. I sat there eating my tattered sandwich and trying to relax, then the telephone rang. It was for my daughter, who was in the bathroom, she called down to me that I should get the person's name and number. As soon as I sat down again, someone knocked on the door, It was a neatly dressed couple with bright eyes who wanted to talk with me about a higher power in life. I politely got rid of them and went back to finish lunch. I thought I would relax over my coffee, I had to break up a fight between my two young sons about which television channel to watch. As a last bit of frustration, my daughter came downstairs and asked me to drive her over to a friend's house before I went back to work.

Regular and Irregular Verbs

This chapter will review the principal characteristics of regular and irregular verbs.

Key Terms

irregular verb: a verb that has an irregular form in the past tense and past participle. For example, *choose* becomes *chose* or *chosen*.

past participle: one of the principal parts of every verb; formed by adding *-d* or *-ed* to the present; used with the helping verbs *have, has,* or *had,* or with a form of *be* (with passive verbs).

present participle: one of the principal parts of every verb; formed by adding *-ing* to the present.

principal parts of verbs: the four parts of every verb: present, past, past participle, and present participle.

verb tense: the times shown by verbs: present, past, and future.

Regular Verbs

A Brief Review of Regular Verbs

Every verb has four principal parts: *present, past, past participle*, and *present participle*. These parts can be used to build all the verb *tenses*—the times shown by verbs.

Most verbs in English are regular. The past and the past participle of regular verbs are formed by adding *-d* or *-ed* to the present. The *past participle* is the form of the verb used with the helping verbs *have, has*, or *had* (or some form of *be* with passive verbs). The *present participle* is formed by adding *-ing* to the present.

For a more in-depth look at verb tense and helping verbs, refer to Chapters 27 and 28.

Here are the principal parts of some regular verbs:

Present	Past	Past Participle	Present Participle
shout	shouted	shouted	shouting
prepare	prepared	prepared	preparing
surprise	surprised	surprised	surprising
tease	teased	teased	teasing
frighten	frightened	frightened	frightening

Nonstandard Forms of Regular Verbs

Many people have grown up in communities where nonstandard forms of regular verbs are used in everyday speech. Instead of saying, for example, "That girl *looks* tired," a person using a community dialect might say, "That girl *look* tired." Instead of saying, "Yesterday I *fixed* the car," a person using a community dialect might say, "Yesterday I *fix* the car." Community dialects have richness and power but are a drawback in college and in the world of work, where regular English verb forms must be used.

The following chart compares the nonstandard and the regular verb forms of the verb *work*.

Nonstandard Verb Form		Regular Verb Form	
(Do *not* use in your writing)		(Use for clear communication)	
Present tense			
I works	we works	I work	we work
you works	you works	you work	you work
he, she, it work	they works	he, she, it works	they work
Past tense			
I work	we work	I worked	we worked
you work	you work	you worked	you worked
he, she, it work	they work	he, she, it worked	they worked

To avoid nonstandard usage, memorize the forms shown above for the regular verb *work*. Then use the activities that follow to help make the inclusion of verb endings a writing habit.

Present Tense Endings

The verb ending -*s* or -*es* is needed with a regular verb in the present tense when the subject is *he, she, it,* or any one person or thing.

>He reads every night.

>She watches television every night.

>It appears they have little in common.

Some verbs in the sentences that follow need -*s* or -*es* endings. Cross out each nonstandard verb form and write the standard form in the space provided.

ACTIVITY 1

_____ 1. My radio wake me up every morning with soft music.

_____ 2. Sonya always rave about the beaches in Costa Rica.

_____ 3. My wife watch our baby in the morning, and I take over afternoons.

_____ 4. Alexander live on Puget Sound in Tacoma, Washington.

_____ 5. My brain work much better at night than it does in early morning.

Past Tense Endings

The verb ending -*d* or -*ed* is needed with a regular verb in the past tense.

>This morning I completed my research paper.

>The recovering hospital patient walked slowly down the corridor.

>Some students hissed when the new assignment was given out.

Some verbs in the sentences that follow need -*d* or -*ed* endings. Cross out each nonstandard verb form and write the standard form in the space provided.

ACTIVITY 2

_____ 1. In 1609, an Italian astronomer named Galileo use the telescope to view the moons of Jupiter.

_____ 2. At one time, the F. W. Woolworth Company own more than one thousand five-and-dime stores across the United States.

_____ 3. We realize a package was missing when we got back from shopping.

_____ 4. Bill was incorrect when he said that Henry Ford invent the automobile.

_____ 5. The driver edge her car into the intersection while the light was still red.

Irregular Verbs

Irregular verbs have irregular forms in past tense and past participle. For example, the past tense of the irregular verb *choose* is *chose;* its past participle is *chosen.*

Almost everyone has some degree of trouble with irregular verbs. When you are unsure about the form of a verb, you can check the following list of irregular verbs. (The present participle is not shown on this list because it is formed simply by adding *-ing* to the base form of the verb.) Or you can check a dictionary, which gives the principal parts of irregular verbs.

A List of Irregular Verbs

PRESENT	PAST	PAST PARTICIPLE
arise	arose	arisen
awake	awoke *or* awaked	awoken *or* awaked
be (am, are, is)	was (were)	been
become	became	become
begin	began	begun
bend	bent	bent
bite	bit	bitten
blow	blew	blown
break	broke	broken
bring	brought	brought
build	built	built
burst	burst	burst
buy	bought	bought
catch	caught	caught
choose	chose	chosen
come	came	come
cost	cost	cost
cut	cut	cut

continued

PRESENT	PAST	PAST PARTICIPLE
do (does)	did	done
draw	drew	drawn
drink	drank	drunk
drive	drove	driven
eat	ate	eaten
fall	fell	fallen
feed	fed	fed
feel	felt	felt
fight	fought	fought
find	found	found
fly	flew	flown
freeze	froze	frozen
get	got	got *or* gotten
give	gave	given
go (goes)	went	gone
grow	grew	grown
have (has)	had	had
hear	heard	heard
hide	hid	hidden
hold	held	held
hurt	hurt	hurt
keep	kept	kept
know	knew	known
lay	laid	laid
lead	led	led
leave	left	left
lend	lent	lent
let	let	let
lie	lay	lain
light	lit	lit
lose	lost	lost
make	made	made
meet	met	met

continued

PRESENT	PAST	PAST PARTICIPLE
pay	paid	paid
ride	rode	ridden
ring	rang	rung
run	ran	run
say	said	said
see	saw	seen
sell	sold	sold
send	sent	sent
shake	shook	shaken
shrink	shrank	shrunk
shut	shut	shut
sing	sang	sung
sit	sat	sat
sleep	slept	slept
speak	spoke	spoken
spend	spent	spent
stand	stood	stood
steal	stole	stolen
stick	stuck	stuck
sting	stung	stung
swear	swore	sworn
swim	swam	swum
take	took	taken
teach	taught	taught
tear	tore	torn
tell	told	told
think	thought	thought
wake	woke *or* waked	woke *or* waked
wear	wore	worn
win	won	won
write	wrote	written

Cross out the incorrect verb form in each of the following sentences. Then write the correct form of the verb in the space provided.

EXAMPLE

_____*flown*_____ After it had ~~flew~~ into the picture window, the dazed bird huddled on the ground.

_____ 1. Before they bought their first house, my parents had chose to live with my grandparents in order to save money.

_____ 2. Before we could find seats, the theater darkened and the opening credits begun to roll.

_____ 3. To be polite, I drunk the slightly sour wine that my grandfather poured from his carefully hoarded supply.

_____ 4. In 1803, the United States payed France fifteen million dollars for the Louisiana Territory.

_____ 5. After crossing over land, the power of the hurricane shrinked significantly.

_____ 6. After a day on the noisy construction site, Sam's ears rung for hours with a steady hum.

_____ 7. Because Sylvia had been stinged by wasps, she was taken to the hospital.

_____ 8. If I had went to work ten minutes earlier, I would have avoided being caught in the gigantic traffic snarl.

_____ 9. After the bicycle hit a patch of soft sand, the rider was throwed into the thorny bushes along the roadside.

_____ 10. Anne Sullivan teached Helen Keller to speak and read.

Nonstandard Forms of Three Common Irregular Verbs

People who use nonstandard forms of regular verbs also tend to use nonstandard forms of three common irregular verbs: *be, have,* and *do.* Instead of saying, for example, "My neighbors *are* nice people," a person using a nonstandard form might say, "My neighbors *be* nice people." Instead of saying, "She doesn't agree," they might say, "She *don't* agree." Instead of saying, "We have tickets," they might say, "We *has* tickets."

The following charts compare the nonstandard and the standard forms of *be, have,* and *do.*

Be

Community Dialect (Do *not* use in your writing)		Standard English (Use for clear communication)	
Present tense			
~~I be~~ (*or* is)	~~we be~~	I am	we are
you be	you be	you are	you are
~~he, she, it be~~	~~they be~~	he, she, it is	they are
Past tense			
~~I were~~	~~we was~~	I was	we were
you was	you was	you were	you were
~~he, she, it were~~	~~they was~~	he, she, it was	they were

Have

Community Dialect (Do *not* use in your writing)		Standard English (Use for clear communication)	
Present tense			
~~I has~~	~~we has~~	I have	we have
you has	you has	you have	you have
~~he, she, it have~~	~~they has~~	he, she, it has	they have
Past tense			
~~I has~~	~~we has~~	I had	we had
you has	you has	you had	you had
~~he, she, it have~~	~~they has~~	he, she, it had	they had

Do

Community Dialect (Do *not* use in your writing)		Standard English (Use for clear communication)	
Present tense			
~~I does~~	~~we does~~	I do	we do
you does	you does	you do	you do
~~he, she, it do~~	~~they does~~	he, she, it does	they do

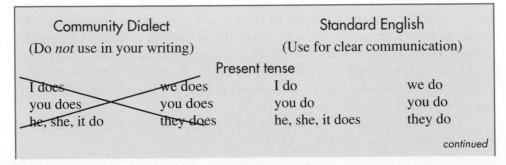

continued

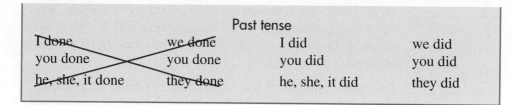

Past tense			
~~I done~~	~~we done~~	I did	we did
you done	you done	you did	you did
~~he, she, it done~~	~~they done~~	he, she, it did	they did

TIP   Many people have trouble with one negative form of *do*. They will say, for example, "He don't agree," instead of, "He doesn't agree," or they will say, "The door don't work," instead of, "The door doesn't work." Be careful to avoid the common mistake of using *don't* instead of *doesn't*.

Cross out the nonstandard verb form in each sentence. Then write the standard form of *be, have,* or *do* in the space provided.

ACTIVITY 4

_____ 1. My boss don't believe that I am sick today.

_____ 2. She be very unfair about missing work.

_____ 3. Last week, I was late because my tires was flat.

_____ 4. They has been fixed now.

_____ 5. My friend were absent for a week because of a funeral.

_____ 6. She be out of a job now.

_____ 7. I has been giving her money to help pay rent.

_____ 8. She be really grateful.

_____ 9. I does hope that she will get a job soon.

_____ 10. I has my own bills to pay.

REVIEW TEST 1

Cross out the incorrect verb form or tense in each sentence. Then write the correct form or tense in the space provided.

Academic

EXAMPLE

___*is*___ The National World War I museum ~~be~~ located in Kansas City, Missouri.

_____ 1. In 1918, at the end of World War I, concerned citizens in Kansas City begin the Liberty Memorial Association.

_____   2. R. A. Long, the founding president, said the memorial would be "a living expression for all time of the gratitude of a grateful people to those who offered and who gives their lives in defense of liberty and our country."

_____   3. Once the members of the association beginned fundraising, it took only ten days to raise $2.5 million dollars.

_____   4. H. Van Buren Magonigle winned the competition to design the memorial.

_____   5. When the site for the memorial were dedicated, Admiral David Beatty of Great Britain, General Armando Diaz of Italy, Marshal Ferdinand Foch of France, Lieutenant General Baron Jacques of Belgium, and General John J. Pershing of the United States, the supreme Allied commanders, spoke to the crowd of people.

_____   6. In 1994, the memorial was closed because its structure had deteriorated and safety had became a concern.

_____   7. In the late 1990s, concerned citizens in Kansas City once again rally to restore the memorial.

_____   8. After an additional sales tax was initiated, enough money is raised to restore the memorial and to expand the museum.

_____   9. The museum is now an 80,000 square-foot facility that housed over 75,000 items.

_____   10. The National Museum received its official status as the United States' official World War I museum in 2004 after Congress had gave it the designation.

_____   11. Visitors to the museum enter by crossing a bridge over a field of nine thousand poppies; each poppy stands for one thousand combatant deaths, representing the nine million who die during the war.

_____   12. A favorite item of many visitors be the 1917 Harley Davidson motorcycle.

_____   13. Children especially enjoyed the interactive displays that explain the war on a level they can understand.

_____   14. Many of the exhibits, like the walk through the crater, allow visitors to experience what the soldiers and civilians experience during and after the devastating war.

_____   15. A visit to Kansas City and the National World War I Museum be an educational experience.

Write short sentences that use the form requested for the following verbs.

EXAMPLE

Past of *think* _I thought I would purchase a car this week._

1. Past participle of *bring* _____

2. Past of *choose* _____

3. Present of *speak* _____

4. Past of *teach* _____

5. Present of *hide* _____

6. Past participle of *shrink* _____

7. Past of *light* _____

8. Past of *lend* _____

9. Past participle of *hurt* _____

10. Present of *spend* _____

Subject-Verb Agreement

Subject-verb agreement is the correspondence in number between the subject and the verb of a sentence; plural subjects take plural verbs, and singular subjects take singular verbs. This chapter will review the necessity for subject-verb agreement.

Incorrect:

The crinkly lines around Joan's mouth gives her a friendly look.

The subject "crinkly lines" is a plural, so the verb should be "give," not "gives."

Correct:

The crinkly lines around Joan's mouth give her a friendly look.

The verb "give" agrees with the plural "crinkly lines."

Key Terms

compound subject: two subjects separated by a joining word such as *and*.

indefinite pronoun: a word that refers to people and things that are not named or are not specific. Many indefinite pronouns (such as *one, nobody, nothing,* and *each*) take a singular verb; others, such as *both* or *few,* take plural verbs.

A verb must agree with its subject in number. A *singular subject* (one person or thing) takes a singular verb. A *plural subject* (more than one person or thing) takes a plural verb. Mistakes in subject-verb agreement are sometimes made in the following situations:

1. When words come between the subject and the verb
2. When a verb comes before the subject
3. With compound subjects
4. With indefinite pronouns

Each of these situations is explained in this chapter.

Words between Subject and Verb

Words that come between the subject and the verb do not change subject-verb agreement. In the sentence

The sharp fangs in the dog's mouth look scary.

the subject *(fangs)* is plural, and so the verb *(look)* is plural. The words that come between the subject and the verb are a prepositional phrase: *in the dog's mouth*. They do not affect subject-verb agreement. (A list of prepositions can be found on page 443.)

To help find the subject of certain sentences, you should cross out prepositional phrases.

The lumpy salt ~~in the shakers~~ needs to be changed.

An old chair ~~with broken legs~~ has sat in our basement for years.

Underline the subject and lightly cross out any words that come between the subject and the verb. Then double-underline the verb in parentheses that you believe is correct.

1. Some members of Abraham Lincoln's cabinet (was, were) his political rivals.

2. The Prado, one of the world's greatest art museums, (is, are) located in Madrid, Spain.

3. Elena's bike, with fat tires, a basket covered in flowers, and a big bell, (is, are) an Electra cruiser.

4. The Grand Canyon, with its deep valleys and colorful rock formations, (is, are) a popular place for hikers to visit.

5. In my opinion, an ocean-side resort that has rooms with balconies overlooking the ocean (make, makes) the perfect place to vacation.

Verb before Subject

A verb agrees with its subject even when the verb comes *before* the subject. Words that may precede the subject include *there, here,* and, in questions, *who, which, what,* and *where.*

Here are some examples of sentences in which the verb appears before the subject:

There are wild dogs in our neighborhood.

In the distance was a billow of black smoke.

Here <u>is</u> the <u>newspaper</u>.

Where <u>are</u> the <u>children's coats</u>?

If you are unsure about the subject, ask *who* or *what* of the verb. With the first example above, you might ask, "*What* are in our neighborhood?" The answer, *wild dogs,* is the subject.

ACTIVITY 2

Write the correct form of each verb in the space provided.

(is, are)

(was, were)

(do, does)

(was, were)

(is, are)

1.   There _____ several reasons that Americans won the Revolution.

2.   Near the top of the hill _____ two gigantic pines covered with snow.

3.   Bethani _____ her grocery shopping every Sunday afternoon.

4.   There _____ four cats eating out of our garbage can last night.

5.   Lance and Landon _____ fraternal twins.

Compound Subjects

A *compound subject* is two subjects separated by a joining word, such as *and.* Subjects joined by *and* generally take a plural verb.

A patchwork <u>quilt</u> and a sleeping <u>bag</u> <u>cover</u> my bed in the winter.

<u>Clark</u> and <u>Lois</u> <u>are</u> a contented couple.

When subjects are joined by *either . . . or, neither . . . nor, not only . . . but also,* the verb agrees with the subject closer to the verb.

Neither the <u>negotiator</u> nor the union <u>leaders</u> <u>want</u> the strike to continue.

The nearer subject, *leaders,* is plural, and so the verb is plural.

Neither the union <u>leaders</u> nor the <u>negotiator</u> <u>wants</u> the strike to continue.

In this version, the nearer subject, *negotiator,* is singular, so the verb is singular.

ACTIVITY 3

Write the correct form of the verb in the space provided.

1.   A watchtower and several cabins _____ over the valley.   (look, looks)

2.   Spidery cracks and a layer of dust _____ the ivory keys   (cover, covers)
     on the old piano.

3.   Not only France and Great Britain but also Italy _____   (belong,
     to NATO.   belongs)

4. In eighteenth-century France, makeup and high heels _____ worn by men.   (was, were)

5. Neither the director nor the writers of this film _____ ever received an Academy Award.   (has, have)

Indefinite Pronouns

The following words, known as *indefinite pronouns,* always take singular verbs:

(-*one* words)	(-*body* words)	(-*thing* words)	
one	nobody	nothing	each
anyone	anybody	anything	either
everyone	everybody	something	neither
someone	somebody	everything	

TIP   *Both* always takes a plural verb.

Write the correct form of the verb in the space provided.

ACTIVITY 4

1. Neither of the essays _____ plagiarized.   (was, were)

2. Somebody without much sensitivity always _____ my birthmark.   (mention, mentions)

3. Both countries _____ great coffee.   (produce, produces)

4. Everyone _____ the college kite-flying contest in the spring.   (enter, enters)

5. One of the students in my history class _____ Polish.   (speak, speaks)

REVIEW TEST 1

In the space provided, write the correct form of the verb shown in the margin.

(are, is)

1. Yellowstone National Park, located in Wyoming, Idaho, and Montana, _____ home to Old Faithful, the world's most famous geyser.

(was, were)

2. Each of their children _____ given a name picked at random from a page of the Bible.

(were, was)

3. Near the top of the company's organizational chart _____ the vice president for sales and the director of personnel.

(is, are)

4. Envelopes, file folders, and a telephone book _____ jammed into Lupe's kitchen drawers.

(contains, contain)

5. Neither of the main dishes at tonight's dinner _____ any meat.

(decrease, decreases)

6. A drop in the price of gasoline and other fuels _____ the chances that bus fares will go up soon.

(appear, appears)

7. Many people in my neighborhood _____ to be recycling paper, cans, glass, and plastic.

(make, makes)

8. A good grounding in mathematics _____ it easier to learn physics.

(cleans, clean)

9. In exchange for reduced rent, Karla and James _____ the dentist's office beneath their second-floor apartment.

(is, are)

10. One of the hospital's delivery rooms _____ furnished with bright carpets and curtains to resemble a room at home.

REVIEW TEST 2

Double-underline the correct verb in parentheses. In addition, underline the subject that goes with the verb.

1. According to Hasbro, the game of MONOPOLY (was created, were created) in 1935, and over 200 million copies have been sold since it first entered the market.

2. When Mr. Charles B. Darrow first presented the game to the Parker Brothers game company, they rejected it because "fifty-two errors" (was found, were found).

3. The inventor then produced the game on his own and (was able, were able) to sell five thousand handmade sets to a department store in Philadelphia.

4. Mr. Darrow contacted Parker Brothers a second time and, by that point, the game (was, were) so popular that the company decided to produce it.

5. Since 1935, the Parker Brothers company (have manufactured, has manufactured) more than 5,120,000,000 little green plastic houses.

6. During World War II, Allied forces (was able, were able) to hide escape maps, files, compasses, and real money inside MONOPOLY game boards that were smuggled into POW camps.

7. Over the years, players (have landed, has landed) on three squares—GO, B&O Railroad, and Illinois Avenue—most often.

8. The total amount of money in a standard MONOPOLY game (is, are) $15,140.

9. Since the 1970s, international MONOPOLY tournaments (occurs, occur) every four years.

10. The documentary *Under the Boardwalk: The MONOPOLY Story* (focuses, focus) on the international tournaments and the stories behind the players.

11. Multiple versions of MONOPOLY (have been, has been) created since it first started.

12. Some of the special editions of MONOPOLY (is, are) *Disney*, *SpongeBob SquarePants*, *Star Wars: Clone Wars*, and *James Bond*.

13. MONOPOLY (continues, continue) to have such a strong following that multiple Facebook pages have been dedicated to the game.

14. Currently, MONOPOLY (is, are) published in twenty-seven languages and is licensed in more than eighty-one countries.

15. Multiple online and computer versions of MONOPOLY (is, are) also available.

Additional Information about Verbs

PERSONALIZED LEARNING

This chapter will provide additional information about verbs, specifically:

- verb tense
- helping verbs
- verbals

Key Terms

gerund: a verbal; the *-ing* form of the verb used as a noun. Example: I love *dancing*.

infinitive: a verbal; *to* plus the base form of the verb. Example: I love *to dance*.

participle: a verbal; the *-ing* or *-ed* form of the verb used as an adjective. Example: I love *dancing* bears.

verbals: words formed from verbs that often express action; these include gerunds, infinitives, and participles.

Verb Tense

As mentioned in Chapter 26, the time that a verb shows is usually called *tense*. The most common tenses are the simple present, past, and future. In addition, nine other tenses enable us to express more specific ideas about time than the simple tenses do.

Tenses	Examples
Present	I *work*.
	Tony *works*.
Past	Ellen *worked* on her car.
Future	You *will work* on a new project next week.

continued

Tenses	Examples
Present perfect	He *has worked* on his term paper for a month. They *have worked* out a compromise. *Note:* The present perfect tense is used for an action that began in the past and continues in the present.
Past perfect	The nurse *had worked* two straight shifts. *Note:* The past perfect tense is used for a past action that came *before* another past action.
Future perfect	Next Monday, I *will have worked* here exactly two years.
Present progressive	I *am working* on my speech for the debate. You *are working* too hard. The tape recorder *is* not *working* properly.
Past progressive	He *was working* in the basement. The contestants *were working* on their talent routines.
Future progressive	My son *will be working* in our store this summer.
Present perfect progressive	Sarah *has been working* late this week.
Past perfect progressive	Until recently, I *had been working* nights.
Future perfect progressive	My mother *will have been working* as a nurse for forty-five years by the time she retires.

On a separate sheet of paper, write twelve sentences using the twelve verb tenses.

ACTIVITY 1

Helping Verbs

These common verbs can either stand alone or "help" other verbs.

be (am, are, is, was, were, being, been)
have (has, having, had)
do (does, did)

Here are examples of the helping verbs:

USED ALONE	USED AS HELPING VERBS
I *was* angry.	I *was growing* angry.
Sue *has* the key.	Sue *has forgotten* the key.
He *did* well in the test.	He *did fail* the previous test.

Nine helping verbs (traditionally known as *modals,* or *modal auxiliaries*) are always used in combination with other verbs. Here are the nine verbs and a sentence example of each:

can	I *can see* the rainbow.
could	I *could* not *find* a seat.
may	The game *may be postponed.*
might	Cindy *might resent* your advice.
shall	I *shall see* you tomorrow.
should	He *should get* his car serviced.
will	Tony *will want* to see you.
would	They *would* not *understand.*
must	You *must* visit us again.

Note from the examples that these verbs have only one form. They do not, for instance, add an *-s* when used with *he, she, it,* or any one person or thing.

ACTIVITY 2   On a separate sheet of paper, write nine sentences using the nine helping verbs.

Verbals

Verbals are words formed from verbs. Verbals, like verbs, often express action. They can add variety to your sentences and vigor to your writing style. The three kinds of verbals are *infinitives, participles,* and *gerunds.* Additional information about infinitives can be found in Chapter 24 and Chapter 45. Additional information about participles and gerunds can be found in Chapters 24, 33, and 45.

Infinitive

An infinitive is *to* and the base form of the verb.

I love *to dance.*

Lina hopes *to write* for a newspaper.

I asked the children *to clean* the kitchen.

Participle

A participle is a verb form used as an adjective (a descriptive word). The present participle ends in *-ing*. The past participle ends in *-ed* or has an irregular ending.

> *Peering* into the cracked mirror, the *crying* woman wiped her eyes.

> The *astounded* man stared at his *winning* lottery ticket.

> *Swinging* a sharp ax, Omar split the *rotted* beam.

Gerund

A gerund is the *-ing* form of a verb used as a noun.

> *Swimming* is the perfect exercise.

> *Eating* junk food is my diet downfall.

> Through *doodling,* people express their inner feelings.

ACTIVITY 3

PART A

On a separate sheet of paper, write three sentences using infinitives, three sentences using participles, and three sentences using gerunds.

PART B

Identify the infinitives, participles, and gerunds in the following sentences. Write *I* for infinitive, *P* for participle, and *G* for gerund above each of them.

_____   1. To teach mathematics is her overwhelming ambition.

_____   2. Leaping toward his students, the fencing coach demonstrated the art of lunging.

_____   3. Sleeping is one of my favorite activities, but I don't get to indulge in it very often.

_____   4. Receiving an award for her work with the homeless was the last thing Marge expected.

_____   5. Entering the hotdog-eating contest, Steven hoped to break last year's record, but his stomach had other ideas.

Pronoun Agreement and Reference

This chapter will provide information on pronoun agreement and reference.

Incorrect:

Miriam was annoyed when they failed her car for a faulty turn signal.

In this case, "they" should be replaced by a specific noun, such as "the inspectors," so the reader knows who the word "they" refers to.

Correct:

Miriam was annoyed when the inspectors failed her car for a faulty turn signal.

Now it is made clear that it was the inspectors who failed the car.

Key Terms

indefinite pronouns: a word that refers to people and things that are not named or are not specific. Many indefinite pronouns (such as *one, nobody, nothing,* and *each*) take a singular verb; others, such as *both* or *few,* take plural verbs.

nouns: words that name persons, places, or things.

pronoun: words that take the place of nouns. Pronouns are short-cuts that keep you from unnecessarily repeating words in writing.

pronoun agreement: correspondence in number between the pronoun and the noun it replaces. Example: *Students enrolled in the art class must prove that they can paint.*

pronoun reference: the relationship between the pronoun and the noun in the sentence to which it refers. A sentence may be confusing if a pronoun appears to refer to more than one noun or does not appear to refer to any specific noun. Example: See above "Incorrect" and "Correct" example sentences.

Nouns name persons, places, or things. *Pronouns* are words that take the place of nouns. In fact, the word *pronoun* means "for a noun." Pronouns are shortcuts that keep you from unnecessarily repeating words in writing. Here are some examples of pronouns:

Eddie left *his* camera on the bus.

(*His* is a pronoun that takes the place of *Eddie's*.)

Elena drank the coffee even though *it* was cold.

(*It* replaces *coffee*.)

As I turned the newspaper's damp pages, *they* disintegrated in my hands.

(*They* is a pronoun that takes the place of *pages*.)

This chapter presents rules that will help you avoid two common mistakes people make with pronouns. The rules are the following:

1. A pronoun must agree in number with the word or words it replaces.

2. A pronoun must refer clearly to the word it replaces.

Pronoun Agreement

A pronoun must agree in number with the word or words it replaces. If the word a pronoun refers to is singular, the pronoun must be singular; if that word is plural, the pronoun must be plural. (Note that the word a pronoun refers to is known as the *antecedent*.)

Marie showed me her antique wedding band.

Students enrolled in the art class must provide their own supplies.

In the first example, the pronoun *her* refers to the singular word *Marie;* in the second example, the pronoun *their* refers to the plural word *Students*.

Write the appropriate pronoun (*their, they, them, it*) in the blank space in each of the following sentences.

ACTIVITY 1

EXAMPLE

I opened the wet umbrella and put _____*it*_____ in the bathtub to dry.

1. Kate and Omar left for the movies earlier than usual because _____ knew the theater would be packed.

2. The clothes were still damp, but I decided to fold _____ anyway.

3. Many people immigrate to America to make a better life for _____ families.

4. Paul's grandparents renewed _____ marriage vows at a huge fiftieth wedding anniversary celebration.

5. The area around San Jose, California, produces fine wines, but _____ is also the home of many high-technology companies.

Indefinite Pronouns

The following words, known as *indefinite pronouns,* are always singular.

(-one words)	(-body words)	
one	nobody	each
anyone	anybody	either
everyone	everybody	neither
someone	somebody	

If a pronoun in a sentence refers to one of these singular words, the pronoun should be singular.

Somebody left her shoulder bag on the back of a chair.

One of the busboys just called and said he would be an hour late.

Everyone in the club must pay his dues next week.

Each circled pronoun is singular because it refers to an indefinite pronoun.

There are two important points to remember about indefinite pronouns:

1. In the last example, if everyone in the club was a woman, the pronoun would be *her*. If the club had women and men, the pronoun would be *his or her:*

    Everyone in the club must pay his or her dues next week.

    Traditionally, writers used *his* to refer to both women and men; however, most writers now use *his* or *her* to avoid an implied gender bias. To avoid using *his* or the somewhat awkward *his or her,* a sentence can often be rewritten in the plural:

    Club members must pay their dues next week.

2. In informal spoken English, *plural* pronouns are often used with the indefinite pronouns. Many people would probably not say,

    Everybody has his or her own opinion about the election.

Instead, they would be likely to say,

> Everybody has their own opinion about the election.

Here are other examples:

> Everyone in the choir must buy their robes.
>
> Everybody in the line has their ticket ready.
>
> No one in the class remembered to bring their books.

In such cases, the indefinite pronouns are clearly plural in meaning, and using *them* helps people avoid the awkward *his or her*. In time, the plural pronoun may be accepted in formal speech or writing. Until then, however, you should use the grammatically correct singular form in your writing.

Underline the correct pronoun.

ACTIVITY 2

1. Each of the three sisters was willing to donate (her, their) inheritance to charity.
2. Everybody should bring (his or her, their) own camera to class next week.
3. Neither of the teachers had set up (his or her, their) classroom for the new school year.
4. All new skiers should expect (his or her, their) muscles to ache the next day.
5. Not one of the men had finished painting (his, their) section of the fence by the time it began to rain.

Pronoun Reference

A sentence may be confusing and unclear if a pronoun appears to refer to more than one word or does not refer to any specific word. Look at this sentence:

> Miriam was annoyed when they failed her car for a faulty turn signal.

Who failed her car? There is no specific word that *they* refers to. Be clear:

> Miriam was annoyed when the inspectors failed her car for a faulty turn signal.

Here are sentences with other faulty pronoun references. Read the explanations of why they are faulty and look carefully at how they are corrected.

FAULTY	CLEAR
Peter told Alan that his wife was unhappy. (Whose wife is unhappy: Peter's or Alan's? Be clear.)	Peter told Alan, "My wife is unhappy."

FAULTY	CLEAR
Kia is really a shy person, but she keeps it hidden.	Kia is really a shy person, but she keeps her shyness hidden.
(There is no specific word that *it* refers to. It would not make sense to say, "Kia keeps shy hidden.")	
Marsha attributed her success to her husband's support, which was generous.	Generously, Marsha attributed her success to her husband's support.
(Does *which* mean that Marsha's action was generous or that her husband's support was generous?)	*Or:* Marsha attributed her success to her husband's generous support.

ACTIVITY 3

Working with a fellow classmate, rewrite each of the following sentences to make clear the vague pronoun reference. Add, change, or omit words as necessary.

EXAMPLE

> Susan's mother wondered if she was tall enough to be a model.
> *Susan's mother wondered if Susan was tall enough to be a model.*

1. Jim is a talkative person; sometimes he just can't control it.

   _____

2. At that fast-food restaurant, they give you free glasses with your soft drinks.

   _____

3. Sallie told Anna that she had just been promoted to assistant manager.

   _____

4. Dipping her spoon into the pot of simmering spaghetti sauce, Helen felt it slip out of her hand.

   _____

5. Pete visited the tutoring center because they can help him with his economics course.

   _____

Underline the correct word in parentheses. Then, in the space provided, write whether the issue is one of pronoun agreement or of pronoun reference.

EXAMPLE

p. agreement   My sister's major was English literature; (she, they) had to read a lot of novels.

_____ 1. Many students in English literature courses have to read the works of the Brontë sisters, who spent (her, their) lives writing poems, stories, and novels.

_____ 2. Charlotte Brontë was born in 1816 and is most famous for (her, their) novel, *Jane Eyre*.

_____ 3. Jane is an orphan who is treated poorly by her cruel aunt, oppressive teachers, and initially Mr. Rochester, but she eventually gets away from (them, her aunt and teachers) and finds love with Mr. Rochester.

_____ 4. Emily Brontë was born in 1818 and is most known for (her, their) novel, *Wuthering Heights*.

_____ 5. In *Wuthering Heights,* Heathcliff and Hindley lead cruel, revenge-filled lives, and (he, Heathcliff) eventually slips into insanity.

_____ 6. Anne Brontë was born in 1820 and is famous for (her, their) poetry and the novel, *The Tenant of Wildfell Hall*.

_____ 7. Anne's novel is not as famous as her sisters' novels, but (it, she) was more progressive and controversial.

_____ 8. The main character, Helen, abandons (her, their) abusive, alcoholic husband and lives as a widow.

_____ 9. By leaving her husband, Helen breaks both the social conventions and English law of the 1800s because even if (they, women) were beaten and abused, they were not allowed to leave or divorce their husbands.

_____ 10. More than 150 years later, the Brontë sisters' books are still read by thousands of literature majors and bibliophiles everywhere because of (their, the works') timeless themes.

Pronoun Types

This chapter will describe some common types of pronouns:

- subject pronouns
- object pronouns
- possessive pronouns
- demonstrative pronouns

Key Terms

demonstrative pronouns: pronouns that point to or single out a person or thing. The four demonstrative pronouns are *this, that, these,* and *those.*

object pronouns: pronouns that function as the objects of verbs or prepositions. Example: *Tony helped me.*

possessive pronouns: pronouns that show ownership or possession. Example: *The keys are mine.*

subject pronouns: pronouns that function as the subjects of verbs. Example: *He is wearing an artificial arm.*

Subject and Object Pronouns

Most pronouns change their form depending on what place they occupy in a sentence. In the box that follows is a list of subject and object pronouns.

Subject Pronouns	Object Pronouns
I	me
you	you (no change)
he	him
she	her
it	it (no change)
we	us
they	them

Subject Pronouns

Subject pronouns are subjects of verbs.

> *He* served as a soldier during the war in Iraq. (*He* is the subject of the verb *served*.)
>
> *They* are moving into our old apartment. (*They* is the subject of the verb *are moving*.)
>
> *We* students should have a say in the decision. (*We* is the subject of the verb *should have*.)

Following are several rules for using subject pronouns—and several kinds of mistakes people sometimes make with subject pronouns.

Rule 1

Use a subject pronoun when you have a compound subject (more than one subject).

INCORRECT	CORRECT
My brother and *me* are Bruce Springsteen fanatics.	My brother and *I* are Bruce Springsteen fanatics.
Him and *me* know the lyrics to all of Bruce's songs.	*He* and *I* know the lyrics to all of Bruce's songs.

> **TIP** *Rule 1*
>
> If you are not sure what pronoun to use, try each pronoun by itself in the sentence. The correct pronoun will be the one that sounds right. For example, "Him knows the lyrics to all of Bruce's songs" does not sound right; "He knows the lyrics to all of Bruce's songs" does.

Rule 2

Use a subject pronoun after forms of the verb *be*. Forms of *be* include *am, are, is, was, were, has been, have been,* and others.

> It was *I* who left the light on.
>
> It may be *they* in that car.
>
> It is *he*.

The sentences above may sound strange and stilted to you because they are seldom used in conversation. When we speak with one another, forms such as "It was me,"

"It may be them," and "It is him" are widely accepted. In formal writing, however, the grammatically correct forms are still preferred.

 TIP *Rule 2*

You can avoid having to use a subject pronoun after *be* by simply rewording a sentence. Here is how the preceding examples could be reworded:

I was the one who left the light on.

They may be in that car.

He is here.

Rule 3

Use subject pronouns after *than* or *as*. The subject pronoun is used because a verb is understood after the pronoun.

You play better than I (play). (The verb *play* is understood after *I*.)

Jenny is as bored as I (am). (The verb *am* is understood after *I*.)

We don't need the money as much as they (do). (The verb *do* is understood after *they*.)

TIP *Rule 3*

Avoid mistakes by mentally adding the "missing" verb at the end of the sentence.

Object Pronouns

Object pronouns (me, him, her, us, them) are the objects of verbs or prepositions. (*Prepositions* are connecting words like *for, at, about, to, before, by, with,* and *of.* See also page 443.)

Tony helped me. (*Me* is the object of the verb *helped.*)

We took *them* to the college. (*Them* is the object of the verb *took.*)

Leave the children with *us.* (*Us* is the object of the preposition *with.*)

I got in line behind *him.* (*Him* is the object of the preposition *behind.*)

People are sometimes uncertain about what pronoun to use when two objects follow a verb.

INCORRECT	CORRECT
I gave a gift to Ray and *she*.	I gave a gift to Ray and *her*.
She came to the movie with Bobbie and *I*.	She came to the movie with Bobbie and *me*.

TIP   If you are not sure what pronoun to use, try each pronoun by itself in the sentence. The correct pronoun will be the one that sounds right. For example, "I gave a gift to she" does not sound right; "I gave a gift to her" does.

Underline the correct subject or object pronoun in each of the following sentences. Then show whether your answer is a subject or object pronoun by circling the S or O in the margin.

ACTIVITY 1

S   O   1. The clothes that Jane gave my sister and (I, me) were too small.

S   O   2. Andrew and (she, her) visited the Tower of London during their trip to England.

S   O   3. The senator praised her opponent by saying that no one had ever run a cleaner campaign than (he, him).

S   O   4. Your piano performance proved that you practiced more than (they, them).

S   O   5. (We, Us) students spent over three weeks painting the sets for the school play.

S   O   6. Jonah and (him, he) did the editing on the class film.

S   O   7. The teachers told (they, them) not to run in the hallways.

S   O   8. Reading about the ancient Greeks became an obsession for Molly and (him, he).

S   O   9. (She, Her) and Lizzie love to bake cookies.

S   O   10. The professor told Quinn and (I, me) that our project was well done.

Possessive Pronouns

Here is a list of possessive pronouns:

my, mine	our, ours
your, yours	your, yours
his	their, theirs
her, hers	
its	

Possessive pronouns show ownership or possession.

Adam revved up *his* motorcycle and blasted off.

The keys are *mine*.

TIP A possessive pronoun *never* uses an apostrophe. (See also page 543.)

INCORRECT

That coat is *hers'*.

The card table is *theirs'*.

CORRECT

That coat is *hers*.

The card table is *theirs*.

ACTIVITY 2 Cross out the incorrect pronoun form in each of the sentences below. Write the correct form in the space at the left.

EXAMPLE

      Those gloves are ~~hers'~~.

_____ 1. I discovered that my car had somehow lost its' rear license plate.

_____ 2. Are those seats theirs'?

_____ 3. The mayor said that the task of cutting the budget was not hers' alone.

_____ 4. The prize-winning entry in the science fair was our's.

_____ 5. These books are yours' if you want them.

Demonstrative Pronouns

Demonstrative pronouns point to or single out a person or thing. There are four demonstrative pronouns:

this	these
that	those

Generally speaking, *this* and *these* refer to things close at hand; *that* and *those* refer to things farther away. The four demonstrative pronouns are also commonly used as demonstrative adjectives.

Is anyone using *this* spoon?

I am going to throw away *these* magazines.

I just bought *that* black pickup truck at the curb.

Pick up *those* toys in the corner.

> **TIP** Do not use *them, this here, that there, these here,* or *those there* to point to or single out. Use only *this, that, these,* or *those.*

Cross out the incorrect form of the demonstrative pronoun, and write the correct form in the space provided.

ACTIVITY 3

EXAMPLE

Those   ~~Them~~ tires look worn.

_____ 1. This here map is out of date.

_____ 2. Leave them keys out on the coffee table.

_____ 3. Them two movies are about life in early New England.

_____ 4. Jack entered that there dog in an obedience contest.

_____ 5. Where are them concert tickets I left here?

Read the paragraph and underline the correct word in the parentheses.

Ben & Jerry's ice cream is a multi-million dollar business that has quite an interesting history. Ben and Jerry opened (their, their's) first shop in 1978 in Burlington, Vermont. (That, That there) shop was housed in an old gas station that (they, them) renovated using scraps of aluminum to fix the roof and second-hand items to furnish the store. By 1981, Ben & Jerry's had grown very popular, and the first franchise opened (its', its) doors in Shelburne, Vermont. In 1983, Ben & Jerry's ice cream was used "to build the world's largest ice cream sundae." (That, These) same year, pints of the ice cream began to be sold in Boston. In 1984, Ben & Jerry's went head-to-head against Haagen-Dazs in a campaign known as "What's the Doughboy Afraid Of?" The following year, Ben & Jerry's began building (its', its) first ice cream manufacturing plant. In 1987, "Cherry Garcia" was introduced. Jerry Garcia was the guitarist for the Grateful Dead; the ice cream was named after (he, him). Also in 1987, the waste from the manufacturing plant began to be used as pig feed and the pigs went wild for almost every flavor. However, (they, them) didn't like "Mint with Oreo® Cookie" because pigs don't like mint. In 1988, Ben & Jerry's gave 7.5 percent of (it's, its) pre-tax income to non-profit organizations, winning (this, this here) company an award for giving. The company also started a non-profit group that is now known as the Business for Social Responsibility. Ben and Jerry were socially conscious when (they, them) chose to renovate the old building. (They, them) continued to be socially conscious as (their, their') company grew larger. In 2005, to protest drilling for oil in the Arctic National Wildlife Refuge, Ben & Jerry's created a nine-hundred-pound Baked Alaska dessert from "Fossil Fuel" ice cream. (That there, That) dessert was served up on the lawn of the U.S. Capital. For over thirty years, Ben & Jerry's has been giving back to (its', its) communities and customers. One of the most popular celebrations is Free Cone Day, an annual event since 1979, because everyone gets a free scoop of ice cream.

Adjectives and Adverbs

This chapter will describe the principal characteristics of adjectives and adverbs.

Key Terms

adjectives: words that describe nouns or pronouns. Example: Yoko is a *wise* woman.

adverbs: words that describe verbs, adjectives, or other adverbs. Example: I walked *quickly* to the store.

Adjectives

What Are Adjectives?

Adjectives describe nouns (names of persons, places, or things) or pronouns.

> Yoko is a *wise* woman. (The adjective *wise* describes the noun *woman*.)
>
> She is also *funny*. (The adjective *funny* describes the pronoun *she*.)
>
> I'll carry the *heavy* bag of groceries. (The adjective *heavy* describes the noun *bag*.)
>
> It is *torn*. (The adjective *torn* describes the pronoun *it*.)

Adjectives usually come before the word they describe (as in *wise* woman and *heavy* bag). But they also come after forms of the verb *be* (*is, are, was, were,* and so on). They also follow verbs such as *look, appear, seem, become, sound, taste,* and *smell*.

> That road is *slippery*. (The adjective *slippery* describes the road.)
>
> The dogs are *noisy*. (The adjective *noisy* describes the dogs.)
>
> Those customers were *impatient*. (The adjective *impatient* describes the customers.)
>
> Your room looks *neat*. (The adjective *neat* describes the room.)

Using Adjectives to Compare

Adjectives are often used to compare things or people. Use the comparative form of the adjective if two people or things are being compared. Use the superlative form of the adjective if three or more people or things are being compared.

For all one-syllable adjectives and some two-syllable adjectives, add *-er* when comparing two things and *-est* when comparing three or more things.

> Phil's beard is *longer* than mine, but Lee's is the *longest*.

> Meg may be the *quieter* of the two sisters; but that's not saying much, since they're the *loudest* girls in school.

For some two-syllable adjectives and all longer adjectives, use *more* when comparing two things and *most* when comparing three or more things.

> Liza Minnelli is *more famous* than her sister; but their mother, Judy Garland, is still the *most famous* member of the family.

> The red letters on the sign are *more noticeable* than the black ones, but the Day-Glo letters are the *most noticeable*.

You can usually tell when to use *more* and *most* by the sound of a word. For example, you can probably tell by its sound that "carefuller" would be too awkward to say and that *more careful* is thus correct. But there are many words for which both *-er* or *-est* and *more* or *most* are equally correct. For instance, either "a more fair rule" or "a fairer rule" is correct.

To form negative comparisons, use *less* and *least*.

> During my first dance class, I felt *less graceful* than an injured elephant.

> When the teacher came to our house to complain to my parents, I offered her the *least* comfortable chair in the room.

Points to Remember about Comparing

Point 1

Use only one form of comparison at a time. That is, do not use both an *-er* ending and *more* or both an *-est* ending and *most*:

INCORRECT	CORRECT
My mother's suitcase is always *more heavier* than my father's.	My mother's suitcase is always *heavier* than my father's.
Psycho is still the *most frighteningest* movie I've ever seen.	*Psycho* is still the *most frightening* movie I've ever seen.

Point 2

Learn the irregular forms of the words shown below.

	COMPARATIVE (For Comparing Two Things)	SUPERLATIVE (For Comparing Three or More Things)
bad	worse	worst
good, well	better	best
little (in amount)	less	least
much, many	more	most

Do not use both *more* and an irregular comparative or *most* and an irregular superlative.

INCORRECT	CORRECT
It is *more better* to give than to receive.	It is *better* to give than to receive.
Last night I got the *most worst* snack attack I ever had.	Last night I got the *worst* snack attack I have ever had.

Add to each sentence the correct form of the word in the margin.

ACTIVITY 1

EXAMPLES

The solutions that Mary offered were ___*better*___ than mine.   good

The Rockies are the world's ___*most beautiful*___ mountains.   beautiful

1. Javon makes the _____ blueberry crumble I have ever tasted.   good

2. Shannon and her sister, Elle, are twins; Shannon is the _____ one.   old

3. Megan and Nolan are the _____ spellers in the class.   bad

4. Lily painted the _____ scene in the class.   unusual

5. The three-legged cat was _____ than the dog.   ferocious

Adverbs

What Are Adverbs?

Adverbs describe verbs, adjectives, or other adverbs. They usually end in *-ly*.

The father *gently* hugged the sick child. (The adverb *gently* describes the verb *hugged*.)

Newborns are *totally* innocent. (The adverb *totally* describes the adjective *innocent*.)

The lecturer spoke so *terribly* fast that I had trouble taking notes. (The adverb *terribly* describes the adverb *fast*.)

A Common Mistake with Adverbs and Adjectives

People often mistakenly use an adjective instead of an adverb after a verb.

INCORRECT	CORRECT
Sam needs a haircut *bad*.	Sam needs a haircut *badly*.
She gets along *easy* with others.	She gets along *easily* with others.
You might have lost the race if you hadn't run so *quick* at the beginning.	You might have lost the race if you hadn't run so *quickly* at the beginning.

ACTIVITY 2   Underline the adjective or adverb needed.

HINT   Remember that adjectives describe nouns, and adverbs describe verbs and other adverbs.

1. As Mac danced, his earring bounced (rapid, rapidly).

2. We back up all of our files in case there is a (sudden, suddenly) power surge that could damage our computers.

3. I hiccuped (continuous, continuously) for fifteen minutes.

4. The detective opened the door (careful, carefully).

5. The Salvation Army is (heavy, heavily) dependent upon donations from the public.

Well and *Good*

Two words that are often confused are *well* and *good*. *Good* is an adjective; it describes nouns. *Well* is usually an adverb; it describes verbs. But *well* (rather than *good*) is used as an adjective when referring to health.

Team up with a fellow classmate and write *well* or *good* in each of the sentences that follow.

1. Miami fared _____ during the last hurricane because the people took adequate precautions.

2. The governor commended the literacy volunteers for the _____ work they had accomplished.

3. In high school, Jessica always did _____ in history.

4. After Jameson won the lottery, he discovered who his _____ friends really were.

5. Grant and Alyssa organized the fundraiser so _____ that everything went perfectly.

Underline the correct word in parentheses.

1. We could not have asked for a (more good, better) teacher in math.

2. The Beatles seemed to burst onto the scene very (quick, quickly), but they had been singing for years before they became so popular.

3. John Roebling's prediction that he could build a bridge across New York's East River turned out (good, well); today that structure is known as the Brooklyn Bridge.

4. The cleaner was very (abrasive, abrasively) and scratched my countertops.

5. As soon as I set down the food, the puppy (hungry, hungrily) wolfed it down.

6. The (stranger, strangest) of the two pictures featured an owl with three eyes.

7. The young boy was the (lazier, laziest) one in the whole family and refused to move off the couch.

8. William took his classes very (serious, seriously) and studied several hours a day.

9. Emma told the (more clever, most clever) jokes I've ever heard.

10. As the little boy (gentle, gently) snuggled the tiny kitten, the kitten purred.

REVIEW TEST 2

There are ten adjective and adverb errors in the paragraph below. In the spaces between the lines, correct the mistakes.

Academic

The Disney Corporation has been producing films since 1937. One of the most earliest films was *Snow White and the Seven Dwarfs*. *Fantasia* followed soon after and is still considered to be a real iconic, groundbreaking film. Two other films, *Saludos Amigos* and *The Three Caballeros*, targeted Latin American audiences; they are not known as good. In 1950, *Cinderella* was released and is believed to be Walt Disney's most favoritest film. *Alice in Wonderland* was released short after *Cinderella* and introduced the beloved novel, *Alice's Adventures in Wonderland*, to a new audience. In 1960, another deep loved novel of younger audiences, *Swiss Family Robinson*, was brought to the screen; however, it was not animated. In 1995, Pixar Studios released *Toy Story* as part of a three-picture deal with Disney. Pixar's computer animation and innovatively technicians forever changed the way that animated films are made. Films such as *Ratatouille* and *Up* mesmerized audiences by their high detailed animations that were extreme realistic and life-like. As technology advances, audiences can look forward to even more creative designed 2-D and 3-D films produced by Disney and Pixar.

Misplaced Modifiers

This chapter will describe misplaced modifiers, which are words that, because of awkward placement, do not describe what the author intended them to describe.

Incorrect:

George couldn't drive to work in his sports car with a broken leg.

The sentence makes it sound as if the car has the broken leg, not George.

Correct:

With his broken leg, George couldn't drive to work in his sports car.

The phrase "with a broken leg" has been moved so that it is closer to "George"; now it is clearer whose leg is broken.

Misplaced modifiers are words that, because of awkward placement, do not describe what the writer intended them to describe. A misplaced modifier can make a sentence confusing or unintentionally funny. To avoid this, place words as close as possible to what they describe.

MISPLACED WORDS	CORRECTLY PLACED WORDS
George couldn't drive to work in his small sports car *with a broken leg*. (The sports car had a broken leg?)	With a broken leg, George couldn't drive to work in his small sports car. (The words describing George are now placed next to *George*.)
The toaster was sold to us by a charming salesman *with a money-back guarantee*. (The salesman had a money-back guarantee?)	The toaster with a money-back guarantee was sold to us by a charming salesman. (The words describing the toaster are now placed next to it.)

MISPLACED WORDS	CORRECTLY PLACED WORDS
He *nearly* brushed his teeth for twenty minutes every night. (He came close to brushing his teeth but in fact did not brush them at all?)	He brushed his teeth for nearly twenty minutes every night. (The meaning—that he brushed his teeth for a long time—is now clear.)

ACTIVITY 1

Underline the misplaced word or words in each sentence. Then rewrite the sentence, placing related words together and thereby making the meaning clear.

EXAMPLES

Frozen shrimp lay in the steel pans <u>that were thawing rapidly</u>.

Frozen shrimp that were thawing rapidly lay in the steel pans.

The speaker discussed the problem of crowded prisons <u>at the college</u>.

At the college, the speaker discussed the problem of crowded prisons.

1. The patient talked about his childhood on the psychiatrist's couch.

   _____

2. The crowd watched the tennis players with swiveling heads.

   _____

3. Vonnie put four hamburger patties on the counter, which she was cooking for dinner.

   _____

4. Steve carefully hung the new suit that he would wear to his first job interview in the bedroom closet.

   _____

5. The novel was about a pioneer family that Annie had borrowed from her cousin.

   _____

6. The latest Denzel Washington movie has almost opened in 2,200 theaters across the country.

   _____

7. To be cooked properly, the chef advised us to place the casserole in a pre-heated oven.

_____

8. The tenants left town in a dilapidated old car owing two months' rent.

_____

9. The plan was to construct a church on an acre of land made of brick and stone.

_____

10. I discovered an unusual plant in the greenhouse that oozed a milky juice.

_____

REVIEW TEST 1

Write MM for *misplaced modifier* or C for *correct* in the space provided for each sentence.

_____ 1. I nearly napped for twenty minutes during the biology lecture.

_____ 2. I napped for nearly twenty minutes during the biology lecture.

_____ 3. The spacecraft traveled nearly 142 million miles to reach Mars.

_____ 4. The spacecraft nearly traveled 142 million miles to reach Mars.

_____ 5. My grandfather prepared breakfast for his family wearing his bathrobe.

_____ 6. Wearing his bathrobe, my grandfather prepared breakfast for his family.

_____ 7. We couldn't read the advertisement on the water tower written in tiny letters.

_____ 8. We couldn't read the advertisement written in tiny letters on the water tower.

_____ 9. I ordered a new telephone from the mail-order catalog shaped like a cartoon character.

_____ 10. I ordered from the mail-order catalog a new telephone shaped like a cartoon character.

REVIEW TEST 2

Make the changes needed to correct the misplaced modifier in each sentence.

1. Henry Wadsworth Longfellow was born a poet and professor in 1907 in Portland, Maine.

   _____

   _____

2. One of Longfellow's most famous poems during the Revolutionary War is "Paul Revere's Ride," depicting an historically important night.

   _____

   _____

3. Longfellow wrote that rainbows are flowers that have died and gone to heaven in a poem.

   _____

   _____

4. Longfellow's wife, Frannie, died when her dress caught fire from terrible burns.

   _____

   _____

5. Eighteen years later, in the sonnet, "The Cross of Snow," Longfellow never fully recovered and commemorated his wife's death.

   _____

   _____

Dangling Modifiers

This chapter will describe dangling modifiers—descriptive words that open a sentence but do not describe what the author intended them to describe.

> **Incorrect:**
>
> *While reading the newspaper, my dog sat with me on the steps.*
>
> The sentence misleadingly states that the dog was reading the newspaper.
>
> **Correct:**
>
> *While I was reading the newspaper, my dog sat with me on the steps.*
>
> The sentence makes it clear that the subject "I" was reading the newspaper.

A modifier that opens a sentence must be followed immediately by the word it is meant to describe. Otherwise, the modifier is said to be dangling, and the sentence takes on an unintended meaning. For example, in the sentence

> While reading the newspaper, my dog sat with me on the front steps.

the unintended meaning is that the *dog* was reading the newspaper. The writer should have said,

> While reading the newspaper, *I* sat with my dog on the front steps.

The dangling modifier could also be corrected by placing the subject within the opening word group:

> While *I* was reading the newspaper, my dog sat with me on the front steps.

DANGLING	CORRECT
Shaving in front of the steamy mirror, the razor nicked Ed's chin. (*Who* was shaving? The subject *Ed* must be added.)	Shaving in front of the steamy mirror, *Ed* nicked his chin with the razor. *Or* When *Ed* was shaving in front of the steamy mirror, he nicked his chin with a razor.
While turning over the bacon, hot grease splashed my arm. (Who was turning over the bacon? *I* was, not the *hot grease*. The subject *I* must be added.)	While *I* was turning over the bacon, hot grease splashed my arm. *Or* While turning over the bacon, *I* was splashed with hot grease.
To impress the interviewer, punctuality is essential. (Who is to impress the interviewer? You are, not *punctuality*.)	To impress the interviewer, *you* must be punctual. *Or* For *you* to impress the interviewer, punctuality is essential.

The examples above show two ways to correct a dangling modifier.

1. Place the subject *within* the opening word group:

   When *Ed* was shaving in front of the steamy mirror, he nicked his chin.

> **TIP** In some cases, a subordinating word such as *when* must be added, and the verb may have to be changed.

2. Place the subject right *after* the opening word group:

   Shaving in front of the steamy mirror, *Ed* nicked his chin.

ACTIVITY 1

Look at the opening words in each sentence and ask *who* or *what*. The subject that answers the question should be nearby in the sentence. If it is not, provide the logical subject by using either method of correction described above.

EXAMPLE

While pitching his tent, a snake bit Tony on the ankle.

While Tony was pitching his tent, a snake bit him on the ankle.

OR

While pitching his tent, Tony was bitten on the ankle by a snake.

1. Applying a salve to the burn on my leg, the pain soon subsided.

_____

_____

2. Marching across the field, a distant river could be seen by the soldiers.

_____

_____

3. Practicing relaxation techniques daily, stress can be relieved.

_____

_____

4. Avoiding foods high in fat and calories, Paul's health drastically improved.

_____

_____

5. Lit by several floodlights, the audience was able to see the stage clearly.

_____

_____

6. Running through the rain, the puddles soaked my pants.

_____

_____

7. Crammed tightly in the elevator, the doors wouldn't close.

_____

_____

8. Hoping to make his employees more comfortable, a dozen new chairs were purchased by the new boss.

_____

_____

9. Fixing the potholes, the roadway was smooth.

_____

_____

10. Screaming loudly, the roller coaster scared the young children.

_____

_____

REVIEW TEST 1

Write DM for *dangling modifier* or C for *correct* in the space provided for each sentence.

_____ 1. Having considered several models, the Ford Mustang was finally agreed upon.

_____ 2. Having considered several models, we finally agreed upon the Ford Mustang.

_____ 3. After eating shellfish for the first time, Jim had a frightening allergic reaction.

_____ 4. After eating shellfish for the first time, Jim's allergic reaction was frightening.

_____ 5. At sixteen, my parents bought me a car.

_____ 6. When I was sixteen, my parents bought me a car.

_____ 7. Waddling slowly along the path, the overweight cat made the girls laugh.

_____ 8. Waddling slowly along the path, the young girls laughed at the overweight cat.

_____ 9. Large and impressive, I was amazed by the size of the tree.

_____ 10. Large and impressive, the tree amazed me by its size.

REVIEW TEST 2

Make the changes needed to correct the dangling modifier in each sentence.

1. Hoping to achieve higher test scores, SAT and other standardized tests are sometimes taken by one top-performing student for other students.

_____

_____

2. Embarrassed by the widespread cheating, tighter rules have been introduced by the testing companies.

_____

_____

3. Required to upload verified photo ID pictures when they register and take the exam, the testing companies have set stricter identification standards for students.

_____

_____

4. Stored in databases, high school and college admissions personnel can access the photos.

_____

_____

5. Cheating on the SAT and ACT, the new rules have made it harder.

_____

_____

REVIEW TEST 3

Complete the following so that a logical subject follows the opening words.

EXAMPLE

Looking through the door's peephole, *I couldn't see who rang the doorbell.*

_____

1. Noticing the light turn yellow, _____

2. Being fragile, _____

3. While washing the car, _____

4. Graduating at the top of her class, _____

5. Driving past the cemetery, _____

SECTION PREVIEW

Chapter 34
Manuscript Form

Chapter 35
Capital Letters

Chapter 36
Numbers and Abbreviations

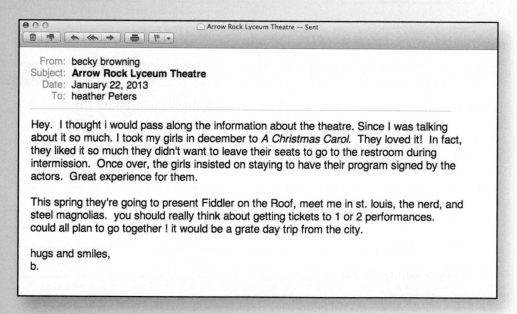

People often forget to apply sentence skills to their writing when composing e-mails. Identify the sentence-skills mistakes in the e-mail pictured here. How could you correct them? Do you think such mistakes should be excusable in e-mails?

Manuscript Form

This chapter will describe manuscript from: the required format for any paper you hand in.

Key Terms

format: the formal characteristics of a manuscript, comprising such things as paper size, margins, spacing, and font.

manuscript: literally, a paper written by hand; in this text, any paper handed in for a grade.

When you hand in a paper for any course, it will probably be judged first by its format. It is important, then, to make the paper look attractive, neat, and easy to read. Here is a checklist you should use when preparing a paper for an instructor:

_____ • Is the paper full-size, 8½ by 11 inches?

_____ • Are there wide margins (1 to 1½ inches) all around the paper? In particular, have you been careful not to crowd the right-hand or bottom margin?

_____ • If the paper is handwritten, have you

   used a blue or black pen?

   been careful not to overlap letters or to make decorative loops on letters?

   made all your letters distinct, with special attention to *a, e, i, o,* and *u*—five letters that people sometimes write illegibly?

   kept all your capital letters clearly distinct from small letters?

_____ • Have you centered the title of your paper on the first line of page 1? Have you been careful *not* to put quotation marks around the title and *not* to underline it? Have you capitalized all the words in the title except short connecting words like *of, for, the, and, in,* and *to*?

_____ • Have you skipped a line between the title and the first line of your paper?

_____ • Have you indented the first line of each paragraph about five spaces (half an inch) from the left-hand margin?

_____ • Have you made commas, periods, and other punctuation marks firm and clear? If you are typing, have you left a double space after a period?

_____ • If you have broken any words at the end of a line, have you been careful to break only between syllables?

_____ • Have you put your name, the date, and other information at the end of the paper (or wherever your instructor has specified)?

Also ask yourself these important questions about the title and the first sentence of your paper:

_____ • Is your title made up of several words that tell what the paper is about? (The title should be just several words, not a complete sentence.)

_____ • Does the first sentence of your paper stand independent of the title? (The reader should *not* have to use the words in the title to make sense of the opening sentence.)

ACTIVITY 1

Use the checklist to locate the seven mistakes in format in the following lines from a student paper. Explain the mistakes in the spaces provided. One mistake is described for you as an example.

	"Being alone"	
	This is something that I simply cannot tolerate, and I will predi-	
	ctably go to great lengths to prevent it. For example, if I know that everyone is	

1. *Hyphenate only between syllables (predict-ably, not predi-ctably).* _____

2. _____

3. _____

4. _____

5. _____

6. _____

7. _____

_____

Capital Letters

This chapter will describe

- the main uses of capital letters

- secondary uses of capital letters

- unnecessary use of capital letters

Incorrect:

The Bank is located on the corner.

"The" is capitalized correctly because it appears at the beginning of the sentence, but "bank" is not the building's official, specific name.

Correct:

The bank is located on the corner.

"The" is capitalized to start the sentence, but "bank" is left lowercase.

Main Uses of Capital Letters

Capital letters are used with

1. First word in a sentence or direct quotation

2. Names of persons and the word *I*

3. Names of particular places

4. Names of days of the week, months, and holidays

5. Names of commercial products

6. Titles of books, magazines, newspapers, articles, stories, poems, films, television shows, songs, papers that you write, and the like

7. Names of companies, associations, unions, clubs, religious and political groups, and other organizations

Each use is illustrated in this chapter.

First Word in a Sentence or Direct Quotation

The corner grocery was robbed last night.

The alien said, "Take me to your leader."

"If you need help," said Teri, "call me. I'll be over in no time."

In the third example above, *If* and *I'll* are capitalized because they start new sentences. But *call* is not capitalized, because it is part of the first sentence.

Names and Titles

Names of Persons and the Word I

Last night, I saw *Elf,* a hilarious movie starring Will Ferrell and James Caan.

Names of Particular Places and Institutions

Although Bill dropped out of Port Charles High School, he eventually earned his degree and got a job with Atlas Realty Company.

But Use small letters if the specific name is not given.

Although Bill dropped out of high school, he eventually earned his degree and got a job with a real estate company.

Names of Days of the Week, Months, and Holidays

On the last Friday afternoon in May, the day before Memorial Day, my boss is having a barbecue for all the employees.

But Use small letters for the seasons—summer, fall, winter, spring.

Most people feel more energetic in the spring and fall.

Names of Commercial Products

Keith installed a new Sony stereo and a Motorola cell phone into his old Ford Ranger pickup.

But Use small letters for the *type* of product (stereo, cell phone, pickup, and so on).

Titles of Books, Magazines, Newspapers, Articles, Stories, Poems, Films, Television Shows, Songs, Papers That You Write, and the Like

We read the book *Hiroshima*, by John Hersey, for our history class.

In the doctor's waiting room, I watched *All My Children*, read an article in *Reader's Digest*, and leafed through the *Miami Herald*.

Names of Companies, Associations, Unions, Clubs, Religious and Political Groups, and Other Organizations

Joe Naples is a Roman Catholic, but his wife is a Methodist.

The Hilldale Square Dancers' Club has won many competitions.

Brian, a member of Bricklayers Local 431 and the Knights of Columbus, works for Ace Construction.

ACTIVITY 1

Underline the words that need capitals in the following sentences. Then write the capitalized form of each word in the space provided. The number of spaces tells you how many corrections to make in each case.

EXAMPLE

Sammy's <u>pizza</u> and <u>pub</u>, which is located at 19 <u>federal</u> <u>street</u>, has phenomenal pizzas. ___*Pizza*___ ___*Pub*___ ___*Federal*___ ___*Street*___

1. We visited several theme parks in orlando, florida, including disney world.

   _____ _____ _____ _____

2. Stan was a big eater. For lunch he had a mcdonald's quarter-pounder, a big mac, and a large coke.

   _____ _____ _____ _____ _____

3. Melissa's favorite download from *born and raised* is "shadow days."

   _____ _____ _____ _____

4. Eddie and brianna had a baby this july; his name is connor matteo campbell.

   _____ _____ _____ _____ _____

5. Kaia is a huge fan of the black eyed peas and has several t-shirts, concert stubs, and a pair of fergie's shoes.

_____ _____ _____ _____ _____

6. My children, rory, maggie, and noah, love to read *highlights* magazine.

_____ _____ _____ _____

7. Martha's vineyard—especially the town of west chop—is a great place to vacation.

_____ _____ _____

8. Since my mother is the leader of our daisy troop, she holds the meetings at cedar creek elementary, which is where she works.

_____ _____ _____ _____ _____

9. Thomas went to visit dr. landown to find out was what causing his wrist pain.

_____ _____

10. The first day of classes was on the tuesday following labor day that year, and I had to report to moore hall to register.

_____ _____ _____ _____ _____

Other Uses of Capital Letters

Capital letters are used with

1. Names that show family relationships
2. Titles of persons when used with their names
3. Specific school courses
4. Languages
5. Geographic locations
6. Historical periods and events
7. Races, nations, and nationalities
8. Opening and closing of a letter

Each use is illustrated on the following pages.

Names and Titles

Names That Show Family Relationships

All his life, Father has been addicted to gadgets.

I browsed through Grandmother's collection of old photographs.

Aunt Florence and Uncle Bill bought a mobile home.

But Do not capitalize words like *mother, father, grandmother, grandfather, uncle, aunt,* and so on when they are preceded by a possessive word (such as *my, your, his, her, our, their*).

All his life, my father has been addicted to gadgets.

I browsed through my grandmother's collection of old photographs.

My aunt and uncle bought a mobile home.

Titles of Persons When Used with Their Names

I contributed to Senator McGrath's campaign fund.

Is Dr. Gomez on vacation?

Professor Adams announced that there would be no tests in the course.

But Use lowercase letters when titles appear by themselves, without specific names.

I contributed to my senator's campaign fund.

Is the doctor on vacation?

The professor announced that there would be no tests in the course.

Specific School Courses

The college offers evening sections of Introductory Psychology I, Abnormal Psychology, Psychology and Statistics, and Educational Psychology.

But Use lowercase letters for general subject areas.

The college offers evening sections of many psychology courses.

Miscellaneous Categories

Languages

My grandfather's Polish accent makes his English difficult to understand.

Geographic Locations

He grew up in the Midwest but moved to the South to look for a better job.

But Use lowercase letters in directions.

Head west for five blocks and then turn south on State Street.

Historical Periods and Events

During the Middle Ages, the Black Death killed over one-quarter of Europe's population.

Races, Nations, and Nationalities

The questionnaire asked whether the head of our household was Caucasian, African American, Asian, Latino, or Native American.

Tanya has lived on army bases in Germany, Italy, and Spain.

Denise's beautiful features reflect her Chinese and Mexican parentage.

Opening and Closing of a Letter

Dear Sir: Sincerely yours,

Dear Ms. Henderson: Truly yours,

Capitalize only the first word in a closing.

Underline the words that need capitals in the following sentences. Then write the capitalized forms of each words in the spaces provided. The number of spaces tells you how many corrections to make in each case.

ACTIVITY 2

1. The boston tea party was an act of defiance against the british government's policy of taxation in the american colonies.

   _____ _____ _____ _____ _____

2. On their job site in korea, the french, swiss, and chinese coworkers used English to communicate.

   _____ _____ _____ _____

3. When uncle harvey got the bill from his doctor, he called the American Medical Association to complain.

   _____ _____

4. Dr. Freeling of the business department is offering a new course called introduction to web design.

   _____ _____ _____

5. A new restaurant featuring vietnamese cuisine has just opened on the south side of the city.

   _____

Unnecessary Use of Capitals

ACTIVITY 3

Many errors occur when capitalization is used when it is not needed. Working with a fellow classmate, underline the incorrectly capitalized words in the following sentences, and write the correct forms in the spaces provided. The number of spaces tells you how many corrections to make in each sentence.

1. Minnesota is bordered by the Canadian Provinces of Manitoba and Ontario to the North, by Wisconsin to the East, and by North and South Dakota to the West.

   _____   _____   _____   _____

2. North America is the World's third largest Continent. It includes Canada, the United States, Mexico, the Countries of Central America, and the island Nations of the Caribbean.

   _____   _____   _____   _____

3. Einstein's theory of relativity, which he developed when he was only twenty-six, led to the invention of the Electron Microscope, Television, and the Atomic bomb.

   _____   _____   _____   _____

4. Homer's Poem, *The Iliad,* is an Epic Poem and tells about the battle between King Agamemnon and the Warrior Achilles.

   _____   _____   _____   _____

5. The *Star Wars* Saga comprises six films depicting the Rise and Fall of Anakin Skywalker and the Empire.

   _____   _____   _____

REVIEW TEST 1

Academic

Add capitals where needed and remove unnecessary capitals in the following sentences.

EXAMPLE:

         A   *R*   *c*

    The ~~a~~merican ~~r~~evolution began in 1775 when the ~~C~~olonists decided that they

                                         E

    were tired of the taxes ~~e~~ngland was imposing.

1. The colonies set up a new government in 1776, and with the aid of the french

   were able to defeat the british government.

2. Not long after the defeat of the british and the establishment of the united states of america, the french also had a Revolution.

3. The majority of the french population consisted of merchants and peasants and were known as the third estate; They were tired of paying taxes to the upper class, also known as the first estate.

4. In july 1789, a parisian mob stormed the bastille, a political prison.

5. Unfortunately, the abolishment of the Monarchy didn't lead to peace right away, and the time known as the reign of terror began in 1792.

6. a slightly more peaceful france was restored when napoleon Bonaparte rose to power in 1799.

7. However, he quickly declared himself emperor napoleon I, and in 1812 led a french invasion of russia.

8. Russia and the european alliance defeated napoleon twice, first in 1814 and again in 1815.

9. Despite Napoleon's defeat, his ideals helped create a spirit of Nationalism throughout europe.

10. After Napoleon was defeated, the congress of vienna met to restore legitimate Monarchs to their thrones; the regulations set up by this congress kept europe largely at peace until the end of the Nineteenth Century.

REVIEW TEST 2

On separate paper, write

1. Seven sentences demonstrating the seven main uses of capital letters.
2. Eight sentences demonstrating the eight other uses of capital letters.

CHAPTER 36

Numbers and Abbreviations

PERSONALIZED LEARNING

This chapter will describe the proper use of numbers and abbreviations.

Incorrect:

It took us 5 weeks to find an apt. we both liked.

"5" can be written as one word ("five") so it should be spelled out. "Apartment" can be abbreviated on an envelope, but should be written out in a sentence.

Correct:

It took us five weeks to find an apartment we both liked.

Spelling out "five" and "apartment" is correct in this format.

Incorrect:

We'll have the report for you in 72 hours.

"72" can be written out as "seventy-two," which is fewer than three words.

Correct:

We'll have the report for you in seventy-two hours.

Because the number can be expressed in fewer than three words, it is spelled out.

Key Term

abbreviations: shortened forms of words, often used for convenience in writing. Certain abbreviations (such as *Mr.*, A.M., and *e.g.*) are acceptable in formal writing; in general, however, the complete form of words is preferred.

Numbers

Here are three helpful rules for using numbers.

Rule 1

Spell out numbers that take no more than two words. Otherwise, use the numbers themselves.

> In Jody's kitchen is her collection of seventy-two cookbooks.
>
> Jody has a file of 350 recipes.
>
> It will take about two weeks to fix the computer database.
>
> Since a number of people use the database, the company will lose over 150 workdays.
>
> Only twelve students have signed up for the field trip.
>
> Nearly 250 students came to the lecture.

Rule 2

Be consistent when you use a series of numbers. If some numbers in a sentence or paragraph require more than two words, then use numbers for the others, too.

> After the storm, maintenance workers unclogged 46 drains, removed 123 broken tree limbs, and rescued 3 kittens who were stuck in a drainpipe.

Rule 3

Use numbers to show dates, times, addresses, percentages, and chapters of a book.

> The burglary was committed on October 30, 2012, but was not discovered until January 2, 2013.
>
> Before I went to bed, I set my alarm for 6:45 A.M. (But spell out numbers before *o'clock*. For example: I didn't get out of bed until seven o'clock.)
>
> The library is located at 45 West 52nd Street.
>
> When you take the skin off a piece of chicken, you remove about 40 percent of the fat.
>
> The name of the murderer is revealed in Chapter 8 on page 290.

ACTIVITY 1

Cross out the mistakes in numbers and write the corrections in the spaces provided.

1. The Puerto Rican Pride Parade will begin at three-thirty in front of the newspaper office at one sixteen South Forty-Second Street.

   _____ . _____   _____

2. The governor is scheduled to arrive at four o'clock, but she is going to be twenty minutes late.

   _____   _____

3. We expect to have fifty percent of the work completed by March tenth.

   _____   _____

Abbreviations

Using abbreviations can save you time when you take notes. In formal writing, however, you should avoid most abbreviations. Listed below are some of the few abbreviations that are considered acceptable in compositions. Note that a period is used after most abbreviations.

1. Mr., Mrs., Ms., Jr., Sr., Dr. when used with names:

   Mrs. Johnson   Dr. Garcia   Howard Kelley Jr.

2. Time references:

   A.M.   P.M.   B.C., A.D.

3. Initials in a person's name:

   J. Edgar Hoover   John F. Kennedy   Michael J. Fox

4. Organizations, technical words, and company names known primarily by their initials:

   IBM   UNICEF   ABC   IRS   NBA   AIDS

ACTIVITY 2

Cross out the words that should not be abbreviated, and correct them in the spaces provided.

1. Between mid-Nov. and the beginning of Jan., I typically gain about five lbs.

   _____   _____   _____

2. I have an appointment this A.M., but I can meet you for lunch in the caf. at noon.

_____   _____

3. I stopped at the p.o. at about twenty min. past ten and bought five dol. worth of stamps.

_____   _____   _____   _____

REVIEW TEST 1

Rewrite the following e-mail to correct problems with numbers and abbreviations.

From: Thomas S.

Sent: Saturday, September 14, 2013

To: Prof. Michael Hatzenberg

Subject: Psychology 2 Schedule, Weeks 2–four

Hi Prof. Hatzenberg:

I wanted to make sure I had our assignments clear for the next

3 weeks in our Psych. class. By Sept. twenty, I am supposed to

understand how Psych drs. study behavior with exp. methods and read

Chapters One & 2 in the textbook. In the 3rd week of class, I will need to

read Chapters 5 and 6 and complete the 7 exercises on pg. fifty-six. In the

fourth week of class, I will need to visit Saint Louis Children's Hosp. from

9:30 A.M. until one-thirty P.M. each day. During the visit, I am to observe the

ped. psych dept. Is this right?

Thx,

Tom

SECTION

III

Punctuation

SECTION PREVIEW

Chapter 37
Apostrophe

Chapter 38
Quotation Marks

Chapter 39
Comma

Chapter 40
Other Punctuation Marks

Is there a punctuation error in the sign pictured here? If so, how would you correct it?

Apostrophe

This chapter will describe the two main uses of the apostrophe. The sentences below will introduce you to one of these uses—to show ownership or possession. The other main use, to form contractions, is defined below.

Incorrect:

Because of the dogs constant barking, I could not sleep all night.

An apostrophe is needed before the s in dogs to show possession of the constant barking.

Correct:

Because of the dog's constant barking, I could not sleep all night.

With the apostrophe included it is clear that the dog is the possessor of the constant barking.

Key Terms

apostrophe: a punctuation mark generally used in order to (1) show the omission of one or more letters in a contraction, and to (2) show ownership or possession.

contraction: the combination of two words through omission of one or more letters and use of an apostrophe. Example: *hasn't* (for *has not*)

The two main uses of the apostrophe are

1. To show the omission of one or more letters in a contraction
2. To show ownership or possession

Apostrophe in Contractions

A contraction is formed when two words are combined. An apostrophe shows where letters are omitted.

> have + not = haven't (the *o* in *not* has been omitted)
>
> I + will = I'll (the *wi* in *will* has been omitted)

Following are some other common contractions:

I + am = I'm	it + is = it's
I + have = I've	it + has = it's
I + had = I'd	is + not = isn't
who + is = who's	could + not = couldn't
do + not = don't	I + would = I'd
did + not = didn't	they + are = they're
	we + are = we're

Will + not has an unusual contraction: won't.

ACTIVITY 1

Write the contractions for the words in parentheses.

1. (Are not) _____ the reserve books in the library kept at the circulation desk?

2. If (they are) _____ going to Israel, they (do not) _____ want to miss visiting Jerusalem.

3. (I am) _____ the kind of student (who is) _____ extremely nervous before tests.

4. (Who is) _____ the clerk who discovered that (it is) _____ cheaper

   to buy supplies online? (We are) _____ always interested in recognizing employees with good ideas.

5. I (cannot) _____ remember if (there is) _____ gas in the car or not.

> ### TIP
> Even though contractions are common in everyday speech and in written dialogue, it is often best to avoid them in formal writing.

Apostrophe to Show Ownership or Possession

To show possession, we can use such words as *belongs to,* or *possessed by.*

> the umbrella that belongs to Mark
>
> the toys possessed by children
>
> the tape recorder owned by the school
>
> the gentleness of my father

But the apostrophe and *s* (if the word doesn't end in *s*) is often the easiest way to do this.

> Mark's umbrella
>
> the children's toys
>
> the school's tape recorder
>
> my father's gentleness

Points to Remember

1. The 's goes with the owner or possessor (in the examples given, *Mark, children, the school, my father*). What follows is the person or thing possessed (in the examples given, *the umbrella, the toys, the tape recorder, gentleness*).

2. There should always be a break between the word and *'s.*

    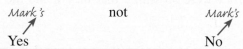

    Mark's   not   Mark's
    Yes   No

3. An apostrophe and *s* are used to show possession with a singular word even if the word already ends in *s:* for example, Doris's purse (the purse belonging to Doris).

ACTIVITY 2

Working in groups of two or three, rewrite the *italicized* part of each of the sentences below, using *'s* to show possession. Remember that the *'s* goes with the owner or possessor.

EXAMPLE

The wing of the bluejay was broken.

The bluejay's wing was broken. _____

1. *The capital of Great Britain* is London.

   _____

2. *One of the major attractions of New York City* is the Empire State Building.

   _____

3. *The three official languages of Switzerland* are German, French, and Italian.

   _____

4. *The piano belonging to the Previn family* was once used in a symphony orchestra.

   _____

5. *The computer belonging to John* was a top-of-the-line Apple.

   _____

6. A cat ran out in front of *the car belonging to Libby.*

   _____

7. *In the window of the bakery* was the largest cupcake I had ever seen.

   _____

8. *The apartment belonging to Caden* was located in an old converted warehouse.

   _____

9. *The tennis shoes owned by Brock* were so stinky that they made the whole room smell awful.

   _____

10. Keenan offered to paint *the house of Whitney Parker.*

    _____

Add *'s* to each of the following words to make it the possessor or owner of something. Then write sentences using the words. The first one is done for you.

1. The railroad conductor _The railroad conductor's_

   The railroad conductor's announcement reassured the passengers that they would arrive on time.

2. The government _____

   _____

3. Annalise _____

   _____

4. The grocery store _____

   _____

5. The golden retriever _____

   _____

6. The ski resort _____

   _____

Apostrophe versus Possessive Pronouns

Do not use an apostrophe with possessive pronouns. They already show ownership. Possessive pronouns include *his, hers, its, yours, ours,* and *theirs.*

INCORRECT	CORRECT
The sun warped his' albums.	The sun warped his albums.
The restored Model T is theirs'.	The restored Model T is theirs.
The decision is yours'.	The decision is yours.
The lion charged its' prey.	The lion charged its prey.

Apostrophe versus Simple Plurals

To make a word plural, add only *s,* not an apostrophe. For example, the plural of the word *movie* is *movies,* not *movies'.*

   Look at this sentence:

   Tim coveted his roommate's collection of cassette tapes and compact discs.

The words *tapes* and *discs* are simple plurals, meaning more than one tape, more than one disc. The plural is shown by adding *s* only. On the other hand, the *'s* after *roommate* shows possession—that the roommate owns the tapes and discs.

ACTIVITY 4

Insert an apostrophe where needed to show possession in the following sentences. Write *plural* above words where the *s* ending simply means more than one. Then, compare your answers with that of a classmate.

EXAMPLE

                      plural   *plural*
  Arlenes tinted contact lenses protect her eyes from glare.

1. Harry grasped his wifes arm as she stood on in-line skates for the first time.

2. Vonettes decision to study computer science is based on predictions of good opportunities for women in that field.

3. Pablo Picassos paintings are displayed in museums all over the world.

4. At the doctors request, Lyndon pulled up his shirt and revealed the zipperlike scars from his operation.

5. Of all the peoples names in all the worlds countries, the most common is Muhammad.

6. Sevilles many attractions include the beautiful Alcazar district built by the Moors, who ruled this Spanish city for five centuries.

7. The childrens shouts of delight grew louder as the clown added eggs, lightbulbs, and a bowling ball to the items he was juggling.

8. Tinas camping handbook suggests that we bring water purification tablets and nylon ropes.

9. *Black Beauty,* a childrens novel, has entertained young readers for more than a hundred years.

10. The rattlesnakes head has a sensitive pit below the eyes, capable of detecting the body heat of warm-blooded prey.

Apostrophe with Plurals Ending in *s*

Plurals that end in *s* show possession simply by adding the apostrophe, rather than an apostrophe and *s*.

the Thompsons' porch

the players' victory

her parents' motor home

the Rolling Stones' last CD

the soldiers' hats

Add an apostrophe where needed.

ACTIVITY 5

1. Several campers tents collapsed during the storm.

2. Both of the Johnsons daughters have become attorneys.

3. Many cities subway and bus systems provide inexpensive and efficient transportation.

4. The twins habit of dressing alike was started by their mother when they were children.

5. At the crowded intersection, several young men rushed out to wash the cars windshields.

REVIEW TEST 1

In the paragraph below, underline the words that either need apostrophes or have misused apostrophes. Then, in the spaces between the lines, correct the mistakes.

Academic

Learning the fifty state's capital's can often be a difficult task, but by using mnemonic devices and practicing, students can find success. Virginias capital is Richmond; a student can picture a rich man and his wife Virginia dancing at a ball to remember this capital. The capital of Maine is Augusta. This wouldnt be hard to forget if a student pictured a huge lion basking in the sun, while a gust of wind tussles the lions mane. Kentuckys capital is Frankfurt, easily remembered by picturing two boys' named Ken and Tuck sharing a hotdog. Connecticuts capital is Hartford, so a student could picture a heart connected to a Ford truck. Arkansas' capital, Little Rock, can be remembered by picturing a huge ark that is hit by a bunch of little rocks'. A fun way to remember Washington States capital, Olympia, is to picture George Washington receiving a gold medal at the Olympics. Mnemonic devices are creative ways to remember information and can help insure students success in school.

Quotation Marks

PERSONALIZED LEARNING

Quotation marks are punctuation marks that indicate exact words or the titles of short works. This chapter will describe the two main uses of quotation marks. The sentences below will introduce you to one of these uses—to set off the exact words of a speaker or writer. The other main use is listed below.

Incorrect:

I'm giving up smoking tomorrow said Jason.

Because it is a direct quote, what Jason said should be in quotation marks.

Correct:

"I'm giving up smoking tomorrow," said Jason.

Jason's words are directly attributed by the quotation marks.

The two main uses of quotation marks are

1. To set off the exact words of a speaker or writer
2. To set off the titles of short works

> TIP Quotation marks are also used in research papers to signify material that has been directly quoted from a source. See Chapter 22.

Quotation Marks to Set Off the Words of a Speaker or Writer

Use quotation marks to show the exact words of a speaker or writer.

Ben Franklin once wrote, "To lengthen thy life, lessen thy meals."(Quotation marks set off the exact words that Ben Franklin wrote.)

"Did you know," said the nutrition expert, "that it's healthier to be ten pounds overweight?"

(Two pairs of quotation marks are used to enclose the nutrition expert's exact words.)

The biology professor said, "Ants are a lot like human beings. They farm their own food and raise smaller insects as livestock. And like humans, ants send armies to war."

(Note that the end quotation marks do not come until the end of the biology professor's speech. Place quotation marks before the first quoted word and after the last quoted word. As long as no interruption occurs in the speech, do not use quotation marks for each new sentence.)

> **TIP** In the three examples above, notice that a comma sets the quoted part off from the rest of the sentence. Also, observe that commas and periods at the end of a quotation always go *inside* quotation marks.

Complete the following statements, which explain how capital letters, commas, and periods are used in quotations. Refer to the four examples above as guides.

1. Every quotation begins with a _____ letter.

2. When a quotation is split (as in the sentence about the nutrition expert), the second part does not begin with a capital letter unless it is a

   _____ sentence.

3. _____ are used to separate the quoted part of a sentence from the rest of the sentence.

4. Commas and periods that come at the end of a quotation go _____ the quotation marks.

The answers are *capital, new, Commas,* and *inside.*

Place quotation marks around the exact words of a speaker or writer in the sentences that follow.

1. Several people have been credited with saying, The more I see of people, the more I like dogs.

2. Let nature be your teacher, advised the poet William Wordsworth.

3. According to the Bible, The laborer is worthy of his hire.

4. The ballot, said Abraham Lincoln, is stronger than the bullet.

5. When chefs go to great lengths, the woman at the diet center said, I go to great widths.

6. My friend said that when she dies, she wants her headstone to read, She lived life to the fullest!

7. I apologize that my homework is tattered and stained, said the child, but I dropped it in a mud puddle.

8. Marilyn Monroe said, I restore myself when I'm alone.

9. The article warned residents, Severe weather is expected to arrive within the next two days.

10. Although he is most known for being funny, when Robin Williams said, No matter what people tell you, words and ideas can change the world, he was giving serious advice.

ACTIVITY 2

1. Write a sentence in which you quote a favorite expression of someone you know. In the same sentence, identify the person's relationship to you.

   EXAMPLE

   My grandfather loves to say, "It can't be as bad as all that."

   _____

   _____

   _____

2. Write a quotation that contains the words *Pablo asked Teresa*. Write a second quotation that includes the words *Teresa replied*.

   _____

   _____

   _____

   _____

   _____

3. Quote an interesting sentence or two from a book or magazine. In the same sentence, identify the title and author of the work.

   EXAMPLE *In The Dilbert Desk Calendar, by Scott Adams, the cartoon character Dilbert says, "I can please only one person per day. Today isn't your day, and tomorrow isn't looking good either."*

   _____

_____
_____
_____
_____
_____

4. Write a sentence in which the speaker of a quotation is identified in the middle of the quotation.

EXAMPLE *"Ralph ate a pound of pasta, six meatballs, and a slice of chocolate cake," said his wife, Alice, "but he was still hungry!"*

_____
_____
_____
_____
_____

Indirect Quotations

An indirect quotation is a rewording of someone else's comments rather than a word-for-word direct quotation. The word *that* often signals an indirect quotation.

DIRECT QUOTATION

The nurse said, "Some babies cannot tolerate cow's milk."
(The nurse's exact spoken words are given, so quotation marks are used.)

Vicky's note to Dan read, "I'll be home by 7:30."
(The exact words that Vicky wrote in the note are given, so quotation marks are used.)

INDIRECT QUOTATION

The nurse said that some babies cannot tolerate cow's milk.
(We learn the nurse's words indirectly, so no quotation marks are used.)

Vicky left a note for Dan saying that she would be home by 7:30.
(We learn Vicky's words indirectly, so no quotation marks are used.)

ACTIVITY 3   Rewrite the following sentences, changing words as necessary to convert the sentences into direct quotations. The first one has been done for you as an example.

1. Teddy asked Margie whether she wanted to see his spider collection.

   Teddy asked Margie, "Do you want to see my spider collection?"

   _____

2. According to Monica, her grandmother has been the role model for several women in her family.

   _____

   _____

3. Angelo said that he wanted a box of the extra-crispy chicken.

   _____

   _____

4. My history professor told us that tomatoes were first grown in Peru.

   _____

   _____

5. The instructor announced that Thursday's test had been canceled.

   _____

   _____

Quotation Marks to Set Off Titles of Short Works

Titles of short works are usually set off by quotation marks, while titles of long works are italicized. Use quotation marks to set off titles of such short works as articles in books, newspapers, or magazines; chapters in a book; short stories; poems; and songs. But you should italicize titles of books, newspapers, magazines, plays, movies, CDs, and television shows. Following are some examples.

QUOTATION MARKS	ITALICS
the essay "On Self-Respect"	in the book *Slouching Towards Bethlehem*
the article "The Problem of Acid Rain"	in the newspaper the *New York Times*

the article "Living with Inflation"	in the magazine *Newsweek*
the chapter "Chinese Religion"	in the book *Paths of Faith*
the story "Hands"	in the book *Winesburg, Ohio*
the poem "When I Have Fears"	in the book *Complete Poems of John Keats*
the song "Ziggy Stardust"	in the CD *Changes*
	the television show *60 Minutes*
	the movie *High Noon*

> ## TIP
> When you are typing a paper, you should always italicize longer works; however, if you are handwriting a paper, you should underline longer works. For example, *Catching Fire* by Suzanne Collins would be handwritten <u>Catching Fire</u> by Suzanne Collins.

Use quotation marks as needed. Underline titles that should be italicized. Review your answers with a partner.

ACTIVITY 4

1. In her short story A Sea Worry, Maxine Hong Kingston describes a group of teenage surfers and a mother who tries to understand them.

2. The January issue of Discover magazine included an article entitled Lost Cities of the Amazon.

3. We read the chapter Pulling Up Roots in Gail Sheehy's book Passages.

4. Raymond gave me a copy of last month's National Geographic magazine, which featured a story called Saving Energy: It Starts at Home.

5. The movie Casablanca, which starred Humphrey Bogart, was originally cast with Ronald Reagan in the leading role.

6. One of my grandfather's favorite old TV shows was Thriller, a horror series hosted by Boris Karloff, the man who starred in the 1931 movie Frankenstein.

7. When the Beatles' movie A Hard Day's Night was first shown, fans screamed so much that no one could hear the songs or the dialogue.

8. Pinned on Jeffery's wall is the cover of a recent issue of Rolling Stone. The cover has a photo of the British rock group The Rolling Stones.

9. The sociology test will cover the first two chapters: Culture and Diversity and Social Stratification.

10. An article in Consumer Reports called Which Cereal for Breakfast? claims that children can learn to like low-sugar cereals like Cheerios and Wheaties.

Other Uses of Quotation Marks

Quotation marks are also used as follows:

1. To set off special words or phrases from the rest of a sentence:

   In grade school, we were taught a little jingle about the spelling rule "*i* before *e*."

   What is the difference between "it's" and "its"?

   (In this and other books, *italics* are often used instead of quotation marks to set off words.)

2. To mark off a quotation within a quotation:

   The physics professor said, "For class on Friday, do the problems at the end of the chapter titled 'Work and Energy.'"

   Brendan remarked, "Did you know that Humphrey Bogart never actually said, 'Play it again, Sam,' in the movie *Casablanca*?"

> **TIP** A quotation within a quotation is indicated by *single* quotation marks, as shown above.

REVIEW TEST 1

Directions: Insert quotation marks where needed in the sentences that follow. One sentence is correct; mark that sentence with a C.

1. In *Monty Python and the Holy Grail*, John Cleese famously says, I fart in your general direction. Your mother was a hamster and your father smelt of elderberries.

2. In *The Usual Suspects*, Verbal Kint (Kevin Spacey) claims, The greatest trick the devil ever pulled was convincing the world he didn't exist.

3. In the short story The Death of Ivan Ilych, Leo Tolstoy writes, In place of death there was light.

4. Remember to let her into your heart is one of the memorable lines from the Beatles' song, Hey Jude.

5. Tom Hanks plays a coach in *A League of Their Own*, but it certainly isn't his finest moment when he yells at one of his players, "Are you crying? There's no crying! There's no crying in baseball!"

6. *Forrest Gump* includes many quotable lines, such as, "Run, Forrest, run. Run, Forrest!" and Mama says, 'Stupid is as stupid does.'

7. Richard Wilbur opens his poem, The Writer, with these lines, In her room at the prow of the house/Where light breaks, and the windows are tossed with linden,/My daughter is writing a story.

8. Emily Blunt's character in *The Devil Wears Prada* explains, I'm just one stomach flu away from my goal weight.

9. Find a truly original idea. It is the only way I will ever distinguish myself. It is the only way I will ever matter, John Nash moans in *A Beautiful Mind*.

10. Robin Williams inspires his students in *Dead Poets Society* when he says, . . . But if you listen real close, you can hear them whisper their legacy to you. Go on, lean in. Listen, you hear it? Carpe—hear it?—Carpe, *Carpe diem*. Seize the day, boys. Make your lives extraordinary.

REVIEW TEST 2

In a newspaper's comic section find an amusing comic strip. Choose one where two or more characters speak to each other. Write a description that enables people who have not read the comic strip to appreciate its humor. Describe the setting and action in each panel, and enclose the speakers' words in quotation marks.

Comma

This chapter will describe the six main uses of the comma. The sentences below will introduce you to one of these uses—to set a direct quotation off from the rest of the sentence. The other five main uses of the comma are included below.

Incorrect:

The journalist pleaded "Just one more question."

A comma is needed to set the direct quotation off from the rest of the sentence.

Correct:

The journalist pleaded, "Just one more question."

With the comma included, the direct quotation is properly set off from the rest of the sentence.

Six Main Uses of the Comma

Commas are used mainly as follows:

1. To separate items in a series
2. To set off introductory material
3. On both sides of words that interrupt the flow of thought in a sentence
4. Between two complete thoughts connected by *and, but, for, or, nor, so, yet*
5. To set off a direct quotation from the rest of a sentence
6. For certain everyday material

You may find it helpful to remember that the comma often marks a slight pause or break in a sentence. Read aloud the sentence examples given for each rule, and listen for the minor pauses or breaks that are signaled by commas.

Comma between Items in a Series

Use commas to separate items in a series.

> The street vendor sold watches, necklaces, and earrings.
>
> The pitcher adjusted his cap, pawed the ground, and peered over his shoulder.
>
> The exercise instructor told us to inhale, exhale, and relax.
>
> Joe peered into the hot, still-smoking engine.

A. The final comma in a series is optional, but it is often used. If you use a final comma in one series in an essay, use one in all the other series in the same essay.

B. A comma is used between two descriptive words in a series only if *and* inserted between the words sounds natural. You could say:

> Joe peered into the hot *and* still-smoking engine.

But notice in the following sentence that the descriptive words do not sound natural when *and* is inserted between them. In such cases, no comma is used.

> Tony wore a pale green tuxedo. (A pale *and* green tuxedo does not sound right, so no comma is used.)

Place commas between items in a series.

ACTIVITY 1

1. The American alligator lives in southern swamps streams lakes and other bodies of water.

2. Rudy stretched out on the swaying hammock popped open a frosty can of soda and balanced it carefully on his stomach.

3. The children splashed through the warm deep swirling rainwater that flooded the street.

4. The police officer's warm brown eyes relaxed manner and pleasant smile made her easy to talk to.

5. The soft warm woolen blankets comforted us as we heard the cold north wind blow through the pines.

Comma after Introductory Material

Use a comma to set off introductory material.

> Just in time, Sherry applied the brakes and avoided a car accident.
>
> Muttering under his breath, Hassan reviewed the terms he had memorized.
>
> In a wolf pack, the dominant male holds his tail higher than the other pack members.

Although he had been first in the checkout line, Deion let an elderly woman go ahead of him.

After the fire, we slogged through the ashes of the burned-out house.

> **TIP** If the introductory material is brief, the comma is sometimes omitted. In the activities here, you should include the comma.

ACTIVITY 2

Place commas after introductory material. Once you have completed the activity, review your answers with a partner.

1. Although it cannot kill certain bacteria penicillin is still a useful antibiotic.

2. His heart pounding wildly Jesse opened the letter that would tell him whether he had been accepted at college.

3. Passing through fourteen states the Appalachian trail is over two thousand miles long.

4. When the band hadn't taken the stage forty-five minutes after the concert was supposed to begin the audience members started shouting and stamping their feet.

5. Along the side of the brook we noticed a newborn fawn speckled brown and red.

Comma around Words That Interrupt the Flow of Thought

Use a comma on both sides of words or phrases that interrupt the flow of thought in a sentence.

The vinyl car seat, sticky from the heat, clung to my skin.

Marty's computer, which his wife got him as a birthday gift, occupies all his spare time.

The hallway, dingy and dark, was illuminated by a bare bulb hanging from a wire.

Usually, by reading a sentence aloud, you can hear the words that interrupt the flow of thought. In cases where you are not sure if certain words are interrupters, remove them from the sentence. If it still makes sense without the words, you know that the words are interrupters and that the information they give is nonessential. *Such nonessential or extra information is set off with commas.*

In the sentence

Sue Dodd, who goes to aerobics class with me, was in a serious car accident.

the words *who goes to aerobics class with me* are extra information not needed to identify the subject of the sentence, *Sue Dodd*. Commas go around such nonessential information. On the other hand, in the sentence

The woman who goes to aerobics class with me was in a serious accident.

the words *who goes to aerobics class with me* supply essential information—information needed for us to identify the woman being spoken of. If the words were removed from the sentence, we would no longer know exactly who was in the accident: "The woman was in a serious accident." Here is another example:

Watership Down, a novel by Richard Adams, is the most thrilling adventure story I've ever read.

Here the words *a novel by Richard Adams* could be left out, and we would still know the basic meaning of the sentence. Commas are placed around such nonessential material. But in the sentence

Richard Adams's novel *Watership Down* is the most thrilling adventure story I've ever read.

the title of the novel is essential. Without it the sentence would read, "Richard Adams's novel is the most thrilling adventure story I've ever read." We would not know which of Richard Adams's novels was so thrilling. Commas are not used around the title, because it provides essential information.

Most of the time you will be able to hear which words interrupt the flow of thought in a sentence and will not have to think about whether the words are essential or nonessential.

Use commas to set off interrupting words.

ACTIVITY 3

1. Two large pines swaying in the wind, signaled that cooler weather was coming.
2. Hawaii which became the fiftieth state in 1959 is made up of eight major islands.
3. Liam Bage an avid football fan watches college football on Saturdays and professional football on Sundays.
4. The weather windy and wild created twenty-foot swells on the lake.
5. A talented actress who has starred in many plays lives across the street.

Comma between Complete Thoughts

Use a comma between two complete thoughts connected by *and, but, for, or, nor, so, yet*.

> Sam closed all the windows, but the predicted thunderstorm never arrived.
>
> I like wearing comfortable clothing, so I buy oversize shirts and sweaters.
>
> Peggy doesn't envy the skinny models in magazines, for she is happy with her own well-rounded body.

A. The comma is optional when the complete thoughts are short.

> The Ferris wheel started and Wilson closed his eyes.
>
> Many people left but the band played on.
>
> I made a wrong turn so I doubled back.

B. Be careful not to use a comma to separate two verbs that belong to one subject. The comma is used only in sentences made up of two complete thoughts (two subjects and two verbs). In the sentence

> The doctor stared over his bifocals and lectured me about smoking.

there is only one subject (*doctor*) and a double verb (*stared* and *lectured*). No comma is needed. Likewise, the sentence

> Dean switched the lamp on and off and then tapped it with his fingers.

has only one subject (*Dean*) and a double verb (*switched* and *tapped*); therefore, no comma is needed.

ACTIVITY 4

Place a comma before a joining word that connects two complete thoughts (two subjects and two verbs). Remember, do *not* place a comma within a sentence that has only one subject and a double verb. Some items are correct as given. For these items, write "Correct" at the end of the sentence.

1. The television sitcom was interrupted for a special news bulletin and I poked my head out of the kitchen to listen to the announcement.

2. Before he led Confederate troops in the Civil War, General Robert E. Lee had fought in the Mexican War and had been superintendent at West Point.

3. The eccentric woman brought all her own clips and rollers to the beauty parlor for she was afraid to use the ones there.

4. Orangutans are ideally suited for living in trees and they rarely climb down to the ground.

5. Plastic surgery was developed to repair damaged tissue but today it is often used to improve one's appearance.

6. Ruth was tired of summer reruns so she visited the town library to pick up some interesting books.

7. You can spend hours driving all over town to look for a particular type of camera or you can telephone a few stores to find it quickly.

8. Many people strolled among the exhibits at the comic book collectors' convention and stopped to look at a rare first edition of *Superman*.

9. Our neighborhood crime patrol escorts elderly people to the local bank and installs free dead-bolt locks on their apartment doors.

10. Brendan tapped the small geraniums out of their pots and carefully planted them on his grandfather's grave.

Comma with Direct Quotations

Use a comma to set off a direct quotation from the rest of a sentence.

The carnival barker cried, "Step right up and win a prize!"

"Now is the time to yield to temptation," my horoscope read.

"I'm sorry," said the restaurant hostess. "You'll have to wait."

"For my first writing assignment," said Scott, "I have to turn in a five-hundred-word description of a stone."

> **TIP** Commas and periods at the end of a quotation go inside quotation marks. See also page 547.

Use commas to set off direct quotations from the rest of the sentence.

ACTIVITY 5

1. The child heard her mother whisper "Ladybird, ladybird, fly away home."

2. "My heart is bursting" said Stella. "How can I ever repay you for all you've done?"

3. The teacher announced "Tomorrow will be our last day of state testing."

4. "I know you did it" the detective accused the murderer "and I can prove it!"

5. "Please remember to watch the gap" the conductor warned.

Comma with Everyday Material

Use a comma when a person is spoken to.

Persons Spoken To

If you're the last to leave, Paul, please switch off the lights.

Fred, I think we're on the wrong road.

Use a comma after the salutation of a friendly letter and after the salutation and closing of a friendly and a formal letter.

Openings and Closings of Letters

Dear Allie,   Sincerely yours,

Dear Roberto,   Yours truly,

> **TIP** In formal letters, a colon is used after the opening: Dear Sir: *or* Dear Madam: *or* Dear Allan: *or* Dear Ms. Mohr:

Use commas in numbers of four digits or more, except for years and street numbers.

Numbers

In 2008, the insurance agent sold me a $50,000 term life insurance policy.

Use commas in dates and in addresses as illustrated.

Dates

Addresses

July 4, 1980, is my brother's birthday.

The Brown Elementary School is located at 20 Milk Street, Wareham, Massachusetts 02571.

> **TIP** No comma is used before a ZIP code.

 ACTIVITY 6

Place commas where needed.

1. The City of Dublin Maggie is the capital of the Republic of Ireland.

2. On July 15 2009, Philip Vassallo opened a legal office at 2600 Woodbridge Avenue Fort Myers Florida.

3. An estimated 875000 African American men participated in the Million Man March on Washington on October 16 1995.

4. The mileage chart shows Elaine that we'll have to drive 1231 miles to get to Sarasota Florida.

5. The coupon refund address is 2120 Industrial Highway Great Plains Minnesota 55455.

REVIEW TEST 1

Insert commas where needed. In the space provided below each sentence, summarize briefly the rule that explains the comma or commas used.

1. "Kleenex tissues" said the history professor "were first used as gas mask filters in World War I."

2. The large juicy Bartlett pear that I bit into was sweet cold and refreshing.

3. While waiting to enter the movie theater we studied the faces of the people just leaving to see if they had liked the show.

4. I had left my wallet on the store counter but the clerk called me at home to say that it was safe.

5. The demonstrators protesting nuclear arms carried signs reading "Humans have never invented a weapon that they haven't used."

6. Large cactus plants which now sell for very high prices are being stolen from national parks and protected desert areas.

7. At the age of twenty-one Tiger Woods won the 1997 Masters Tournament with the highest margin of victory in the golfing tournament's history.

8. Tucson a large city in Arizona is quite near the border with Mexico.

9. The North African nation of Algeria is bordered by five other countries: Tunisia Libya Niger Mali and Mauritania.

10. Cats and dogs like most animals love the taste of salt and will lick humans' hands to get it.

REVIEW TEST 2

Insert commas where needed. Mark the one sentence that is correct with a C.

1. Before leaving for the gym Nikki added extra socks and a tube of shampoo to the gear in her duffel bag.

2. My father said "Golf isn't for me. I can't afford to buy lots of expensive sticks so that I can lose lots of expensive white balls."

3. Reviewed by a committee of college faculty Jason's application for scholarship aid was approved unanimously.

4. Oscar took a time-exposure photo of the busy highway so the cars' taillights appeared in the developed print as winding red ribbons.

5. A line of dancing numerals on *Sesame Street* kicked across the screen like a chorus line.

6. During the summer graduation ceremony students fanned themselves with commencement programs and parents hid in the shade of trees.

7. Leaving seven astronauts dead the space shuttle *Columbia* broke apart as it returned to Earth on February 1 2003.

8. "When I was little" said Ernie "my brother told me it was illegal to kill praying mantises. I still don't know if that's true or not."

9. The Cloisters a museum of medieval art which is part of the New York Metropolitan Museum of Art includes buildings brought to the United States from Europe.

10. On June 24 1948 the Soviet Union closed the German city of Berlin to traffic from the West. However this ill-fated venture lasted only until May 11 1949 when the Soviets were forced to reopen the city.

REVIEW TEST 3

In the following passage, there are ten missing commas. Add the commas where needed. The types of mistakes to look for are shown in the box below.

> 3 commas missing between items in a series
>
> 2 commas missing after introductory material
>
> 2 commas missing between complete thoughts
>
> 2 commas missing around interrupting words
>
> 1 comma missing with a direct quotation

Instructor Performance Review: Ms. J. Thompson

It is evident that Ms. Thompson is well liked by her students engenders an atmosphere of fun in her classroom, and has continued to improve as an instructor. During Ms. Thompson's evaluation she presented a lesson on creating parallelism in writing. Students then partnered up, read their essays, and tried to incorporate parallel statements in their own pieces of writing. Most students except two remained focused during the activity and Ms. Thompson quickly addressed both students "Either pay attention and complete the activity, or remove yourself from the class." She then continued to walk about the classroom and used her presence to remind the class to stay focused. When students finished this activity they moved to a discussion about the English Portfolio Assessment. Students presented their portfolios and Ms. Thompson offered insight and advice. Students' portfolios were very innovative and included items such as a "Bucket List," creative covers that reflected something about the contents of the portfolio and a bio-poem. Although Ms. Thompson's students exhibited success in their approaches, Ms. Thompson should refocus her course goals to include more academic and longer pieces that follow the outcomes laid out in the faculty handbook. These pieces should demonstrate expressive, expository and persuasive writing techniques that use the principles of organization, unity, coherence, and theme development. It is suggested that Ms. Thompson work with a tenured professor chosen by the English department to reconfigure her syllabus to meet the course outcomes as laid out by the college.

REVIEW TEST 4

On separate paper, write six sentences, one illustrating each of the six main comma rules.

Other Punctuation Marks

This chapter will describe other punctuation marks including the colon, the dash, the hyphen, parentheses, and the semicolon.

Key Terms

colon: punctuation mark used at the end of a complete statement to introduce a list, a long quotation, or an explanation.

dash: punctuation mark used to signal a pause longer than that of a comma but not as long as that of a period.

hyphen: punctuation mark used with two or more words that act as a single unit or to divide a word at the end of a line.

parentheses: punctuation marks used to set off extra or incidental information from the rest of a sentence.

semicolon: punctuation mark used to mark a break between two complete thoughts or to mark off items in a series when the items themselves contain internal punctuation (such as commas).

Colon (:)

Use the colon at the end of a complete statement to introduce a list, a long quotation, or an explanation.

1. List:

    The store will close at noon on the following dates: November 26, December 24, and December 31.

2. Quotation:

    In his book *Life Lines,* Forrest Church maintains that people should cry more: "Life is difficult. Some people pretend that it is not, that we should be able to breeze through. Yet hardly a week passes in which most of us don't have something worth crying about."

3. Explanation:

    Here's a temporary solution to a dripping faucet: tie a string to it, and let the drops slide down the string to the sink.

Place colons where needed in the sentences below:

1. There are eight parts of speech noun, pronoun, verb, adjective, adverb, preposition, conjunction, and article.

2. There's a reason the Italian lira and the German mark are no longer used in 1999, the official currency of many European countries became the euro.

3. T.S. Eliot, an American-born poet, had an insightful comment about education "It is in fact a part of the function of education to help us to escape, not from our own time—for we are bound by that—but from the intellectual and emotional limitations of our time."

Semicolon (;)

The main use of the semicolon is to mark a break between two complete thoughts, as explained on page 564. Another use is to mark off items in a series when the items themselves contain commas. Here are some examples:

> Maya's children are named Melantha, which means "black flower"; Yonina, which means "dove"; and Cynthia, which means "moon goddess."

> My parents' favorite albums are *Rubber Soul,* by the Beatles; *Songs in the Key of Life,* by Stevie Wonder; and *Bridge over Troubled Water,* by Simon and Garfunkel.

Working with a partner, place semicolons where needed in the sentences below.

1. There are three major Hindu gods: Brahma, the power that creates Shiva, the power that destroys and Vishnu, the power that restores.

2. My new cell phone has a camera my last phone didn't even have voicemail.

3. I made enough money last summer to pay for my college textbooks: by babysitting, I earned $200 by selling lemonade, $100 and by cleaning homes, $600.

Dash (—)

A dash signals a pause longer than a comma but not as complete as a period. Use a dash to set off words for dramatic effect:

> I was so exhausted that I fell asleep within seconds—standing up.

> He had many good qualities—sincerity, honesty, and thoughtfulness—yet he had few friends.

> The pardon from the governor finally arrived—too late.

> **TIPS**
> a. A dash can be formed using a keyboard by striking the hyphen twice (--). Computer software also has a symbol for the dash. In handwriting, a dash is as long as two letters would be.
> b. Be careful not to overuse dashes.

ACTIVITY 3

Place dashes where needed in the following sentences.

1. The victim's leg broken in three places lay twisted at an odd angle on the pavement.

2. On September 17, 2008, a phone call from the Lottery Commission changed the Richardsons' lives they were informed they had won ten million dollars.

3. After nine days of hiking in the wilderness, sleeping under the stars, and communing with nature, I could think of only one thing a hot shower.

Parentheses ( )

Parentheses are used to set off extra or incidental information from the rest of a sentence:

> In 1913, the tax on an annual income of four thousand dollars (a comfortable wage at that time) was one penny.

> Arthur C. Clarke, author of science fiction books (including *2001: A Space Odyssey*), was inspired as a young man by the magazine *Astounding Stories*.

> **TIP**   Do not use parentheses too often in your writing.

ACTIVITY 4

Add parentheses where needed.

1. Ukraine became independent the country had been part of the Soviet Union since 1922, in 1990, after the fall of communism in Eastern Europe.

2. In the series, *Murder She Wrote,* Jessica Fletcher solved murders for twelve seasons 1984–1996.

3. When I finished *Harry Potter and the Sorcerer's Stone* Book 1, I immediately began the second book, *Harry Potter and the Chamber of Secrets.*

Hyphen (-)

1. Use a hyphen with two or more words that act as a single unit describing a noun.

   > The light-footed burglar silently slipped open the sliding glass door.

   > While being interviewed on the late-night talk show, the quarterback announced his intention to retire.

   > With a needle, Rich punctured the fluid-filled blister on his toe.

2. Use a hyphen to divide a word at the end of a line of writing or typing. When you need to divide a word at the end of a line, divide it between syllables. Use your dictionary to be sure of correct syllable divisions.

   > Selena's first year at college was a time filled with numerous new pres-sures and responsibilities.

TIPS

a. Do not divide words of one syllable.

b. Do not divide a word if you can avoid dividing it.

Working with a partner, place hyphens where needed.

ACTIVITY 5

1. The blood red moon hanging low on the horizon made a picture-perfect atmosphere for Halloween night.

2. We walked by a beautiful lily covered pond, then through a sweet smelling pine forest, and finally up to the mountain's sun-bathed summit.

3. The well written article in *Newsweek* described the nerve racking experiences of a journalist who infiltrated the mob.

REVIEW TEST 1

At the appropriate spot, place the punctuation mark shown in the margin.

1. An A on my English paper, a raise in pay at the Dairy Delight, and the birth of my first nephew it's been a great week!   —

2. My sister who will be six next week started school today.   ( )

3. Mrs. Richardson offered advice to her students "Always do your homework to the best of your ability."   :

4. Lauren's favorite drink is a cherry flavored limeade.   -

( )   5. Fermium named after Italian physicist Enrico Fermi, who helped develop the atomic bomb is a radioactive element discovered in 1952.

;   6. The winners of the race were Reagan, a first-grader Coby, a third-grader and Courtney, a fourth-grader.

—   7. There are only two ways to get an A in Professor Callahan's class read the material carefully and write good papers.

-   8. My maternal grandmother is the most warm hearted person I know.

;   9. Many students like to study in large groups other students prefer to study alone.

:   10. There are three ways to clean a toilet hire someone, assign the chore to a son or daughter, or do it yourself while wearing a full hazmat suit.

Word Use

SECTION PREVIEW

Chapter 41
Spelling Improvement

Chapter 42
Commonly Confused Words

Chapter 43
Effective Word Choice

Chapter 44
Editing Tests

Chapter 45
ESL Pointers

What is it about these signs that makes them funny? How could each one be fixed so that its message is clearer?

Spelling Improvement

This chapter will list six steps toward improving your spelling:

  Step 1: Use a Dictionary

  Step 2: Keep a Personal Spelling List

  Step 3: Master Commonly Confused Words

  Step 4: Learn Key Words in Major Subjects

  Step 5: Study a Basic Word List

  Step 6: Use Electronic Aids

Key Term

personal spelling list: a list of words you misspell written on the back page of a frequently used notebook or on a separate sheet of paper.

Poor spelling can be corrected. If you can write your name without misspelling it, you can learn to spell any word in the English language. You can use the next six steps to improve your spelling.

Step 1: Use a Dictionary

When writing a paper, leave time to look up the spelling of all words you are unsure about. Don't overlook the value of this step. Using a dictionary will help you improve your spelling significantly!

Step 2: Keep a Personal Spelling List

Keep a list of words you misspell, and study them regularly. Write the list on the back page of a frequently used notebook or on a separate sheet of paper entitled "Personal Spelling List."

  1. Write down hints to help you remember a word's spelling. For example, note that *occasion* is spelled with two *c*'s or that *all right* is two words, not one.

2. Study a word by saying and spelling it. Write the word one or more times.

3. Break a long word into syllables. *Inadvertent* can be divided into four syllables: *in ad ver tent. Consternation* can be spelled easily if you hear its four syllables in turn: *con ster na tion.*

4. Review and repeatedly test yourself. When learning a series of words, go back after studying each new word and review all preceding ones.

Step 3: Master Commonly Confused Words

Master the meanings and spellings of the commonly confused words on pages 575–584. Your instructor may assign twenty words for you to study at a time and give you a series of quizzes until you have mastered the words.

Step 4: Learn Key Words in Major Subjects

Make up and master lists of words central to the vocabulary of your major subjects. For example, a list of key words in business might include *economics, management, resources, scarcity, capitalism, decentralization, productivity, enterprise,* and so on; in psychology, *behavior, investigation, experimentation, frustration, cognition, stimulus, response, organism,* and so on. Set aside a specific portion of your various course notebooks to be used only for such lists, and study them using the methods described above for learning words.

Step 5: Study a Basic Word List

Following is a list of 250 English words that are often misspelled. Study their spellings. Your instructor may assign 25 or 50 words for you to study at a time and give you a series of quizzes until you have mastered the entire list.

The 250 English Words Most Often Misspelled

absence	appearance		believe
ache	appetite		beneficial
achieve	attempt	25	bottom
acknowledge	attendance		breathe
advice	autumn		brilliant
aisle	awful		bureau
all right	bachelor		business
already	balance		cafeteria
amateur	bargain		calendar
answer	basically		candidate
anxious	beautiful		category

continued

ceiling	existence	lightning
cemetery	familiar	likely
chief	fascinate	livelihood
choose	February	loneliness
cigarette	financial	loose
citizen	foreign	magazine
college	forty	making
column	**75** friend	maintain
comfortable	furniture	marriage
committed	government	material
completely	grammar	mathematics
conceit	grieve	medicine
conscience	guidance	minute
conscious	hammer	mortgage
conversation	handkerchief	muscle
cruelty	harass	naturally
50 daughter	height	necessary
deceit	hospital	neither
definite	hundred	nickel
deposit	husband	niece
dictionary	imitation	ninety
disastrous	incredible	noise
disease	independent	obedience
distance	instant	**125** obstacle
doctor	instead	occasion
doubt	intelligence	occur
efficient	interest	occurrence
eighth	interfere	omission
either	interrupt	opinion
emphasize	irresistible	opportunity
entrance	January	optimist
environment	kindergarten	ounce
exaggerate	**100** leisure	outrageous
examine	library	pageant

continued

pamphlet
people
perform
persistent
physically
picnic
plausible
pleasant
policeman
possible
precede
prefer
preference
prejudice
150 prescription
probably
psychology
pursue
quantity
quarter
quiet
quiz
raise
really
recede
receive
recognize
recommend
reference
region
relieve
religion
representative
resistance

restaurant
rhythm
ridiculous
right
175 safety
said
salary
scarcely
scholastic
science
scissors
secretary
seize
separate
sergeant
several
severely
shriek
siege
similar
sincerely
sophomore
straight
succeed
suppress
telephone
temperature
tenant
tendency
200 tenth
than
theater
though
thousand

through
tomorrow
tongue
tonight
tournament
toward
transferred
trousers
truly
twelfth
unanimous
until
unusual
usage
used
usual
usually
vacuum
valuable
variety
225 vegetable
vengeance
view
villain
vision
visitor
voice
Washington
wear
weather
Wednesday
weight
weird
welcome

continued

whether	won't	yesterday
which	writing	yolk
woman	written	your
women	wrong 250	you're

Step 6: Use Electronic Aids

There are several electronic aids that can help your spelling. An electronic spell-checker looks like a pocket calculator, which has a tiny keyboard. You type the word the way you think it is spelled. Then the checker provides the correct spelling of related words. As part of the word-processing program in a computer, a spell-checker identifies incorrect words and suggests correct spellings.

Commonly Confused Words

This chapter will list homonyms and other commonly confused words and provide activities to help you learn to distinguish them.

Key Term

homonym: words such as *brake* and *break* that have the same sounds but different meanings.

Homonyms

Some words are commonly confused because they have the same sounds but different meanings and spellings; such words are known as *homonyms*. Following are a number of homonyms. Complete the activity for each set of words. Check off and study the words that give you trouble.

all ready	completely prepared
already	previously; before

It was *already* four o'clock by the time I thought about lunch.

My report was *all ready,* but the class was canceled.

Fill in the blanks: Tyrone was _____ to sign up for the course when he discovered that it had _____ closed.

brake	stop
break	come apart

The mechanic advised me to add *brake* fluid to my car.

During a commercial *break,* Marie lay on the floor and did fifty sit-ups.

Fill in the blanks: I didn't want to _____ my promise, but since the _____ on my bike wasn't working, I couldn't take my son biking.

course	part of a meal; a school subject; direction
coarse	rough

At the movies, I tried to decide on a *course* of action that would put an end to the *coarse* language of the man behind me.

Fill in the blanks: Over the _____ of time, jagged, _____ rocks will be polished to smoothness by the pounding waves.

hear	perceive with the ear
here	in this place

I can *hear* the performers so well from *here* that I don't want to change my seat.

Fill in the blanks: "_____ is the best place to _____ the birds," said Reagan as she pointed out a shaded spot near the river.

hole	an empty spot
whole	entire

A *hole* in the crumbling brick mortar made a convenient home for a small bird and its *whole* family.

Fill in the blanks: It took a _____ weekend for the two men to dig a _____ for the new waterfall and pond.

its	belonging to it
it's	shortened form (contraction) of "it is" or "it has"

The tall giraffe lowered *its* head (the head belonging to the giraffe) to the level of the car window and peered in at us.

It's (it is) too late to sign up for the theater trip to New York.

Fill in the blanks: I decided not to take the course because _____ too easy; _____ content offers no challenge whatsoever.

knew	understood; past form of *know*
new	not old

No one *knew* our *new* phone number, but the obscene calls continued.

Fill in the blanks: Bryan and Courtney _____ that having a _____ car was a luxury they couldn't afford.

| know | to understand |
| no | a negative |

By the time students complete that course, they *know* two computer languages and have *no* trouble writing their own programs.

Fill in the blanks: The students _____ that anytime the teacher says _____, they need to listen.

| passed | went by; succeeded in; handed to |
| past | a time before the present; by, as in "I drove past the house" |

As Yvonne *passed* exit six on the interstate, she knew she had gone *past* the correct turnoff.

Fill in the blanks: Lewis asked for a meeting with his boss to learn why he had been _____ over for promotion twice in the _____ year.

| peace | calm |
| piece | a part |

The best *piece* of advice she ever received was to maintain her own inner *peace*.

Fill in the blanks: I will have _____ of mind once I know this expensive _____ of jewelry is in the safe-deposit box.

| plain | simple |
| plane | aircraft |

The *plain* box contained a very expensive model *plane* kit.

Fill in the blanks: After studying and practicing for months, Pierce finally executed a solo landing of his _____ on the highway near his _____ brown house.

| principal | main; a person in charge of a school |
| principle | a law or standard |

If the *principal* ingredient in this stew is octopus, I'll abandon my *principle* of trying everything at least once.

Fill in the blanks: The _____ of the school announced that the _____ behind exams was to test students' learning.

| right | correct; opposite of "left" |
| write | to put words on paper |

Without the *right* amount of advance planning, it is difficult to *write* a good research paper.

Fill in the blanks: Connie wanted to send for the CDs offered on TV, but she could not _____ fast enough to get all the _____ information down before the commercial ended.

| than | (thăn) used in comparisons |
| then | (thĕn) at that time |

I made more money *then,* but I've never been happier *than* I am now.

Fill in the blanks: I wanted to attend New York University more _____ the University of Chicago, but _____ I was offered a scholarship to the University of Chicago, so that is where I wound up.

their	belonging to them
there	at that place; a neutral word used with verbs like *is, are, was, were, have,* and *had*
they're	contraction of "they are"

The tenants *there* are complaining because *they're* being cheated by *their* landlord.

Fill in the blanks: _____ hoping to move _____ campsite over _____ near the tall oak tree.

| threw | past form of *throw* |
| through | from one side to the other; finished |

As the inexperienced pizza-maker *threw* the pie into the air, he punched a hole *through* its thin crust.

Fill in the blanks: As the president moved slowly _____ the cheering crowd, the Secret Service agent suddenly _____ himself at a man waving a small metal object.

to	verb part, as in *to smile;* toward, as in "I'm going *to* heaven."
too	overly, as in "The pizza was *too* hot"; also, as in "The coffee was hot, *too.*"
two	the number 2

I ran *to* the car *to* roll up the windows. (The first *to* means "toward"; the second *to* is a verb part that goes with *roll*.)

That amusement park is *too* far away; I hear that it's expensive, *too* (The first *too* means "overly"; the second *too* means "also.")

The *two* players (2 players) jumped up to tap the basketball away.

Fill in the blanks: I wanted _____ take the _____ young girls to see the roses at the botanical garden, but the girls were _____ interested in the Japanese garden _____ comply.

| wear | to have on |
| where | in what place |

Where I will *wear* a purple feather boa is not the point; I just want to buy it.

Fill in the blanks: My husband and son like to go to parties _____ they can _____ colorful ties and suits.

| weather | atmospheric conditions |
| whether | if it happens that; in case; if |

Although meteorologists are *weather* specialists, even they can't predict *whether* a hurricane will change course.

Fill in the blanks: I didn't know _____ to wear long pants or shorts because the _____ kept changing so suddenly.

| whose | belonging to whom |
| who's | contraction of "who is" and "who has" |

"*Who's* the patient *whose* filling fell out?" the dentist's assistant asked.

Fill in the blanks: _____ the salesperson _____ customers are always complaining about his high-pressure tactics?

| your | belonging to you |
| you're | contraction of "you are" |

You're making a fool of yourself; *your* Elvis imitation isn't funny.

Fill in the blanks: If _____ having trouble filling out _____ tax return, why don't you call the IRS's toll-free hot line?

Other Words Frequently Confused

Not all frequently confused words are homonyms. Here is a list of other words that people often confuse. Complete the activities for each set of words. Check off and study the words that give you trouble.

a, an   Both *a* and *an* are used before other words to mean, approximately, "one."

Generally you should use *an* before words starting with a vowel (*a, e, i, o, u*) or a vowel sound:

> an orange   an umbrella   an indication   an ape   an effort
> an hour   an Xray

Generally you should use *a* before words starting with a consonant (all other letters) or a consonant sound:

> a genius   a movie   a speech   a study   a typewriter
> a unique   a useless

Fill in the blanks: Mrs. Surface's classroom had _____ old, comfy couch and _____ plush easy chair for the students to enjoy while reading.

accept   (ăk sĕpt′)   to receive; agree to
except   (ĭk sĕpt′)   excluding; but

> It was easy to *accept* the book's plot, *except* for one unlikely coincidence at the very end.

Fill in the blanks: Ved would _____ the position, _____ that it would add twenty minutes to his daily commute.

advice   (ăd vīs′)   noun meaning "an opinion"
advise   (ăd vīz′)   verb meaning "to counsel, to give advice"

> I have learned not to take my sister's *advice* on straightening out my life.
>
> A counselor can *advise* you about the courses you'll need next year.

Fill in the blanks: The professor often liked to _____ his students, but they didn't always welcome his _____.

affect   (uh fĕkt′)   verb meaning "to influence"
effect   (ĭ fĕkt′)   verb meaning "to cause something"; noun meaning "result"

> The bad weather will definitely *affect* the outcome of the election.
>
> If we can *effect* a change in George's attitude, he may do better in his courses.
>
> One *effect* of the strike will be dwindling supplies in the supermarkets.

Fill in the blanks: People who diet often have the side _____ of hunger, which can _____ their moods.

among   implies three or more

between   implies only two

> After the team of surgeons consulted *among* themselves, they decided that the bullet was lodged *between* two of the patient's ribs.

Fill in the blanks: _____ halves, one enthusiastic fan stood up _____ the crowd of equally fanatic spectators and took off his coat and shirt.

beside   along the side of

besides   in addition to

> *Besides* doing daily inventories, I have to stand *beside* the cashier whenever the store gets crowded.

Fill in the blanks: _____ my glass of water and book, I always place my glasses on the table _____ my bed.

fewer   used with things that can be counted

less   refers to amount, value, or degree

> I've taken *fewer* classes this semester, so I hope to have *less* trouble finding time to study.

Fill in the blanks: Since I am working _____ hours, I am making _____ money than I used to.

former   refers to the first of two items named

latter   refers to the second of two items named

> Sue yelled at her sons, Greg and John, when she got home; the *former* (Greg) had left the refrigerator open and the *latter* (John) had left wet towels all over the bathroom.

Fill in the blanks: Eddy collects coupons and parking tickets; the _____ saves him money and the _____ is going to cost him a great deal of money someday.

learn   to gain knowledge

teach   to give knowledge

> I can't *learn* a new skill unless someone with lots of patience *teaches* me.

Fill in the blanks: My philosophy professor likes to _____ about the great philosophers of the past, and I have enjoyed this opportunity to _____ about the brilliant minds behind my favorite theories.

| loose | (lo͞os) | not fastened; not tight-fitting |
| lose | (lo͞oz) | to misplace; fail to win |

In this strong wind, the house may *lose* some of its *loose* roof shingles.

Fill in the blanks: The _____ screw caused us to _____ a wheel on our garden wagon, thus making our vegetables spill all over the yard.

| quiet | (kwī′ ĭt) | peaceful |
| quite | (kwīt) | entirely; really; rather |

Jennifer seems *quiet* and demure, but she has *quite* a temper at times.

Fill in the blanks: I am _____ certain that _____, relaxing mornings are the perfect way to start a day.

ACTIVITY 1

These sentences check your understanding of *its, it's; there, their, they're; to, too, two;* and *your, you're.* Underline the two incorrect spellings in each sentence. Then spell the words correctly in the spaces provided.

_____   1. "Its not a very good idea," yelled Alexandra's boss, "to tell

_____   you're customer that the striped dress she plans to buy makes

                her look like a pregnant tiger."

_____   2. You're long skirt got stuck in the car door, and now its

_____   sweeping the highway.

_____   3. When your young, their is a tendency to confuse a crush with

_____   true love.

_____   4. After too hours of typing, Lin was to tired to type any

_____   longer.

_____   5. In its' long history, the island of Sicily has been a colony of

_____   Greece, a Norman kingdom, and an Arab emirate; today its

                part of the Republic of Italy.

_____   6. The vampires bought a knife sharpener in order too sharpen

_____   there teeth.

_____   7. Your never alone if your loved ones are in you're

_____   heart.

_____ 8. When the children get to quiet, Clare knows their getting

_____   into trouble.

_____ 9. There friendship developed into love as the years passed, and

_____   now, in midlife, their newlyweds.

_____ 10. It is to far to swim too Nantucket Island—the Massachusetts

_____   mainland is twenty-five miles away.

REVIEW TEST 1

Read the following paragraph to find the twelve incorrectly used words. Draw a line through those words. In the space between the lines, write the correct word.

Academic

    Woodrow Wilson served as the twenty-eighth president of the United States from 1913–1921. President Wilson earned his doctorate at Johns Hopkins University and then began a academic career. In 1902, he became the president of Princeton University. In 1910, he ran for governor of New Jersey, and, in 1912, was nominated as the Democratic candidate in the presidential race. The race of 1912 was very important because three candidates with very different ideologies ran against each other. Wilson's policy stood for the principals of individualism and states' writes with a platform called the Knew Freedom. The incumbent, President Taft, was the conservative Republican candidate who represented big business. Theodore Roosevelt was the Bull Moose Party (Progressive) candidate, representing the reform-minded majority of America. Even though Wilson received only 42 percent of the popular vote, he won the electoral vote too become president. While in office, he managed to get the Federal Reserve Act past and established the Federal Trade Commission. He was able two win a second election in 1916 with the slogan, "He kept us out of war." However, in 1917, he had to ask Congress for a declaration of war. America than entered World War I. In 1918, the Treaty of Versailles was signed by the League of Nations; the affect of this treaty was an end to the war and a tentative worldwide piece. Congress wouldn't except Wilson's support of the treaty and would not agree to sign the treaty. This greatly devastated President Wilson. As he campaigned to gain public support for the United States to enter into agreement with the League of Nations, he suffered a massive stroke. President Wilson was cared for by his second wife and died a quite death in 1924.

REVIEW TEST 2

On separate paper, write short sentences using the ten words shown below.

1. accept
2. its
3. you're
4. too
5. then
6. course
7. their
8. passed
9. fewer
10. all ready

Effective Word Choice

This chapter will give you practice in avoiding slang, clichés, and pretentious words.

Key Terms

cliché: an expression that has been worn out through constant use. Example: *short but sweet*

pretentious language: artificial or stilted expressions that more often obscure meaning than communicate it clearly. Example: *It was a splendid opportunity to obtain some slumber* could be more simply expressed as *It was a good chance to get some sleep.*

slang: nonstandard language particular to a time and often to a specific locale; acceptable in everyday speech, slang should be avoided in formal contexts and, with few exceptions, in writing. Example: *I'm going to have to sweat it out for the next couple of days until the test results are posted* would be more appropriately expressed as *I'm going to have to wait anxiously for the next couple of days until the test results are posted.*

Choose your words carefully when you write. Always take the time to think about your word choices rather than simply use the first word that comes to mind. You want to develop the habit of selecting words that are precise and appropriate for your purpose. One way you can show sensitivity to language is by avoiding slang, clichés, and pretentious words.

Slang

We often use slang expressions when we talk because they are so vivid and colorful. However, slang is usually out of place in formal writing. Here are some examples of slang:

Someone *ripped off* Ken's new Adidas running shoes from his locker.

After the game, we *stuffed our faces* at the diner.

I finally told my parents to *get off my case.*

The movie really *grossed me out.*

Slang expressions have a number of drawbacks. They go out of date quickly, they become tiresome if used excessively in writing, and they may communicate clearly to some readers but not to others. Also, the use of slang can be an evasion of the specific details that are often needed to make one's meaning clear in writing. For example, in "The movie really grossed me out," the writer has not provided the specific details about the movie necessary for us to clearly understand the statement. Was it acting, special effects, or violent scenes that the writer found so disgusting? In general, then, you should avoid slang in your writing. If you are in doubt about whether an expression is slang, it may help to check a recently published hardbound or an electronic dictionary.

ACTIVITY 1   Rewrite the following sentences, replacing the italicized slang words with more formal ones.

EXAMPLE

When we told the neighbors to *can the noise,* they *freaked out.*
When we told the neighbors to be quiet, they got upset.

1. When our car *died,* the *cops* were very *cool;* they called a tow truck, which got there *in a flash.*

   _____

   _____

   _____

2. I was *like really freaked out* when I saw the *'rents* dancing to rock music at my cousin's anniversary *bash.*

   _____

   _____

   _____

3. Theo was so *wiped out* after his workout at the gym that he couldn't *get it together* to defrost a frozen dinner.

   _____

   _____

   _____

4. When Rick tried to *put the moves on* Lola at the school party, she told him to *shove off.*

_____

_____

_____

5. The entire town was *psyched* that the corrupt mayor *got busted.*

_____

_____

_____

Clichés

A *cliché* is an expression that has been worn out through constant use. Here are some typical clichés:

short but sweet	at a loss for words
drop in the bucket	taking a big chance
had a hard time of it	took a turn for the worse
word to the wise	singing the blues
it dawned on me	in the nick of time
sigh of relief	too close for comfort
too little, too late	saw the light
last but not least	easier said than done
work like a dog	on top of the world
all work and no play	time and time again
it goes without saying	make ends meet

Clichés are common in speech but make your writing seem tired and stale. Also, they are often an evasion of the specific details that you must work to provide in your writing. You should, then, avoid clichés and try to express your meaning in fresh, original ways.

ACTIVITY 2

Underline the cliché in each of the following sentences. Then substitute specific, fresh words for the trite expression. Partner with a classmate and go over your answers together.

EXAMPLE

My boyfriend has stuck with me <u>through thick and thin.</u>

through good times and bad.

1. As the only girl in an otherwise all-boy family, I got away with murder.

   _____

2. I was on top of the world when the doctor told me I was as healthy as a horse.

   _____

3. My suggestion is just a shot in the dark, but it's better than nothing.

   _____

4. Janice got more than she bargained for when she offered to help Larry with his math homework.

   _____

5. A stone's throw from the Colosseum in Rome are some restaurants, where the food is as good as it gets.

   _____

6. On a hot, sticky midsummer day, iced tea or any frosty drink really hits the spot.

   _____

7. Nadia thanks her lucky stars that she was born with brains, beauty, and humility.

   _____

8. Anything that involves mathematical ability has always been right up my alley.

   _____

9. The Montessori system of education is old hat now but, when it came upon the scene, it raised a few eyebrows.

   _____

10. Even when we are up to our eyeballs in work, our boss wonders if we have enough to do.

    _____

Write a short paragraph describing the kind of day you had. Try to put as many clichés as possible into it. For example, "I got up at the crack of dawn, ready to take on the world. I grabbed a bite to eat. . . ." By making yourself aware of clichés in this way, you should lessen the chance that they will appear in your writing.

ACTIVITY 3

Pretentious Words

Some people feel that they can improve their writing by using fancy, elevated words rather than simple, natural words. They use artificial, stilted language that more often obscures their meaning than communicates it clearly. This frequently occurs when students attempt to use a dictionary or thesaurus, but just pick words at random to replace the simpler words. Using college-level vocabulary is a way to improve your writing, but you must be careful in choosing words. Not only can certain choices sound artificial, but another problem may arise when words are chosen without enough thought. Since many words can act as nouns, verbs, adjectives, and adverbs, using the wrong part of speech often leads to obscured meaning.

Here are some unnatural-sounding sentences:

It was a marvelous gamble to procure some slumber.

We relished the delectable noon-hour repast.

The officer apprehended the imbibed operator of the vehicle.

The female had an affectionate spot in her heart for domesticated canines.

The same thoughts can be expressed more clearly and effectively by using plain, natural language, as below:

It was an excellent chance to get some sleep.

We enjoyed the delicious lunch.

The officer arrested the drunk driver.

The woman had a warm spot in her heart for dogs.

Here are some other inflated words and simpler words that could replace them:

Inflated Words	Simpler Words
amplitude	fullness or abundance
terminate	finalize or finish
delineate	describe or explain
facilitate	assist or help
moribund	dying or wasting away

continued

Inflated Words	Simpler Words
manifested	established or shown
to endeavor	to attempt or to try
habituated	accustomed or familiar

ACTIVITY 4

Cross out the inflated words in each sentence. Then substitute clear, simple language for the inflated words.

EXAMPLE

The ~~conflagration~~ was ~~initiated~~ by an arsonist.

... fire was started by an arsonist.

1. Rico and his brother do not interrelate in a harmonious manner.

     _____

2. The meaning of the movie's conclusion eluded my comprehension.

     _____

3. The departmental conference will commence promptly at two o'clock.

     _____

4. Utilization of the left lane is proscribed except for buses.

     _____

5. When my writing implement malfunctioned, I asked the professor for another.

     _____

REVIEW TEST 1

Certain words are italicized in the following paragraph. These words are either clichés, slang, or inflated. In the space between the lines, replace the italicized words with more effective diction. In a few cases, the italicized words are not needed at all. Simply cross those words out.

Immigration in the United States has some costs and risks, but it can be *strategically advantageous* for the country *time and time again*. Many people fear or resent *persons who have emigrated from foreign lands,* afraid that they may be bringing in drugs, planning terrorist acts, or simply *purloining* jobs from American citizens. Thinking about immigrants within these *nullifying* terms ignores all the *indisputably wonderful augmentations* that immigrants have made to our country. In fact, it is often said that this country wouldn't exist if it weren't for immigrants. Over the many past decades, millions of average citizens, as well as some of our most influential residents, have immigrated to the United States. Henry Kissinger, fifty-sixth Secretary of State and 1973 Nobel Peace Prize winner, was born in Germany and immigrated in 1938 when he was fifteen. Ang Lee, writer and director, was born in Taiwan, moved to the United States, *and got his act together* to study at the University of Illinois at Urbana-Champaign and to complete his Master's degree in Film Production at New York University. Without immigration, people like Albert Einstein, Madeline Albright, and I.M. Pei wouldn't have had *the golden opportunities that come once in a lifetime* to affect American society as they did. Without immigration, American palates would not know *the delectations of the palatableness* of salsa, foie gras, paprika-based dishes, or pizza. Without immigration about 25 percent of American *physicians of medicine* would not be in the United States. Without immigration, the United States of America would not have the history it does. *Last but not least,* when the discussion of immigration comes up, people *should be cognizant that it isn't an either-or issue.*

Editing Tests

This chapter will give you practice in editing, or revising, to correct sentence-skills mistakes.

Key Terms

editing: revising to correct sentence-skills mistakes.

proofreading: carefully examining written text to correct typographical mistakes and other related errors.

proofreading symbols: shorthand notations intended to call attention to typographical mistakes and other related errors.

The ten editing tests in this chapter will give you practice in revising to correct sentence-skills mistakes. Remember that if you don't edit carefully, you run the risk of sabotaging much of the work you have put into a paper. If readers see too many surface flaws, they may assume that you don't place much value on what you have to say, and they may not give your ideas a fair hearing. Revising to eliminate sentence-skills errors is a basic part of clear, effective writing.

In five of the tests, the spots where errors occur have been underlined; your job is to identify and correct each error. In the other five tests, you must locate as well as identify and correct the errors.

EDITING HINTS

1. Have at hand two essential tools: a good dictionary and a sentence-skills handbook (you can use Chapter 5 and Part Four of this book).

2. Use a sheet of paper to cover your essay so that you will expose only one sentence at a time. Look for errors in grammar, spelling, and typing. It may help to read each sentence out loud. If a sentence does not read clearly and smoothly, chances are something is wrong.

3. Pay special attention to the kinds of errors you tend to make. For example, if you tend to write run-ons or fragments, be especially on the lookout for those errors.

4. Proofreading symbols that may be of particular help are the following:

_e_	omit	draw two ~~two~~ conclusions _e_	
^	insert missing letter or word	achíeve	
cap, lc	add a capital (or a lowercase) letter	My <u>e</u>nglish Ȼlass (lc)	

EDITING TEST 1

In the spaces at the bottom, write the numbers of the eight word groups that contain fragments or run-ons. Then, in the spaces between the lines and in the margin, edit by making necessary corrections.

Academic

[1] Filming a television show is much more difficult than many viewers know. [2] On screen, viewers may see one or two hosts, but behind the scenes, dozens of people are working hard to create the show. [3] The person with the money behind the show is the executive producer. [4] Whose role is to oversee the work of the producer. [5] The producer, on the other hand, coordinates and supervises all aspects of the production. [6] Production assistants perform various tasks. [7] Like office work, cleaning up, organizing people, and doing whatever the producer needs. [8] The best boy is the primary electrician on

continued

the crew, he or she coordinates all the lighting technicians, the logistics,
organizes the equipment, and keeps track of the paperwork. [9]The lighting
supervisor works with the script and the lighting department to set up the
studio's lighting for overall design. [10]As the title implies, the camera operator
operates the camera. [11]But not alone as he or she is often aided by several
camera assistants. [12]The director is the person responsible for getting the
script to the screen. [13]And getting the actors to perfect their roles. [14]The film
editor actually assembles all the footage he or she then organizes it into
the final product. [15]Researchers do a variety of jobs like checking facts,
developing ideas, and checking for possible legal issues. [16]Script supervisors
sit on set and observe every shot closely they take detailed notes on the script
to help ensure that the final production has verbal and visual continuity. [17]These
are but a few of the many jobs that intertwine to produce the comedies, news
shows, and dramas that people enjoy. [18]Watching on their televisions.

1. _____   3. _____   5. _____   7. _____

2. _____   4. _____   6. _____   8. _____

EDITING TEST 2

Identify the ten sentence-skills mistakes at the underlined spots in the student
paper that follows. From the box below, choose the letter that describes each
mistake and write that letter in the space provided. (The same kind of mistake
may appear more than once.) Then, in the spaces between the lines, edit and correct each mistake.

a. fragment
b. run-on
c. inconsistent verb tense
d. dangling modifier
e. missing comma
f. spelling mistake

George Washington was a land <u>surveyor during</u> the French and Indian
1

Wars, he led the Virginia militia. Twenty years later, when the American

Revolution <u>broke out. Washington</u> commanded the Continental armies. In
2

1776, <u>after blockading Boston,</u> the city was taken from the British. Later,
3

however, Washington yielded New York City to the <u>enemy, he</u> retreated
4

to Pennsylvania. In December, he boosted the sagging morale of

<u>his men crossing</u> the Delaware River on Christmas night he <u>attacks</u> Trenton,
5   6

where Hessians (British allies) were <u>stationed. Then</u> went on to <u>defeet</u> a
7   8

British army at Princeton. In 1777–1788, the army spent a miserable

winter at <u>Valley Forge Pennsylvania.</u> Later, however, it defeated the British
9

at Monmouth, New Jersey. This battle marked a turning point. In 1781, by

winning the battle of <u>Yorktown Washington</u> brought the war to an end.
10

1. _____   3. _____   5. _____   7. _____   9. _____
2. _____   4. _____   6. _____   8. _____   10. _____

EDITING TEST 3

Identify the ten sentence-skills mistakes at the underlined spots in the student paper
that follows. From the box below, choose the letter that describes each mistake and
write that letter in the space provided. (The same kind of mistake may appear more
than once.) Then, in the spaces between the lines, edit and correct each mistake.

a. run-on	d. wordiness
b. mistake in subject-verb agreement	e. cliché
c. faulty parallelism	f. fragment

It is this writer's opinion that taking care of the environment is not a
                    ‾‾‾‾‾‾‾‾‾‾‾‾‾‾‾‾‾‾‾‾‾‾‾‾‾‾‾‾‾‾
                                1
political issue, but an ethical issue. The environment is not simply pretty

mountains, fields of wild grass, and glacial ice; it is the air we breathe,

the drinking water, and the food we eat. Our air is more polluted than it were
‾‾‾‾‾‾‾‾‾‾‾‾‾‾‾‾   ‾‾‾‾
        2   3
one hundred years ago. We have added cars, factories, and refineries to

the world. It goes without saying that as we have built up cities, we have cut
          ‾‾‾‾‾‾‾‾‾‾‾‾‾‾‾‾‾‾‾
                   4
down trees. Thereby upsetting the earth's natural balance. The water we drink
          ‾‾‾‾‾‾‾
             5
is not only at risk of being overly polluted as more and more people need
                                ‾‾‾‾‾‾‾‾‾
                                    6
water, it is also becoming a rare resource. Too many people waste water

as they unnecessarily leave faucets running and water lawns too frequently.

Another threat to healthy drinking water is the run-off from all the fertilizers and

pesticides that people are using on lawns, gardens, and farms. The polluted

air, polluted water, and overcrowded world are all also affecting the food we
                                           ‾‾‾
                                            7
eat. Not only is it going to be increasingly difficult to produce the amount of

food needed to feed the world, the quality of food is also becoming poorer. If
                        ‾‾‾‾‾
                          8
humans doesn't start taking better care of the environment soon, it will be too
      ‾‾‾‾‾‾‾‾‾‾‾‾‾‾   ‾‾‾‾‾‾
             9
little too late.
‾‾‾‾‾‾‾‾‾‾‾
   10

1. _____   3. _____   5. _____   7. _____   9. _____
2. _____   4. _____   6. _____   8. _____   10. _____

EDITING TEST 4

Identify the eight sentence-skills mistakes at the underlined spots in the student
paper that follows. From the box below, choose the letter that describes each mistake
and write that letter in the space provided. (The same kind of mistake may appear
more than once.) Then in the spaces between the lines, edit and correct each mistake.

a. fragment	e. dangling modifier
b. run-on	f. missing comma
c. mistake in pronoun-antecedent agreement	g. wordiness
d. misplaced modifier	h. cliché

Academic

Anyone who doubts the possibility of <u>falling in love at first sight</u> without
                                                    1
meeting in person should reconsider <u>their</u> beliefs. John G. Neihardt and
                                        2
his wife, Mona Martinson, fell in love through the magic of letters. Mona,

a sculptor who studied with Auguste Rodin, first heard of Neihardt.

<u>When she read his book of poetry, *A Bundle of Myrhh*.</u> <u>Shortly after reading
                                 3   4
the book,</u> Neihardt received her first letter, and a correspondence between

the two ensued. They finally met six months after the first letter exchange. <u>Their

love had grown, they married the next day.</u> For the next fifty <u>years</u> the couple
                                  5   6
remained faithful to each other. They had four daughters, Enid, Sigurd, Hilda,

and Alice. When Neihardt died, his ashes were mixed and scattered over

the Missouri River <u>with Mona's.</u> <u>Therefore, one could make the observation
                        7   8
that long</u> before e-mail, Match.com, and eHarmony, people were falling

in love by writing letters and getting to know each other without actually

meeting.

1. _____   3. _____   5. _____   7. _____

2. _____   4. _____   6. _____   8. _____

EDITING TEST 5

Identify the ten sentence-skills mistakes at the underlined spots in the paper that follows. From the box below, choose the letter that describes each mistake and write that letter in the space provided. (The same kind of mistake may appear more than once.) Then in the spaces between the lines, edit and correct each mistake.

a. fragment	e. mistake in pronoun point of view
b. run-on	f. spelling error
c. mistake in subject-verb agreement	g. missing comma
d. mistake in verb tense	

Academic

College should be a time to expand horizons by meeting new people, getting exposure to new ideas and becoming a better critical thinker. Meeting
___1___
new people are one of the best parts about college. Many colleges have
___2___
students from around the country, as well as from diffrent countries. For
___3___
example, college students in Texas may meet and perhaps room with students from New York City, Seattle, London, and Tokyo. Getting to know new people is not only exciting because of possible new friendships. But it also
___4___
helps expose you to new ideas. People who grow up in different cultures
___5___
often look at things differently. A student from London will have a very different perspective on European politics from a student who lives in Seattle. Meeting new people however, is not the only way college students get exposed to
___6___
new ideas. Every class that a college student took exposes him or her to
___7___
new ideas. Whether its American Indian Literature or College Algebra 101,
___8___

continued

the professor instructing the class will introduce concepts and methods that

will be new to students. These new ideas, along with new friendships and

relationships, will help students become critical thinkers. With each new

experience, students will need <u>too</u> make decisions and form reactions. Many
9

students think they should know everything when they enter <u>college they</u>
10

should be prepared for all the new people, ideas, and experiences that

await them.

1. _____   3. _____   5. _____   7. _____   9. _____

2. _____   4. _____   6. _____   8. _____   10. _____

EDITING TEST 6

Identify the ten sentence-skills mistakes at the underlined spots in the student paper that follows. From the box below, choose the letter that describes each mistake and write that letter in the space provided. (The same kind of mistake may appear more than once.) Then, in the spaces between the lines, edit and correct each mistake.

a. fragment	e. missing capital letter
b. run-on	f. dangling modifier
c. mistake in subject-verb agreement	g. homonym mistake
	h. missing apostrophe
d. missing comma	i. cliché

At one time doctors believed that diseases generated spontaneously—
1
on their own. Louis Pasteur (1822–95), a french scientist, disproved that.
2
Demonstrating that germs cause many diseases. Pasteur worked like a dog
3   4
to convince doctors to sterilize their instruments and wash their hands

before delivering a baby. Pasteur new this would reduce the chances of
5
infection as a result, it would save the lives of many women who otherwise
6
would have died giving birth. Another of Pasteurs discoveries was a vaccine
7
for rabies. Retarding the progress of the disease, a boy bitten by a rabid dog

was saved. Finally, Pasteur is responsible for a process that stop the growth
8   9
of bacteria in wine and milk, it now bears his name: pasteurization.
10

1. _____   3. _____   5. _____   7. _____   9. _____

2. _____   4. _____   6. _____   8. _____   10. _____

EDITING TEST 7

Locate the ten sentence-skills mistakes in the following passage. The mistakes are listed in the box below. As you locate each mistake, write the number of the word group in the space provided. Then, in the space between the lines, edit and correct each mistake.

---

1   fragment _____

1   run-on _____

1   mistake in verb tense _____

1   nonparallel structure _____

1   dangling modifier _____

1   mistake in pronoun point of
    view _____

1   missing comma after
    introductory material _____

2   missing quotation
    marks _____   _____

1   missing apostrophe _____

---

¹The greatest of my everyday fears is technology. ²Beginning when I couldn't master bike riding and extending to the present day. ³Fear kept me from learning to operate a jigsaw, start an outboard motor, or even using a simple tape recorder. ⁴I almost didn't learn to drive a car. ⁵ At age sixteen, Dad lifted the hood of our Chevy and said, All right, you're going to start learning to drive. ⁶Now, this is the distributor . . . ⁷When my eyes glazed over, he shouted, Well, I'm not going to bother if youre not interested! ⁸Fortunately, the friend who later taught me to drive skipped what goes on under the hood. ⁹My most recent frustration is the digital camera, I would love to take professional-quality pictures, but all the buttons and tiny electronic menus confuse me. ¹⁰As a result, my unused camera is hidden away on a shelf in my closet. ¹¹Just last week, my sister gives me a beautiful digital watch for my birthday. ¹²I may have to put it on the shelf with the camera—the alarm keeps going off, and you can't figure out how to stop it.

EDITING TEST 8

Locate the ten sentence-skills mistakes in the following passage. The mistakes are listed in the box below. As you locate each mistake, write the number of the word group in the space provided. Then, in the space between the lines, edit and correct each mistake.

<table>
<tr><td>2</td><td>fragments _____ _____</td><td>2</td><td>apostrophe mistakes</td></tr>
<tr><td>1</td><td>run-on _____</td><td></td><td>_____ _____</td></tr>
<tr><td>1</td><td>mistake in subject-verb</td><td>3</td><td>missing commas</td></tr>
<tr><td></td><td>agreement _____</td><td></td><td></td></tr>
<tr><td>1</td><td>nonparallel structure _____</td><td></td><td>_____ _____ _____</td></tr>
</table>

¹Most products have little or nothing to do with sex a person would never know that by looking at ads'. ²A television ad for a headache remedy, for example shows the product being useful because it ends a womans throbbing head pain just in time for sex. ³Now she will not say "Not tonight, honey." ⁴Another ad features a detergent that helps a single woman meet a man in a laundry room. ⁵When it comes to products that do relate to sex appeal advertisers often present more obvious sexuality. ⁶A recent magazine ad for women's clothing, for instance, make no reference to the quality of or how comfortable are the company's clothes. ⁷Instead, the ad features a picture of a woman wearing a low-cut sleeveless T-shirt and a very short skirt. ⁸Her eyes are partially covered by semi-wild hair. ⁹And stare seductively at the reader. ¹⁰A recent television ad for perfume goes even further. ¹¹In this ad, a boy not older than twelve reaches out to a beautiful woman. ¹²Sexily dressed in a dark room filled with sensuous music. ¹³With such ads, it is no wonder that young people seem preoccupied with sex.

EDITING TEST 9

Locate the ten sentence-skills mistakes in the following passage. The mistakes are listed in the box below. As you locate each mistake, write the number of the word group in the space provided. Then, in the space between the lines, edit and correct each mistake.

1 fragment _____	2 missing apostrophes
1 run-on _____	_____ _____
1 mistake in subject-verb agreement _____	1 nonparallel structure _____
	1 dangling modifier _____
2 missing commas after introductory material	1 mistake in pronoun point of view _____
_____ _____	

Work

¹Being a waitress is an often underrated job. ²A waitress needs the tact of a diplomat, she must be as organized as a business executive, and the ability of an acrobat. ³Serving as the link between customers and kitchen, the most demanding diners must be satisfied, and the often temperamental kitchen help must be kept tamed. ⁴Both groups tend to blame the waitress whenever anything goes wrong. ⁵Somehow, she is held responsible by the customer for any delay (even if it's the kitchens fault), for an overcooked steak, or for an unavailable dessert. ⁶While the kitchen automatically blames her for the diners who change their orders or return those burned steaks. ⁷In addition she must simultaneously keep straight who ordered what at each table, who is yelling for the check, and whether the new arrivals want cocktails or not. ⁸She must be sure empty tables are cleared, everyone has refills of coffee, and no one is scowling because a request for more rolls are going unheard. ⁹Finally, the waitress must travel a hazardous route between the busy kitchen and the crowded dining room, she has to dodge a diners leg in the aisle or a swinging kitchen door. ¹⁰And you must do this while balancing a tray heaped with steaming platters. ¹¹The hardest task of the waitress, though, is trying to maintain a decent imitation of a smile on her face—most of the time.

EDITING TEST 10

Locate the ten sentence-skills mistakes in the following passage. The mistakes are listed in the box below. As you find each mistake, write the number of the word in the space provided. Then, in the space between the lines, correct each mistake.

2	fragments _____ _____	1	mistake in pronoun point of view _____
1	run-on _____		
1	mistake in verb tense _____	1	mistake in pronoun agreement _____
1	misplaced modifier _____		
2	missing capital letters _____ _____	1	mistake in subject-verb agreement _____

¹The earliest type of paper appeared about five thousand years ago in Egypt it took its name from the papyrus plant. ²The fibers of which were used in its manufacture. ³The kind of paper that you use today probably originated in china in the second century. ⁴However, some historians argue that paper have been invented in that country hundreds of years earlier. ⁵Made of hemp fiber and tree bark, the Arabs brought this new paper to Europe in the fifteenth century via spain. ⁶A country they controlled at the time. ⁷When printing was invented, the manufacture of paper increased greatly. ⁸Today, most paper consist of wood fiber, but they may also contain cotton and other textiles.

ESL Pointers

This chapter will cover rules useful for speakers of English as a second language (ESL).

Incorrect:

The ball was thrown by the boy.

The verb is expressed in the passive voice.

Correct:

The boy threw the ball.

The action is attributed directly to the boy.

Key Terms

active voice: mode of expression in which the subject performs the action expressed by the verb.

count nouns: words that name people, places, things, or ideas that can be counted and made into plurals, such as *teacher, restroom,* and *joke.*

idiomatic: particular to a certain language.

noncount nouns: words that refer to things or ideas that cannot be counted, such as *water, bravery,* and *snow.*

qualifier: a word that expresses the quantity of a noncount noun. Example: *some* water

This section covers rules that most native speakers of English take for granted but that are useful for speakers of English as a second language (ESL).

Articles with Count and Noncount Nouns

Articles are noun markers—they signal that a noun will follow. (A noun is a word used to name something: a person, place, thing, or idea.) The indefinite articles are *a* and *an*. (Use *a* before a word that begins with a consonant sound: **a c**ar, **a p**iano, **a u**niform—the *u* in *uniform* sounds like the consonant *y* plus *u*. Use *an* before a word beginning with a vowel sound: **an e**gg, **an o**ffice, **an h**onor—the *h* in *honor* is silent.) The definite article is *the*. An article may immediately precede a noun: **a** smile, **the** reason. Or it may be separated from the noun by modifiers: **a** slight smile, **the** very best reason.

To know whether to use an article with a noun and which article to use, you must recognize count and noncount nouns.

Count nouns name people, places, things, or ideas that can be counted and made into plurals, such as *teacher, restroom,* and *joke (one teacher, two restrooms, three jokes).*

Noncount nouns refer to things or ideas that cannot be counted, such as *flour, history,* and *truth.* The following box lists and illustrates common types of noncount nouns.

> **TIP**   There are various other noun markers besides articles, including quantity words *(some, several, a lot of)*, numerals *(one, ten, 120)*, demonstrative adjectives *(this, these)*, possessive adjectives *(my, your, our)*, and possessive nouns *(Jaime's, the school's)*.

Common Noncount Nouns

Abstractions and emotions: anger, bravery, health, pride, truth

Activities: baseball, jogging, reading, teaching, travel

Foods: bread, broccoli, chocolate, cheese, flour

Gases and vapors: air, helium, oxygen, smoke, steam

Languages and areas of study: Korean, Spanish, algebra, history, physics

Liquids: blood, gasoline, lemonade, tea, water

Materials that come in bulk form: aluminum, cloth, dust, sand, soap

Natural occurrences: magnetism, moonlight, rain, snow, thunder

Other things that cannot be counted: clothing, furniture, homework, machinery, news, transportation, vocabulary, work

The quantity of a noncount noun can be expressed with a word or words called a **qualifier,** such as *some, a lot of, a unit of,* and so on. (In the following two examples, the qualifiers are shown in *italic* type, and the noncount nouns are shown in **boldface** type.)

Please have *some* **patience.**

We need to buy *two bags of* **flour** today.

Some words can be either count or noncount nouns, depending on whether they refer to one or more individual items or to something in general.

Certain **cheeses** give some people a headache.
(This sentence refers to individual cheeses; *cheese* in this case is a count noun.)
Cheese is made in almost every country where milk is produced.
(This sentence refers to cheese in general; in this case, *cheese* is a non-count noun.)

Using *a* or *an* with Nonspecific Singular Count Nouns

Use *a* or *an* with singular nouns that are nonspecific. A noun is nonspecific when the reader doesn't know its specific identity.

A left-hander faces special challenges with right-handed tools.
(The sentence refers to any left-hander, not a specific one.)

Today, our cat proudly brought **a** baby bird into the house.
(The reader isn't familiar with the bird. This is the first time it is mentioned.)

Using *the* with Specific Nouns

In general, use *the* with all specific nouns—specific singular, plural, and noncount nouns. Certain conditions make a noun specific and therefore require the article *the*.

A noun is specific in the following cases:

• When it has already been mentioned once

Today, our cat proudly brought a baby bird into the house.
Luckily, **the** bird was still alive.
(*The* is used with the second mention of *bird*.)

• When it is identified by a word or phrase in the sentence

The pockets in the boy's pants are often filled with sand and dirt.
(*Pockets* is identified by the words *in the boy's pants*.)

- When its identity is suggested by the general context

  At Willy's Diner last night, **the** service was terrible and **the** food was worse.
  (The reader can conclude that the service and food being discussed were at Willy's Diner.)

- When it is unique

  There will be an eclipse of **the** moon tonight.
  (Earth has only one moon.)

- When it is preceded by a superlative adjective *(best, biggest, wisest)*

  The best way to store broccoli is to refrigerate it in an open plastic bag.

Omitting Articles

Omit articles with nonspecific plurals and noncount nouns. Plurals and noncount nouns are nonspecific when they refer to something in general.

Pockets didn't exist until the end of the 1700s.

Service is as important as **food** to a restaurant's success.

Iris serves her children homemade **lemonade.**

Using *the* with Proper Nouns

Proper nouns name particular people, places, things, or ideas and are always capitalized. Most proper nouns do not require articles; those that do, however, require *the*. Following are general guidelines about when and when not to use *the*.

1. Do not use *the* for most singular proper nouns, including names of the following:

    - *People and animals* (Benjamin Franklin, Fido)

    - *Continents, states, cities, streets, and parks* (North America, Illinois, Chicago, First Avenue, Washington Square)

    - *Most countries* (France, Mexico, Russia)

    - *Individual bodies of water, islands, and mountains* (Lake Erie, Long Island, Mount Everest)

2. Use *the* for the following types of proper nouns:

    - *Plural proper nouns* (the Turners, the United States, the Great Lakes, the Rocky Mountains)

- *Names of large geographic areas, deserts, oceans, seas, and rivers* (the South, the Gobi Desert, the Atlantic Ocean, the Black Sea, the Mississippi River)
- *Names with the format* the _____ of _____ (the Fourth of July, the People's Republic of China, the University of California)

Underline the correct form of the noun in parentheses.

ACTIVITY 1

1. (A library, Library) is a valuable addition to a town.
2. This morning, the mail carrier brought me (a letter, the letter) from my cousin.
3. As I read (a letter, the letter), I began to laugh at what my cousin wrote.
4. The Boy Scouts had to carry a great deal of (equipment, equipments) when they marched out of camp.
5. Every day, Melissa reminds me that (jogging, joggings) can help me keep trim.
6. (Acrobatics, The acrobatics) requires a great deal of motor coordination.
7. The soldiers in battle showed a great deal of (courage, courages).
8. A famous sight in Arizona is (Grand Canyon, the Grand Canyon).
9. My son would like to eat (the spaghetti, spaghetti) at every meal.
10. It is dangerous to stare directly at (the sun, sun).

Underline the correct form of the noun in parentheses.

ACTIVITY 2

1. Last night, I went to (a restaurant, the restaurant) with my best friend.
2. (The restaurant, A restaurant) was a more expensive place than we had expected.
3. Jeremy was told he had been accepted to (the University, University) of Pennsylvania.
4. A newspaper reporter is supposed to write a story with (the honesty, honesty).
5. Armando was honored by (Republic of Italy, the Republic of Italy.)
6. Long-distance runners need lots of (determination, determinations) to succeed.
7. A hurricane crossed (Atlantic Ocean, the Atlantic Ocean) before it hit the United States.
8. (The Chilean, Chilean) sea bass at Emilio's Restaurant is the best I have ever tasted.
9. (Jupiter, The Jupiter) is the largest planet in our solar system.
10. Computers have been programmed to play (the chess, chess) and can now beat most human players.

Subjects and Verbs

Avoiding Repeated Subjects

In English, a particular subject can be used only once in a clause. Don't repeat a subject in the same clause by following a noun with a pronoun.

> Incorrect: The *manager he* asked Dmitri to lock up tonight.
>
> Correct: The **manager** asked Dmitri to lock up tonight.
>
> Correct: **He** asked Dmitri to lock up tonight.

Even when the subject and verb are separated by a long word group, the subject cannot be repeated in the same clause.

> Incorrect: The *girl* who danced with you *she is* my cousin.
>
> Correct: The **girl** who danced with you **is** my cousin.

Including Pronoun Subjects and Linking Verbs

Some languages may omit a pronoun as a subject, but in English, every clause other than a command must have a subject. In a command, the subject *you* is understood: (**You**) Hand in your papers now.

> Incorrect: The Grand Canyon is in Arizona. *Is* 217 miles long.
>
> Correct: The Grand Canyon is in Arizona. **It is** 217 miles long.

Every English clause must also have a verb, even when the meaning of the clause is clear without the verb.

> Incorrect: Angelita's piano teacher very patient.
>
> Correct: Angelita's piano teacher **is** very patient.

Including *There* and *Here* at the Beginning of Clauses

Some English sentences begin with *there* or *here* plus a linking verb (usually a form of *to be: is, are,* and so on). In such sentences, the verb comes before the subject.

> **There are** masks in every culture on Earth.
>
> The subject is the plural noun *masks,* so the plural verb *are* is used.
>
> **Here is** your driver's license.
>
> The subject is the singular noun *license,* so the singular verb *is* is used.

In sentences like those above, remember not to omit *there* or *here*.

> Incorrect: *Are* several chickens in the Bensons' yard.
> Correct: **There are** several chickens in the Bensons' yard.

> ## TIP
> The topic of subjects and verbs is covered more comprehensively in Chapter 23, "Subjects and Verbs," and Chapter 27, "Subject-Verb Agreement."

Not Using the Progressive Tense of Certain Verbs

The progressive tenses are made up of forms of *be* plus the *-ing* form of the main verb. They express actions or conditions still in progress at a particular time.

> George **will be taking** classes this summer.

However, verbs for mental states, the senses, possession, and inclusion are normally not used in the progressive tense.

> Incorrect: All during the movie they *were hearing* whispers behind them.
> Correct: All during the movie they **heard** whispers behind them.
> Incorrect: That box *is containing* a surprise for Pedro.
> Correct: That box **contains** a surprise for Pedro.

Common verbs not generally used in the progressive tense are listed in the following box.

> ### Common Verbs Not Generally Used in the Progressive
>
> *Thoughts, attitudes, and desires:* agree, believe, imagine, know, like, love, prefer, think, understand, want, wish
> *Sense perceptions:* hear, see, smell, taste
> *Appearances:* appear, seem
> *Possession:* belong, have, own, possess
> *Inclusion:* contain, include

Using Only Transitive Verbs for the Passive Voice

Only transitive verbs—verbs that need direct objects to complete their meaning—can have a passive form (one in which the subject receives the action instead of performing it). Intransitive verbs cannot be used in the passive voice.

Incorrect: If you don't fix those brakes, an accident *may be happened*. (*Happen* is an intransitive verb—no object is needed to complete its meaning.)

Correct: If you don't fix those brakes, an accident **may happen.**

If you aren't sure whether a verb is transitive or intransitive, check your dictionary. Transitive verbs are indicated with an abbreviation such as *tr. v.* or *v. t.* Intransitive verbs are indicated with an abbreviation such as *intr. v.* or *v. i.*

Using Gerunds and Infinitives after Verbs

A gerund is the *-ing* form of a verb that is used as a noun: For Walter, **eating** is a daylong activity. An infinitive is *to* and the basic form of the verb (the form in which the verb is listed in the dictionary): **to eat.** The infinitive can function as an adverb, an adjective, or a noun. Some verbs can be followed by only a gerund or only an infinitive; other verbs can be followed by either. Examples are given in the following lists. There are many others; watch for them in your reading.

Verb + gerund (admit + **stealing**)
Verb + preposition + gerund (apologize + for + **yelling**)

Some verbs can be followed by a gerund but not by an infinitive. In many cases, there is a preposition (such as *for, in,* or *of*) between the verb and the gerund. Following are some verbs and verb-preposition combinations that can be followed by gerunds but not by infinitives:

admit	deny	look forward to
apologize for	discuss	postpone
appreciate	dislike	practice
approve of	enjoy	suspect of
avoid	feel like	talk about
be used to	finish	thank for
believe in	insist on	think about

Incorrect: He must *avoid to jog* until his knee heals.

Correct: He must **avoid jogging** until his knee heals.

Incorrect: The instructor *apologized for to be* late to class.

Correct: The instructor **apologized for being** late to class.

Verb + infinitive (agree + to leave)

Following are common verbs that can be followed by an infinitive but not by a gerund:

agree	decide	plan
arrange	have	refuse
claim	manage	wait

Incorrect: The children *want going* to the beach.

Correct: The children **want to go** to the beach.

Verb + noun or pronoun + infinitive (cause + them + to flee)

Below are common verbs that are followed first by a noun or pronoun and then by an infinitive (not a gerund):

cause	force	remind
command	persuade	warn

Incorrect: The coach *persuaded Yasmin studying* harder.

Correct: The coach **persuaded Yasmin to study** harder.

Following are common verbs that can be followed either by an infinitive alone or by a noun or pronoun and an infinitive:

ask	need	want
expect	promise	would like

Dena asked to have a day off next week.

Her boss asked her to work on Saturday.

Verb + gerund or infinitive (begin + packing *or* begin + to pack)

Following are verbs that can be followed by either a gerund or an infinitive:

begin	hate	prefer
continue	love	start

The meaning of each of the above verbs remains the same or almost the same whether a gerund or an infinitive is used.

Faith hates **being** late.

Faith hates **to be** late.

With the verbs below, the gerunds and the infinitives have very different meanings.

forget	remember	stop

Esta **stopped to call** home.
(She interrupted something to call home.)

Esta **stopped calling** home.
(She discontinued calling home.)

> **TIP**   The topic of verbs is covered more comprehensively in Chapter 26, "Regular and Irregular Verbs," Chapter 27, "Subject-Verb Agreement," and Chapter 28, "Additional Information about Verbs."

ACTIVITY 3

Underline the correct form in parentheses.

1. The day was sunny but a little cool. (It was, Was) the perfect day to run a marathon.

2. (Are several art galleries, There are several art galleries) in Florence, Italy.

3. The township committee (plans voting, plans to vote) on the new proposal Tuesday.

4. When I am sad, I feel like (to eat, eating).

5. Some students at my school (they study, study) every day in the library.

6. Many young boys (enjoy to play, enjoy playing) baseball.

7. The trees in California's Redwood Forest (enormous, are enormous).

8. The suitcase (is containing, contains) my clothes for vacation.

9. The conductor (asked me, she asked me) for my ticket.

10. The computer (finished printing, finished to print) my assignment quickly.

ACTIVITY 4

Underline the correct form in parentheses.

1. My grandparents (are, they are) in their nineties.

2. The pizza is two days old. (Is, It is) dry and stale.

3. (Is, There is) no excuse for not seeking tutoring at our college; the learning center is open 18 hours a day.

4. The manager (owns, is owning) two SUVs: a Honda and a Ford.

5. The package will not (be arrived, arrive) until Friday morning.

6. During World War II, (there were, were) many countries that declared their neutrality.

7. Most adults need (to sleep, sleeping) at least seven hours each night.

8. Our new puppy (wants to be chewing, wants to chew) all the furniture in our apartment.

9. On their wedding day, the bride and groom (they seemed, seemed) very happy.

10. Whenever she hears music, Sara feels like (to dance, dancing).

Adjectives

Following the Order of Adjectives in English

Adjectives modify nouns and pronouns. In English, an adjective usually comes directly before the word it describes or after a linking verb (a form of *be* or a "sense" verb such as *look*, *seem*, and *taste*), in which case it modifies the subject. In each of the following two sentences, the adjective is **boldfaced** and the noun it describes is *italicized*.

That is a **false** *story*.

The *story* is **false**.

When more than one adjective modifies the same noun, the adjectives are usually stated in a certain order, though there are often exceptions. Following is the typical order of English adjectives:

Typical Order of Adjectives in a Series

1. **Article or other noun marker:** a, an, the, Lee's, this, three, your

2. **Opinion adjective:** dull, handsome, unfair, useful

3. **Size:** big, huge, little, tiny

4. **Shape:** long, short, round, square

5. **Age:** ancient, medieval, old, new, young

continued

Typical Order of Adjectives in a Series

6. **Color:** blue, green, scarlet, white
7. **Nationality:** Italian, Korean, Mexican, Vietnamese
8. **Religion:** Buddhist, Catholic, Jewish, Muslim
9. **Material:** cardboard, gold, marble, silk
10. **Noun used as an adjective:** house (as in *house call*), tea (as in *tea bag*), wall (as in *wall hanging*)

Here are some examples of the above order:

a long cotton scarf

the beautiful little silver cup

your new lavender evening gown

Ana's sweet Mexican grandmother

In general, use no more than two or three adjectives after the article or another noun marker. Numerous adjectives in a series can be awkward: **the beautiful big new blue cotton** sweater.

Using the Present and Past Participles as Adjectives

The present participle ends in *-ing*. Past participles of regular verbs end in *-ed* or *-d;* a list of the past participles of many common irregular verbs appears on pages 476–478. Both types of participles may be used as adjectives. A participle used as an adjective may precede the word it describes: That was an **exciting** *ball game*. It may also follow a linking verb and describe the subject of the sentence: The *ball game* was **exciting.**

While both present and past participles of a particular verb may be used as adjectives, their meanings differ. Use the present participle to describe whoever or whatever causes a feeling: an **embarrassing** *incident* (the incident is what causes the embarrassment). Use the past participle to describe whoever or whatever experiences the feeling: the **embarrassed** *parents* (the parents are the ones who are embarrassed).

The long day of holiday shopping was **tiring.**

The shoppers were **tired.**

Following are pairs of present and past participles with similar distinctions:

annoying/annoyed   confusing/confused

boring/bored   depressing/depressed

exciting/excited	frightening/frightened
exhausting/exhausted	surprising/surprised
fascinating/fascinated	

> **TIP** The topic of adjectives is covered more comprehensively in Chapter 31, "Adjectives and Adverbs."

Underline the correct form in parentheses.

ACTIVITY 5

1. The Renaissance was an era in which Europeans made (intellectual significant, significant intellectual) advances.
2. The audience became (exciting, excited) when the president was announced.
3. There is a (Thai popular, popular Thai) restaurant near the college I attend.
4. The bride's dress was made of (long white silk, white silk long).
5. After running the marathon, I was (exhausted, exhausting).

Underline the correct form in parentheses.

ACTIVITY 6

1. My mother is an (excellent public, public excellent) speaker.
2. The ancient Maya of Central America built (large stone, stone large) temples that can still be seen today.
3. The bridges of Madison County, Iowa, are well known because they are all (old wooden, wooden old) bridges.
4. The audience found the horror film (frightening, frightened).
5. They moved to a (large yellow, yellow large) house last week.

Prepositions Used for Time and Place

The use of prepositions in English is often idiomatic—a word that means "peculiar to a certain language"—and there are many exceptions to general rules. Therefore, correct preposition use must be learned gradually through experience. Following is a chart showing how three of the most common prepositions are used in some customary references to time and place:

Use of *on, in,* and *at* to Refer to Time and Place

Time

On a specific day: on Monday, on January 1, on your anniversary

In a part of a day: in the morning, in the daytime (but at night)

In a month or a year: in December, in 1776

In a period of time: in an hour, in a few days, in a while

At a specific time: at 10:00 A.M., at midnight, at sunset, at dinnertime

Place

On a surface: on the desk, on the counter, on a ceiling

In a place that is enclosed: in my room, in the office, in the box

At a specific location: at the mall, at his house, at the ballpark

ACTIVITY 7

Underline the correct preposition in parentheses.

1. I found my winter coat (in, at) my closet.

2. The cat liked to sit (on, in) my desk by my computer.

3. My meeting with my professor is (on, at) 3:00 P.M. this Monday.

4. The flour and sugar are (on, in) the cupboard.

5. My favorite show starts at 9:00 P.M. (on, at) Monday evenings.

ACTIVITY 8

Underline the correct preposition in parentheses.

1. Tina's husband always sends her flowers (on, at) her birthday.

2. The patients (at, in) the waiting room at the dentist's office all looked uneasy.

3. Let's meet (on, at) the coffee shop after work.

4. The bank is open (in, on) Thursday evenings, but only until six.

5. The Great Depression began when the stock market crashed (in, at) 1929.

REVIEW TEST 1

Underline the correct form in parentheses.

1. During the storm, I was startled by the loud (thunder, thunders).

2. The people (on, in) my community (are often working, often work) together to keep our streams, rivers, and lakes clean.

3. The ending of the movie was very (surprised, surprising).

4. Many animals that sleep all day are active (at, in) night.

5. (The people, People) in the photograph are my mother's relatives.

6. The city streets were full of (big yellow, yellow big) taxis.

7. Between the end of World War II and the fall of communism, (there were, were) two Germanys.

8. In the West, New Year's Day is celebrated (in, on) January 1.

9. If I were in London right now, I would certainly (consider, consider to) visiting the British Museum.

10. Most (cheese, cheeses) are made from cow's milk, but others are made from the milk of sheep or goats.

REVIEW TEST 2

Underline the correct form in parentheses.

1. (The computers, Computers) have revolutionized our society.

2. (There was, Was) hardly anything left to do after the children cleaned up the kitchen and swept the floor.

3. The credit card company (agreed, agreeing) to refund the fraudulent charges.

4. The Internet connection kept (to disconnect, disconnecting).

5. The car slid down the icy road and stopped (in, at) my front gate.

6. A (huge angry, angry huge) dog attacked my friend.

7. We (planned to buy, planned buying) the concert tickets.

8. (On, In) November, my family always gets together to celebrate Thanksgiving.

9. I had to pay a fine to (the library, library) because my book was overdue.

10. I was so (insulting, insulted) by the comedian's joke that I (was complaining, complained) to the club owner.

Correction Symbols

Here is a list of symbols the instructor may use when marking papers. The numbers in parentheses refer to the pages that explain the skill involved.

Agr	Correct the mistake in agreement of subject and verb (484–489) or pronoun and the word the pronoun refers to (494–499)
Apos	Correct the apostrophe mistake (539–545)
Bal	Balance the parts of the sentence so they have the same (parallel) form (111–112)
Cap	Correct the mistake in capital letters (526–533)
Coh	Revise to improve coherence (84–94, 152–155)
Comma	Add a comma (554–563)
CS	Correct the comma splice (460–472)
DM	Correct the dangling modifier (517–521)
Det	Support or develop the topic more fully by adding details (62–66)
Frag	Attach the fragment to a sentence or make it a sentence (447–459)
Ital	*Italics* (549–550)
lc	Use a lowercase (small) letter rather than a capital (526–533)
MM	Correct the misplaced modifier (513–516)
¶	Indent for a new paragraph
No¶	Do not indent for a new paragraph
Pro	Correct the pronoun mistake (494–499)
Quot	Correct the mistake in quotation marks (546–533)
R-O	Correct the run-on (460–472)
Sp	Correct the spelling error (570–574)
Trans	Supply or improve a transition (87–91)
Verb	Correct the verb or verb form (473–483, 490–493)
Wordy	Omit needless words (121–123)
WW	Replace the word marked with a more accurate one
?	Write the illegible word clearly
/	Eliminate the word, letter, or punctuation mark so slashed
^	Add the omitted word or words
; /: /- /—	Add semicolon (565), colon (564), hyphen (567), or dash (565)
✓	You have something fine or good here: an expression, a detail, an idea

Readings for Writers

PART 5

PREVIEW

Introduction to the Readings

Eighteen Reading Selections

Reading Comprehension Chart

"I spend a great deal of my time thinking about the power of language—the way it can evoke an emotion, a visual image, a complex idea, or a simple truth."
Amy Tan, in "Mother Tongue," 1990

Do you agree with writer Amy Tan (The Joy Luck Club) about the power of language? What are some other ways language can be powerful? Can you think of a student essay in this book, a fellow student's writing, or a professional reading that affected you in such a way? What was it about the writing that made it powerful?

The eighteen reading selections in Part Five will help you find topics for writing. (Note that there are also nine professional essays in Part Two.) These selections deal in various ways with interesting, often thought-provoking concerns or experiences of contemporary life. Subjects of the essays include the shame of poverty; the power of family and self; life goals; practical advice on surviving the first year of college; ways the media influence our attitudes; ways people change society; and the challenges of everyday life. The varied subjects should inspire lively class discussions as well as serious individual thought. The selections should also provide a continuing source of high-interest material for a wide range of writing assignments.

The selections serve another purpose as well. They will help develop reading skills, with direct benefits to you as a writer. One benefit is that, through close reading, you will learn how to recognize the thesis in a selection and to identify and evaluate the supporting material that develops the thesis. In your own writing, you will aim to achieve the same essential structure: an overall thesis followed by detailed, valid support for that thesis. A second benefit is that close reading will also help you explore a selection and its possibilities thoroughly. The more you understand about what is said in a piece, the more ideas and feelings you may have about writing on an assigned topic or a related topic of your own. A third benefit of close reading is that you will become more aware of authors' stylistic devices—for example, their introductions and conclusions, and their ways of presenting and developing a point, their use of transitions, their choice of language to achieve a particular tone. Recognizing these devices in other people's writing will help you enlarge your own range of ideas and writing techniques.

The Format of Each Selection

Each selection begins with a short overview that gives helpful background information as well as a brief idea of the topic of the reading. The selection is followed by three sets of questions:

- First, ten "Reading Comprehension" questions help you measure your understanding of the material. These questions involve several important reading skills: understanding vocabulary in context, recognizing a subject or topic, determining a thesis or main idea, identifying key supporting points, and making inferences. Answering the questions will enable you and your instructor to quickly check your basic understanding of a selection. More significantly, as you move from one selection to the next, you will sharpen your reading skills as well as strengthen your thinking skills—two key factors in making you a better writer.

- Following the comprehension questions are four questions on "Structure and Technique" that focus on aspects of a writer's craft, and four questions on "Critical Reading and Discussion" that involve you in reading carefully and thinking actively about a writer's ideas.

- Finally, several writing assignments accompany each selection. The assignments range from personal narratives to expository and persuasive essays about issues in the world at large. Many assignments provide detailed guidelines on how to proceed, including suggestions for prewriting and appropriate methods of development. When writing your essay responses to the readings, you will have opportunities to apply all the methods of development presented in Part Two of this book.

How to Read Well: Four General Steps

Skillful reading is an important part of becoming a skillful writer. Following is a series of four steps that will make you a better reader—of the selections here and in your reading at large.

1. Concentrate As You Read

To improve your concentration, follow these tips:

- First, read in a place where you can be quiet and alone. Don't choose a spot where there is a TV or stereo on or where friends or family are talking nearby.

- Next, sit upright when you read. If your body is in a completely relaxed position, sprawled across a bed or nestled in an easy chair, your mind is also going to be completely relaxed. The light muscular tension that comes from sitting in a straight chair promotes concentration and keeps your mind ready to work.

- Third, consider using your index finger (or a pen) as a pacer while you read. Lightly underline each line of print with your index finger as you read down a page. Hold your hand slightly above the page and move your finger at a speed that is a little too fast for comfort. This pacing with your index finger, like sitting upright in a chair, creates a slight physical tension that will keep your body and mind focused and alert.

2. Skim Material before You Read It

In skimming, you spend about two minutes rapidly surveying a selection, looking for important points and skipping secondary material. Follow this sequence when skimming:

- Begin by reading the overview that precedes the selection.

- Then study the title of the selection for a few moments. A good title is the shortest possible summary of a selection; it often tells you in several words—or even a single word—just what a selection is about. For example, the title "Shame" suggests that you're going to read about a deeply embarrassing condition or incident in a person's life.

- Next, form a question (or questions) based on the title. For instance, for the selection titled "Shame," you might ask, What exactly is the shame? What caused the shame? What is the result of the shame? Using a title to form questions is often a key to locating a writer's thesis, your next concern in skimming.

- Read the first and last couple of paragraphs in the selection. Very often a writer's thesis, *if* it is directly stated, will appear in one of these places and will relate to the title. For instance, in "What's Wrong with Schools?" the author says in his second paragraph that "many students are turned off because they have little power and responsibility for their own education."

- Finally, look quickly at the rest of the selection for other clues to important points. Are there any subheads you can relate in some way to the title? Are there any words the author has decided to emphasize by setting them off in *italic* or **boldface** type? Are there any major lists of items signaled by words such as *first, second, also, another*, and so on?

3. Read the Selection Straight Through with a Pen in Hand

Read the selection without slowing down or turning back; just aim to understand as much as you can the first time through. Write a check or star beside answers to basic questions you formed from the title and beside other ideas that seem important. Number lists of important points: 1, 2, 3, and so on. Circle words you don't understand. Write question marks in the margins next to passages that are unclear and that you will want to reread.

4. Work with the Material

Go back and reread passages that were not clear the first time through. Look up words that block your understanding of ideas and write their meanings in the margin. Also, reread carefully the areas you identified as most important; doing so will enlarge your understanding of the material. Now that you have a sense of the whole, prepare a short written outline of the selection by answering these questions:

- What is the thesis?
- What key points support the thesis?
- What seem to be other important ideas in the selection?

By working with the material in this way, you will significantly increase your understanding of a selection. Effective reading, just like effective writing, does not happen all at once. Rather, it must be worked on. Often you begin with a general impression of what something means, and then, by working at it, you move to a deeper level of understanding.

How to Answer the Comprehension Questions: Specific Hints

The ten reading comprehension questions that follow each selection involve several important reading skills:

- understanding vocabulary in context
- summarizing the selection in a title
- determining the main idea
- recognizing key supporting details
- making inferences

The following hints will help you apply each of these reading skills:

- *Vocabulary in context*. To decide on the meaning of an unfamiliar word, consider its context. Ask yourself, Are there any clues in the sentence that suggest what this word means?

- *Subject or title*. Remember that the title should accurately describe the entire selection. It should be neither too broad nor too narrow for the material in the selection. It should answer the question "What is this about?" as specifically as possible. Note that you may at times find it easier to answer the title question after the main-idea question.

- *Main idea*. Choose the statement that you think best expresses the main idea—also known as the *central point,* or *thesis*—of the entire selection. Remember that the title will often help you focus on the main idea. Then ask yourself, Does most of the material in the selection support this statement? If you can answer yes, you have found the thesis.

- *Key details*. If you were asked to give a two-minute summary of a selection, the key, or major, details are the ones you would include in that summary. To determine the key details, ask yourself, What are the major supporting points for the thesis?

- *Inferences*. Answer these questions by drawing on the evidence presented in the selection and your own common sense. Ask yourself, What reasonable judgments can I make on the basis of the information in the selection?

On page 763 is a chart on which you can keep track of your performance as you answer the ten comprehension questions for each selection. The chart will help you identify reading skills you need to strengthen.

from Self-Reliance

Ralph Waldo Emerson

PREVIEW

Ralph Waldo Emerson was born on May 25, 1803, in Boston, Massachusetts. He is known as an essayist, poet, and the "philosophical voice of the nineteenth century in America." He graduated from Harvard Divinity School and was ordained as a minister, but resigned after the death of his first wife. After his marriage to his second wife, Emerson settled into a life of reading, writing, and lecturing. He died of pneumonia in 1882. This excerpt from *Self-Reliance* demonstrates Emerson's philosophy of individualism.

1 There is a time in every man's education when he arrives at the conviction that envy is ignorance; that imitation is suicide; that he must take himself for better for worse as his portion; that though the wide universe is full of good, no kernel of nourishing corn can come to him but through his toil bestowed on that plot of ground which is given to him to till. . .

2 Trust thyself: every heart vibrates to that iron string. Accept the place the divine providence has found for you, the society of your contemporaries, the connection of events. Great men have always done so, and confided themselves childlike to the genius of their age, betraying their perception that the absolutely trustworthy was seated at their heart, working through their hands, predominating in all their being. . . .

3 Whoso would be a man, must be a nonconformist. He who would gather immortal palms must not be hindered by the name of goodness, but must explore if it be goodness. Nothing is at last sacred but the integrity of your own mind. Absolve you to yourself, and you shall have the suffrage of the world. I remember an answer which when quite young I was prompted to make to a valued adviser, who was wont to importune me with the dear old doctrines of the church. On my saying, "What have I to do with the sacredness of traditions, if I live wholly from within?" my friend suggested,—"But these impulses maybe from below, not from above." I replied, "They do not seem to me to be such; but if I am the Devil's child, I will live then from the Devil." No law can be sacred to me but that of my nature. Good and

bad are but names very readily transferable to that or this; the only right is what is after my constitution, the only wrong what is against it. . .

What I must do is all that concerns me, not what the people think. This rule, 4 equally arduous in actual and in intellectual life, may serve for the whole distinction between greatness and meanness. It is the harder because you will always find those who think they know what is your duty better than you know it. It is easy in the world to live after the world's opinion; it is easy in solitude to live after our own; but the great man is he who in the midst of the crowd keeps with perfect sweetness the independence of solitude. . .

For nonconformity the world whips you with its displeasure. And therefore a 5 man must know how to estimate a sour face. The by-standers look askance on him in the public street or in the friend's parlor. If this aversion had its origin in contempt and resistance like his own he might well go home with a sad countenance; but the sour faces of the multitude, like their sweet faces, have no deep cause, but are put on and off as the wind blows and a newspaper directs. . .

The other terror that scares us from self-trust is our consistency; a reverence 6 for our past act or word, because the eyes of others have no other data for computing our orbit than our past acts, and we are loath to disappoint them. . .

A foolish consistency is the hobgoblin of little minds, adored by little states- 7 men and philosophers and divines. With consistency a great soul has simply nothing to do. He may as well concern himself with his shadow on the wall. Speak what you think now in hard words, and tomorrow speak what tomorrow thinks in hard words again, though it contradict every thing you said today.—"Ah, so you shall be sure to be misunderstood."—Is it so bad, then, to be misunderstood? Pythagoras was misunderstood, and Socrates, and Jesus, and Luther, and Copernicus, and Galileo, and Newton, and every pure and wise spirit that ever took flesh. To be great is to be misunderstood.

READING COMPREHENSION

1. The word *bestowed* in "through his toil bestowed on that plot of ground" (paragraph 1) means

   a. used or shared

   b. given as a gift

   c. provided with housing

   d. taken

2. The word *predominating* in "working through their hands, predominating in all their being" (paragraph 2) means

   a. to have advantages in numbers

   b. to have insignificance

    c. to exert controlling influence

    d. to dominate

3. The word *absolve* in "Absolve you to yourself" (paragraph 3) means

    a. blame

    b. free from guilt

    c. release from sin

    d. to incriminate

4. Which of the following would be a good alternative title for this selection?

    a. Inconsistency Is Key

    b. Be Understood

    c. Good vs. Bad

    d. Don't Conform

5. Which sentence best expresses the main idea of the selection?

    a. People should trust in themselves and say what they truly believe, regardless of what others think.

    b. People should conform to the standards set by the church and great philosophers.

    c. People should do everything they can to avoid being misunderstood.

    d. People should always act to do good and never do wrong.

6. According to Emerson, what is the main source of greatness in a person?

    a. religion

    b. beauty

    c. a person's individuality

    d. conforming among people

7. Emerson refers to the "integrity of your own mind" (paragraph 3) and defines it within the paragraph. Which of the following is part of his definition?

    a. following the teachings of the church

    b. following the teachings of the Devil

    c. following one's conscience

    d. following the teaching of great philosophers

8. *True or False?* _____ Emerson values traditional wisdom over original thoughts.

9. Emerson calls "foolish consistency" the "hobgoblin of little minds." What does he mean by this?

   a. People need to remain consistent in their beliefs forever.

   b. People should never remain consistent in their beliefs.

   c. People who stay consistent in their beliefs, despite new knowledge, could make mistakes.

   d. People should change their beliefs every time they learn new ideas.

10. According to Emerson's essay, which virtue does society demand the most?

   a. self-reliance

   b. conformity

   c. consistency

   d. truth

STRUCTURE AND TECHNIQUE

1. Emerson begins his second paragraph with "Trust thyself: every heart vibrates to that iron string." What does he mean by this? Why do you think he placed it this early in the essay?

2. Emerson uses several metaphors in his essay. Find one that you identify with and explain your connection.

3. Emerson ends his essay by listing important historical figures who were misunderstood. What is his purpose in ending on such an important note?

4. A title can offer interesting insights into an essay, especially if the title acquires unexpected meanings. Before reading this essay, what did you think the title *Self-Reliance* might refer to? What additional meaning have you gleaned after reading the essay?

CRITICAL READING AND DISCUSSION

1. What does Emerson mean by "envy is ignorance; . . . imitation is suicide"?

2. Emerson states that "the only right is what is after my constitution; the only wrong what is against it." Do you think he means that people can be totally selfish and do whatever they want? Explain your answer.

3. In paragraph 4, Emerson says "it is easy in the world to live after the world's opinion; it is easy in solitude to live after our own." What does he mean by this? What is his purpose in making this statement?

4. What does Emerson say is a consequence of being a nonconformist and why does he feel this consequence shouldn't put you off?

WRITING ASSIGNMENTS

Assignment 1

Respond to Emerson's essay and his central idea that all people have the potential to be great, if they trust themselves. Do you agree or disagree with what he says? Explain your reaction to his ideas.

Assignment 2

Emerson mentions several accomplished men in his essay. Choose one of the men mentioned, research about his life, and then explain how he fits the statement at the end of the essay: "To be great is to be misunderstood." Alternately, choose a person who has lived since Emerson's time who fits the statement and is known for his/her accomplishments.

Assignment 3

The promise of the American Dream prevails, but many people think it is a right, not an earned privilege. Most people who have achieved the American Dream have worked hard and haven't simply waited for someone to hand them the prize. People like Steve Jobs and Bill Gates started out working long hours in their garages, taking risks when necessary (often with dire consequences), and pushed themselves to achieve. Write an essay in which you use the principles laid out in *Self-Reliance* as a guide for achieving the dream. You may want to incorporate examples of people who have demonstrated these principles as extra support.

Three Passions

Bertrand Russell

PREVIEW

Bertrand Russell (1872–1970), a philosopher and mathematician, was a controversial figure on the world stage. He was imprisoned twice, first in 1918 for his outspoken criticism of British involvement in World War I, and again in 1961 for "inciting civil disobedience" while campaigning for nuclear disarmament. His writings on social, political, and educational issues led to his winning the Nobel Prize for Literature in 1950. "Three Passions" is taken from the prologue to his autobiography.

Three passions, simple but overwhelmingly strong, have governed my life: the longing for love, the search for knowledge, and unbearable pity for the suffering of mankind. These passions, like great winds, have blown me hither and thither, in a wayward course, over a deep ocean of anguish, reaching to the very verge of despair. 1

I have sought love, first, because it brings ecstasy—ecstasy so great that I would often have sacrificed all the rest of life for a few hours of this joy. I have sought it, next, because it relieves loneliness—that terrible loneliness in which one shivering consciousness looks over the rim of the world into the cold unfathomable lifeless abyss. I have sought it, finally, because in the union of love I have seen, in a mystic miniature, the prefiguring vision of the heaven that saints and poets have imagined. This is what I sought, and though it might seem too good for human life, this is what—at last—I have found. 2

With equal passion I have sought knowledge. I have wished to understand the hearts of men. I have wished to know why the stars shine. And I have tried to apprehend the Pythagorean power by which number holds sway above the flux. A little of this, but not much, I have achieved. 3

Love and knowledge, so far as they were possible, led upward toward the heavens. But always pity brought me back to earth. Echoes of cries of pain reverberate in my heart. Children in famine, victims tortured by oppressors, helpless old people a hated burden to their sons, and the whole world of loneliness, poverty, and pain make a mockery of what human life should be. I long to alleviate the evil, but I cannot, and I too suffer. 4

This has been my life. I have found it worth living, and would gladly live it again if the chance were offered me. 5

READING COMPREHENSION

1. The word *alleviate* in "I long to alleviate the evil, but I cannot, and I too suffer" means

   a. increase.

   b. tolerate.

   c. enjoy.

   d. relieve.

2. Which of the following would be a good alternative title for this selection?

   a. The Forces Driving Me

   b. The Truth about Love

   c. The Anguish of Life

   d. The Power of Knowledge

3. What sentence best expresses the main idea of the selection?

   a. People's inhumanity to other humans has been a source of great pain in the author's life.

   b. The author wishes he had his life to live over again.

   c. The author sees his life driven by three passions.

   d. The author has found life's struggle to be painful but ultimately rewarding.

4. Russell compares his life's passions to

   a. great winds.

   b. the stars.

   c. a bottomless abyss.

   d. a boundless ocean.

5. Which of the following is *not* a reason that Russell sought love?

   a. It relieves loneliness.

   b. It leads to marriage.

   c. It brings ecstacy.

   d. It provides a glimpse of heaven.

6. *True or False?* _____ Russell believes that he has gained considerable knowledge in life.

7. When Russell uses the metaphor of a "deep ocean" to describe his anguish, he implies that it is

   a. cold.

   b. without life.

    c. almost bottomless.

    d. lacking in color.

8. Russell implies that loneliness, at its core, is

    a. a self-defeating impulse.

    b. impossible to avoid.

    c. a sign of selfishness.

    d. a fear of death.

9. Russell implies that life for him has been

    a. passionately complex.

    b. simpler than he would have imagined.

    c. so troubled that it has increased his faith in God.

    d. more materialistic than he would have wished.

10. We can conclude that the author would agree with which statement?

    a. He regrets that he could not free himself of pity.

    b. Human love is ultimately disappointing.

    c. Heaven is merely a poetic invention.

    d. A loving person naturally wants to relieve the suffering of others.

STRUCTURE AND TECHNIQUE

1. Does this essay follow the frequently used one-three-one essay model of introduction, support, and conclusion? How would you outline the essay?

2. This essay primarily is organized in terms of three causes and their overall effect. What is the effect and what are the causes? The essay can also be seen as an exemplification essay. What examples does the author provide to help the reader understand each of his lifelong passions?

3. What kind of transitional signals—time, space, or addition—does Russell employ in the second paragraph? List the transitions you find there.

4. Russell is a master of the use of metaphorical language. For instance, as has already been seen, he compares his anguish to an "ocean." What other examples of metaphorical language can you find? Why do you think Russell chose to use such imaginative language, rather than write in plainspoken terms?

CRITICAL READING AND DISCUSSION

1. Can you identify one or two passions—or at least strong influences—that have, in Russell's words, governed your life? What examples can you provide of how those passions have affected you?

2. Do you think that many people are influenced by the same passions as Russell: love, knowledge, then pity? Or do you feel that many people spend their lives influenced by other factors? What other passions or influences do people live by, in your experience?

3. Russell writes, "[I]n the union of love I have seen, in a mystic miniature, the prefiguring vision of the heaven that saints and poets have imagined" (paragraph 2). Most people, whether they believe in heaven in a religious sense or not, have a concept of an ideal place of perfect love and harmony. What on earth—perhaps a place, a relationship, an individual, or a situation—comes closest to giving you a "prefiguring vision" of heaven? What is it about that place, person, or thing that seems heavenly to you?

4. Overall, do you find Russell's statement an uplifting or a saddening one? What elements of each do you find within it? What makes one element outweigh the other, in your mind?

WRITING ASSIGNMENTS

Assignment 1

Write an essay in which you identify three passions that have strongly influenced your life. Like Russell, explain why each of them has been so important to you, and provide examples of how those passions have played out in your life.

Alternatively, select one particular passion, and write about three areas of your life in which this passion has influenced you.

If you choose the first alternative, your thesis statement might be something like this:

The love of family, a rebellious streak, and affection for the outdoors are three passions that have governed my life.

If you choose the second alternative, this is how your thesis might look:

My rebellious streak has strongly influenced my family life, my performance in school, and my choice of career.

Assignment 2

Write an essay in which you describe three earthly things you've observed or experienced that have given you something like Russell's "prefiguring vision of heaven." In other words, they have given you a sense of something ideal, pure, perfect, and beautiful. Describe your observations or experiences in rich detail so that your reader will understand why you found them so special, and explain what effect they have had on you. Here is a sample thesis for such an essay:

In the faces of my newborn niece, my elderly grandmother, and a seriously ill friend, I have glimpsed something like Russell's "prefiguring vision of heaven."

Assignment 3

Clearly, "love" is a multifaceted emotion. People might say they love their spouses, love their children, love their friends, and love humankind in general, but they mean quite different things in each case. Write an essay in which you divide and classify three types of love. Give detailed examples that illustrate how each type of love is demonstrated.

Shame

Dick Gregory

PREVIEW

In this selection, Dick Gregory—the comedian and social critic—narrates two painful experiences from his boyhood. Although the incidents show graphically what it can be like to grow up black and poor, the essay also deals with universal emotions: shame, embarrassment, and the burning desire to hold on to one's self-respect.

I never learned hate at home, or shame. I had to go to school for that. I was about   1
seven years old when I got my first big lesson. I was in love with a little girl named
Helene Tucker, a light-complexioned little girl with pigtails and nice manners. She
was always clean and she was smart in school. I think I went to school then mostly
to look at her. I brushed my hair and even got me a little old handkerchief. It was
a lady's handkerchief, but I didn't want Helene to see me wipe my nose on my
hand. The pipes were frozen again, there was no water in the house, but I washed
my socks and shirt every night. I'd get a pot, and go over to Mister Ben's grocery
store, and stick my pot down into his soda machine. Scoop out some chopped ice.
By evening the ice melted to water for washing. I got sick a lot that winter because
the fire would go out at night before the clothes were dry. In the morning I'd put
them on, wet or dry, because they were the only clothes I had.

Everybody's got a Helene Tucker, a symbol of everything you want. I loved   2
her for her goodness, her cleanness, her popularity. She'd walk down my street and
my brothers and sisters would yell, "Here comes Helene," and I'd rub my tennis
sneakers on the back of my pants and wish my hair wasn't so nappy and the white
folks' shirt fit me better. I'd run out on the street. If I knew my place and didn't
come too close, she'd wink at me and say hello. That was a good feeling. Sometimes I'd follow her all the way home, and shovel the snow off her walk and try to
make friends with her Momma and her aunts. I'd drop money on her stoop late at

night on my way back from shining shoes in the taverns. And she had a Daddy, and he had a good job. He was a paper hanger.

I guess I would have gotten over Helene by summertime, but something happened 3 in that classroom that made her face hang in front of me for the next twenty-two years. When I played the drums in high school it was for Helene and when I broke track records in college it was for Helene and when I started standing behind microphones and heard applause I wished Helene could hear it, too. It wasn't until I was twenty-nine years old and married and making money that I finally got her out of my system. Helene was sitting in that classroom when I learned to be ashamed of myself.

It was on a Thursday. I was sitting in the back of the room, in a seat with a 4 chalk circle drawn around it. The idiot's seat, the troublemaker's seat.

The teacher thought I was stupid. Couldn't spell, couldn't read, couldn't do 5 arithmetic. Just stupid. Teachers were never interested in finding out that you couldn't concentrate because you were so hungry, because you hadn't had any breakfast. All you could think about was noontime, would it ever come? Maybe you could sneak into the cloakroom and steal a bite of some kid's lunch out of a coat pocket. A bite of something. Paste. You can't really make a meal of paste, or put it on bread for a sandwich, but sometimes I'd scoop a few spoonfuls out of the big paste jar in the back of the room. Pregnant people get strange tastes. I was pregnant with poverty. Pregnant with dirt and pregnant with smells that made people turn away, pregnant with cold and pregnant with shoes that were never bought for me, pregnant with five other people in my bed and no Daddy in the next room, and pregnant with hunger. Paste doesn't taste too bad when you're hungry.

The teacher thought I was a troublemaker. All she saw from the front of the 6 room was a little black boy who squirmed in his idiot's seat and made noises and poked the kids around him. I guess she couldn't see a kid who made noises because he wanted someone to know he was there.

It was on a Thursday, the day before the Negro payday. The eagle always flew 7 on Friday. The teacher was asking each student how much his father would give to the Community Chest. On Friday night, each kid would get the money from his father, and on Monday he would bring it to the school. I decided I was going to buy a Daddy right then. I had money in my pocket from shining shoes and selling papers, and whatever Helene Tucker pledged for her Daddy I was going to top it. And I'd hand the money right in. I wasn't going to wait until Monday to buy me a Daddy.

I was shaking, scared to death. The teacher opened her book and started calling 8 out names alphabetically.

"Helene Tucker?"   9

"My Daddy said he'd give two dollars and fifty cents."   10

"That's very nice, Helene. Very, very nice indeed."   11

That made me feel pretty good. It wouldn't take too much to top that. I had 12 almost three dollars in dimes and quarters in my pocket. I stuck my hand in my pocket and held on to the money, waiting for her to call my name. But the teacher closed her book after she called everybody else in the class.

I stood up and raised my hand.   13

"What is it now?"   14

"You forgot me?"   15

She turned toward the blackboard. "I don't have time to be playing with you, 16
Richard."

"My Daddy said he'd . . . "   17

"Sit down, Richard, you're disturbing the class."   18

"My Daddy said he'd give . . . fifteen dollars."   19

She turned around and looked mad. "We are collecting this money for you and 20
your kind, Richard Gregory. If your Daddy can give fifteen dollars you have no
business being on relief."

"I got it right now, I got it right now, my Daddy gave it to me to turn in today, 21
my Daddy said . . . "

"And furthermore," she said, looking right at me, her nostrils getting big and her 22
lips getting thin and her eyes opening wide, "we know you don't have a Daddy."

Helene Tucker turned around, her eyes full of tears. She felt sorry for me. Then 23
I couldn't see her too well because I was crying, too.

"Sit down, Richard."   24

And I always thought the teacher kind of liked me. She always picked me to 25
wash the blackboard on Friday, after school. That was a big thrill; it made me feel
important. If I didn't wash it, come Monday the school might not function right.

"Where are you going, Richard!"   26

I walked out of school that day, and for a long time I didn't go back very often. 27
There was shame there.

Now there was shame everywhere. It seemed like the whole world had been in- 28
side that classroom, everyone had heard what the teacher had said, everyone had
turned around and felt sorry for me. There was shame in going to the Worthy Boys
Annual Christmas Dinner for you and your kind, because everybody knew what a
worthy boy was. Why couldn't they just call it the Boys Annual Dinner—why'd they
have to give it a name? There was shame in wearing the brown and orange and white
plaid mackinaw[1] the welfare gave to three thousand boys. Why'd it have to be the
same for everybody so when you walked down the street the people could see you
were on relief? It was a nice warm mackinaw and it had a hood, and my Momma beat
me and called me a little rat when she found out I stuffed it in the bottom of a pail full
of garbage way over on Cottage Street. There was shame in running over to Mister
Ben's at the end of the day and asking for his rotten peaches, there was shame in asking Mrs. Simmons for a spoonful of sugar, there was shame in running out to meet the
relief truck. I hated that truck, full of food for you and your kind. I ran into the house
and hid when it came. And then I started to sneak through alleys, to take the long way
home so the people going into White's Eat Shop wouldn't see me. Yeah, the whole
world heard the teacher that day—we all know you don't have a Daddy.

---

[1] *mackinaw:* a short, heavy woolen coat, usually plaid and double-breasted.

It lasted for a while, this kind of numbness. I spent a lot of time feeling sorry **29** for myself. And then one day I met this wino in a restaurant. I'd been out hustling all day, shining shoes, selling newspapers, and I had googobs of money in my pocket. Bought me a bowl of chili for fifteen cents, and a cheeseburger for fifteen cents, and a Pepsi for five cents, and a piece of chocolate cake for ten cents. That was a good meal. I was eating when this old wino came in. I love winos because they never hurt anyone but themselves.

The old wino sat down at the counter and ordered twenty-six cents worth of **30** food. He ate it like he really enjoyed it. When the owner, Mister Williams, asked him to pay the check, the old wino didn't lie or go through his pocket like he suddenly found a hole.

He just said: "Don't have no money."   **31**

The owner yelled: "Why in hell did you come in here and eat my food if you **32** don't have no money? That food cost me money."

Mister Williams jumped over the counter and knocked the wino off his stool **33** and beat him over the head with a pop bottle. Then he stepped back and watched the wino bleed. Then he kicked him. And he kicked him again.

I looked at the wino with blood all over his face and I went over. "Leave him **34** alone, Mister Williams. I'll pay the twenty-six cents."

The wino got up, slowly, pulling himself up to the stool, then up to the counter, **35** holding on for a minute until his legs stopped shaking so bad. He looked at me with pure hate. "Keep your twenty-six cents. You don't have to pay, not now. I just finished paying for it."

He started to walk out, and as he passed me, he reached down and touched **36** my shoulder. "Thanks, sonny, but it's too late now. Why didn't you pay it before?"

I was pretty sick about that. I waited too long to help another man.   **37**

READING COMPREHENSION

1. The words *pregnant with* in "pregnant with poverty" (paragraph 5) mean
   a. full of.
   b. empty of.
   c. sick of.
   d. satisfied with.

2. The word *hustling* in "I'd been out hustling all day" (paragraph 29) means
   a. learning.
   b. stealing.
   c. making friends.
   d. working hard.

3. Which of the following would be a good alternative title for this selection?

    a. Helene Tucker

    b. The Pain of Being Poor

    c. Losing a Father

    d. Mr. Williams and the Wino

4. Which sentence best expresses the main idea of the selection?

    a. Richard felt that being poor was humiliating.

    b. Richard liked Helene Tucker very much.

    c. Richard had to work hard as a child.

    d. The wino refused Richard's money.

5. The teacher disliked Richard because he

    a. was dirty.

    b. liked Helene.

    c. was a troublemaker.

    d. ate paste.

6. *True or False?* _____ Helene Tucker felt sorry for Richard when the teacher embarrassed him.

7. Richard had trouble concentrating and learning in school because he was

    a. poor and hungry.

    b. distracted by Helene.

    c. lonely.

    d. unable to read.

8. Gregory implies that in his youth, he

    a. was not intelligent.

    b. was proud.

    c. had many friends.

    d. and Helene became friends.

9. The author implies that

    a. Mr. Williams felt sorry for the wino.

    b. Richard's teacher was insensitive.

    c. Richard liked people to feel sorry for him.

    d. Richard's father was dead.

10. The author implies that

    a. the mackinaws were poorly made.

    b. Helene was a sensitive girl.

c. Helene disliked Richard.

d. the wino was ashamed of his poverty.

STRUCTURE AND TECHNIQUE

1. In paragraphs 1 and 2, Gregory mentions several steps he took to impress Helene Tucker. What were they? Why does he include them in his essay?

2. A metaphor is a suggested comparison. What metaphor does Gregory use in paragraph 5, and what is its purpose? What metaphor does he use in the second sentence of paragraph 7, and what does it mean?

3. In narrating the incidents in the classroom and in the restaurant, Gregory chooses to provide actual dialogue rather than merely to tell what happened. Why?

4. At the end of the essay, Gregory shifts his focus from the classroom to the scene involving the wino at the restaurant. What is the connection between this closing scene and the rest of the essay?

CRITICAL READING AND DISCUSSION

1. When Gregory writes, "I never learned hate at home, or shame. I had to go to school for that" (paragraph 1), he is using irony—an inconsistency between what is expected and what actually occurs. What does he mean by these two statements? What is the effect of his irony?

2. What are Gregory's feelings about his teacher? What were your feelings about her as you read this essay? What could the teacher have done or said that would *not* have made Gregory feel ashamed?

3. Gregory shows how a childhood incident taught him shame. What other important lessons does Gregory learn in this essay? Explain.

4. At the end of his essay, Gregory says, "I waited too long to help another man." Why do you think he waited so long to assist the wino? What are some reasons people do not always help others who are in need (for example, ignoring a homeless person seated on the sidewalk)?

WRITING ASSIGNMENTS

Assignment 1

Dick Gregory tells us in "Shame" that he was ashamed of his poverty and of being on welfare—to the point that he threw away the warm hooded mackinaw he had been given simply because it was obvious proof that he and his family were on relief. Do you think Gregory was justified in feeling so ashamed of his situation? How about other people who are on welfare? Are they justified if they feel ashamed? Choose either of the following thesis statements and develop it in an essay of several paragraphs:

People on welfare are justified in feeling ashamed.

People on welfare should not feel ashamed.

Then develop your thesis by thinking of several reasons to support the statement you have chosen. You might think along the following lines:

availability of jobs

education or lack of education

number of young children at home requiring care

illness, physical disability

psychological factors—depression, work habits, expectations, mental illness

society's attitude toward people on welfare

Assignment 2

At some time in your life, you probably had an experience like Dick Gregory's in "Shame"—something that happened in a classroom, a group of friends or peers, or a family situation that proved to be both embarrassing and educational. At the time, the experience hurt you very much, but you learned from it. Write a narrative paragraph in which you retell this experience. Try to include vivid details and plenty of conversation so that the incident will come to life.

Assignment 3

Write an essay about three basic things that people must have to feel self-respect. In your thesis statement, name these three necessities and state that a person must possess them to feel self-respect. Here are some ideas to consider:

a certain number of material possessions

a job

a loving family or a special person

a clear conscience

a feeling of belonging

freedom from addictions

In your supporting paragraphs, discuss the factors you have chosen, showing specifically why each is so important. To avoid falling into the trap of writing generalities, you may want to give examples of people who lack these necessities and show how such people lose self-respect. Your examples may be drawn from personal experience, or they may be hypothetical.

I Became Her Target

Roger Wilkins

PREVIEW

Any newcomer in school often has an awkward time breaking the ice with classmates. For Roger Wilkins, being the only black student in his new school made the situation considerably worse. He could easily have become the focus of the other students' prejudice and fear. Instead, help came in the form of a teacher who quickly made it clear how she saw him—as a class member with something to contribute.

My favorite teacher's name was "Deadeye" Bean. Her real name was Dorothy. She 1 taught American history to eighth-graders in the junior high section of Creston, the high school that served the north end of Grand Rapids, Michigan. It was the fall of 1944. Franklin D. Roosevelt was president; American troops were battling their way across France; Joe DiMaggio was still in the service; the Montgomery bus boycott was more than a decade away, and I was a twelve-year-old black new-comer in a school that was otherwise all white.

My mother, who had been a widow in New York, had married my stepfather, 2 a Grand Rapids physician, the year before, and he had bought the best house he could afford for his new family. The problem for our new neighbors was that their neighborhood had previously been pristine[1] (in their terms) and that they were ignorant about black people. The prevailing wisdom in the neighborhood was that we were spoiling it and that we ought to go back where we belonged (or alternatively, ought not intrude where we were not wanted). There was a lot of angry talk among the adults, but nothing much came of it.

But some of the kids, those first few weeks, were quite nasty. They threw 3 stones at me, chased me home when I was on foot and spat on my bike seat when I was in class. For a time, I was a pretty lonely, friendless and sometimes frightened kid. I was just transplanted from Harlem, and here in Grand Rapids, the dominant culture was speaking to me insistently. I can see now that those youngsters were bullying and culturally disadvantaged. I knew then that they were bigoted, but the culture spoke to me more powerfully than my mind and I felt ashamed for being different—a nonstandard person.

---

[1] *pristine:* pure.

I now know that Dorothy Bean understood most of that and deplored it. So 4 things began to change when I walked into her classroom. She was a pleasant-looking single woman, who looked old and wrinkled to me at the time, but who was probably about forty. Whereas my other teachers approached the problem of easing in their new black pupil by ignoring him for the first few weeks, Miss Bean went right at me. On the morning after having read our first assignment, she asked me the first question. I later came to know that in Grand Rapids, she was viewed as a very liberal person who believed, among other things, that Negroes were equal.

I gulped and answered her question and the follow-up. They weren't brilliant 5 answers, but they did establish the facts that I had read the assignment and that I could speak English. Later in the hour, when one of my classmates had bungled an answer, Miss Bean came back to me with a question that required me to clean up the girl's mess and established me as a smart person.

Thus, the teacher began to give me human dimensions, though not perfect ones 6 for an eighth-grader. It was somewhat better to be an incipient[2] teacher's pet than merely a dark presence in the back of the room onto whose silent form my class-mates could fit all the stereotypes they carried in their heads.

A few days later, Miss Bean became the first teacher ever to require me to 7 think. She asked my opinion about something Jefferson had done. In those days, all my opinions were derivative.[3] I was for Roosevelt because my parents were, and I was for the Yankees because my older buddy from Harlem was a Yankee fan. Besides, we didn't have opinions about historical figures like Jefferson. Like our high school building or old Mayor Welch, he just was.

After I had stared at her for a few seconds, she said: "Well, should he have 8 bought Louisiana or not?"

"I guess so," I replied tentatively.   9

"Why?" she asked   10

Why! What kind of question was that, I groused silently. But I ventured an 11 answer. Day after day, she kept doing that to me, and my answers became stronger and more confident. She was the first teacher to give me the sense that thinking was part of education and that I could form opinions that had some value.

Her final service to me came on a day when my mind was wandering and I 12 was idly digging my pencil into the writing surface on the arm of my chair. Miss Bean impulsively threw a hunk of gum eraser at me. By amazing chance, it hit my hand and sent the pencil flying. She gasped, and I crept mortified after my pencil as the class roared. That was the icebreaker. Afterward, kids came up to me to laugh about "Old Deadeye Bean." The incident became a legend, and I, a part of that story, became a person to talk to. So that's how I became just another kid in school and Dorothy Bean became "Old Deadeye."

---

[2] *incipient:* about to become.
[3] *derivative:* not original.

READING COMPREHENSION

1. The word *deplored* in "But some of the kids, those first few weeks, were quite nasty. . . . Dorothy Bean understood most of that and deplored it" (paragraphs 3–4) means
   a. supported.
   b. imitated.
   c. often taught.
   d. disapproved of.

2. The word *groused* in "Why! What kind of question was that, I groused silently" (paragraph 11) means
   a. complained.
   b. agreed.
   c. answered.
   d. yelled.

3. Which of the following would be a good alternative title for this selection?
   a. Education in the Forties
   b. A True Teacher's Pet
   c. Eighth Grade
   d. Teacher's Help

4. Which of the following sentences best expresses the main idea of the selection?
   a. After moving from Harlem to Grand Rapids, Michigan, the author had numerous adjustments to make.
   b. Eighth grade can be a challenging time for a new student.
   c. Using unusual methods, Miss Bean helped her eighth-grade students learn to think for themselves.
   d. A teacher helped the first black student in school to be accepted and to learn to think for himself.

5. After moving to Grand Rapids, Wilkins felt ashamed of
   a. having a stepfather.
   b. being smart.
   c. having lived in Harlem.
   d. being different.

6. By involving Wilkins in class discussion, Miss Bean helped the other students see him as more than a

   a. stereotype.

   b. liberal.

   c. legend.

   d. bigot.

7. Wilkins writes that before entering Miss Bean's class, he held

   a. no opinions.

   b. no original opinions.

   c. opinions based on careful thought.

   d. opinions on various historical figures.

8. The author implies that some of the bigotry in Grand Rapids was the result of

   a. anger about the war.

   b. ignorance about black people.

   c. his youth.

   d. ignorance about physicians.

9. In stating "the teacher began to give me human dimensions, though not perfect ones for an eighth-grader" (paragraph 6), the imperfection that Wilkins refers to is his

   a. different race.

   b. inadequate answers.

   c. becoming a teacher's pet.

   d. coming from another state.

10. We can conclude that Dorothy Bean threw an eraser at the author because she

   a. knew the event would become an icebreaker for him.

   b. wanted to knock the pencil from his hand.

   c. wanted to ask his opinion about something.

   d. wanted him to pay attention in class.

STRUCTURE AND TECHNIQUE

1. Which pattern of development—comparison, narration, or description—does Wilkins use in most of his essay? Explain.

2. Which kind of transition signal—addition, time, or space—does Wilkins use to move his essay smoothly from one event to the next? Find at least four different words that are examples of this signal.

3. In the first paragraph, Wilkins chooses to provide some historical background for his story. Why do you think he chose the specific details mentioned there? What might have been lost if these details had been excluded from the essay?

4. A title can offer interesting insights into an essay, especially if the title acquires unexpected meanings. Before reading this essay, what did you think the title "I Became Her Target" might refer to? What additional meanings do you think Wilkins intended?

CRITICAL READING AND DISCUSSION

1. What does Wilkins mean by the term *nonstandard person* (paragraph 3)? Do you think he later felt more like a "standard" person? Why or why not?

2. Wilkins mentions several ways Miss Bean treated him differently from the way he was treated by the other teachers at Creston. How did her approach differ from theirs? What does this approach reveal about Miss Bean—as a teacher and as a person?

3. Wilkins says that initially he was Miss Bean's "incipient teacher's pet" (paragraph 6). But how did Miss Bean's behavior toward him go beyond mere favoritism? In what way did her treatment of Wilkins affect how his peers regarded him?

4. In paragraph 7, Wilkins says, "Miss Bean became the first teacher ever to require me to think." Before Miss Bean's class, what do you suspect Wilkins—and his classmates—were being taught to do in school? Describe a teacher who gave you "the sense that thinking was part of education." In your opinion, what can teachers do to get students to think?

WRITING ASSIGNMENTS

Assignment 1

Dorothy Bean, Wilkins's favorite teacher, obviously had an important influence on him in more ways than one. She helped him become accepted by the other students, she strengthened his self-image, and she helped him learn to think for himself. Write an essay on one of your favorite teachers and the ways he or she influenced you.

Like Wilkins, dramatize specific incidents to show how this teacher affected you. Provide whatever background is necessary to put the teacher's influence into perspective. Your thesis will be a general statement that summarizes the teacher's impact on your life, such as this one: "Mrs. Croson, my sixth-grade teacher, helped me in ways that strengthened all of the rest of my education." Then go on in your introduction to list three specific ways the teacher influenced you. An example of such a plan of development is "She gave me confidence and taught me the joys of reading and writing."

Alternatively, write an essay on three of your favorite teachers. Your thesis might be about the characteristics the three teachers shared or how they influenced you.

Assignment 2

Wilkins suggests that the students in his new school misjudged him because at first they saw him only as a stereotype, a stranger with no particular personal character-istics. Perhaps we are all subject to prejudging people, if not because of their race, then for another reason. Did a person who made a good impression on you ever turn out to be boring and mean? Did a boss you thought was overly strict ever turn out to be supportive and teach you a lot? Write an essay about someone who was really quite different from what you initially thought he or she would be. You may wish to consider the following characteristics, which often lead people to prejudge each other:

age

gender

race

sexual preference

size

clothing

job

Begin your essay by explaining in vivid detail your first impression and what caused it. Then go on to narrate some experiences you had with the person and how these experiences changed your mind about him or her.

Alternatively, write about an individual or individuals who have prejudged you. Explain what those people thought of you and why, and describe how they treated you. If they came to change their minds, explain why and how your rela-tionship changed.

Assignment 3

Write an essay in which you contrast your best teacher and your worst teacher. Make a list of the qualities that made one teacher excellent and the other ineffective or worse. Focus on three pairs of contrasting qualities, using either a *one-side-at-a-time* or a *point-by-point* method of development (see pages 282–284). Following are some elements of teaching to consider as you plan your essay:

grasp of the subject

ability to communicate

ability to motivate

interest in students

classroom presentation

sense of humor

In addition, consider what you or other students learned or did not learn, such as the following:

subject matter

ways to learn

ways to think

self-confidence

methods of cooperation

Stepping into the Light

Tanya Savory

PREVIEW

What would you do if you were convinced that people would reject, even despise you if they knew who you really were? Would you dare to be yourself and risk their condemnation? Or would you do your best to conform to their expectations? In this selection, Tanya Savory tells how she came to terms with her identity as a gay woman. In doing so, she draws a parallel between fair treatment for gays and the civil rights struggles of her youth.

One night in April when I was barely seven years old, my mother told me to put 1
on my Sunday dress—Dad was taking the family to a church across town. None of
this made sense to me. After all, it was a Thursday, it was nearly bedtime, and our
church was right next door. Dad was the minister, so all we did was walk across a
parking lot to get to church. Why were we going across town?

After what seemed like an endless drive, we were winding slowly through a 2
neighborhood I'd never seen before. Suddenly we were in front of a big wooden
building with no windows. Streams of people were pouring in, all of them quiet
and many of them hugging or holding hands. When our family walked into the
church, many people turned to stare at us for a moment—nearly everyone in the
church was black, and we were white. But then a friend of my father's, a young
black minister, rushed over to greet us and led us to a pew.

Throughout that evening, the tall black woman sitting next to me turned to smile 3
at me again and again even though there were tears in her eyes. I was amazed by her
hat full of flowers and even some bird feathers, so I smiled back. No one wore hats
like that in our church. I gazed at her hat until I became drowsy and drifted in and
out of sleep, occasionally waking up to hear voices joined in song. Many songs were
sung that night that I knew, but at the end of the service everyone joined hands and
sang a slow, moving song that I'd never heard before: *We shall overcome, we shall
overcome, we shall overcome some day. . . .* The tall woman next to me put one arm
around me and lifted the other into the air, tears streaming down her face.

It was April 4th, 1968, and Martin Luther King Jr. had been shot and killed just 4
five hours earlier.

When I was a senior in high school, I sat on the front porch with my dad one 5
warm South Carolina afternoon and asked him about that night.

"Weren't you afraid?" I asked   6

"Afraid? Of what?" my dad asked, giving me a kind of funny look.   7

"Well, you know," I said awkwardly, "afraid of the kind of white people who 8 hate blacks. What if they had found out that we were at that service that night? Weren't you afraid of what they might think or do?"

My dad stared at me for a long moment before he answered. "Your mother 9 and I have never been *afraid* of what bigots think of us. And we certainly weren't going to be bullied into hiding the way we felt just because some racists thought we were wrong."

"Yeah, but when everyone found out, you lost a lot of friends. Even Aunt Jo 10 still doesn't speak to you," I pointed out.

"Not a lot of friends—a few. But that's a small price to pay to be true to your- 11 self. I'm sorry to lose some friends, but I'd be sorrier to be living my life according to how other people think I should live it."

"Really? I asked. "You really think that?"   12

"Yes. I really *know* that," my dad answered.   13

That night I lay awake for hours thinking about what my dad had said. I knew 14 he was right, but I was 100% afraid to be true to myself. I was in a small town in the South in 1978, and I was afraid, very afraid, that I was someone that even open-minded people would despise. Someone who, if I *were* true to myself, would be laughed at, abandoned by my friends, and worse. Someone whose own mother and father might turn against her. I was afraid I was gay.

This was decades before gay characters on TV or in the movies had become 15 commonplace. The words "gay marriage" would only have been heard in a punch line to a joke, and, in fact, most people still believed that homosexuality was a mental illness or a crime. In the town where I grew up, it was illegal to be gay— police used to stake out a little rundown cinderblock bar on the other side of the tracks where, supposedly, gay men gathered. It was not uncommon for the police to rough up and handcuff men they saw coming out of this bar. Then they were thrown in the jail for the night for little or no real reason. Most of the townspeople thought this was a good idea.

Every day in the halls at school, I would wonder and worry if my classmates 16 could tell by looking at me. I pretty much looked and acted like any other seventeen-year-old girl. I passed notes in geometry, wore too much mascara, and worried about what I would wear to the prom in April. And like most of my friends, I had a boyfriend that I loved. But something had begun to creep into my consciousness about a year earlier—something like the slightest pinprick of light that had grown just a bit brighter every day until I was sure that everyone could see it like a spotlight on me: I didn't love my boyfriend, Mark, the same way I loved my best friend, Karla. I loved her more—I was *in* love with her. Midway through my senior year in high school, I became so afraid and confused about how I felt that I simply made the choice to stop being friends with Karla. The way I saw it, if I turned off the spotlight, no one would be able to see the real me.

In the darkness, it was easier to hide. I made new friends that I didn't really 17 care too much about. I lost interest in anything that was special or unique about me, not wanting to draw attention to who I was. I went entirely overboard in my devotion to Mark, even suggesting that we get married as soon as we graduated from high school. College and my future no longer mattered to me. All that mattered was escaping the light, the fear of who I really was. It didn't matter that I was confused and miserable as long as I was hidden.

Strange as it may sound today, I was actually relieved when, one Sunday morn- 18 ing, I came across a short and angry article in a Christian magazine that insisted that homosexuality was a sin and that it was a choice. Apparently, all one had to do was change his or her mind about who they loved, *choose* to hate that kind of love, and everything would be okay. Supposedly it was as simple as deciding not to rob a bank or choosing not to eat too much pie. Choose heterosexuality and you get heaven. Otherwise, you get hell. I had made the right choice! In a burst of satisfaction, I decided to tell my father everything I had been through and how I had made the right decision. After all, he was a minister. Surely he'd be proud of me.

Thankfully, he was not.   19

"Is your decision based on who you really are or who you want people to think 20 you are?" was my dad's first question.

I was stunned. This was not how I had expected my father to respond at all. 21 No one I knew had ever said anything about it being okay to be gay. In fact, no one ever talked about it at all except to make fun of it. I paused for a long time before answering. Finally, I quietly said, "I'm not sure."

I don't remember what else was said, but my father hugged me. And that was 22 a great turning point, a great source of light in my life.

Decades later, I look back on that year as a strange, murky time full of confu- 23 sion about myself and about the world around me. Luckily, I had parents who, though they worried about how the world around me would treat me, did not try to change me. They never once suggested that there was anything "wrong" with me. But most of the gay people I know who grew up in that same era were not so lucky: One friend tells a story of his seventy-five-year-old grandmother chasing him down the street with a shotgun when she found out he was gay. "She thought I'd be better off dead," he explained. "Luckily, her aim was bad." Another friend describes how her parents changed the locks on the doors, leaving a note that simply read, "Don't come back." Perhaps worst of all was a friend whose own family boycotted his funeral when he died of AIDS.

It's hard to imagine where that kind of hate comes from. What is it about love 24 between two people of the same sex that creates such anger and hostility? Some people, like my friend's seventy-five-year-old grandmother, have an uninformed idea of what gay people are like. They believe all the ridiculous stereotypes that they've read about or seen on TV or in the movies. The stereotypes are frightening to them—and fear is always one step away from hate. To them, gay people are a big group of creepy and weird outcasts full of prissy men who wear dresses and angry women who look like lumberjacks. In reality, of course, gay people are no different from anyone else. We work in the same jobs, eat the same foods, have the same worries, and experience the same joys and sorrows as any other human beings.

Other people, like the parents who locked their daughter out of their house, feel that it is immoral—that it is just plain wrong for two people of the same sex to fall in love. They feel that it is best to just lock it out and hope it goes away. This, in fact, was the same way many people felt about black and white people falling in love years ago. It just seemed wrong and it made people feel uneasy. They didn't want to have to see it or think about it. So until 1948, it was against the law in the United States for interracial couples to marry. But laws designed to keep people from loving one another, and labeling something "immoral" just because it makes some people uncomfortable are always bad ideas. **25**

Still other people, like the family that refused to attend their own son's funeral, claim that God doesn't approve of homosexuality. Like the author of the article I had read so many years ago, they feel it's a sin. There is rarely any argument one can present that can change the minds of people who point to the Bible as their reason for disliking, even hating, gay people. But using religion to justify the way we can mistreat other people, however, is nothing new. In the past, the Bible has been used to justify slavery, segregation, and even denying women the right to vote. As the daughter of a minister, all of this seems strange to me. Like my father, I would like to think that religion is better suited to promoting love—not hate. **26**

Luckily, things are changing. It is definitely not the same dark and mysterious world for a young gay person that it was when I was seventeen. Being gay is actually discussed, and it is no longer considered cool or socially acceptable to make fun of gay people or tell jokes about them. And the majority of Americans say that they think homosexuals should be accepted the same as anyone else. It is no longer unusual to hear about gay actors, singers, athletes, ministers, teachers, firefighters, senators, or even a gay wizard in *Harry Potter*! Even so, there is a long road ahead. In many states it is still legal to fire an employee simply because he or she is gay. And nearly every day there are acts of violence directed at gay people who refuse to hide who they are. **27**

But somewhere in the future, there will certainly come a day when no one has to worry about "coming out" any longer because no one will really care one way or the other about sexual orientation. It will become a non-issue. As it is, gay people rarely spend their time focusing on the fact that they are gay, regardless of how big a deal the media likes to make of a celebrity or politician who has suddenly come out. As talk show host Ellen Degeneres once explained, "I never think about being gay, you know? I'm just living my life . . . I don't wake up every morning and say, 'I'm gay!'" Like any minority, gay people are not looking for special **28** recognition—just fair treatment and the same rights everyone has that make it possible just to live one's life.

Not long ago, I read a story that made me very angry. In a small town in the 29 Midwest, an elderly woman named Sarah had just lost her partner of forty-two years, Laura, to leukemia. As Laura lay dying in the hospital, Sarah pleaded with the hospital staff to allow her to see Laura, but the staff refused—only family was allowed in the rooms of critical patients. That was the law. Laura died alone, and Sarah never got to tell her goodbye.

Within a couple days of Laura's death, Laura's only surviving relative, a 30 nephew who hadn't seen his great-aunt in twenty years, came to claim possession of the home Sarah and Laura had shared for decades. The home was in Laura's name, so now the law said it belonged to the nephew. Additionally, the nephew was happy to be legally entitled to all of the home's possessions and all of the money in his aunt's savings. Sarah was left with nothing—no laws protected her because no laws recognized her relationship with Laura. Legally, Sarah and Laura were no more than strangers to one another. Sarah would spend her remaining years in a rundown facility for penniless elderly people.

And, legally, Sarah could even have been denied the right to attend her part- 31 ner's funeral if the nephew hadn't wanted her there. However, the nephew had no interest in attending the service once he secured the deed to the house.

On a cold April morning, Sarah and a handful of friends gathered at Laura's 32 gravesite. But just as the service began, shouts were heard. Ten members of an anti-gay hate group had gathered across the road from the rural cemetery. Somehow, they had gotten wind of the fact that a gay person was about to be buried. Standing in a line and holding signs with slogans such as "Fags Burn in Hell" and "God Hates Homos," the group shouted cruel and angry comments throughout the funeral service. *Legally,* they had the right to do this.

As I read this story and looked at the pictures of the faces of those holding 33 the signs and yelling, I felt hate. I felt like jumping in my car and driving nonstop to that little town and giving them a dose of their own darkness. I wanted to pay them back for all the despair their kind of hatred brought to gay teens who were, like I had once been, lost and confused. I wanted to spew venom right back at this group.

But then, near the end of the story, a comment by the elderly woman, Sarah, 34 stopped me in my tracks. Reporters, who had crassly rushed to the scene, asked Sarah how she felt about the group picketing across the street. "Well," she had said, "I'm sorry they feel that way. But it won't do no good to hate them back."

And suddenly, Sarah's words were like a light—a light that seemed to shine 35 all the way back to nearly forty years ago. To a night in April amidst a group of mourners who chose to sing and hold hands in response to hate and violence. A group that was certainly angry and weary of being treated unfairly. And surely, somewhere during that evening, the young black minister who had led us to a seat must have reminded the congregation of Dr. King's own words: "Darkness can not drive out darkness; only light can do that. Hate can not drive out hate; only love can do that."

READING COMPREHENSION

1. The word *crassly* in "Reporters, who had crassly rushed to the scene, asked Sarah how she felt about the group picketing across the street" (paragraph 34) means

   a. crudely.

   b. sensitively.

   c. violently.

   d. cleverly.

2. Which of the following would be a good alternative title for this selection?

   a. The Bigots Among Us

   b. An Unusual Church Service

   c. How I Learned to Love Myself—and My Neighbor

   d. Special Rights for Gays

3. Which sentence best expresses the main idea of the selection?

   a. The author had a difficult time growing up in a small town in the South.

   b. Attitudes toward homosexuality have changed over the past several years.

   c. Over time, the author learned to accept her gayness and love her enemies.

   d. Gays have often been the target of cruel and unfair treatment.

4. When Savory read an article in a Christian magazine about being gay, she decided

   a. that the author didn't know what he was talking about.

   b. she had made the right decision in choosing to be heterosexual.

   c. she must keep her homosexuality a secret from everyone.

   d. to reveal that she was a homosexual to her father.

5. According to the article, the majority of Americans

   a. despise homosexuals.

   b. think of gays as a big group of creepy and weird outcasts.

   c. believe in gay marriage.

   d. think homosexuals should be accepted the same as anyone.

6. The hospital staff told Sarah she could not see her partner Laura because
   a. Laura had a highly contagious disease.
   b. Sarah was not a family member.
   c. Sarah was gay.
   d. Laura didn't want any visitors.

7. We can infer that the author would agree that
   a. gay couples should have the same rights as heterosexual couples.
   b. while some people are born gay, others choose to be gay.
   c. it's useless to try to change people's minds about homosexuality.
   d. gay couples should be given special rights.

8. Based on paragraphs 18–22, we can infer that the author's dad
   a. believed that people could choose to be gay or heterosexual.
   b. did not think homosexuality was sinful.
   c. had little to do with his daughter after she came out as a gay woman.
   d. knew a lot of gay people.

9. In telling the story of Sarah and Laura, the author implies that
   a. Sarah should have inherited Laura's home, possessions, and money.
   b. Laura's nephew didn't care about her, just her money.
   c. Sarah is a forgiving person.
   d. all of the above.

10. We can infer that the picketers at the funeral
   a. will some day change their minds about homosexuality.
   b. were basically decent people.
   c. used religion to support their hateful views.
   d. may have been gay themselves.

STRUCTURE AND TECHNIQUE

1. What method of introduction—brief story, stating importance of topic, or broad-to-narrow—does Savory use? Why do you think she chose this way to begin her essay?

2. Which pattern of development—comparison, narration, or description—does Savory use in most of her essay? Explain.

3. A symbol is something that represents something else. In the title and throughout the selection, Savory uses light in a symbolic sense. What does light represent to her? What does the absence of light represent?

4. Savory concludes her essay by going back to where it began—her childhood. In your opinion, is this an effective way to conclude her essay? Why or why not?

CRITICAL READING AND DISCUSSION

1. How does Savory's attitude toward homosexuality change in the course of the selection? What incident marks the turning point in her attitude toward her own sexuality?

2. According to the Christian magazine that Savory read as a youth, people can choose to be heterosexual in the same way that they can decide not to rob a bank or eat too much pie. In your view, is homosexuality a choice or not? Explain.

3. What did Savory feel was so unjust about the story of Sarah and Laura? If you agree with her attitude toward the couple, what steps could be taken to make sure that unfortunate situations like these no longer occur?

4. In paragraph 28, Savory states that there will come a day when no one will really care one way or the other about sexual orientation. Do you agree or disagree with her belief? Explain.

WRITING ASSIGNMENTS

Assignment 1

Clearly, Savory's minister father was an important figure in her life. Not only did he show her that it was important to stand up for one's beliefs and to treat others with respect, but he made it easier for her to accept her own sexuality. Write an essay about a person in your life who has had a positive influence on you. Provide whatever background is necessary to put the person's influence into perspective. Your thesis will be a general statement that summarizes the person's impact on your life, such as this one: "_____ helped me in ways that affected my life." Then go on in your introduction to list three specific ways that person influenced you. An example of such a plan of development is, "He helped me to believe in myself, showed me that it was important to listen to others, and taught me the value of hard work."

Assignment 2

Savory was outraged by the picketers who appeared at Laura's funeral. Although most of us have probably not experienced this level of hatred, we've all seen or heard about situations that have awakened our sense of injustice. Write an essay about three situations you've experienced or learned about that awakened your sense of injustice. In your essay, devote each supporting paragraph to one such anecdote, describing the incident in detail and your response to it. Like Savory, the incident you describe could be something you read about or saw on TV. If you wish, you may suggest ways in which similar incidents might be avoided. Your thesis for the essay might be similar to the following:

In my life, three incidents in particular have awakened my sense of injustice.

Assignment 3

Although, as Savory points out, gay people are now more accepted by society than they once were, the question of gay marriage is still a controversial topic. Write an essay that takes as its thesis one of the following statements:

Gay marriage is an idea whose time has come.

The word *marriage* should apply only to a union between a man and a woman.

Support your thesis with several points, each developed in its own paragraph. Before you begin, you may wish to research arguments for and against gay marriage on the Internet. To access the Internet, use the very helpful search engine Google (www.google.com) and refer to Chapter 21, "Using the Library and the Internet."

A Hanging

George Orwell

PREVIEW

You are about to attend an execution. In this essay George Orwell (author of *Animal Farm* and *1984*) recalls a hanging he witnessed when he was an English police officer stationed in Burma. Orwell's senstivity and vividly descriptive wrting will make you see and feel what it is like to take the seemingly endless walk from cell to gallows. You will share the guards' uneasiness and the prisoner's terror. And after you finish the selection, you may also share Orwell's views on capital punishment.

It was in Burma, a sodden morning of the rains. A sickly light, like yellow tinfoil, 1 was slanting over the high walls into the jail yard. We were waiting outside the condemned cells, a row of sheds fronted with double bars, like small animal cages. Each cell measured about ten feet by ten and was quite bare within except for a plank bed and a pot of drinking water. In some of them brown silent men were squatting at the inner bars, with their blankets draped round them. These were the condemned men, due to be hanged within the next week or two.

One prisoner had been brought out of his cell. He was a Hindu, a puny wisp 2 of a man, with a shaven head and vague liquid eyes. He had a thick, sprouting moustache, absurdly too big for his body, rather like the moustache of a comic man on the films. Six tall Indian warders were guarding him and getting him ready for the gallows. Two of them stood by with rifles with fixed bayonets, while the others handcuffed him, passed a chain through his handcuffs and fixed it to their belts, and lashed his arms tight to his sides. They crowded very close about him, with their hands always on him in a careful, caressing grip, as though all the while feeling him to make sure he was there. It was like men handling a fish which is still alive and may jump back into the water. But he stood quite unresisting, yielding his arms limply to the ropes, as though he hardly noticed what was happening.

Eight o'clock struck and a bugle call, desolately thin in the wet air, floated 3 from the distant barracks. The superintendent of the jail, who was standing apart from the rest of us, moodily prodding the gravel with his stick, raised his head at the sound. He was an army doctor, with a grey toothbrush moustache and a gruff voice. "For God's sake hurry up, Francis," he said irritably. "The man ought to have been dead by this time. Aren't you ready yet?"

Francis, the head jailer, a fat Dravidian in a white drill suit and gold spectacles, 4 waved his black hand. "Yes sir, yes sir," he bubbled. "All iss satisfactorily prepared. The hangman iss waiting. We shall proceed."

"Well, quick march, then. The prisoners can't get their breakfast till this job's 5 over."

We set out for the gallows. Two warders marched on either side of the prisoner, 6 with their files at the slope; two others marched close against him, gripping him by arm and shoulder, as though at once pushing and supporting him. The rest of us, magistrates and the like, followed behind. Suddenly, when we had gone ten yards, the procession stopped short without any order or warning. A dreadful thing had happened—a dog, come goodness knows whence, had appeared in the yard. It came bounding among us with a loud volley of barks, and leapt round us wagging its whole body, wild with glee at finding so many human beings together. It was a large woolly dog, half Airedale, half pariah. For a moment it pranced round us, and then, before anyone could stop it, it had made a dash for the prisoner, and jumping up tried to lick his face. Everyone stood aghast, too taken aback even to grab at the dog.

"Who let that bloody brute in here?" said the superintendent angrily. "Catch 7 it, someone!"

A warden, detached from the escort, charged clumsily after the dog, but it 8
danced and gambolled just out of his reach, taking everything as part of the game.
A young Eurasian jailer picked up a handful of gravel and tried to stone the dog
away, but it dodged the stones and came after us again. Its yaps echoed from the
jail walls. The prisoner, in the grasp of the two warders, looked on incuriously, as
though this was another formality of the hanging. It was several minutes before
someone managed to catch the dog. Then we put my handkerchief through its collar and moved off once more, with the dog still straining and whimpering.

It was about forty yards to the gallows. I watched the bare brown back of the 9
prisoner marching in front of me. He walked clumsily with his bound arms, but
quite steadily, with that bobbing gait of the Indian who never straightens his knees.
At each step his muscles slid neatly into place, the lock of hair on his scalp danced
up and down, his feet printed themselves on the wet gravel. And once, in spite of
the men who gripped him by each shoulder, he stepped slightly aside to avoid a
puddle on the path.

It is curious, but till that moment I had never realised what it means to destroy 10
a healthy, conscious man. When I saw the prisoner step aside to avoid the puddle,
I saw the mystery, the unspeakable wrongness, of cutting a life short when it is in
full tide. This man was not dying; he was alive just as we were alive. All the organs of his body were working—bowels digesting food, skin renewing itself, nails
growing, tissues forming—all toiling away in solemn foolery. His nails would still
be growing when he stood on the drop, when he was falling through the air with
a tenth of a second to live. His eyes saw the yellow gravel and the grey walls, and
his brain still remembered, foresaw, reasoned—reasoned even about puddles. He
and we were a party of men walking together, seeing, hearing, feeling, understanding the same world; and in two minutes, with a sudden snap, one of us would be
gone—one mind less, one world less.

The gallows stood in a small yard, separate from the main grounds of the 11
prison, and overgrown with tall prickly weeds. It was a brick erection like three
sides of a shed, with planking on top, and above that two beams and a crossbar
with the rope dangling. The hangman, a grey-haired convict in the white uniform
of the prison, was waiting beside his machine. He greeted us with a servile crouch
as we entered. At a word from Francis the two warders, gripping the prisoner more
closely than ever, half led, half pushed him to the gallows and helped him clumsily
up the ladder. Then the hangman climbed up and fixed the rope round the prisoner's neck.

We stood waiting, five yards away. The warders had formed in a rough circle 12
round the gallows. And then, when the noose was fixed, the prisoner began crying
out to his god. It was a high, reiterated cry of "Ram! Ram! Ram! Ram!" not urgent
and fearful like a prayer or a cry for help, but steady, rhythmical, almost like the
tolling of a bell. The dog answered the sound with a whine. The hangman, still
standing on the gallows, produced a small cotton bag like a flour bag and drew it

down over the prisoner's face. But the sound, muffled by the cloth, still persisted, over and over again: "Ram! Ram! Ram! Ram! Ram!"

The hangman climbed down and stood ready, holding the lever. Minutes 13 seemed to pass. The steady, muffled crying from the prisoner went on and on, "Ram! Ram! Ram!" never faltering for an instant. The superintendent, his head on his chest, was slowly poking the ground with his stick; perhaps he was counting the cries, allowing the prisoner a fixed number—fifty, perhaps, or a hundred. Everyone had changed colour. The Indians had gone grey like bad coffee, and one or two of the bayonets were wavering. We looked at the lashed, hooded man on the drop, and listened to his cries—each cry another second of life; the same thought was in all our minds: oh, kill him quickly, get it over, stop that abominable noise!

Suddenly the superintendent made up his mind. Throwing up his head he made 14 a swift motion with his stick. "Chalo!" he shouted almost fiercely.

There was a clanking noise, and then dead silence. The prisoner had vanished, and 15 the rope was twisting on itself. I let go of the dog, and it galloped immediately to the back of the gallows; but when it got there it stopped short, barked, and then retreated into a corner of the yard, where it stood among the weeds, looking timorously out at us. We went round the gallows to inspect the prisoner's body. He was dangling with his toes pointed straight downwards, very slowly revolving, as dead as a stone.

The superintendent reached out with his stick and poked the bare body; it 16 oscillated,[1] slightly. "*He's* all right," said the superintendent. He backed out from under the gallows, and blew out a deep breath. The moody look had gone out of his face quite suddenly. He glanced at his wristwatch. "Eight minutes past eight. Well, that's all for this morning, thank God."

The warders unfixed bayonets and marched away. The dog, sobered and con- 17 scious of having misbehaved itself, slipped after them. We walked out of the gallows yard, past the condemned cells with their waiting prisoners, into the big central yard of the prison. The convicts, under the command of warders armed with lathis,[2] were already receiving their breakfast. They squatted in long rows, each man holding a tin pannikin,[3] while two warders with buckets marched round ladling out rice; it seemed quite a homely, jolly scene, after the hanging. An enormous relief had come upon us now that the job was done. One felt an impulse to sing, to break into a run, to snicker. All at once everyone began chattering gaily.

The Eurasian boy walking beside me nodded towards the way we had come, 18 with a knowing smile: "Do you know, sir, our friend (he meant the dead man), when he heard his appeal had been dismissed, he pissed on the floor of his cell. From fright.—Kindly take one of my cigarettes, sir. Do you not admire my new silver case, sir? From the boxwallah,[4] two rupees eight annas. Classy European style."

---

[1]*oscillated:* swung back and forth.
[2]*lathis:* long, heavy sticks, usually of bamboo and bound with iron.
[3]*pannikin:* small metal (usually tinned iron) drinking vessel.
[4]*boxwallah:* expert box-maker.

Several people laughed—at what, nobody seemed certain.   19

Francis was walking by the superintendent, talking garrulously: "Well, sir, all 20
hass passed off with the utmost satisfactoriness. It wass all finished—flick! like
that. It iss not always so—oah, no! I have known cases where the doctor wass
obliged to go beneath the gallows and pull the prisoner's legs to ensure decease.
Most disagreeable!"

"Wriggling about, eh? That's bad," said the superintendent.   21

"Ach, sir, it iss worse when they become refractory! One man, I recall, clung 22
to the bars of hiss cage when we went to take him out. You will scarcely credit, sir,
that it took six warders to dislodge him, three pulling at each leg. We reasoned with
him. 'My dear fellow,' we said, 'think of all the pain and trouble you are causing to
us!' But no, he would not listen! Ach, he wass very troublesome!"

I found that I was laughing quite loudly. Everyone was laughing. Even the 23
superintendent grinned in a tolerant way. "You'd better all come out and have a
drink," he said quite genially. "I've got a bottle of whisky in the car. We could do
with it."

We went through the big double gates of the prison, into the road. "Pulling at 24
his legs!" exclaimed a Burmese magistrate suddenly, and burst into a loud chuck-
ling. We all began laughing again. At that moment Francis's anecdote seemed ex-
traordinarily funny. We all had a drink together, native and European alike, quite
amicably. The dead man was a hundred yards away.

READING COMPREHENSION

1. The word *gambolled* in "[the dog] danced and gambolled just out of his reach"
   (paragraph 8) means
   a. crawled.
   b. limped.
   c. leaped.
   d. stood.

2. The word *amicably* in "We all had a drink together, . . . quite amicably" (paragraph 24) means
   a. with hostility.
   b. unnecessarily.
   c. quietly.
   d. in a friendly way.

3. Which of the following would be a good alternative title for this selection?
   a. A Burmese Prisoner
   b. Methods of Capital Punishment

    c. The Necessity of Execution

    d. The Difficulty of Taking a Life

4. Which sentence best expresses the main idea of the selection?

    a. Capital punishment is unpleasant to carry out, but it is necessary in some cases.

    b. Executions in Burma were done in an inefficient and amateurish way.

    c. Taking another person's life is morally wrong.

    d. No one cared about the Burmese prisoner who was hanged.

5. Just before he was executed, the prisoner

    a. protested his innocence.

    b. cried out to his god.

    c. tried to escape from the gallows.

    d. said a quiet prayer.

6. *True or False?* _____ The author says that the prisoner had been convicted of murder.

7. After the execution, the author and the other officials

    a. felt relief.

    b. became very depressed.

    c. chased away the dog.

    d. couldn't speak for a long while.

8. The author implies that

    a. the dog that interrupted the march to the gallows belonged to the prisoner.

    b. no one has the right to take another person's life.

    c. the authorities knew the prisoner was innocent.

    d. other methods of execution are more humane than hanging.

9. The author implies that

    a. the prisoner would have escaped if he had not been so heavily guarded.

    b. the prisoner did not die immediately.

    c. the hangman had volunteered for the job.

    d. the superintendent of the jail was nervous and upset about the hanging.

10. The author implies that

    a. the people who witnessed the hanging later laughed and joked to cover up the uneasiness they felt.

    b. the native people and the Europeans felt differently about the hanging.

    c. he had become friends with the prisoner before the execution.

    d. Burmese officials were corrupt.

STRUCTURE AND TECHNIQUE

1. Paragraphs 1, 2, and 3 contain vivid descriptions of the people and things surrounding the author on the morning of the execution. What details does he use that appeal to readers' senses of sight, hearing, and touch? What is the effect of all these details?

2. "A Hanging" takes place in Burma, and Orwell occasionally uses regional terms such as *lathis* and *boxwallah* in the course of his essay. Why do you think Orwell chose to include these foreign terms rather than translate them into English?

3. In part, Orwell uses dialogue to tell his story, giving the actual words of numerous individuals. What does the essay gain or lose from this technique? Explain.

4. In paragraph 10, Orwell provides a series of details about the bodily organs of the condemned man. List these details. How do they relate to Orwell's larger point in "A Hanging"?

CRITICAL READING AND DISCUSSION

1. Why does everyone stand "aghast" when the stray dog licks the prisoner's face? Why is this incident important?

2. The author has a moment of understanding when the prisoner steps "slightly aside to avoid a puddle on the path" (paragraph 9). What realization does Orwell come to? How is this insight related to the small incident of avoiding a puddle?

3. The character of the superintendent evolves in the course of this narrative. How do the words he speaks (and the tone of voice he speaks them in) reflect the emotional changes he goes through?

4. The author's thesis is most clearly stated in paragraph 10: "When I saw the prisoner step aside to avoid the puddle, I saw the mystery, the unspeakable wrongness, of cutting a life short when it is in full tide." Do you agree that capital punishment is always wrong? Explain your answer.

WRITING ASSIGNMENTS

Academic

Assignment 1

Use examples and details from "A Hanging" to support the following thesis statement:

In "A Hanging," George Orwell constantly contrasts death with life to show us how wrong it is to kill another human being.

You might organize your paragraphs by showing how death is contrasted with life (1) on the way to the gallows, (2) at the gallows, and (3) after the hanging.

To get started, reread the selection closely, noting words and incidents that seem to be closely related to either death or life. For example, in paragraph 2, Orwell describes the prisoner as "quite unresisting, yielding his arms limply to the ropes." It is as if the prisoner is already dead. In contrast, the guards are filled with life and action: they handcuff the prisoner, lash his arms, and keep a "careful, caressing grip" on him. At many other points in the story, this strong contrast between death and life is described.

Use a point-by-point method of contrast in developing your essay. You may want to look first at the example of this method on pages 283–284.

Assignment 2

Find out (1) if capital punishment is legal in your state, and if so, (2) which method of execution is used. (You could find this information by calling your city or county library.) Then imagine that a statewide vote will soon be taken to find out if voters want to change this law. Decide if you would (or would not) change the law. Give reasons for your decision. For example, if your state does have capital punishment, and you would vote not to change the law, you might give the reasons in the following essay outline:

Thesis: Our state law allows a jury to vote for "death by lethal injection" for convicted criminals, and I would not vote to change this law.

Topic sentences:

(a) First of all, the death penalty saves thousands of tax dollars that would be spent to keep criminals in prison for life.
(b) In addition, the punishment acts as a deterrent to other criminals.
(c) Most important, death is an appropriate punishment for someone who commits a terrible crime.

To avoid writing in vague, general terms, you may want to use specific examples of cases or crimes currently being discussed in the news. You may also need facts and statistics. You can find these by typing "capital punishment law" and the name of your state into an Internet search engine.

Assignment 3

On the basis of the knowledge you have gained by reading this selection, write an essay with *either* of the thesis statements below:

Executions today are as brutal as the one described in "A Hanging."

Executions today are humane compared with the one described in "A Hanging."

In your supporting paragraphs, you may want to write about each of the following:

methods of execution and atmosphere in which executions are conducted

kinds of people who are executed

fairness of the trials and judges

EXECUTION OF REV. STEPHEN BURROUGHS.

How does capital punishment today differ from the hangings that took place during the Salem witch trials in 1692? After doing some research on both, write a comparison or contrast essay. You may refer to Chapter 21 for tips on using the library and the Internet to conduct your research.

What Your Closet Reveals about You

Amy Tan

PREVIEW

Amy Tan is a well-known author who was born in California to Chinese immigrants. Much of her work focuses on the Chinese immigrant experience, American-Chinese culture, and mother-daughter relationships. She has written numerous books that include *The Joy Luck Club*, *The Bonesetter's Daughter*, and *Saving Fish from Drowning*. She has also won an Emmy for her animated series, *Sagwa*. This article, in which Tan discusses what clothes reveal about a person, first appeared in *Harper's Bazaar* in 2006.

1 A few months back I attended a benefit luncheon at the home of a venture capitalist in Silicon Valley whose art collection adorned nearly every vertical surface of her Bauhaus house. While freshening up, I was amused to see she had artwork even in her bathroom and, as I then saw, her vault-size closet. I stepped in, ostensibly to examine the painting, and there I experienced a life-changing revelation.

2 At first glance the interior of the closet and its cabinetry of bird's-eye maple were merely impressive. An Eames bench sat in the center, where one might sit as if resting among exhibits at a costume museum. Cashmere sweaters and scarves, arranged by tonality, were aligned on sliding trays. Segregated sections contained jackets, black-tie gowns, cocktail-party dresses, business suits, and golfing attire-phalanxes of fashion organized by function, color, and texture, all of it hanging on the erect shoulders of identical mahogany hangers, a precision team at the ready for any occasion.

3 And then there was this: four banks of shelves housing four dozen shoe boxes, which had been wrapped in rough hemp mesh and coated with a thin layer of gouache. Affixed to the front of each was a small stainless-steel nameplate, on which appeared the names of the various conceptual artists: Giorgio Armani, Manolo Blahnik, and Jimmy Choo. In smaller type were notes with numbers and letters; those, I discerned through similar coding found in other parts of her closet, referred to the black-tie, cocktail, and business attire that coordinated with the shoes. This was the temple into which the woman entered to consider the existential question we all face each day: I am what I wear, I wear what I am. Who am I today?

You don't have to be a psychiatrist to recognize that the matching hangers 4
and labeled shoe boxes were clinical signs of a mental-health disorder. Obsessive-
compulsive sprang to mind. Although she was only in her 30s, I knew she would
never marry. This was clearly someone who was so inflexible she allowed no wrinkles in her life, certainly no man with uncoded shoe boxes.

As I made this smug assessment, I had a sudden and terrible realization that 5
my own closet had served for others as an amusing window into my psyche.
I could picture it: the overflowing drawers of socks and stockings, long dresses
mingling with old blouses and skirts, winter clothes with summer, many of the
outfits dangling by one shoulder off skewed plastic and wire hangers. My rack
of clothes was far from looking like a precision team; it was the unruly lineup of
people waiting to deplane after a red-eye flight. Under the clothes rack and pushed
against the wall were various bags from my latest round of travels, half packed
with clean and dirty clothes as well as items I had thought were necessities and
turned out not to be. Clearly, anyone would conclude that my life was a mess, that
I had no concept of boundaries and often did not know if I was coming or going.
My closet was a repository of foibles and fetishes, an archive of my personality
and life history.

It occurred to me that closet analysis should be part of any psychotherapy 6
sessions with a Freudian. The ego: That would be the clothes representing the private side—say, the comfort clothes a woman wears when she is alone and sick at
home with the flu, when she is her essential miserable self. In my case, that would
be the oversize fleecewear and the babydoll dress I bought a dozen years ago that
reminded me of the babydoll dress I wore when I was fourteen and questioned
almost nothing told to me. Among the comfort clothes I wear—and I know this will
sound sick—are the pink pajamas my mother wore the last week of her life. In that
vein, there are also the wool Bavarian slipper socks that were a Christmas present
from a friend who died too young, the nightgown I wore the night after my father
died, and the six sweaters my mother knitted the following year and gave me when
I gladly escaped her clutches and started college a year early. Those were the sweaters I never wore again until my thirties, when I found them stuffed in a cardboard
box of old clothes.

As for the superego, those are the clean clothes a person wears in public as 7
an adaptation to a social setting, situation, or purpose—the fashions that make a
woman look sexy to a suitor, younger at a reunion, or sensibly boring to a future
mother-in-law. They are the suits that have already proven their worth during successful interviews and speeches, the clingy top that led to a pleasantly consummated
dalliance, the pants that fit after six months of exercise. Often those outfits are advanced front and center. But they are always subject to demotion; once they fail at
their intended purpose, they're shoved to the back, along with impulse items never
worn, whose price tags had once made them irresistible and now remind us how
little we value our intelligence. To throw them away only magnifies the stupidity.

At the farthest reaches of the closet—the corners of the topmost shelves, squeezed behind uncoded shoe boxes, crammed at the back of drawers, or hidden under a pile of flip-flops and unused running shoes—resides the id. This is the underwear you will have on when you wake up in the ambulance, the permanently stained clothing, and other ghastly things you would disclose only under hypnosis.

I tried to rationalize the untidy personality within my closet as complex and **8** not twisted like the wire hangers I got for free from the dry cleaner's.

If my personality lies in my closet, I further justified, then it is disorganized be- **9** cause I find it impossible to live an orderly life when it is chaos and confusion that serve me best as a writer. Messiness is the impetus, the disarray is the wellspring, even the shameful parts—especially those. I dredge them up and salvage them over and over again. I cannot discard clothes if they were gifts, no matter how hideous. To do so would make me feel ungrateful for friendship. The clutter within a closet is fond memories, hard-learned mistakes, comfort for future cold nights. That was my excuse, anyway. Until recently.

Today, if you were to open my closet door, you would see blouses hung in **10** one section, jackets in another. Long skirts are partitioned from long dresses. One shelf is labeled "long-sleeved tops," another "short-sleeved tops," and a third "no sleeves." The shoes are in shoe caddies or on wire racks, and they are separated by season and function. The drawers contain socks and underwear, even the old ones, folded as nicely as those in fine lingerie stores. The nightgowns are placed in two drawers according to fabric weight.

How did I come to see the light? It was really quite simple and unexpected. **11** My old housekeeper retired and recommended a new one, a woman with common sense and a way to apply it to the interior life of other people. When I returned from one of my travels, I saw that my closet had been transformed. When she presented me with the receipts for storage containers and other equipment, I was amazed to see how little matching hangers cost. For so little money, a girl can have a precision team at her beck and call.

Through such objective orderliness, I saw some of my foibles exposed: six **12** skirts that were almost identical in fabric, color, and length. Why do I buy the same thing over and over again? What ingrained insecurity or needless pattern does that signify? I began to pare down and wound up with a dozen bagfuls—the useless jean jackets of my youth, the meaningless impulse buys, the excess of unused base-ball caps and T-shirts emblazoned with the names of bookstores, book festivals, writers' conferences, annual events, cities visited, and tour attractions toured. My housekeeper gladly took those clothes, and for this, I too was grateful.

In reducing the chaos, I found what I had misplaced and buried. Among them **13** were my mother's wedding jacket, a favorite blouse that I wrongfully assumed a girl at a party had stolen, the velveteen vest that was the first expensive present my then boyfriend and now husband gave me more than thirty years ago. And that, I realized, is also the kind of discovery I make when writing stories. In wading through the mess, I gradually put aside what is no longer meaningful, what is over-used, what is overly sentimental. And what is left is the essentials: both a sense of who I am and memories of what helped me become that way.

READING COMPREHENSION

1. The word *tonality* in "Cashmere sweaters and scarves, arranged by tonality, were aligned . . . " (paragraph 1) means

   a. an arrangement of tones and chords.

   b. the scheme or interrelation of the tones in a painting.

   c. the overall scheme of colors and tones.

   d. the relationship between the elements of harmony and melody.

2. The word *phalanxes* in "phalanxes of fashion organized by function, color, and texture . . . " (paragraph 12) means

   a. arranged in strict order like a military formation.

   b. a number of individuals united for a common purpose.

   c. any group of people gathered for a celebration.

   d. assembled randomly like a spontaneous crowd.

3. The word *gouache* in " . . . rough hemp mesh and coated with a thin layer of gouache" (paragraph 13) means

   a. a method of painting with opaque watercolors.

   b. a picture painted with watercolors.

   c. an opaque water-base paint prepared with gum.

   d. an oil paint that is used to seal hemp.

4. Which of the following would be a good alternative title for this selection?

   a. A Vault-Size Closet

   b. The Psychology of Clothing

   c. Obsessive-Compulsive Disorders

   d. Cleaning Out My Closet

5. Which sentence best expresses the main idea of the selection?

   a. By looking at your own closet, you can learn a lot about yourself.

   b. By visiting other people's closets, you can learn a lot about those people.

   c. When a person decides to organize a closet, it is important to hire a professional to help.

   d. Although it seems like organizing a closet would be expensive, it really can be done inexpensively.

6. Why was the narrator in the private vault-size closet?

    a. She was being nosy.

    b. She had been told to look around.

    c. She was looking at the art collection.

    d. She wanted to get some ideas for her own closet.

7. What conclusion did the narrator come to regarding the owner of the closet?

    a. She was incredibly wealthy and happy.

    b. She had a lot of hired help to keep her organized.

    c. She must have a wonderful husband who bought her things.

    d. She would probably be single her entire life.

8. What did the narrator mean when she said her "closet was a repository of foibles and fetishes"?

    a. Her closet was disorganized and contained *every* item she had ever purchased—foolish purchases, loved purchases, and fads.

    b. Her closet was where she would go to write in her diary about her mistakes, successes, and wishes.

    c. Her closet was poorly organized.

    d. Her closet was an embarrassment to her.

9. By reading paragraph 6, we can infer that the author believes

    a. most people have too many clothes.

    b. most people like clean clothes only when out in public.

    c. people like to wear clothes given as Christmas presents only in private.

    d. most people dress differently if they are going to be out in public than if they are staying home.

10. The author compares writing to

    a. discovering forgotten items.

    b. cleaning out a closet.

    c. making a salad.

    d. buying new clothes.

STRUCTURE AND TECHNIQUE

1. Which patterns of development are the most dominant in the essay?

2. Tan mentions several famous names in design like Eames, Bauhaus, Armani, and Blahnik. What is her purpose in "dropping names" like this in her essay?

3. Tan employs the use of alliteration throughout her essay. Find several examples of alliteration that you believe are especially effective.

4. Tan breaks conventions and shifts from first person point-of-view to second person point-of-view. Why do you think she does this? Is it effective?

CRITICAL READING AND DISCUSSION

1. Why do you think Tan believed that the owner of the closet would probably never marry?

2. React to Tan's statements that outfits are "shoved, to the back, along with impulse items never worn, whose price tags had once made them irresistible and now remind us how little we value our intelligence. To throw them away only magnifies the stupidity." Do you agree or disagree? Explain your answer.

3. Tan states that her foibles were exposed by her six skirts that were almost identical and then questions why she continued to buy this type of skirt. Why do you think she had purchased so many similar skirts? What does this say about her? Think about a foible that you have and be prepared to discuss it with your class.

4. Tan mentions several items of clothing that are especially important to her because they represent meaningful moments. Why do you think people place such importance on items like "a favorite blouse" or a "velveteen vest"?

WRITING ASSIGNMENTS

Assignment 1

Look through your closet and choose three items of clothing that represent important moments in your life. Use details to create a colorful picture of each piece of clothing, how you felt when wearing the clothing, and why that piece is so representative of the specific moment. For instance, if you are writing about your wedding dress, you might say that the "gorgeous silk skimmed my body in waves of beauty, much like the day was filled with waves of happiness." If you are writing about a bad memory, you could say "the horrible scratchiness of the polyester sleeves caused me to tug constantly, adding misery to an already awful day."

Assignment 2

Tan refers to the id, ego, and superego in her essay. These three elements of personality, according to Sigmund Freud, work together to create each person's individual complex behavior. The id is generally considered to be the pleasure principle, the part of the brain that wants instant gratification. Babies rely on the id to get their needs—food, diaper changes, sleep—immediately met. The ego is the part of the personality that is responsible for reality; it tries to meet the needs of the id, but always takes into account social appropriateness. The superego is the part of the personality that holds our morals, standards, and guidelines for making good judgments. Using Tan's essay (especially paragraphs 6 and 7) as a guide, analyze your closet and determine what you have in there that represents your id, ego, and superego.

Assignment 3

Tan's essay focuses on personal closets, but businesses also have closets, cubicles, and offices that represent the psyche of their owners. For this assignment, you are to write a report that analyzes your work space and makes recommendations to improve the work space. Perhaps your work area has a kitchen that is currently growing mold and other "science experiments." If so, you could propose a cleaning schedule for your co-workers. Or, if the company has had to cut back on cleaning costs, you could propose a way for the employees to pitch in and keep the offices clean. Another approach might focus on cubicles in your area that are very bland and personality-free. In this case, you might suggest to your boss that workers be allowed to add some personal items, within certain limitations, and/or to decorate the work space in other ways.

The Professor Is a Dropout

Beth Johnson

PREVIEW

After being mistakenly labeled "retarded" and humiliated into dropping out of first grade, Lupe Quintanilla knew she wanted nothing more to do with formal education. Life as a wife and mother would satisfy her—and it did, until she saw her own children being pushed aside as "slow learners." Driven to help them succeed, Lupe took steps that dramatically changed her life.

Guadalupe Quintanilla is an assistant professor at the University of Houston. She is president of her own communications company. She trains law enforcement officers all over the country. She was nominated to serve as the U.S. Attorney General. She's been a representative to the United Nations.

That's a pretty impressive string of accomplishments. It's all the more impressive when you consider this: "Lupe" Quintanilla is a first-grade dropout. Her school records state that she is retarded, that her IQ is so low she can't learn much of anything.

How did Lupe Quintanilla, "retarded" nonlearner, become Dr. Quintanilla, respected educator? Her remarkable journey began in the town of Nogales, Mexico, just below the Arizona border. That's where Lupe first lived with her grandparents. (Her parents had divorced.) Then an uncle who had just finished medical school made her grandparents a generous offer. If they wanted to live with him, he would support the family as he began his medical practice.

Lupe, her grandparents, and her uncle all moved hundreds of miles to a town in southern Mexico that didn't even have paved roads, let alone any schools. There, Lupe grew up helping her grandfather run his little pharmacy and her grandmother keep house. She remembers the time happily. "My grandparents were wonderful," she said. "Oh, my grandfather was stern, authoritarian, as Mexican culture demanded, but they were also very kind to me." When the chores were done, her grandfather taught Lupe to read and write Spanish and do basic arithmetic.

When Lupe was twelve, her grandfather became blind. The family left Mexico 5 and went to Brownsville, Texas, with the hope that doctors there could restore his sight. Once they arrived in Brownsville, Lupe was enrolled in school. Although she understood no English, she was given an IQ test in that language. Not surprisingly, she didn't do very well.

Lupe even remembers her score. "I scored a sixty-four, which classified me as 6 seriously retarded, not even teachable," she said. "I was put into first grade with a class of six-year-olds. My duties were to take the little kids to the bathroom and to cut out pictures." The classroom activities were a total mystery to Lupe—they were all conducted in English. And she was humiliated by the other children, who teased her for being "so much older and so much dumber" than they were.

After four months in first grade, an incident occurred that Lupe still does not 7 fully understand. As she stood in the doorway of the classroom waiting to escort a little girl to the bathroom, a man approached her. He asked her, in Spanish, how to find the principal's office. Lupe was delighted. "Finally someone in this school had spoken to me with words I could understand, in the language of my soul, the lan-

guage of my grandmother," she said. Eagerly, she answered his question in Spanish. Instantly her teacher swooped down on her, grabbing her arm and scolding her. She pulled Lupe along to the principal's office. There, the teacher and the principal both shouted at her, obviously very angry. Lupe was frightened and embarrassed, but also bewildered. She didn't understand a word they were saying.

"Why were they so angry? I don't know," said Lupe. 8 "Was it because I spoke Spanish at school? Or that I spoke to the man at all? I really don't know. All I know is how humiliated I was."

Guadalape
Quintanilla today

When she got home that day, she cried miserably, begging her grandfather not 9 to make her return to school. Finally he agreed.

From that time on, Lupe stayed at home, serving as her blind grandfather's 10 "eyes." She was a fluent reader in Spanish, and the older man loved to have her read newspapers, poetry, and novels aloud to him for hours.

Lupe's own love of reading flourished during these years. Her vocabulary was 11 enriched and her imagination fired by the novels she read—novels which she learned later were classics of Spanish literature. She read *Don Quixote,* the famous story of the noble, impractical knight who fought against windmills. She read thrilling accounts of the Mexican revolution. She read *La Prensa,* the local Spanish-language paper, and *Selecciones,* the Spanish-language version of *Reader's Digest.*

When she was just sixteen, Lupe married a young Mexican-American dental 12 technician. Within five years, she had given birth to her three children, Victor, Mario, and Martha. Lupe's grandparents lived with the young family. Lupe was quite happy with her life. "I cooked, sewed, cleaned, and cared for everybody," she said. "I listened to my grandmother when she told me what made a good wife. In the morning I would actually put on my husband's shoes and tie the laces—anything to make his life easier. Living with my grandparents for so long, I was one generation behind in my ideas of what a woman could do and be."

Lupe's contentment ended when her children started school. When they 13 brought home their report cards, she struggled to understand them. She could read enough English to know that what they said was not good. Her children had been put into a group called "Yellow Birds." It was a group for slow learners.

At night in bed, Lupe cried and blamed herself. It was obvious—not only was 14 she retarded, but her children had taken after her. Now they, too, would never be able to learn like other children.

But in time, a thought began to break through Lupe's despair: Her children 15 didn't seem like slow learners to her. At home, they learned everything she taught them, quickly and easily. She read to them constantly, from the books that she herself had loved as a child. *Aesop's Fables* and stories from *1,001 Arabian Nights* were family favorites. The children filled the house with the sounds of the songs, prayers, games, and rhymes they had learned from their parents and grandparents. They were smart children, eager to learn. They learned quickly—in Spanish.

A radical idea began to form in Lupe's mind. Maybe the school was wrong 16 about her children. And if the school system could be wrong about her children—maybe it had been wrong about her, too.

Lupe visited her children's school, a daring action for her. "Many Hispanic 17 parents would not dream of going to the classroom," she said. "In Hispanic culture, the teacher is regarded as a third parent, as an ultimate authority. To question her would seem most disrespectful, as though you were saying that she didn't know her job." That was one reason Lupe's grandparents had not interfered when Lupe was classified as retarded. "Anglo teachers often misunderstand Hispanic parents, believing that they aren't concerned about their children's education because they don't come visit the schools," Lupe said. "It's not a lack of concern at all. It's a mark of respect for the teacher's authority."

At her children's school, Lupe spoke to three different teachers. Two of them told 18 her the same thing: "Your children are just slow. Sorry, but they can't learn." A third offered a glimmer of hope. He said, "They don't know how to function in English. It's possible that if you spoke English at home they would be able to do better."

Lupe pounced on that idea. "Where can I learn English?" she asked. The teacher 19 shrugged. At that time there were no local English-language programs for adults. Finally he suggested that Lupe visit the local high school. Maybe she would be permitted to sit in the back of a classroom and pick up some English that way.

Lupe made an appointment with a counselor at the high school. But when the 20 two women met, the counselor shook her head. "Your test scores show that you are retarded," she told Lupe. "You'd just be taking space in the classroom away from someone who could learn."

Lupe's next stop was the hospital where she had served for years as a volunteer. **21** Could she sit in on some of the nursing classes held there? No, she was told, not without a diploma. Still undeterred, she went on to Texas Southmost College in Brownsville. Could she sit in on a class? No; no high-school diploma. Finally she went to the telephone company, where she knew operators were being trained. Could she listen in on the classes? No, only high-school graduates were permitted.

That day, leaving the telephone company, Lupe felt she had hit bottom. She **22** had been terrified in the first place to try to find an English class. Meeting with rejection after rejection nearly destroyed what little self-confidence she had. She walked home in the rain, crying. "I felt like a big barrier had fallen across my path," she said. "I couldn't go over it; I couldn't go under it; I couldn't go around it."

But the next day Lupe woke with fresh determination. "I was motivated by **23** love of my kids," she said. "I was not going to quit." She got up; made breakfast for her kids, husband, and grandparents; saw her children and husband off for the day; and started out again. "I remember walking to the bus stop, past a dog

Lupe enjoys a story with her twin grandchildren, Alyssa and Christian, and a visiting friend.

that always scared me to death, and heading back to the college. The lady I spoke to said, 'I told you, we can't do anything for you without a high-school degree.' But as I left the building, I went up to the first Spanish-speaking student I saw. His name was Gabito. I said, 'Who really makes the decisions around here?' He said, 'The registrar.'" Since she hadn't had any luck in the office building, Lupe decided to take a more direct approach. She asked Gabito to point out the registrar's car in the parking lot. For the next two hours she waited beside it until its owner showed up.

Impressed by Lupe's persistence, the registrar lis- **24** tened to her story. But instead of giving her permission to sit in on a class and learn more English, he insisted that she sign up for a full college load. Before she knew it, she was enrolled in four classes: basic math, basic English, psychology, and typing. The registrar's parting words to her were, "Don't come back if you don't make it through."

With that "encouragement," Lupe began a semester that was part nightmare, part **25** dream come true. Every day she got her husband and children off to school, took the bus to campus, came home to make lunch for her husband and grandparents, went back to campus, and was home in time to greet Victor, Mario, and Martha when they got home from school. In the evenings she cooked, cleaned, did laundry, and got the children to bed. Then she would study, often until three in the morning.

"Sometimes in class I would feel sick with the stress of it," she said. "I'd go to **26** the bathroom and talk to myself in the mirror. Sometimes I'd say, 'What are you doing here? Why don't you go home and watch *I Love Lucy?*'"

But she didn't go home. Instead, she studied furiously, using her Spanish- 27 English dictionary, constantly making lists of new words she wanted to understand. "I still do that today," she said. "When I come across a word I don't know, I write it down, look it up, and write sentences using it until I own that word."

Although so much of the language and subject matter was new to Lupe, one 28 part of the college experience was not. That was the key skill of reading, a skill Lupe possessed. As she struggled with English, she found the reading speed, comprehension, and vocabulary that she had developed in Spanish carrying over into her new language. "Reading," she said, "reading was the vehicle. Although I didn't know it at the time, when I was a girl learning to love to read, I was laying the foundation for academic success."

She gives credit, too, to her Hispanic fellow students. "At first, they didn't 29 know what to make of me. They were eighteen years old, and at that time it was very unfashionable for an older person to be in college. But once they decided I wasn't a 'plant' from the administration, they were my greatest help." The younger students spent hours helping Lupe, explaining unfamiliar words and terms, coaching her, and answering her questions.

That first semester passed in a fog of exhaustion. Many mornings. Lupe doubted 30 she could get out of bed, much less care for her family and tackle her classes. But when she thought of her children and what was at stake for them, she forced herself on. She remembers well what those days were like. "Just a day at a time. That was all I could think about. I could make myself get up one more day, study one more day, cook and clean one more day. And those days eventually turned into a semester."

To her own amazement perhaps as much as anyone's, Lupe discovered that 31 she was far from retarded. Although she sweated blood over many assignments, she completed them. She turned them in on time. And, remarkably, she made the dean's list her very first semester.

After that, there was no stopping Lupe Quintanilla. She soon realized that the 32 associate's degree offered by Texas Southmost College would not satisfy her. Continuing her Monday, Wednesday, and Friday schedule at Southmost, she enrolled for Tuesday and Thursday courses at Pan American University, a school 140 miles from Brownsville. Within three years, she had earned both her junior college degree and a bachelor's degree in biology. She then won a fellowship that took her to graduate school at the University of Houston, where she earned a master's degree in Spanish literature. When she graduated, the university offered her a job as director of the Mexican-American studies program. While in that position, she earned a doctoral degree in education.

How did she do it all? Lupe herself isn't sure. "I hardly know. When I think 33 back to those years, it seems like a life that someone else lived." It was a rich and exciting but also very challenging period for Lupe and her family. On the one hand, Lupe was motivated by the desire to set an example for her children, to prove to them that they could succeed in the English-speaking academic world. On the other hand, she worried about neglecting her family. She tried hard to attend important activities, such as parents' meetings at school and her children's sporting events. But things didn't always work out. Lupe still remembers attending a baseball game that her older son, Victor, was playing in. When Victor came to bat, he hit a home run. But as the crowd cheered and Victor glanced proudly over at his mother in the stands, he saw she was studying a textbook. "I hadn't seen the home run," Lupe admitted. "That sort of thing was hard for everyone to take."

Lupe surrounded by her children: Martha, Victor, and Mario.

Although Lupe worried that her children would 34 resent her busy schedule, she also saw her success reflected in them as they blossomed in school. She forced herself to speak English at home, and their language skills improved quickly. She read to them in English instead of Spanish—gulping down her pride as their pronunciation became better than hers and they began correcting her. (Once the children were in high school and fluent in English, Lupe switched back to Spanish at home, so that the children would be fully comfortable in both languages.) "I saw the change in them almost immediately," she said. "After I helped them with their homework, they would see me pulling out my own books and going to work, In the morning, I would show them the papers I had written. As I gained confidence, so did they." By the next year, the children had been promoted out of the Yellow Birds.

Even though Victor, Mario, and Martha all did well academically, Lupe real- 35 ized she could not assume that they would face no more obstacles in school. When Mario was in high school, for instance, he wanted to sign up for a debate class. Instead, he was assigned to woodworking. She visited the school to ask why. Mario's teacher told her, "He's good with his hands. He'll be a great carpenter, and that's a good thing for a Mexican to be." Controlling her temper, Lupe responded, "I'm glad you think he's good with his hands. He'll be a great physician someday, and he is going to be in the debate class."

Today, Lupe Quintanilla teaches at the University of Houston, where she has developed several dozen courses concerning Hispanic literature and culture. Her cross-cultural training for law enforcement officers, which helps bring police and firefighters and local Hispanic communities closer together, is renowned throughout the country. Former President Ronald Reagan named her to a national board that keeps the White House informed of new programs in law enforcement.

36

Two members of the Houston police department learn job-specific Spanish phrases from Lupe. Lupe also trains the officers in cultural awareness.

She has received numerous awards for teaching excellence, and there is even a scholarship named in her honor. Her name appears in the Hispanic Hall of Fame, and she has been co-chair of the White House Commission on Hispanic Education.

The love of reading that her grandfather instilled in Lupe is still alive. She 37 thinks of him every year when she introduces to her students one of his favorite poets, Amado Nervo. She requires them to memorize these lines from one of Nervo's poems: "When I got to the end of my long journey in life, I realized that I was the architect of my own destiny." Of these lines, Lupe says, "That is something that I deeply believe, and I want my students to learn it before the end of their long journey. We create our own destiny."

Her love of reading and learning has helped Lupe create a distinguished des- 38 tiny. But none of the honors she has received means more to her than the success of her own children, the reason she made that frightening journey to seek classes in English years ago. Today Mario is a physician. Victor and Martha are lawyers, both having earned doctor of law degrees. And so today, Lupe likes to say, "When someone calls the house and asks for 'Dr. Quintanilla,' I have to ask, 'Which one?' There are four of us—one retarded and three slow learners."

READING COMPREHENSION

1. The word *flourished* in "Lupe's own love of reading flourished during these years. Her vocabulary was enriched and her imagination fired by the novels she read" (paragraph 11) means

   a. grew.

   b. stood still.

   c. was lost.

   d. remained.

2. The word *instilled* in "The love of reading that Lupe's grandfather instilled in Lupe is still alive" (paragraph 37) means

   a. frightened.

   b. established.

   c. forced.

   d. forgot.

3. Which of the following would be a good alternative title for this selection?

   a. Difficulties Facing Spanish-Speaking Students

   b. Unfair Labeling

   c. Balancing School and Family

   d. A Courageous Mother's Triumph

4. Which sentence best expresses the main idea of the selection?

   a. Lupe, a first-grade dropout, eventually earned a doctoral degree and created a professional career.

   b. Lupe Quintanilla's experience proves that the educational system has been set up to accommodate non-English-speaking children.

   c. Through hard work and persistence combined with a love of reading and learning, Lupe has created a distinguished career and helped her children become professionals.

   d. In school, Spanish-speaking students may experience obstacles as they aim for professional careers.

5. Lupe realized that her children were not retarded when

   a. they got good grades at school.

   b. she saw how quickly they learned at home.

   c. they were put in the group called "Yellow Birds."

   d. they read newspapers, poetry, and novels to her.

6. Lupe's training for law enforcement officers

   a. teaches them to speak Spanish.

   b. teaches Hispanic literature and culture.

   c. offers a scholarship named in her honor.

   d. brings police, firefighters, and local Hispanic communities together.

7. According to Lupe, Hispanic parents rarely visit their children's schools because they

   a. do not consider schoolwork important.

   b. think doing so would be disrespectful to the teacher.

   c. are ashamed of their English language skills.

   d. are usually working during school visitation hours.

8. "Once they arrived in Brownsville, Lupe was enrolled in school. Although she understood no English, she was given an IQ test in that language. Not surprisingly, she didn't do very well" (paragraph 5). From these sentences, we might conclude that

   a. an IQ test in a language that the person tested doesn't know is useless.

   b. although Lupe was not very intelligent at first, she became more intelligent once she learned English.

   c. Lupe really did know English.

   d. there are no IQ tests in Spanish.

9. We might conclude from the reading that
   a. a school system's judgment about an individual is always accurate.
   b. it is often better for a child to stay home rather than attend school.
   c. by paying attention and speaking up, parents may remove obstacles to their children's education.
   d. working parents should accept the fact that they cannot attend important events in their children's lives.

10. The last line of the reading suggests that
   a. retarded people can become successful professionals.
   b. people should not blindly accept other people's opinions of them.
   c. Lupe's children are smarter than she is.
   d. all of the above

STRUCTURE AND TECHNIQUE

1. Johnson begins the essay by listing Lupe Quintanilla's accomplishments, then revealing that Quintanilla was once classified as retarded. What introductory technique is Johnson employing? Why is it effective here?

2. Paragraphs 3–11 are devoted to the first fifteen years of Lupe's life. But the next decade or so is covered in only two paragraphs (12–13). Why might Johnson have presented Lupe's earlier life in so much more detail? Do you agree with her decision?

3. In paragraph 2, Johnson writes that "[Lupe's] school records state that she is retarded . . . ." But in the next sentence, she writes, "How did Lupe Quintanilla; 'retarded' nonlearner, become Dr. Quintanilla, respected educator?" Why does Johnson put the word "retarded" in quotation marks in the second sentence; but not in the first? What is she implying? Can you find another place where Johnson makes similar use of quotation marks?

4. At one point, Johnson switches from the topic of Lupe's success in college to the topic of the challenges that continued to face her children in school. In what paragraph does she make that switch? What transitional words does she use to alert the reader to her new direction?

CRITICAL READING AND DISCUSSION

1. In the course of the essay, what characteristics and attitudes does Lupe suggest are typical of Hispanic culture? Does she seem sympathetic, critical, or neutral about those qualities or attitudes? How has she dealt with cultural expectations in her own life?

2. How has Lupe handled the question of what language to use with her children? If you grew up in a two-language household, how did your family deal with the issue? How would you approach the issue with children of your own?

3. Do you think Lupe's grandfather was right in allowing her to quit school? What factors do you imagine might have gone into his decision?

4. Lupe credits her fellow Hispanic students with giving her valuable support in college. Is there anyone in your life—a teacher, family member, or friend— who has helped you through challenging times in your education? Explain what obstacles you faced and how this person helped you overcome them.

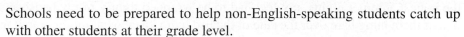

WRITING ASSIGNMENTS

Assignment 1

Write an essay that takes as its thesis one of the following statements:

> Schools need to be prepared to help non-English-speaking students catch up with other students at their grade level.

> The responsibility for catching non-English-speaking students up to their grade level rests solely with the students and their families.

> Support your thesis with several points, each developed in its own paragraph.

Assignment 2

Lupe Quintanilla is an outstanding example of someone who has taken charge of her life. She has been, to echo the poet whose work she teaches, the architect of her own destiny. Choose a person you know who, in your opinion, has done a fine job of taking charge of his or her own destiny. Write an essay about this person. You might describe three areas of life in which the person has taken control. Alternatively, you might narrate three incidents from the person's life that illustrate his or her admirable self-determination.

Assignment 3

Lupe had to struggle in order to balance her school responsibilities with her duties as a wife and mother. Write an essay in which you identify aspects of your life that you need to juggle along with your responsibilities as a student. They may include a job, a spouse or significant other, children, housekeeping duties, pets, extracurricular activities, a difficult living situation, or anything else that poses a challenge to your academics. Provide vivid, real-life illustrations of how each of those responsibilities sometimes conflicts with your studies.

The Certainty of Fear

Audra Kendall

PREVIEW

What are you afraid of? Were your fears different five years ago? Will they change as you grow older? In this selection, Audra Kendall shows us that every stage of life brings its own fears—and that all fears revolve around the threat of loss. Do your fears fit the pattern?

I had all the usual childhood fears. I couldn't go to sleep unless the light in my 1 bedroom closet was on. I dreaded that someday when my mother was distracted, Crazy Betty (our local small-town oddball) would grab me in the grocery store. On the hottest summer nights, my feet had to be wrapped tightly in my bedsheets; if one of them hung bare over the side of the bed, who knew what might grab it in its cold, slimy claw?

But all other frights paled before the Great Fear, the *Titanic* of my childhood 2 terrors. That fear—and I admit, I feel a tightening in my stomach typing the words even today—was that something would happen to Monk-Monk.

Looking at Monk-Monk today, you wouldn't see what I see. You'd see a torn, 3 discolored sock monkey, very much past his prime, stuffing leaking from his stumpy tail, holes on his sock-body inexpertly stitched up with thread that doesn't match. I see my dearest childhood friend, my companion of a thousand nights. When I was only two and very ill, an aunt made him for me and delivered him to the hospital. I bonded with him fiercely and rarely let him out of my sight. When no one else was around, Monk-Monk played endless games with me, soaked up my tears, and listened to my secrets.

And then Uncle Ken came to visit. I didn't know Uncle Ken well, and I didn't 4 like him very much. I had the feeling he didn't really like me, either. He clearly thought it was pretty silly that a big first-grader was dragging a sock monkey around, and he teased me by saying he thought he'd take Monk-Monk home to Ohio with him. I clutched Monk-Monk more tightly.

I was at school a few days later when Uncle Ken left. When I came home, I 5 couldn't find Monk-Monk anywhere. I can hardly describe the depths of my panic. I don't think I cried; my terror was beyond that. I could barely breathe. My thoughts raced like a wild animal in a tiny cage. Where was Monk-Monk? What had Uncle Ken done to him? Was he safe somewhere, or had Uncle Ken (and this thought made my heart nearly stop) thrown him out the car window? Was Monk-Monk lying in a weedy strip along the interstate, lonely and cold, never to be loved again?

When we found Monk-Monk wedged behind the sofa (could Uncle Ken really **6** have been mean enough to do that? I never found out), I was limp with relief. For days afterwards I was shaken, crying at the least provocation.

As far as I can remember, that near-loss of Monk-Monk was my first encounter **7** with real, deep-down fear. I felt the threatened loss of something precious to me. And that, I think, is the essence of fear—the threat of loss.

Small children fear the loss of a favorite toy. The fears of adolescents are dif- **8** ferent. Above almost anything, adolescents fear losing their cool—looking "stupid." They will risk almost anything in order to maintain the illusion that they are cool, composed and in control.

Let me give you an example. A friend of mine had the opportunity to work **9** in Florence, Italy, for a few months. While he was gone, he arranged for his two teenage sons to visit him for a week. The excited boys arrived at the airport and checked in. After sitting down to wait for their flight, one nudged the other. "Look at the tickets," he told his brother. "They don't say 'Florence.'" Indeed, the tickets did not list Florence as the destination. They said "Firenze."

Now, it so happens that Firenze is the Italian name for Florence, so everything **10** was fine. But the boys didn't know that. They thought that through some error, they were being put on the wrong plane for the wrong destination.

So what did they do?   **11**

Nothing.   **12**

At the appointed time, they unhappily boarded the plane for Firenze, sat **13** down, and worried silently for six hours that they were going to end up in, oh, maybe South America. Possibly Asia. They had no idea. But the thought of admitting to a ticket agent that they didn't know what "Firenze" meant was more terrifying than the prospect of being dumped, alone, in a strange city on an unknown continent.

The fear of being conspicuous does not usually land teenagers on jet airplanes **14** bound for unknown destinations. But for many adolescents, it rules their daily lives. Such fear is rooted in the enormous self-consciousness that afflicts many adolescents. Psychologist David Elkind has come up with what he calls the "Imaginary Audience Theory" to help explain this period of life.

During adolescence, Elkind says, kids are changing so much so fast (physically, **15** mentally, and emotionally) that they become intensely self-centered. It is literally difficult for them to remember that other individuals have their own lives, thoughts, and feelings, and that they are not focusing their attention on the adolescents. According to Elkind, the adolescent feels as though he or she is on an enormous stage before a watchful audience that is noticing every aspect of his or her behavior. As a result, the adolescent is terrified of doing or saying something that will attract scorn or criticism. As a result, we end up with the teenager whose life is "ruined" by an outbreak of acne; an adolescent who won't leave the house on a bad hair day, or the teen who refuses to return to school after making an embarrassing slip during a speech.

In general, typical adolescent fears don't do great harm. Kids mature and eventu- 16 ally realize a moment's embarrassment isn't that big a deal, and that, in fact, most people aren't paying much attention to them at all. But the fear of being conspicuous can have serious, even tragic results. Adolescents can be so fearful of being criticized that they sometimes go along with the crowd when it is in their best interests not to. Teens get into cars with obviously intoxicated drivers; they go along with the crowd on a shoplifting expedition; they engage in risky sexual behavior, etc., in large part because they are afraid to speak up and risk the scorn of the "audience."

In midlife, we generally become more confident and less obsessed with what 17 others are thinking of us. But underneath that veneer of confidence, a new kind of fear grips many middle-aged people. That fear has been expressed in timeless fashion by the Italian poet Dante in his famous poem *The Inferno:* "In the middle of the road, I found myself in a dark wood, with no clear path through."

The key word here is "middle." As people enter middle age, they face the un- 18 settling fact that their lives are halfway over. They are no longer youngsters, looking ahead at decades filled with unlimited potential. In looking back at what they have accomplished, many people feel unsatisfied. They may not have achieved the career success they had hoped for. They fear they do not have time to reach goals that they had once dreamed of. They become critical of their own aging bodies. As their parents die and their children grow up and leave home, they feel adrift, no longer certain of their roles in life. Frightening thoughts press in: "My life is heading downhill. I'm running out of time."

The result of all this inner turmoil is what is often termed a midlife crisis. Mov- 19 ies and sitcoms often present such a crisis in tragicomic style: the middle-aged guy dumps his wife, dyes his hair, buys a sports car, and begins romancing a woman young enough to be his daughter. The middle-aged woman gets liposuction and a facelift and has an affair with a young personal trainer.

There is plenty of evidence that such behavior does occur. Many long-term 20 marriages break up as a result of one or both partners' midlife crisis. The panicky feelings that can result from thinking "Is this all there is?" can make even a formerly happy marriage seem suffocating.

However, most midlife crises do not have such dramatic results. More typi- 21 cally, the midlife crisis is a time of inner exploration, of reconsidering one's priorities. It may involve a period of depression, but, fortunately, most people emerge from a midlife crisis feeling relatively satisfied. They come to terms with the idea that youth and its promise are behind them, and learn to appreciate the perhaps quieter joys of mature life.

Those joys and a sense of certainty about life's priorities often carry over into the 22 elderly years. Senior citizens self-knowledge often allows them to state their opinions and explore new interests in a way they did not feel free to in their younger years.

But along with the relief from self-consciousness comes another set of fears 23 for the elderly. Those fears center around the increasing frailty of the body and the accompanying loss of independence.

Some years ago, a television ad featured an elderly woman saying, "Help! I've **24** fallen and I can't get up." The ad became the punch line of many jokes, but the message was serious. Many elderly people report falling as their greatest fear. They are not simply concerned with the injury they might suffer. They worry that a fall might lead to being institutionalized, a step that many elderly people fear deeply. After a lifetime of independence and, often, of taking care of others, they dread the idea of being helpless, even a burden to their families.

As a result, many elderly people—especially after having suffered a fall or **25** another injury—become increasingly reluctant to go out into the world to try new things and keep up with friends. Afraid of being hurt, they become hermit-like, staying within the confines of their homes. Ironically, this isolation and lack of exercise can actually hasten the dreaded loss of independence. Mental and physical activity are both key elements in keeping elderly people in good health.

Benjamin Franklin once wrote, "In this world nothing is certain but death and **26** taxes." Franklin might have added, "and fears." Every stage of life brings them; while we may say goodbye to childish fears, there are always others in the wings, waiting to take their place. By being aware of them, we can keep their dark shadows from adversely affecting our lives.

READING COMPREHENSION

1. The word *turmoil* in "The result of all this inner turmoil is what is often termed a midlife crisis" (paragraph 19) means
   a. confusion.
   b. calmness.
   c. sickness.
   d. anger.

2. The word *frailty* in "Those fears center around the increasing frailty of the body and the accompanying loss of independence" (paragraph 23) means
   a. physical weakness.
   b. restlessness.
   c. tiredness.
   d. slowness.

3. Which of the following would be a good alternative title for this selection?
   a. Don't Let Fear Rule Your Life
   b. The *Titanic* of My Childhood Fears
   c. Death, Taxes, and Fears
   d. Every Stage of Life Brings Fear

4. Which of the following sentences best expresses the main idea of the selection?

    a. It is impossible to be totally fearless.

    b. Many people allow their fears to negatively affect their behavior.

    c. People fear different things at different stages in their lives.

    d. Some people handle fear better than others.

5. According to the selection, the thing that adolescents fear most of all is

    a. looking "stupid."

    b. flying to overseas destinations.

    c. appearing to be self-conscious.

    d. engaging in risky behavior.

6. The author states that elderly people

    a. are better off leading a quiet existence.

    b. need both mental and physical activity to stay healthy.

    c. sometimes feel relief when they are institutionalized.

    d. have less to fear than adolescents and middle-aged people.

7. Many elderly report their greatest fear to be

    a. fear of outliving their spouse.

    b. fear of falling.

    c. fear of getting cancer.

    d. fear of becoming deaf and blind.

8. The author infers that Uncle Ken was

    a. an insensitive, mean-spirited man.

    b. kind-hearted, but silly.

    c. wise to conclude that a first-grader should not be dragging around a sock monkey.

    d. probably a child molester.

9. On the basis of paragraphs 20–21, we can infer that the author

    a. strongly disapproves of middle-aged people who have affairs with younger partners.

    b. respects middle-aged people who do new things, like taking up with younger partners, buying sports cars, and having plastic surgery.

    c. is not yet middle-aged.

    d. believes it is important for middle-aged people to learn to appreciate the quieter joys of mature life.

10. Paragraph 26 suggests that

    a. recognizing our fears helps us to keep them from becoming crippling.

    b. Ben Franklin was himself fearless.

    c. all fears are childish.

    d. it is possible, with effort, to become completely fearless.

STRUCTURE AND TECHNIQUE

1. The author uses the first-person approach to introduce her topic. Why do you think she uses this approach? Do you think this approach is effective?

2. In paragraph 5, Kendall writes a series of four questions. Why does she employ this technique? Do you think it is effective?

3. Which kind of transition signal—addition, change of direction, or illustration—does Kendall use to move from a discussion of adolescent fears to a discussion of fears that occur in middle age? From midlife fears to fears of the elderly? Which transitional word does she use in each case?

4. In paragraph 2, Kendall begins a personal anecdote about her own greatest childhood fear. Starting in paragraph 9, she relates another anecdote about the teenage sons of a friend of hers. What do these anecdotes contribute to the essay? How do they relate to the larger point she is trying to make?

CRITICAL READING AND DISCUSSION

1. Kendall calls her greatest childhood fear "the *Titanic* of my childhood terrors." What does the use of this metaphor add to her essay? What was your own greatest childhood fear? Did it actually happen?

2. According to Kendall, different stages of life are characterized by different fears. Which fears accompany which stages? Based upon your observations, is Kendall's thesis accurate? Why or why not?

3. The author writes, "And that, I think, is the essence of fear—the threat of loss." Do you agree with her? What are some examples you can think of in which fears are caused by the threat of loss? If you disagree with her statement, what other fears can you think of that would lie outside this description?

4. What do you think of psychologist David Elkind's "Imaginary Audience Theory" of adolescence? Did you feel the kind of self-consciousness he describes when you were an adolescent? Do you observe that kind of behavior in other teens?

WRITING ASSIGNMENTS

Assignment 1

Clearly, the loss of Monk-Monk was a frightening incident in Kendall's childhood. Write an essay about a frightening incident that occurred during your childhood. Begin by providing some background information about yourself. How old were you when this incident occurred? Where did it take place? Was another person involved besides you? Was this incident something you had feared might happen or did it happen unexpectedly? Then organize your supporting paragraphs into two or three time phases. First, you may want to review Chapter 9 on the narrative essay (pages 203–221). You might conclude your essay by summing up what this incident says about childhood fears in general.

Alternatively, write an essay in which you describe in detail three of your childhood fears. The thesis of your essay might be similar to this:

Like Audra Kendall in "The Certainty of Fear," I had my own childhood fears.

Assignment 2

Kendall writes about fears that characterize different life stages. Think of some people you know of different ages. Then write an essay about three of them who exhibit fears characteristic of their age group. The thesis of your essay might be similar to this:

It is clear to me that my little brother Ben, my thirteen-year-old cousin Ted, and my grandmother Rose have fears that are specific to their age group.

A supporting paragraph about a little brother, for instance, might begin, "Since I'm often around him, I've come to realize that my little brother Ben has some typical childhood fears."

Assignment 3

Often the things we fear never happen, such as the fear the teens in the selection had of landing someplace other than in Florence, Italy. Write an essay in which you contrast your fears about *what could have happened* on three different occasions with what actually happened. Below are a few possible situations you might describe:

starting school	learning a new skill
going on a first date	beginning a new job
making a class presentation or	giving birth
giving a speech	playing a sport
going on a job interview	taking an exam
performing on stage	

What's Wrong with Schools? Teacher Plays Student, Learns to Lie and Cheat

Casey Banas

PREVIEW

A teacher pretends to be a student and sits in on several classes. What does she find in the typical class? Boredom. Routine. Apathy. Manipulation. Discouragement. If this depressing list sounds familiar, you will be interested in the following analysis of why classes often seem to be more about killing time than about learning.

Ellen Glanz lied to her teacher about why she hadn't done her homework; but, of 1 course, many students have lied to their teachers. The difference is that Ellen Glanz was a twenty-eight-year-old high school social studies teacher who was a student for six months to improve her teaching by gaining a fresh perspective of her school.

She found many classes boring, students doing as little as necessary to pass tests 2 and get good grades, students using ruses to avoid assignments, and students manipulating teachers to do the work for them. She concluded that many students are turned off because they have little power and responsibility for their own education.

Ellen Glanz found herself doing the same things as the students. There was the 3 day when Glanz wanted to join her husband in helping friends celebrate the purchase of a house, but she had homework for a math class. For the first time, she knew how teenagers feel when they think something is more important than homework.

She found a way out and confided: "I considered my options: Confess openly 4 to the teacher, copy someone else's sheet, or make up an excuse." Glanz chose the third option—the one most widely used—and told the teacher that the pages needed to complete the assignment had been ripped from the book. The teacher accepted the story, never checking the book. In class, nobody else did the homework; and student after student mumbled responses when called on.

"Finally," Glanz said, "the teacher, thinking that the assignment must have 5 been difficult, went over each question at the board while students copied the problems at their seats. The teacher had 'covered' the material and the students had listened to the explanation. But had anything been learned? I don't think so."

Glanz found this kind of thing common. "In many cases," she said, "people 6 simply didn't do the work assignment, but copied from someone else or manipulated the teacher into doing the work for them."

"The system encourages incredible passivity," Glanz said. "In most classes 7 one sits and listens. A teacher, whose role is activity, simply cannot understand the passivity of the student's role," she said. "When I taught," Glanz recalled, "my mind was going constantly—figuring out how to best present an idea, thinking about whom to call on, whom to draw out, whom to shut up; how to get students involved, how to make my point clearer, how to respond; when to be funny, when serious. As a student, I experienced little of this. Everything was done to me."

Class methods promote the feeling that students have little control over or 8 responsibility for their own education because the agenda is the teacher's, Glanz said. The teacher is convinced the subject matter is worth knowing, but the student may not agree. Many students, Glanz said, are not convinced they need to know what teachers teach, but they believe good grades are needed to get into college.

Students, obsessed with getting good grades to help qualify for the college of 9 their choice, believe the primary responsibility for their achievement rests with the teacher, Glanz said. "It was his responsibility to teach well rather than their responsibility to learn carefully."

Teachers were regarded by students, Glanz said, not as "people," but as "role- 10 players" who dispensed information needed to pass a test. "I often heard students describing teachers as drips, bores, and numerous varieties of idiots," she said. "Yet I knew that many of the same people had traveled the world over, conducted fascinating experiments or learned three languages, or were accomplished musicians, artists, or athletes."

But the sad reality, Glanz said, is the failure of teachers to recognize their 11 tremendous communication gap with students. Some students, she explained, believe that effort has little value. After seeing political corruption they conclude that honesty takes a back seat to getting ahead any way one can, she said. "I sometimes estimated that half to two-thirds of a class cheated on a given test," Glanz said. "Worse, I've encountered students who feel no remorse about cheating but are annoyed that a teacher has confronted them on their actions."

Glanz has since returned to teaching at Lincoln-Sudbury. Before her stint as 12 a student, she would worry that perhaps she was demanding too much. "Now I know I should have demanded more," she said. Before, she was quick to accept the excuses of students who came to class unprepared. Now she says, "You are responsible for learning it." But a crackdown is only a small part of the solution.

The larger issue, Glanz said, is that educators must recognize that teachers 13 and students, though physically in the same school, are in separate worlds and have an ongoing power struggle. "A first step toward ending this battle is to convince students that what we attempt to teach them is genuinely worth knowing," Glanz said. "We must be sure, ourselves, that what we are teaching is worth knowing." No longer, she emphasized, do students assume that "teacher knows best."

READING COMPREHENSION

1. The word *ruses* in "students using ruses to avoid assignments" (paragraph 2) means
   a. questions.
   b. sicknesses.
   c. parents.
   d. tricks.

2. The word *agenda* in "the agenda is the teacher's" (paragraph 8) means
   a. program.
   b. boredom.
   c. happiness.
   d. book.

3. Which of the following would be a good alternative title for this selection?
   a. How to Get Good Grades
   b. Why Students Dislike School
   c. Cheating in Our School System
   d. Students Who Manipulate Teachers

4. Which sentence best expresses the main idea of the selection?
   a. Ellen Glanz is a burned-out teacher.
   b. Ellen Glanz lied to her math teacher.
   c. Students need good grades to get into college.
   d. Teachers and students feel differently about schooling.

5. How much of a class, according to the author's estimate, would often cheat on a test?
   a. One-quarter or less
   b. One-half
   c. One-half to two-thirds
   d. Almost everyone

6. *True or False?* _____ As a result of her experience, Glanz now accepts more of her students' excuses.

7. Glanz found that the school system encourages an incredible amount of

   a. enthusiasm.

   b. passivity.

   c. violence.

   d. creativity.

8. The author implies that

   a. few students cheat on tests.

   b. most students enjoy schoolwork.

   c. classroom teaching methods should be changed.

   d. Glanz had a lazy math teacher.

9. The author implies that

   a. Glanz should not have become a student again.

   b. Glanz is a better teacher than she was before.

   c. Glanz later told her math teacher that she lied.

   d. social studies is an unimportant subject.

10. The author implies that

   a. most students who cheat on tests are caught by their teachers.

   b. most teachers demand too little of their students.

   c. students who get good grades in high school also do so in college.

   d. students never question what teachers say.

STRUCTURE AND TECHNIQUE

1. Which method of introduction—broad-to-narrow, anecdote, or questions—does Banas use in his essay? Why do you think he chose this approach?

2. List the time transitions that Banas uses in paragraph 12. How do they help Banas make his point?

3. Throughout "What's Wrong with Schools?" Banas shifts between summarizing Ellen Glanz's words and quoting Glanz directly. Find an instance in the essay in which both direct and indirect quotations are used in the same paragraph. What does Banas gain or lose from using this technique? (Refer to pages 549–550 for definitions and examples of direct and indirect quotations.)

4. Parallel structures are often used to emphasize similar information. They can create a smooth, readable style. For example, note the series of *-ing* verbs in the following sentence from paragraph 2: " . . . students **doing** as little as necessary to pass tests and get good grades, students **using** ruses to avoid assignments, and students **manipulating** teachers to do the work for them." Find two other uses of parallelism, one in paragraph 4 and one in paragraph 7.

CRITICAL READING AND DISCUSSION

1. After reading this essay, what do you think Glanz's attitude is? Is she pro- or anti-teacher? Pro- or anti-student? Provide evidence for your position.

2. Banas suggests that many students are in school to get good grades—not to learn. Explain whether or not you agree with this assessment. Do you find that getting a good grade isn't always the same as really learning?

3. The author ends with Glanz's view of "the larger issue": "We must be sure, ourselves, that what we are teaching is worth knowing." What was taught in your high school classes that you feel is worth knowing or not worth knowing? Explain why. Also, what is being taught in your college classes that you feel is worth knowing or not worth knowing, and why?

4. Much of this essay contrasts the behavior of students with that of teachers. In what ways does Glanz see their behavior and views differing? What do you think each group should be doing differently?

WRITING ASSIGNMENTS

Assignment 1

Play the role of student observer in one of your college classes. Then write an essay with *either* of the following theses:

> In my _____ class, students are turned off.
>
> In my _____ class, students are active and interested.

In each supporting paragraph, state and detail one reason why the atmosphere in that particular class is either boring or interesting. You might want to consider areas such as these:

Instructor: presentation, tone of voice, level of interest and enthusiasm, teaching aids used, ability to handle questions, sense of humor, and so on

Students: level of enthusiasm, participation in class, attitude (as shown by body language and other actions), and so on

Other factors: conditions of classroom, length of class period, noise level in classroom, and so on

Assignment 2

Glanz says that students like to describe their teachers as "drips, bores, and numerous varieties of idiots." Write a description of one of your high school teachers or college instructors who either *does* or *does not* fit that description. Show, in your essay, that your teacher or instructor was weak, boring, and idiotic—or just the opposite (dynamic, creative, and bright). In either case, your focus should be on providing specific details that *enable your readers to see for themselves* that your thesis is valid.

Assignment 3

How does the classroom situation Ellen Glanz describes compare with a classroom situation with which you are familiar—either one from the high school you attended or one from the school in which you are presently enrolled? Select one class you were or are a part of, and write an essay in which you compare or contrast your class with the ones Ellen Glanz describes. Here are some areas you might wish to include in your essay:

how interesting the class was

how many of the students did their assignments

what the teaching methods were

how much was actually learned

how active the teacher or instructor was

how passive the students were

what the students thought of the teacher or instructor

Choose any three of the above areas or three other areas. Then decide which method of development you will use: *one side at a time* or *point by point* (see pages 282–284).

Propaganda Techniques in Today's Advertising

Ann McClintock

PREVIEW

Advertisers want your business, and they will use a variety of clever ad slogans to get it. If you've ever responded to ads, you have been swayed by the effective use of propaganda. You may associate the word *propaganda* with the tactics used by strong-arm governments. But Ann McClintock provides evidence that we are the targets of propaganda every day and that it shapes many of our opinions and decisions.

Americans, adults and children alike, are being seduced. They are being brain- 1
washed. And few of us protest. Why? Because the seducers and the brainwashers are the advertisers we willingly invite into our homes. We are victims, content—even eager—to be victimized. We read advertisers' propaganda messages in newspapers and magazines; we watch their alluring images on television. We absorb their messages and images into our subconscious. We all do it—even those of us who claim to see through advertisers' tricks and therefore feel immune to advertising's charm. Advertisers lean heavily on propaganda to sell products, whether the "products" are a brand of toothpaste, a candidate for office, or a particular political viewpoint.

Propaganda is a systematic effort to influence people's opinions, to win them 2
over to a certain view or side. Propaganda is not necessarily concerned with what is true or false, good or bad. Propagandists simply want people to believe the messages being sent. Often, propagandists will use outright lies or more subtle deceptions to sway people's opinions. In a propaganda war, any tactic is considered fair.

When we hear the word "propaganda," we usually think of a foreign menace: 3
anti-American radio programs broadcast by a totalitarian regime or brainwashing tactics practiced on hostages. Although propaganda may seem relevant only in the political arena, the concept can be applied fruitfully to the way products and ideas are sold in advertising. Indeed, the vast majority of us are targets in advertisers' propaganda war. Every day, we are bombarded with slogans, print and Internet pop-up ads, commercials, packaging claims, billboards, trademarks, logos, and designer brands—all forms of propaganda. One study reports that each of us, during an average day, is exposed to over *five hundred* advertising claims of various

types. This saturation may even increase in the future, since current trends include ads on movie screens, shopping carts, videocassettes, and even public television.

What kind of propaganda techniques do advertisers use? There are seven basic 4
types:

1. Name Calling.   Name calling is a propaganda tactic in which negatively 5
charged names are hurled against the opposing side or competitor. By using such names, propagandists try to arouse feelings of mistrust, fear, and hate in their audiences. For example, a political advertisement may label an opposing candidate a "loser," "fence-sitter," or "warmonger." Depending on the advertiser's target market, labels such as "a friend of big business" or "a dues-paying member of the party in power" can be the epithets that damage an opponent. Ads for products may also use name calling. An American manufacturer may refer, for instance, to a "foreign car" in its commercial—not an "imported" one. The label of foreignness will have unpleasant connotations in many people's minds. A childhood rhyme claims that "names can never hurt me," but name calling is an effective way to damage the opposition, whether it is another car maker or a congressional candidate.

2. Glittering Generalities.   Using glittering generalities is the opposite of name call- 6
ing. In this case, advertisers surround their products with attractive—and slippery—words and phrases. They use vague terms that are difficult to define and that may have different meanings to different people: *freedom, democratic, all-American, progressive, Christian,* and *justice.* Many such words have strong affirmative overtones. This kind of language stirs positive feelings in people, feelings that may spill over to the product or idea being pitched. As with name calling, the emotional response may overwhelm logic. Target audiences accept the product without thinking very much about what the glittering generalities mean—or whether they even apply to the product. After all, how can anyone oppose "truth, justice, and the American way"?

The ads for politicians and political causes often use glittering generalities 7
because such "buzzwords" can influence votes. Election slogans include high-sounding but basically empty phrases like the following:

"He cares about people." (That's nice, but is he a better candidate than his opponent?)

"Vote for progress." (Progress by whose standards?)

"They'll make this country great again." (What does "great" mean? Does "great" mean the same thing to others as it does to me?)

"Vote for the future." (What kind of future?)

"If you love America, vote for Phyllis Smith." (If I don't vote for Smith, does that mean I don't love America?)

Ads for consumer goods are also sprinkled with glittering generalities. 8
Product names, for instance, are supposed to evoke good feelings: *Luvs* diapers.

Stayfree feminine hygiene products, *Joy* liquid detergent, *Loving Care* hair color, *Almost Home* cookies, *Yankee Doodle* pastries. Product slogans lean heavily on vague but comforting phrases: . . . General Electric "brings good things to life," and Dow Chemical "lets you do great things." Chevrolet, we are told, is the "heartbeat of America," and Chrysler boasts cars that are "built by Americans for Americans."

3. Transfer. In transfer, advertisers try to improve the image of a product by associating it with a symbol most people respect, like the American flag or Uncle Sam. The advertisers hope that the prestige attached to the symbol will carry over to the product. Many companies use transfer devices to identify their products: Lincoln Insurance shows a profile of the president; Continental Insurance portrays a Revolutionary War minuteman; Amtrak's logo is red, white, and blue; Liberty Mutual's corporate symbol is the Statue of Liberty; Allstate's name is cradled by a pair of protective, fatherly hands. 9

Corporations also use the transfer technique when they sponsor prestigious shows on radio and television. These shows function as symbols of dignity and class. Kraft Corporation, for instance, sponsored a "Leonard Bernstein Conducts Beethoven" concert, while Gulf Oil is the sponsor of *National Geographic* specials and Mobil supports public television's *Masterpiece Theater*. In this way, corporations can reach an educated, influential audience and, perhaps, improve their public image by associating themselves with quality programming. 10

Political ads, of course, practically wrap themselves in the flag. Ads for a political candidate often show either the Washington Monument, a Fourth of July parade, the Stars and Stripes, a bald eagle soaring over the mountains, or a white-steepled church on the village green. The national anthem or "America the Beautiful" may play in the background. Such appeals to Americans' love of country can surround the candidate with an aura of patriotism and integrity. 11

4. Testimonial. The testimonial is one of advertisers' most-loved and most-used propaganda techniques. Similar to the transfer device, the testimonial capitalizes on the admiration people have for a celebrity to make the product shine more brightly—even though the celebrity is not an expert on the product being sold. 12

Print and television ads offer a nonstop parade of testimonials: here's William Shatner for Priceline.com; here's basketball star Michael Jordan eating Wheaties; a slew of well-known people (including pop star Madonna) advertise clothing from the Gap; and Jerry Seinfeld assures us he never goes anywhere without his American Express card. Testimonials can sell movies, too; newspaper ads for films often feature favorable comments by well-known reviewers. And, in recent years, testimonials have played an important role in pitching books; the backs of paperbacks frequently list complimentary blurbs by celebrities. 13

Political candidates, as well as their ad agencies, know the value of testimonials. Barbra Streisand lent her star appeal to the presidential campaign of Bill 14

Clinton, while Arnold Schwarzenegger endorsed George Bush. Even controversial social issues are debated by celebrities. The nuclear freeze, for instance, starred Paul Newman for the pro side and Charlton Heston for the con.

As illogical as testimonials sometimes are (Pepsi's Michael Jackson, for in-   15 stance, was a health-food adherent who does not drink soft drinks), they are effective propaganda. We like the *person* so much that we like the *product* too.

5. Plain Folks.   The plain folks approach says, in effect, "Buy me or vote for me.   16 I'm just like you." Regular folks will surely like Bob Evans's Down on the Farm Country Sausage or good old-fashioned Countrytime Lemonade. Some ads emphasize the idea that "we're all in the same boat." We see people making long-distance calls for just the reasons we do—to put the baby on the phone to Grandma or to tell Mom we love her. And how do these folksy, warmhearted (usually saccharine[1]) scenes affect us? They're supposed to make us feel that AT&T—the multinational corporate giant—has the same values we do. Similarly, we are introduced to the little people at Ford, the ordinary folks who work on the assembly line, not to bigwigs in their executive offices. What's the purpose of such an approach? To encourage us to buy a car built by these honest, hardworking "everyday Joes" who care about quality as much as we do.

Political advertisements make almost as much use of the "plain folks" ap-   17 peal as they do of transfer devices. Candidates wear hard hats, farmers' caps, and assembly-line coveralls. They jog around the block and carry their own luggage through the airport. The idea is to convince voters that the candidates are average people, not the elite—not wealthy lawyers or executives but common citizens.

6. Card Stacking.   When people say that "the cards were stacked against me,"   18 they mean that they were never given a fair chance. Applied to propaganda, card stacking means that one side may suppress or distort evidence, tell half-truths, oversimplify the facts, or set up a "straw man"—a false target—to divert attention from the issue at hand. Card stacking is a difficult form of propaganda both to detect and to combat. When a candidate claims that an opponent has "changed his mind five times on this important issue," we tend to accept the claim without investigating whether the candidate had good reasons for changing his mind. Many people are simply swayed by the distorted claim that the candidate is "waffling" on the issue.

Advertisers often stack the cards in favor of the products they are pushing.   19 They may, for instance, use what are called "weasel words." These are small words that usually slip right past us, but that make the difference between reality and illusion. The weasel words are underlined in the following claims:

"Helps control dandruff symptoms." (The audience usually interprets this as stops dandruff.)

---

[1] *saccharine:* exaggeratedly sentimental.

"Most dentists surveyed recommend sugarless gum for their patients who chew gum." (We hear the "most dentists" and "for their patients," but we don't think about how many were surveyed or whether or not the dentists first recommended that the patients not chew gum at all.)

"Sticker price $1,000 lower than most comparable cars." (How many is "most"? What car does the advertiser consider "comparable"?)

Advertisers also use a card stacking trick when they make an unfinished claim. **20** For example, they will say that their product has "twice as much pain reliever." We are left with a favorable impression. We don't usually ask, "Twice as much pain reliever as what?" Or advertisers may make extremely vague claims that sound alluring but have no substance: Toyota's "Oh, what a feeling!"; Vantage cigarettes' "the taste of success"; "The spirit of Marlboro"; Coke's "the real thing." Another way to stack the cards in favor of a certain product is to use scientific-sounding claims that are not supported by sound research. When Ford claimed that its LTD model was "400% quieter," many people assumed that its LTD must be quieter than all other cars. When taken to court, however, Ford admitted that the phrase referred to the difference between the noise level inside and outside the LTD. Other scientific-sounding claims use mysterious ingredients that are never explained as selling points: Retsyn, "special whitening agents," "the ingredient doctors recommend."

7. Bandwagon.   In the bandwagon technique, advertisers pressure, "Everyone's **21** doing it. Why don't you?" This kind of propaganda often succeeds because many people have a deep desire not to be different. Political ads tell us to vote for the "winning candidate." The advertisers know we tend to feel comfortable doing what others do; we want to be on the winning team. Or ads show a series of people proclaiming, "I'm voting for the senator. I don't know why anyone wouldn't." Again, the audience feels under pressure to conform.

In the marketplace, the bandwagon approach lures buyers. Ads tell us that **22** "nobody doesn't like Sara Lee" (the message is that you must be weird if you don't). They tell us that "most people prefer Brand X two to one over other leading brands" (to be like the majority, we should buy Brand X). If we don't drink Pepsi, we're left out of "the Pepsi generation." To take part in "America's favorite health kick," the National Dairy Council asks us, "Got Milk?" And Honda motorcycle ads, praising the virtues of being a follower, tell us, "Follow the leader. He's on a Honda."

Why do these propaganda techniques work? Why do so many of us buy the **23** products, viewpoints, and candidates urged on us by propaganda messages? They work because they appeal to our emotions, not to our minds. Often, in fact, they capitalize on our prejudices and biases. For example, if we are convinced that environmentalists are radicals who want to destroy America's record of industrial growth and progress, then we will applaud the candidate who refers to them as "treehuggers." Clear thinking requires hard work: analyzing a claim, researching the facts, examining both sides of an issue, using logic to see the flaws in an argument. Many of us would rather let the propagandists do our thinking for us.

Because propaganda is so effective, it is important to detect it and understand 24 how it is used. We may conclude, after close examination, that some propaganda sends a truthful, worthwhile message. Some advertising, for instance, urges us not to drive drunk, to become volunteers, to contribute to charity. Even so, we must be aware that propaganda is being used. Otherwise, we have consented to handing over to others our independence of thought and action.

READING COMPREHENSION

1. The word *epithets* in "labels such as 'a friend of big business' or 'a dues-paying member of the party in power' can be the epithets that damage an opponent" (paragraph 5) means

   a. courtesies.

   b. descriptive labels.

   c. assurances.

   d. delays.

2. The words *capitalizes on* in "the testimonial capitalizes on the admiration people have for a celebrity" (paragraph 12) mean

   a. reports about.

   b. ignores.

   c. cuts back on.

   d. takes advantage of.

3. Which of the following would be a good alternative title for this selection?

   a. The World of Advertising

   b. Common Persuasion Techniques in Advertising

   c. Propaganda in Politics

   d. Common Advertising Techniques on Television

4. Which sentence best expresses the main idea of the selection?

   a. Americans may be exposed daily to over five hundred advertising claims of some sort.

   b. The testimonial takes advantage of the admiration people have for celebrities, even though they have no expertise on the product being sold.

   c. People should detect and understand common propaganda techniques, which appeal to the emotions rather than to logic.

   d. Americans need to understand that advertising, a huge industry, affects their lives in numerous ways.

5. The propaganda technique in which a product is associated with a symbol or image most people admire and respect is
    a. glittering generalities.
    b. transfer.
    c. testimonials.
    d. bandwagon.

6. The technique in which evidence is withheld or distorted is called
    a. glittering generalities.
    b. bandwagon.
    c. plain folks.
    d. card stacking.

7. The technique that makes a political candidate seem to be just like the people an ad is aimed at is
    a. glittering generalities.
    b. bandwagon.
    c. plain folks.
    d. card stacking.

8. A way to avoid being taken in by propaganda is to use
    a. our emotions.
    b. name calling.
    c. clear thinking.
    d. our subconscious.

9. The author implies in paragraph 16 that
    a. most Americans do not frequently call their grandmothers.
    b. multinational corporations do not have the same values as average citizens.
    c. Bob Evans is an American celebrity.
    d. executives at AT&T and Ford are hardworking and honest.

10. From paragraphs 23 and 24, we can conclude that the author feels
    a. we are unlikely to analyze advertising logically unless we recognize it as propaganda.
    b. propaganda should not be allowed.
    c. if we don't want to hand over to others our independence, we should ignore all propaganda.
    d. we should not support the "products, viewpoints, and candidates urged on us by propaganda messages."

STRUCTURE AND TECHNIQUE

1. In paragraph 1, McClintock's choice of words reveals her attitudes toward both propagandists and the public. What specific words reveal her attitudes, and what attitudes do they represent?

2. What key term does McClintock define in paragraph 2? Why does she define it here? Where else in the essay does she use the technique of definition?

3. McClintock uses parentheses in two lists, the ones in paragraphs 7 and 19. What purpose do these parentheses serve?

4. McClintock provides abundant examples throughout her essay. Why does she provide so many examples? What does she accomplish with this technique?

What propaganda technique (or techniques) does this advertisement use? Is it effective? Why or why not?

CRITICAL READING AND DISCUSSION

1. Some of the propaganda techniques listed in the selection have contrasting appeals. How do name-calling and glittering generalities contrast with each other? Testimonials and plain folks?

2. Why are ads that use the bandwagon approach so effective? What ads have you seen recently that use that approach?

3. The author states, "Americans, adults and children alike, are being seduced" (paragraph 1). What might be the differences between the ways adults and children react to the seductions of advertising?

4. McClintock states, "We are victims, content—even eager—to be victimized" (paragraph 1). Do you agree? Is this article likely to change how you view ads in the future? Why or why not?

WRITING ASSIGNMENTS

Assignment 1

Imagine that you work for an ad agency and have been asked to come up with at least three possible campaigns for a new product (for example, a car, a perfume, a detergent, jeans, beer, a toothpaste, a deodorant, or an appliance). Write an essay in which you describe three different propaganda techniques that might be used to sell the product and how these claims could persuade the public to buy. Be specific about the general looks, the character, and the wording of your ads and about how they fit with the techniques you suggest.

Assignment 2

Choose three ads currently appearing on television or in print. Show that each ad uses one or more of the propaganda techniques McClintock discusses. Be specific about product names, what the ad looks like, kinds of characters in the ad, and so on. Don't forget that all your specific details should back up your point that each ad uses a certain propaganda technique (or techniques) to sell a product. Your thesis will make some overall statement about the three ads, such as either of these:

> Beer advertisements use a variety of propaganda techniques.

> Glittering generalities are used to sell very different types of products.

Assignment 3

Do some informal "market research" on why people buy the products they do. Begin by asking at least ten people why they bought a particular brand-name item. You might question them about something they're wearing (designer jeans, for example). Or you might ask them what toothpaste they use, what car they drive, what pain reliever they take, or what chicken they eat—or ask about any other product people use. Take notes on the reasons people give for their purchases.

Then write an essay with the thesis "My research suggests that people often buy products for three reasons." Include in your introductory paragraph your plan of development—a list of the three reasons that were mentioned most often by the people you interviewed. Develop your supporting paragraphs with examples drawn from the interviews. As part of your support, use quotations from the people you spoke with.

Chief Seattle's Speech of 1854

Chief Seattle

PREVIEW

Chief Seattle was member of the Duwamish tribe through his mother. Although he is referred to as "Chief," his tribe didn't have hereditary chiefs; instead the tribe had leaders who were respected and followed. Chief Seattle was noted for his leadership skills, his oratorical expertise, and his ability to understand the intentions of white settlers. In December 1854, Chief Seattle gave a speech during treaty negotiations. This version is based on the notes of Dr. Henry A. Smith, a settler and amateur poet who was present at the speech.

Yonder sky that has wept tears of compassion on our fathers for centuriesuntold, **1** and which, to us, looks eternal, may change. Today it is fair, tomorrow it may be overcast with clouds. My words are like the stars that never set. What Seattle says, the great chief, Washington . . . can rely upon, with as much certainty as our pale-face brothers can rely upon the return of the seasons.

The son [a reference to Territorial Governor Stevens] of the White Chief says **2** his father sends us greetings of friendship and good will. This is kind, for we know he has little need of our friendship in return, because his people are many. They are like the grass that covers the vast prairies, while my people are few, and resemble the scattering trees of a storm-swept plain.

The great, and I presume also good, white chief sends us word that he wants to **3** buy our lands but is willing to allow us to reserve enough to live on comfortably. This indeed appears generous, for the red man no longer has rights that he need respect, and the offer may be wise, also, for we are no longer in need of a great country.

There Was a Time

When our people covered the whole land, as the waves of a wind-ruffled sea cover **4** its shell-paved floor. But that time has long since passed away with the greatness of tribes now almost forgotten. I will not mourn over our untimely decay, nor reproach my pale-face brothers for hastening it, for we, too, may have been some-what to blame.

When our young men grow angry at some real or imaginary wrong, and dis- 5 figure their faces with black paint, their hearts, also, are disfigured and turn black, and then their cruelty is relentless and knows no bounds, and our old men are not able to restrain them.

But let us hope that hostilities between the red-man and his pale-face brothers 6 may never return. We would have everything to lose and nothing to gain.

True it is, that revenge, with our young braves, is considered gain, even at 7 the cost of their own lives, but old men who stay at home in times of war, and old women, who have sons to lose, know better.

Our great father Washington, for I presume he is now our father, as well as 8 yours, since George [a reference to King George III, i.e., Great Britain] has moved his boundaries to the north; our great and good father, I say, sends us word by his son, who, no doubt, is a great chief among his people, that if we do as he desires, he will protect us. His brave armies will be to us a bristling wall of strength, and his great ships of war will fill our harbors so that our ancient enemies far to the northward, the Simsiams [Tsimshian] and Hydas [Haidas], will no longer frighten our women and old men. Then he will be our father and we will be his children.

But Can This Ever Be?

Your God loves your people and hates mine; he folds his strong arms lovingly 9 around the white man and leads him as a father leads his infant son, but he has forsaken his red children; he makes your people wax strong every day, and soon they will fill the land; while my people are ebbing away like a fast-receding tide, that will never flow again. The white man's God cannot love his red children or he would protect them. They seem to be orphans who can look nowhere for help. How then can we become brothers? How can your father become our father and bring us prosperity and awaken in us dreams of returning greatness?

Your God seems to us to be partial. He came to the white man. We never saw 10 Him; never even heard His voice; He gave the white man laws but He had no word for His red children whose teeming millions filled this vast continent as the stars fill the firmament. No, we are two distinct races and must remain ever so. There is little in common between us. The ashes of our ancestors are sacred and their final resting place is hallowed ground, while you wander away from the tombs of your fathers seemingly without regret.

Your religion was written on tables of stone by the iron finger of an angry God, 11 lest you might forget it. The red man could never remember nor comprehend it.

Our religion is the traditions of our ancestors, the dreams of our old men, given 12 them by the great Spirit, and the visions of our sachems, and is written in the hearts of our people.

Your dead cease to love you and the homes of their nativity as soon as they pass 13 the portals of the tomb. They wander far off beyond the stars, are soon forgotten, and never return. Our dead never forget the beautiful world that gave them being. They still love its winding rivers, its great mountains and its sequestered vales, and they ever yearn in tenderest affection over the lonely hearted living and often return to visit and comfort them.

Day and night cannot dwell together. The red man has ever fled the approach 14 of the white man, as the changing mists on the mountain side flee before the blazing morning sun.

However, your proposition seems a just one, and I think my folks will accept 15 it and will retire to the reservation you offer them, and we will dwell apart and in peace, for the words of the great white chief seem to be the voice of nature speaking to my people out of the thick darkness that is fast gathering around them like a dense fog floating inward from a midnight sea.

It matters but little where we pass the remainder of our days.   16

They Are Not Many

The Indian's night promises to be dark. No bright star hovers above the horizon. 17 Sad-voiced winds moan in the distance. Some grim Nemesis of our race is on the red man's trail, and wherever he goes he will still hear the sure approaching footsteps of the fell destroyer and prepare to meet his doom, as does the wounded doe that hears the approaching footsteps of the hunter. A few more moons, a few more winters, and not one of all the mighty hosts that once filled this broad land or that now roam in fragmentary bands through these vast solitudes will remain to weep over the tombs of a people once as powerful and as hopeful as your own.

But why should we repine? Why should I murmur at the fate of my people? Tribes 18 are made up of individuals and are no better than they. Men come and go like the waves of a sea. A tear, a tamanawus, a dirge, and they are gone from our longing eyes forever. Even the white man, whose God walked and talked with him, as friend to friend, is not exempt from the common destiny. We *may* be brothers after all. We shall see.

We will ponder your proposition, and when we have decided we will tell you. 19 But should we accept it, I here and now make this the first condition: That we will not be denied the privilege, without molestation, of visiting at will the graves of our ancestors and friends. Every part of this country is sacred to my people. Every hillside, every valley, every plain and grove has been hallowed by some fond memory or some sad experience of my tribe.

Even the Rocks

That seem to lie dumb as they swelter in the sun along the silent seashore in solemn 20 grandeur thrill with memories of past events connected with the fate of my people, and the very dust under your feet responds more lovingly to our footsteps than to yours, because it is the ashes of our ancestors, and our bare feet are conscious of the sympathetic touch, for the soil is rich with the life of our kindred.

The sable braves, and fond mothers, and glad-hearted maidens, and the little 21 children who lived and rejoiced here, and whose very names are now forgotten, still love these solitudes, and their deep fastnesses at eventide grow shadowy with the presence of dusky spirits. And when the last red man shall have perished from the earth and his memory among white men shall have become a myth, these shores shall swarm with the invisible dead of my tribe, and when your children's children shall think themselves alone in the field, the store, the shop, upon the highway or in the silence of the woods they will not be alone. In all the earth there is no place dedicated to solitude. At night, when the streets of your cities and villages shall be silent, and you think them deserted, they will throng with the returning hosts that once filled and still love this beautiful land. The white man will never be alone. Let him be just and deal kindly with my people, for the dead are not altogether powerless.

READING COMPREHENSION

1. The word *ebbing* in " . . . while my people are ebbing away like a fast-receding tide, that will never flow again" (paragraph 3) means

   a. a rising or upswing in something.

   b. the reflux of the tide toward the sea.

   c. a periodic variation in the surface level of the oceans.

   d. a decreasing over time.

2. The word *sequestered* in " . . . its great mountains and its sequestered vales . . . " (paragraph 13) means

   a. hidden or secluded.

   b. retired.

   c. set apart or segregated.

   d. placed in custody.

3. The word *repine* in "But why should we repine?" (paragraph 18) means

   a. to rejoice or delight.

   b. to express dejection or discontent.

   c. to long for.

   d. to accept.

4. Which of the following would be a good alternative title for this selection?

   a. Go Ahead, Take Our Land

   b. Why I Hate the White Man

   c. On One Condition

   d. A Terrible Proposition

5. Which sentence best expresses the main idea of the selection?

   a. Chief Seattle accepts that his people will have to move to a reservation but only if they can maintain rights to visit their ancestors.

   b. Chief Seattle believes that the proposition offered by the U.S. government is completely fair and just.

   c. Chief Seattle believes that the white man's God is more powerful than the gods of the red man.

   d. Chief Seattle envisions a time when white men and red men will harmoniously live side by side.

6. Who is the "great chief" to whom Chief Seattle addresses his remarks?

   a. Dr. Henry Smith

   b. the white man's God

   c. Territorial Governor Stevens

   d. the President

7. According to Chief Seattle, "our young men" often grow

   a. tall.

   b. slowly.

   c. angry.

   d. weary.

8. Who are the Simsiams and Hydas?

   a. allies of Chief Seattle's people

   b. ancient enemies of Chief Seattle's people

   c. ancient enemies of the United States government

   d. tribes who have become extinct

9. What is the proposition to which Chief Seattle is responding?

   a. The U.S. government wants Chief Seattle's people to enroll in a public school system.

   b. The U.S. government wants Chief Seattle's people to religiously convert.

   c. The U.S. government wants to move Chief Seattle's people to a reservation.

   d. The U.S. government wants to purchase Chief Seattle's property.

10. The speaker implies that

    a. the U.S. government is a good government that will produce a great country.

    b. his people may be losing this battle, but the same fate will fall upon the white man at some point.

    c. young people are always much wiser than older people.

    d. U.S. citizens would be much better off if they listened to those in power.

STRUCTURE AND TECHNIQUE

1. What is the tone of Chief Seattle's speech? Explain why you think Chief Seattle chose to speak in this way.

2. Which patterns of development does Chief Seattle employ in his speech?

3. Chief Seattle contrasts his people's fate with that of the white man by saying "... one of all the mighty hosts ... .will remain to weep over the tombs of a people once as powerful and as hopeful as your own." What is his purpose in making this statement?

4. Chief Seattle employs the use of simile and metaphor throughout his speech. Find some examples that you feel are particularly effective and list them.

CRITICAL READING AND DISCUSSION

1. What do you believe is Chief Seattle's overall goal in this speech? Be prepared to demonstrate how you have come to this conclusion.

2. How does Chief Seattle feel about the actions of the younger tribal members? Use examples from the speech to support your ideas.

3. According to the speech, what does Chief Seattle believe will eventually happen to his people? What does he believe will eventually happen to the white man?

4. Read the last two lines of Chief Seattle's speech. What you think he means? Be prepared to support your ideas.

WRITING ASSIGNMENTS

Personal

Assignment 1

Chief Seattle uses many images and strong statements throughout his speech to support his purpose. Choose a quote that you identify with and, in an essay, explain why it is meaningful to you. Possibilities might include "day and night cannot dwell together" (paragraph 14), "they are not many" (paragraph 17), or "the white man will never be alone" (paragraph 21).

Remember that to create a good essay, you must start with a good introduction, which should include the title of the work you are responding to, necessary background information, and a thesis statement describing your topic and your claim. One way you could write your thesis would be to state the quotation and explain why it is significant to you:

> I was saddened when I read Chief Seattle's words, "No, we are two distinct races and must remain ever so," because I believe that all humans should be able to live harmoniously with one another.

Another method for your introduction would be to lead off with the quotation and then make a general reference to it in the thesis statement. Thus, after the quotation, you might write:

> Chief Seattle's words indicate that humans are not infallible, and if we don't start listening to our elders, we will eventually destroy ourselves.

Once you have created a strong introduction and thesis, your essay will need detailed support. Just as Chief Seattle provides specific reasons for his feelings and beliefs, you will need to do the same. For example, if you are arguing that we need to start listening to the lessons our elders offer, you could include a lesson you learned from your grandmother:

> My grandmother warned me years ago that water was a resource that should not be wasted. When my city implemented water rationing because our water plant had become contaminated, and water had to be brought in, I quickly discovered that I wasted my allotted amount on taking showers, leaving the water running while I was brushing my teeth, and cleaning the dishes. This left no water for me to drink or cook with. Through this experience, I learned how careless I had been and gained a new perspective about the importance of water.

You will need to include multiple paragraphs that each contain detailed support for your thesis statement to create a strong, persuasive essay. Your final paragraph should restate your thesis and draw your essay to a conclusion.

Assignment 2

Chief Seattle's speech is very persuasive and passionate because he is arguing for a cause in which he fervently believes. He appeals to his audience by offering both arguments and counterarguments. Think about something you believe in strongly enough to fight for. Like Chief Seattle, you might be passionate about the environment and want people to take better care of it. Maybe you believe a specific book should be taught at your town's elementary school, or you might believe that a local official needs to introduce a new city policy. Write an essay that is inspiring and persuasive enough that it will motivate your reader to take action.

Depending on your chosen topic, you may need to do additional research that will require proper integration and citation. For instance, if you are writing to persuade a local school board to increase the amount of physical exercise and outdoor activity students are permitted, you will want to provide evidence that supports the importance of daily exercise in improving students' health, behavior, and school performance. You will also need to think about possible counterarguments—like the amount of time spent outside the classroom—that the board may have and address those arguments. Your chosen topic will also dictate what format your essay will take. Again, if you are addressing the local school board, you may want to write your essay as a formal letter or present it as a speech.

Just as Chief Seattle considered his audience, you will need to use the right tone and language. This may mean that your tone will be more factual than emotional to support your point. In all instances, you will need to include the right details and support to persuade your audience to agree with your position.

Assignment 3

Even in the face of defeat, Chief Seattle calmly negotiates his people's right to visit the graves of their ancestors. The ability to negotiate is a critical skill in life, in school, and in the work place. Write a persuasive essay aimed at negotiating an important issue with your boss. You may want to negotiate fewer hours to accommodate your class schedule, or you may want to negotiate a raise. You might even try negotiating a better work environment.

Like Chief Seattle, you must use strong supporting details to make your appeal. Instead of complaining to your boss that your office is cold and unfriendly, suggest specific ways to improve the atmosphere. As you put your ideas together, remember that negotiation means that you don't get everything without conceding something. In this spirit, you will need to offer your boss ideas that show you are willing to help—for example, by having employees volunteer to bring in plants from home or offering to keep the coffee station filled themselves.

Negotiating also means carefully choosing your language. Chief Seattle was obviously unhappy at having to move his people onto a reservation, but instead of resorting to name-calling and rancor, he calmly stated, "The great, and I presume also good, white chief. . . .appears generous," and later asserted, "We will ponder your proposition, and when we have decided. . . . ." In this same manner, you will want to choose the words you use carefully and remain as positive as possible. If your thesis is that you need fewer office hours in order to study more, then merely complaining about your current schedule won't advance your argument. However, if you offer measured specific support about how you believe that cutting back on your hours will make you both a better employee and a better student, your boss is more likely to consider your request seriously.

Single-Sex Schools: An Old Idea Whose Time Has Come

Diane Urbina

PREVIEW

If you attended a public high school, most likely it was coeducational. But what happens when girls and boys are educated separately? According to many researchers, the results include better grades, stronger self-confidence, and more fulfilling careers. In this essay, Diane Urbina argues that single-sex schools should be an option available to all students, not just those attending private schools.

In 1972, single-sex public schools were made illegal by Title IX, the federal law 1 that prohibits sex discrimination in education. Since that time, boys' and girls' schools (and men's and women's colleges) have been limited to private schools whose high tuition fees are paid by students and their parents. The result is that single-sex education has become available to only a small percentage of students, and primarily those from well-off families. For most people, single-sex schools are thought of as something antique: a quaint remnant of the distant past. And that's a shame. For there is increasingly persuasive evidence that single-sex education offers students—particularly girls—advantages that they cannot get in coed settings.

It has been demonstrated time and time again that students who attend 2 single-sex schools perform better academically. In the biggest study of its kind, researchers in Australia measured the academic performance of 270,000 students over a period of twenty years. The boys and girls who attended single-sex schools performed between 15 and 22 percentage points higher on standardized tests than students attending coed schools. A separate study in Britain looked at 979 elementary schools and 2,954 high schools. Its results showed that the highest-achieving students were girls in single-sex schools, followed by girls in coed schools. Next came boys in single-sex schools. The lowest-achieving group was made up of boys in coed schools. Another study showed that girls who attend all-girl high schools are six times more likely to major in math or science in college.

Why would students perform better when in school with only those of their 3 own gender? Researchers, teachers, and the students themselves have offered a variety of explanations. Some of the most convincing arguments have come from David Sadker and the late Myra Sadker, social scientists who spent twenty years looking at gender bias in education. They are the authors of *Failing at Fairness: How Our Schools Cheat Girls*. Although as the title suggests, the Sadkers' findings focus on how girls are short-changed by coeducational schools, they suggest that boys as well are better served by single-sex schools.

The advantages to single-gender schools are entangled and difficult to sepa-   4
rate. A clearly defined one, however, is that girls and boys literally learn differently. This is not the same as the erroneous idea that boys and girls are "by nature" better suited to different fields of study (and, later, careers). That belief is a loaded one that has been used as a weapon against granting equal opportunities in education and employment. And the fact is *not* that boys are "just better" at math and sciences, while girls are "just better" at English and foreign languages.

Why, then, do standardized tests seem to show that boys have the edge in some   5
fields and girls in others? There are several factors at play here. First, boys mature more slowly. According to Dr. Leonard Sax, author of *Why Gender Matters,* the part of the brain that governs language in a typical five-year-old boy is two or three years' less developed than that of a typical five-year old girl. An average fourteen-year-old boy is even further behind—four or five years.

Eventually the boy's language ability catches up with the girl's, but it's easy   6
to see that in those ensuing years a lot of problems can occur in the classroom. Girls, typically, learn to read earlier and more easily. Boys are pushed to learn to read at an age when many of them are unprepared to do so, and later, to keep up with their female classmates. The results are ones almost everyone has observed: lots of boys who dislike reading and think they're no good at it, and lots of people who take it for granted that girls are "just better" at reading, writing, and other language skills.

And what about the girls? Again, according to Sax and other researchers, while   7
girls' brains are on the fast track developing their language centers, they are on a less hurried schedule developing the areas that govern spatial relationships and geometry. These areas in boys' brains mature more quickly. The result? Girls who are thrown together with boys in school quickly conclude that they're "dumb at math and science."

In single-sex schools, the classroom curriculum could be designed with girls'   8
and boys' learning differences in mind. In reading class, boys would be expected to keep pace with other boys, not with girls who seem impossibly more advanced. They could concentrate on reading material of particular interest to boys of their ages, rather than the stories and literature that are often selected by (mostly female) teachers for their (mostly female) enthusiastic readers. Girls could be introduced to math and science concepts in ways that particularly appeal to them. Girls are typically less interested in pure math at an early age, but they often

enjoy learning the practical, problem-solving aspects of math. Teachers who understood and could appeal to the boys' or girls' learning style would have a far better chance of reaching more students than those who are trying to do "one size fits all" teaching.

Another great advantage of single-sex schools is that they take into account a **9** very basic fact of life: Boys and girls act differently in each others' presence. Anyone who has observed a group of quietly talking boys turn into posturing, shoving, guffawing loudmouths when girls come into view, or a group of sensible girls start giggling, shrieking, and preening when boys approach recognizes the truth of this statement.

There's nothing wrong with this flirting, attention-getting behavior. It's as old **10** as the Neanderthals, and nothing is going to keep people from flirting with those who they find attractive. The problem is that this perfectly normal social behavior creates at least two serious obstacles to learning. The first is simple: Flirting takes up a lot of time and energy that could be better used in the classroom. It's terribly difficult to concentrate on the difference between "ser" and "estar" in Spanish class when you're trying to figure out how to accidentally bump into the hunk in the second row after class. And boys and girls being boys and girls, such social plotting often becomes the focus of the school day. Both genders burn up the phone lines at night, not comparing notes on classes, but on who said what to whom and if anyone has a date for Saturday night.

The second, related, problem is that the presence of the opposite sex often **11** influences students to act, well, stupid. Think again about the first point raised in this paper—the misconception that girls are naturally "good" at reading but "bad" at math, with the opposite being true for boys. If students believe that, then that "badness" becomes a sexual characteristic, just as a girl's curvy figure or a boy's deep voice is. A girl may think she seems "girlier," more feminine, more attractive, if she makes a point of being clueless in math class. A boy may think he's more macho, more alluring to girls if he loudly proclaims that he hates to read. As a result, students may deliberately flaunt their weaknesses in order to impress the opposite sex. In general, mixed classes tend to encourage such potentially harmful gender differences. In the presence of guys, many girls give in to the stereotype that says girls are "nice," quiet, passive, and nonathletic. Around girls, guys feel compelled to be "jocks," noisy, disruptive, and overbearing. In a single-sex school, none of this behavior would be necessary. Students could concentrate on learning, rather than competing with each other for the attention of a cute guy or girl, or demeaning him or her self in order to catch someone's eye. They could develop their individual talents, without the constant concern of how they were coming off to the cute girl or guy in the next seat.

A final reason that single-sex schools are advantageous concerns the behavior **12** of teachers. As the Sadkers were compiling their twenty years of research, they took many hours of videotape of classrooms in action. When they played those tapes back, many of the teachers were surprised—and horrified—by what they saw. A few examples:

- Boys were eight times more likely to call out in class without raising their hands. In general, teachers accepted their behavior.   13
- Teachers were twice as likely to pick out boys in the class as role models.
- When boys raised their hands, they were five times more likely to be called on than girls.
- Teachers memorized boys' names more quickly than the names of girls.
- When a boy gave a wrong answer, teachers would spend time praising him, encouraging him, and trying to lead him to the right answer. When a girl gave a wrong answer, teachers generally just moved on to another student.

No one assumes that the teachers involved "liked" boys better than girls. 14 Rather, it is apparent than teachers as well as students are very much influenced by gender stereotypes. Because girls are (in general) less disruptive and demanding in a mixed-class setting, they receive less attention and affirmation. In general, the Sadkers concluded, girls in coed settings become the "audience," rather than the "players."

But in single-sex schools, girls and guys can play *all* the roles—scientist, 15 writer, musician, basketball player, artist, math whiz, track star. Without the presence of voices (spoken and unspoken) saying "Boys don't do that" or "Girls aren't good at that," they can develop their own gifts and talents, irrespective of gender. Without the constant pressure to impress the opposite sex, boys and girls can channel their energies into becoming the best people they can be, rather than forcing themselves into stereotypical molds. Single-sex schools could be the very best thing to ever happen to many students. It's time to bring them back.

READING COMPREHENSION

1. The word *flaunt* in "As a result, students may deliberately flaunt their weaknesses in order to impress the opposite sex" (paragraph 11) means

   a. hide.

   b. investigate.

   c. show off.

   d. ignore.

2. Which of the following would be a good alternative title for this selection?

   a. Coed Schools Are Short-Changing Our Children

   b. Girls and Boys *Do* Learn Differently

   c. Popular Misconceptions about Education

   d. Gender Stereotypes in Schools

3. Which sentence best expresses the main idea of the selection?

   a. In contrast to coeducational schools, single-sex schools can design the curriculum with girls' and boys' learning differences in mind.

   b. When boys and girls attend the same school, they tend to distract each other from academic pursuits.

   c. Single-sex schools would benefit both girls and boys because girls and boys learn differently and their behavior gets worse when they attend the same schools.

   d. Many studies have concluded that boys and girls learn best in single-sex schools.

4. According to the author, girls who attend all-girl high schools are

   a. often very good at languages.

   b. likely to believe that they are stupid at science and math.

   c. likely to wish they were enrolled in mixed-class schools.

   d. six times more likely to major in math or science in college.

5. According to the selection, a very basic fact of life is that

   a. girls are better at reading than boys are.

   b. boys do better in math and science than girls do.

   c. boys and girls act differently in each other's presence.

   d. there is nothing wrong with flirting.

6. According to researchers, girls in coed settings

   a. are more likely to do well in math and science.

   b. become the "audience," rather than the players.

   c. know that teachers like boys better than girls.

   d. are less disruptive than girls in single-sex schools.

7. According to researchers, girls receive less attention from teachers because

   a. teachers don't want to be seen as favoring girls.

   b. girls are less disruptive and demanding in mixed-class settings.

   c. teachers, who are mostly female, like boys better than girls.

   d. girls almost always have a better grasp of subject matter than boys do.

8. The author implies that
   a. there is something wrong with students who flirt in class.
   b. it is possible to keep male and female students from flirting in coed settings.
   c. single-sex schools would benefit girls but not boys.
   d. single-sex schools would be good for our society.

9. The author implies that
   a. traditional gender roles are very limiting.
   b. most students would choose to attend single-sex schools, if given the choice.
   c. most girls are naturally passive while most boys are naturally disruptive and overbearing.
   d. it's natural for boys to do better than girls in math and science.

10. We can infer from paragraph 11 that many girls believe that boys
   a. really like to read.
   b. are clueless in math class.
   c. are turned off by assertive and athletic girls and those who are good in math.
   d. are turned off by quiet, passive, and nonathletic girls.

STRUCTURE AND TECHNIQUE

1. Urbina begins her essay by providing some background information on the decline of single-sex schools in our society. Then she declares that this decline is "a shame." What introductory technique—broad-to-narrow, contrast, or anecdote—is she employing? Why is it effective here?

2. Does the author clearly state her thesis? If so, where is it stated, and how?

3. Urbina's essay is an argument in favor of single-sex public schools. What argumentation techniques does she employ? (See pages 343–364 for information on argumentation.)

4. How does Urbina conclude her essay—with a summary and final thought, a prediction or recommendation, or with a question?

CRITICAL READING AND DISCUSSION

1. According to researchers, why do girls perform better in single-sex schools? Why do boys perform better in single-sex schools?

2. According to the article, there are some differences in the way girls and boys learn. What are they? What does Urbina suggest educators do to take into account these differences?

3. Urbina presents a number of advantages to attending single-sex schools. What might be some disadvantages to attending single-sex schools? If you were a parent, would you want your child or children to attend single-sex or coed schools? Why?

4. In your experience, do teachers treat boys and girls differently in the class-room? In what ways?

WRITING ASSIGNMENTS

Assignment 1

In this selection, Urbina presents a strong argument in favor of single-sex schools. But not everyone agrees that single-sex public schools are a good idea. Use the Internet to research the arguments of people who oppose single-sex public schools. To access the Internet, use the very helpful search engine Google (www.google.com) and refer to Chapter 21, "Using the Library and the Internet." Try entering "single-sex public schools" or "against single-sex public schools." Then write an essay that summarizes the views of those who are opposed to single-sex public schools. Your thesis for the essay might be similar to the following:

> Unlike Diane Urbina, there are those who believe that single-sex public schools are *not* a good idea.

Each of your supporting paragraphs, then, would present evidence opposing single-sex public schools.

Assignment 2

Write an essay in which you describe in detail a typical classroom in the high school you attended. If you attended a coed school, did the students conform to the social roles that Urbina describes in her essay? Did the teacher tend to call on the boys more often than the girls? Were the boys the "players" and the girls the "audi-ence"? One way to organize your paper would be by describing the behavior of the boys, the behavior of the girls, and the teacher's behavior. Alternatively, you could describe three different classrooms and how teachers, boys, and girls interacted. In either case, your thesis might be something like the following:

> Looking back on my high school years, it is clear to me that the boys were the players and the girls were the audience.

Assignment 3

Urbina believes that the goal of public schools should be "to enable boys and girls to channel their energies into becoming the best people they can be." Thinking back on your high school education, write an essay in which you describe a class that did this for you. Your thesis, for example, might be similar to the following:

> A dynamic teacher, bright students, and interesting subject matter combined to make U.S. History I the best class I ever took.

Alternatively, you may wish to describe the worst class you ever took. In that case, your thesis might be similar to the following:

> A boring teacher, lazy students, and dull subject matter combined to make U.S. History II the worst class I ever took.

Here's to Your Health

Joan Dunayer

PREVIEW

Joan Dunayer contrasts the glamorous "myth" about alcohol, as presented in advertising and popular culture, with the reality—which is often far less appealing. After reading her essay, you will be more aware of how we are encouraged to think of alcohol as being tied to happiness and success. You may also become a more critical observer of images presented by advertisers.

As the only freshman on his high school's varsity wrestling team, Tod was anxious 1 to fit in with his older teammates. One night after a match, he was offered a tequila bottle on the ride home. Tod felt he had to accept, or he would seem like a sissy. He took a swallow, and every time the bottle was passed back to him, he took another swallow. After seven swallows, he passed out. His terrified teammates carried him into his home, and his mother then rushed him to the hospital. After his stomach was pumped, Tod learned that his blood alcohol level had been so high that he was lucky not to be in a coma or dead.

Unfortunately, drinking is not unusual among high-school students or, for 2 that matter, in any other segment of our society. And that's no accident. There are numerous influences in our society urging people to drink, not the least of which is advertising. Who can recall a televised baseball or basketball game without a beer commercial? Furthermore, alcohol ads appear with pounding frequency in magazines, on billboards, and in college newspapers. According to industry estimates, brewers spend more than $600 million a year on radio and TV commercials and another $90 million on print ads. In addition, the liquor industry spends about $230 million a year on print advertising, and since 1966 it has greatly expanded its presence on cable and independent broadcast stations. Just recently, NBC became the first network station to accept hard liquor ads for broadcast.

To top it all off, this aggressive advertising of alcohol fosters a harmful myth 3 about drinking.

Part of the myth is that liquor signals professional success. In a slick men's 4 magazine, one full-page ad for Scotch whiskey shows two men seated in an elegant restaurant. Both are in their thirties, perfectly groomed, and wearing expensive-looking gray suits. The windows are draped with velvet, the table with spotless white linen. Each place-setting consists of a long-stemmed water goblet, silver utensils, and thick silver plates. On each plate is a half-empty cocktail glass. The two men are grinning and shaking hands, as if they've just concluded a business deal. The caption reads, "The taste of success."

Contrary to what the liquor company would have us believe, drinking is 5 more closely related to lack of success than to achievement. Among students, the heaviest drinkers have the lowest grades. In the work force, alcoholics are frequently late or absent, tend to perform poorly, and often get fired. Although alcohol abuse occurs in all economic classes, it remains most prevalent among the poor.

Another part of the alcohol myth is that drinking makes you more attractive 6 to the opposite sex. "Hot, hot, hot," one commercial's soundtrack begins, as the camera scans a crowd of college-age beachgoers. Next it follows the curve of a woman's leg up to her bare hip and lingers there. She is young, beautiful, wearing a bikini. A young guy, carrying an ice chest, positions himself near to where she sits. He is tan, muscular. She doesn't show much interest—until he opens the chest and takes out a beer. Now she smiles over at him. He raises his eyebrows and, invitingly, holds up another can. She joins him. This beer, the song concludes, "attracts like no other."

Beer doesn't make anyone sexier. Like all alcohol, it lowers the levels of male 7 hormones in men and of female hormones in women—even when taken in small amounts. In substantial amounts, alcohol can cause infertility in women and impotence in men. Some alcoholic men even develop enlarged breasts.

The alcohol myth also creates the illusion that beer and athletics are a perfect 8 combination. One billboard features three high-action images: a sprinter running at top speed, a surfer riding a wave, and a basketball player leaping to make a dunk shot. A particular light beer, the billboard promises, "won't slow you down."

"Slow you down" is exactly what alcohol does. Drinking plays a role in over 9 six million injuries each year—not counting automobile accidents. Even in small amounts, alcohol dulls the brain, reducing muscle coordination and slowing reaction time. It also interferes with the ability to focus the eyes and adjust to a sudden change in brightness—such as the flash of a car's headlights. Drinking and driving, responsible for over half of all automobile deaths, is the leading cause of death among teenagers. Continued alcohol abuse can physically change the brain, permanently impairing learning and memory. Long-term drinking is related to malnutrition, weakening of the bones, and ulcers. It increases the risk of liver failure, heart disease, and stomach cancer.

Finally, according to the myth, alcohol is the magic ingredient for social suc- 10 cess. Hundreds of TV and radio ads have echoed this message in recent years. In one commercial, for instance, an overweight man sits alone in his drab living room. He reaches into a cooler, pulls out a bottle of beer, and twists off the bottle cap. Instantly dance music erupts, and dozens of attractive young adults appear in a shower of party streamers and confetti. "Where the party begins," a voice says. The once lonely man, now a popular guy with lots of male and female friends, has found the answer to his social problems—beer.

Relationships based on alcohol are unlikely to lead to social success and 11 true friendships. Indeed, studies show that when alcohol becomes the center of a social gathering, it may lead to public drunkenness and violence. The ad's image of the man's new friends ignores an undeniable reality: that alcohol ruins—not creates—relationships. In addition to fighting and simple assault, drinking is linked to two-thirds of domestic violence incidents. Rather than leading to healthy social connections, alcohol leads to loneliness, despair, and mental illness. Over a fourth of the patients in state and county mental hospitals have alcohol problems; more than half of all violent crimes are alcohol-related; the rate of suicide among alcoholics is fifteen times higher than among the general population.

Advertisers would have us believe the myth that alcohol is part of being suc- 12 cessful, sexy, healthy, and happy; but those who have suffered from it—directly or indirectly—know otherwise. For alcohol's victims, "Here's to your health" rings with a terrible irony when it is accompanied by the clink of liquor glasses.

READING COMPREHENSION

1. The word *impairing* in "Continued alcohol abuse can physically alter the brain, permanently impairing learning and memory" (paragraph 9) means

   a. postponing.

   b. doubling.

   c. damaging.

   d. teaching.

2. The word *fosters* in "this aggressive advertising of alcohol fosters a harmful myth about drinking" (paragraph 3) means

    a. avoids.

    b. delays.

    c. promotes.

    d. discourages.

3. Which one of the following would be a good alternative title for this selection?

    a. The Taste of Success

    b. Alcohol and Your Social Life

    c. Too Much Tequila

    d. Alcohol: Image and Reality

4. Which sentence best expresses the main idea of the selection?

    a. Sports and alcohol don't mix.

    b. The media and our culture promote false images about success and happiness.

    c. The media and our culture promote false beliefs about alcohol.

    d. Liquor companies should not be allowed to use misleading ads.

5. According to the selection, drinking can

    a. actually unify a family.

    b. lower harmone levels.

    c. temporarily improve performance in sports.

    d. increase the likelihood of pregnancy.

6. *True or False?* _____ Alcohol abuse is most severe among middle-class people.

7. *True or False?* _____ The leading cause of death among teenagers is drinking and driving.

8. From the first paragraph of the essay, we can conclude that

    a. even one encounter with alcohol can lead to death.

    b. tequila is the worst type of alcohol to drink.

    c. wrestlers tend to drink more than other athletes.

    d. by the time students reach high school, peer pressure doesn't influence them.

9. *True or False?* _____ The author implies that one or two drinks a day are probably harmless.

10. The author implies that heavy drinking can lead to

    a. poor grades.

    b. getting fired.

    c. heart disease.

    d. all of the above.

STRUCTURE AND TECHNIQUE

1. What method of introduction does Dunayer use? What effect do you think she hoped to achieve with this introduction?

2. Dunayer begins her criticism of alcohol with "Part of the myth is . . . " (See the first sentence of paragraph 4.) What additional transitions does she use to introduce each of the three other parts of the myth (in the first sentences of paragraphs 6, 8, and 10)? What is gained by the use of these transitions?

3. The body of Dunayer's essay is made up of four pairs of paragraphs (paragraphs 4 and 5; 6 and 7; 8 and 9; 10 and 11). What is the relationship between the paragraphs in each pair? In which of the two paragraphs does Dunayer present her own perspective? Why do you think she puts her own perspective in that paragraph?

4. In her essay, Dunayer provides vivid descriptions of alcohol advertisements, particularly in paragraphs 4 and 6. What vivid details does she provide? How do these details support her main point?

CRITICAL READING AND DISCUSSION

1. Dunayer presents and then rebuts four "myths" about alcohol. What are these four myths? According to Dunayer, what is the reality behind each myth?

2. Dunayer concludes, "'Here's to your health' rings with a terrible irony when it is accompanied by the clink of liquor glasses" (paragraph 12). What is the "terrible irony" she refers to? How does this irony—already signaled in her essay's title—relate to her main point?

3. Do you think Dunayer's essay is one-sided or balanced? Explain. What additional points could be used to support her point or to rebut it?

4. Advertisers often create myths or use false ideas to get people to buy their products. Besides alcohol ads, what are some other examples of manipulative or deceptive advertising? Do you think advertisers should be permitted to use such tactics to sell products?

WRITING ASSIGNMENTS

Assignment 1

Describe and analyze the print advertisements for beer and liquor below. Argue whether the ads are socially responsible or irresponsible in the way that they portray drinking. Your thesis might be something like one of the following examples:

> In two recent ads, ad agencies and liquor companies have acted irresponsibly in their portrayal of alcohol.

> In two recent ads, ad agencies and liquor companies have acted with a measure of responsibility in their portrayal of alcohol.

Alternatively, write about what you consider responsible or irresponsible advertising for some other product or service. Cigarettes, weight loss, and cosmetics are possibilities to consider.

Assignment 2

If you have a friend, relative, or classmate who drinks a lot, write a letter warning him or her about the dangers of alcohol. If appropriate, use information from Dunayer's essay. Remember that since your purpose is to get someone you care about to control or break a dangerous habit, you should make your writing very

personal. Don't bother explaining how alcoholism affects people in general. Instead, focus directly on what you see it doing to your reader.

Divide your argument into at least three supporting paragraphs. You might, for instance, talk about how your reader is jeopardizing his or her relationship with three of the following: family, friends, boss and coworkers, instructors and classmates.

Assignment 3

Dunayer describes how alcohol advertisements promote false beliefs, such as the idea that alcohol will make you successful. Imagine that you work for a public service ad agency given the job of presenting the negative side of alcohol. What images would you choose to include in your ads?

Write a report to your boss in which you propose in detail three anti-alcohol ads. Choose from among the following:

    ad counteracting the idea that alcohol leads to success

    ad counteracting the idea that alcohol is sexy

    ad counteracting the idea that alcohol goes well with athletics

    ad counteracting the idea that alcohol makes for happy families

Mayor of Rust

Sue Halpern

PREVIEW

Sue Halpern, a former Rhodes Scholar and Guggenheim Fellow, has a Ph.D. from Oxford University, has taught at Columbia University's College of Physicians and Surgeons, and is currently a scholar-in-residence at Middlebury College. She is also the director of Face of Democracy, a non-profit project that teaches documentary journalism to high school students. In this article, which appeared in *The New York Times Magazine*, she profiles a young man who is trying to make a difference in his town.

At the Aspen Ideas Festival in Colorado last July, John Fetterman, the mayor of 1 Braddock, a small Pennsylvania town ten miles upriver from Pittsburgh, was introduced by Dana Gioia, former chairman of the National Endowment for the Arts, as a man who demonstrates "how ideas can change the world." It was four days into the weeklong festival, and Fetterman, a forty-one-year-old, 6-foot-8 white man with a shaved head, a fibrous black beard, and tattoos up one arm and down the other, was presenting a slideshow about how art could bring social change to a town where one-third of its 2,671 residents, a majority of whom are African-American and female, live in poverty. Fetterman projected pictures of old, bustling Braddock, which steel made until the middle of the twentieth century and unmade throughout the rest. Its main street was packed with shoppers, its storefronts filled with wares. Then he turned to Braddock as it is today.

"We've lost 90 percent of our population and 90 percent of our buildings," he 2 said. "Ninety percent of our town is in a landfill. So we took a two-pronged approach. We created the first art gallery in the four-town region, with artists' studios. We did public art installations. And, I don't know if you consider it arts, exactly, but I consider growing organic vegetables in the shadow of a steel mill an art, and that has attracted homesteading."

Fetterman displayed a picture of a furniture store, which the nonprofit he 3 founded bought in 2009 for $15,000, and an abandoned church, which is being turned into a community center, and former building lots that are now green spaces, and an outdoor pizza oven, made with bricks from a demolished building, and a house belonging to two of the homesteaders who have moved to Braddock from "all over the country."

"They bought this house for $4,300," Fetterman told the crowd, "and put in a 4 lot of sweat equity, and now it looks like something you'd see in a magazine." The audience was enchanted. Here was a guy in biker boots bringing the Park Slope (Aspen, Marin, Portland, Santa Fe) ethos—organic produce, art installations, an outdoor bread oven—to the disenfranchised. "What was Braddock like before we took office? Braddock was a notorious community that was steeped in violence. But as of—knock on wood—today, we are now twenty-seven months without a homicide." The audience began to clap and didn't stop for a long time.

As the event wound down, Gioia asked Fetterman to explain the numbers tat- 5 tooed on his arms. "This one," the mayor said, holding out his right forearm, "is the Braddock ZIP code, 15104. And this one," he said, switching arms, "are the dates of the five people we lost to senseless violence in Braddock since I took office." The audience clapped again. When the applause died out, people swarmed the mayor. A woman from a foundation in Dallas wanted to make a grant. "Whatever you're interested in, we have projects up the wazoo," he said. A sculptor offered one of her pieces. "We use art to combat the dark side of capitalism," Fetterman replied. A man asked how many people had made the move to Braddock. "It's the same as 4,000 people moving into Pittsburgh," Fetterman said, not offering a real number. Then Lynn Goldsmith, a photographer known for her portraits of rock stars, asked if she could take his picture, and in the shade of the building, the mayor struck a pose, unsmiling, arms out.

With appearances this past year or so on "The Colbert Report," CBS News 6 Sunday Morning, PBS, and CNN, John Fetterman has become the face of Rust

Belt renewal. He was dubbed America's "coolest mayor" by *The Guardian* and the Mayor of Hell by *Rolling Stone*. *The Atlantic* included him in its "Brave New Thinkers" issue of 2009. In contrast to urban planners caught up in political wrangling, budget constraints, and bureaucratic shambling, Fetterman embraces a do-it-yourself aesthetic and a tendency to put up his own money to move things along. He has turned a thirteen-block town into a sampling of urban renewal trends: land-banking (replacing vacant buildings with green space, as in Cleveland); urban agri-culture (Detroit); championing the creative class to bring new energy to old places (an approach popularized by Richard Florida); "greening" the economy as a path out of poverty (as Majora Carter has worked to do in the South Bronx); embracing depopulation (like nearby Pittsburgh). Thrust into the national spotlight, Fetterman has become something of a folk hero, a Paul Bunyan of hipster urban revival, with his own Shepard Fairey block print—the Fetterman mien with the word "mayor" underneath. *This*, the poster suggests, is what a mayor should be.

I met Mayor John, as he likes to be called, for the first time on a warm summer **7** day. We sat on the porch of a former convent, across the street from Andrew Carnegie's first American steel mill, the Edgar Thomson Steel Works, which now employs fewer than one-tenth of the workers it used to and was sending a steady cloud of steam and particulates into a perfect blue sky. Next door, at a school-turned-gallery, two New York artists were taking down a show. Nearby, on a parcel of land called Braddock Farms run by the Pittsburgh nonprofit Grow Pittsburgh, a lone young man pulled weeds. Behind the convent, students from a charter school a couple of towns over were tending a bee colony. Mayor John, who wore low-hanging jeans and a black T-shirt, said the bees were found in one of the town's many abandoned buildings and "repurposed."

Had I sat there all day, as the beekeepers and artists and farmers wandered in **8** and out of view, listening to Fetterman explain how the population of Braddock had gone from 20,000 people crammed into houses built fast and cheap in 1920, to less than 2,700 now, and how, as the population dwindled, the stores all closed, too, and how he paid a guy out of his own pocket to drive around town giving out ice cream to poor kids because their town was "a food desert," and taken in his explanation that Braddock was gentrification-proof because "even if housing prices tripled, which they'd never do, a house would still only cost $15,000," I might have been so convinced of the answer that I would have forgotten to ask the question: Is Braddock a model for bringing a Rust Belt town back to life?

Urban decline has been around just about as long as there have been cities, **9** but the degeneration of America's industrial heartland, because it cuts across a wide swath of the country and is as much about jobs as it is about habitation, has seemed both intractable and inevitable. Earlier efforts to address it involved razing whole neighborhoods and erecting Robert Moses-inspired projects. But in places like Youngstown, Detroit, and Pittsburgh, as well as satellites like Braddock, where urban blight was not just a matter of run-down neighborhoods but of manufactur-ing plants packing up and moving away, even such radical solutions offered little hope. It's one thing to replace substandard housing stock, quite another to reinvent an economy.

Typically, when John Fetterman talks about his town, he starts with the long list 10 of businesses that once lined its main street. "In 2010," Fetterman then invariably says, "those numbers have dropped to zero." It is a stunning, almost unfathomable decline, and it suggests why Braddock has become a favorite media stand-in for Rust Belt devastation, even if what Fetterman says is not precisely true. A medical clinic, auto garages, a florist, an optometrist, three markets, a preschool, a parochial school, a dollar store, and Carnegie's first public library continue to do business alongside empty buildings wrapped in barbed wire.

John Fetterman showed up in Braddock in 2001. He had tried the family busi- 11 ness, insurance, but it didn't take, and he ended up joining AmeriCorps and moving to Pittsburgh in the late '90s. After a two-year interlude at Harvard's Kennedy School studying education and social policy, Fetterman was hired to start a program for at-risk youth in Braddock, a town beset by violence. Two years later, Fetterman bought the church that he planned to turn into a community center; it was part of his Aspen slideshow, which he planned to turn into a community center. He squatted in the church for a while, then, entranced by the town's "malignant beauty," bought the warehouse next door and turned it into a Dwell-worthy loft, topped by two remodeled shipping containers for additional living space. Four years after arriving in town, he ran for mayor.

In Braddock, executive decisions are made by an elected six-person borough 12 council, and day-to-day municipal affairs are run by a nonelected borough manager. The mayor, who works for a salary of $150 a month, has two main functions: to break a tie and to oversee the police (he has veto power but can be overruled by a majority council vote). Fetterman knew this, of course, but he thought being mayor would give him a "bully pulpit." Fetterman made no attempt to hide his belief that most of the borough council members had little interest in furthering the fortunes of the town and were using their positions mainly to benefit themselves. The borough manager, Ella B. Jones (who was later charged with forgery and theft of $178,000 of the town's money, a charge to which she pleaded not guilty), considered Fetterman to be a wealthy interloper, the "great white hope" of Braddock, as Jones put it. "Council makes the laws," Jones said in 2006. "They do it all. They have the vote. They make the rules. And he doesn't."

So Fetterman built a back door—he started a nonprofit organization called 13 Braddock Redux, financed until recently primarily by family money. (His father is its largest individual donor.) Because Fetterman is the head of a nonprofit that uses Fetterman money, and because for the longest time it had only two other members, Jeb Feldman, a friend, and Helen Wachter, the head of the countywide KEYS-AmeriCorps program (which supplied volunteers to the nonprofit, including an assistant for Fetterman), Braddock Redux is known around town as John's Nonprofit. Before it became part of Braddock Redux, the Fettermans put up the money for the church next to the mayor's house, which is popularly called John's

Church. Braddock Redux owns the convent across the street from the steel mill, which is known as John's Convent. Feldman has the title to the convent school, which is known as Jeb's School. The church houses the county's summer program, the Braddock Youth Project, among other things. The convent sometimes serves as a hostel for potential "urban pioneers," and the middle school as a gallery and studio space. By heading a nonprofit that is a major property owner, the mayor was able to advance what he calls his "social-justice agenda" without having much political power, or the burden of it, either.

In 2009, when the Levi's jeans company wanted to use Braddock to promote 14 a line of work clothes, it approached Fetterman, not the borough council. The million and a half dollars Levi's offered in exchange went to John's Nonprofit, for John's Church and community center, rather than the town's coffers. It was a closed loop that didn't sit well with some of the mayor's constituents, even those who voted for him in the last election, in 2009, which he won, 294 to 103.

"I came back to Braddock because I was interested in what John was doing," 15 Pat Morgan, a church musician told me one evening after a borough council meeting. "But he doesn't play well with others. He decides we need a youth center, and he's going to put it here, but I never hear him come to one of these council meetings and say, 'You know what, I've got some money, what should we do with it?' If you're casting yourself as the mayor who speaks for Braddock, we want him to at least pretend that we have a say in any of this."

It was a sentiment I would hear numerous times, from longtime residents like 16 the filmmaker Tony Buba ("John's idea of grass roots is Astroturf") as well as from transplants. Because he ran a nonprofit, Fetterman operated with limited public accountability. It was efficient—Braddock Redux could buy a building and get the H. J. Heinz Company Foundation to donate $100,000 to put a green roof on it and bypass the pesky part where people debate the pros and cons. But as a consequence, no matter how sincere Fetterman's "social justice agenda," it is, in the end, often perceived as his.

"The key to urban reclamation is citizen participation," David Lewis told me 17 when I visited him in Homestead, another struggling Mon Valley borough across the river from Braddock. An architect and urban planner known for his emphasis on community participation, Lewis was instrumental in a massive redevelopment project there called the Waterfront. "You start with the people," Lewis said.

Fetterman, who did convene a group of residents to plan the community center, 18 likes to say that he won the last election 2 to 1. "The election was a referendum on the things I've done," he said.

Levi's Braddock ad campaign had its debut in movie theaters across the coun- 19 try on July 4th weekend. "We were taught how the pioneers went into the West. They opened their eyes and made up what things could be," a girl intoned. "A long time ago, things got broken here. People got sad and left. Maybe the world breaks on purpose so we can have work to do. People think there aren't frontiers anymore. They can't see how frontiers are all around us."

That same weekend, billboards with Braddock, PA, along the bottom appeared 20 in Times Square and across the country. They featured portraits of some of the finer-looking denizens of the town, like Dave Rosenstraus, whose company, Fossil Free Fuel, was the one new business in town (which recently spawned another, still with the same partners); Jack Samuel, a member of a straight-edge-vegan-punk-rock collective; and Deanne Dupree, whose boyfriend was the last homicide in town. They carried the affirming slogan "Everybody's Work Is Equally Important," which had a touch of irony in a place where so many people cannot find jobs.

The urban-pioneer motif in the Levi's ads was part of the Braddock revival 21 story from the beginning. One of the first things Fetterman did when he took office was offer free studio space to artists. "It's hard to appreciate how big a leap of faith it was," the mayor told me. "No way artists are going to come out to Braddock" from Pittsburgh "at nine at night for studio space. The perception was that it was too dangerous." It was easy to segue from there to offering—or at least pointing to the availability of—cheap housing to anyone willing to make up what could be. Still, according to Fetterman, "we have never tried to bring people in. It's just like media interest. They've just found us."

That media interest was itself an invitation, and it began with a colorful spread 22 in 2007 in the magazine *ReadyMade*. In the accompanying article, the mayor declared: "We need to get people excited about living in Braddock again. For D.I.Y.-ers, this town is a dream." The article, which highlighted Fetterman's own rugged homesteading experience, flew around the Internet and was picked up by the mainstream media. The *Daily Beast* did a "live chat." *The New York Times* published three separate articles. Japanese and Swiss television crews showed up. So did the curious, the adventurous, the idealistic. "Braddock would not be possible if it were not for the Internet," Fetterman said. "To be able to type in 'Braddock' and pull up this wealth of information and you can draw your own beliefs on it—it's impossible to overstate that."

In Aspen, when Fetterman was asked how many "modern pioneers" had moved 23 to Braddock, he framed his answer as an equivalence: it was like 4,000 people moving to Pittsburgh, he said, which sounded like a lot. The actual number is currently twenty-three, in ten households. Modern pioneering turns out to be harder than just fixing a wrecked house, which turns out to be hard enough. Gutting and renovating a structure that wasn't built well the first time can easily compete with having a regular job. In Braddock, a successful modern pioneer typically requires family money, savings, or another outside means of support, and even then it's often a stretch.

And, for "urban pioneers" and longtime residents, it can be challenging to live 24 in a place that is getting so much attention. They resent their town being cast as a wasteland. They resent hearing that it "broke on purpose." They resent that some of the good things done by groups not affiliated with the mayor, like a new, state-of-the-art senior housing complex, or the thirty-six new homes and rental units built by the Mon Valley Initiative, which house eighty-nine people and have brought an influx of working families to Braddock (most headed by women employed in a range of jobs in the area), rarely find their way into the prevailing narrative. And they resent that one man's vision is represented as their collective vision, even while acknowledging that some of his actions, like planting fruit trees in abandoned lots, using Levi's money to finance a children's librarian and helping to get a new playground donated to the town make Braddock a more appealing, and most likely safer, place.

"I get jealous reading those stories because I want to live in that place," Jodi **25** Morrison said. Morrison grew up a few towns over and moved to Braddock from Brooklyn in 2008 after learning about its progressive mayor. Morrison, who is thirty-three, was showing me the colossal bank building she bought almost three years ago for $125,000. At the time, Morrison wasn't sure what she was going to do with it but figured it didn't matter. She'd come to Braddock, and the spirit of the place would move her. Not long after that, the roof sprang a massive leak. "My life here has become reactionary," Morrison said. "It's whatever crisis has come up that week that I have to fix. I'm way overwhelmed. I don't know how I am going to do this alone."

A few blocks away, Morrison's friends Jenny and Kevin Fremlin are not just **26** overwhelmed; they're angry. The couple, who are in their thirties, moved here from Juneau, Alaska, after an exploratory visit. They liked what they saw: arts groups working with kids, a potluck at a neighbor's house and the 17,000-square-foot former Chevy dealership that Fetterman's sister, Kristin, and her partner, Joel Rice, were converting (for about $250,000) into a magnificent furniture workshop, loft, greenhouse and textile studio. The Fremlins were eager to buy a $5,000 house but agreed to manage John's Convent in exchange for free housing on its third floor. By the time they arrived from Alaska, dog and possessions in tow, it had been declared uninhabitable.

Paradoxically, it can be difficult to find a home in Braddock. Many buildings **27** are slated for demolition, and there is a relatively profitable Section 8 rental market for those that aren't. Eventually, with the mayor's help, the Fremlins found a house on one of the more crime-ridden streets.

That was more than two years ago. Their $5,000 house has now cost them nearly **28** $60,000, and they are broke. There was drive-by shooting out front. They own a shotgun because it is more intimidating than a handgun. "Most people come here because of the hype that you can get houses cheap and fulfill your dreams," said Jenny, who runs an online communications design business. "We came here so we could work less and do the projects we wanted, and we're working more than we ever did."

Kevin, her husband, agreed. "We've spent every dime we had and then some," **29** he said. "It's a hard pill to swallow when you realize you have squandered your nest egg. Squandered. It's gone."

Scale is a tricky variable when it pertains to turning around a city, especially **30** one as small as Braddock. From 2000 to 2009, the population has declined by 241; about 600 jobs were lost last year alone when the University of Pittsburgh Medical Center closed the local hospital. Those are big numbers in a small place, and they represent a tide that even a personality as large as Fetterman's is unable to hold back. Nonetheless, tearing down a single abandoned building and returning the lot to green space, or renovating a dilapidated house, has its own significance: it suggests something else is possible.

"We have made our lives here, started a family and support local events and 31 fundraisers, even if we aren't always happy about living here and hope to move out," Jenny Fremlin wrote in a recent e-mail. On their own, she and Jodi Morrison are starting a "friends of the library group" and hope someday to open a used bookstore in an unused part of the library.

For the mayor, though, fostering civic engagement is not a necessary corol- 32 lary to urban homesteading. "If someone wants to buy a house and live their life and pay their taxes, that's fine," Fetterman said. "Ninety percent of old Braddock walked away. That left a lot of chaos in town."

Which raises the question: Is urban renewal just a matter of showing up?   33

On Wood Street, Jack Samuel, the twenty-five-year-old straight-edge vegan 34 punk rocker and Levi's model, was hanging out in one of the two houses he and the six other members of the Some Ideas Collective bought last year. The group wanted an inexpensive "live-work" space where they could play music, write, and work on bikes. They bought a house for $6,000 from a filmmaker who was moving on. It was run-down, but for kids whose goal was to "make life cheap enough" so they could "binge work and then be free," it was just fine.

"My goal is to build for myself a life that meets my needs most effectively," 35 Samuel explained last summer. "So that means the lowest possible overhead costs day to day. If you qualify for food stamps, that's that much less money you have to make. I've been on food stamps for the last few months."

Samuel and his collective did not move to Braddock with the intent of "fixing it." 36 That idea, he said, "is potentially very colonial or paternalistic." "I got a little blinded by the image of Braddock that has been portrayed by the media, that all this place is is an artist's compound. And then getting here, it's like, 'Oh, there are just people who live here.' This is home for a lot of people, a lot of low-income people in particular."

James Smith, a thirty-two-year-old Braddock native, often hangs out in the 37 dollar-store parking lot with a group of friends. A graduate of the local high school, Smith can find only temp work, like cleaning Heinz Stadium after Steelers' games. The weekly farmers' market in Braddock is OK, Smith says, but even if he wanted to shop there, he couldn't afford it. Jobs and public transportation to get to them remain in short supply. Nothing that was happening in Braddock—not the green roof on the old furniture store, not the screen printing studio run by members of a social-lyconscious arts collective, not beehives, not the Shepard Fairey art installation on a nearby wall, not the Levi's ad campaign—has changed the most essential facts of his life: he is poor and without prospects. "The mayor is doing good things for the kids, and that does matter most, the future," he told me. "But what about the future that was neglected? Our generation, the generation before us. There is nothing for us."

One afternoon at the mayor's house, the former warehouse he shares with **38** his wife and young son, I asked him how having seven underemployed twenty-somethings move to town was a strategy for change. "What's better, having a group of kids like Jack buy a house, or waiting another six years till the buildings fall in on themselves?" the mayor asked.

A few weeks later I got an e-mail from Fetterman. "I know I am not Braddock's **39** savior, never felt that way, and never will," he wrote. "There's no 'Rudy-style ending' waiting for me where I get carried off the field and everything turns out OK for me or for Braddock," he continued, referring to the Notre Dame football legend.

I'd heard the mayor use that analogy a number of times before; it had seemed **40** like a throwaway line. Reading it now, though, I realized that it went some way toward explaining why the mayor of such a small town had got so much attention. The Braddock story has the appeal of an inspirational sports movie: we want this guy to win the game against all odds. We want to believe that all it takes to fix a town is—to borrow a phrase from Samuel and his friends—"some ideas."

READING COMPREHENSION

1. The word *disenfranchised* in "Here was a guy in biker boots bringing the Park Slope ethos . . . to the disenfranchised" (paragraph 5) means
   a. not interested, disengaged.
   b. independent.
   c. deprived of power, marginalized.
   d. forbidden to vote.

2. The word *reclamation* in "The key to urban reclamation is citizen participation" (paragraph 17) means
   a. change.
   b. restoration.
   c. decline.
   d. revision.

3. Which of the following would be a good alternative title for this selection?
   a. Grow Pittsburgh
   b. Biker Boy Buys Votes
   c. A Disastrous Mayor
   d. Finding a Future

4. Which sentence best expresses the main idea of the selection?
   a. Everyone in Braddock is excited about the mayor's vision.
   b. The mayor is trying to revitalize his town, despite the obstacles.

    c. More and more towns in America are dying because of the lack of jobs.

    d. People who don't want to work should move to towns like Braddock.

5. What do the tattoos on Fetterman's arm stand for?

    a. the birthdates of his children

    b. the important fraternity dates from his college days

    c. the number of people killed in Braddock since he took office and the address of City Hall

    d. the dates of the people killed in Braddock since he took office and the zip code of Braddock

6. What qualifications does Fetterman have to be mayor?

    a. past experience working in insurance

    b. attendance at Harvard's Kennedy School studying social policy

    c. running a program for at-risk youth

    d. all of the above

7. Halpern uses the term "Rust Belt town" to describe Braddock. Based on contextual clues, what does this term mean?

    a. A dirty, dingy town with lots of rusty buildings.

    b. A town that no longer produces any type of industrial product and now focuses on green products.

    c. A town that used to thrive by manufacturing industrial products, but now has multiple factories that are shut down.

    d. A town that used to create a lot of products, but has now focused on producing only one type of product.

8. Why does Fetterman believe his position offers him a "bully pulpit"?

    a. He doesn't feel the city council has revitalization of Braddock at the forefront of its agenda, so he believes his position is to "bully" the council into making revitalization its top priority.

    b. He wants to run and dominate the town, so he feels that becoming mayor will allow him to do whatever he wants.

    c. Bullying has been a problem in Braddock, so the mayor feels that his position will now allow him to eradicate all forms of bullying.

    d. The city council has had a history of bullying the residents into participating in projects they don't like, so Fetterman sees his position as the one to put a stop to this bullying.

9. What does Halpern mean by "Fetterman built a back door" (paragraph 13)?

    a. He figured out how to fix most of the run-down buildings.

    b. He figured out a way to work with the city council.

    c. He started a non-profit organization.

    d. He figured out a way around all the red tape of the city council.

10. The author implies that

    a. many of the current residents of Braddock have been surprised by what real life is like in the town.

    b. the mayor of Braddock is a con artist.

    c. only someone with a degree from an elite college could take on such a project.

    d. the film about Braddock was a joke.

STRUCTURE AND TECHNIQUE

1. What method of introduction—brief story, stating importance of topic, or broad-to-narrow—does Halpern use? Why do you think she chose this way to begin her article?

2. Halpern employs the use of dialogue throughout her article. Why do you think she does this, and do you find it effective?

3. What pattern(s) of development does Halpern use in her article?

4. Analyze how the tone changes throughout the article.

CRITICAL READING AND DISCUSSION

1. What is Halpern's purpose in using these details—shaved head, tattoos, 6-foot-8—in her description of Fetterman ?

2. The slogan, "Everybody's Work Is Equally Important," was featured on billboards across the country. The author stated that this slogan was ironic when applied to Braddock because so many were out of work. Why do you think this slogan was featured? Do you agree that it is ironic, or might it have a different purpose? Explain your reasoning.

3. Not all the people interviewed are happy with Fetterman and the way he is running things, yet he has been reelected. Why do you think Fetterman is handling the revitalization of Braddock in the manner he is?

4. The article ends on a realistic, rather than a happy, note. Instead of touting Fetterman as the savior of Braddock, Halpern portrays the reality of trying to save a dying town. Why wouldn't Halpern want to end her article on a more positive note? Do you think she supports Fetterman? Do you think she condones his actions?

WRITING ASSIGNMENTS

Assignment 1

Fetterman has spent personal money to help revitalize Braddock. You are to write an essay explaining what you would do if you were given a million dollars, with the stipulation that it had to be used to benefit others in your community. You will want to explain in detail what you would do with the money, how it would benefit your community, and your reasons for selecting certain causes and not others.

Assignment 2

In paragraph 14, Halpern refers to the Levi's ad campaign: "A long time ago, things got broken here. People got sad and left. Maybe the world breaks on purpose so we can have work to do. People think there aren't frontiers anymore. They can't see how frontiers are all around us." Respond to this quote. Do you agree/disagree? Why?

Assignment 3

Fetterman sometimes bypassed the city council to get things done—much to the annoyance of many of the members. Most people, however, have to work through proper channels. Write a letter to your city council discussing something that needs to be done to improve your community or discussing the need to streamline a process, such as applying for a permit to demolish a blighted building, improving a playground, or getting speed bumps installed to slow traffic.

How to Make It in College, Now That You're Here

Brian O'Keeney

PREVIEW

The author of this selection presents a compact guide to being a successful student. He will show you how to pass tests, how to avoid becoming a student zombie, how to find time to fit in everything you want to do, and how to deal with personal problems while keeping up with your studies. These and other helpful tips have been culled from the author's own experience and his candid interviews with fellow students.

Today is your first day on campus. You were a high school senior three months ago. 1
Or maybe you've been at home with your children for the last ten years. Or maybe you work full time and you're coming to school to start the process that leads to a better job. Whatever your background is, you're probably not too concerned today with staying in college. After all, you just got over the hurdle (and the paperwork) of applying to this place and organizing your life so that you could attend. And today, you're confused and tired. Everything is a hassle, from finding the classrooms to standing in line at the bookstore. But read my advice anyway. And if you don't read it today, clip and save this article. You might want to look at it a little further down the road.

By the way, if this isn't your very first day, don't skip this article. Maybe you 2 haven't been doing as well in your studies as you'd hoped. Or perhaps you've had problems juggling your work schedule, your class schedule, and your social life. If so, read on. You're about to get the inside story on making it in college. On the basis of my own experience as a final-year student, and after dozens of interviews with successful students, I've worked out a no-fail system for coping with college. These are the inside tips every students needs to do well in school. I've put myself in your place, and I'm going to answer the questions that will cross (or have already crossed) your mind during your stay here.

What's the Secret of Getting Good Grades?

It all comes down to getting those grades, doesn't it? After all, you came here for 3 some reason, and you're going to need passing grades to get the credits or degree you want. Many of us never did much studying in high school; most of the learning we did took place in the classroom. College, however, is a lot different. You're really on your own when it comes to passing courses. In fact, sometimes you'll feel as if nobody cares if you make it or not. Therefore, you've got to figure out a study system that gets results. Sooner or later, you'll be alone with those books. After that, you'll be sitting in a classroom with an exam sheet on your desk. Whether you stare at that exam with a queasy stomach or whip through it fairly confidently depends on your study techniques. Most of the successful students I talked to agreed that the following eight study tips deliver solid results.

1. Set Up a Study Place.   Those students you see "studying" in the cafeteria or 4 game room aren't learning much. You just can't learn when you're distracted by people and noise. Even the library can be a bad place to study if you constantly find yourself watching the clouds outside or the students walking through the stacks. It takes guts to sit, alone, in a quiet place in order to study. But you have to do it. Find a room at home or a spot in the library that's relatively quiet—and boring. When you sit there, you won't have much to do except study.

2. Get into a Study Frame of Mind.   When you sit down, do it with the attitude 5 that you're going to get this studying done. You're not going to doodle in your notebook or make a list for the supermarket. Decide that you are going to study and learn *now,* so that you can move on to more interesting things as soon as possible.

3. Give Yourself Rewards.   If you sweat out a block of study time, and do a good 6 job on it, treat yourself. You deserve it. You can "psych" yourself up for studying by promising to reward yourself afterward. A present for yourself can be anything from a favorite TV show to a relaxing bath to a dish of double chocolate ice cream.

4. Skim the Textbook First.   Lots of students sit down with an assignment like 7 "Read chapter five, pages 125–150" and do just that. They turn to page 125 and start to read. After a while, they find that they have no idea what they just read. For the last ten minutes, they've been thinking about their five-year-old or what they're going to eat for dinner. Eventually, they plod through all the pages but don't remember much afterward.

In order to prevent this problem, skim the textbook chapter first. This means: 8 look at the title, the subtitles, the headings, the pictures, the first and last paragraphs. Try to find out what the person who wrote the book had in mind when he or she organized the chapter. What was important enough to set off as a title or in bold type? After skimming, you should be able to explain to yourself what the main points of the chapter are. Unless you're the kind of person who would step into an empty elevator shaft without looking first, you'll soon discover the value of skimming.

5. Take Notes on What You're Studying.   This sounds like a hassle, but it 9 works. Go back over the material after you've read it, and jot down key words and phrases in the margins. When you review the chapter for a test, you'll have handy little things like "definition of rationalization" or "example of assimilation" in the margins. If the material is especially tough, organize a separate sheet of notes.

Write down definitions, examples, lists, and main ideas. The idea is to have a single sheet that boils the entire chapter down to a digestible lump.

6. Review after You've Read and Taken Notes.   Some people swear that talking 10 to yourself works. Tell yourself about the most important points in the chapter. Once you've said them out loud, they seem to stick better in your mind. If you can't talk to yourself about the material after reading it, that's a sure sign you don't really know it.

7. Give Up.   This may sound contradictory, but give up when you've had enough. 11 You should try to make it through at least an hour, though. Ten minutes here and there are useless. When your head starts to pound and your eyes develop spidery red lines, quit. You won't do much learning when you're exhausted.

8. Take a College Skills Course If You Need It.   Don't hesitate or feel embar- 12 rassed about enrolling in a study skills course. Many students say they wouldn't have made it without one.

How Can I Keep Up with All My Responsibilities without Going Crazy?

You've got a class schedule. You're supposed to study. You've got a family. You've got 13 a husband, wife, boyfriend, girlfriend, child. You've got a job. How are you possibly going to cover all the bases in your life and maintain your sanity? This is one of the toughest problems students face. Even if they start the semester with the best of intentions, they eventually find themselves tearing their hair out trying to do everything they're supposed to do. Believe it or not, though, it is possible to meet all your responsibilities. And you don't have to turn into a hermit or give up your loved ones to do it.

The secret here is to organize your time. But don't just sit around half the 14 semester planning to get everything together soon. Before you know it, you'll be confronted with midterms, papers, family, and work all at once. Don't let yourself reach that breaking point. Instead, try these three tactics.

1. Monthly Calendar.   Get one of those calendars with big blocks around the 15 dates. Give yourself an overview of the whole term by marking down the due dates for papers and projects. Circle test and exam days. This way those days don't sneak up on you unexpectedly.

2. Study Schedule.   Sit down during the first few days of this semester and make 16 up a sheet listing the days and hours of the week. Fill in your work and class hours first. Then try to block out some study hours. It's better to study a little every day than to create a huge once-or-twice-a-week marathon session. Schedule study hours for your hardest classes for the times when you feel most energetic. For example, I battled my tax law textbook in the mornings; when I looked at it after 7:00 P.M., I might as well have been reading Chinese. The usual proportion, by the way, is one hour of study time for every class hour.

In case you're one of those people who get carried away, remember to leave 17 blocks of free time, too. You won't be any good to yourself or anyone else if you don't relax and pack in the studying once in a while.

3. "To Do" List.   This is the secret that, more than any other, got me through 18 college. Once a week (or every day if you want to), write a list of what you have to do. Write down everything from "write English paper" to "buy cold cuts for lunch." The best thing about a "to do" list is that it seems to tame all those stray "I have to" thoughts that nag at your mind. Just making the list seems to make the tasks "doable." After you finish something on the list, cross it off. Don't be compulsive about finishing everything; you're not Superman or Wonder Woman. Get the important things done first. The secondary things you don't finish can simply be moved to your next "to do" list.

What Can I Do If Personal Problems Get in the Way of My Studies?

One student, Roger, told me this story: 19

> Everything was going OK for me until the middle of the spring semester. I went through a terrible time when I broke up with my girlfriend and started seeing her best friend. I was trying to deal with my ex-girlfriend's hurt and anger, my new girlfriend's guilt, and my own worries and anxieties at the same time. In addition to this, my mother was sick and on a medication that made her really irritable. I hated to go home because the atmosphere was so uncomfortable. Soon, I started missing classes because I couldn't deal with the academic pressures as well as my own personal problems. It seemed easier to hang around my girlfriend's apartment than to face all my problems at home and at school.

Another student, Marian, told me: 20

> I'd been married for eight years and the relationship wasn't going too well. I saw the handwriting on the wall, and I decided to prepare for the future. I enrolled in college, because I knew I'd need a decent job to support myself. Well, my husband had a fit because I was going to school. We were arguing a lot anyway, and he made it almost impossible for me to study at home. I think he was angry and almost jealous because I was drawing away from him. It got so bad that I thought about quitting college for a while. I wasn't getting any support at home, and it was just too hard to go on.

Personal troubles like these are overwhelming when you're going through 21 them. School seems like the least important thing in your life. The two students above are perfect examples of this. But if you think about it, quitting or failing school would be the worst thing for these two students. Roger's problems, at least with his girlfriends, would simmer down eventually, and then he'd regret having left school. Marian had to finish college if she wanted to be able to live independently. Sometimes, you've just got to hang tough.

But what do you do while you're trying to live through a lousy time? First of 22 all, do something difficult. Ask yourself, honestly, if you're exaggerating small problems as an excuse to avoid classes and studying. It takes strength to admit this, but there's no sense in kidding yourself. If your problems are serious, and real, try to make some human contacts at school. Lots of students hide inside a miserable shell made of their own troubles and feel isolated and lonely. Believe me, there are plenty of students with problems. Not everyone is getting A's and having a fabulous social and home life at the same time. As you go through the term, you'll pick up some vibrations about the students in your classes. Perhaps someone strikes you as a compatible person. Why not speak to that person after class? Share a cup of coffee in the cafeteria or walk to the parking lot together. You're not looking for a best friend or the love of your life. You just want to build a little network of support for yourself. Sharing your difficulties, questions, and complaints with a friendly person on campus can make a world of difference in how you feel.

Finally, if your problems are overwhelming, get some professional help. Why 23 do you think colleges spend countless dollars on counseling departments and campus psychiatric services? More than ever, students all over the country are taking advantage of the help offered by support groups and therapy sessions. There's no shame attached to asking for help, either; in fact, almost 40 percent of college students (according to one survey) will use counseling services during their time in school. Just walk into a student center or counseling office and ask for an appointment. You wouldn't think twice about asking a dentist to help you get rid of your toothache. Counselors are paid—and want—to help you with your problems.

Why Do Some People Make It and Some Drop Out?

Anyone who spends at least one semester in college notices that some students give 24 up on their classes. The person who sits behind you in accounting, for example, begins to miss a lot of class meetings and eventually vanishes. Or another student comes to class without the assignment, doodles in a notebook during the lecture, and leaves during the break. What's the difference between students like this and the ones who succeed in school? My survey may be nonscientific, but everyone I asked said the same thing: attitude. A positive attitude is the key to everything else—good study habits, smart time scheduling, and coping with personal difficulties.

What does "a positive attitude" mean? Well, for one thing, it means avoiding 25 the zombie syndrome. It means not only showing up for your classes, but also doing something while you're there. Really listen. Take notes. Ask a question if you want to. Don't just walk into a class, put your mind in neutral, and drift away to never-never land.

Having a positive attitude goes deeper than this, though. It means being ma- 26 ture about college as an institution. Too many students approach college classes like six-year-olds who expect first grade to be as much fun as *Sesame Street*. First grade, as we all know, isn't as much fun as *Sesame Street*. And college classes can sometimes be downright dull. If you let a boring class discourage you so much that you want to leave school, you'll lose in the long run. Look at your priorities. You want a degree, or a certificate, or a career. If you have to, you can make it through a less-than-interesting class in order to achieve what you want. Get whatever you can out of every class. But if you simply can't stand a certain class, be determined to fulfill its requirements and be done with it once and for all.

After the initial high of starting school, you have to settle in for the long haul. 27 If you follow the advice here, you'll be prepared to face the academic crunch. You'll also live through the semester without giving up your family, your job, or *Monday Night Football*. Finally, going to college can be an exciting time. You do learn. And when you learn things, the world becomes a more interesting place.

READING COMPREHENSION

1. The word *queasy* in "with a queasy stomach" (paragraph 3) means
   a. strong.
   b. healthy.
   c. full.
   d. nervous.

2. The word *tactics* in "try these three tactics" (paragraph 14) means
   a. proofs.
   b. problems.
   c. methods.
   d. questions.

3. Which of the following would be a good alternative title for this selection?
   a. Your First Day on Campus
   b. Coping with College
   c. How to Budget Your Time
   d. The Benefits of College Skills Courses

4. Which sentence expresses the main idea of the selection?
   a. In high school, most of us did little homework.
   b. You should give yourself rewards for studying well.

    c. Sometimes personal problems interfere with studying.

    d. You can succeed in college by following certain guidelines.

5. According to the author, "making it" in college means

    a. studying whenever you have any free time.

    b. getting a degree by barely passing your courses.

    c. quitting school until you solve your personal problems.

    d. getting good grades without making your life miserable.

6. If your personal problems seem overwhelming, you should

    a. drop out for a while.

    b. exaggerate them to teachers.

    c. avoid talking about them.

    d. get help from a professional.

7. Which of the following is *not* described by the author as a means of time control?

    a. monthly calendar

    b. to-do list

    c. study schedule

    d. flexible job hours

8. We can infer that the writer of this essay

    a. cares about college students and their success.

    b. dropped out of college.

    c. is very disorganized.

    d. is an A student.

9. From the selection we can conclude that

    a. college textbooks are very expensive.

    b. it is a good practice to write notes in your textbook.

    c. taking notes on your reading takes too much time.

    d. a student should never mark up an expensive book.

10. The author implies that

    a. fewer people than before are attending college.

    b. most college students experience no problems during their first year.

    c. all college students experience overwhelming problems.

    d. coping with college is difficult.

STRUCTURE AND TECHNIQUE

1. O'Keeney uses a highly structured format in his essay. What are some of the features of this format? Why do you think O'Keeney structured his essay in this way?

2. Does the author clearly state his thesis? If so, where is it stated, and how?

3. What method of introduction does the author use in the section on personal problems (starting with paragraph 19)? What is the value of using this method?

4. In his essay, O'Keeney addresses his audience in the second person—using the word *you*. How does such a technique advance his main point?

CRITICAL READING AND DISCUSSION

1. What, according to O'Keeney, is the secret of getting good grades? Have you used any of O'Keeney's study methods? If so, how useful do you think they have been for you? Are there any that you haven't used but might try? Explain your answer.

2. What does O'Keeney recommend students do to manage their time and responsibilities more effectively? Which of these suggestions are you most likely to use? Which are you least likely to use? Why?

3. What is the secret the author says got him through college? What do you think is the most helpful or important suggestion the author makes in the selection? Give reasons for your choice.

4. Do you agree with the author that Roger and Marian should stay in school? Are there any situations in which it would be better for students to quit school or leave, at least temporarily? Explain, giving examples to support your answer.

WRITING ASSIGNMENTS

Assignment 1

Write an essay similar to the one you've just read that explains how to succeed in some other field—for example, a job, a sport, marriage, child rearing. First, brainstorm three or four problem areas a newcomer to this experience might encounter. Then, under each area you have listed, jot down some helpful hints and techniques for overcoming these problems. For example, a paper on "How to Succeed as a Waitress" might describe the following problem areas:

developing a good memory

learning to do tasks quickly

coping with troublesome customers

Each supporting paragraph in this paper would discuss specific techniques for dealing with these problems. Be sure that the advice you give is detailed and specific enough to really help a person in such a situation. You may find it helpful to look over the essays in Chapter 11.

Assignment 2

Write a letter to Roger or Marian, giving advice on how to deal with the personal problem mentioned in the article. You might recommend the following:

Make other contacts at school. (How? Where?)

See a counselor. (Where? What should this person be told?)

Realize that the problem is not so serious. (Why not?)

In your introductory paragraph, explain why you are writing the letter. Include a thesis statement that says what plan of action you are recommending. Then, in the rest of the paper, explain the plan of action in detail.

Assignment 3

Write an essay contrasting college *as you thought it would be* with college *as it is.* You can organize the essay by focusing on three specific things that are different from what you expected. Or you can cover three areas of difference. For instance, you may decide to contrast your expectations about (1) a college dorm room, (2) your roommate, and (3) dining-hall food with reality. Or you could contrast your expectations about (1) fellow students, (2) college professors, and (3) college courses with reality.

Refer to the section in Chapter 13 on methods of developing comparison or contrast essays to review point-by-point and one-side-at-a-time development. Be sure to make an outline of your essay before you begin to write.

College Lectures: Is Anybody Listening?

David Daniels

PREVIEW

College students are doodling in their notebooks or gazing off into space as their instructor lectures for fifty minutes. What is wrong with this picture? Many would say that what is wrong is the students. However, the educator and author David Daniels would say that the lecture itself is the problem. As you read this article, see if you agree with Daniels's analysis of lectures and their place in a college education.

A former teacher of mine, Robert A. Fowkes of New York University, likes to tell the **1** story of a class he took in Old Welsh while studying in Germany during the 1930s. On the first day the professor strode up to the podium, shuffled his notes, coughed, and began, "*Guten Tag, Meinen Damen und Herren*" ("Good day, ladies and gentlemen"). Fowkes glanced around uneasily. He was the only student in the course.

Toward the middle of the semester, Fowkes fell ill and missed a class. When **2** he returned, the professor nodded vaguely and, to Fowkes's astonishment, began to deliver not the next lecture in the sequence but the one after. Had he, in fact, lectured to an empty hall in the absence of his solitary student? Fowkes thought it perfectly possible.

Today, American colleges and universities (originally modeled on German ones) **3** are under strong attack from many quarters. Teachers, it is charged, are not doing a good job of teaching, and students are not doing a good job of learning. American businesses and industries suffer from unenterprising, uncreative executives educated not to think for themselves but to mouth outdated truisms[1] the rest of the world has long discarded. College graduates lack both basic skills and general culture. Studies are conducted and reports are issued on the status of higher education, but any changes that result either are largely cosmetic or make a bad situation worse.

One aspect of American education too seldom challenged is the lecture sys- **4** tem. Professors continue to lecture and students to take notes much as they did in the thirteenth century, when books were so scarce and expensive that few students

---

[1] *truisms:* self-evident truths.

could own them. The time is long overdue for us to abandon the lecture system and turn to methods that really work.

To understand the inadequacy of the present system, it is enough to follow a **5** single imaginary first-year student—let's call her Mary—through a term of lectures on, say, introductory psychology (although any other subject would do as well). She arrives on the first day and looks around the huge lecture hall, taken a little aback to see how large the class is. Once the hundred or more students enrolled in the course discover that the professor never takes attendance (how can he?—calling the role would take far too much time), the class shrinks to a less imposing size.

Some days Mary sits in the front row, from where she can watch the professor **6** read from a stack of yellowed notes that seem nearly as old as he is. She is bored by the lectures, and so are most of the other students, to judge by the way they are nodding off or doodling in their notebooks. Gradually she realizes the professor is as bored as his audience. At the end of each lecture he asks, "Are there any questions?" in a tone of voice that makes it plain he would much rather there weren't. He needn't worry—the students are as relieved as he is that the class is over.

Mary knows very well she should read an assignment before every lecture. **7** However, as the professor gives no quizzes and asks no questions, she soon realizes she needn't prepare. At the end of the term she catches up by skimming her notes and memorizing a list of facts and dates. After the final exam, she promptly forgets much of what she has memorized. Some of her fellow students, disappointed at the impersonality of it all, drop out of college altogether. Others, like Mary, stick it out, grow resigned to the system and await better days when, as juniors and seniors, they will attend smaller classes and at last get the kind of personal attention real learning requires.

I admit this picture is overdrawn—most universities supplement lecture courses **8** with discussion groups, usually led by graduate students; and some classes, such as first-year English, are always relatively small. Nevertheless, far too many courses rely principally or entirely on lectures, an arrangement much loved by faculty and administrators but scarcely designed to benefit the students.

One problem with lectures is that listening intelligently is hard work. Reading **9** the same material in a textbook is a more efficient way to learn because students can proceed as slowly as they need to until the subject matter becomes clear to them. Even simply paying attention is very difficult; people can listen at a rate of four hundred to six hundred words a minute, while the most impassioned[2] professor talks at scarcely a third of that speed. This time lag between speech and comprehension leads to daydreaming. Many students believe years of watching television have sabotaged their attention span, but their real problem is that listening attentively is much harder than they think.

---

[2]*impassioned:* enthusiastic.

Worse still, attending lectures is passive learning, at least for inexperienced lis- 10 teners. Active learning, in which students write essays or perform experiments and then have their work evaluated by an instructor, is far more beneficial for those who have not yet fully learned how to learn. While it's true that techniques of active listening, such as trying to anticipate the speaker's next point or taking notes selectively, can enhance the value of a lecture, few students possess such skills at the beginning of their college careers. More commonly, students try to write everything down and even bring tape recorders to class in a clumsy effort to capture every word.

Students need to question their professors and to have their ideas taken seri- 11 ously. Only then will they develop the analytical skills required to think intelligently and creatively. Most students learn best by engaging in frequent and even heated debate, not by scribbling down a professor's often unsatisfactory summary of complicated issues. They need small discussion classes that demand the common labors of teacher and students rather than classes in which one person, however learned, propounds his or her own ideas.

The lecture system ultimately harms professors as well. It reduces feedback to 12 a minimum, so that the lecturer can neither judge how well students understand the material nor benefit from their questions or comments. Questions that require the speaker to clarify obscure points and comments that challenge sloppily constructed arguments are indispensable to scholarship. Without them, the liveliest mind can atrophy. Undergraduates may not be able to make telling contributions very often, but lecturing insulates a professor even from the beginner's naive question that could have triggered a fruitful line of thought.

If lectures make so little sense, why have they been allowed to continue? Ad- 13 ministrators love them, of course. They can cram far more students into a lecture hall than into a discussion class, and for many administrators that is almost the end of the story. But the truth is that faculty members, and even students, conspire with them to keep the lecture system alive and well. Lectures are easier on everyone than debates. Professors can pretend to teach by lecturing just as students can pretend to learn by attending lectures, with no one the wiser, including the participants. Moreover, if lectures afford some students an opportunity to sit back and let the professor run the show, they offer some professors an irresistible forum for showing off. In a classroom where everyone contributes, students are less able to hide and professors less tempted to engage in intellectual exhibitionism.

Smaller classes in which students are required to involve themselves in discus- 14 sion put an end to students' passivity. Students become actively involved when forced to question their own ideas as well as their instructor's. Their listening skills improve dramatically in the excitement of intellectual give-and-take with their instructors and fellow students. Such interchanges help professors do their job better because they allow them to discover who knows what—before final exams, not after. When exams are given in this type of course, they can require analysis and synthesis from the students, not empty memorization. Classes like this require energy, imagination, and commitment from professors, all of which can be exhausting. But they compel students to share responsibility for their own intellectual growth.

Lectures will never entirely disappear from the university scene both because   15
they seem to be economically necessary and because they spring from a long tradition in a setting that values tradition for its own sake. But the lectures too frequently come at the wrong end of the students' educational careers—during the first two years, when they most need close, even individual, instruction. If lecture classes were restricted to junior and senior undergraduates and to graduate students, who are less in need of scholarly nurturing and more able to prepare work on their own, they would be far less destructive of students' interests and enthusiasms than the present system. After all, students must learn to listen before they can listen to learn.

READING COMPREHENSION

1. The word *enhance* in "techniques of active listening . . . can enhance the value of a lecture" (paragraph 10) means

   a. ruin.

   b. ignore.

   c. increase.

   d. claim.

2. The word *atrophy* in "Without [questions and comments], the liveliest mind can atrophy" (paragraph 12) means

   a. waste away.

   b. be unchanged.

   c. compete.

   d. strengthen.

3. Which of the following would be a good alternative title for this selection?

   a. How to Benefit from Lecture Classes

   b. The Necessity of Classroom Lecturing

   c. Problems with Lecture Classes

   d. College Lectures: An Inspirational Tradition

4. Which sentence best expresses the main idea of the selection?

   a. American colleges and universities are being attacked from many sides.

   b. Colleges and universities should offer interactive, not lecture, classes to first-year and second-year students.

   c. College graduates lack basic skills and general culture.

   d. American colleges and universities are modeled on German ones.

5. According to the author, the lecture system

   a. encourages efficient learning.

   b. encourages students to ask questions.

   c. helps professors teach better.

   d. discourages students' attendance and preparation.

6. An example of passive learning is

   a. attending lectures.

   b. writing essays.

   c. doing experiments.

   d. debating a point.

7. To develop their thinking skills, students do not need to

   a. bring tape recorders to class.

   b. question professors.

   c. debate.

   d. attend small discussion classes.

8. The author implies that large lecture classes

   a. require students to have well-developed listening skills.

   b. encourage participation.

   c. are more harmful for juniors and seniors than for first-year students.

   d. are a modern invention.

9. *True or False?* _____ Daniels suggests that small classes demand greater effort from both faculty and students.

10. The author implies that administrators love lectures because

   a. students learn better in lectures.

   b. professors teach better through lecturing.

   c. schools make more money on lecture classes.

   d. professors can show off in lectures.

STRUCTURE AND TECHNIQUE

1. Daniels begins his essay with an anecdote about a former teacher of his. How does this introduction relate to his thesis?

2. Does Daniels directly state his thesis? If so, where is it stated?

3. In describing Mary's classroom experience (paragraphs 5–7), Daniels provides numerous details. What are some of these details? How do they relate to the essay's main idea?

4. Daniels's essay is an argument against the lecture system of education. What argumentation techniques does he employ? (See pages 343–364 for information on argumentation.)

CRITICAL READING AND DISCUSSION

1. Daniels states that "listening intelligently is hard work" (paragraph 9) and "[a]ctive learning . . . is far more beneficial for those who have not yet fully learned how to learn" (paragraph 10). Why might Daniels feel that listening is so hard? And why does he feel that active learning is so good?

2. In paragraph 8, Daniels acknowledges that he has exaggerated Mary's negative classroom experience, saying, "I admit this picture is overdrawn." Does this admission strengthen or weaken his argument? Explain.

3. According to Daniels, the lecture system harms professors by reducing feedback from students to a minimum. What is useful about feedback from students?

4. How do your experiences in both lecture classes and smaller classes compare with Daniels's descriptions? As a student, which type of class do you prefer? Why? If you were an instructor, which type of class would you prefer to teach? Why?

WRITING ASSIGNMENTS

Personal

Assignment 1

Write an essay in which you contrast a lecture class with a smaller, more interactive class. First make a list of the differences between the two classes. Following are some possible areas of difference you might consider:

opportunities for asking questions

opportunities for discussions

quality of feedback from the instructor

Choose three of the differences you found, and then decide which class you learned more in. You will then have the basis for a thesis statement and three supporting topic sentences. An example of a thesis statement for this essay is

> Because of the different approaches to students' questions, class discussion, and feedback from the instructor in grading papers, I learned a lot more in my first-year English class than in my business lecture class.

That thesis statement could be shortened to

> I learned a lot more in my first-year English class than in my business lecture class.

The three supporting points for this thesis statement are about

> different approaches to students' questions.
>
> class discussion.
>
> personal feedback on assignments.

Change each of the points listed above into a sentence, and you have your three topic sentences. A topic sentence based on the last point above might be "While my English instructor gave me a lot of useful feedback on my assignments, my business instructor put only a grade on papers." Use specific details from your experience to develop your supporting paragraphs.

Assignment 2

In this selection, Daniels has given some disadvantages of lectures. Write an essay on the advantages of lectures. To support your points, use examples from your personal experience and the experiences of others. Begin by jotting down a list of advantages. Then choose the advantages you have the most to say about and develop those in your essay.

Assignment 3

Which teachers or instructors have you had who were not in a rut, who conducted classes that made you glad to learn? Write a description of your idea of a very good teacher or instructor. Your description may be of someone who actually taught you, or it may be of a fictional person who combines all the traits you have enjoyed (or missed) in your teachers and instructors through the years. Be sure to include plenty of specific examples of classroom activities and their effects on students. Here are a few aspects of teaching that you may wish to use in your description:

> mastery of subject matter
>
> ability to excite students about subject
>
> types of activities used

Is Sex All That Matters?

Joyce Garity

PREVIEW

From the skimpy clothing in ads to the suggestive themes in many of today's TV comedies, our young people are bombarded with sexuality. How does the constant stream of sexual images influence their behavior and dreams? In considering that question, social worker Joyce Garity focuses on one young woman named Elaine, alone and pregnant with her second child.

A few years ago, a young girl lived with me, my husband, and our children for 1 several months. The circumstances of Elaine's coming to us don't matter here; suffice it to say that she was troubled and nearly alone in the world. She was also pregnant—hugely, clumsily pregnant with her second child. Elaine was seventeen. Her pregnancy, she said, was an accident; she also said she wasn't sure who had fathered her child. There had been several sex partners and no contraception. Yet, she repeated blandly, gazing at me with clear blue eyes, the pregnancy was an accident, and one she would certainly never repeat.

Eventually I asked Elaine, after we had grown to know each other well enough 2 for such conversations, why neither she nor her lovers had used birth control. She blushed—porcelain-skinned girl with one child in foster care and another swelling the bib of her fashionably faded overalls—stammered, and blushed some more. Birth control, she finally got out, was "embarrassing." It wasn't "romantic." You couldn't be really passionate, she explained, and worry about birth control at the same time.

I haven't seen Elaine for quite a long time. I think about her often, though. 3 I think of her as I page through teen fashion magazines in the salon where I have my hair cut. Although mainstream and relatively wholesome, these magazines trumpet sexuality page after leering page. On the inside front cover, an advertisement for Guess jeans features junior fashion models in snug denim dresses, their legs bared to just below the crotch. An advertisement for Liz Claiborne fragrances shows a barely clad young couple sprawled on a bed, him painting her toenails. An advertisement for Obsession cologne displays a waif-thin girl draped stomach-down across a couch, naked, her startled expression suggesting helplessness in the face of an unseen yet approaching threat.

I think of Elaine because I know she would love these ads. "They're so beauti- 4 ful," she would croon, and of course they are. The faces and bodies they show are lovely. The lighting is superb. The hair and makeup are faultless. In the Claiborne ad, the laughing girl whose toenails are being painted by her handsome lover is obviously having the time of her life. She stretches luxuriously on a bed heaped with clean white linen and fluffy pillows. Beyond the sheer blowing curtains of her room, we can glimpse a graceful wrought-iron balcony. Looking at the ad, Elaine could only want to be her. Any girl would want to be her. Heck, *I* want to be her.

But my momentary desire to move into the Claiborne picture, to trade lives 5 with the exquisite young creature pictured there, is just that—momentary. I've lived long enough to know that what I see is a marketing invention. A moment after the photo session was over, the beautiful room was dismantled, and the models moved on to their next job. Later, the technicians took over the task of doctoring the photograph until it reached full-blown fantasy proportions.

Not so Elaine. After months of living together and countless hours of watching 6 her yearn after magazine images, soap-opera heroines, and rock goddesses, I have a pretty good idea of why she looks at ads like Claiborne's. She sees the way life—her life—is supposed to be. She sees a world characterized by sexual spontaneity, playfulness, and abandon. She sees people who don't worry about such unsexy details as birth control. Nor, apparently, do they spend much time thinking about such pedestrian topics as commitment or whether they should act on their sexual impulses. Their clean sunlit rooms are never invaded by the fear of AIDS, of unwanted pregnancy, of shattered lives. For all her apparent lack of defense, the girl on the couch in the Obsession ad will surely never experience the brutality of rape.

Years of exposure to this media-invented, sex-saturated universe have done 7 their work on Elaine. She is, I'm sure, completely unaware of the irony in her situation: She melts over images from a sexual Shangri-la,[1] never realizing that her attempts to mirror those images left her pregnant, abandoned, living in the spare bedroom of a stranger's house, relying on charity for rides to the welfare office and supervised visits with her toddler daughter.

Of course, Elaine is not the first to be suckered by the cynical practice of using sex 8 to sell underwear, rock groups, or sneakers. Using sex as a sales tool is hardly new. At the beginning of this century, British actress Lily Langtry shocked her contemporaries by posing, clothed somewhat scantily, with a bar of Pear's soap. The advertisers have always known that the masses are susceptible to the notion that a particular product will make them more sexually attractive. In the past, however, ads used euphemisms, claiming that certain products would make people "more lovable" or "more popular." What is a recent development is the abandonment of any such polite double-talk. Advertising today leaves no question about what is being sold along with the roasted peanuts or artificial sweetener. "Tell us about your first time," coyly invites the innuendo[2]-filled magazine advertisement for Campari liquor. A billboard for Levi's shows two jeans-clad young

[1] *Shangri-la:* an imaginary paradise on earth (the name of a beautiful faraway place in the novel *Lost Horizon*).
[2] *innuendo:* subtle suggestion.

men on the beach, hoisting a girl in the air. The boys' perfect, tan bodies are matched by hers, although we see a lot more of hers: bare midriff, short shorts, cleavage. She caresses their hair; they stroke her legs. A jolly fantasy where sex exists without consequences.

But this fantasy is a lie—one which preys on young people. Studies show that 9 by the age of twenty, 75 percent of Americans have lost their virginity. In many high schools—and an increasing number of junior highs—virginity is regarded as an embarrassing vestige of childhood, to be disposed of as quickly as possible. Young people are immersed from their earliest days in a culture that parades sexuality at every turn and makes heroes of the advocates of sexual excess. Girls, from toddlerhood on up, shop in stores packed with clothing once thought suitable only for streetwalkers—lace leggings, crop tops, and wedge-heeled boots. Parents drop their children off at concerts featuring simulated on-stage masturbation or pretended acts of copulation. Young boys idolize sports stars like the late Wilt Chamberlain, who claimed to have bedded 20,000 women. And when the "Spur Posse," eight California high school athletes, were charged with systematically raping girls as young as ten as part of a "scoring" ritual, the beefy young jocks were rewarded with a publicity tour of talk shows, while one father boasted to reporters about his son's "manhood."

In a late, lame attempt to counterbalance this sexual overload, most schools 10 offer sex education as part of their curriculums. (In 1993, forty-seven states recommended or required such courses.) But sex ed classes are heavy on the mechanics of fertilization and birth control—sperm, eggs, and condoms—and light on any discussion of sexuality as only one part of a well-balanced life. There is passing reference to abstinence as a method of contraception, but little discussion of abstinence as an emotionally or spiritually satisfying option. Promiscuity is discussed for its role in spreading sexually transmitted diseases. But the concept of rejecting casual sex in favor of reserving sex for an emotionally intimate, exclusive, trusting relationship—much less any mention of waiting until marriage—is foreign to most public school settings. "Love and stuff like that really wasn't discussed" is the way one Spur Posse member remembers his high school sex education class.

Surely teenagers need the factual information provided by sex education courses. 11 But where is "love and stuff like that" talked about? Where can they turn for a more balanced view of sexuality? Who is telling young people like Elaine, my former houseguest, that sex is not an adequate basis for a healthy, respectful relationship? Along with warnings to keep condoms on hand, is anyone teaching kids that they have a right to be valued for something other than their sexuality? Madison Avenue, Hollywood, and the TV, music, and fashion industries won't tell them that. Who will?

No one has told Elaine—at least, not in a way she comprehends. I haven't seen 12 her for a long time, but I hear of her occasionally. The baby boy she bore while living in my house is in a foster home, a few miles from his older half-sister, who is also in foster care. Elaine herself is working in a local convenience store—and she is pregnant again. This time, I understand, she is carrying twins.

READING COMPREHENSION

1. The word *dismantled* in "A moment after the photo session was over, the beautiful room was dismantled, and the models moved on to their next job" (paragraph 5) means

   a. used.

   b. photographed.

   c. taken apart.

   d. perfected.

2. The word *vestige* in "In many high schools—and an increasing number of junior highs—virginity is regarded as an embarrassing vestige of childhood" (paragraph 9) means

   a. reversal.

   b. activity.

   c. remainder.

   d. error.

3. Which of the following would be a good alternative title for this selection?

   a. Teens and Birth Control

   b. The Use of Sex to Sell Products

   c. An Unbalanced View of Sexuality

   d. The Advantages of Casual Sex

4. Which sentence best expresses the main idea of the selection?

   a. Sexual images have helped our society become more open and understanding about a natural part of life.

   b. We live in a society ruled by Madison Avenue, Hollywood, and the TV, music, and fashion industries.

   c. Sex education courses, required in most states, have not done enough to teach our children about sexuality and responsible behavior.

   d. Nothing, not even sex education, is counteracting the numerous sexual images in our society that encourage irresponsible, casual sex.

5. According to the author, Elaine may look at sexy magazine ads because

   a. she doesn't have high moral standards.

   b. she wishes she could afford the products being advertised.

   c. they portray the kind of life she'd like to lead.

   d. they remind her of her life before she had children.

6. In contrast to Elaine, the author
   a. understands that most ads portray an unreal world.
   b. finds ads like the Claiborne ad distasteful.
   c. never looks at fashion magazines.
   d. does not have children.

7. Elaine
   a. wanted to become pregnant.
   b. thinks birth control isn't romantic.
   c. never finished high school.
   d. has a healthy fear of AIDS.

8. We can conclude the author believes that
   a. sex is a private matter that should not be discussed.
   b. many young people view sex as an adequate basis for a relationship.
   c. Madison Avenue, Hollywood, and the TV, music, and fashion industries have completely destroyed all morality in America.
   d. virginity is an embarrassing vestige of childhood.

9. The author implies that
   a. sexy ads should be illegal.
   b. schools should teach contraception at an earlier age.
   c. sex should be reserved for an exclusive, loving relationship.
   d. casual sex is sometimes, though not always, a good idea.

10. The author suggests that sex education classes
    a. are a major cause of casual, unprotected sex.
    b. should include the role of sex in a meaningful relationship.
    c. should not include the mechanics of fertilization and birth control.
    d. have taken over a role that rightfully belongs to parents.

STRUCTURE AND TECHNIQUE

1. To support her views about sexuality in popular culture, Garity presents the case of Elaine. Why has the author chosen to focus so much of her essay on Elaine? What would have been lost if Garity had omitted Elaine?

2. List the details that Garity provides as she describes the Claiborne ad. Why does she go to such lengths to describe it? Why might she think it important for the reader to see it so clearly?

3. Garity uses a number of examples to support her claim about the prevalence of sex in popular culture. Cite some of these examples and explain how they support her argument.

4. Throughout paragraph 11, Garity poses a series of questions. What does she gain by using this technique?

CRITICAL READING AND DISCUSSION

1. How do you think Garity felt about Elaine? Affectionate? Scornful? Resentful? Disapproving? Pitying? Explain your answer. Use evidence from the text.

2. In paragraph 7, the author says that Elaine is "completely unaware of the irony in her situation." In an ironic situation, there is an inconsistency between what might be expected and what actually happens. What about Elaine's situation is ironic?

3. The author lists numerous examples to illustrate and support her claim that "young people are immersed from their earliest days in a culture that parades sexuality at every turn and makes heroes of advocates of sexual excess." What examples can you think of to add to her list? Describe and explain them.

4. In arguing against the emphasis on sexuality in our culture, Garity focuses on potential dangers to young women. How do you think this highly sexualized culture affects young men? Are they also at risk? Explain.

WRITING ASSIGNMENTS

Assignment 1

Garity accuses the advertising, film, TV, music, and fashion industries of contributing to our sex-saturated society by parading "sexuality at every turn." Choose one industry from that list and write your own essay about how it portrays sexuality.

There is more than one way you can approach this assignment. In an essay on the fashion industry, for instance, you could focus on types of clothing being promoted, ads in print, and ads on TV. In an essay on the music industry, you might discuss three musicians and how their lyrics and their performances promote a particular view of sex. Whatever your choice, include specific, colorful descriptions, as Garity does when discussing ads and fashions. (See, for example, paragraphs 3 and 8.)

Assignment 2

Garity suggests that sex education courses should include more than the " mechanics of fertilization and birth control" (paragraph 10). Write an essay describing several ways you feel sex education classes could incorporate "love and stuff like that." Begin by selecting three general approaches that could be used in a sex education class to get students to think about what makes a rich, balanced romantic relationship. For example, you might focus on three ideas such as the following:

discussion of the lyrics of a popular song

bringing into class a psychologist who deals with problems in relationships

bringing into class one or more couples who have been together for many years

Discuss each method you choose in a separate paragraph. Describe in detail how the method would work, using hypothetical examples to illustrate your points.

Assignment 3

Advertisements represent many elements of our society. Choose an element other than sexuality and analyze the way ads of any kind (in magazines and newspapers, on billboards and buses, on TV and radio, and on the Internet) portray that subject. For example, you might choose family life, looks, or health.

In analyzing an ad, consider what images and words are used, how they are intended to appeal to the audience, and what values they promote. Use the conclusion you come to as the thesis of your essay. For example, an essay on men's roles might make this point: "Many of today's TV ads promote participation of fathers in domestic activities."

Support your conclusion with colorful descriptions of several ads. Make your descriptions detailed enough so that your readers can "see" the elements of ads you refer to. Be sure to focus on the parts of the ads that support the point you are trying to make. You could organize your essay by devoting a paragraph each to three significant ads. Or you could devote each supporting paragraph to one of several important points about the subject you've chosen. For instance, an essay about fathers helping at home might discuss child care, cleaning, and cooking. A paragraph on each of those topics might refer to two or more ads.

Reading Comprehension Chart

Write an X through the numbers of any questions you missed while answering the comprehension questions for each selection in Part Five, "Readings for Writers." Then write in your comprehension score. If you repeatedly miss questions in any particular skill, the chart will make that clear. Then you can pay special attention to that skill in the future.

Selection	Vocabulary in Context	Title and Main Idea	Key Details	Inferences	Comprehension Score
Emerson	1 2 3	4 5	6 7	8 9 10	%
Russell	1	2 3	4 5 6	7 8 9 10	%
Gregory	1 2	3 4	5 6 7	8 9 10	%
Wilkins	1 2	3 4	5 6 7	8 9 10	%
Savory	1	2 3	4 5 6	7 8 9 10	%
Orwell	1 2	3 4	5 6 7	8 9 10	%
Tan	1 2 3	4 5	6 7	8 9 10	%
Johnson	1 2	3 4	5 6 7	8 9 10	%
Kendall	1 2	3 4	5 6 7	8 9 10	%
Banas	1 2	3 4	5 6 7	8 9 10	%
McClintock	1 2	3 4	5 6 7 8	9 10	%
Seattle	1 2 3	4 5	6 7 8	9 10	%
Urbina	1	2 3	4 5 6 7	8 9 10	%
Dunayer	1 2	3 4	5 6 7 8	9 10	%
Halpern	1 2	3 4	5 6	7 8 9 10	%
O'Keeney	1 2	3 4	5 6 7 8	9 10	%
Daniels	1 2	3 4	5 6 7	8 9 10	%
Garity	1 2	3 4	5 6 7	8 9 10	%

CREDITS

Text Credits

p. 1: "Have Yourself a Merry Little Christmas." Words and Music by Hugh Martin and Ralph Blane. © 1943 (Renewed) Metro-Goldwyn-Mayer, Inc. © 1944 (Renewed) EMl FEIST Catalog Inc. All rights controlled by EM! FEIST Catalog. Inc. (Publishing) and Alfred Publishing Co., Inc. (Print), All rights reserved. Used by permission.

p. 192: Beth Johnson. "Lou's Place." Reprinted by permission of the author.

p. 214: The Yellow Ribbon © [2010] by Pete Hamill. Used by permission. All rights reserved.

p. 233: Andrew Malcolm. "Dad." Reprinted by permission.

p. 251: Glenda Davis, "How to Do Well on a Job Interview." Used by permission of Townsend Press.

p. 269: "Taming the Anger Monster," by Anne Davidson. Used by permission of Townsend Press.

p. 293: Camille Lewis, "Born to Be Different?" Used by permission of Townsend Press.

p. 313: "Cookies or Heroin?" from *THE PLUG-IN DRUG*, REVISED AND UPDATED-25TH ANNIVERSARY EDITION by Marie Winn, copyright © 1977, 1985, 2002 by Marie Winn Miller. Used by permission of Viking Penguin, a division of Penguin Group (USA) Inc.

p. 334: Copyright © 1987 Tom Bodett. Reprinted by permission of Da Capo Press, a member of the Perseus Books Group.

p. 356: Molly Ivins, "Ban the Things. Ban Them All," *The Washington Post,* March 16, 1993. Copyright © Molly Ivins. Used by permission of the Estate of Molly Ivins.

p. 421: Jane Brody, "New Respect for the Nap," *The New York Times*, January 4, 2000. © 2000 *The New York Times*. All rights reserved. Used by permission and protected by the Copyright Laws of the United States. The printing, copying, redistribution, or retransmission of the Material without express written permission is prohibited.

Readings

p. 627: from *Self-Reliance* by Ralph Waldo Emerson—1841.

p. 632: from "Three Passions," *The Autobiography of Bertrand Russell.* Copyright © 2000. Reproduced by permission of Taylor & Francis Books, UK. Used by permission of Cengage Learning Services Limited, UK.

p. 636: from *Nigger: An Autobiography* by Dick Gregory, copyright © 1964 by Dick Gregory Enterprises, Inc. Used by permission of Dutton, a division of Penguin Group (USA) Inc.

p. 643: Roger Wilkins, "I Became Her Target," *Newsday,* September 6, 1987. Reprinted by permission of the author

p. 650: Tanya Savory, "Stepping into the Light." Used by permission of Townsend Press.

p. 658: George Orwell, "A Hanging," from *Shooting an Elephant and Other Essays,* Copyright © George Orwell 1931 and copyright 1950 by Sonia Brownell Orwell and renewed 1978 by Sonia Pitt-Rivers. Reprinted by permission of Houghton Mifflin Harcourt Publishing Company and by Bill Hamilton as the Literary Executor of the estate of the late Sonia Brownell Orwell and Seeker & Warburg Ltd.

p. 667: Amy Tan, "What Your Closet Reveals About You," *Harper's Bazaar*, March 2006, pp. 241, Issue 3532. Copyright © 2006 by Amy Tan. Reprinted by permission of Sandra Dijkstra Literary Agency.

p. 674: Beth Johnson, "The Professor is a Dropout." Reprinted by permission of the author.

p. 684: Audra Kendall, "The Certainty of Fear." Used by permission of Townsend Press.

p. 691: Casey Banas, "What's Wrong With Schools?" *The Chicago Tribune,* August 5, 1979. Copyright © 1979, Chicago Tribune Company. All rights reserved. Used by permission and protected by the Copyright Laws of the U.S. The printing, copying. redistribution, or retransmission of the Material without express written permission is prohibited. www.chicagotribune.com.

p. 697: Ann McClintock, "Propaganda Techniques in Today's Advertising." Used by permission of Townsend Press.

p. 707: Chief Seattle's Speech of 1854.

p. 715: Diane Urbana. "Single-Sex Schools: An Old Idea Whose Time Has Come." Used by permission of Townsend Press.

p. 722: Joan Dunayer, "Here's to Your Health." Used by permission of Townsend Press.

p. 728: Sue Halpern "Mayor of Rust," *The New York Times*, February 11, 2011. Used by permission of the author.

p. 739: Brian O'Keeney, "How to Make it in College." Used by permission of Townsend Press.

p. 748: David Daniels. "College Lectures: Is Anybody Listening?" Reprinted by permission of David Daniels.

p. 755: Joyce Garity, "Is Sex All That Matters?" Used by permission of Townsend Press.

Photo Credits

Chapter Opener 1: © Stock Image/SuperStock; 14: © Jamie Grill/Corbis RF; CO 2: © Purestock/SuperStock RF; CO 3: © Jiang Jin/SuperStock; p. 82: © Comstock Select/Corbis RF; CO 4: © Tim Pannell/Corbis; p. 101: © Getty RF; CO 5: © Image Source/Corbis RF; p. 119: © Paul Barton/Corbis; CO 6: © Yomiuri Shimbun/AFP/Getty Images; Part Opener 2a: © Lawrence Manning/Corbis RF; PO2b: © Newsies Media/Alamy; PO2c: Courtesy of Yahoo; PO2c (Yosemite): © Doug Sherman/Geofile RF; PO2c (Smoking): © Image100/Corbis RF; PO2c (Woman and Flag): © David Buffington/Blend Images LLC RF; CO 7: © M4OS Photos/Alamy; CO 8: © Photographers Choice RF/SuperStock; p. 201: © Wildroze/Getty Images RF; CO 9: © James Leynse/Corbis; CO 10: © AP Photo/James Nachtwey/VII; p. 237: © James Woodson/Getty Images RF; CO 11: © Mike Watson Images/Corbis RF; p. 255: © Bloomimage/Corbis RF; CO 12: Photo: Craig Sjodin/© ABC/Courtesy Everett Collection; p. 276: © PhotoAlto/Sigrid Olsson/Getty Images RF; p. 280: © Jerry McCrea/Star Ledger/Corbis; CO 13 (top): © vario images GmbH & Co.KG/Alamy; CO 13 (bottom): © Photodisc/SuperStock RF; p. 300 (top): © Brand X Pictures/PunchStock RF; p. 300 (bottom): © Peter M. Fisher/Corbis; CO 14: © Digital Vision/Getty RF; p. 319 (top): © BananaStock/SuperStock RF; p. 319 (bottom): © Roberto Westbrook/Blend Images LLC; CO 15: Library of Congress; p. 326: © BananaStock/SuperStock RF; p. 335: © John Gress/Reuters/Corbis; p. 338: © Fancy Photography/Veer RF; CO 16: © Bill Aron/PhotoEdit; p. 346: © Mary Kate Denny/PhotoEdit; p. 362: © Bananastock/Imagestate RF; Part Opener 3: © Steve Boyle/NewSport/Corbis; CO 17: © Comstock/Imagestate RF; CO 18: © Bill Aron/PhotoEdit; CO 19: © The New York Review of Books; CO 20: © Kayte M. Deioma/PhotoEdit; CO 21: © Mika/Corbis; p. 409: © Google; CO 22: © Alan D. Monyelle/U.S.Navy/Handout/Reuters/Corbis; p. 414, p. 415: Courtesy of Barnes & Noble; p. 437: © Zave Smith/Corbis RF; PO 4: © Natalie Hummel; Section Opener I: © Bill Aron/PhotoEdit; SO II: Editorial Image, LLC; SO III: © Jamie Carstairs/Alamy; SO IV (top): © Photri MicroStock™/A.Kaplan; SO IV (bottom): © Danny Letham; PO 5: © Joe Tabacca/AP Photo; p. 627: Library of Congress; p. 631: © Tony Avelar/AFP/Getty Images; p. 632: © Bettmann/Corbis; p. 636: © Reuters NewMedia Inc./Corbis; p. 643: © Cynthia Johnson/Time Life Pictures/Getty Images; p. 649: © Mike Watson Images/Corbis RF; p. 658: © Popperfoto/Getty Images; p. 666: © North Wind Picture Archives/Alamy; p. 674: Courtesy of Beth Johnson; p. 675 - p. 679: Courtesy of John Langan; p. 691: © Chicago Tribune/Landov LLC; p. 697: Courtesy of John Langan; p. 704: © Brigette Sullivan/PhotoEdit; p. 722: Library of Congress; p. 727 (left): © Kayte M. Deioma/PhotoEdit; p. 727 (right): © Susanne Oehlschlaeger/VISUM/The Image Works; p. 728: © Sophie McKibben; p. 738: © AP Photo/Andrew Rush; p. 748: Courtesy of David Daniels.

INDEX

Abbreviations, 534, 536–537
Abstract. *See* Summary
Active verbs, 120–121
Active voice, 605
Added detail fragments, 453–455
Addition signals, 87
Adequate details, 65–66
Adjectives
  defined, 507
  ESL pointers, 615–617
  in series, 129–130
  using to compare, 508–509
Adverbs, 507, 509–511
Anecdotes, 229
Apostrophe
  in contractions, 540–541
  defined, 539
  to show ownership or possession,
    541–545
Argument essays
  "Ban the Things, Ban Them All"
    (Ivins), 356–359
  defined, 180, 343–344
  essay development, 351–355
  strategies, 344–347
  student essays, 347–351
Articles (pieces of writing), finding on
    research topic, 404–406, 408
Articles (parts of speech), with count
    and noncount nouns, 606–609
Audience
  changing writing to suit, 13
  knowing in essay development, 176
Auxiliary verbs, 439

"Ban the Things, Ban Them All"
    (Ivins), 356–359
Banas, Casey, 691–696
Bodett, Tom, 334–337
Book stacks, 403–404
"Born to Be Different?" (Lewis),
    293–298
Brainstorming, 26–28

Call number, 401
Capital letters
  main uses, 526–529
  other uses, 529–531
  unnecessary use, 532
Catchphrase, 368

Cause and effect essays
  defined, 180, 260–261
  essay development, 264–269
  student essays, 261–264
  "Taming the Anger Monster"
    (Davidson), 269–275
"The Certainty of Fear" (Kendall)
  content, 684–687
  critical reading and discussion, 689
  preview, 684
  reading comprehension, 687–689
  structure and technique, 689
  writing assignments, 690–691
Change-of-direction signals, 87
"Chief Seattle's Speech of 1854"
    (Seattle)
  content, 707–710
  critical reading and discussion, 712
  preview, 707
  reading comprehension, 710–712
  structure and technique, 712
  writing assignments, 712–714
Chronological order, 84
Citing sources, 423–426
Classification. *See* Division-
    classification essays
Clause, 460
Cliché, 585, 587–589
Clustering
  to limit thesis, 53–54
  as prewriting technique, 28–29
Coherence, 84, 152–155
"College Lectures: Is Anybody
    Listening?" (Daniels)
  content, 748–751
  critical reading and discussion, 753
  preview, 748
  reading comprehension, 751–752
  structure and technique, 752–753
  writing assignments, 753–755
Colon, 564–565
Comma,
  after introductory material, 555–556
  around words that interrupt the flow
    of thought, 556–557
  between complete thoughts, 558–559
  between items in a series, 555
  with direct quotations, 559
  main uses, 554
  other uses, 560

Comma splice, 460–461
Communication, writing as a
    means of, 13
Comparison and/or contrast essays
  "Born to Be Different?" (Lewis),
    293–298
  defined, 180, 282
  essay development, 282–284,
    289–292
  student essays, 284–288
Complex sentence, 125–127
Compound subject, 484, 486–487
Comprehension questions, answering,
    625–626
Computer, using to write, 15–17
Concise words, 121–123
Concluding paragraph, 9–10,
    97–100
Conclusion
  methods of, 98–100
  signals for, 87
Conjunctive adverb, 88
Connecting words, 91–94
Content, revising, 34
Contraction, 539–541
Contrast. *See* Comparison and/or
    contrast essays
Coordination, 124–125
Correction symbols, 620
Count nouns, 605–609
Cover letter writing, 396–398

"Dad" (Malcolm), 233–236
Dangling modifiers, 517–519
Daniels, David, 748–755
Dash, 564, 565–566
Davidson, Anne, 269–275
Davis, Glenda, 251–255
Definition essays
  defined, 180, 304
  essay development, 308–313
  student essays, 305–308
  "Television Addiction" (Winn),
    313–316
Demonstrative pronouns, 500, 505
Dependent clause, 460
Dependent statement, 448
Dependent thought, 125–127
Dependent-word fragments,
    447–450

Description essays
    defined, 180, 182–183
    essay development, 187–192
    "Lou's Place" (Johnson), 192–197
    student essays, 183–187
Details
    adequate, 65–66
    specific, 62–64
Development, plan of, 7
Diagramming, as prewriting
        technique, 28–29
Dialogue, 208–210
Direct quotation, 417–418. *See also*
        Quotation and Quotation marks
Direction words, 369–371
Division-classification essays
    defined, 180, 326
    essay development, 330–333
    student essays, 326–329
    "Wait Divisions" (Bodett), 334–337
Documentation of sources, 423–426
Dunayer, Joan, 722–728

-*ed* words, 127
Editing
    defined, 592
    hints, 593
    sentences, 130–131, 593–604
    using computer for, 17
    in writing process, 35–37
Effects. *See* Cause and effect essays
Emerson, Ralph Waldo, 627–631
Emphatic order, 85
ESL pointers
    adjectives, 615–617
    articles with count and noncount
        nouns, 605–609
    prepositions for time and place,
        617–618
    subjects and verbs, 610–615
Essay development
    argument, 351–355
    cause and effect, 264–269
    definition, 308–313
    description, 187–192
    determining point of view,
        176–178
    division-classification, 330–333
    exemplification, 228–233
    knowing purpose and audience, 176
    knowing subject, 175
    narration, 203–204, 208–213
    patterns of, 180–181
    process, 242, 246–250

understanding assignment, 175
    comparison and/or contrast,
        282–284, 289–292
Essay exams
    anticipate probable questions,
        367–368
    outline answer, 368–369, 371–372
    plan answer before writing, 369–372
    write essay, 372–374
Essays
    benefits of writing, 11
    coherence, 152–155
    connecting evidence, 87–94
    defined, 5
    diagram of, 10
    introductory paragraph, 94–97
    organizing evidence, 84–87
    parts of, 7–10
    point and support in, 5–6
    support, 148–152
    thesis statement (*see* Thesis and
        thesis statements)
    traditional structure of, 6–11
    unity, 145–148
Evidence
    connecting, 87–94
    organizing, 84–87
    revising for, 148–152
    supporting thesis with, 60–66
Exemplification essays
    "Dad" (Malcolm), 233–236
    defined, 180, 222–223
    essay development, 228–233
    student essays, 223–228
Exposition essays, 180

Final outline, 422
First draft
    on computer, 16
    in writing process, 31–33
First-person approach, 176–177
Focusing a thesis, 52–57
Format, 523
Fragments
    added detail fragments, 453–455
    defined, 447
    dependent-word fragments,
        447–450
    -*ing* and *to* fragments, 451–453
    missing-subject fragments, 455–456
Freewriting
    on computer, 15–16
    as prewriting technique, 23–25
Fused sentences, 460–461

Garity, Joyce, 755–762
Gerund, 490, 493, 612–614
Grammar
    adjectives and adverbs, 507–511
    dangling modifiers, 517–519
    fragments, 447–459
    helping verbs, 491–492
    misplaced modifiers, 513–515
    pronoun agreement and reference,
        494–498
    pronoun types, 500–505
    regular and irregular verbs,
        473–481
    run-on sentences, 460–472
    subject-verb agreement, 484–487
    subjects and verbs, 439–446
    verb tense, 473, 490–491
    verbals, 492–493
Gregory, Dick, 636–642

Halpern, Sue, 728–738
Hamill, Pete, 214–217
"A Hanging" (Orwell)
    content, 659–662
    critical reading and discussion, 664
    preview, 658
    reading comprehension, 662–663
    structure and technique, 664
    writing assignments, 664–666
"Here's to Your Health" (Dunayer)
    content, 722–724
    critical reading and discussion, 726
    preview, 722
    reading comprehension, 724–726
    structure and technique, 726
    writing assignments, 727–728
Homonyms, 575–579
"How to Do Well on a Job Interview"
        (Davis), 251–255
"How to Make It in College, Now That
        You're Here" (O'Keeney)
    content, 739–744
    critical reading and discussion, 746
    preview, 739
    reading comprehension, 744–745
    structure and technique, 746
    writing assignments, 746–747
Hyphen, 564, 567

"I Became Her Target" (Wilkins)
    content, 643–644
    critical reading and discussion, 647
    preview, 643
    reading comprehension, 645–646

structure and technique, 646–647
writing assignments, 647–649
Idiomatic, 605
Illustration signals, 87
Indefinite pronoun, 484, 487, 494,
  496–497
Independent clause, 460
Indirect quotations, 549–550
Infinitive, 490, 492, 612–614
-ing and *to* fragments, 451–453
-ing words, 127
Internet
  evaluating sources, 408–410
  online periodical databases,
    405–406, 408
  using for research, 407–408, 414–415
Introduction, in research paper, 422
Introductory paragraph, 7–8, 94–97
Irregular verbs, 473, 476–481
Ivins, Molly, 356–359

Job application
  cover letters, 396–398
  résumés, 392–396
Johnson, Beth, 192–195, 674–683
Journal keeping, 14–15
Journals, 404–406, 408

Keeping a journal, 14–15
Kendall, Audra, 684–691
Key words, 368

Letters
  capitalization in, 531
  job applications and, 396–398
Lewis, Camille, 293–298
Library
  book stacks, 403–404
  library catalog, 400–402
  main desk, 400
  periodicals, 404–406
  in research, 400, 413–414
Library of Congress, 107
Limiting a thesis, 52–57
Linking sentences, 91
Linking verbs, 439, 610
List making, as prewriting technique,
  26–28
"Lou's Place" (Johnson), 192–197
-ly words, 127

Magazines, 404–406, 408
Making a list, as prewriting technique,
  26–28

Malcolm, Andrew H., 233–236
Manuscript, 523
Manuscript form, 523–525
Mapping, as prewriting technique, 28–29
"Mayor of Rust" (Halpern)
  content, 728–735
  critical reading and discussion, 737
  preview, 728
  reading comprehension, 735–737
  structure and technique, 737
  writing assignments, 737–738
McClintock, Ann, 697–706
Mechanics
  capital letters, 526–532
  manuscript form, 523–525
  numbers and abbreviations, 534–537
Misplaced modifiers, 513–515
Missing-subject fragments, 455–456
Modifiers
  dangling, 517–519
  misplaced, 513–515

Narration essays
  defined, 180, 203–204
  essay development, 208–213
  student essays, 204–208
  "The Yellow Ribbon" (Hamill),
    214–217
Newspapers, 404–406
Noncount nouns, 605–609
Note-taking, 417–419
Nouns
  articles with, 606–609
  defined, 494–495
Numbers, 535–536

Object pronouns, 500–503
O'Keeney, Brian, 739–747
One side at a time method of developing
  comparison/contrast essay, 282–283
One-three-one essay, 10
Online databases for periodicals, 405–406
Orwell, George, 658–666
Outlines
  different from summaries, 375–376
  for essay exams, 368–369, 371–372
  importance of, 42
  in peer review, 178–179
  as prewriting technique, 29–31
  for research paper, 416–417, 422

Paragraphs
  concluding, 9–10, 97–100
  defined, 4
  introductory, 7–8, 94–97

point and support in, 4–5
supporting, 8–9
Paraphrase, 417–418
Parentheses, 564, 566
Participle, 490, 493
Past participle, 473, 616–617
Peer review, 178–179
Periodicals, 404–406, 408
Personal spelling list, 570–571
Plagiarism, 419–422
Plan of development, 7
Plural subject, 484
Point and support, 3–6. *See also* Thesis
  and thesis statements
Point by point method of developing
  comparison/contrast essay, 283–284
Point of view, determining, 176–178
Possessive pronouns, 500, 504
Précis. *See* Summary
Prediction, in conclusions, 99
Preface, summary writing and, 386
Preposition, 439, 617–618
Prepositional phrase, 128
Present participle, 473, 616–617
Pretentious language, 585, 589–590
Prewriting
  clustering, 28–29
  computers and, 15–16
  freewriting, 23–25
  list making, 26–28
  questioning, 25–26
  scratch outline, 29–31
Principal parts of verbs, 473
Process essays
  defined, 180, 242
  essay development, 246–250
  "How to Do Well on a Job
    Interview" (Davis), 251–255
  student essays, 243–246
"The Professor Is a Dropout" (Johnson)
  content, 674–680
  critical reading and discussion,
    682–683
  preview, 674
  reading comprehension, 680–682
  structure and technique, 682
  writing assignments, 683
Progressive tense, 611
Pronoun agreement, 494, 495–496
Pronoun reference, 494, 497–498
Pronouns
  as connecting words, 92
  consistency with, 114
  defined, 494–495

Pronouns—*Contd.*
  indefinite, 496–497
  pronoun agreement, 495–496
  pronoun reference, 497–498
  types, 500–505
Proofreading
  computers and, 17
  defined, 132, 592
  sentences, 132–133
  symbols, 132, 620
Proofreading symbols
  defined, 592
  list of, 620
"Propaganda Techniques in Today's
    Advertising" (McClintock)
  content, 697–702
  critical reading and discussion, 705
  preview, 697
  reading comprehension, 702–703
  structure and technique, 704
  writing assignments, 705–706
Proximate cause, 265
Punctuation
  apostrophe, 539–545
  comma, 554–560
  other punctuation marks, 564–567
  quotation marks, 546–552
Purpose
  changing writing to suit, 13
  knowing in essay development, 176

Qualifier, 605, 607
Questioning, as prewriting technique,
    25–26
Quotation
  commas with, 559
  in concluding paragraphs, 98
  indirect, 549–550
  in introductory paragraphs, 96
  taking notes on for research paper,
    417–418
Quotation marks
  defined, 546
  dialogue and, 209
  other uses, 552
  to set off titles of short works,
    550–551
  to set off words of speakers or
    writers, 546–549

Reaction, including in report writing,
    387–388
*Readers' Guide to Periodical
    Literature*, 404–405

Reading Comprehension Chart, 763
Reading well, 623–625
Rebuttal, 347
Recommendations in conclusions, 99
Regular verbs, 473–476
Repeated words, 92
Report writing, 387–391
Research
  using the internet, 407–410
  using the library, 400–407
Research paper
  citing sources, 423–426
  limiting topic, 415–416
  model paper, 427–436
  note-taking, 417–419
  outline for paper, 416–417, 422
  plagiarism, 419–422
  topic selection, 413–415
  writing the paper, 422
Résumé writing, 392–396
Revising
  for coherence, 152–155
  on computer, 16–17
  for content, 34
  for sentence skills, 155–159
  for support, 148–152
  for unity, 145–148
  varying sentence structure, 124–130
  in writing process, 33–34
Revising sentences
  use active verbs, 120–121
  use concise words, 121–123
  use consistent point of view,
    113–116
  use parallelism, 111–112
  use specific words, 116–119
Run-on sentences
  correcting with comma and joining
    word, 463–466
  correcting with period and capital
    letter, 462–463
  correcting with a semicolon,
    466–468
  defined, 460–461
  subordination, 469
Russell, Bertrand, 632–636

Savory, Tanya, 650–658
Scratch outline
  in peer review, 178–179
  as prewriting technique, 29–31
  for research paper, 416–417
Seattle, Chief, 707–714
Second-person approach, 177

Self-Reliance (Emerson)
  content, 627–628
  critical reading and discussion, 630
  preview, 627
  reading comprehension, 628–630
  structure and technique, 630
  writing assignments, 631
Semicolon, 466–468, 564, 565
Sentence fragments
  added detail fragments, 453–455
  defined, 447
  dependent-word fragments, 447–450
  -ing and *to* fragments, 451–453
  missing-subject fragments, 455–456
Sentence outline, 422
Sentence skills
  use active verbs, 120–121
  use concise words, 121–123
  use consistent point of view,
    113–116
  use parallelism, 111–112
  use specific words, 116–119
  see also Grammar, Mechanics,
    Punctuation, Word Use
Sentences
  editing, 130–131, 593–604
  parallelism, 111–112
  proofreading, 132–133
  variation, 124–130
  see also Revising sentences
"Is Sex All That Matters?"
  content, 755–758
  critical reading and discussion, 760
  preview, 755
  reading comprehension, 758–759
  structure and technique, 760
  writing assignments, 760–762
"Shame" (Gregory)
  content, 636–639
  critical reading and discussion, 641
  preview, 636
  reading comprehension, 639–641
  structure and technique, 641
  writing assignments, 641–642
"Single-Sex Schools: An Old Idea
    Whose Time Has Come" Urbina
  content, 715–718
  critical reading and discussion,
    720–721
  preview, 715
  reading comprehension, 718–720
  structure and technique, 720
  writing assignments, 721–722
Singular subject, 484

Slang, 585–587
Sources, citing for research paper, 423–426
Space signals, 87
Specific details, 62–64
Spelling improvement, 570–574
"Stepping into the Light" (Savory)
    content, 650–655
    critical reading and discussion, 657
    preview, 650
    reading comprehension, 655–656
    structure and technique, 656–657
    writing assignments, 657–658
Subject
    agreement with verbs, 484–487
    defined, 439
    ESL pointers, 610–615
    finding in a sentence, 440
    more about, 443–444
Subject headings, 401
Subject pronouns, 500–503
Subordination, 125–127, 469
Subtitle, 376
Summary
    of article, 376–385
    of book, 385–386
    defined, 375, 418
    in report writing, 387–388
Support
    adequate details, 65–66
    need for in writing, 3–6
    revising for, 148–152
    specific evidence, 60–63
Supporting paragraph, 8–9
Synonyms, as connecting words, 92–93

Table of contents, 385
"Taming the Anger Monster" (Davidson), 269–275
Tan, Amy, 621, 667–673
"Television Addiction" (Winn), 313–316
Tense, verb, 473, 490–491
Thesis and thesis statements
    avoiding common mistakes, 57–60
    defined, 5, 51–52
    in introductory paragraph, 7, 94–97
    limiting and focusing, 52–57
    in research paper, 422
    supporting with specific evidence, 60–66

Third-person approach, 177–178
"Three Passions" (Russell)
    content, 632
    critical reading and discussion, 634–635
    preview, 632
    reading comprehension, 633–634
    structure and technique, 634
    writing assignments, 635–636
Time order, 84
Time signals, 87
Titles
    capitalization of, 528
    defined, 100
    summary writing and, 376, 385
    writing, 100–101
to and *–ing* fragments, 451–453
To word group, 128
Topic, selecting and limiting for research paper, 413–416
Topic outline, 422
Topic sentence
    defined, 4
    in supporting paragraphs, 8
Transitional phrase, 88
Transitional sentences, 91
Transitional words, 467–468
Transitions, 87–91
Transitive verbs, 611–612

Ultimate cause, 265
Unity, 145–148
Urbina, Diane, 715–722

Verb tense, 473, 490–491
Verbals, 490, 492–493
Verbs
    active, 120–121
    agreement with subject, 484–487
    consistency with, 113
    defined, 439
    ESL pointers, 610–615
    finding in a sentence, 440–443
    helping verbs, 491–492
    irregular, 473, 476–481
    more about, 443–444
    regular, 473–476
    in series, 129–130
    verb tense, 473, 490–491
    verbals, 492–493

"Wait Divisions" (Bodett), 334–337
"What Your Closet Reveals About You" (Tan)
    content, 667–670
    critical reading and discussion, 672
    preview, 667
    reading comprehension, 670–671
    structure and technique, 671–672
    writing assignments, 672–673
"What's Wrong with Schools? Teacher Plays Student, Learns to Lie and Cheat" (Banas)
    content, 691–693
    critical reading and discussion, 695
    preview, 691
    reading comprehension, 693–694
    structure and technique, 694–695
    writing assignments, 695–696
Wilkins, Roger, 643–649
Winn, Marie, 313–316
Word use
    commonly confused words, 575–582
    editing tests, 592–604
    effective word choice, 585–590
    ESL pointers, 605–618
    spelling improvement, 570–574
Wordiness, 121
Writing inventory, 38–39
Writing process
    editing, 35–37
    first draft, 31–33
    prewriting (*see* Prewriting)
    revising, 33–34
Writing
    connecting evidence, 87–94
    difference from talking, 3–4
    as means of communication, 13
    organizing evidence, 84–87
    point and support, 3–6
    as a process of discover, 12–13
    as a skill, 11–12
    thesis statement (*see* Thesis statement)
    using computers for, 15–17

"The Yellow Ribbon" (Hamill), 214–217